EXPERIMENTAL CINEMA,
THE FILM READER

1 Reader brings together key writings on American avant-garde
? tradition of underground filmmaking from its origins in the 1920s
iry film and video artists.

e development of major movements such as the New American
id the Structuralist films of the 1970s, examining the work of key
ering neglected filmmakers. Contributors focus on the ways in which
ve explored issues of gender, sexuality, and race, and foreground
novations such as the use of Super 8mm and video.

ires an editor's introduction setting debates in their context. Sections

nerican avant-garde cinema – explores the influence of European movements
of experimental film, and considers the early work of filmmakers such as

perimental cinema explosion – traces the development of the New American
mining the influence and work of key filmmakers such as Kenneth Anger, Jack
Warhol, Stan Brakhage, and collage filmmaker Bruce Conner
in the 1970s – identifies and discusses the main figures in Structuralist film
chael Snow and Hollis Frampton
nemas – examines the work of recent filmmakers such as Isaac Julien, Julie
arbara Hammer, and considers the future of experimental film

rs. Daryl Chin, Wheeler Winston Dixon, David Ehrenstein, Gwendolyn Audrey Foster,
Ganguly, Gloria Gibson, Peter Gidal, Kate Haug, Chris Holmlund, Jan-Christopher
Philip Lopate, Scott MacDonald, Judith Mayne, Jonas Mekas, Kobena Mercer, Yoko
uren Rabinovitz, P. Adams Sitney, Juan A. Suarez, Jerry Tartaglia, Reva Wolf.

W ston Dixon is Ryan Professor of Film Studies, Chair of the Film Studies Program,
Don Gr ssc glish at the University of Nebraska. His publications include *The Exploding
Disas d Memory* (1998), and *The Second Century of Cinema* (2000)

Gwendolyn Audrey Foster is Associate Professor in the Department of English and a member
of the Film Studies Program at the University of Nebraska. Her publications include *Women
Film Directors: An International Bio-Critical Dictionary* (1995), *Women Filmmakers of the African and
Asian Diaspora: Decolonizing the Gaze, Locating Subjectivity* (1997), and *Captive Bodies: The Postcolonial
Subjectivity in Cinema* (1999).

In Focus: Routledge Film Readers
Series Editors: Steven Cohan (Syracuse University) and Ina Rae Hark (University of South Carolina)

The In Focus series of readers is a comprehensive resource for students on film and cinema studies courses. The series explores the innovations of film studies while highlighting the vital connection of debates to other academic fields and to studies of other media. The readers bring together key articles on a major topic in film studies, from marketing to Hollywood comedy, identifying the central issues, exploring how and why scholars have approached it in specific ways, and tracing continuities of thought among scholars. Each reader opens with an introductory essay setting the debates in their academic context, explaining the topic's historical and theoretical importance, and surveying and critiquing its development in film studies.

Exhibition, The Film Reader
Edited by Ina Rae Hark

Hollywood Musicals, The Film Reader
Edited by Steven Cohan

Horror, The Film Reader
Edited by Mark Jancovich

Experimental Cinema, The Film Reader
Edited by Wheeler Winston Dixon and Gwendolyn Audrey Foster

Marketing, The Film Reader
Edited by Justin Wyatt

Forthcoming Titles:

Hollywood Comedians, The Film Reader
Edited by Frank Krutnik

Movie Music, The Film Reader
Edited by Kay Dickinson

Reception, The Film Reader
Edited by Barbara Klinger

Stars, The Film Reader
Edited by Marcia Landy and Lucy Fischer

EXPERIMENTAL CINEMA,
THE FILM READER

Edited by Wheeler Winston Dixon
and Gwendolyn Audrey Foster

Routledge
Taylor & Francis Group

LONDON AND NEW YORK

First published 2002
by Routledge
11 New Fetter Lane, London EC4P 4EE

Simultaneously published in the USA and Canada
by Routledge
29 West 35th Street, New York, NY 10001

Routledge is an imprint of the Taylor & Francis Group

© 2002 Selection and editorial, Wheeler Winston Dixon and
Gwendolyn Audrey Foster; individual chapters to their authors

Designed and typeset in Novarese and Scala Sans
by Keystroke, Jacaranda Lodge, Wolverhampton
Printed and bound in Great Britain
by The Cromwell Press, Trowbridge, Wiltshire

British Library Cataloguing in Publication Data
A catalogue record for this book is available from the British Library

Library of Congress Cataloging in Publication Data
has been applied for

ISBN 0–415–27786–8 (hbk)
ISBN 0–415–27787–6 (pbk)

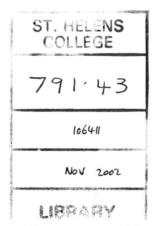

Contents

Acknowledgments

The editors extend their grateful permission to the following copyright holders for permission to reprint the essays included in *Experimental Cinema: The Film Reader*, edited by Wheeler Winston Dixon and Gwendolyn Audrey Foster.

Introduction: "The Experimental Cinema," Wheeler Winston Dixon, Gwendolyn Audrey Foster. Based on an original essay by Wheeler Winston Dixon entitled "Performativity in 1960s American Experimental Cinema: The Body as Site of Ritual and Display," *Film Criticism* 23.1 (Fall 1998), pages 48–60. Reprinted by permission of Lloyd Michaels, editor.

Horak, Jan-Christopher. "The First American Film Avant-garde, 1919–1945." *Lovers of Cinema: The First American Film Avant-garde 1919–1945*, pages 14–66. Copyright © 1995 the University of Wisconsin Press. Reprinted by permission of The University of Wisconsin Press.

Mekas, Jonas. "Notes on the New American Cinema," *Film Culture* 24 (Autumn 1962), pages 6–16. Reprinted by permission of Robert Haller, Editor, *Film Culture*.

Rabinovitz, Lauren. "The Woman Filmmaker in the New York Avant-garde," *Points of Resistance: Women, Power and Politics in the New York Avant-garde Cinema, 1943–1971*, pages 1–12. Copyright © 1991 by the Board of Trustees of the University of Illinois. Used with permission of the University of Illinois Press.

Mayne, Judith. "Women in the Avant-garde: Germaine Dulac, Maya Deren, Agnès Varda, Chantal Akerman and Trinh T. Minh-ha." Original essay title: "Revising the 'Primitive.'" *The Woman at the Keyhole: Feminism and Women's Cinema*, pages 184–222. Indiana University Press, 1990. Reprinted by permission of Indiana University Press.

Suarez, Juan A. "Pop, Queer, or Fascist? The Ambiguity of Mass Culture in Kenneth Anger's *Scorpio Rising*." *Bike Boys, Drag Queens and Superstars: Avant-garde, Mass Culture and Gay Identities in the 1960s Underground Cinema*, pages 141–180. Indiana University Press: 1996. Reprinted by permission of Indiana University Press.

Ganguly, Suranjan. "Stan Brakhage—The 60th Birthday Interview," *Film Culture* 78 (Summer 1994), pages 18–38. Reprinted by permission of Robert Haller, Editor, *Film Culture*.

ACKNOWLEDGMENTS

Tartaglia, Jerry. "The Perfect Queer Appositeness of Jack Smith," *Quarterly Review of Film and Video* 18.1. (Fall 2001), pages 39–53. Copyright © 2001 Jerry Tartaglia. Reproduced by permission of Taylor and Francis.

Haug, Kate. "An Interview with Carolee Schneemann," *Wide Angle* 20.1 (January 1998), pages 20–49. Reprinted by permission of Johns Hopkins University Press.

Wolf, Reva. "*The Flower Thief*: The 'Film Poem,' Warhol's Early Films, and the Beat Writers," *Andy Warhol, Poetry, and Gossip in the* 1960s, pages 125–148. Chicago: University of Chicago Press, 1997. Reprinted by permission of The University of Chicago Press.

Chin, Daryl. "Walking on Thin Ice: The Films of Yoko Ono." *The Independent* (April 1989), pages 19–23. Copyright © 1989 Daryl Chin; reprinted by permission of Daryl Chin.

Ono, Yoko. "Yoko Ono on Yoko Ono." *Film Culture* 48/49 (Winter/Spring 1970), pages 32–33. Reprinted by permission of Robert Haller, Editor, *Film Culture*.

Sitney, P. Adams. "Structural Film," *Film Culture* 47 (Summer 1969), pages 1–10. Reprinted by permission of Robert Haller, Editor, *Film Culture*.

MacDonald, Scott. "Interview with Michael Snow," *A Critical Cinema 2: Interviews with Independent Filmmakers*, pages 51–76. Copyright © 1992 the Regents of the University of California. Reprinted by permission of University of California Press.

Lopate, Philip. "The Films of Warren Sonbert," *Film Culture* 70–71 (Winter 1983), pages 177–184. Reprinted by permission of Robert Haller, Editor, *Film Culture*.

Ehrenstein, David. "Warren Sonbert Interview," *Film Culture* 70–71 (Winter 1983), pages 185–196. Original essay title: "Warren Sonbert Interviewed by David Ehrenstein, December 1978." Reprinted by permission of Robert Haller, Editor, *Film Culture*.

Gidal, Peter. "An Interview with Hollis Frampton," *Structural Film Anthology*. Peter Gidal, ed. BFI, 1976, pages 64–72. Copyright © 1972, 2002 Peter Gidal. Reprinted by permission of Peter Gidal.

Foster, Gwendolyn Audrey. "Re/Constructing Lesbian Auto/Biographies in *Tender Fictions* and *Nitrate Kisses*," *Post Script* 16.3 (Summer, 1997) pages 3–16. Original essay title: "Barbara Hammer, an Interview: Re/Constructing Lesbian Auto/Biographies in *Tender Fictions* and *Nitrate Kisses*." Reprinted by permission of Gerald Duchovnay, Editor, *Post Script*.

Holmlund, Chris. "The Films of Sadie Benning and Su Friedrich," Original essay title: "When Autobiography Meets Ethnography and Girl Meets Girl: The 'Dyke Docs' of Sadie Benning and Su Friedrich," pages 127–143. *Between the Sheets, In the Streets: Queer, Lesbian and Gay Documentary*. Chris Holmlund and Cynthia Fuchs, eds. University of Minnesota Press: 1997. Reprinted by permission of University of Minnesota Press.

Gibson, Gloria J. "Black Women's Independent Cinema," Original essay title: "Aspects of Black Feminist Cultural Ideology in Films by Black Women Independent Artists," pages 365–379. *Multiple Voices in Feminist Film Criticism*. Diane Carson, Linda Dittmar and Janice R. Welsch, eds. University of Minnesota Press: 1994. Reprinted by permission of University of Minnesota Press.

Mercer, Kobena. "Dark and Lovely Too: Black Gay Men in Independent Film," *Queer Looks: Perspectives on Lesbian and Gay Film and Video*. Martha Gever, Pratibha Parmar and John Greyson eds. New York: Routledge, 1993, pages 238–256. Copyright © 1993 Kobena Mercer. Reprinted by permission of Routledge Books.

All illustrations, unless otherwise noted, are from the collection of Anthology Film Archives; reprinted by permission. Our thanks to Robert Haller of Anthology Film Archives for his help in this matter. The stills from Trinh T. Minh-ha's *Reassemblage* (1982) and Ayoka Chenzira's *Hair Piece* (1985) appear through the courtesy of Women Make Movies, Inc.

ACKNOWLEDGEMENTS

Experimental Cinema,
The Film Reader

Introduction: Toward a New History of the Experimental Cinema

There is little room for playfulness or experimentation in contemporary mainstream filmmaking. The stakes are simply too high; the average film costs between $50 and $100 million, and all commercial films must recoup their backers' investment. Thus, the box-office driven spectacles produced by Hollywood are triumphs of marketing, not imagination. Art-house films and independent films have little hope of finding an audience because of changes in distribution patterns (VHS, DVD, and cable) and the increasing conglomeration of Hollywood. Nevertheless, there is and always has been a body of film art that exists outside the confines of commercial production. Experimental cineastes don't set out to please an audience of marketing executives: they give no thought to the pressures of opening-weekend grosses, nor do they try to manipulate, or even please, the masses. Their films find their own audiences and operate entirely outside of the value system that we have come to know as the Hollywood construct.

Robert Bresson writes that there are two types of films, "those that use the camera in order to *reproduce*; and those that employ the resources of cinematography to *create*" (1975: 2). Creativity requires breathing room for its playfulness. Perhaps nothing liberates the film artist more than freedom from the obligation to please market researchers and massive audiences. Filmic creativity is often actually fueled by a lack of resources. A case in point is Sadie Benning, who, at the age of 15, picked up a children's toy—a Fisher Price Pixelvision camera—and invented an entirely new type of personal experimental film that used the inherent image distortion of the primitive video camera as an artistic asset. Often less *is* more, if one respects the individual creative spirit rather than adheres to the constraints of genre.

In the late 1800s, when the cinema was first invented, filmmakers toyed with the new art form they had created. They hand cranked the film at variable speeds through the camera and discovered the magic that the cinema had to offer. People and objects could be made to disappear, fly through the air, and change shape at will. Inanimate objects could come to life through the magic of stop-motion animation. Alice Guy Blaché and other early filmmakers experimented with frame-by-frame hand tinting to create color films and experimented with sound; early attempts at sound recording were made using a wax cylinder to synchronize picture and sound. The surrealists also stretched the supposed limitations of the new art form, constructing radically inventive editing techniques and ignoring the requirements of conventional narrative, to create "cinepoems" of anarchic beauty. Dziga Vertov and his students in the former Soviet Union invented rapid montage editing out of necessity. Denied access to raw stock to shoot new films, they learned how to cut film by re-editing D. W. Griffith's *Birth of A Nation* (1915) in short bursts of hyperedited frames, a style of editing that would become the hallmark of Soviet silent cinema.

Experimental filmmakers physically "attacked the film" by scratching it, baking it, dyeing it, using outdated stock—both when economically necessary and by deliberate design—to create a tactile viewing experience that would repeatedly remind the audience throughout the projection that they were witnessing a plastic construct, a creation of light and shadow, in which the syntactical properties of the cinematic medium were always an aesthetic consideration. Filmmakers will always find ways of playing with film and video. For those unfamiliar with the large body of work in experimental cinema, there exists a treasure trove of film to be experienced, a deeply personal cinema that is as varied as it is playful and imaginative. These films are self-distributed or distributed by a small but dedicated group of truly independent distributors. They are regularly screened at museums, in classrooms, in living rooms, and on the web.

Mainstream filmmakers know about these films but do little to promote their existence; each of these films represents the individual vision of one person and is not the product of a media conglomerate's edict. Commercial filmmakers have borrowed from experimentalists many innovative approaches to filmmaking and cinematography, but what they usually appropriate is merely *style* rather than *content*. Creative artistry is thus transformed into a wholly commercial product. A good case in point is the manner in which MTV and television commercials regularly use editing and graphic design techniques that were invented by experimental filmmakers, without the subtext inherent in the original films. The difference is that these images and techniques are used not for a *purpose* but for a stylized effect on MTV. Commercial television and cinema increasingly offer viewers a digitized universe, a product designed solely for consumption rather than for contemplation or enlightenment. This exploitation of experimental film makes it even more essential that it is studied, understood, and supported.

This book brings together a wide range of critical essays on American and European experimental cinema but focuses, for the most part, on American developments within the movement while placing them within the larger context of the European and Russian experimental cinema that predated and, to a large degree, informed the American movement. The intent of the volume, which traces the movement from the 1920s to the present, using critical and historical essays, as well as interviews with key figures in the movement, is to represent diverse critical approaches to experimental cinema. The reader is divided into four parts: Part One, Origins of the American Avant-garde Cinema, 1920–1959, traces the rise of the American experimental cinema from its birthplace in France, Germany, and Russia and then moves on to the avant-garde American filmmakers who, between 1921 and 1943, were working in response to the European movement of the 1920s. The rest of the first section is a series of essays covering American experimental filmmaking, on both the East and West Coasts, in the 1940s and 1950s. These essays lead to a detailed examination of the 1960s American experimental cinema as a whole, from its early romantic and anarchic roots through the formalist structuralism of Michael Snow and others in the late 1960s and early 1970s in Part Two, The 1960s Experimental Cinema Explosion, and Part Three, Structuralism in the 1970s. Finally, the volume concludes with Part Four, Alternative Cinemas, 1980–2000, a series of essays and interviews covering more recent experimental cinema, particularly African-American and queer cinema from the 1980s to the present.

While this reader covers many of the experimental movement's major figures, including Stan Brakhage, Kenneth Anger, Maya Deren, Michael Snow, Jonas Mekas, and others, the volume also examines American experimental filmmakers whose work is often excluded from the experimental film canon, including Barbara Rubin, Robert Nelson, Ben Van Meter, Gerard Malanga, Jud Yalkut, Scott Bartlett, and many others. All of these film artists share one thing: a highly personal and deeply felt vision of a new and anarchic way of looking at film and video, fueled by the inexhaustible romanticism of the era and by the fact that film and video were both very "cheap" media in which to work during the 1940s through the 1960s. The camera of choice for the experimental filmmaker was the Bolex, a lightweight, spring-wound camera, which was sturdy, portable, and capable of yielding professional results in the right hands. Film was inexpensive: a 100-foot roll of black-and-white film was $2; color film, $5. Processing cost two or three cents per foot. Filmmakers would often band together to purchase raw stock in bulk, or they would use outdated film that professional companies would simply throw away. Many experimental films were shot completely silent, with soundtracks of music and effects added later.

Thus, even in the late 1960s, one could make a 16mm 15-minute black-and-white sound film for as little as $200; if one had the *desire* to do it, anyone could make a film. These filmmakers also disdained, for the most part, the Hollywood model of slick professionalism in lighting, acting, sets, costume design, and other physical production details. The avant-garde filmmakers of the 1920s and 1940s aspired to a certain level of studio gloss in their work, but by the 1950s and 1960s, the "Beat" and "underground" filmmakers in New York, San Francisco, and Los Angeles were all embracing the idea that avant-garde films should be rough, raw, and imperfect. These were outlaw works, created at the margins of society. It seemed perfectly natural to make a film for *oneself* as the audience and to ignore both the established film critics and the normal distribution channels. Thus, throughout the history of experimental cinema, various communities developed, each of which provided distribution facilities, screening venues, and the spiritual and financial support necessary to the communal enterprise of filmmaking.

Beginnings of the Avant-garde

In the 1920s and 1930s, the work of a community of French surrealists and dadaists, such as Jean Cocteau, Man Ray, Marcel Duchamp, and René Clair, inspired the American experimental filmmakers to abandon the constraints of narrative and to create something more ambitious: the cinepoem. Man Ray's *Le Retour à la raison* (1923), Dimitri Kirsanov's *Ménilmontant* (1926), Fernand Léger's *Ballet mécanique* (1924), Marcel Duchamp's *Anémic cinéma* (1926), and René Clair's *Entr'acte* (1924) heralded the birth of a new freedom in the cinema, wherein narrative became secondary to visual poetry and the individual concerns of the artist.

Man Ray's *Le Retour à la raison*, for example, was created by sprinkling salt and pepper, along with thumbtacks and whatever other materials might be handy, directly onto the unexposed film with some fragmentary photographed visuals spliced in at random intervals. Kirsanov's *Ménilmontant*, a highly poetic tale of two young women struggling to survive in the slums of Paris, opens with a staggering display of editing in which an ax murder is depicted in a series of rapid shots that directly mimic the violence of the act itself, prefiguring in many ways Alfred Hitchcock's handling of similar material in *Psycho* (1960). Léger's *Ballet mécanique*, with its incessant loops of a woman walking up a flight of stairs, repeated again and again until the human body itself becomes a mere mechanism, endlessly replicating the same movements, prefigured the structuralist films that would eventually blossom in the late 1960s. Clair's *Entr'acte*, in which a funeral procession famously becomes a chase and eventually a roller-coaster ride, is another collection of absurdist segments in a film that deliberately seeks to avoid concrete interpretation, leaving it to the audience to divine the filmmaker's true intent.

The sense of liberation created by these early experimentalists was soon transported through the medium of international screenings to ciné clubs in the United States, where independent filmmakers eagerly embraced this newfound freedom, even as Hollywood, predictably, stuck to direct, narrative-driven representational films, which mainstream audiences had come to expect from the major studios. All of these independent artists shared one trait: although they screened their films for each other and assisted each other with production chores, each filmmaker was guided solely by her or his own vision, not by the desire to create a film for an audience. Each filmmaker had an individual style and approach to the material that made her or his films uniquely that filmmaker's alone. Thus, these films resist categorization and do not fall within the confines of established genres. The independent filmmaker creates films because of an internal drive to do so; the films discussed in this volume are the unique creations of artists who fought to express their vision on the screen, using whatever equipment came to hand, working on nonexistent budgets.

Jan-Christopher Horak, in his essay in this volume, "The First American Film Avant-garde, 1919–1945," goes into great detail on the lives and works of these early American experimentalists, demonstrating that this first community of avant-garde filmmakers had a range and depth of cinematic discourse that has often been ignored. Charles Sheeler and Paul Strand created *Manhatta* (1921), an impressionist view of New York City, using distorting lenses and rapid cuts to convey the frenzy of the metropolis. In 1928, émigrés Slavko Vorkapich and Robert Florey directed the groundbreaking American experimental short silent film *The Life and Death of 9413— A Hollywood Extra*, which documented how the dreams of an aspiring actor are destroyed by the crushing weight of the studio system, on a minuscule budget. Ironically, both Vorkapich and Florey later became part of the Hollywood community, along with their photographer on the film, the legendary Gregg Toland, who eventually photographed Orson Welles's *Citizen Kane* (1941). James Watson and Melville Webber created *The Fall of the House of Usher* (1928) and their first sound film, *Lot in Sodom* (1933), by using abstraction, symbolic structures, and experimental sound techniques to create harrowingly personal visions of societal collapse.

From the early 1940s to the late 1950s, numerous independent filmmakers created a series of personal and uncompromising films that would define a new generation. Jonas Mekas's essay, "Notes on the New American Cinema," captures much of the energy of this turbulent era, while Lauren Rabinovitz, in "The Woman Filmmaker in the New York Avant-garde," demonstrates that the movement was not as egalitarian as it seemed at first glance. Judith Mayne also offers a feminist counterperspective in her essay "Women in the Avant-garde: Germaine Dulac, Maya Deren, Agnès Varda, Chantal Akerman, and Trinh T. Minh-ha," demonstrating that women and men have continually pursued differing avenues of expression in their works. Maya Deren, for example, became the first independent filmmaker to successfully exhibit her work, including perhaps her most famous film, *Meshes of the Afternoon* (1943), a sexual meditation on the role of women in the domestic sphere of 1940s America. In creating these early expressionist works, Deren was joined by a community of filmmakers who also sought to bring their own vision to the screen.

Marie Menken began her career as a filmmaker during World War II, working for the Signal Corps between 1941 and 1945. During her tenure in the military, Menken created and photographed miniature sets for military training films. She later created the animated chess sequence for filmmaker Maya Deren's *At Land* (1944), and photographed *Geography of the Body* (1943) for her husband, Willard Maas. As the fifties progressed, Menken made an entrancing series of short films, including *Dwightiana* (1959), a brief animated short film in which beads, stones, and other everyday objects take on a life of their own; *Hurry! Hurry!* (1957), in which human sperm die in the attempt to replicate human life, set to a soundtrack of continuous bombing; and the lyrical and graceful *Glimpse of the Garden* (1957), in which Menken's camera sweeps through a small backyard garden as if imitating the point of view of a bird; the soundtrack of the film is comprised solely of continual birdsong (Brakhage 1989: 33–48).

Mary Ellen Bute was the first filmmaker to use electronically generated images, utilizing the output of a cathode ray oscilloscope. She named this process "abstronics," which signified a wedding of abstract and electronic forms (Foster 1995: 58–60). Many contemporary developments in computer technology in the cinema represent direct outgrowths of Bute's work. Sara Kathryn Arledge, working on the West Coast in the 1940s, created *Introspection* (1941–46), an abstract vision of the human body that has much in common with works by Menken and Maas. Arledge's 1958 film *What Is a Man?* is an exploration of the relationships between women and men in life and art. The film presents the viewer with then-revolutionary images of the nude human body as a site of performance and pleasure with a directness that is fresh and original. Arledge was a pioneer in this area, making films that were uncompromising in their graphic nudity, depicting sexuality as a basic human fact rather than relegating physical desire to the pornographic zone of the forbidden. Arledge's work directly tackles the issues of filmed sexual performativity and transcends the mere documentation of human sexuality through the mediation of her humanist gaze (Dixon 1997: 10–16). In addition, animator Harry Smith created a series of remarkable abstract animations in the late 1940s, and Kenneth Anger made his debut as a filmmaker with *Fireworks* (1947). The groundbreaking work done by these filmmakers freed the cinema of many of its imagistic and narrative constraints, but a new wave of filmmakers took this liberating impulse even further in the late 1950s, as part of the Beat cinema.

The Beat Filmmakers

The Beats were a group of poets, musicians, painters, sculptors, and filmmakers who rejected the materialism of post-World War II America in favor of a simpler lifestyle, living in cheap apartments, staging poetry readings, happenings, and film screenings almost as clandestine affairs for members of their closed community. As with the 1920s and 1940s experimental film communities, the Beat artists flourished on both coasts in the late 1950s and early 1960s, with the centers of activity located in New York City and San Francisco.

The archetypal West Coast Beat film, *The Flower Thief* (1960), directed by Ron Rice, exemplifies this rejection of conventional values in every aspect of its production. Shot on a nonexistent budget, using severely outdated 50-foot cartridges of World War II surplus gunnery film as raw stock, *The Flower Thief* follows actor-performer Taylor Mead, the Charlie Chaplin of the 1960s underground, on a series of picaresque adventures in and around San Francisco. The film has little plot and needs none; the title of the film derives from a random incident in which Mead steals a flower from a street vendor and then fantasizes that the police are about to arrest him for his crime. Escaping down the steep San Francisco streets in a Radio Flyer—a child's wagon— desperately clutching his much-abused teddy bear, Mead is at once pathetic and endearing, projecting an image of holy foolishness on the screen. As the film progresses through its 75-minute running time, Mead interacts with groups of roving beatniks, schoolchildren, jazz musicians, and North Beach hustlers to create a portrait of a man unfettered by the constraints of society. The soundtrack is an asynchronous mélange of Beat poetry, jazz music, and Serge Prokofiev's *Peter and the Wolf*, recorded on a primitive reel-to-reel tape machine. Considered perhaps the most uncompromising and genuinely avant-garde feature film of the early 1960s, *The Flower Thief* is a paean to the plight of the outsider in a world that is both unresponsive and unyielding.

Vernon Zimmerman's satiric *Lemon Hearts* (1960) is a 16mm 30-minute film produced on the astoundingly low budget of $50 (Sargeant 1997: 88). Taylor Mead plays *eleven* roles in this entirely improvised film, as he drifts aimlessly through the ruins of a series of soon-to-be-demolished Victorian houses, sometimes appearing in drag, sometimes in blue jeans and a sweatshirt. The soundtrack is once again pirated from jazz records, interspersed with Mead's own Beat poetry ("Oh God, oh God, my feet smell . . . I pissed on Jane Wyman's picture"). With his gracefully languid nymphlike body and a blissfully blank expression, Mead creates the perfect picture of absolute innocence in a hopelessly corrupt universe. Other Beat films from this period include Dick Higgins's *Flaming City* (1963), a hard-edged epic about Manhattan life on the margins, and Christopher MacLaine's short films *Beat* (1958), *The Man Who Invented Gold* (1957), *Scotch Hop* (1959), and *The End* (1953), which document the San Francisco Beat milieu. All of these films provide a tantalizing peek into the world of a vanished yet still influential subculture (Brakhage 1989: 115–28) and prefigured the major work that was to come in the following decade.

The 1960s Explosion

The 1960s are justly celebrated as a veritable renaissance period in experimental cinema, in which some of the most influential avant-garde works were produced. The Kennedy assassination and the advent of the Beatles and the Rolling Stones, together with the influence of such counter-culture figures as Allen Ginsberg, Timothy Leary, Lenore Kandel, and Abbie Hoffman, signaled a new openness in American culture. People began to reassess 1950s values, which had once been unquestioningly accepted, and an entire new wave of experimental cinema was born. Filmmakers in the 1960s, working in New York, Los Angeles, and San Francisco, created sophisticated distribution and screening outlets, especially the Filmmakers' Cooperative (a distribution facility) and the Filmmakers' Cinematheque (a film theatre, which changed locations numerous times) in New York, and Canyon Cinema in San Francisco. Both Canyon Cinema and the Filmmakers' Cooperative had one guiding principle in their initial bylaws: anyone could become a member simply by placing his or her films in distribution. There were no censorship or "selection" criteria of any kind, and anyone who had a film to screen was welcomed, regardless of the film's content, style, or production values. Thus, Canyon and the Cooperative acknowledged that, above all, the 1960s experimental cinema artist was a free agent, answerable only to her/himself. Previously applied standards were swept away, and an entirely new style of raw, tactile, "funk" filmmaking appeared.

Again filmmakers physically attacked the film, scratching it, baking it, dyeing it, using outdated stock when economically necessary or by deliberate design, to create a tactile viewing experience that reminded the audience repeatedly throughout the projection that they were witnessing a plastic construct, a creation of light and shadow, in which the syntactical properties of the cinematic medium were always an aesthetic consideration. Many mainstream approaches to commercial filmmaking and cinematography are appropriated from experimental filmmakers, including light flares, punch holes, leader streaking, and the defiant sloppiness of the 1960s avant-garde, when filmmakers sought to embrace the mistakes in their work and delighted in unexpected superimpositions and the chance manipulations of random editing, echoing the syntactical structures popularized by the composer John Cage and others. In addition, these filmmakers tackled themes of race relations, sexuality, drugs, social conventions, and other topics that the conventional cinema consciously avoided. More than anything else, the experimental cinema of the 1960s was an advocate for social change and complete artistic freedom.

Major figures of the 1960s are individually examined in the essays included in Part II of this reader: in "Pop, Queer, or Fascist? The Ambiguity of Mass Culture in Kenneth Anger's *Scorpio Rising*," Juan A. Suarez discusses Kenneth Anger's *Scorpio Rising* (1963); Suranjan Ganguly interviews the prolific filmmaker Stan Brakhage in "Stan Brakhage: The 60th Birthday Interview"; Jerry Tartaglia examines the pioneering queer vision of filmmaker Jack Smith in "The Perfect Queer Appositeness of Jack Smith"; Kate Haug offers "An Interview with Carolee Schneemann," the performance artist; Reva Wolf's contribution, "*The Flower Thief*: The 'Film Poem,' Warhol's Early Films, and the Beat Writers," demonstrates how Andy Warhol's films owed a debt to the spiritual freedom personified by the Beat filmmakers; and Daryl Chin, in "Walking on Thin Ice: The Films of Yoko Ono," and Yoko Ono herself, in "Yoko Ono on Yoko Ono," discuss Ono's films.

Yet in addition to these artists, there were a number of other influential figures in the 1960s who deserve mention. Since these artists are not examined in detail in the text of this volume, we offer a few brief observations on their works here. As was the case with members of the previous experimental communities, each of these filmmakers had an entirely original way of dealing with the possibilities the medium afforded; some were animators, some romantic diarists, and some pop satirists. Their visual styling is unique and immediately recognizable, and although they all worked during the same era, their films are one of a kind. Unlike the Hollywood genres, such as the western, the musical, the horror film, the war film, and the like, avant-garde films belong to no specific genre and thus make unique demands upon their audiences.

New York animator Robert Breer's works, for example, are elaborately structured free form affairs that either tease the audience with abstractions that gradually take on recognizable form or assault the audience with a collage of single-frame imagery, in which each image is entirely unrelated to the one preceding or succeeding it. Breer's first film using unrelated, continuous images was *Images by Images I* (1954); a mere 10 seconds long, the film is a succession of 240 stills. *Jamestown Baloos* (1957) is a collage film that incorporates seemingly disparate images into a mysteriously coherent whole; *A Man and His Dog out for Air* (1957) offers the viewer a pulsating, abstract line drawing that momentarily metamorphoses into an image of a man walking his dog at the film's conclusion. *Homage to Jean Tinguely's Homage to New York* (1968) is a document of Jean Tinguely's self-destructing sculpture performance in the garden of the Museum of Modern Art. Breer returned to line animations with *Inner and Outer Space* (1960) and to image-collage films with *Blazes* (1961), *Horse over Teakettle* (1962), *Pat's Birthday* (1962), *Breathing* (1963), *Fist Fight* (1964), and *66* (1966). Breer's *69* (1969) remains one of the artist's most accomplished works. Basic geometric shapes are rotated against a background of constantly changing colors. As the film progresses, the drawings intertwine, forming new configurations, interspersed with sections of black leader that divide the film into stylistic segments (Renan 1967: 129–133).

The works of New York 1960s artists Shirley Clarke and Maya Deren are well known and discussed in detail in this volume, but the films of one of their most talented contemporaries,

Storm de Hirsch, are often marginalized. De Hirsch's *Goodbye in the Mirror* (1964), to pick just one film from de Hirsch's considerable body of work, is a 35mm feature film shot in Rome that deals with the lives of three young American women living abroad. Other de Hirsch films include the brief abstract animation film *Trap Dance* (1968), in which the images are scratched directly onto the film with surgical instruments; and *Shaman: A Tapestry for Sorcerers* (1966), which extends the filmmaker's body into the performance space of the film frame as de Hirsch photographs herself, nude, through a variety of prismatic lenses and diffusion filters, presenting her body to the audience as the site of ritualistic display (Dixon 1997: 42–45).

The poet Gerard Malanga, perhaps best known as Andy Warhol's right-hand man during Warhol's most prolific and influential period as a filmmaker and painter, created a series of deeply romantic and poetic films of his own. In them, Malanga's onscreen persona of "the young poet" is foregrounded in each frame. Where Warhol's gaze was clinical and detached, Malanga's extravagant vision bursts forth in such films as *In Search of the Miraculous* (1967), an emotional, vivid poem of adoration for his then-fiancée, Bennedetta Barzini. One of Malanga's most ambitious works, the 60-minute, split-screen, two-projector, stereo-sound *Pre-Raphaelite Dream* (1968), documents the filmmaker's friends and extended family in Cambridge, Massachusetts, as they perform their lives for the camera (Dixon 1997: 107–112; Renan 1967: 203–205). Ed Emshwiller's dance films, especially *Dance Chromatic* (1959), *Lifelines* (1960), *Thanatopsis* (1962), and his epic film *Relativity* (1966), center on the body in motion, and particularly on dance as a location of celebration of the human desire for physical pleasure and self-expression.

New Yorker Barbara Rubin's *Christmas on Earth* (1963), created when the filmmaker was only 18, is a 30-minute 16mm double-projection film in which two separate reels of images of the human body in the act of making love are superimposed, one on the other, to create a landscape of desire that remains one of the most audacious cultural statements of the 1960s. Rubin photographed the images for the film in a free-form, documentary manner and then cut the developed reels of film into short strips, threw them into a basket, and drew the individual shots out one by one, splicing them together in random order. When the film was completed, Rubin instructed the projectionist to run the reels in any order, forward or backward, and put colored strips of plastic in front of the projector lens at random intervals during screenings of the work (Mekas 1972: 174–175).

Jud Yalkut's *Kusama's Self Obliteration* (1967) offers us a vision of the Japanese performance artist Yayoi Kusama engaged in a "self-obliteration" ritual, in which she paints dots of color on leaves, animals, various other objects, and finally on a group of people ecstatically copulating in one of Kusama's endlessly mirrored "Infinity Chambers"; they carry on making love, seemingly oblivious to Kusama's painterly brushstrokes being applied to their naked skin. By linking nature in the form of trees, flowers, grass, and animals to the human experience of performative re/production, Kusama demonstrates that individual identity is mediated by the performative act of "self-obliteration," in which individuality is subsumed in the larger fabric of shared existence (Dixon 1997: 193–194).

Stan Vanderbeek's experimental films anticipated many of the techniques we now take for granted in the cinema: computer imagery, the use of specialized projection environments in which to show his films and videotapes, collage animation from newspaper and magazine cutouts (which later became a staple on the *Monty Python* series), and compilation filmmaking, to name just a few of his contributions to the technological advancement of cinema. Vanderbeek even went so far as to build his own film theater, which he dubbed the "Moviedrome," a spherical structure in the woods near Stony Point, New York, where multiple projector presentations of his works played for rapt audiences in the 1960s. Vanderbeek's early films include *What Who How* (1957), *Mankinda* (1957), *One* (1957), *Astral Man* (1957), *Ala Mode* (1958), *Three-Screen-Scene* (1958), and *Science Fiction* (1959), all films using collage cutout techniques to satirize the American consumer dream. *Achoo Mr Keroochev* (1959) is a 2-minute black-and-white sound film lampooning Soviet dictator Nikita Khrushchev: whenever Khrushchev starts to speak during a parade or at the United Nations, he gets hit over the head with a hammer (Dixon 1997: 164–172).

In San Francisco, pioneering video and film artist Scott Bartlett created a series of challenging and evocative films in the mid to late 1960s, fusing video and film techniques in such early classics as *Metanomen* (1966), *Off/On* (1967), and *Moon 1969* (1969). Often neglected today, Bartlett's work was revolutionary both in style and in content and pushed the limits of film and video in new and often unexpected directions. In *Metanomen*, he used black-and-white high-contrast cinematography to create a hauntingly bleak boy-meets-girl antinarrative set to a sitar soundtrack. *Off/On*, an abstract, nonnarrative cinepoem that is at once haunting and mysteriously seductive, is the first experimental film that truly combines film and video imagery in a coherent whole. *Off/On* is for the most part comprised of a series of repeating film and video loops, which Bartlett manipulates through various rephotographing and video colorization techniques to create an intense cybernetic journey that challenges both the physical consciousness and the aesthetic sensibilities of the viewer. In Bartlett's next film, *Moon 1969*, he explores the sensory limits of the viewer: the beginning moves slowly from complete blackness and blankness to glaring white, with aerial footage of an airport runway at night slowly washing in and out. *Moon 1969* proceeds through a series of tempo changes until it reaches stroboscope intensity in its final minutes; the film triumphantly concludes with a long shot of the sun reflected in the sand at the edge of a beach (Dixon 1997: 21–25; Youngblood 1970: 318–312).

West Coast funk filmmaker Robert Nelson's first film was the intentionally primitive *Plastic Haircut* (1963), a 15-minute black-and-white short thrown together from a large quantity of material that Nelson shot of himself and his friends Ron Davis and William Wiley. This work was followed by Nelson's most famous film, *Oh Dem Watermelons* (1965), an 11-minute film featuring members of the San Francisco Mime Troupe in a brutal burlesque of American racism. For the film's sound track, Steve Reich created a collage of stereotypically racist Stephen Foster songs, coupled with a repetitive chant of "Oh Dem Watermelons," as a series of watermelons are destroyed, disemboweled, and exploded by the multiracial cast on the screen to the general delight and amusement of the film's participants (Renan 1967: 171–174). Also working in San Francisco, Bruce Conner created a series of frenzied collage films, using bits of old newsreels, cartoons, timing leader, and other scraps of film to create the landmark film *Cosmic Ray* (1961), which many observers consider to be the first true music video, scored to the beat of Ray Charles's pop song "What'd I Say?" Conner's films *A Movie* (1958), which is composed entirely of stock footage from old newsreels, and *Report* (1963–1967), which documents the assassination of John F. Kennedy in harrowing fashion through the use of archival footage, created a new style of frenzied montage that became associated in the minds of many with the films of the American avant-garde (Brakhage 1989: 128–147). West Coast artist Bruce Baillie created a series of gently pastoral films during the early days of the Canyon Cinema Cooperative (which Baillie helped found), such as *To Parsifal* (1963), *Mass for the Dakota Sioux* (1963–1964) and *Quixote* (1964–1965), all of which celebrate indigenous American culture.

Finally, Ben Van Meter, a West Coast filmmaker most active in the 1960s, created a gorgeous series of films that celebrate the human body: *The Poon-Tang Trilogy* (1964), *Colorfilm* (1964–1965), *Olds-Mo-Bile* (1965), and his epic *Acid Mantra: Re-Birth of a Nation* (1966–1968),

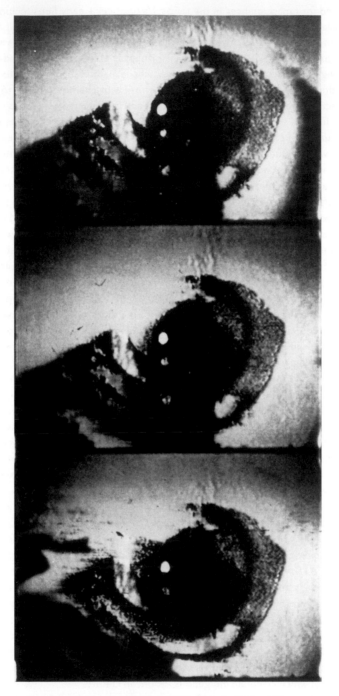

1. Scott Bartlett's *Off/On* (1967). Courtesy Anthology Film Archives; reprinted by permission.

a 47-minute color and black-and-white work of such propulsive energy and intensity that viewing it is almost an exhausting experience. Starting with footage of various rock bands in concert, including the Velvet Underground and the Grateful Dead, the film superimposes as many as 10 layers of images simultaneously to engulf the viewer in a cornucopia of sight and sound, all leading up to a climactic orgy during a summer picnic at a party in the Bay area countryside. As the couples engage in ecstatic sexual unions, Van Meter hand drips blobs of colored paint directly on the film, as if to suggest the intensity of the energy that is being released by his performers. As the film ends, we see family units in the nude, swimming, playing Frisbee, relaxing, and walking in the tall grass (Dixon 1997: 172–176).

In all of these films, we see the element of *celebration* as key to the works' construction. Many of these films, especially Malanga's and Van Meter's, are deliberately anarchic, using over- and underexposure, multiple superimpositions, color and black-and-white film intercut at random intervals, and other aggressive visual strategies to delight and seduce the viewer. In addition, most of these filmmakers, both in New York and in Los Angeles, explored issues of sexuality with a candor that seems revolutionary even today, and made their films with a rough-and-ready abandon that recalls the "anything goes" strategy of Rice's film *The Flower Thief*. In many cases, these films were cut in the camera, with not one frame of film wasted in the editing process; the filmmakers would simply string the reels of exposed film together to form a longer work and then present it with an accompanying soundtrack. Other artists, such as Conner and Breer, took a more meticulous approach to their work, crafting their brief films with a sculptural intensity that was at that time unprecedented. Conner's *Cosmic Ray*, for example, contains numerous levels of superimposition throughout its 3-minute running time, and each level is edited with an almost manic intensity.

The Structuralist Movement

In New York in the late 1960s and early 1970s, a new form of filmmaking began to take precedence over the more anarchic, romantic 1960s experimentalists. Dubbed "structuralism," the movement had numerous precedents, including the often motionless work of Andy Warhol in his early films. But structuralism pushed Warhol's motionless-camera strategy even further; Warhol used a "star" system, and his films were often driven by the sheer force of his performers' personalities. For the structuralist filmmakers, form *became* content, and the editorial and visual method of presenting the image often took precedence over the content of the film itself. P. Adams Sitney, in his landmark essay included in this volume, "Structural Film," examines the early works of a number of structuralist filmmakers whose most influential productions were created between the late 1960s and the early 1980s.

Michael Snow, the Canadian-born film artist who created his most influential works in New York in the late 1960s and early 1970s, became the key figure of the structuralist movement. As Scott MacDonald notes in "Interview with Michael Snow" in Part Three of this volume, Snow came to filmmaking not through an apprenticeship in the cinema but rather through an interest in painting, sculpture, and photography. Snow's breakthrough film was *Wavelength* (1967), which took the art world by storm and introduced a series of formalist cinematic strategies that would dominate experimental film production for the next decade. In *Wavelength*, a camera zooms with excruciating slowness across an empty loft with four windows, starting with a wide-angle shot of the space and ending 45 minutes later with a close-up of a photograph on the far wall of the room. Color filters are used throughout the film, along with different film stocks and a series of ghostly superimpositions. The jagged progress of Snow's zoom is interrupted by four actions: a cabinet is brought into the room; two women enter and listen to "Strawberry Fields Forever" on the radio; a man (Hollis Frampton) enters the frame space and then crumples to the floor, dead; finally, a young woman walks into the room, sees the man on the floor, and calls a friend to find out what she should do. Throughout the film there is a rising electronic pitch on the soundtrack, described by Snow as a "glissando," mixed in with the live sync-sound.

The critical impact of *Wavelength* was overwhelming. Many theoreticians considered it the most audaciously original experimental film ever produced and praised its rigorous attention to framing, color, and spatial detail. In Snow's subsequent films, including *One Second in Montreal* and *Back and Forth* (both 1969), Snow refined these strategies even further. *One Second in Montreal*, which is silent, is essentially a series of still photographs in which motion is imperceptible but nevertheless seems to occur over a long period of time. The shots lengthen in duration as the film progresses but then become shorter as the film concludes. The end result is mysterious and remarkable; it seems as if we have returned from a journey to a place where time and space have been immeasurably lengthened to create another dimension. *Back and Forth* is a much more brutal affair; for 52 minutes, the camera pans mechanically from left to right, then right to left, presenting the viewer with an ironic image of an empty classroom; as the film progresses, the pendulum motion of the camera speeds up until the classroom is simply a blur as the camera keeps whipping back and forth through space evermore frenetically. Just as the camera movement reaches its zenith, Snow cuts to a shot of the camera performing the same rapid back-and-forth pan motion, but this time from top to bottom and back again. Gradually, the camera slows down to show us the empty room as we saw it at the beginning of the film. Snow's next film was *La Region Central* (1971), a 3-hour epic in which Snow transported a specially designed camera on a moving crane to a mountaintop, turned the camera on, and then departed, leaving the camera to sweep through space photographing the sky, the earth, the sky, and the earth in a seemingly endless series of figure-eight configurations for the duration of the film. Much of the time, there is little or no image on the screen, and the unceasing movement of the camera makes the screen a space of constant, transfixing motion (Dixon 1997: 156–158).

Other members of the structuralist group include Hollis Frampton, Ernie Gehr, Warren Sonbert, and Joyce Wieland. Philip Lopate, in his essay, "The Films of Warren Sonbert," examines Sonbert's shift from a romantic diarist in the early 1960s to his more rigorous films of the 1970s and 1980s; while David Ehrenstein, in "Warren Sonbert Interview," allows Sonbert to discuss his evolution as an independent filmmaker. In the final essay of Part Three, Peter Gidal, a structuralist filmmaker in his own right, engages in a dialogue with filmmaker Hollis Frampton on his epic film *Zorns Lemma* (1970) in "An Interview with Hollis Frampton," and examines the film's carefully considered genesis in detail.

Punk, Feminist, and Lesbian Cinema

As structuralism flourished, a backlash was building and brought about yet another radical shift in avant-garde experimental cinema practice. Super 8mm filmmakers Beth B. and Scott B., Nick Zedd, and other late 1970s–early 1980s punk cineastes created self-consciously brutal and anarchic films, which echoed the nihilist attitudes of such singers and pop groups as Patti

Smith and The Ramones. Punk films were made with minimal budgets and structured with deliberate technical crudity to alienate and/or enrage the spectator. Video cameras were in their infancy, but Super 8mm sound equipment was just starting to become available and at a fraction of the cost of 16mm. These new punk Super 8mm films were thus different in one essential factor from their 1960s 16mm ancestors: they were usually shot with lip-synchronous sound, a luxury that few independent filmmakers could previously have afforded. The image quality of Super 8mm was, naturally, not as clear as that of 16mm, but this, too, became part of the appeal; the punk films were raw, unrefined, and confrontational. Not surprisingly, the punk movement was based, for the most part, in New York City.

Nick Zedd, in particular, saw his films as a reaction to the work of the structuralists and consciously made "trash" films in Super 8mm with such titles as *They Eat Scum* (1979), *The Bogus Man* (1980), *Geek Maggot Bingo* (1983), and *The Wild World of Lydia Lunch* (1983). Punk filmmakers Beth B. and Scott B.'s *Letters to Dad* (1979) cuts across the norms of spectator pleasures as 19 people look and talk directly to the viewer, who, in effect, becomes "Dad." At the end of the film, the filmmakers reveal that the actors have been reading actual portions of letters to Jim Jones that were written just before the mass suicide at Jonestown. *Black Box* (1978) is a brutal allegory in which an anonymous man is abducted from his apartment and thrown into a hermetically sealed torture device that assaults him with loud noises and flashing lights, creating a hell from which he (and the viewer) can never escape (Foster 1995: 29–31).

In 1979, punk filmmaker Bette Gordon directed *Exchanges*, one of her first films to represent women as sexual subjects not objectified by a male gaze. In *Exchanges*, women exchange clothes with one another in a performance that displaces voyeuristic pleasure as it deconstructs the representation of the striptease. *Empty Suitcases* (1980) concerns a multidimensional female subject—a professor, mistress, terrorist, and suffering artist. Gordon takes on the ultimate objectification of women, pornography, in *Variety* (1983), scripted by novelist Kathy Acker. In *Variety*, Gordon turns the gendered subject–object position around and constructs a woman voyeur of male voyeurs. The woman in the film becomes obsessed with pornography because she works selling tickets in a porno theatre (Foster 1995: 151–154).

But the punk movement was not the only new wave in 1970s experimental cinema. Many feminist experimental films of the 1970s and 1980s are responses to Laura Mulvey's article, "Visual Pleasure and the Narrative Cinema," which called for interventionist strategies against voyeuristic pleasure, the objectifying male gaze, and the objectified female body. Yvonne Rainer is a New York-based lesbian filmmaker who has been actively dedicated to feminist countercinema since the 1960s. In *Lives of Performers* (1972) and *Film about a Woman Who . . .* (1974), Rainer plays with the language of dominant narrative cinema. *Lives of Performers* centers around a man and two women who play themselves as dancers working for an experimental filmmaker (not coincidentally) named Yvonne Rainer. Intertitles break up the narrative flow by self-reflectively calling into question our spectatorship position. The performers confront us with questions of identification, asking at one point, "Which woman is the director most sympathetic to?" Rainer's involvement in the criticism of spectatorship is directly linked to feminist critiques of traditional cinema's positioning of woman as object and man as spectator.

Rainer's later films, such as *The Man Who Envied Women* (1985) and *Privilege* (1990), move beyond purely cerebral investigation of spectatorship into a critique of pleasure in film viewing. *The Man Who Envied Women* makes reference to psychoanalytic and poststructural theorists, such as Michel Foucault and Fredric Jameson, within references to François Truffaut's film *The Man Who Loved Women* (1977) and Luis Buñuel's *Un Chien Andalou* (1928), for example, to displace pleasurable viewing and move the audience into a critical stance. *Privilege* addresses film pleasure in the context of a discussion on menopause, lesbian sexuality, and women's community. Intertitles throughout the film display Rainer's distinct philosophical sense of humor: "Utopia: the more impossible it seems, the more necessary it becomes" (Foster 1995: 313–316).

Barbara Hammer made her first 16mm film, *I Was/I Am*, in 1973. The film re-enacts Hammer's coming out, showing her in a "feminine" gown wearing a crown and then as a "motorcycle dyke." In these early films, Hammer was directly influenced by the dream imagery of pioneering feminist filmmaker Maya Deren. *Dyketactics* (1974), *X* (1974), *Women I Love* (1976), and *Double Strength* (1978) loosely fall into the category of diary films of lesbian sexualities. Hammer's erotic films were some of the first images of lesbian lovemaking made by and for lesbian spectators. One of her best-known works is *Multiple Orgasm* (1977), which shows a woman masturbating. Hammer appears as the filmmaker subject/object of her own camera gaze, using a hand-held camera to record the film's images. *Sanctus* (1990) and *Vital Signs* (1991) use manipulated images culled from found footage, including archival X-ray footage and clips from Alain Resnais's *Hiroshima mon amour* (1959), intertwined with excerpts from Michel Foucault's text *The Birth of the Clinic* (Foster 1995: 168–173). In an interview with Gwendolyn Audrey Foster included in Part Four of this volume, "Re/Constructing Lesbian Auto/Biographies in *Tender Fictions* and *Nitrate Kisses*," Hammer discusses her 1992 and 1995 films.

The films of Sadie Benning and Su Friedrich blur the boundaries of autobiography, documentary, and fantasy. Benning's disturbing video *A Place Called Lovely* (1991) captures the filmmaker's childhood memories of her violent neighborhood, while *Living Inside* (1989) examines the difficulties of being queer in a small town. *It Wasn't Love* (1992) is a send-up of such Hollywood movies as *Bonnie and Clyde* (1967). The narrative focuses on two young girls running away together in defiance of patriarchal social norms. Characters in Benning's feature-length film, *Flat Is Beautiful* (1995), wear handmade paper masks throughout the film. The unnerving mixture of live action with the artifice of the grotesque masks makes the film at once surreal and directly accessible to the viewer.

Su Friedrich displays an uncanny ability to play with cinematic norms. Her early works are autobiographical and stylistically innovative, with frequent use of hand-scratched titles on black leader and appropriated female imagery. The autobiographical *Sink or Swim* (1990) is told through the point of view of a girl who recounts memories of her childhood. Friedrich juxtaposes images from family vacations with a voice-over of the young woman, who comes to the conclusion that her father cared more for his career than for his family. *The Ties That Bind* (1984) examines the life of Friedrich's mother, who lived in Nazi Germany during the war. The mother's voice provides the running voice-over narrative, which Friedrich punctuates with etch-lettered questions from the daughter. *Damned If You Don't* (1987) is an experimental narrative film exploring a nun's losing battle with her own lesbian sexual desire. Chris Holmlund, in her essay "The Films of Sadie Benning and Su Friedrich," dubs the work of Benning and Friedrich "dyke docs" and examines their importance as representations of lesbian cinema.

Alternative Cinemas

In the 1980s and 1990s, African-American experimental women filmmakers began to make significant inroads into experimental film production. African-American women were involved in independent film production as early as the 1930s, when Eloyce Gist, a black evangelist, directed and self-distributed such films as *Hell Bound Train* (1932) and *Verdict Not Guilty* (1932–1933). Such scholars as Pearl Bowser, Jacqueline Bobo, and Alexandra Juhasz are actively uncovering the lineage of previously unknown, neglected, forgotten, or marginalized black women directors. Grouping black women directors may seem essentialist at first glance; however, as Gloria J. Gibson demonstrates in her essay, "Black Women's Independent Cinema," these films display a consistent black feminist cultural ideology, even as they are drawn from a multiplicity of personal and cultural experiences. One commonality that black women filmmakers face, however, is essentialist by nature: race and gender discrimination. Another commonality among black women filmmakers is the desire to represent images that are oppositional and corrective to Hollywood stereotypes, silences, and omissions. Zora Neale Hurston, for example, studied anthropology and subsequently made a series of independent experimental documentary films on the lives of African-Americans. Her films break the rules of observational documentary as she interacts with her subjects as a coparticipant. Similarly, Camille Billops developed a performative and deeply personal approach to personal documentary with such films as *Finding Christa* (1991) and *Suzanne, Suzanne* (1982), both codirected with James V. Hatch.

Michelle Parkerson released *Storme: The Lady of the Jewel Box* (1987), a portrait of female-to-male drag king Storme DeLarverie. In 1979, Alile Sharon Larkin self produced *A Different Image*, with the aid of the Black Filmmakers' Foundation, which she cofounded. Larkin's experimental films explore the history of black female representation, as do the films of Maureen Blackwood, a black British director who cofounded Sankofa, a black British film collective. Blackwood's *Perfect Image?* (1988) uses experimental film techniques to explore and expose stereotypes of black women (Dixon 1995–1996: 131–143). One of the strongest voices in this area is that of Ngozi Onwurah, another black British filmmaker, whose *And Still I Rise* (1993) critiques colonialist documentary practice. *Coffee Colored Children* (1988) and *The Body Beautiful* explore black corporeal space as they blur boundaries between experimental, autobiographical, and documentary cinema (Foster 1997a: 24–42).

During the 1980s and 1990s, queer cinema also saw a rise in production and distribution. Derek Jarman's highly personal and experimental films, including *The Last of England* (1987), *Queer Edward II* (1991), and *Caravaggio* (1986), consolidated his reputation as one of the foremost queer cinema artists of the twentieth century. Richly detailed and vividly colorful (Jarman began his career as a production designer for director Ken Russell), Jarman's films synthesize Super 8mm home movies, gay erotica, and staged narrative sequences, moving easily across time and space to create multilevel works that are at once theatrical and intensely visual. Diagnosed with AIDS in the early 1990s, Jarman faced his own impending blindness with *Blue* (1993), a film composed solely of a fixed blue screen accompanied by Jarman's autobiographical narration. Jarman's death in 1994 dealt a great blow to the experimental film world and the gay, lesbian, bisexual, and transgendered community. Nevertheless, his films continue to inform and inspire the work of other filmmakers (see Lippard 1996).

Queer cinema in the 1990s was energized by gay collectivism, activism, and the fight against AIDS. Perhaps no films have been as controversial as those of Isaac Julien and Marlon Riggs. The final essay of Part Four, Kobena Mercer's "Dark and Lovely Too: Black Gay Men in Independent Film," explores identity issues in the films of Marlon Riggs and Isaac Julien. Mercer, like many queer theorists, dislodges essentialist and overdetermined categories of identity. Mercer explains that identities are not necessarily biologically constructed, but rather culturally performed. Experimental filmmakers and queer theorists have been wrestling with identity markers and their meanings because of the rise of political activism and alliances across such identity markers as race, class, and sexuality, especially at the turn of the twenty-first century.

Because of the rise in experimental filmmaking in the 1990s and the early years of the twenty-first century, it would be impossible to mention every significant experimental filmmaker of the contemporary era, just as it is impossible to catalogue the enormous number of deeply personal, experimental, and independent filmmakers of the past. Instead, this volume is designed to offer the reader some signposts to guide them through the plethora of experimental films and their makers. As this introduction demonstrates, independent filmmakers thrive where there is community. In the digital age, experimental filmmakers are finding one another in enclaves in New York, Amsterdam, Berlin, Paris, and in small towns and communities around the world. While distribution still poses significant challenges, self-distribution on the web is on the rise. Museums and colleges are responding to a renewed interest from young people who are searching for an authentic personal cinema and finding out about experimental films and filmmakers.

What we hope to accomplish with this volume, then, is an introduction to the debate and practice of experimental cinema, from the 1920s to the present, demonstrating how it remains always slightly ahead of the curve, tackling subjects that the mainstream cinema finds either taboo or unprofitable. The experimental cinema is a cinema of poets and artists who strive to create personal works in a medium that is both expensive and ephemeral. But the vitality of their vision can be measured by the influence their films have on those who view these alternative visions, which show us a life beyond that offered by the commercial cinema. Experimental cinema, finally, is the domain of the personal, rather than the corporate, vision. It is this individuality and uncompromising honesty that this reader explores and celebrates.

PART ONE

ORIGINS OF THE AMERICAN AVANT-GARDE CINEMA, 1920–1959

Introduction

The essays in this section describe and define the origins of experimental film practice from both historical and theoretical perspectives. In the first piece, "The First American Film Avant-garde, 1919–1945," Jan-Christopher Horak notes that many filmmakers who are now routinely classified as experimental or avant-garde artists actually thought of themselves as "amateurs" or "dabblers" in film. Their self-description as amateurs implied artistic integrity and was predicated on a self-definition in opposition to the commercial film industry. Only later would these same filmmakers come to be known as the first wave of the American avant-garde. These filmmakers, Horak argues, were largely pioneers of film abstraction, animation, parody, symbolism, and surrealism. From the earliest days of what is now known as avant-garde filmmaking, filmmakers relied on communities that were loosely connected to distribution and exhibition venues. Horak considers the importance of amateur film clubs and cinema clubs, as well as the first journals that promoted film experimentation, such as *Close-up* and *Film Art*. In addition, Horak notes that such exhibition venues as the Museum of Modern Art, the first to have a film department (in 1935), were largely Eurocentric in their programming. Nevertheless, the works of European cinepoets, such as Germaine Dulac and René Clair, were shown alongside those of American filmmakers, such as Slavko Vorkapich and Robert Florey.

The second article in this section, "Notes on the New American Cinema" by filmmaker Jonas Mekas, provides an important contrast and complement to Horak's essay. Mekas's essay reads like a manifesto, a call to arms, whose audience is the experimental film community. Jonas Mekas, who cofounded the film journal *Film Culture*, calls for critics to keep out of the emerging art form, which he poetically terms a "new bud." Implicit in his essay is the fear that too much emphasis on criticism—with its aesthetic labels, privilege of form over content, and tendency toward canon formation—is a menace to the New American Cinema. Mekas calls for purist cinema, and he sees the New American Cinema as an *ethical* movement more than as a conscious anti-Hollywood movement. In "Notes on the New American Cinema," Mekas distinguishes himself from critics and their abstract theories. Mekas cites Siegfried Kracaeur as a model for the "living thing" he calls the New American Cinema, a cinema free of literary and theatrical ideas. Mekas champions the work of Stan Vanderbeek, Marie Menken, Ron Rice, and John Cassavetes in this egalitarian manifesto. He finds a *morality* in trying new approaches. It is important for the reader to be aware that Jonas Mekas has had an immense impact on the distribution and dissemination of independent cinema, from his long-running column "Movie Journal" in the *Village Voice* to his cofounding of the Filmmakers' Cooperative and later the Anthology Film Archives, which now houses and screens the world's largest collection of experimental cinema.

Lauren Rabinovitz's essay, "The Woman Filmmaker in the New York Avant-garde," moves the reader into a feminist perspective of the origins of the New American Cinema. Rabinovitz, writing from the perspective of a late twentieth-century critic and feminist historian, begins with the story of a baby shower for Bebe Baron, an experimental music artist. The shower, hosted by Maya Deren, was attended by Anaïs Nin, Shirley Clarke, Betty Ferguson, Storm de Hirsch, and other members of a community of women who supported one another and, as Rabinovitz argues, provided role models for one another in a male-dominated arena. Rabinovitz uses the baby shower as a central motif in her study of the cultural contradictions of being an artist and a traditional female, a mother, a nurturer. One of the most important points in Rabinovitz's essay is that female artists and filmmakers found points of resistance even within a system that constructed their identities from a patriarchal perspective. Though being an artist was considered masculine, Rabinovitz argues, Maya Deren managed to portray herself as the romantic type; Shirley Clarke took on the role of the female beatnik; and Joyce Wieland, to some extent, became the Earth Mother that she was labeled. Nevertheless, as Rabinovitz carefully notes, their films "articulated positions for a *refusal* of the male gaze." Though contained and categorized, excluded and sometimes marginalized, Deren, Clarke, and Wieland ultimately triumphed in that their works provide a legacy of feminist avant-garde film practice.

The final essay in Part One, "Women in the Avant-garde: Germaine Dulac, Maya Deren, Agnès Varda, Chantal Akerman, and Trinh T. Minh-ha" by Judith Mayne, is another contemporary feminist approach to the work and aesthetics of women directors. Mayne, like Rabinovitz, combines a historical and theoretical methodology to discuss a shared tradition she finds in the films of Dulac, Deren, Akerman, Varda, Minh-ha, and other women filmmakers. Mayne uses the work of Tom Gunning as a jumping-off point. While Gunning discusses the relationship between early "primitive" cinema and the avant-garde, Mayne finds the "primitive" mode of representation in use as female "primitive" narration across a variety of women filmmakers' works. Careful to articulate her use of the word *primitive*, Mayne notes that her use of the term evokes both early filmmaking and ritualistic traditional female activities. The playfulness and originality that Mekas called for in his manifesto is clearly manifested in the narrative style of a number of women filmmakers of seemingly disparate backgrounds, as Mayne makes clear.

Taken together, the essays in this section sketch not only the history of experimental film but challenge the very notion of a concrete history. There are multiple ways of historicizing avant-garde practice, and these essays demonstrate that experimental film history is continually evolving with each new wave of filmmakers and video artists.

The First American Film Avant-garde, 1919–1945

1

JAN-CHRISTOPHER HORAK

A history of amateurs

Contrary to the standard histories of American avant-garde cinema, numerous American avant-garde artists produced films in the 1920s, 1930s, and early 1940s. They include: Sara Arledge, Roger Barlow, Josef Berne, Thomas Bouchard, Irving Browning, Francis Bruguière, Rudy Burkhardt, Paul Burnford, Mary Ellen Bute, Joseph Cornell, Stanley Cortez, Douglass Crockwell, Boris Deutsch, Emlen Etting, Paul Fejos, Robert Flaherty, Robert Florey, John Flory, Roman Freulich, Jo Gerson, Dwinell Grant, Harry Hay, Jerome Hill, Louis Hirshman, John Hoffman, Theodore Huff, Lewis Jacobs, Elia Kazan, Charles Klein, Francis Lee, Jay Leyda, M.G. MacPherson, Jean D. Michelson, Dudley Murphy, Ted Nemeth, Warren Newcombe, Lynn Riggs, LeRoy Robbins, Henwar Rodakiewicz, Joseph Schillinger, Mike Siebert, Stella Simon, Ralph Steiner, Seymour Stern, Paul Strand, Leslie Thatcher, William Vance, Charles Vidor, Slavko Vorkapich, James Sibley Watson, Melville Webber, Herman Weinberg, Orson Welles, and Christopher Young.[1] Supporting these filmmakers was a network of exhibition outlets, art theaters, and amateur film clubs, as well as film publications. Together these filmmakers and attendant phenomena constitute an avant-garde film movement of more than marginal significance. Indeed, the sheer volume of activity demands attention.

To understand the dynamics of the 1920s and 1930s avant-garde in comparison with its post-World War II American successors, the different self-perceptions and material conditions of the two generations must be recognized. Both defined themselves in opposition to commercial, classical narrative cinema, privileging the personal over the pecuniary. However, the 1950s avant-gardists proclaimed themselves to be independent filmmakers, actively engaged in the production of "art," while the earlier generation viewed themselves as cineastes, as lovers of cinema, as "amateurs" willing to work in any arena furthering the cause of film art, even if it meant working for hire.

The aesthetic position of the second American film avant-garde, defined exclusively in terms of personal expression, led this generation to reject any collaboration with commercial or public interests, any utilitarian usage of the medium, be it commercial, instructional, or ideological. Ironically, their self-conscious declarations about their roles as film artists indicated a romanticized professionalization of the avant-garde project. Of his own generation Jonas Mekas noted: "To former generations film art was something still new and exotic, but for this generation it is part of our lives, like bread, music, trees, or steel bridges."[2] This professionalization of avant-garde filmmaking was, of course, possible only because the institutions providing material support for the avant-garde had expanded to include university film courses (offering filmmakers a place to earn money while making their films), government and foundation grants (allowing them to finance production), and nontheatrical film exhibition within the institutional framework of museums, archives, and media centers (offering filmmakers a place to show their work).

Earlier filmmakers, on the other hand, thought of themselves primarily as film amateurs rather than as professionals. The professional was an employee in Hollywood, producing for hire a profit benefiting the corporate hierarchy, while the amateur was concerned with the cause of film art. Given this self-image, the agenda of the first American film avant-garde could be much broader: to improve the quality of all films, whether personal or professional, to create structures for distribution and exhibition, and to further reception through publications. These cineastes moved freely between avant-garde film and other endeavors: documentary, industrials, experimental narrative, film criticism, film exhibition, painting, and photography. Many were primarily painters or photographers who only "dabbled" in film.

Lewis Jacobs, as a member of a Philadelphia amateur film club, noted of his group: "Our club is composed of painters, dancers, and illustrators. . . . It is our aim to emphasize a direction that will result in cinematic form."[3] As a paradigmatic example of the contemporary 1920s cineaste, one might fruitfully look at the career of Herman Weinberg: in the late 1920s and early 1930s, he worked as a manager for a "little theater" in Baltimore, wrote film criticism for various magazines, and made avant-garde shorts.[4] This range of activities in different cinematic endeavors was of course economically determined, since no single effort offered a livelihood.

For Weinberg, the avant-garde constituted itself everywhere beyond the realm of classical Hollywood narrative. The amateur film enthusiast, "the lover of cinema," was seen as the most ardent supporter of an avant-garde. As Col. Roy W. Winton, managing director of the Amateur Cinema League, noted: "We are concerned about where this Eighth Art is going and we are concerned about it aesthetically as well as socially and ethically."[5] In making avant-garde works, even the professional could become an amateur, as Weinberg explained in the case of Robert Florey: "It was only when he was working on his own, after studio hours, with borrowed equipment, scanty film, a volunteer cast and the most elemental of props, that, released from the tenets of the film factories, he was able to truly express himself in cinematic terms."[6]

Ironically, the desire to improve the status of the film medium on many different fronts was characteristic of both the 1920s European avant-garde—a fact that has been often suppressed by later historians[7]—and the first American avant-garde. Both European and American avant-gardists entered film as amateurs because economics dictated it. At the same time, amateurs-turned-professionals, like Walter Ruttmann, Hans Richter, and René Clair, among others, thought of their contract and personal work as of a piece. Whether "city films" by Joris Ivens or Wilfried Basse or scientific views of sea life by Jan Mol, these documentaries were considered to constitute avant-garde cinema. Thus, Europeans and Americans shared a broader, inclusionist rather than exclusionist view of independent cinema.

While the first avant-garde pioneered alternative forms that survived on the fringes of institutional power, it was only sporadically able to support itself economically. The avant-garde itself had not yet been embraced by institutions that could have created the material conditions for its continued survival. As a result of such factors, it is extremely difficult, for example, to separate avant-garde film production from the production of some documentary films in the 1930s. Roger Barlow, Paul Strand, Willard Van Dyke, LeRoy Robbins, Irving Lerner, Henwar Rodakiewicz, Ralph Steiner, and others not only earned their livelihood during the Great Depression through organizational, governmental, and private documentary film production, but actually perceived such activity as continuing their experimentation with cinematic form. A history of the early American avant-garde, then, cannot help but broaden its definition to include other noncommercial film forms (e.g., amateur and documentary films), as well as unrealized film projects, film criticism, and film reception.

In its earliest phases the American avant-garde movement cannot be separated from a history of amateur films. Indeed, the avant-garde and a growing amateur film movement were two alternative discourses on the fringes of the commercial mainstream that for at least a few years overlapped.[8] As C. Adolph Glassgold wrote programmatically in 1929: "The artistic future of the motion picture in America rests in the hands of the amateur."[9] Both avant-garde and amateur film initiatives received a boost after the Eastman Kodak Company's introduction in 1924 of 16mm film and the easy-to-use Cine-Kodak 16mm camera. The new technology was not only cheaper and safer than 35mm nitrate film; it was also in many ways more versatile, allowing for hand-held camera work and shooting on location and under ambient light conditions. The CineKodak made Everyman and Everywoman a potential film artist, and while some avant-garde filmmakers preferred 35mm, others, like Theodore Huff, could not have made films without the low-cost 16mm alternative. Thus technology played an important role in the development of this first avant-garde, as it did in the experimental film movements after World War II.

The first avant-garde defined itself in opposition to the commercial industry not only aesthetically, but also economically, producing films at minimal expense. Instead of large crews and expensive sets, avant-garde filmmakers worked with modest expenditures of money and materials, their films subject to the personal budgets of an amateur. When Slavko Vorkapich and Robert Florey completed The Life and Death of 9413—A Hollywood Extra (1928), the press continually mentioned that the film cost a mere $97.50;[10] Florey's The Love of Zero (1928) was produced for approximately $120.00, and Charles Vidor's The Bridge (1929) for approximately $250.00, plus sound work.[11] Roman Freulich produced Broken Earth (1936) for $750.00, after earning a net profit of $200.00 on his first short, Prisoner (1934).[12] Two independent features, Paul Fejos' The Last Moment (1928) and Josef von Sternberg's The Salvation Hunters (1925), were both released for under $15,000. Roger Barlow made a film for supposedly no more than four dollars.[13]

The cause of the avant-garde and amateurs was given a concrete organizational form with the founding of the Amateur Cinema League in 1926, led in its early years by the inventor Hiram Percy Maxim. By June 1927 there were an estimated thirty thousand amateur filmmakers in the United States alone.[14] In 1928 more than a hundred amateur cinema clubs existed in the United States and abroad, while the Amateur Cinema League had more than twenty-three hundred members, all of whom were producing amateur films.[15]

Amateur, avant-garde groups sprang up all over the country, some shooting in 35mm, some in 16mm, some only spinning grandiose dreams. In New York, Merle Johnson, an amateur cameraman, shot Knee Deep in Love (1926), an avant-garde narrative in which the faces of the protagonists/lovers are never visible.[16] In Burbank, California, the experimental production group "Artkino" was founded in 1925 by two amateurs, Jean D. Michelson and M.

G. MacPherson, the name suggesting a homage to Soviet cinema. They apparently produced at least half a dozen films, including *War Under the Sea* (1929), *The Trap* (1930), *The Power of Suggestion* (1930), and *Oil—A Symphony in Motion* (1933), of which only the last-named title seems to survive in any form. According to Arthur Gale:

> This interesting amateur unit has made experiments of a wider range than any other similar group and has the most original list of titles to its credit. In all instances, experimentation has been concentrated on continuity structure, camera treatment and lighting effects rather than upon camera tricks.[17]

In New York, the founding of Eccentric Films was announced in 1929. "The first avant-garde production unit in America," they planned the production of an expressionist film with action "harking back to Freud's notebooks."[18] In upstate New York the "Cinema Club of Rochester" was formed in 1928 under the chairmanship of Dr. James Sibley Watson. In Philadelphia, Lewis Jacobs, Jo Gerson, and Louis Hirshman belonged to "The Cinema Crafters of Philadelphia", founded in early 1928 to realize "pioneer experiments in the new field of photoplay production."[19]

Professionalism was equated with commercialism, while amateurism connoted artistic integrity. This discourse also identifies personal expression with formal experimentation, a dualism repeated continually in contemporary aesthetic manifestoes and reviews, and echoed in the polemics of the second American avant-garde. The emphasis on formalism is apparent in Frederick Kiesler's comment: "In the film, as in every other art, everything depends on *how* its mediums (means) are utilized and not on *what* is employed."[20] Lewis Jacobs concurred: "Such stuff as story, acting and sets are merely contributing factors to the more important element, form. We are trying to make film something restless, fluent and dynamic."[21]

Avant-garde Exhibition and Reception

Just as avant-garde film production created an alternative discourse on filmmaking, the "Little Cinema" movement provided both an exhibition outlet for avant-garde and European art films and an alternative to the commercial cinema chains dominated by the major Hollywood studios. The establishment of art cinemas was apparently first suggested in March 1922 by the magazine of the National Board of Review of Motion Pictures, *Exceptional Photoplays*,[22] which specifically tied the founding of a little cinema movement to the growth of avant-garde cinema:

> The showing of experimental pictures in a special theatre or series of theatres, and the building up of an audience, would naturally be followed by the actual making of experimental pictures. Directors and actors, stimulated by what they had seen in this theatre and encouraged by the reception of new work, would feel impelled to try their hand.[23]

Three years later the "Little Cinema" movement took off when the newly founded Screen Guild in New York showed a series of Sunday films at the Central Theater and at the George M. Cohan organized by Symon Gould. Other series were programed by Montgomery Evans at the Klaw Theatre (New York) in March 1926, and by Tamar Lane, who formed the Hollywood

Film Guild in the same month.[24] Gould, meanwhile, began the first continuous art film program, also in March 1926, at the Cameo Theatre, sponsored by the International Film Arts Guild.[25] Seating 540 persons, the Cameo scheduled many European and American films that had been failures in their first run because they were not "popular" enough.

In a speech before the Society of Motion Picture Engineers, Gould noted that the film art movement "had dedicated itself to the task of reviving and keeping alive classic motion pictures, as well as those films that may be noteworthy for the best elements." He concluded: "There is no doubt that this is the age of celluloid. We are only standing on the threshold of unforeseen developments in this momentous field."[26]

Meanwhile, in October 1926 Joseph Fleisler, Michael Mindlin, and the Screen Guild, acting as the Film Associates, Inc., took over the 5th Avenue Playhouse at 66 Fifth Avenue, proclaiming it the "first succinctly art cinema house in America."[27] The first film on the program of the new cinema was the re-released *Das Cabinet des Dr. Caligari* (1919), often credited with initiating a film art movement in the United States.[28] Within a few years "little cinemas" sprang up all over the country. The Art Cinema League, meanwhile, remodeled a barn and presented experimental shorts.[29]

In spring 1927 the Little Theatre of the Motion Picture Guild, under the management of John Mulligan, was opened in Washington, D.C., the first "little cinema" outside New York City. This was followed by the Little Theatre of the Movies in Cleveland in late 1927, and almost immediately by the Playhouse in Chicago. A. W. Newman, director of the Cleveland cinema, specifically referred to the exhibition of short films that "represent important experimentation" as a part of its mandate.[30]

In Hollywood the Filmarte was founded in 1928 by Ms. Regge Doran;[31] other little theaters were located in Boston (Fine Arts Theatre), Rochester (Little Theatre), New York (Carnegie Playhouse), Newark (Little Theatre), Buffalo (Motion Picture Guild), Baltimore (Little Theatre),[32] Philadelphia (Motion Picture Guild), Brooklyn (St. George's Playhouse/Brooklyn Film Guild), and East Orange, N.J. (Oxford Theatre).[33] The Motion Picture Guild, under the direction of Robert F. Bogatin, operated the theaters in Philadelphia, Buffalo, Cleveland, and Rochester. Michael Mindlin had his own subway circuit with the 55th Street Playhouse in New York, the St. George in Brooklyn, and the Playhouse in Chicago.

In February 1929 Symon Gould opened the Film Guild Cinema on Eighth Street. Designed by Frederick Kiesler, it was in the eyes of its architect the "first 100 per cent cinema in the world."[34] The New York Film Art Guild's inaugural screening in 1929, which was attended by numerous dignitaries, including Theodore Dreiser, presented two avant-garde films by Americans, *The Fall of the House of Usher* (1928, Watson/Webber) and *Hands* (1928, Stella Simon), along with a Soviet feature, *Two Days* (1927). The premiere led the National Board of Review to name *The Fall of the House of Usher* in its "a Calendar of Progress," noting that: "Amateur experimentation reaches a sudden peak in this abstract film."[35]

The Little Theatre in Rochester opened on 17 October 1929, with seating for 299. The opening-night program featured the French/Italian silent, *Cyrano de Bergerac* (1923), with a three-man orchestra in the balcony providing musical accompaniment. With its slogan "The House of Shadow Silence," the Little Theatre consciously set itself against large commercial theatres, by now all wired for sound. It was dedicated to showing "art films that appeal to the intelligent and the sophisticated."[36] In early 1931 the theater was turned over to Ben and Florence Belinson, who ran it for the next thirty-five years. Today the Little Theatre is the oldest functioning art cinema in the United States.

Not surprisingly, art cinema programs often paired American avant-garde films with European, especially German and Russian, features. Dreiser commented on this mixture in the Film Guild's inaugural program brochure, which referred to "the little cinema theatres, which should, and I hope will, act as havens for artistic American as well as European productions and such experimental efforts of 'amateurs' here as many have the real interests of the screen as art truly at heart."[37]

The Life and Death of 9413—A Hollywood Extra played at the Philadelphia Motion Picture Guild with the German/Indian production, *Die Leuchte Asiens/Light of Asia* (1926), while Robert Florey's second film, *The Love of Zero*, was billed at the Los Angeles Filmarte Theater with Gösta Ekman's *Klöven* (1927).[38] *The Story of a Nobody* (1930, Gerson/Hirshman) was exhibited with Paul Fejos' arty Universal feature, *The Last Performance* (1929),[39] while Charles Vidor's *The Bridge* premiered at the Hollywood Filmarte Theatre with another European feature.[40] Roman Freulich's *Prisoner* was shown at the Little Theatre in Baltimore with *Sweden, Land of the Vikings* (1934).

Ironically, obituaries for the Little Cinema movement appeared as early as 1929, when the movement was far from spent. John Hutchins' article in *Theatre Arts Monthly* noted in September 1929:

> That their bright day is done and they are for the dark, within only four years of their inception, is the unhappy comment on an art movement that from the first was characterized not so much by art as by a truly astonishing lack of foresight, and later by merely bad business methods.[41]

The fact that Hutchins wrongly proclaims the demise of at least two cinemas, and overlooks the imminent opening of two others in Rochester and Baltimore in October 1929, suggests that another agenda is at work. In fact, the author finds many of the foreign films distasteful, "static and inferior" (a consistent criticism of European "art" films from allies of the American film industry), argues that the Little Cinemas had "little or nothing to offer," and accuses Gould's Film Guild, for example, of showing too many Russian films. Indeed, it would not be inferior foreign films, but rather a worsening economic climate, that would eventually contribute to the demise of many Little Cinemas. But that would take several more years.

Art galleries were another potential site for avant-garde exhibitions. In many cases gallery organizers screened the films of the artists whose works in other media they represented. Marius de Zayas' New York gallery showed Strand and Sheeler's *Manhatta* (1921) in 1922, after exhibiting Sheeler's photography, drawings, and painting. Jay Leyda's *A Bronx Morning* (1931) was premiered at the Julien Levy Gallery in New York, as was Lynn Riggs's *A Day in Santa Fe* (1931), Henwar Rodakiewicz's *Portrait of a Young Man* (1932), and Joseph Cornell's *Rose Hobart* (1936). Presenting European films as well, Julien Levy in fact built up a substantial collection of avant-garde films, which he hoped "to display on request."[42] Rodakiewicz's and Leyda's films were also shown at Alfred Stieglitz's An American Place, occasional showcase for American avant-garde films.[43]

Another exhibition outlet from 1930 through mid-decade was the Workers Film and Photo League, which was allied with the Communist Party, USA. Apart from its film production and photography activities, the League also set up local 16mm film distribution systems and, in 1934, a national one.[44] Presenting to its membership Soviet feature films, newsreels concerning left-wing political actions, and evenings of avant-garde films, the League was instrumental in developing an audience for art films, especially at the Hollywood chapter, which had an ambitious exhibition program under the directorship of Bill Miller.[45] League member Tom Brandon founded Garrison Films in 1932 to distribute to League organizations.[46]

The largest audiences were undoubtedly the Amateur Cinema League's local clubs in countless American cities. The ACL had begun to organize a lending library as early as 1927, in order, Arthur Gale wrote, to "provide an adequate distribution of amateur photoplays, secure a dependable event for club programs and, as well, encourage new groups to undertake amateur productions."[47] Its distribution catalogue included The Fall of the House of Usher, The Tell-Tale Heart (1928, Charles Klein), H_2O (1929, Ralph Steiner), as well as Portrait of a Young Man (1932, Henwar Rodakiewicz), Lot in Sodom (1933, Watson/Webber), Mr. Motorboat's Last Stand (1933, Huff/John Flory), and Another Day (1934, Leslie P. Thatcher), all of which were screened extensively throughout the United States. The Fall of the House of Usher, one of the most popular, was screened hundreds of times in ACL clubs.[48] Although ACL's interests turned in the 1930s increasingly to travelogues and other forms of home movies, these avant-garde films were still available through the League in the early 1950s.

The ACL awarded yearly film prizes, adding the winners to its library. Photoplay and Liberty magazine also staged amateur film contests, which offered public exposure to independent filmmakers. For example, Photoplay awarded its first prize in 1929 to Ralph Steiner's H_2O, which in turn led to a review in the National Board of Review Magazine.[49] In 1937 an amateur film contest announced in Liberty magazine was the occasion for LeRoy Robbins, Roger Barlow, and Harry Hay to produce Even As You and I (1937).

Other kinds of distribution were haphazard, usually dependent on the filmmaker's renting the film to individual exhibition outlets. Symon Gould, the founder of the Cinema Guild, apparently set up some kind of distribution network, renting films to both the little cinemas and commercial theaters. However, any profits realized never made their way back to the filmmakers. Strand and Sheeler, for example, complained that their film Manhatta disappeared after Gould got the print for a screening at the Cameo Theatre in 1926. Robert Florey was even more specific about promises made to him:

> Early in 1928, Mr. Simon [Sic] Gould, then manager of the 5th Street Cinema Playhouse [Sic] in New York offered to give World Wide exploitation to my experimental shorts . . . and to that effect I gave him all the negatives and prints that I had I regret to say that I have not heard from Mr. Gould since 1929, I have never received an account of the rentals or sales of my pictures.[50]

When Frank Stauffacher, programmer for the "Art in Cinema" series at the San Francisco Museum of Modern Art (1946–1951), asked Gould in 1950 about the existence of certain avant-garde prints, Gould answered (on Film Guild letterhead) that he would be glad to undertake a search, for a twenty-five-dollar fee.[51]

Several film magazines were dedicated to promoting art films: Close Up, published in Switzerland in English; Film Art, published in London; Experimental Cinema, edited by Seymour Stern and Lewis Jacobs; and the National Board of Review Magazine, successor to the board's Exceptional Photoplays. The first three journals functioned briefly as critical voices in the discourse around both European and American art film, while the last continued its battle for better films for many years.

Close Up, in particular through its American contributors, Harry A. Potamkin and Herman Weinberg, documented the achievements of the American avant-garde from 1928 to 1934. The journal was initially impressed with the ability of the American avant-garde to produce low-cost films of high artistic merit, as evidenced in Kenneth MacPherson's editorial on Robert Florey's *Life and Death of* 9413—*A Hollywood Extra.*[52] In later issues, *Close Up* regularly published stills from new American avant-garde films, as well as reviews and news of future (sometimes unrealized) projects.

Film Art, published in London from 1933 to 1937, continued where *Close Up* left off, with many of the same contributors—Weinberg, Rudolf Arnheim, Oswell Blakeston. The journal, published more or less quarterly, printed not only reviews of American avant-garde films but also stills from films by Lewis Jacobs and Joe Berne and information about new productions.

Experimental Cinema, published between 1931 and 1934, concerned itself primarily with leftist filmmaking but also considered avant-garde efforts. In issue number 5, for example, the magazine published stills from Steiner's *Pie in the Sky* (1935), Jacobs' unfinished *As I Walk* (1934), and Joseph Schillinger and Mary Ellen Bute's equally unfinished *Synchronmy* (1934), as well as a series of notes on various avant-garde efforts, including the Group Theatre project, *Cafe Universal* (1934).[53]

The *National Board of Review Magazine* reviewed not only commercial Hollywood films, but also European art films, and occasionally American avant-garde films.[54] Shortly after the magazine's founding in 1926, the journal published a series of articles on the Little Cinema movement. Its coverage of avant-garde films was more sporadic, since it apparently limited itself to reviewing films that were being distributed commercially.

Amateur Movie Makers, the official organ of the Amateur Cinema League, on the other hand, originally focused on amateurs, among them avant-gardists, but shifted away from the latter in the mid-1930s. As the organization became aesthetically more conservative, its members increasingly preferred polished travelogues and Hollywood's professional discourse to formal experimentation. In its early phase, though, articles by Theodore Huff, Jay Leyda, Henwar Rodakiewicz, and Herman Weinberg encouraged amateurs to experiment with film form. The magazine also published reports on local amateur cinema club activities, including screenings of films from the ACL library.

Thus, while the first American avant-garde relied on an institutional framework that was less well developed than that of the postwar avant-garde, their efforts did not exist in a complete vacuum, as has been previously assumed. Avant-garde filmmakers, while working essentially in isolation, were able to screen their films through a number of outlets and saw them reviewed in a variety of magazines. A public discourse on the nature and viability of amateur and avant-garde film first appeared in that period.

To be sure, as the 1930s progressed and the Depression deepened, possibilities for film production, as well as distribution and exhibition, steadily declined. By the late 1930s the ACL had turned completely to travelogues, a number of the Little Cinemas had failed, and money and jobs were scarce. Filmmakers emerging after 1935, like Sara Arledge, Rudy Burkhardt, Joseph Cornell, and Francis Lee, produced their films essentially in a void, until they were discovered by the second American avant-garde. Roger Barlow, LeRoy Robbins, Paul Strand, Willard Van Dyke, Ralph Steiner, and others turned to government- or politically-sponsored social documentary as a means of expanding the borders of cinematic language.

It was, of course, at this very moment, in 1935, that the Film Department of the Museum of Modern Art (MOMA) was founded. Under its first curator, Iris Barry, the department's outlook was essentially Eurocentric: it exhibited the classic art and avant-garde films of the 1920s and 1930s, as well as the great silents, giving a new generation a film historical education. MOMA preserved the Berlin-produced avant-garde film, *Hands* (1928) by Stella Simon, but it also allowed the original and only surviving print of Jo Gerson and Louis Hirshman's *Story of a Nobody* to decompose in its vaults.[55]

Relegated to the dustbin of history, the first American avant-garde was not thought worthy of preservation. Many of the films produced by that avant-garde have been lost; others still await preservation. This survey must necessarily remain fragmentary.

Early Avant-garde Film Production

Although European art and avant-garde films aroused intense interest in America and resulted in a degree of emulation, American avant-garde films were unique products of American culture. The very fact that they were born out of the *reception* of European avant-garde films *in America* inscribed their position: while often borrowing or quoting the formal techniques of the European avant-garde, they demonstrated a certain wild eclecticism, innovativeness, and at times naiveté that was only possible for American filmmakers working far from Paris and Berlin, the centers of Western high culture. Contemporary critics condemned this eclecticism, as when Kirk Bond wrote of *Lot in Sodom*: "But by any worthwhile standard it is a chaos of conflicting mediums. Nothing is thought out in terms of any one, but the directors, like a painter with his colors, dip by turn into each, following the turn of the story."[56] Rather than denigrating American eclecticism, it might be fruitful to look at the early American avant-garde with a postmodern sensibility, appreciating the hodgepodge of styles (Expressionism, Cubism, Art Nouveau) and philosophical currents that make up the first American avant-garde.

The first American avant-garde—like the second, and unlike the European avant-garde—seems to have had an extremely contradictory relationship to the modernist project. Its utilization of modernist form in connection with expressions of highly romantic, even antimodernist, sentiments is symptomatic of this ambivalence toward modernism. A particularly American romanticism, which manifests itself in a longing for (wo)man's reunification with nature, informs the early American avant-garde's visualization of the natural environment and the urban sprawl. This kind of romanticism was quite absent from most of its European predecessors, with the possible exception of the French film Impressionists around Louis Delluc.[57] In European modernist films nature is seen at best as an abstraction, as an ideal aesthetic construct, not as a primordial force from which human society has been forcibly separated. While the European avant-garde is proudly modernist in its celebration of urbanism and the machine age, American avant-garde films are much more ambivalent, viewing the separation from nature with a degree of dread. This romantic view not only separates the early American avant-garde from its European models, but also connects it directly to filmmakers of the second American avant-garde, such as Stan Brakhage, James Broughton, and Ed Emschwiller.

Even within the first American avant-garde, differences can be ascertained. Avant-garde filmmakers in the 1920s produced experiments with the hope of distributing them through commercial channels; avant-garde filmmakers after 1929 produced their work with the expansion of the amateur film movement in view. While the former were often film professionals, working on their own time outside the commercial film industry, the latter were usually true amateurs. This loose division is also marked by the professional use of 35mm film stock versus amateurs' general use of 16mm at the very end of the decade and into the 1930s. Thus, filmmakers of the first generation, like Warren Newcombe, Boris Deutsch, Robert Flaherty, Charles Klein, Robert Florey, and Dudley Murphy, produced their avant-garde films and simultaneously or subsequently worked in the film industry in a professional capacity.

In 1929 Hans Richter created the first topology of avant-garde film for his seminal exhibition, "Film und Foto," held in Stuttgart, Germany.[58] In that exhibition, Richter differentiated between absolute *cinema pur* documentary and narrative *art cinema*.[59] Twenty-five years later, Jonas Mekas developed his own topology in his article on the American avant-garde. It included film drama, film poem, cineplastics, and document film.[60] P. Adams Sitney's topology in *Visionary Film* divides the avant-garde into five types: trance, lyrical, mythopoetic, structural, and poetic.[61] Dana Polan has rightly criticized this typology as incomplete and lacking "the kind of metacommentary that could concretize its categories in history."[62] Polan himself has suggested a typology that would take into consideration the "stances the films take (consciously or not) toward social experience."[63] He goes on to define the social and the lyrical, the structural and the physiological in avant-garde cinema, but ultimately admits that no topology can contain the diversity of avant-garde practice.

It might be useful to look at all avant-garde films as discursive practices in opposition to classical cinema. We might also fruitfully think of avant-garde cinema as "pedagogical interventions, as works that allow us to see cinema again, in places and at levels where we had ceased to see it."[64] Looking at the avant-garde in this way allows us to see these films as critiques of mainstream, classical narrative, and as cinematic discourses on a whole range of issues. The subheadings below reflect this range of issues and can be divided into sets of polarities, depending on their referents: urbanism/nature, painting/dance, fiction/parody, and poetry. Clearly the theoretical question of topology remains unanswered, but such a project would demand an extended theoretical discussion that is not possible here.

The Poetics of Urban Space

Paul Strand and Charles Sheeler's *Manhatta* (1921) was not only the first avant-garde film produced in the United States, and a model for subsequent "city films" in Europe and America, but also a highly contradictory film in terms of its modernist text. Previous readings of the film have failed to take into account *Manhatta*'s romantic subtext, which is visible both in the inter-titles, taken from the poetry of Walt Whitman, and in the film's overall narrative construction.

Manhatta was released commercially as a "scenic," a quasi travelogue, shown in cinemas as a short before the feature presentation, as was Robert Flaherty's so-called scenic, *Twenty-Four Dollar Island* (1927). Financed by Pictorial Clubs of America, and released by Pathé, Flaherty's homage to New York City, ostensibly completed for the three hundredth anniversary of the landing of the Dutch in 1626, was in many ways less rigorous in its formal construction than *Manhatta*.[65] Flaherty's film was eventually used as a moving-image backdrop for a stage show at New York's Roxy Theatre titled "The Sidewalks of New York."[66]

The film begins with etchings of the Dutch buying Manhattan from the island's Native American inhabitants in 1624, then proceeds with a series of drawings and maps of what the Dutch called "Neiuw Amsterdam." Flaherty next cuts to an aerial view of the city, taken three centuries later. The following images, mostly held in long shot, and often taken from skyscrapers high above the city, focus on construction: cranes and excavators digging, a dredger working the river, bulldozers, workers blowing out bedrock with dynamite. Intercut with these images are shots of traffic and bridges on the Hudson and East rivers, on the one hand, and skyscrapers, on the other. Through the use of telephoto lenses and his bird's eye view, Flaherty collapses spaces, creating canyons of concrete and iron and giving the city a feeling of incredible density and power.

Unlike *Manhatta*, then, which ultimately attempts a visual symbiosis of city and country, man and nature, Flaherty, the romantic chronicler of "primitive cultures" in *Nanook of the North* (1922) and *Moana* (1926), here presents urban civilization as completely overpowering and destructive of nature, as when a lone tree is seen against a backdrop of the concrete jungle. The people of New York play no part in the film. Instead, as Flaherty himself noted, it was "not a film of human beings, but of skyscrapers which they had erected, completely dwarfing humanity itself."[67] The natural environment, then, has been replaced by an artificially constructed, primordial environment. Only the film's final image, an extreme long shot of Central Park, brings the film back to the first shots of the Dutch invaders and Native Americans, reminding the audience of that great absence that informs the film—the separation from the natural environment.

Much more celebratory of the city and also more humanistic in its view of city dwellers is Jay Leyda's *A Bronx Morning*, a tribute to one of his favorite photographers, Eugene Atget. It is a lyrical look at his Bronx neighborhood in the early morning hours before traffic and pedestrians crowd the street.[68]

An important city portrait from the early 1930s was Irving Browning's *City of Contrasts* (1931). Released commercially by Sol Lesser with a superficial "comic" narration to improve its box-office potential, the film nevertheless merits recognition in terms of its cinematography and sophisticated montage.[69] Browning, a photographer by trade, visually juxtaposes images both formally, contrasting light, shade, and form through extreme camera angles, and semantically, contrasting various ethnic neighborhoods, skyscrapers, and city parks, the wealthy at Riverside Drive and the shantytown at Hooverville on the Hudson.[70] Its editing is thus much more ambitious than its soundtrack, creating a "New Realist" montage of the city's contradictions. The contradictory social forces and conditions visualized in the film are accepted as endemic to urban life. The unserious narration, added against the artist's intentions, positions the subject as a tourist, appealing to a desire for the exotic without forcing him or her to confront or analyze the juxtaposition of rich and poor, African-American and European.

The critic, film historian, and cinema manager Herman Weinberg produced at least two avant-garde films on the subject of the city, although the first, *A City Symphony* (1930),[71] was apparently chopped up to provide footage for the second, *Autumn Fire* (1931).[72] According to Weinberg, the latter film was a *romance sentimentale*, made not for public exhibition, but as a means of courting a woman he then married.[73] The film subjectively portrays two lovers who suffer through their separation until they are united at the end. Utilizing a Russian montage style, Weinberg intercuts continually between the two, juxtaposing their environments, identifying the young woman symbolically with nature and the man with the city (New York). That woman is identified with images of nature implies a whole set of textual referents: walking along the beach, gazing out her window at a field of flowers, she is inscribed as "the waiting woman," consumed by the emotional desire of man, an object of the male gaze. This gendered dichotomy is bridged by the film's reunification scene in a railroad station, which posits a form of narrative closure, cross-cutting images of nature (flowing water) with the station.[74] Thus, the film mixes elements of the city film with a portrait of nature, expressing a romantic longing for man's lost connection with the wilderness.

In the 1930s Lewis Jacobs also turned to documenting the city. While shooting footage for the Film and Photo League and working in New York as a cutter for advertising films, Jacobs began a project, As I Walk, which remained unfinished. It was to be a two-reel documentary of a working-class section of New York, following the "general trend of independent films to show the disgusting social conditions which exist in large and small cities."[75] A fragment, called Footnote to Fact (1934), was finished. A portrait of a young woman, it expressed in images the thoughts and scenes flashing through her mind: documentary shots of street life in New York. Jacobs' inter-cutting between shots of the woman and her subjective views of reality accelerates until the film comes to a climax.[76] The film's other three parts were to be called Highway 66, Faces in the Street, and Night Between the Rivers. According to Jacobs, the whole was to be post-synchronized, "using sound in a stream of consciousness technique, including snatches of jazz, natural sounds, modern poetry and inner monologues."[77] The articulation of subjectivity was to become a lifelong preoccupation for Jacobs, as demonstrated by his later film, Case History (1956).[78]

American avant-garde films about the city, then, always seem to be about man and nature in the city. Such ambivalence toward urban spaces is nowhere as evident as in Willard Van Dyke, Henwar Rodakiewicz, and Ralph Steiner's government-sponsored documentary, The City (1939), possibly the last of the real "city films." From the very beginning the film sets up a country/city dichotomy, juxtaposing the opening "New England" sequence to the following scenes of heavy industry.[79] The metropolis is seen here as overcrowded, noisy, polluted, and unhealthy; images of smokestacks, traffic jams, and substandard industrial housing predominate. Only in the latter half of the film is a new vision presented: a city without a cityscape, a city in harmony with the environment, a city replicating a small-town feeling, the urban jungle miraculously metamorphized into suburbs. The film advocates a form of city planning where living spaces and work spaces are strictly divided, offering residents of newly constructed, individual houses clean, green suburbs in which the nature they crave and are denied in an urban environment is ever-present. Thus, while The City's montage reproduces the formal aesthetics of earlier city films, its ideological position is far from modernist.

Toward the end of the 1930s, Rudy Burkhardt, a Swiss-born photographer who would become an important avant-garde figure in the 1950s and 1960s, made his first films with a 16mm camera. Burkhardt's city films, however, are not marked by the same ambivalence toward urbanism. Many in fact are conscious reworkings of the amateur travelogue, but constructed with an eye for composition, and for the unexpected, the incongruous, the off-beat. In 1936 Burkhardt shot 145 West 21, a little silent comedy about a domestic quarrel with some of his artist friends as actors. That was followed by Seeing the World—Part One: A Visit to New York (1937), a spoof on travelogues.

Burkhardt lived in New York City, and many of his early films were visual poems to that particular urban landscape. In The Pursuit of Happiness (1940), his second film about the city,[80] Burkhardt's camera focuses on crowds, showing their collective power through fast and slow motion, analyzing their individuality through closeup still photographs of faces. In between we see shops, advertisements, and buildings, but these seem to be mere obstacles for the ever-moving crowds of pedestrians, that flow of humanity which had been so invisible in the avant-garde's first city films. Possibly because Burkhardt was a European, there is much less sense of nature's absence in the city or feeling that subjectivity can only be expressed through a reunification with the environment. Instead, like the European avant-garde, Burkhardt seems comfortable in urban spaces far from nature.

Surprisingly, then, most American "city films" seem to lack the unequivocal celebration of modernism and urbanism found in European "city films." In *Rien que les Heures* (1925, Alberto Cavalcanti), *Berlin: The Symphony of a City* (1926, Walter Ruttmann), and *The Man with a Movie Camera* (1929, Dziga Vertov), to name a few of the best-known feature films in this subgenre, the urban environment is celebrated for its excitement, speed, and modernity, with few references to nature, beyond its role in leisure-time activities for Sunday picnickers. The early American avant-garde, on the other hand, laments its separation from the country, a mood nowhere more evident than in its lyrical documentaries of nature.

Lyrical Nature

If we theorize that many of the city films of the American avant-garde constructed a mixture of modernist formal elements and romantic desires, then the avant-garde's depiction of nature seems to be a more direct expression of American romantic sensibilities. Certainly, the documentation of the natural environment seems to be almost completely absent from the European avant-garde, with its modernist fascination with speed, transportation, and the urban environment. The only exceptions to this rule were the scientific films of Jan Mol in Holland and Jean Painlevé in France, whose microscopic views of sea life coincided with ideas about a new mechanical vision and were thus popular with avant-garde cinema clubs, allowing their very empiricism to be co-opted by the modernist project.

What connected American avant-garde filmmakers to Romanticism, however, was their interest not only in depicting nature, however abstracted, but, more importantly, in utilizing nature as a visual metaphor for the expression of human (mostly male) subjectivity. Henwar Rodakiewicz's supremely romantic *Portrait of a Young Man* (1932) indicates in its very title that this nature film is a reflection of the filmmaker's inner consciousness. There is little interest in documenting nature objectively; rather, it is the abstraction of nature that fascinates the eye, its formal play in an infinite variety of patterns of form, movement, light.

Ralph Steiner's H_2O is a perfect case in point. This twelve-minute film of water, rain, raindrops, pools, brooks, streams, rivers, and oceans moves from very concrete images of water in all its manifestations to extremely abstract images of the way water reflects and refracts light.[81] For Steiner it is in fact the ability of the camera to capture the play of light in water that becomes the film's text. Steiner's *Surf and Seaweed* (1931) is a continuation of his exploration of water and light, with its montage of closeup images of the ocean, low-angle shots of waves crashing against the rocks, and extreme closeups of the swirling patterns of seaweed.

Very similar in terms of its construction, but closer to the modernist project in terms of its thematic concerns, is Steiner's *Mechanical Principles* (1933). Like H_2O and *Surf and Seaweed*, the film's images of reality are iconic. In this case moving engine parts create highly abstract geometric designs, their sense of composition heightened by movement. In the 1960s this kind of film would be called structural, but in the 1930s it was considered an attempt to find the abstract beauty of nature, invisible to the human eye, but accessible to the camera lens.

Mechanical Principles's machine parts are imbued with a strong sense of the anthropomorphic, romantic endeavor to reintegrate technology with the realm of nature.

Much the same can be said for Artkino's *Oil—A Symphony in Motion*, which postulates an even more radical synthesis of nature and technology by discovering the origins of the latter in the former.[82] The film utilizes a first-person monologue (intertitles), spoken by the oil underground: "I am the pulse beat of green jungles stored in the ground beneath your farms." The monologue in intertitles continues throughout the film, as oil narrates its own rise to power as the force behind technological development. The images, mostly held in heroic high-angle shots with objects shot against the open sky, and strongly influenced by Soviet aesthetics, begin with a pastoral landscape of farms, cows, and farmers, slowly giving way (thankfully, since the soil is exhausted) to oil derricks. Yet these derricks are presented almost as natural phenomena willed into existence by the narrating oil, since they, too, are anthropomorphic, functioning with few exceptions independently of humans and sprouting from the ground like the corn that preceded them. The final third of the film is a paean to technology and the speed of modern transportation, as the filmmakers juxtapose antiquated horse-drawn buggies to motor cars, trains, and planes. A closeup of a turning auto tire, superimpositions in criss-cross patterns of fast-moving railroad cars, and high-angle shots of the oil derrick silhouetted against the evening sky become metonymies for a functioning technology in harmony with nature. With its optimistic view of technology and, by extension, economic expansion, it is also very much an expression of male desire in the early twentieth century.

Henwar Rodakiewicz's *Portrait of a Young Man* is, likewise, an intensely romantic film, communicating a desire for union with nature. The young man of the title in fact never appears in the film; instead, the film presents an abstract montage of the sea, clouds, smoke, trees, and man-made machinery, mostly in closeup. The camera eye as an extension of the filmmaker's body constructs male subjectivity. According to Rodakiewicz, the meaning of the whole arises from the sum of its parts: "In creating a film of nature that represents the cameraman's individuality, the importance of selection cannot be overestimated."[83] Divided into three movements, the film's construction and rhythm are modeled on that of a symphony: an adagio layered between two faster-paced sequences.

Another subjective view of the natural environment was presented in Slavko Vorkapich and John Hoffman's *Moods of the Sea* (1942). Vorkapich was an early experimentalist who later made periodic forays into avant-garde film practice (*Millions of Us*, 1935, being a case in point) after establishing himself as a "montage specialist" in the Hollywood studios. Having collaborated with Robert Florey on *The Life and Death of 9413—A Hollywood Extra* (1928), Vorkapich in the 1930s and 1940s created "montages" in countless films, collapsing space and time into a matter of moments, thereby visually circumscribing the meteoric rise of a Broadway star, the cross-country tour of a boxer, or the simple passage of the seasons.[84] While such sequences soon degenerated from the experimental to the conventional, Vorkapich sought creative expression in the production of his own shorts.

Moods of the Sea, a pictorial fantasy, utilizes Felix Mendelssohn's *Fingal's Cave* as musical accompaniment to images of the ocean.[85] Opening with a view from a cave onto the ocean, the film orchestrates images of a powerful natural environment: giant waves breaking on the shore, cliffs towering above the surf, a sea gull in elegant flight, clouds gathering above the ocean, a sunset on the horizon. The images, true to Vorkapich's interest in montage, are cut precisely to the music, each image sequence reaching a rhythmic crescendo with the melodies. The romanticism of Mendelssohn's music contributes to the film's overall romantic quality, but it is both the framed image from the cave entrance at the film's beginning and the constantly moving camera that emphasize the subjective nature of the camera's point of view. Thus, like Rodakiewicz's film, *Moods of the Sea* refers not so much to nature as to the human observer's experience of nature, the moods conjured up through a walk along the sea.[86]

Another film that seems to have existed between the commercial and the avant-garde was John Hoffman's *Prelude to Spring* (1946). Like many of the films discussed above, *Prelude to Spring* hoped to "not speak with words. It talks with images relating an eternal yet ever new story."[87] Presenting a series of shots of mountains, woods, and brooks, as the snow slowly melts, spring arrives, and a storm comes and goes, *Prelude*'s images are composed for their formal beauty. Many of the shots tend toward the abstract, especially the images of flowing water, an effect heightened by high-contrast printing. Unfortunately, the soundtrack's clichéd use of Sergei Prokofiev's *Peter and the Wolf* gives the film a literalness that its often striking images contradict.

Reviewing the gamut of lyrical documentaries of nature, it seems evident that all of these experiments are motivated by a romantic subjectivity that is particularly American in terms of its aesthetics. The level of abstraction may vary, the correspondences established between images and music may be more or less direct, but these films are romantic in mood and seemingly far from the European modernist project.

Painting in Motion

The earliest known American experimental live-action and animated film, *The Enchanted City* (1922) is, like *Manhatta*, informed by romantic and modernist discourses. Made by Warren Newcombe,[88] the film treads an uneasy line between Hollywood kitsch and avant-garde abstraction.[89] Newcombe animates what are essentially a series of paintings, sandwiched between live-action images of a couple sitting at the sea shore.[90] The paintings are highly artificial, seemingly closer to Maxfield Parrish than to modern art. On the other hand, Newcombe's monumentalized spaces, devoid of human life, evidence a primacy of the architectural over the human form, recalling the metaphysical paintings of Giorgio de Chirico.

In its narrative of a quest down a river through an enchanted city, the film inscribes a male spectator looking at woman; it is a journey through dreams, through man's anxieties and fears in reference to female lack, as theorized by Freud. One of the earliest images of stairs, a tower, and a woman's face sets the tone by referencing Freud's conception of the phallic woman and man's fear of castration. This fear of castration is almost obsessively reworked in numerous other images, in shots of phalluses, and in the way views are restricted to a tunnel-like vision, culminating in the image of the voyager being engulfed in a giant waterfall, Freud's metaphor for man's disappearance into the gaping black hole of the womb. There is ultimately an irrationality to the sequencing of images, a narrative that does not so much resolve itself as come to a metaphysical halt, a formal *deus ex machina* dissolving the image of destruction into one of redemption. Thus, *The Enchanted City* too straddles romantic and modernist discourses, its narrative of romantic desire fraught with male *Angst* and unresolved conflicts, which the film's final images of nature cannot contain.

Francis Bruguière, who had collaborated on *Danse Macabre*, had by the late 1920s wandered to Europe, where he produced an abstract film, *Light Rhythms* (1930), in collaboration with *Close*

Up editor Oswell Blakeston. In the film, Bruguière and Blakeston animated static forms solely through the manipulation of light.[91] Running eight minutes, the film presents a highly abstract meditation on the power of light to change perceptions of form. In this sense, the film can be compared to Lázló Moholy-Nagy's *Lichtspiel—Schwarz Weiss Grau* (1930), except that in the latter film, light is bounced off a moving object, whereas in this film the objects themselves never move.[92]

According to her own statements, Mary Ellen Bute began experimenting with abstract animated designs in order to visualize music. Like Oskar Fischinger in Germany, Bute was convinced of the formal possibilities of putting abstract forms to music. She joined forces with a young industrial film cameraman, Theodore Nemeth, to produce a whole series of abstract animated films. Through high-contrast lighting, color, and multiple exposures, Bute produced an effective method of creating animation in the third dimension, the length of the individual shots and their internal movement worked out with mathematical precision to visualize the accompanying music.[93]

Another pioneer of abstract animation was Francis Lee, who began his experimental work in 1939.[94] His *1941* is an emotionally powerful rendering of the Japanese attack on Pearl Harbor, presented in completely abstract form as an animated action painting:[95] an egg is smashed, red color dissolves over a globe floating in blue paint. Broken electric light bulbs litter the phantasmagoric landscape. Lee painted directly on glass, shooting from underneath to a light source above, giving the film's color a strong vibrancy, which is heightened by the extreme saturation of the colors, an effect made possible through Lee's use of the then-new 16mm Kodachrome film stock. As the film progresses, the primary colors of the first images give way to grays, blacks, and browns, as the world is metaphorically turned into a desolate, ashen battlefield.

While this description may seem to give the film a narrative dimension, it must be underscored that all of Lee's early films are essentially abstract, their effect based on the emotional quality of their color and shape rather than any anthropomorphic reality. This also holds true for *Le Bijou* (1946) in which diamonds, red, blue, and gold crystals, and disks seem to move through a barren landscape. The three-dimensional quality of the objects nevertheless increases their anthropomorphic quality, creating an unspoken narrative of pure cinema. *Idyll* (1948) presents a phantasmagoric underwater landscape, using water and oil colors on glass, as in *1941*. Here nature seems to be abstracted, reducing animal and vegetable life to its spiritual essence, where color rather than shape predominates. The vibrant, saturated colors of *Le Bijou* give way in *Idyll* to more pastel hues like chalk colors, the whole underscored by romantic music.

Douglass Crockwell began his experiments at approximately the same time as Lee, and both indeed enjoyed a degree of favor with the second American avant-garde.[96] In 1938 and 1939 Crockwell, who was a well-known and highly paid commercial illustrator for the *Saturday Evening Post*, produced his first animated films. Working with paint on glass, Crockwell created a series of short animated abstractions, which he later compiled into what he called *The Glens Falls Sequence* (1946).[97]

Dwinell Grant began making abstract films in 1940, shortly after Lee and Crockwell.[98] His first film, *Composition 1 (Themis)* (1940), used wood, glass, and paper forms animated with a stop-motion camera. The lines, circles, and squares vary in their shape and movement, as well as in their color, which is limited to primary colors. In many respects this work resembles a constructivist painting in motion—Mondrian on the move. Yet, while the film gives a sense of objects in motion (time), they do not seem to move through anything but a two-dimensional space, and thus lack the kinetic force of other abstract animation.

In *Composition 2 (Contrathemis)* (1941), Grant increases the sense of movement, utilizing pulsating lines that move in circular patterns and seem to breathe as they grow thick or thin.[99] In his next two films, *Composition 3* (1942) and *Composition 4* (1945), Grant began moving into an exploration of three-dimensional space. In *Composition 3* this was accomplished by using three-dimensional media—clay, wooden objects, and such. In *Composition 4* the third dimension was actually created by developing a 3-D film, which used a beam-splitter and was viewed through polaroid glasses.[100]

It seems no accident that a number of the avant-garde filmmakers discussed here were later accepted into the pantheon of the second American avant-garde. Except for Newcombe and Bute, both of whom seemed to be tainted by commercialism, the work of these abstract animators could be subsumed under the aesthetics of Abstract Expressionism, while they simultaneously functioned as legitimate heirs to the European modernist traditions established by Hans Richter and others. For the producers of dance films, on the other hand, such a European modernist tradition was lacking.

Terpsichore on Film

One of America's earliest avant-garde films is *Danse Macabre*. Made in 1922, it was a collaboration between Francis Bruguière, film director Dudley Murphy,[101] and the dancer Adolph Bolm. While at first glance *Danse Macabre* seems to be a simple recording of a ballet set to Saint-Saëns' music, the use of animation in its first scene and of multiple exposures to visualize death's threatening presence bespeak its experimental intentions. At the same time, its final romantic image of love conquering death once again reflects male subjectivity.

Another American avant-garde filmmaker in Europe was Stella Simon. A photographer, Simon had studied with Clarence White in New York in the mid-1920s but, as a woman, was unable to receive any training in motion picture photography. She thus resolved to move to Berlin, where she entered the Technische Hochschule in 1926.[102] There she shot *Hände/Hands*, subtitled "the life and loves of the gentler sex."[103] Unlike Viktor Albrecht Blum's avant-garde documentary of 1928, which shows hands at work, Simon's film is a narrative of hands, dancing through expressionist-influenced miniature sets.[104] The film was successfully presented in Europe and in the United States, although its earnings were never enough to allow Simon to make another film.[105]

The film opens with hands waving in front of black velvet, the implication being that these hands and arms will be synecdoches for whole bodies.[106] In the highly abstracted scenes that follow, the viewer sees the mating of male and female, a "coquette" enticing a group of males, a wild party, an attempted suicide through drowning, and a final reconciliation and celebration of life—in short, a story of a *ménage à trois*. Utilizing abstract sets, which have been reduced to constructivist triangles, squares, and circles, the film's spaces are further limited by numerous variously shaped masks. The film's abstract quality is further strengthened by Marc Blitzstein's abstract twelve-tone music.

Yet, at the same time, the film presents a "melodrama" of female subjectivity and *angst*. It is the drama of a woman who is afraid to lose her mate to another, more desirable woman, the melodrama of a woman who is continually playing out masochistic fantasies of defeat and self-mutilation, ever fearful that she is no longer the object of man's desire. The film's narrative closure, reproducing in its ballet of reunification a Hollywood ending, inscribes woman's desire for sexual harmony, and is indicative of Simon's romantic American approach.

While *Hands* can only be classified as a dance film in the widest sense, *Underground Printer* (1934) seems to have been more of a collaboration between filmmakers and dancers, although with a strong political intent. The film was directed by the photographer Thomas Bouchard in conjunction with the dancer/choreographer John Bovington, while Lewis Jacobs was responsible for photography and editing. Bouchard, who was best known for his photographic portraits of theater personalities, probably brought Jacobs and Bovington together. Bovington appeared in a solo dance in the film, while Jacobs took

> the grotesque movements and broke them up into their essences—mounting his sound and image with percussion shocks, throwing into startling relief the gyrations of the dancer as he spins and whirls as Goebbels, explodes as Goering, and exults as the Communist underground printer preparing his anti-Nazi leaflets.[107]

According to an ancient distribution catalogue, this was to be interpreted as "an artistic attack on the type of machine made thinking which produced the Nazi menace in Europe."[108]

Another early avant-garde filmmaker to attempt the motion picture visualization of dance was Sara Arledge. Like so many filmmakers in this period, Arledge had gone to art school and worked as a painter before beginning her film experiments. In 1936 she bought a 16mm Cine-Kodak Special, taught her husband how to use it, and began experimenting with multiple exposures, negative and positive images, fish-eye lenses, and colored filters.[109] Her first film, *Introspection*, was begun in 1941 but not completed until 1946.[110] It consisted of a series of multiple exposures of male dancers: their heads, legs, arms, moving in layered images.[111] In one sequence a body is wrapped in rags, much like a mummy, the body moving in a slow, dreamlike manner around its own axis. These images are intercut with negative images of hands reaching out and red-tinted images of a faceless body exercising. The repetition of movements, forms, and visual motifs makes the film almost structuralist in its concern with the cinema's formal applications. Unfortunately, as was often the case with avant-garde filmmakers, this beautifully conceived and mystical film was to remain Arledge's only completed film. A second film, *Phantasmagoria* (1946), shot on 16mm Kodachrome and "presenting some of the manifold possibilities of the motion picture as a medium for the dance," was apparently never completed.[112]

Ironically, none of these early dance films, except for the work of Sara Arledge, entered the canon of the second American avant-garde, even though the dance tradition would continue to have its supporters in the coming years, with many dancers (Maya Deren, Shirley Clarke, Kathy Rose) becoming avant-garde filmmakers. Again one might hypothesize that it was the lyrical and romantic elements in these earlier films that made them less fashionable. The same can be said for the experimental narratives produced by the first American avant-garde.

Short Stories

Not all painters experimenting with avant-garde film made abstract animations. One painter at the edge of Hollywood, both geographically and spiritually, was Boris Deutsch, who in

1925 directed a one-reel experimental narrative film, *Lullaby*.[113] Shot in 35mm, *Lullaby* was apparently produced with the participation of the Russian exile community in Los Angeles, including Deutsch's wife, Riva, in the female lead, and the actor Michael Visaroff.[114] Opening on a painted miniature scene of Russian Orthodox church steeples, composed diagonally, almost abstractly, the film cuts to the sitting room of a Russian Kulak and family, drinking and eating happily. In a corner a (Jewish?) maid is rocking the baby of the family. The peasant patriarch mercilessly mistreats the maid, who, as a result, suffers from horrible dreams, including one in which she kills the child. After a brutal beating, the maid flees into the night. In the last image she is happily lying in the arms of an accordion player who had earlier shown her a moment of kindness.

This highly elliptical narrative, shot in two scenes on a very minimal set, is articulated without resorting to any intertitles, while its flashes of interior vision situate the film in the realm of the experimental. These very short shots consist of some of Deutsch's abstract paintings, which spin around their own central axis, denoting the subjective state of the female protagonist. In another scene, reminiscent of *Caligari*, Deutsch's high-contrast paintings of masks dissolve in and out in a subjective vision of paranoia. In fact, the power of the visions, and their stark abstraction and horrific anguish contrasted with the relative realism of the rest of the film, create a narrative excess that the film's final image of tranquility cannot contain.

One of the most important avant-garde filmmakers to come directly out of the Hollywood film industry was Robert Florey. In 1927 he produced *The Life and Death of 9413—A Hollywood Extra* with Slavko Vorkapich. While simultaneously continuing to work on Hollywood film productions, Florey went on to produce *The Love of Zero* (1928) together with William Cameron Menzies, *Johann the Coffin Maker* (1928), and a city film, *Skyscraper Symphony* (1929).[115] The first two films in particular featured expressionistic sets (made almost exclusively in miniature and photographed with live actors through mirrors) and an elliptical narrative.

In 1928 Dr. James Sibley Watson, Jr., collaborated with Melville Webber on *The Fall of the House of Usher*, possibly one of the most highly regarded amateur film productions of its day: the chairman of the National Board of Review considered the film to be "the most outstanding contribution to motion pictures as an art form since *Caligari*."[116]

Watson's second avant-garde film, *It Never Happened/Tomatoes Another Day* (1930), is an unique example of dadaist aesthetics in early sound cinema: a minimalist and virtually expressionless acting style on a claustrophobic set characterizes the melodramatic love triangle. Although It seems extremely modern to today's eye, Watson considered the film a failure and suppressed its existence; it was recently discovered in the nitrate holdings of his estate.[117]

Another collaboration with Melville Webber, *Lot in Sodom*, was also shot in Watson's Prince Street studio, using a homemade optical printer.[118] It premiered at the Little Carnegie Theatre on 25 December 1933, along with Josef Berne's *Dawn to Dawn*, and continued to play in theaters throughout the 1930s and 1940s, becoming in the process probably the most commercially successful avant-garde film of the era.

Edgar Allan Poe was the inspiration for three major avant-garde works in 1928: "The Fall of the House of Usher" was adapted by both Watson and the French experimentalist Jean Epstein, while "The Tell-Tale Heart" was the literary source for an avant-garde short of the same name. Charles Klein's *The Tell-Tale Heart* was another very low budget off-Hollywood production reprising German Expressionist cinema. It is considered one of the most successful art films of the period.[119]

The film opens with a closeup of a pair of eyes superimposed over a handwritten text from Poe's opening paragraph. The film relates an insane young man's killing of an old man, and his eventual mental breakdown and confession to a pair of detectives questioning him. Two particularly interesting devices are the use of words burned into the image (similar to *Caligari*), and the intercutting of single-frame images flashing back to the murder to illustrate the subjective state of the protagonist. Another expressionist device is the extremely distorted closeup of the killer, as seen through a magnifying glass by the detectives, hoping to discover "guilt in his eyes." It is in fact the closeup of the old man's eyes and the superimposition of an image of a beating hammer that become visual tropes for Poe's literary device of the victim's beating heart.

Another experimental narrative, produced by the Cinema Crafters of Philadelphia, Lewis Jacobs, Jo Gerson, and Louis Hirshman, was *Mobile Composition* No. 1 (1928), a film that apparently has not survived. Jacobs describes it as a story about a love affair in which

> significant details, contrast lighting, double exposures, and large close-ups depicted the growing strain of disturbed emotions. In one of the scenes, in which the boy and girl were dancing together, the camera assumed a subjective viewpoint and showed the spinning walls and moving objects of the studio as seen by the boy, emphasizing a specific statuette to suggest the boy's inner disturbance.[120]

Gerson and Hirshman, who were both trained as painters,[121] apparently had a falling out with Jacobs over the conception of their film, because they decided to remake *Mobile Composition* without actors, calling it *The Story of a Nobody* (1930). In the film they attempted to recreate the subjective views of the two lovers, defining them metaphorically through objects, rather than actions. Utilizing a symphonic structure, the film consisted of numerous closeups, which were edited together through dissolves, laps, and quick cutting, depending on the rhythm of the scene.[122] Thus, as in *Portrait of a Young Man*, the camera's gaze becomes its own text, a direct articulation of the filmmaker's male subjectivity.

Charles Vidor's *The Bridge* was an adaptation of Ambrose Bierce's short story "An Occurrence at Owl Creek Bridge." Vidor's film uses a flash-forward technique to visualize the escape fantasy of a World War I Austrian deserter condemned to hang, which metamorphoses into a "life-before-one's-eyes" construction, similar to Fejos' *Last Moment*. Making use of real locations and nonprofessional actors without makeup, the film's quick cutting style, a montage of fantasy and grim reality, effectively created a mixture of objectivity and inner subjectivity, stretching a few moments into a one-reel film.[123]

Adapted by Seymour Stern,[124] Josef Berne's *Dawn to Dawn* (1933), at thirty-five minutes in length, was thought to be an "arty" featurette. It told the story of a young farm girl who comes into conflict with her authoritarian father over a young drifter, leading to the father's death of a stroke after the young man leaves. Presented in only a few scenes with a cast of unknowns without makeup, and virtually silent except for a musical score, the film's strength lay in its lyrical realism, its pastoral scenes on a real farm, which did not suppress the harsh reality of American agriculture before the age of electricity and machinery, and its explicit seduction scene. The film's central narrative conceit, the fear of strangers in a rural environment, struck a chord in the American psyche while almost self-consciously developing a lyrical realist aesthetic that nevertheless incorporated flashes of Expressionism. Eric Knight called the film "one of the most remarkable attempts at independent cinematography in America."[125]

Finally, the Hollywood stills photographer Roman Freulich directed a first short, *Prisoner*, which is apparently lost, although a complete script survives.[126] *Prisoner* opened at the Filmarte in Hollywood in July 1934, and was shown successfully in various little theaters, including Baltimore's.[127] Taking its cue from the last scene of Erich von Stroheim's *Greed*, the film concerns a prisoner (played by George Sari), lost in the desert and chained to a sheriff (Jack Rockwell). He dreams of escape as his captor sleeps, then awakes to find him dead, making freedom possible, although it is clear that the desert will not allow him to escape alive. Shot in an expressionistic style, with subjective images preventing any differentiation between dream and reality, Herman Weinberg rhapsodized about the film: "The world cinema at large can only justify itself to historians when it will give imaginative young men like Freulich a chance to put their theories into practice and, perhaps, help their bit to found an authentic film language."[128]

A remarkable one-reel short, *Broken Earth*, was Freulich's second experimental short narrative. The producer was Edward Spitz, who had produced Fejos' *The Last Moment* and who now planned a whole series of shorts on "Negro life" with Freulich and the African-American actor Clarence Muse.[129] *Broken Earth* related the story of a black sharecropper whose son miraculously recovers from a fever through the father's fervent prayer. Shot on a farm in the South with nonprofessional actors (except for Clarence Muse), the film's early scenes focused in a highly realistic manner on the incredible hardship of black farmers, with plowing scenes as powerful as those in *Dawn to Dawn*. The latter half demonstrated the centrality of the religious experience for a rural African-American population.[130]

It seems to be no coincidence that the experimental narratives discussed here not only attempted to expand aesthetically beyond the narrow confines of Hollywood classical narrative, but were also produced by amateurs or film technicians at the fringes of the film industry who were European-born or educated. Ironically, in the cases of Deutsch, Florey, Klein, Vidor, Berne, and Freulich, their European background and extremely low budgets conspired against what was probably their primary goal—breaking into the commercial film industry—and led them inadvertently to produce experimental narratives that would be valorized in the "art cinema" market. At the same time, these films, like those of the Europhile James Sibley Watson, are not simply copies of European art films. Their thematic concerns are for the most part American, their stylistic sensibilities a mixture of sophistication and naiveté, their aesthetics against the grain of Hollywood narrative. In contrast to these serious narratives, the first American avant-garde also developed a more satirical form of narrative.

Parodies as Avant-garde Critique

While the American avant-garde film of the 1920s seemed to focus more on abstract and formalist experimentation, moving from the modernist vision of Strand and Sheeler's *Manhatta* to the new realist abstraction of Steiner's H_2O, and from Newcombe's animated dreamscapes in *The Enchanted City* to Florey's expressionist *The Love of Zero*, the 1930s avant-garde seemed, in general, to gravitate toward metaphor and parody, possibly a sign of increasingly difficult times.

In contrast to the earnest metaphors of Watson, Webber, and others, parody was the preferred genre of Theodore Huff, another prominent ACL member, who in the early 1930s directed 16mm spoofs of Hollywood genre films. His first two productions, *Hearts of the West*

(1931) and *Little Geezer* (1932), starred children, giving the films an ambiguous sexuality and implicating the subject in the director's slightly perverse gaze, although ostensibly both films merely imitated the conventions, stereotypical characters, and naive plots of silent film.

Mr. *Motorboat's Last Stand* (1933), Theodore Huff and John Flory's 16mm silent Depression comedy, is a much less self-conscious work, an ironic comment on America's inability to deal with the economic catastrophe of the 1930s. Mr. *Motorboat* is, in fact, a humorous allegory on America's economic rise and fall, employing visual metaphor in the manner of medieval morality plays. Images communicate their meaning quite literally, like the bursting bubble that refers to the "exploding prosperity bubble" of the 1920s. After working as a film curator at the Museum of Modern Art, Huff returned to filmmaking in the late 1940s to produce, in collaboration with Kent Munson, *The Stone Children* (1948) and *The Uncomfortable Man* (1948).[131]

The photographer Ralph Steiner, who had made abstract avant-garde films in the late 1920s, contributed his own parody of American economic life with *Panther Woman of the Needle Trades, or The Lovely Life of Little Lisa* (1931), made in collaboration with John Flory.[132] The film opens with Jehovah creating the world out of a test tube and proceeds to present a short history of the universe. The birth of Elizabeth Hawes (1903) introduces the real-life heroine, whose career from child seamstress to Parisian designer of *haute couture*, via a Vassar education, is recounted.[133] Reminiscent of Robert Florey's *Life and Death of 9413—A Hollywood Extra* in terms of its art direction and elliptical narrative style, *Panther Woman* is a parody of the all-American success story, a young woman's fantasy of a glamorous career in an age of diminishing possibilities. Steiner also collaborated on *Pie in the Sky* with Elia Kazan, Irving Lerner, and Molly Day Thatcher.

While most avant-garde films discussed in this section are parodies of mainstream commercial cinema, two films can be seen as parodies of the avant-garde itself. William Vance's *Hearts of the Age* (1934) was, according to Orson Welles, a parody of *Blood of a Poet*.[134] Vance shot the film on 16mm reversal, after completing a parody of *Dr. Jekyll and Mr. Hyde* in 1932. The film opens with a positive and negative image of a bell ringing in a bell-tower. There follows a series of visual non-sequiturs: an old woman ringing a bell, an angel carrying a globe, Death stalking corridors, a Keystone-like cop, a hanged man, a hand beckoning from the grave. Like earlier avant-garde films, *Hearts of the Age* privileges obtuse camera angles, expressionist lighting, and narrative ellipses, utilizing these avant-garde techniques both seriously and with tongue in cheek.[135]

Near the end of the 1930s, Roger Barlow, Harry Hay, and LeRoy Robbins produced their own parody of the avant-garde, *Even As You and I*. The film was shot for the most part in Robbins' home, using leftover film scrounged from the film studios.[136] The three filmmakers began the project after *Liberty* magazine announced a short film contest sponsored by MGM's "Pete Smith Specialties" series. The contest in fact became the frame for the film's narrative.[137] Playfully ironic, almost dadaist in construction, the film narrated the attempts of three unemployed young men to make a film for an amateur film contest. After rejecting numerous "boy meets girl" script ideas, the three discover an article on surrealism and proceed to construct a script randomly out of paper scraps. The film within a film is an anarchistic montage of images, which acknowledges its debt to surrealism, Eugene Atget, Donald Duck, Luis Buñuel's *Un Chien Andalou*, Hans Richter's *Ghosts Before Breakfast*, Sergei Eisenstein's *Potemkin*, René Clair's *Entr'acte*, and Leni Riefenstahl's *Triumph of the Will*. It ends with the three would-be film artists realizing they have missed the deadline for the contest, and then attempting to invent a useful gadget for another competition. Shot silent, the film was performed with selections from George Gershwin's *An American in Paris* and, in the second half, Sergei Prokofiev's *Love of Three Oranges*.[138] Almost postmodern in its use of quotation, *Even As You and* I comments on the pressure of originality when a canon of avant-garde works has already been established, and to the difficulty of becoming a filmmaker and surviving economically in a Depression economy.

As is not surprising in a worldwide Depression, most of these satires have a political dimension, an implicit or explicit critique of social relations in American society and the inability of the economy to meet even the most basic needs. Like their spiritual predecessor, *Entr'acte*, they also question the role of the artist and the intellectual in a society geared toward profit. Unlike European models, though, they are willing to use metaphor overtly, almost naively, in the interest of social critique, their signifiers unambiguously literal. For the surrealist wing of the early American avant-garde, on the other hand, ambiguity is a virtue.

The Symbolic and the Surrealist

Best known as a painter and sculptor, Joseph Cornell produced his first film, *Rose Hobart*, in 1936.[139] A nineteen-minute (at silent speed) re-editing of images from Universal Pictures' fiction feature *East of Borneo* (1931), with a few snippets from scientific instructional films thrown in, Cornell's film, like his famous collage boxes, is essentially a creation out of *objets trouvés*. Completely eliminating any semblance of plot and dialogue, Cornell's montage of the ostensible heroine, hero, and villain has them moving in slow motion through empty rooms, caressing curtains, reacting to unseen events, never meeting. Their looks lead nowhere, their erotic desires careen into a void, while the audience is left with a mystery, as the film's purple-tinted eroticism masks unfulfilled desire. In keeping with the surrealist creed, Cornell subverts not only the standard conventions of Hollywood filmmaking, but also viewer identification, draining the gaze of meaning.

Jerome Hill,[140] later known for his film animation, began his career in the late 1920s, when he purchased a 16mm Cine-Kodak Special to shoot *The Fortune Teller* (1932)[141] in a village in southern France. True to the title, the film has mystical overtones, its narrative constructed from seemingly unconnected images: a young woman hanging wash, a walk in the surf, a consultation with a gypsy fortune teller, a man rising up out of the sea. Apart from their pictorial beauty, the film's images seem to hold some primordial meaning connected to fertility rites, to mystical love and romantic fate, yet they remain ambiguous, like the old gypsy's fortune as visualized in the cards. The film's visual text thus constructs romantically imbued riddles that remain unsolved, the stuff of dreams.

Born in Merion, Pennsylvania, in 1905, the painter and avant-garde filmmaker Emlen Etting graduated from St. George's School and Harvard (1928), then moved to Paris to study painting with André Lhote. He returned to Pennsylvania in 1932, where he started teaching art at the Tyler School of Temple University and making films, including *Oramunde* (1933), *Poem 8* (1933), and *Laureate* (1940), the last a Kodachrome film in collaboration with his wife, Gloria.

Being also a sometime poet and translator of verse by Paul Valéry, Etting combined his visual and literary senses in his films, creating film poems "wherein the picture, their sequence and development are used as in a poem as opposed to the customary story form. . . . In the film poem, music, the dance, the theater and the artist will all work together."[142] Accompanied by Alexander Scriabin's *Poem of Fire* and Gustav Holst's *Saturn* cycle, *Oramunde* presents (mostly in operatic long shots) a mythological Melissande dancing/walking through woods and ocean grottos, searching for her dead lover, Pelleas, and the lost wedding ring of her king and husband, eventually crossing the river Styx in a rowboat with a black-hooded man. *Poem 8* uses a moving, reeling "subjective camera" to signify a male gaze, erotically enticed by several women. The viewer ultimately participates in the murder of a seductress before fleeing through city streets.[143] *Laureate* demonstrates the hand of the painter in its spectacular use of still-lifes and complementary colors, as it metaphorically visualizes a writer's struggle to create poetry by having him (Etting himself) chase and confront various muses (played in classical Greek garb by Gloria Etting and friends of the couple) before receiving his laurels.

Christopher Baughman Young, the son of the landscape artist Charles Morris Young, made his first avant-garde film, *Object Lesson*, in 1941. An avid skier, explorer, and mountain climber, Young was apparently wealthy enough, like Jerome Hill, to finance the film himself. Billing it as "America's first surrealist film," he took over his own distribution after having "most unsatisfactory" dealings with a business partner.[144]

Shot in 35mm, *Object Lesson* begins with the statement: "Let us consider objects. For they tell the story of life. There is nothing without meaning—and the combination of things make new meanings that are too complicated to explain." The film itself opens with a series of natural landscapes in which there appear various objects: the heads and masks of Greek statues, swords, shields, violins, tennis rackets. These objects have been strewn about, out of place in the lush vegetation, creating a surrealist image of incongruence: nature and the detritus of man. In the next sequence, Young presents documentary images of the Empire State Building, hydroelectric plants, and garbage, followed by a metaphorical rendering of war. There is no dialogue or commentary, just an array of musical excerpts, including liturgical music, industrial sounds, Eastern European folksongs, and electronic music.

Virtually all the images are static and extremely well composed, like photographs. This lack of motion or action heightens the film's surrealistic aspect, allowing the viewer to contemplate both the incongruence of the moment and the juxtaposition of images in a syntactical construction. According to Young, "the objects must first be looked at as objects before they can be thought of as symbols," allowing viewers "to imagine their own story."[145] The filmmaker interprets the film's ending, where statues and objects "just have a good time being themselves and not representing anything," as a state where destruction and war have given way to objects and nature without meaning. Thus, Young wants to have the film read two ways: as a surrealist construct (*sans raison*), and as a metaphorical and poetic vision. His film also stresses the conflict between man and nature, articulating ultimately its belief in nature as a dominant and abiding force.

Lacking any kind of narrative cohesion, these seemingly diverse films nevertheless are evidence of authorial voices that foreground the subjectivity of the artist. There seems to be in the works of Hill, Etting, and Young a romantic urge to understand the mysteries of nature, and possibly to escape into a universe in which a natural order once again holds sway. In such a world the role of the artist is productively defined, his creation not a throwaway object of civilization, as in *Object Lesson*. Even Cornell's conscious deconstruction of narrative in the interest of subverting classical modes of address creates a new narrative out of the void, one in which the artist is central. The subtext in all of these surrealist films is avant-garde practice itself.

Notes

1   A first, admittedly incomplete bio-filmography of American avant-garde cinema before Maya Deren (1943) can be found in Jan-Christopher Horak, *Lovers of Cinema: The First American Film Avant-garde* 1919–1945 (Madison: University of Wisconsin Press, 1995) 363–382.

2   Jonas Mekas, "The Experimental Film in America," *Film Culture* 1, no. 3 (May–June 1955): 16.

3   Arthur L. Gale, "Amateur Clubs," *Amateur Movie Makers* 3, no. 2 (February 1928): 100.

4   Herman Weinberg, A *Manhattan Odyssey: A Memoir* (New York: Anthology Film Archives, 1982), p. 28.

5   Roy W. Winton, "For the Love of It," *National Board of Review Magazine* 3, no. 7 (July 1927): 4.

6   Herman Weinberg, "A Paradox of the Photoplay," *Amateur Movie Makers* 4, no. 1 (January 1929): 866.

7   Hans Richter provides a perfect case in point. While his early "avantgarde" films were initially produced as advertising films or prologues to commercial features, they were later exhibited and discussed by Richter and others as pure art films. See Jan-Christopher Horak, "Discovering Pure Cinema: Avant-garde Film in the 1920s." *Afterimage* 8, nos. 1–2 (Summer 1980): 4–7.

8   See Patricia Zimmermann, "The Amateur, the Avant-Garde, and Ideologies of Art," *Journal of Film and Video* 38, nos. 3–4 (Summer/Fall 1986).

9   C. Adolph Glassgold, "THE FILMS: Amateur or Professional?" *The Arts* 15, no. 1 (January 1929): 56.

10 See review of *The Life and Death of* 9413—A *Hollywood Extra*, *Variety*, 20 June 1928; see also Weinberg, "A Paradox of the Photoplay," 866; *Close Up* 2, no. 6 (June 1928): 76.

11 See *Close Up* 7, no. 6 (December 1930): 454.

12 See "Honor Without Peace in Hollywood," *New York Times*, 5 April 1936, Sec. X.

13 Sheldon Renan, *An Introduction to the American Underground Film* (New York: Dutton, 1967), p. 220.

14 "Cranking Your Own," *National Board of Review Magazine* 2, no. 6 (June 1927): 3.

15 See letter, Arthur Gale (Amateur Cinema League consultant) to Marion Gleason, 21 November 1928, Gleason file, George Eastman House (GEH), Rochester, N.Y

16 The film was shown at the Cameo Theatre in New York. See *New York Times*, 26 January 1927, review of *Slums of Berlin*. No print or negative is known to survive.

17 See Arthur Gale, "Oil Film," *Amateur Movie Makers* 5, no. 10 (October 1930): 640; see also "Homemade Locale," *Amateur Movie Makers* 4, no. 12 (December 1929): 797. No trace of the filmmakers has surfaced.

18 Founded by the playwright Lajos N. Egri, Herman Weinberg, the stage designer Robert van Rosen, and the amateur cameraman Merle Johnson, the group failed actually to produce a film, although Weinberg's *City Symphony* (working title *Cosmopolis*) was apparently scheduled for release through Eccentric. See "Expressionism," *Amateur Movie Makers* 4, no. 8 (August 1929): 526; see also *Close Up* 5, no. 4 (October 1929): 338–339.

19 *Amateur Movie Makers* 3, no. 2 (February 1929): 100.

20 Frederick Kiesler, "100 Per Cent Cinema," *Close Up* 3, no. 2 (August 1928): 39–40.

21 *Amateur Movie Makers* 3, no. 2 (February 1928): 100.

22 See O. Spearing, "A Valuable Service," *Exceptional Photoplays* 2 (March 1922); John Hutchins, "L'Enfant Terrible: The Little Cinema Movement," *Theatre Arts Monthly* 13, no. 9 (September

1929): 696. See also Michael Budd, "The National Board of Review and the Early Art Cinema in New York: *The Cabinet of Dr. Caligari* as Affirmative Culture," *Cinema Journal* 26, no. 1 (Fall 1986): 7–8.

23   Quoted in Hutchins, "L'Enfant Terrible," p. 697.

24   See Marguerite Tazelaar, "The Story of the First Little Film Theatre," *Amateur Movie Makers* 3, no. 7 (July 1928): 441.

25   Alfred B. Kuttner, "The Little Motion Picture Theatre," *National Board of Review Magazine* 1, no. 2 (May–June 1926): 3.

26   The full text of Gould's speech was published as "The Little Theatre Movement in the Cinema," *National Board of Review Magazine* 1, no. 5 (September–October 1926): 4–5. See also a report on the speech in "Special Theatres Urged for Artistic Pictures," *New York Times*, 10 October 1926, Sec. VIII.

27   "The Little Cinema Marches On," *New York Times*, 6 February 1938.

28   "The Fifth Avenue Playhouse," *National Board of Review Magazine* 1, no. 6 (November 1926): 4. According to Weinberg, the day-to-day operations of the 5th Avenue Playhouse were handled by Ed Sullivan, Joe Balaben, and Jean Dubany, with Weinberg serving as publicity director. See Weinberg, *Manhattan Odyssey*, p. 28.

29   *New York Times*, 6 February 1938.

30   "More About the Little Theatre," *National Board of Review Magazine* 2, no. 11 (November 1927): 5.

31   "Hollywood Notes," *Close Up* 3, no. 1 (July 1928): 74. While there were reports of the closure of the Filmarte in April 1929, the theater did continue screenings. See "Hollywood Notes," *Close Up* 6, no. 4 (April 1929): 78.

32   The Baltimore "Little Theatre" was founded by the management of the 5th Avenue Playhouse, and Weinberg was sent down to Baltimore to become the new manager. See Weinberg, *Manhattan Odyssey*, pp. 35–36, 47.

33   Letter, Arthur Gale to Marion Gleason, 21 November 1928, Gleason file, GEH.

34   Kiesler, "100 Per Cent Cinema," pp. 35–38; see also "Four Screen Theatre Being Built Here," *New York Times*, 9 December 1928, Sec. II.

35   "The Motion Picture: A Calendar of Progress," *Theatre Arts Monthly* 13, no. 9 (September 1929): 644.

36   See program brochure for twentieth anniversary of the Little Theatre (1929–1949), published by the Civic Association of Rochester, vertical file, GEH.

37   See inaugural program of the Eighth Street Film Guild Cinema, 1 February 1929, vertical file, New York Public Library, Performing Arts Library at Lincoln Center, New York.

38   Brian Taves gives an extensive listing of the playdates of Florey's avant-garde films in Chapter 4 of Jan-Christopher Horak, *Lovers of Cinema: The First American Film Avant-garde 1919–1945* (Madison: University of Wisconsin Press, 1995).

39   Harry A. Potamkin, *Close Up* 6, no. 2 (February 1930): 111.

40   *Close Up* 7, no. 6 (December 1930): 454.

41   Hutchins, "L'Enfant Terrible," p. 694.

42   Lincoln Kirstein, "Experimental Films," *Arts Weekly* 1, no. 3 (25 March 1932): 52.

43   See "Close-Ups," *Amateur Movie Makers* 7, no. 4 (April 1932): 179. See also Elena Pinto Simon and David Stirk, *Jay Leyda: A Chronology*, published in honor of Leyda's memory by the Tisch School of the Arts, New York University, December 1987.

44 Russell Campbell, "Radical Cinema in the 1930s: The Film and Photo League," reprinted in Jump Cut: Hollywood, Politics and Counter Cinema, ed. Peter Steven (New York: Praeger, 1985), p. 131.

45 Interview with Florence Robbins and Harry Hay, 24 May 1991, Escondido, Calif.

46 See William Alexander, Film on the Left: American Documentary Film from 1931 to 1942 (Princeton: Princeton University Press, 1981), pp. 36–38.

47 Letter, Arthur Gale to Marion Gleason, 10 December 1927, Gleason file, GEH.

48 Letter, James W. Moore to Frank Stauffacher, 28 January 1947, "Art in Cinema" files, Pacific Film Archives (PFA), Berkeley, Calif.

49 The panel of judges for the contest was made up of industry members and private individuals, including King Vidor, James R. Quirk (Photoplay), George Pierce Baker (Yale), and Wilton A. Barrett (National Board of Review). See "H$_2$O," National Board of Review Magazine 4, no. 10 (December 1929): 12.

50 Letter, Robert Florey to Frank Stauffacher, 27 February 1947, "Art in Cinema" files, PFA.

51 Letter, Symon Gould to Frank Stauffacher, 1 March 1950, "Art in Cinema" files, PFA. Even in the late 1940s, the field of avant-garde film distribution had not changed substantially. Thus, Stauffacher and Amos Vogel at Cinema 16 in New York could not fall back on established distribution outlets for avant-garde film, but were dependent on personal contacts to find films and filmmakers, usually borrowing directly from the makers for about ten dollars per film.

52 Kenneth MacPherson, "As Is," Close Up 2, no. 6 (June 1928): 5.

53 "Experimental Film in America," Experimental Cinema 1, no. 5 (1934): 54.

54 See e.g. review of Lot in Sodom by James Shelley Hamilton, National Board of Review Magazine 9, no. 2 (February 1934): 14–15.

55 Louis Hirshman, a.k.a. Hershell Louis, donated an original nitrate print to the museum in 1947. It was destroyed through decomposition by 1956.

56 Kirk Bond, "Lot in Sodom," Film Art 1, no. 4 (Summer 1934): 69.

57 See Richard Abel, French Cinema: The First Wave 1915–1929 (Princeton: Princeton University Press, 1984).

58 See Film und Foto der zwanziger Jahre, ed. Ute Eskildsen and Jan-Christopher Horak (Stuttgart: Verlag Gerd Hatje, 1979). See also Horak, "Discovering Pure Cinema," pp. 4–7.

59 Hans Richter, Filmgegner von heute, Filmfreunde von morgen (Halle/Saale: Verlag Wilhelm Knapp, 1929).

60 Mekas, "Experimental Film in America," p. 15.

61 P. Adams Sitney, Visionary Film: The American Avant-Garde 1943–1978 (New York: Oxford University Press, 1979).

62 Dana Polan, The Political Language of Film and the Avant-Garde (Ann Arbor: UMI Research Press, 1985), p. 64.

63 Ibid.

64 Bart Testa, Back and Forth: Early Cinema and the Avant-Garde (Toronto: Art Gallery of Ontario, 1992), p. 19.

65 Long considered lost, a print survives at the Museum of Modern Art (MOMA), but this version of Flaherty's seems to have been seriously compromised by re-editing. Directed and photographed by Flaherty, originally in two reels, the film was cut down to one reel by John D. Pearmain, the business manager of the film's financiers, Mrs. Ada de Acosta

Root and Col. Breckenridge, for its New York release at the Roxy Theatre. See Herman G. Weinberg, *Film Index Series*, No. 6—Robert Flaherty (London: British Film Institute, 1946).

66 See Arthur Calder-Marshall, *The Innocent Eye: The Life of Robert Flaherty* (London: Penguin Books, 1970), p. 122.

67 Quoted in Lewis Jacobs, "Experimental Film in America (Part 1)," *Hollywood Quarterly* 3, no. 2 (Winter 1947–1948): 116. See also Wolfgang Klaue and Jay Leyda, eds., *Robert Flaherty* (East Berlin: Henschelverlag, 1964), pp. 210–211.

68 Before he began production of *A Bronx Morning*, Jay Leyda articulated his ideas on filming urban landscapes in "Tips on Topicals," *Amateur Movie Makers* 6, no. 1 (January 1931): 13–14, 39.

69 MOMA has preserved the original negative, which was a full-aperture silent negative, indicating that Browning had originally intended the film to be silent. See *Travelling* 56 (Fall 1979).

70 A still from the film was reproduced in *Amateur Movie Makers* 7, no. 3 (March 1932): 103.

71 *City Symphony* was first shown at the Little Theatre in Philadelphia in June 1930. See Weinberg biographical file at MOMA, New York.

72 *Autumn Fire* premiered at the Europa Theatre in Baltimore in December 1931. See Weinberg biographical file, MOMA. See also Robert Haller, "Autumn Fire," in *Field of Vision* (Spring 1980), who claims that Weinberg cut up *City Symphony* for his next film. There is some reason to doubt this assertion, whose source may be Weinberg himself, since the former film was shown publicly and it is hard to imagine that a future film historian would intentionally destroy his own film a mere year after its first public screening. On the other hand, William Uricchio in Chapter 12 of Jan-Christopher Horak, *Lovers of Cinema: The First American Film Avant-garde 1919–1945* (Madison: University of Wisconsin Press, 1995), quotes Harry Potamkin, who may have been the impetus for Weinberg to destroy the film. The 35mm negative of *Autumn Fire* was discovered in 1993 and has been preserved at George Eastman House. MOMA has a 16mm negative and reference print.

73 See FIAF notes by Weinberg in *Travelling* 56 (Fall 1979). Given Weinberg's penchant for generating publicity about the production of *City Symphony*, this seems unlikely. In a letter to Frank Stauffacher, 7 March 1947, Weinberg does note that the film was shown throughout Europe and America in the early and mid-1930s, "although it was never intended for public showing, having been made primarily as a personal exercise in cutting." See "Art in Cinema" files, PFA; compare *Close Up* 5, no. 4 (Oct. 1929): 339; *Amateur Movie Makers* 5, no. 6 (June 1930): 377.

74 Weinberg apparently planned a sound film remake, *Rhapsody*: "A poem in picture and sound . . . the rushing emotions of two young people very much in love . . . the parallel in nature . . . the flowering of this romance to an exuberant climax." See note in *Film Art* 1, no. 4 (Summer 1934): 83.

75 See "Comment," *Film Art* 1, no. 3 (Spring 1934): 34.

76 See Robert Allen, "Cine Experimenter," *Home Movies* (1940), clipping in possession of Lewis Jacobs. Thanks to Mr. Jacobs for making his files available to me.

77 Letter, Lewis Jacobs to Frank Stauffacher, 12 November 1946. "Art in Cinema" files, PFA. See also Manuel Komroff, "Lewis Jacobs—Explorer," *Direction* (September 1936): 8.

78 Jacobs described *Case History* as follows: "Most of the sound was to be INNER MONOLOGUE. . . . Realistic street sounds, remembered phrases and thoughts—all exaggerated and distorted to emphasize the stream of consciousness of one's inner—but disturbed—

logic." See *Competition du Film Experimental 21–27.IV.1958*, ed. Jacques Ledoux (Brussels: Cinémathèque de Belgique, 1958), p. 71.

79 Henwar Rodakiewicz describes the film's construction in some detail in "Treatment of Sound in *The City*," in *The Movies as Medium*, ed. Lewis Jacobs (New York: Farrar, Straus & Giroux, 1970), pp. 278–288.

80 Burkhardt went on to make numerous other portraits of his city, including *The Climate of New York* (1948), *Under the Brooklyn Bridge* (1953), *Eastside Summer* (1959), and *Default Averted* (1975).

81 Photographed and composed by Ralph Steiner, 16mm black-and-white, silent, 330 feet. Print preserved at MOMA.

82 A 35mm negative of this film (without a soundtrack) was recently discovered and has been preserved by the UCLA Film and Television Archives. Producer: Artkino; camera and editing: Jean D. Michelson; direction: M. G. MacPherson; music: Lee Zahler; special effects: Leon M. Leon; black-and-white, 945 feet.

83 Henwar Rodakiewicz, "Something More Than a Scenic," *Amateur Movie Makers* 7, no. 6 (June 1932): 249.

84 For Vorkapich's own discussion of his pioneering work in the montage field, see "Montage: A Look Into the Future with Slavko Vorkapich," *Cinema Progress* 2, no. 5 (Dec./Jan. 1937–1938): 18–22.

85 Originally shot in 35mm; a 16mm print (black-and-white, 340 feet) is available at MOMA.

86 Slavko Vorkapich made a second nature film, illustrating woods and wildlife in the style of *Moods of the Sea*, and utilizing Richard Wagner's *Forest Murmurs*. The film was apparently produced for Metro-Goldwyn-Mayer, but probably never distributed. See letter, Slavko Vorkapich to Stauffacher, 29 October 1950, "Art in Cinema" files, PFA.

87 *Prelude to Spring* (1946). Conceived, photographed, and produced by John Hoffman. Production associates: Bror Lansing, Ray Olsen; optical printing: Howard Anderson. 35mm print, 610 feet, at MOMA.

88 Using the same "Newcombe process," Newcombe shot a second film, *The Sea of Dreams* (1923). Born in Waltham, Mass., in 1894, Warren Newcombe worked for over thirty years as head of the special-effects department at MGM, but also had a career as a painter with a series of one-man exhibitions in the late 1920s and 1930s. See Newcombe entry in *Who Was Who in American Art*, ed. Peter Hastings Falk (Madison, Conn.: Soundview Press, 1985), p. 447; see also *The 1938–1939 Motion Picture Almanac* (New York: Quigley Publishing, 1938), p. 561; William Moritz, "Visual Music and Film-As-An-Art in California Before 1950," in *On the Edge of America: California Modernist Art, 1900–1950*, Paul Karlstrom and Ann Karlstrom, eds. (Berkeley: University of California Press, 1996).

89 The film was distributed by the Educational Film Exchange. A print of the film survives at MOMA, and a nitrate original was recently discovered in Argentina, where it was apparently also distributed. According to the credits, the film was presented by E. W. Hammons and produced by Newcombe, "by special arrangement with Howard Estabrook."

90 For a contemporary review see Myron M. Stearns, "The Art of Suggested Motion." *Arts and Decoration* 12, no. 3 (July 1922): 191, 221.

91 See James L. Enyeart, *Bruguière: His Photographs and His Life* (New York: Alfred A. Knopf, 1977), pp. 85–93.

92 Stills from the film were published by Bruguière and Mercurius in *Architectural Review* (March 1930). A 35mm print has been preserved at MOMA.

93 For a general introduction to Bute's work, see *Experimental Animation: An Illustrated Anthology*, ed. Robert Russett and Cecile Starr New York: Van Nostrand Reinhold, 1976), pp. 102–105.

94 A student of Hans Hoffman at the National Academy of Design, Lee finished his first film, 1941, shortly after Pearl Harbor. After spending the next four years in uniform as a combat motion picture photographer, Lee completed *Le Bijou* in 1946, followed by *Idyll* (1948). See Russett and Starr, eds., *Experimental Animation*, pp. 114–115.

95 Completed on 16mm Kodachrome in December 1941, the four-minute film has been preserved by Anthology Film Archives.

96 See Arthur Knight. "Self-Expression," *Saturday Review of Literature*, 27 May 1950, pp. 38–40.

97 The films were acquired by MOMA and shown at the "Art in Cinema" series in 1946, at which time, having just moved to Glens Falls, New York, he christened one group of animations *The Glens Falls Sequence*, "in lieu of any better name." See letter, Douglass Crockwell to Frank Stauffacher, 31 August 1946, "Art in Cinema" files, PFA.

98 Educated at the Dayton Art Institute and the National Academy of Design in New York (like Crockwell), Grant had been an abstract painter since 1933. See Russett and Starr, eds., *Experimental Animation*, p. 111.

99 All of Grant's films are available at Anthology Film Archives.

100 See Dwinell Grant, "Film Notes to Compositions 1–5," in Russett and Starr, eds., *Experimental Animation*, p. 112.

101 Murphy went on to make *Ballet Mécanique* in Paris with Fernand Léger, before eventually returning to the United States to work at the fringes of Hollywood, where he produced off-beat, if not exactly experimental, work. See William Moritz's chapter in Chapter 3 of Jan-Christopher Horak, *Lovers of Cinema: The First American Film Avant-garde 1919–1945* (Madison: University of Wisconsin Press, 1995). A 35mm print has been preserved at GEH.

102 Louis M. Simon, "Stella Simon and Her Film, *Hands*," manuscript (1989), Simon files, MOMA.

103 The official credits list Miklós Bándy as director, Leopold Kutzleb (photographer), and the composer, Marc Blitzstein. The film's original length was 609 meters. A 16mm print is preserved at MOMA. See also Simon file, MOMA, which includes letter from Louis Simon (Stella's son) to Ron Magliozzi.

104 According to Louis Simon his mother was aware of but never saw the Blum film. Letter, L. Simon to J.-C. Horak, 16 October 1989.

103 First shown in Berlin in September 1927, the film was later screened at an all-night soiree of the "Novembergruppe" (16 February 1929), which included Man Ray's *Emak Bakia*, music by George Antheil, a performance of Negro spirituals, and a boxing match.

106 See Oswell Blakeston, "*Hands*," *Close Up* 5, no. 2 (August 1929): 137. Four stills from the film were published in *Close Up* 5, no. 1 (July 1929).

107 See "*Underground Printer*," *Film Art* 3, no, 9 (Autumn 1936): 28.

108 Film Classic Exchange, *16mm ART FILMS*, catalogue, no date (presumably from the late 1940s), vertical file, GEH. Bovington, who apparently financed the film, had a falling out with the two filmmakers, because it was taken out of their hands and re-edited by him. Interview. Lewis Jacobs with J.-C. Horak. New York City, September 1989. See also letter, Eli Willis to Frank Stauffacher, 9 February 1947, "Art in Cinema" files, PFA. Prints of the film are for sale through a distributor, but were too expensive for this project.

109 Barbara Hammer, "Sara Kathryn Arledge," *Cinemanews* 1, no. 6 (1981): 3.

110 Arledge had shot three minutes in 1941, but lacked the funds to complete the film. In the summer of 1946 she shot additional footage, and premiered the film in November 1946 in Hollywood. Letter, Sara Arledge to Richard B. Foster, 9 October 1946, "Art in Film" files, PFA.

111 *Introspection* was planned and directed by Sara Kathryn Arledge; photography by Clyde B. Smith, Don Sykes; dancers: James Mitchell, Bill Martin, Joe Riccard, John R. Baxter; technicians: Don Littlepage, Ida Shapiro. 222 feet, 16mm, color, sound. Available through Canyon Cinema, Berkeley, Calif.

112 Letter, Arledge to Foster, 9 October 1946. A handwritten letter from Arledge to Frank Stauffacher, 25 August 1947, suggests that George Barrati was to write the music for her second film. "Art in Cinema" files, PFA.

113 Born in Lithuania in 1892, Deutsch emigrated to Los Angeles in 1919, via Berlin and Seattle, after breaking off his studies for the rabbinate. See Ralph Flint, "Boris Deutsch," *Creative Art* 8 (June 1931): 430–432; see also *Who Was Who in American Art*, 1985, p. 162.

114 *Lullaby*'s credits list Boris Deutsch for "direction and special effects." No distributor is listed in the print. A 16mm print is stored at GEH. The film can be purchased from Murray Glass Films, Los Angeles, Calif.

115 A still from *Skyscraper Symphony* was reproduced in *Theatre Arts Monthly* 13, no. 9 (September 1929). No print is known to have survived in this country, although it is rumored to exist in Moscow.

116 See "Club Library," *Amateur Movie Makers* 4, no. 7 (July 1929).

117 All the films of James Sibley Watson have been preserved in 35mm from the original nitrate negatives at GEH.

118 The optical printer, as well as Dr. Watson's papers. can be viewed at GEH.

119 See "Hollywood Notes," *Close Up* 3, no. 2 (August 1928): 54. Three stills from the film are reproduced in the same issue. *The Tell-Tale Heart*, 35mm print, black-and-white, 1,825 feet, is housed at GEH. Klein was a German cameraman and director who trained at UFA (Berlin) and Emelka (Munich), before coming to America with Lee DeForest in 1923. He would go on to a short and undistinguished career in Hollywood before returning in the early 1930s to Germany, where he continued his rather mediocre filmmaking activities in the Nazified film industry. This film is somewhat of an anomaly in his *oeuvre*.

120 Lewis Jacobs, *The Rise of the American Film*, 2d ed. (New York: Teachers College Press, 1968), p. 555.

121 Gerson studied art at the University of Pennsylvania in the late 1920s and became an instructor there for a few years. He later worked as a puppeteer with his wife, Mary Gerson. Hirshman studied at the Academy of Fine Arts in Philadelphia, and began his career as a painter, but eventually gravitated to three-dimensional caricatures, which have been widely exhibited.

122 See Harry A. Potamkin in *Close Up* 6, no. 2 (Feb. 1930): 111; see also "Modernist Film by Local Makers," *Philadelphia Inquirer*, 23 February 1930, and unidentified clippings in Gerson file. Theatre Collection, Free Library of Philadelphia.

123 For a shot-by-shot analysis see *From Fiction to Film: Ambrose Bierce's "An Occurrence at Owl Creek Bridge,"* ed. Gerald R. Barrett and Thomas L. Erskine (Encino, Calif.: Dickenson Publishing Co., 1973), pp. 87–106. Vidor apparently tried unsuccessfully to get his film released for some time; finally, in 1931, it was distributed to great acclaim under a new

title, *The Spy*. See Moritz, "Visual Music and Film-As-An-Art," p. 10. A negative without the original soundtrack has been preserved at GEH.

124   Seymour Stern, who later made a "career" out of writing about D. W. Griffith, was not only an editor for *Experimental Cinema*, but was also apparently involved in a number of avant-garde projects with leftist tendencies. Prior to 1932, Stern had worked for a while in Hollywood as a script doctor and second-unit director at Universal. Between 1932 and 1936, Stern worked at MGM. He directed the documentary *Imperial Valley* in 1932. See Ira H. Gallen, "Notes on a Film Historian: Seymour Stern," manuscript (1979), Stern file, MOMA, p. 2.

125   Quoted in *Audio-Brandon Film Catalogue* (1971), p. 444. This film, like *Lot in Sodom* and *The Spy*, was distributed by Brandon from the 1930s through the 1970s.

126   In the mid-1920s Freulich had joined his brother Jack Freulich as a stills photographer at Universal and remained there until 1944, when he became head of the stills department at Republic. See Judith Freulich Caditz, "Roman Freulich—Hollywood's Golden Age Portraitist," *The Rangefinder* (July 1991): 46. Thanks to Ms. Caditz for making a copy of the script for *Prisoner* available to me.

127   See "Notes from the Hollywood Studios," *New York Times*, 5 August 1934; *The Little magazine* 1, no. 5 (14 October 1934), program brochure for Baltimore Little Theatre, vertical files, GEH.

128   Herman Weinberg, "*The Prisoner*," *Film Art* 2, no. 5 (Winter 1934): 39.

129   Freulich noted that in Hollywood blacks were treated as an inferior race, useful only as "comedy relief," while he (not completely free of his own subconscious racism) perceived them to offer a "rich vein of cinematic material. Here is a race with a tragic background, though primitive and elemental, rich especially in folklore and music." See "Herman Weinberg Interviews Roman Freulich," *Film Art* 3, no. 8 (Summer 1936): 41.

130   The film is not mentioned by any of the standard histories of black film, and is misdated by Henry T. Sampson, *Blacks in Black-and-white: A Source Book on Black Films* (Metuchen, N.J.: Scarecrow Press, 1977), p. 272. A short review appeared in *Motion Picture Daily*, 30 March 1936. The film has been preserved by the Southwest Film/Video Archives at Southern Methodist University.

131   See letter, Ted Huff to Frank Stauffacher. 20 June 1949, in which Huff apologizes that his film was "not up to your standard" and demands that it be air-freighted back immediately. "Art in Cinema" files, PFA. All of Huff's films are being preserved at GEH.

132   The cast included Morris Carnovsky (Jehovah), Elizabeth Hawes, Julian Whittlesey, Alice Shepard, and F. Day Tuttle. 16mm print at MOMA.

133   Elizabeth Hawes was in fact the first American *couturière* to have collections shown in Paris. She later married Joseph Losey. See Michel Ciment, *Conversations with Losey* (New York: Methuen, 1985), p. 39.

134   Quoted in Joseph McBride, *Welles* (New York: Viking Press, 1972), p. 26.

133   A 16mm print, black-and-white, 222 feet, can be viewed at MOMA.

136   See Renan. *Introduction to the American Underground Film*, p. 220. Robbins was a photographer on a Works Progress Administration (WPA) Project in California that included Edward, Brett and Chan Weston, Roger Barlow, and Hy Hirsch. In some sources Hy Hirsch is listed in the credits, but the film was produced by Barlow, Hay, and Robbins, with Hirsch only appearing as an actor in two shots. Interview with Florence Robbins and Harry Hay, 23 May 1991, Escadido, Calif. See also letter, Harry Hay to J.-C. Horak, 14 September 1990. 16mm print available at MOMA.

137 *Even As You and* I failed to win any prizes, although it was shown at the Los Angeles Carpenters' Local Hall, along with Paul Strand's *Redes*, and screened by Fred Zinnemann for MGM executives. Interview with F. Robbins and H. Hay, 23 May 1991.

138 Letter, Harry Hay to Frank Stauffacher, 16 September 1949, "Art in Cinema" files, PFA. Robbins, who left a second avant-garde film uncompleted (*Suicide*, 1935–1937), and Barlow both went on to make documentaries after the demise of the WPA photography project in 1939, while Hay later worked as a trade union organizer and gay activist.

139 A 16mm print is preserved at Anthology Film Archives.

140 Born into a wealthy St. Paul family, Hill moved to Europe in 1927, where he was inspired by French surrealist films. See Jerome Hill, "Some Notes on Painting and Filmmaking," *Film Culture* 32 (Spring 1964): 31–32.

141 *The Fortune Teller* and *The Magic Umbrella* were incorporated *in toto* into Jerome Hill's autobiographical compilation/meditation, *Film Portrait* (1972), available through Filmmakers' Coop.

142 Letter, Emlen Etting to Frank Stauffacher. 26 March 1947, "Art in Cinema" files, PFA. After Etting's death, all of his films were donated to George Eastman House, where they are being preserved. For further biographical details, see obituary, *Philadelphia Inquirer*, 18 July 1993.

143 According to Amos Vogel, *Poem 8* "retained a certain poetic vitality and verve" through its early use of the subjective camera. See letter, Amos Vogel to Frank Stauffacher, 7 June 1949, "Art in Cinema" files, PFA.

144 See letter, Rosland Kossoff to Frank Stauffacher, 13 August 1949. See also letter, Christopher Young to Frank Stauffacher, 28 July 1949, "Art in Cinema" files, PFA. The film was screened in the series in 1950, won a prize for best avant-garde film at the Venice Film Festival that same year, and was eventually added to Cinema 16's distribution catalogue. See obituary, Christopher B. Young, *Philadelphia Evening Bulletin*, 2 December 1975, Young file, MOMA.

145 "*Object Lesson*—A Motion Picture by Christopher Young," unpublished program notes to be read before (part 1) and after (part 2) the screening, "Art in Cinema" files, PFA.

Notes on the New American Cinema

2

JONAS MEKAS

Ever since the article on the Cinema of the New Generation appeared (Film Culture 21) there has been continuous discussion on the subject of the new American cinema. Fresh material for this discussion was provided by the Spoleto Film Exposition, Summer 1961, which was devoted exclusively to the American independent filmmakers, and was the most representative program of their work assembled for public scrutiny until now.

Since there has been much misunderstanding concerning this new cinema it is timely to present a fuller and first hand investigation of the ideas, styles and achievements of this new cinema: to inquire into the motivations behind it; to attempt to describe what the new artist feels, how his mind works, why he creates the way he does; why he chooses his particular style to express the physical and psychological realities of his life.

I shall try to understand the new artist instead of telling him what to do. I will leave it for the critics to erect abstract theories and judge the work of the new artist from behind the stools of Culture. I don't want any part of the Big Art game. The new cinema, like the new man, is nothing definitive, nothing final. It is a living thing. It is imperfect, it errs. Nevertheless, it is the artist, with all his imperfections, who is the antenna (e.pound) of his race, not the critic. All a critic can do is to try and understand the artist, interpret him, explain the state of society through the works of its artists—and not vice versa. This is where our critics fail unanimously.

> Painting—any kind of painting, any style of painting—to be painting at all, in fact—is a way of living today, a style of living, so to speak.
>
> Willem de Kooning

> A poet is the combined product of such internal powers as modify the nature of others; and of such external influences as excite and sustain these powers; he is not one, but both. Every man's mind is, in this respect, modified by all the objects which he ever admitted to act upon his consciousness; it is the mirror upon which all forms are reflected, and in which they compose one form. Poets, not otherwise than philosophers, painters, sculptors, and musicians, are, in one sense, the creators, and in another, the creations, of their age. From this subjection the loftiest do not escape.
>
> Shelley, Preface to "Prometheus Unbound"

Part One: Historical Perspective

Helen Levitt, James Agee, Sidney Meyers: From the Studios into the Streets

In the Street (shot in 1948, edited in 1951), by Helen Levitt, Janice Loeb and James Agee, a documentary shot in the streets of New York, and The Quiet One (1949), by Sidney Meyers, a story about a lonely, psychologically disturbed Negro boy—are two films which can be considered the forerunners of the low-budget independent film and the beginnings of a new film style, something that has been often called the New York film school.

Both films dealt with realistic subject matter; both used non-actors; both were shot on actual location, often with concealed cameras. And they both had a spontaneity of action and camera that was very different from their documentary predecessors (Willard Van Dyke, Paul Strand, Pare Lorentz) and the experimental films made at about the same time in New York and San Francisco. Whereas the experimentalists such as Maya Deren, Willard Maas, Hans Richter, and Sidney Peterson were concerned with the exploration of the subconscious, with the development of a universal, abstracted film poetry, free from time and place, this other group of filmmakers were interested in exploring their world in a more prosaic and realistic manner, right here and now.

It is a mistake for the critics to treat these filmmakers as a conscious anti-Hollywood movement. Like the experimentalists, these "stream-of-life" filmmakers did not band together to fight Hollywood. These were single individuals who were quietly trying to express their own cinematic truth, to make their own kind of cinema. Needless to say, on aesthetic grounds they were dissatisfied with the Hollywood style and its themes. In their own films, they wanted to break away from the closed circle of "cinema as a profession," they wanted to make films in a more personal manner. They were not exactly clear how to go about it. However, one thing was clear: they had to move out, no matter where, and learn from actual experience. The low budgets, the small crews, and the visual and technical roughness imposed by the new and unpredictable shooting circumstances, served as an impetus in freeing their work from the conventional, overused visual and dramatic forms, and also forced them to search for new and fresh subject matter, to look at the old things from new angles, and in a new light.

Stylistically and thematically, In the Street and The Quiet One seemed to indicate the proper direction for the new experiments. They perfectly complied with the proposition of James Agee, the man who contributed much to the formulation of an aesthetic basis for the New York Film School:

> The films I most eagerly look forward to will not be documentaries but works of fiction, played against and into, and in collaboration with unrehearsed and uninvented reality.

Morris Engel: The Low-Budget Feature

In The Little Fugitive (1953), a story about a little boy's adventures in Coney Island, Morris Engel pushed the low-budget techniques further into the dramatic film. With sure skill, he used the New York background to convey the humor and the poetry of everyday life. He made a low-budget film that was suitable for a large commercial market and thus, once and for all, destroyed the $1,000,000 production cost myth. Shot on a $50,000 budget—in Hollywood it would have cost ten times more—this film, more than any other, contributed to the growth of low-budget independent feature production in America.

In *Lovers and Lillipops* (1955) and *Weddings and Babies* (1958), Morris Engel expanded his experiments to the camera and sound track. He improved and used with great success the portable camera and the new synchronous sound recording units. Ricky Leacock, himself an explorer of new camera techniques, said:

> Morris Engel's camera was almost totally uninhibited by the usual complications of changing position. It was able to go anywhere with a minimum of preparation and delay. I had the feeling that the camera was able to catch subtleties in the acting that are usually lost under normal conditions of shooting. *Weddings and Babies* is the first theatrical motion picture to make use of a fully mobile, synchronous sound-and-picture system. It should be of enormous interest to filmmakers, because it is precisely in this area that the greatest undeveloped potential of the film is to be found.

Morris Engel also experimented with a plotless, episodic story construction. His films were freer from imposed dramas than those of other filmmakers of the time. Engel concentrated on recognizable, everyday incidents and situations, on basic character relationships, relying much on improvisation, contributing to the destruction of the literary and theatrical conventions in cinema. The importance of Morris Engel films will grow with time—his films being irreplaceable documents of mid-century America. The faithfulness of their detail, the purity of their style, and the objectivity of the camera work sets them apart from other entertainment films of the period.

Lionel Rogosin: Social Engagement

With *On the Bowery* (1956) and *Come Back, Africa* (1958), Lionel Rogosin brought to the independent cinema a strong note of social consciousness. The first film was a plea for Manhattan's skid-row; the second film, in Rogosin's own words, "is concerned essentially with human conditions as they exist in the Union of South Africa under the ruthless policy of the present regime. Art may be indefinable," he continues, "but for me it is important to do something significant. The form must grow from the subject matter and from our times. The artist must be engaged in his times in the strongest way possible."

Formally, one of Rogosin's contributions to the new cinema was an effective dramatization of reality, the use of real life scenes in an organized, planned drama. This blending of the documentary with the dramatic enabled him to record the truth of the situation through the lips of the people who actually live in that situation themselves, and to create a drama which was effective on its own terms.

Lionel Rogosin writes about his method:

> To capture reality spontaneously and to give it life, more is involved of course than simply casting people of the milieu. They must be allowed to be themselves, to express themselves in their own manner but in accordance with the abstractions and themes which you as the director must be able to see in them. This is something quite different

from traditional script writing, in which the ideas and abstractions are essentially the writer's, with professional actors portraying those ideas and abstractions through their personality. The final product of such films is far removed from the reality of the society portrayed, although it may be highly satisfactory as a drama of symbolic ideas in which plot, dialogue and actors are primarily devices for describing the writer's ideas and themes. But for expressing the inner life of people in a particular milieu, I believe the method I followed in my films is a deeper and truer one.

Cassavetes: The Improvisation

Shadows (1958), a workshop project coordinated by John Cassavetes, carried the improvisation techniques in a fictional dramatic film to new heights.

The content sought by Cassavetes and his actors was no longer the surface realism alone, which was well explored by Morris Engel and the neorealists. For the new cinema, Shadows represented a turn inwards—a focusing upon psychological realities. The little bits of plot were used only as loose frameworks to explore and exhibit the actors' own emotions, attitudes, remembrances, reactions. Hence a correct comparison of Shadows to Chekhov's writings. The actors and the director improvized as they went along, searching into their own experiences, listening, without forcing, without dramatizing. It is this immediacy of the drama-less, beginning-less and end-less episode which is the most important aspect of Shadows. The true value of the "immediacy" being not its realism, but its cinematic properties. The film's rhythm, its temperament is not that of the ideas in it, but, primarily, that of the people in it, their faces, their movements, their tone of voice, their stammerings, their pauses—their psychological reality as revealed through the most insignificant daily incidents and situations.

Without knowing it, Cassavetes and his actors created a work that moved freely in what Siegfried Kracauer has called "camera reality"—a film free from literary and theatrical ideas. And it is precisely this "undramatic," "unintelligent," "amoeba-like" camera reality that provokes the most criticism from the old school of critics. One could, in fact, write a long discourse called "In Defense of Stupidity in Cinema," or "The Wisdom of the Camera Reality," or "The Difference, Between Literary- and Camera-Intelligence."

Sidney Meyers: The Naked Camera Eye

The Savage Eye (1959), by Sidney Meyers, Ben Maddow and Joseph Strick, concentrated mainly on camera-eye techniques. Their camera, like that of Dziga-Vertov's thirty years ago in Russia, watched and recorded contemporary American life. There was one essential difference, however, between Dziga-Vertov and Sidney Meyers. Vertov photographed the typical aspects of Soviet life, attempting to reveal the sensations of the usual, ordinary events of the day, whereas Sidney Meyers chose the atypical, the sensational, the exceptional. Sidney Meyers' camera eye is cynical, cold. He laughs at the tragic and the sad with the same detachment that he laughs at the evil, corrupt.

Despite this, The Savage Eye remains a tour-de-force lesson in camera-eye techniques. It was this camera-eye technique, but with a more subjective, personal attitude on the part of the filmmaker, that was developed to perfection by Ricky Leacock during the last few years, revolutionizing much of the independent filmmaking in America.

Ricky Leacock: New Documentary Frontiers—Revolution of the Camera

Cuba Si, Yankee No (1960), Primary (1960), Eddie (1960), by Ricky Leacock, assisted by the brothers Al and David Maysles and Don Pennebaker, demonstrated anew the immense capabilities of the camera to record life, its poetry and its prose—a fact often forgotten since Lumière took his first street shots.

The experiences of Morris Engel with the portable synchronous sound camera, contributed much to this new development. During the past two years, this equipment is being constantly perfected and the experiments have been continuing. These experiments enabled Leacock to reduce the shooting team to one man—the filmmaker himself is now the director, cameraman and, often, sound man, all in one. The filmmaker now can go everywhere, watch the scene unobtrusively and record the drama or the beauty of what he sees, all in perfect sinc and color.

Today there is a bustle of young filmmakers everywhere in America, working on low-budget, independent productions, like never before. There is a feeling in the air that cinema is only beginning; that now cinema is available not only to those who possess a high organizational and group-work talent, but also to those poets who are more sensitive, but often un-communal, who prefer privacy, whose powers of observation and imagination are most active in privacy. An entire area of subject matter, untouched by cinema, is opening before the filmmaker—an area into which he can delve and come up with a new and deeper contribution to the sum total of human experience.

The attitude and the working methods of the new documentary filmmakers could best be described by Ricky Leacock himself:

> Tolstoy envisioned the filmmaker as an observer and perhaps as a participant capturing the essence of what takes place around him, selecting, arranging but never controlling the event. Here it would be possible for the significance of what is taking place to transcend the conceptions of the filmmaker because essentially he is observing that ultimate mystery, the reality. Many filmmakers feel that the aim of the filmmaker is to have complete control. Then the conception of what happens is limited to the conception of the filmmaker. We don't want to put this limit on actuality. What's happening, the action, has no limitations, neither does the significance of what's happening. The filmmaker's problem is more a problem of how to convey it. How to convey the feeling of being there.

Leacock's Camera and the Dramatic Feature

During the last few months, Leacock has turned his interest towards the dramatic feature. We'll soon be able to see the first results. In his first feature length documentary, Eddie (it is also known under the title On the Pole), Leacock has already demonstrated the virtues of his approach. *Eddie* is no longer the usual type documentary. It is a documentary drama. We follow the protagonist, we live with him, we get to know him, we identify with him. But we know all the time that he is not acting his life for the camera (as did the shepherds for Vittorio de Seta in *Banditi a Orgosolo*)—the camera is only a stranger, catching, unobtrusively, glimpses from his life. Using this same technique—leaving the camera completely alone, an independent observer—the acted film drama may gain a new and much needed freedom, a freedom towards which cinema is desperately reaching, as exemplified through such films as *Breathless*, *Chronique d'une été*, *Shadows*. The creative function of the cameraman will play a much greater role in this new type of filmmaking. As a matter of fact, the director will have to become his own cameraman. It is not at all surprising, therefore, that the Nouvelle Vague directors, more author-conscious than Hollywood, have been the first ones to invade Leacock's 43rd Street studio to get acquainted with the new techniques. Leacock's studio suddenly has become a sort of crossroad of the world for the new cinema.

Meanwhile, on their own, below 43rd Street, the students of Ricky Leacock are pushing documentary filmmaking into various unexplored directions.

Dan Drasin: Burton Brothers

In *Sunday* (1961), Dan Drasin's uninhibited camera, zooming in and out and around the action, caught the clash between the folk-singers and the police in New York with an immediacy and aliveness seldom seen in the documentary film or television. Drasin was greatly assisted by his ignorance of certain professional techniques which would have hampered his freedom. He came to cinema completely free of professional inhibitions. He moved with his zoom freely, against all textbook rules, not afraid of shaky movements or garbled sounds. The shooting circumstances didn't even permit much time for perfectionism. He lost the slickness but he gained the truth, both in sound and image.

AFTER SEEING SUNDAY

THE FINAL DEFENSE OF THE AMERICAN IS HIS INTEGRITY, HIS HUMANITY, ITS FLOWERING IS IN HIS CONSCIOUS WILLINGNESS TO DEFEND BOTH, FREE AS MAN & ARTIST.

THIS FILM IS THE CLEAREST ILLUMINATION OF THE BASIC AMERICAN CONFLICT, THE CLASH BETWEEN UNFEELING, BRUTAL, SELF RIGHTEOUS AUTHORITY & THE MOST HUMAN, UNIVERSAL AMERICAN ASPIRATIONS, THE ULTIMATE LIBERATION OF THE AMERICAN SOUL.

THE FOLKSINGERS ARE AMERICA, THE ARTISTS ARE AMERICA, AMERICA IS PEOPLE, NOTHING MORE OR LESS,

GOD BLESS THE *PEOPLE* SINGING, SPEAKING, WALKING, TALKING, SCREAMING, HURTING WITHIN THIS FILM, FREE!

GOD BLESS THE PEOPLE WHO MADE THIS FILM, THE ARTIST UNSEEN, AMERICA WILL TAKE CARE OF THE OTHERS.

BOB KAUFMAN

However, like Cassavetes before him, Drasin seems not to be aware of the true meaning of his own achievement. He is not consciously aware of the true success and the meaning of his film

> As the event fades into the past, I reflect more and more on what a piece of cinema *Sunday* might have been had I, as editor, been less impregnated with the reality of the *event*, and more concerned with the *idea* and the *cinematic* reality. I will probably never make another film like *Sunday*,

writes Drasin in a postscript to the film, not realizing, that this *"idea* and the *cinematic* reality" would have thrown his film back into the literary. The true *cinematic* reality and *idea* was caught in *Sunday* precisely because of his impregnation with the reality of the event. Without it, the film wouldn't exist. Drasin, the artist "unseen" (B. Kaufman), was right.

Michael Burton and Philip Burton followed the same direction in their documentary on the Un-American Activities Committee, *Wasn't That a Time* (1961). Their approach to the new style and the new techniques, however, was a more conscious act. The theme of their film called for the elimination of the formal documentary approach. The sense of informality achieved in *Wasn't That a Time* was neither an accident nor an abstract game in the new style— it was chosen consciously. The free informality of the film was posed against the abstract formality of the government machine. The camera showed us the casual, insignificant moments in the lives of the three protagonists, stressing the everyday, the informal against the official and the formal. The tears rolling down the face of Barbara Sherwood are the first real tears cinema has seen—tears which make the staged film drama look insignificant, pretentious, small.

What is most admirable in the work of Leacock-Maysles-Drasin-Burton is their complete freedom of movement. One could say that only now is the camera becoming conscious of its steps. Until now the camera could move only in a robot-like fashion, on pre-planned tracks, and along indicated lines. Now it is beginning to move freely, by itself, according to its own desires and whims, tracing its own steps. Cinema is groping, cinema is going through its own Actors' Studio period—mumbling, stammering, searching.

Robert Frank, Alfred Leslie: Further Explorations of Improvisation

Turning from the documentary to the fiction film—*Pull My Daisy* (1959), by Robert Frank and Alfred Leslie, a spoof on the beat generation, a nonsense comedy, blended most perfectly the elements of improvisation and conscious planning, both in camera work and directing. The plot-less episode has never been more eloquent than it is in this film. That feeling of "being there," of which Leacock speaks in connection with the documentary, was achieved in this fictional film to the highest degree. Its authenticity is so effective, its style so perfect, that the film has fooled even some very intelligent critics: they speak about it as if it were a slice-of-life film, a piece cut out from the raw stream of life, a documentary. Instead of criticizing the film, they criticize the beat generation. The film's amazing sense of style and form escape through their fingers like a fluid—it is almost invisible, transparent. No other film ever said so much, and in such a pure and condensed manner, about the man of the beat generation.

In *The Sin of Jesus* (1961), Robert Frank continues his documentation of the soul of modern man. Formally, the film is an attempt to merge the best of the old with the best of the new cinema. It can be much criticized on these grounds. Despite its formal faults, the presence of the director is unmistakable.

"If your aim is high, it should be you that comes through the most," says Robert Frank. The self-expression of an artist, however, is a universal act, it expresses a universal content. This is what the modern artist is doing in his "useless," "shapeless," "meaningless" work. The lonely woman's desperate and recriminatory cry in the dark, doomed and desolate fields of New Jersey expresses the despair of our own existence—or, should I say, the American existence Anno 1961. One could say, perhaps, even more: that this pessimism, this desolation, or doom, or despair revealed in *The Sin of Jesus* is the inner landscape of the twentieth-century man, a place that is cold, cruel, heartless, stupid, lonely, desolate—this landscape emerges from Robert Frank's film with a crying, terrifying nakedness. Robert Frank is here as much a documentarist as Robert Flaherty was in *Nanook*.

Shirley Clarke: The Connection

It is a similar spiritual landscape that Shirley Clarke is painting in her first feature, *The Connection* (1961). Again, one could criticize the film on formal grounds, its use of Pirandelloisms, which are more suitable for the stage than the screen. However, such criticism can not minimize the importance of this film as an attempt to put across on the commercial screen the new content, the new reality. The play has been molded into a strong cinematic unity with a singlemindedness of style which makes it merit an important place in the annals of independent cinema. Whether you take it as a piece of "magic realism," the American version of *Waiting for Godot*, or just a simple parable about a group of junkies waiting for a fix—the film remains a unique achievement.

Guns of the Trees: Elimination of the Plot, Film as an Emotional Statement

In my own film, *Guns of the Trees* (1961), I attempted to break away from the last remnants of the traditional manner of story-telling, using single disconnected scenes as parts of an accumulative emotional fresco—like an action painter uses his splashes of paint. The film departs from realism and attempts to reach into the poetic. At a certain point, if one wants to reach down into deeper truths, if one wants to speak indirectly, one has to abandon realism and enter the regions of poetry.

The new content asks for a new mode of artistic expression. The artist is beginning to express his anxiety and discontent in a more open and direct manner. He is searching for a freer form, one which allows him a larger scale of emotional and intellectual statements, explosions of truths, outcries of warnings, accumulations of images—not to carry out an amusing story but to fully express the tremblings of man's unconscious, to confront us, eye-to-eye, with the soul of modern man. The new artist is not interested in entertaining the viewer: he is making personal statements about the world today.

Vanderbeek, Preston: Social-Political Satire—Protest Films

In this context, I should mention the work of Stanley Vanderbeek and Richard Preston, two foremost satirists of the new cinema. During the last three years they have produced a number of short films which in a free, plotless manner, sharply comment on various aspects of contemporary American life. Nothing is spared—the arts, the sciences, the press, television, housewives, presidents, sex. Both use collage and assemblage techniques; both are ingenious manipulators of everyday imagery; both are perfect masters of their medium. Unlike the surrealists of the 1920s, who expressed their dissatisfaction in personal, often indecipherable imagery, these satirists use the everyday objects and textures of modern America as their vocabulary. They are not entertainers nor are they story tellers. They are, rather, modern clowns who splash their discontent and their irony into the face of their public. Their style, like that of other modern artists, is a result of an exploded emotion, an act that couldn't be kept back any longer.

Says Preston:

> I have been in the pillory for years, but now, with the aid of film, I have managed to wriggle one arm free. With this good arm, I can catch and hurl back some of the garbage that has been thrown at me. And by garbage I mean the lies, the distortions, the hypocrisies that are the manipulators' weapons. In short, through film I have discovered power. The will to have power is good only when it is directed to power over things . . . steel, stone, paints, film. It is evil when it is directed to the control and manipulation of other men.

And says Stanley Vanderbeek:

> The purpose of "poetic-politic" satire in my films is to attack some of the aspects of super-reality that has been so hastily, carelessly built around us. It seems desperate and peculiar that today we have so few comic and comic-tragic spokesmen to jibe at the massive involuntary joke of living in a monolithic society and statistical age. If my films have a social ambition, it is to help disarm the social fuse of people living with anxiety, to point out the insidious folly of competitive suicide (by way of rockets). I am trying to evolve a "literagraphic" image, an international sign language of fantasy and satire. There is a social literature through filmic pantomime, that is, non-verbal comedy-satire; a "comic-ominous" image that pertains to our time and interests which Hollywood and the commercial film are ignoring.

In this respect, a significant development is the increasing number of *protest* documentary films. To mention some of the most significant:

Edward Bland's *Cry of Jazz* (1958), a thesis film about the position of the Negro in America today;

John Korty's *Language of Faces* (1961), an antiwar film, based on the peace vigil in front of the White House;

Polaris Action (1962), a group project, edited by Hilary Harris—an anti-war film;

The already mentioned Dan Drasin's *Sunday* and the Burton brothers' *Wasn't That a Time*—two films on freedom of speech.

Notwithstanding the statements of some foreign and local critics who reproach the independent filmmaker for what they call his escapism—the American cinema has never been so deeply grounded in reality, reacting to it, expressing it, and commenting upon it. All filmmakers discussed in this survey take their content and their form from the most direct stream of modern life.

Brakhage, Breer, Menken: The Pure Poets of Cinema

Robert Breer, Stanley Brakhage and Marie Menken, thematically and formally, represent in the new American cinema the best of the tradition of experimental and poetic cinema. Freely, beautifully they sing the physical world, its textures, its colors, its movements; or they speak in little bursts of memories, reflections, meditations. Unlike the early avant-garde films, these films are not burdened by Greek or Freudian mythology and symbolism, their meaning is more immediate, more visual, suggestive. Stylistically and formally their work represents the highest and purest creation achieved in the poetic cinema.

It was a short film by Stanley Brakhage, *Desistfilm* (1954)—still one of the most influential of all modern American films—that started the stylistic revolution which has now reached the documentary and is beginning to be noticeable in the commercial dramatic film. (Truffaut kicks and shakes his camera in *Jules et Jim* to destroy static, "professional," smooth pans and tilts.) Very few other filmmakers have been as preoccupied with style and techniques as has been Brakhage. Ironically enough, it is Brakhage who is usually picked up by the old school critics when they need an example of bad style and bad techniques. They couldn't have chosen a more fallacious example, for Brakhage is truly one of the virtuosos of modern cinema.

Some of Brakhage's attitudes towards film style and techniques can best be illustrated through his own writings:

> So the money vendors have begun it again. To the catacombs then, or rather plant this seed deeper in the underground beyond false nourishing of sewage waters. Let it draw nourishment from hidden uprising springs channeled by gods. . . .Forget ideology, for film unborn as it is has no language and speaks like an aborigine—monotonous rhetoric. . . . Abandon aesthetics. . . . Negate techniques, for film, like America, has not been discovered yet, and mechanization, in the deepest possible sense of the word, traps both beyond measuring even chances. . . . Let film be. It is something . . . becoming.
>
> . . . somewhere, we have an eye capable of any imagining. And then we have the camera eye, its lenses grounded to achieve 19th century Western compositional perspective (as best exemplified by the 19th century architectural conglomeration of details of the "classic" ruin) in bending the light and limiting the frame of the image just so, its standard camera and projector speed for recording movement geared to the feeling of the ideal slow Viennese waltz, and even its tripod head, being the neck it swings on, balled with bearings to permit it that Les Sylphides motion (ideal to the contemplative romance) and virtually restricted to horizontal and vertical movements (pillars and horizon lines) a diagonal requiring a major adjustment, its lenses coated or provided with filters, its light meters balanced, and its color film manufactured to produce that picture post card effect (salon painting) exemplified by those oh so blue skies and peachy skins.

By deliberately spitting on the lens or wrecking its focal intention, one can achieve the early stages of impressionism. One can make this prima donna heavy in performance of image movement by speeding up the motor, or one can break up movement, in a way that approaches a more direct inspiration of contemporary human eye perceptibility of movement, by slowing the motion while recording the image. One may hand hold the camera and inherit worlds of space. One may over- or under-expose the film. One may use the filters of the world, fog, downpours, unbalanced lights, neons with neurotic color temperatures, glass which was never designed for a camera, or even glass which was, but which can be used against specifications, or one may photograph an hour after sunrise or an hour before sunset, those marvelous taboo hours when the film labs will guarantee nothing, or one may go into the night with a specific daylight film or vice versa. One may become vice versa, the supreme trickster, with hatfuls of all the rabbits listed above breeding madly. One may, out of incredible courage, become Méliès, that marvelous man who gave even the "art of film" its beginning in magic.

In his latest film, *Prelude* (1961), Brakhage achieves a synthesis of all his techniques. In this film of exquisite beauty the images become like words, they come back, in little bursts, and disappear, and come back again, like in sentences, creating visual and mental impressions, experiences. Within the abstract context, the flashes of memories of a more personal and temporal nature appear, always in a hinting, oblique, indirect manner—the images of foreboding clouds, memories of the atom bomb, endless cosmic spaces, dreams and fears that constitute the subconscious of modern man. If the contemporaneity of the other filmmakers discussed here is very real, emotional, raw, still a part of our daily experience—in *Prelude* (as in the work of Robert Breer and Marie Menken) this contemporaneity is abstracted, filtered, it becomes a thought, a meditation occurring in a world of its own, in the world of a work of art.

Brakhage, from a letter to a friend (1958), before beginning his work on *Prelude*:

> I am now considering a second feature length film which will dwell cinematically upon the atomic bomb. But as *Anticipation of the Night* is a work of art rather than an indictment of contemporary civilization in terms of the child, so too my prospective film will dream upon the bomb, create it out of, as I envision it, an almost Spinozian world of mathematical theory, visualize the flowering of its form in relation to the beautiful growths as well as to those more intellectually parasitic, and in the wake of its smoke deal with the devastation it leaves in the human mind rather than material devastation, the nightmare and also the "devoutly to be wished" which it engenders, ergo religion— the end, the resolve with death.

There are only one or two other filmmakers working today who can transform reality into art as successfully as Brakhage, Breer, and Menken. A landscape, a face, a blotch of light— everything changes under their eye to become something else, an essence of itself, at the service of their personal vision. To watch, in Brakhage's *Whiteye*, a winter landscape transform itself, through the magic of motion, temperament and light into pure poetry of white, is an unforgettable experience.

2. Marie Menken's *Glimpse of the Garden*
(1957). Courtesy Anthology Film Archives;
reprinted by permission.

Ron Rice, Vernon Zimmerman: The Poetry of the Absurd

The Flower Thief (1960), by Ron Rice, and Lemon Hearts (1961) by Vernon Zimmerman, are two of the latest and most successful examples of post-Pull My Daisy cinema. Both are made with the utmost creative freedom, with the utmost disrespect for the "professional" camera, plot, character conventions. They merge and combine the spontaneous cinema of Pull My Daisy, the freedom of the image of Brakhage, the "uncleanniness" of action painting, the theatre of Happenings (Kaprow) and the sense of humor of Zen. Their imagination, coming from deeply "deranged" and liberated senses, is boundless. Nothing is forced in these films. They rediscover the poetry and wisdom of the irrational, of nonsense, of the absurd—the poetry which comes from regions which are beyond all intelligence, the regions of Zero de Conduite, of Fireworks, of Desistfilm.

Nevertheless, the materials with which they create are embedded in reality. Didn't Rimbaud write his "Illuminations" out of the burning, intensified reality of his own life? Such are the lives of the modern film poets. With their own lives they create a "cinema reality" that is tense to the point of explosion. In a sense, they don't have to "invent": they just have to turn the camera upon themselves, or upon their close friends, and it explodes into the pyrotechnics upon which no imagination could improve.

ODE TO THE EYE

About that time it was decided by the Gods that reality was more important than creation. The reality of anything moves the spirit more than artificial attempts to create motion where there is static.

A drunkard struggling in the alley to remove the cap from the wine bottle strikes the emotions with more force and meaning than any logical sequence of staged events that don't have the fibre of life.

Any scene, no matter what, can evoke more of man to believe and feel than a parallelism which contains logic without reality.

It is better to film anything that is living and real than to film ideas of what should, or might be real.

Ron Rice

The Others

The few films discussed here indicate the main tendencies of the so-called New American Cinema. There are other films which, in one way or another, also have contributed to the growth of the new cinema, and they should be mentioned in any survey of this kind: George Stoney's All My Babies (circa 1953); Bert Stern's Jazz on a Summer's Day (1959); Jerome Hill's The Sand Castle (1960); Peter Kass' Time of the Heathen (1961); Gregory Markopoulos' unfinished film Serenity (1961); Ricky Carrier's Strangers in the City (1961); Irvin Kershner's Stakeout on Dope Street (circa 1958); Stanley Kubrick's Fear and Desire (circa 1953); Denis and Terry Sanders' Time out of War and Crime and Punishment, U.S.A. (1959); John Frankenheimer's The Young Strangers; Tom Laughlin's The Proper Time (1960); Curtis Harrington's Night Tide (1961); Alexander Singer's

A *Cold Wind in August* (1961); Leslie Stevens' *Private Property* (1960); Allen Baron's *Blast of Silence* (1961)—and a few others. Some of these constitute what might be called the "experimental" or "fringe" Hollywood; others are works of young new directors who are trying to find themselves. One could find much unfulfilled exciting promise among these films. I should also mention the experimental filmmakers such as Charles Boultenhouse, Gregory Markopoulos, Carmen D'Avino, Hilary Harris whose work I did not have space enough to discuss but whose contribution to the independent cinema is of great importance.

The independent filmmaker is now at a stage where he feels himself entirely free from the bonds of Hollywood; only now is he becoming truly independent and only now can he say the whole truth and nothing but the truth, be it his personal truth or a social, communal truth—he can say it as freely as the poet with his typewriter. The first phase of the independent cinema is coming to an end and one can state firmly that it has liberated the filmmaker, it has given him self-confidence, and, at the same time, it has created a series of films which are both documents of man's spirit and works of art—films which can serve as an inspiration and a reminder of standards.

Part Two: A Few Statements on the New American Artist as a Man

Like the new poet, the new filmmaker is not interested in public acceptance. The new artist knows that most of what's publicly said today, is corrupt and distorted. He knows that the truth is somewhere else, not in the NY *Times* and not in *Pravda*. He feels that he must do something about it, for his own conscience, that he must rebel against the tightening web of lies.

Some writers from home and abroad have accused the new artist of nihilism and anarchy. The American artist could sing happily and carelessly, with no despair in his voice—but then he would reflect neither his society nor himself, he would be a liar like everybody else. With man's soul being squeezed out in all the four corners of the world today, when governments are encroaching upon his personal being with the huge machinery of bureaucracy, war and mass communications, he feels that the only way to preserve man is to encourage his sense of rebellion, his sense of disobedience, even at the cost of open anarchy and nihilism. The entire landscape of human thought, as it is accepted publicly in the Western world, has to be turned over. All public ideologies, values, and ways of life must be doubted, attacked. "Smell it and get high, maybe we'll all get the answer that way! Don't give up the ship!" exclaims Allen Ginsberg. Yes, the artist is getting high on the death of his civilization, breathing in its poisonous gases. And yes, our art definitely suffers from it. Our art is "confused" and all that jazz, jazz, jazz (Taylor Mead). But we refuse to continue the Big Lie of Culture. To the new artist the fate of man is more important than the fate of art, more important than the temporary confusions of art. You criticize our work from a purist, formalistic and classicist point of view. But we say to you: What's the use of cinema if man's soul goes rotten?

> It seems to me that the entire society of man is bent on destroying that which is alive within its individuals (most contemporarily exemplified by the artist), so that presumably the society can run on and on like the machine it is, to the expense of the humans composing it. I have felt this both personally and in objectively watching the lives of

others alive in their struggles, and most particularly in observing the death of the average human being insisted upon by the society at the time of that human being's adolescence.

Stanley Brakhage

Artists, poets, filmmakers; it is you who are the last inheritors of the world's conscience, the visionaries and prophets of the twentieth century. The voices of our "leaders" are as sound tracks in reverse. The parliaments and the churches of men preach dissension and confusion.

Dick Preston

Part Three: Summing Up—Connecting the Style with the Man

Thus, we can say, that the new independent cinema movement—like the other arts in America today—is primarily an existential movement, or, if you want, an ethical movement, a human act; it is only secondarily an aesthetic one. But then one could say that all art in all times has been, primarily, an existential act. Even when our films seem to be utterly detached from reality, like the works of Robert Breer or Brakhage—they come from a dissatisfaction with the static, outdated concepts of life and art. One could say that there is a *morality in the new*.

A Side Note on the Morality of the New

One may wonder, sometimes, why I am so obsessed with the new, why this hatred for the old.

I believe that true wisdom and knowledge are very old; but this wisdom and this knowledge have been covered with layers and layers of static culture.

If we know anything about man, it is this: he must be allowed to fulfill his own life, to live his life as fully as possible. The cul-de-sac of western culture is stifling the spiritual life of man. His "culture" is misleading his thoughts and his intuitions. My position is this: Everything that keeps man in the molds of western culture prevents him from living his own life. Surely, one of the functions of the artist is to listen to the true voice of man.

The new artist, by directing his ear inward, is beginning to catch bits of man's true vision. By simply being *new* (which means, by listening deeper than their other contemporaries)— Brakhage and Breer contribute to the liberation of man's spirit from the dead matter of culture, they open new vistas for life. In this sense, an old art is immoral—it keeps man's spirit in bondage to Culture. The very destructiveness of the modern artist, his anarchy, as in Happenings, or even action painting, is, therefore, a positive act, a confirmation of life and freedom.

Evil is that which is finite.

Kabbala

A Note on Improvisation

I have heard too often both American and foreign critics laugh at the words "spontaneity" and "improvisation." They say this is not creation, that no art can be created "off-the-cuff." Need I state here that such criticism is pure ignorance, that it represents only a snobbish, superficial understanding of the meaning of "improvisation"? The truth is that improvisation never excludes condensation, or selection. On the contrary, improvisation is the highest form of condensation, it points to the very essence of a thought, an emotion, a movement. It was not without reason that Adam Mickiewicz called his famous Konrad Walenrod soliloquy an Improvisation. Improvisation is, I repeat, the highest form of concentration, of awareness, of intuitive knowledge, when the imagination begins to dismiss the pre-arranged, the contrived mental structures, and goes directly to the depths of the matter. This is the true meaning of improvisation, and it is not a method at all, it is, rather, a state of being necessary for any inspired creation. It is an ability that every true artist develops by a constant and life-long inner vigilance, by the cultivation—yes!—of his senses.

A Note on the "Shaky Camera"

I am sick and tired of the guardians of Cinema Art who accuse the new filmmaker of shaky camera work and bad technique. In like manner, they accuse the modern composer, the modern sculptor, the modern painter of sloppiness and poor technique. I have pity for such critics. They are hopeless. I would rather spend my time in heralding the new. Mayakovski once said that there is an area in the human mind which can be reached only through poetry, and only through poetry which is awake, changing. One could also say that there is an area in the human mind (or heart) which can be reached only through cinema, through that cinema which is always awake, always changing. Only such cinema can reveal, describe, make us conscious, hint at what we really are or what we aren't, or sing the true and changing beauty of the world around us. Only this kind of cinema contains the proper vocabulary and syntax to express the true and the beautiful. If we study the modern film poetry, we find that even the mistakes, the out-of-focus shots, the shaky shots, the unsure steps, the hesitant movements, the over-exposed, the under-exposed bits, have become part of the new cinema vocabulary, being part of the psychological and visual reality of modern man.

The Second Note on Improvisation

It was in his quest for inner freedom that the new artist came to improvisation. The young American filmmaker, like the young painter, musician, actor, resists his society. He knows that everything he has learned from his society about life and death is false. He cannot, therefore, arrive at any true creation, creation as revelation of truth, by re-working and re-hashing ideas, images and feelings that are dead and inflated—he has to descend much deeper, below all that clutter, he has to escape the centrifugal force of everything he has learned from his society. His spontaneity, his anarchy, even his passivity are his acts of freedom.

On Acting

The fragile, searching acting style of the early Marion Brando, a James Dean, a Ben Carruthers is only a reflection of their unconscious moral attitudes, their anxiety to be—and these are important words—honest, sincere, truthful. Film truth needs no words. There is more truth and real intelligence in their "mumbling" than in all the clearly pronounced words on Broadway in five seasons. Their incoherence is as expressive as one thousand words.

The young actor of today doesn't trust any other will than his own, which, he knows, is still too frail and, thus, harmless—it is no will at all, only the distant, deep waves and motions and voices and groans of a Marlon Brando, a James Dean, a Ben Carruthers, waiting, listening (the same way Kerouac is listening for the new American word and syntax and rhythm in his improvisations; or Coltrane in his jazz; or De Kooning in his paintings). As long as the "lucidly minded" critics will stay out, with all their "form," "content," "art," "structure," "clarity," "importance,"—everything will be all right, just keep them out. For the new soul is still a bud, still going through its most dangerous, most sensitive stage.

Closing Remarks

Several things should be clear by now:

The new American artist can not be blamed for the fact that his art is in a mess: he was born into that mess. He is doing everything to get out of that mess.

His rejection of "official" (Hollywood) cinema is not always based on artistic objections. It is not a question of films being bad or good artistically. It is a question of the appearance of a new attitude towards life, a new understanding of man.

It is irrelevant to ask the young American artist to make films like those made in Russia or France or Italy; their needs are different, their anxieties are different. Content and form in art cannot be transplanted from country to country like beans.

To ask the American artist to make "positive" films, to clean out—at this time—all the anarchic elements from his work, means to ask him to accept the existing social, political and ethical order of today.

The films being made by the new American artist, that is, the independents, are by no means in the majority. But we must remember that it is always the few, the most sensitive ones who are the spokesmen of the true feelings, the truths of any generation.

And, finally, the films we are making are not the films we want to make forever, they are not our ideal of art: these are the films we *must* make if we don't want to betray ourselves and our art, if we want to move forwards. These films represent only one specific period in the development of our lives and our work.

I can think of various arguments the critics or the readers of these notes may throw against me or against the young American artist of today as he is described here. Some may say that he is on a dangerous road, that he may never get out of his confusion in one piece; that he may succeed in destroying everything, that he will have nothing new to offer in its place, etc. etc.—the usual arguments that are thrown against anything young, budding, unknown.

I, however, I look at the new man with trust. I believe in the truth (victory) of the new.

Our world is too cluttered with bombs, newspapers, TV antennae—there is no place for a subtle feeling or a subtle truth to rest its head. But the artists are working. And with every word, every image, every new musical sound, the confidence in the old is shaken, the entrance to the heart is widened.

Natural processes are uncertain, in spite of their lawfulness. Perfectionism and uncertainty are mutually exclusive.

Research without mistakes is impossible. All natural research is, and was, from its very beginning, explorative, "unlawful," labile, externally reshaping, in flux, uncertain and unsure, yet still in contact with real natural processes. For these objective natural processes are in all their basic lawfulness variable to the highest degree, free in the sense of irregular, incalculable, and unrepeatable.

Wilhelm Reich,
"Orgonomic Functionalism"

The Woman Filmmaker in the New York Avant-garde

3

LAUREN RABINOVITZ

One autumn afternoon in 1961, a dozen women assembled in a Greenwich Village apartment in New York City. The hostess welcomed her guests and served them tea. The guest of honor unwrapped colorful boxes and held up for view a succession of tiny infant's garments. The women's overlapping voices responded in harmonious, conversational rhythms that framed the visual display of gifts. The baby shower, like countless others across the country in the 1950s and 1960s, celebrated women's bonding while it affirmed the traditional importance of motherhood and childbirth in a woman's life.

But this baby shower, conventional enough in practice, also strained some of the social conventions to which it appeared to adhere. Amidst the clutter of wrapping paper, the women sat cross-legged on the floor of a Greenwich Village apartment filled with cat odor and Haitian music. Rather than an array of ready-to-wear fashions, the guests presented an odd visual assortment of bohemian costumes.

These women were known not for their support but for their renunciation of women's traditional sex roles and their celebrations of women's sexuality. Among them was author Anaïs Nin, who wrote erotic stories and flaunted her sensual lifestyle to a degree that would have appalled most bourgeois matrons. Another of the guests, independent filmmaker Shirley Clarke, had just completed a feature-length movie about a group of "junkies," and her fourteen-year marriage to Bert Clarke was in the divorce courts while she lived with an African-American actor several years her junior. Marie Menken was well known in New York City for her experimental films, and she soon acquired a different kind of notoriety as one of the regulars at Andy Warhol's Factory. The guest of honor, Bebe Barron, was a composer working in the male-dominated area of electronic music. Barron and the other guests (who included filmmakers Storm De Hirsch and Betty Ferguson and film organization activists Marcia Vogel and Cecile Starr) were all artists who were part of Greenwich Village's avant-garde.

The one, perhaps, who looked and played her part as a bohemian artist to the fullest was the hostess, filmmaker Maya Deren. More often than not, she appeared colorfully dressed for her parties wearing a peasant blouse, hoop earrings, jangling bracelets, and a long flowing skirt so that she could easily break into impromptu dancing. Deren was a beautiful woman whose curly dark hair formed a mane around her face. She was charismatic, opinionated, and outspoken—a leader in the avant-garde who championed filmmaking as an art form that was the equal of painting, modern dance, or poetry.

Deren frequently invited all sorts of people to the Greenwich Village apartment that she shared with her husband, composer Teiji Ito. She collected dancers, choreographers, filmmakers, poets, writers, art critics, and musicians in what could be considered a bohemian salon. Amidst her sizable collections of Haitian drums, Caribbean masks, primitive figures, contemporary paintings, and eighteen cats whose odor permeated the room no matter how filled with cigarette smoke it became, Deren held court.

If Deren and her parties were well known in Greenwich Village, her baby shower for Bebe Barron became legendary. For one thing, it was the last time many of her friends saw Deren; she died shortly afterward, at 44. A baby shower, overripe with associations of the conventional female roles of motherhood and housewifery, may not have been the one last party for which Deren would have wanted to be remembered. But this humorous irony may have strengthened the event's image as a Greenwich Village legend, making this baby shower a romantic remembrance of women artists banding together and supporting each other.

The Deren-Barron baby shower was simplified into a protofeminist gathering as it was retold to succeeding generations of women filmmakers. Filmmaker Joyce Wieland recalled hearing about it as early as 1963, and she later thought about it as an example of the way that Deren led the women artists in a mutual support group.[1] However much dramatic and political color the occasion later offered artists as well as historians in the 1970s and 1980s, such contemporary depictions of the event project feminist concerns onto the meaning of the gathering. Once the discovery of available women models and mentors spurred new women's histories in the 1970s and 1980s, artists and critics alike made this baby shower a political metaphor removed from its social and cultural context.

The image of the baby shower, however, seems to illustrate more fully the cultural contradictions that Deren and the other women experienced. The baby shower evolved within the American ideology of the 1950s that idealized an all-consuming motherhood, linking childbearing and child-rearing to women's fulfillment. At the same time, white bourgeois women who increasingly entered the job market faced both their inability to live up to notions of the ideal mother and the possibility of individual fulfillment outside home and family.

The baby shower is more appropriately a female ritual that reconciles a woman's desire for independence from the family with her belief that she be selflessly devoted to familial needs. The shower itself represents a woman's leisure time selfishly devoted to socializing with other women primarily for her individual pleasure. At the same time, it allows her to fulfill a familial role of selfless devotion to home and children as she prepares for a new baby by receiving gifts and advice that will aid her in the future. Thirdly, the baby shower serves an important economic function, providing the woman and her family with material goods that will lessen the financial burden of infant care. One may further claim that such collective celebration of economic consumption associated with impending motherhood has an ideological value as a means for valorizing a woman's traditional role as the primary consumer in the family. As a ritual—the function of which is to resolve symbolically those beliefs that cannot actually be reconciled—the baby shower gives outward visible form to these contradictory impulses.

Deren's and her friends' psychic lives as artists might seem to have required little need for the baby shower's ritualistic function. Their actions outwardly opposed the dominant ideology of the 1950s. They were the exceptional women who balked enough at the conventions that they achieved a measure of success in artistic areas usually considered "masculine"—the erotic novel, electronic music, and filmmaking. But they did so without entirely understanding how the cultural institutions, including the family, constructed and organized women's social subordination.

Whereas the women may have individually prided themselves on the ways that their bohemian lifestyles and artistic pursuits subverted bourgeois appearances, they were also identifiable, as a group, as the wives of highly respected artists. In several instances, their relation to male filmmakers or artists was a condition of their entrance into the arts.[2] Deren had learned filmmaking from her second husband, Alexander Hammid. Bebe Barron's career began as a collaborator with her husband, composer Louis Barron. Marcia Vogel, likewise, was a film activist largely in collaborative efforts with Amos Vogel. Anaïs Nin's initial literary successes were intertwined with those of her celebrated husband, Henry Miller. Even Shirley Clarke, who became a filmmaker through both her financial and professional independence from her husband, still depended upon her marriage as a psychological precondition to a professional career as an artist. She married Bert Clarke because he supported her desire and calmed her fears about an artistic career.[3]

The stereotypical woman artist whose success depends upon her relationship to a male artist has a historical basis. Rozsika Parker and Griselda Pollock argue that only in the last two hundred years have women been so systematically denied access to the social institutions necessary for an arts career that they have had to depend more regularly upon familial relationships to overcome institutional restraints.[4] In addition, Parker's and Pollock's argument also suggests that modern art histories have implicitly perpetuated the stereotype by either omitting the existence of working women artists or dismissing as insignificant those they do acknowledge.

Such histories themselves are part of the modern definition of the artist that, since the nineteenth century, has equated artistic creativity with masculinity and male social roles so that Woman becomes excluded as a subject from this domain. Responding to Linda Nochlin's 1972 essay, "Why Have There Been No Great Women Artists?" and its query from a defensive, negative point of view, Parker and Pollock demand a reformulation for inquiries about women artists, "Each woman's work is different, determined by the specific factors of sex, class and place in particular historical periods. . . . But because of the economic, social and ideological effects of sexual difference in a western, patriarchal culture, women have spoken and acted from a different place within that society and culture."[5]

Constructed as synonymous with structures of femininity, Woman is a social category. As Simone de Beauvoir said in the heralded statement that has become a slogan for contemporary radical feminism, "One is not born a woman, but becomes one." Women occupy particular positions—economic, social, and ideological—within patriarchy, positions marked by unequal relations to the structures of power. As Parker and Pollock note, "Power is not only a matter of coercive forces. It operates through exclusions from access to those institutions and practices through which dominance is exercised. One of these is language, by which we mean . . . positions from which to speak."[6] Art is a language in these terms of representations and sign systems as well as a cultural, ideological practice. As such, it constitutes a discourse by which power relations are sustained on several cultural levels, and it reproduces those relations in language and in images. In short, art presents the world from points of view that represent positions of and relations to power of sexes, classes, and races.

As female pioneers in their "masculine" fields of endeavor, women artists remained prisoners of an ideology that even constructed their positions of resistance within traditional social roles. As Parker and Pollock assert, "The phrase 'woman artist' does not describe an artist of the female sex, but a kind of artist that is distinct and clearly different from the great artist."[7] The bohemian realm of the Greenwich Village scene in the 1940s through the 1960s celebrated the male artist as a Romantic hero while configuring women's roles only in relation to the male artist's greatness—as either wives or lovers. The large, familial atmosphere typically describing Greenwich Village's legendary artists' parties was structurally an enclave consisting of artists, wives, and mistresses. In this environment, bohemian male artists were exempt from the bourgeois morals and demands of marriage but women were not.

If the woman artist's dilemma was as simple as radical feminist theorist Shulamith Firestone's belief that women's oppression stems from the "natural handicap" of pregnancy, then one could easily claim that Deren and her friends unwittingly celebrated at the baby shower the source of their oppression.[8] But from a materialist point of view that identifies a social—rather than biological—source for women's oppression, the position of the shower guests was more contradictory. As French feminist Christine Delphy points out, "Society does much to make us think that the material conditions of periods [menstruation] or motherhood derive from the physical event: that these *socially constructed* conditions are *natural* conditions. . . . There are thus not one but *two* cultural interventions: 1—the devaluation of women's bodies and physiology; 2—the material handicap created by the social conditions."[9] The baby shower—itself a ritual that eased women's conflicting tensions without erasing them—encapsulated the complex web of emotions associated with women's class and status while it affirmed their dependency upon the family for their social identity and position.

Indeed, the whole issue of childbirth and motherhood as a material condition of women's cultural worth raised conflicts and contradictory desires among women artists seeking measures of professional value. Maya Deren never had a child, although she began to express a desire for one in the late 1950s when she was past forty. Shirley Clarke had a daughter early in her adult life, but suffered recurring bouts of guilt over her ambivalence toward motherhood, over an abortion in the late 1940s, and over her decision to pursue a professional career rather than to be a full-time mother. Even among the next generation of women filmmakers, Joyce Wieland was resolutely silent about her inability to bear children, and her silence on the subject itself may be a mark of the degree to which society has equated a socially constructed condition with a biological one.

Acknowledging the contradictory state of relations that these women represent provides the means by which one may begin to understand women's impact on the art world after World War II. Women filmmakers played an especially significant role in shaping the film avant-garde. Avant-garde, or independent, cinema offered women greater opportunities for artistic success because arts institutions initially accorded cinema only marginal status. Feminist film scholar Annette Kuhn explains, "Low investments of money and 'professionalism' have meant that avant-garde cinema has historically been much more open than the film industry to women."[10] The independent filmmaker individually or with a small group controlled the production process using inexpensive technology in what has become known as an artisanal mode of production. Pam Cook has noted that this cinema, concerned as it is with personal expression (the autobiographical, the intimate, the domestic), was especially appealing to women.[11]

Three women in particular explored cinema as a means for personal expression, and they successively represent the woman filmmaker's evolving function in the American avant-garde. Maya Deren, Shirley Clarke, and Joyce Wieland made films that ranged from psychonarration to social realism to feminist polemic—a progression that establishes the dominant direction of independent cinema after World War II. They supported their films through unifying their activities in movie production, distribution, and exhibition. Through lectures, printed interviews, published articles, and books, they shaped the receptions for their films and for independent cinema and identified the avant-garde cinema as an important contemporary means of self-expression.

It is perhaps significant that each woman had decided to become an artist and had already made a personal commitment to a career as an artist before she became a filmmaker. Maya Deren moved to film in 1943 from involvement in the New York dance theater and in writing poetry; Shirley Clarke moved from modern dance to film in the early 1950s; and Joyce Wieland gradually turned from drawing and painting to filmmaking in the late 1950s and early 1960s. The fact that each was already active in the avant-garde arts and had already become identified with an unconventional, even socially unacceptable position for a woman in the 1940s and 1950s may explain the ease with which all three achieved visibility in a medium that frequently intimidated young women unaccustomed and unacculturated to working with movie technology.[12] Because the three had already faced social pressures regarding the propriety of their chosen careers, their transitions to a newer medium may have presented fewer challenges to them than to other women who have embarked on filmmaking careers.

Maya Deren made her first film, *Meshes of the Afternoon* (1943), with documentary filmmaker Alexander Hammid. Deren's initial cinematic interest was in an individual woman's psychological experiences and in presenting a female subjective voice. But she expanded her interest from the individual woman to women's collective experience and its celebration in myths and rituals. Her short, modernist films both adapted strategies from other art forms and rhetorically challenged the aesthetic ideology of Hollywood filmmaking.

Since she was unable to secure continued financial backing for her films, Deren assumed the roles of lecturer, teacher, publicist, and organizational administrator to create and promote a more sympathetic climate for independent filmmaking. She developed organized economic bases for the production and reception of a radical film aesthetic. In the decade following World War II, Deren argued for artist-controlled organizations as a means for achieving a discourse of cinema art that would promote and celebrate independent films. Against the norms of New York City practice, she insisted that the contemporary artist must be more than a specialist in artistic production and must assume social and economic responsibility for artistic reception.

Deren set an example for many young filmmakers and, for Shirley Clarke in particular, she was a role model. The two women became friendly in the early 1950s when Clarke was an aspiring dancer studying with the renowned modern dancer and choreographer Hanya Holm. When it became clear to Clarke that her career as a dancer had limited possibilities for individual success, she began making dance films.[13] Clarke's first effort, *Dance in the Sun* (1953), reminded her friends of Deren's work, so they suggested that the two meet. After visiting Deren and seeing her films, Clarke applied Deren's ideas of poetic editing to short films that used nondance subjects.

Deren's strong sense of identity as a woman artist and her filmic philosophy shaped Clarke's political commitment to the independent cinema. Clarke's fierce campaigns for the independent cinema paid off in the New American Cinema movement of the 1960s. The New American Cinema advocated low-budget, starkly realistic films that addressed social rather than psychological issues, and it emerged temporarily in the 1960s as an alternative to

Hollywood cinema. As a leader of the New American Cinema, Clarke made feature movies that critiqued patriarchal structures of knowledge—*The Connection* (1961), *The Cool World* (1963), *Portrait of Jason* (1967). She also applied and adapted Deren's model of economic organization and artist-participation. She preserved Deren's vision of an alternative cinema in the 1960s but extended it to a commercial cinematic system that included more diverse types of filmmaking than those envisioned by Deren.

Clarke met Joyce Wieland in 1963 when Clarke was at the height of her career in the New American Cinema and Wieland was a newly arrived painter-filmmaker in New York City. Wieland approached the independent, or underground, film community rather than any of the established art institutions because she was intimidated by the intensely competitive nature of the more prestigious art gallery system. After being encouraged by the filmmakers' open, friendly atmosphere, Wieland concentrated more on her filmmaking. Wieland admired Clarke's artist-defined role as an advocate for independent economic practices as well as for politically informed aesthetics. She, too, addressed culturally constructed ways of seeing in such experimental films as *Water Sark* (1965), *Hand Tinting* (1967), and *Rat Life and Diet in North America* (1968). Wieland emulated Clarke's move from experimental to documentary films, seeking a more politically expedient format for social critiques and, in the early 1970s, she introduced an explicitly feminist identification in such films as *Solidarity* (1973) and her feature-length melodrama, *The Far Shore* (1976).

Each woman worked under constant social and psychological constraints because of her status as a woman. For example, male art critics from Wieland's hometown of Toronto angrily dismissed Wieland's explicit psychosexual art solely because they felt women should not publicly address sexual pleasure. Deren's male peers made fun of a woman having intellectual theories regarding film as an art form. Clarke's business associates only invested in her films when she found male producers. The social relations that shaped the women's lives encouraged their trivialization or marginalization as artists as a means for containing them within dominant ideology.

Deren, Clarke, and Wieland were aware of their problematic position among filmmakers and artists. Clarke announced to an interviewer in 1967, "I have to deal with myself as a woman, then as a director."[14] In the same year, Wieland said, "I looked at a lot of men's art . . . but I thought: where is my tradition, where is my life? . . . I still had to look into the lives of women who had made independent statements."[15] Clarke also remembered Deren's words: "We [women] get everything we want by raising hell except what we want most."[16]

But, more than other women filmmakers working throughout the 1950s and 1960s in New York City, each of these women achieved public acclaim that went beyond the independent cinema community. The popular discourses about each woman focus on the female artist's body in a way that they might not for a man. Deren is represented as the embodiment of the exotic, Romantic woman, a mysterious and much talked about figure among the Greenwich Village art crowd. A decade later, Clarke delighted the popular press because she represented to them the eccentric Beat girl. Descriptions portray her as a diminutive, pixielike woman whose sleek dancer's body dramatically contrasted her intensity and spoken strings of profanities; she embodied the cool, hip attitude associated with the Beat generation of the early 1960s. A generation younger, Wieland came of age as an artist and political activist during the height of the counterculture in the middle and late 1960s. Journalists represented her as a plump woman with a round Madonna face, and they often photographed her wearing fashionably long, flowing cotton dresses that gave her an earth mother appearance.

Whether the women knowingly or unknowingly manipulated such poses is not the issue. They may have individually discovered that they were successful publicity ploys, or they may have wanted to protect the privacy of their identities, but their respective images fit the fashionable myths of femininity of their times, rendering the women culturally acceptable stereotypes within dominant ideology. Whereas these images helped to draw popular attention to artists and their causes as points of resistance, they also contradictorily popularized the idea that such women artists were still feminine.

The public construction of these three filmmakers may or may not be representative of public discourses surrounding women filmmakers and artists as a group in the 1940s through the 1960s. These women were certainly not the only individual artists contained by feminine stereotyping and language. In the same city in the 1950s, Helen Frankenthaler's stain-and-soak paintings were either dismissed or discussed in relation to metaphors, historical references, and literary analogies of the "eternal feminine."[17] Parker and Pollock describe such critical discourse surrounding Frankenthaler as "oozing notions of femininity from every pore."[18]

In the case of the three women filmmakers, it is especially important that they were contained and categorized because the films that they made consistently articulated positions for a *refusal* of the male gaze. The fact that, in the course of promoting their films and art practices, the filmmakers themselves were repetitively positioned as the sexual objects and stereotypes of male reporters' gazes is significant for telling what can and cannot be said about women artists and their work in the postwar era. Unable to discuss the women simply as artists and their films as breaking new ground within existing film movements, the discourse shifts the terms and focuses rhetorically on the filmmakers as women. It is an important condition for the reception of their films, always prefiguring the possibility for containment of their more radical filmic practices.

The troubled and troublesome nature of the woman filmmaker's continuing position in the American avant-garde was ultimately ruptured in the late 1960s when the art establishment noticed the independent cinema because of its successful programs. Museums and universities began carving out whole territories for independent cinema as a part of their institutional programs. Film production grants, filmmaking curricula taught by newly appointed filmmaker-professors, art journal coverage of film, collection development, and exhibition—the entire support system that Deren originally had envisioned—became inscribed within visual arts institutions. As institutional support for independent film increased, a rigid hierarchy concerning economic practices and political goals developed within the institutions that excluded women artists from the positions of authority and privileged their male counterparts. Women filmmakers—including Clarke and Wieland—lost their voices in the discursive and economic systems they helped establish. Such exclusion radicalized them, and they identified their experience in political terms of sexual and social power.

Clarke and Wieland felt so keenly betrayed that they both dropped out of the New York scene. Clarke first resumed work on private, short 8mm films, and then she turned to the newer medium of video. She subsequently moved to California and worked as a film instructor. She has only recently renewed her ties to documentary and feature film practices. Wieland returned to Toronto in 1971, where she became an important leader in feminist and nationalist artists' groups. She continued to experiment with the creation of an alternative cinema system and, learning from her New York City experiences, she attempted to create a

3. Maya Deren filming in the 1940s. Courtesy Anthology Film Archives; reprinted by permission.

more politically radical cinema for popular audiences. But after the commercial failure of her feminist feature film, *The Far Shore*, Wieland quit cinema and returned primarily to painting and drawing. She, too, has lately pursued filmmaking interests concentrating on the kind of short, intimate, artisanal films with which she began her film career.

As Deren, Clarke, and Wieland created an avant-garde cinema, their conflicting successes and failures forged connections among women, women's films and art, and women's lives in social institutions. Each one encouraged another to build upon the same strategies, creating a continuous chain of alternative film practices in spite of the frequency with which their efforts flagged and their films publicly failed. Constantly challenged in their attempts to control production and dissemination, they demonstrated that the means by which they financed, marketed, and exhibited their films were politically crucial to stopping their suppression. Deren's, Clarke's, and Wieland's struggles demonstrate that relationships among women's sexuality, power, and economics were important both to independent cinema's position as a subversive program of American cinema and to independent cinema's institutional implantation in dominant arts organizations.

Notes

1 Joyce Wieland, interview with author, Toronto, Ontario, 15 Nov. 1979.
2 Several scholars, including Germaine Greer and Eleanor Munro, have identified women painters' relations as daughters or lovers of famous male artists as a social condition for their success. Many New York City painters in the 1950s who became acknowledged as leading artists only in the 1970s and 1980s were more likely to be known in the 1950s as the wives of major painters. More recent accounts of the professional careers of Lee Krasner (married to Jackson Pollock), Elaine de Kooning (married to Wilhelm de Kooning), and Helen Frankenthaler (married to Robert Motherwell) are replete with anecdotes and examples of how their marriages exacerbated the contradictory position of a woman as a professional artist. For general historical examples, see Germaine Greer, *The Obstacle Race: The Fortunes of Women Painters and Their Work* (New York: Farrar, Straus, and Giroux, 1979). For a discussion of American women painters in the 1950s, see Eleanor Munro, *Originals: American Women Artists* (New York: Simon and Schuster, 1979).
3 Shirley Clarke, interview with author, Chicago, Illinois, 24 Sept. 1981.
4 Rozsika Parker and Griselda Pollock, *Old Mistresses: Women, Art and Ideology* (New York: Pantheon, 1981), 82–113.
5 Ibid., 49; Linda Nochlin, "Why Have There Been No Great Women Artists?" *Art News* 69, no. 9 (January 1971): 22–39, 67–71.
6 Parker and Pollock, Old Mistresses, 49.
7 Ibid., 114.
8 Shulamith Firestone, *The Dialectics of Sex: The Case for Feminist Revolution* (New York: Morrow, 1970).
9 Christine Delphy, *Close to Home: Materialist Analysis of Women's Oppression*, trans. and ed. Diana Leonard (London: Hutchinson, 1984), 195.
10 Annette Kuhn, *Women's Pictures: Feminism and Cinema* (Boston: Routledge and Kegan Paul, 1982), 185.

11 Pam Cook, "The Point of Self-expression in Avant-garde Film" in *Theories of Authorship*: A *Reader*, ed. John Caughie (Boston: Routledge and Kegan Paul, 1981), 271–281.

12 As Deren said to an interviewer in 1947, "[It] always comes as a little bit of a shock to men when a woman is doing something in a field that has to do with machinery and with creating in terms of inventing with a machine." "Interview with Maya Deren," WGXR-Radio, New York City, 1947, Audio tape collection, School of the Art Institute of Chicago, Chicago, Illinois.

13 Shirley Clarke, interview with author.

14 Albert Bermel, "Young Lady with a Camera," *Escapade* 10, no. 5 (May 1967): 78.

15 Barrie Hale, "Joyce Wieland: Artist, Canadian, Soft, Tough, Woman!" *Toronto Telegram*, 11 Mar. 1967.

16 Maya Deren, as quoted in "Maya Deren," Shirley Clarke TS, November 1966, Shirley Clarke papers, Wisconsin Center for Film and Theater Research, University of Wisconsin-Madison, and the State Historical Society of Wisconsin, Madison. Quoted with the permission of Shirley Clarke.

17 Parker and Pollock, *Old Mistresses*, 149.

18 Ibid.

Women in the Avant-garde

Germaine Dulac, Maya Deren, Agnès Varda, Chantal Akerman, and Trinh T. Minh-ha

JUDITH MAYNE

In this chapter, I will discuss three different contexts of women's filmmaking where explorations of the 'primitive" both cite the example of early film and examine relationships between different meanings of the term *primitive*. The first context includes two films, Maya Deren's *Meshes of the Afternoon* (codirected with Alexander Hammid, 1943) and Suzan Pitt's *Asparagus* (1974), in which the style of "primitive" filmmaking is appropriated. While these two films are closest to the kind of avant-garde filmmaking influenced by early film that Tom Gunning discusses, they take as their primary point of departure not just the "primitive" style of filmmaking, but also and especially the "primitive" representation of the female body and its relationship to other definitions of the so-called primitive. While both of these films excavate "primitive" narration—and the "primitive" narrator, in Pitt's film—the second group of films is more specifically concerned with the *narrative* implications of the "primitive" in terms of early cinema, of gender, and—in the case of Akerman's film—of psychoanalysis.

In Germaine Dulac's *The Smiling Madame Beudet* (*La Souriante Madame Beudet* [1922]), Agnès Varda's *Cleo from 5 to 7* (*Cléo de 5 à 7* [1962]), and Chantal Akerman's *Jeanne Dielman, 23 Quai du Commerce, 1080 Bruxelles* (1975), a form of "primitive" narration is associated specifically with a female character, and the narration of the films both incorporates and distances itself from it. In each case, "primitive" narration evokes simultaneously the realm of early film-making and the realm of traditional female activities. That all three of these films are in the French language is suggestive, as well, of a shared tradition, one split between their connections with the movements with which they are associated (impressionism in the case of Dulac, the New Wave in the case of Varda; less specifically defined, in the case of Akerman, is the contemporary European narrative film) and with each other.

Finally, the third context involves the relationship between women, a "primitive" mode of representation, and the cultural meanings of "primitivism" in an anthropological sense. Trinh T. Minh-ha's *Reassemblage* (1982) and Laleen Jayamanne's *A Song of Ceylon* (1985) are meditations upon the construction of otherness, and their evocations of the "primitive" range across documentary cinema and anthropology, as well as the modernist appropriation of primitivism and the cinematic avant-garde. Both of these films were made by women who quite literally have crossed thresholds separating "West" and "East"; Trinh T. Minh-ha is a Vietnamese woman who works in the U.S., and Jayamanne, born in Sri Lanka, now works in Australia.

Tom Gunning's discussion of the relationship between early cinema and the avant-garde does not focus exclusively on male filmmakers; Maya Deren is mentioned as one filmmaker influenced by Méliès, and a scene in *Meshes of the Afternoon*, where a group of Maya Derens sit around a dining table, is cited as influenced by Méliès's preoccupation with multiplications of his own body.[1] The reverberations of the "primitive" in Deren's work provide an excellent example of the relationship between early cinema and the context of gender and female identity. Deren's relationship to different configurations of the "primitive" involves, at one point at least, an inquiry into exhibitionism which, while quite different from the context in which Gunning uses the term, nonetheless suggests a similar preoccupation with alterity.

In the 1947 notebooks describing her most ambitious and never-realized project, a film which would compare the rituals and gestures of various non-Western cultures, Deren described the sense of "otherness" she encountered in examining footage of Balinese dance made available to her by the anthropologists Gregory Bateson and Margaret Mead. Noting the "complete lack of identification between audience and performer" in Balinese dance, Deren writes: "In our culture the tension between exhibitionist and spectator is one of identification: the spectator either would like to be capable of the acts of the performer or identifies himself temporarily, and this enviable and envied 'model' role is the incentive for the performer." Deren goes on to question whether the polarities of exhibitionist and onlooker are even pertinent to Balinese dance: "A condition of exhibitionism is an acute consciousness of exhibiting oneself, and this the little girls in amnesic trance certainly are not. Nor do they have 'memories' of their moments of glory, so to speak—trunks of souvenirs, or the dress they performed in the night the Prince of Wales sat in the right box. No— *exhibitionism* is the wrong word."[2]

Deren's fascination with Balinese dance, like her well-known interest in Haitian culture, is characterized by a questioning of some of the oppositions which form the very basis of Western identity, and a preoccupation with the logocentric dualities of Western consciousness runs throughout her work. The relationship between performer and spectator is one such opposition, and much of Deren's attraction to non-Western cultures had to do with the possibilities of other formulations of difference. She notes with glee that "Freud wouldn't do so well in Bali. Hooray for the Balinese."[3] That Freud has done fairly well within feminist film theory suggests, perhaps, at least one of the reasons why Maya Deren's film work has not received the sustained critical attention one might expect within feminist film studies, particularly given her status in the history of the American avant-garde.[4] Deren's work is informed by a utopian sensibility, a desire not just to rethink the categories of opposition but to discard and surpass them, and in this sense her work has much in common with those films that have been central in feminist writing on film. Yet her rethinking of opposition focused more explicitly on cultural differences and less on sexual ones. Thus, Deren explored so-called primitive cultures. Her film project on comparative rituals was never completed. Perhaps Western dualities are so integral to the cinema that the radical otherness which Deren hoped to capture and explore was virtually unrepresentable on film. However, that desire does inform virtually all of the films that Deren did complete, as well as many of her writings on film.

Indeed, it is in the category of the "primitive," and particularly in the cross-referencing between different meanings of the "primitive," that Deren's work occupies a difficult and challenging area of inquiry for feminist film theory. For the notion of the "primitive" foregrounds the often unacknowledged connections between the feminine and the culturally exotic, and unless those connections are explored, feminist film theory risks perpetuating a female subject fully consonant with white, Western notions of the self. Now the immediate temptation, in Deren's case, is to characterize her outright celebration of the "primitive," her distrust of Western rationality, and her attention to the spiritual side of creation as "essentialist." Such a categorization and implicit dismissal obscure, however, the extent to which her work involves a significant inquiry into cultural and historical difference. Although Deren herself does not often refer specifically to a female (or much less feminist) investment in such an inquiry, such connections are suggested in some of her writing and certainly in her films.

Deren's interest in "primitive" cultures is characterized by a criticism of those who have adopted "primitivism" as a way of describing art work that in fact shares little with the cultures in question, as well as a frustration with the lack of attention to the larger cultural context that shapes "primitive" art and rituals. A section of her 1946 pamphlet *An Anagram of Ideas on Art, Form, and Film*, for instance, is devoted to just such a criticism:

> I am certain that thoughtful critics do not use the term "primitive" without definition and modification. But its general usage, and as a category title for exhibits, reveals a comparative ideal based on the superficial similarity between the *skilled simplicity* of artists whose culture was limited in information and crude in equipment; and the *crude simplifications* of artists whose culture is rich in information and refined in its equipment.[5]

In an earlier essay, Deren compares the trance state characteristic of ritual dance in "primitive" cultures with hysteria.[6] Noting that both are motivated by "psychic conflicts and insults" and characterized by "suggestibility and hypnotism, and hypnoid trances," she observes as well that "hysteria, as possession also, occurs only within social context, when there are one or more witnesses to the scene. In other words, the role of the community as a necessary frame of reference may include an audience function similar to that of the audience in cases of hysteria." This comparison between possession and hysteria should not be read as a simple equation, since Deren is again careful to stress the radical difference in social context, and the fact that they are "parallel, rather than identical phenomena."[7] What Deren does not foreground is the common association between women and hysteria, and the therefore implicit assumption that the cultural conditions for the production of hysteria and the subsequent parallelism with possession and trance states are particularly relevant to women.

Given the extent to which Deren's films focus on the dreams and anxieties and perceptions of women, however, one might extend the comparison she makes in more gender-specific terms. Some of Deren's film work—like the never-completed film on Balinese dance referred to above—explores quite literally the affiliation with "primitive" cultures. In her better-known films, including *Meshes of the Afternoon*, another, quite different affiliation with the "primitive" emerges, one more along the lines of the relationship Gunning explores between early film and the avant-garde. *Meshes of the Afternoon* is structured by the repetition of a series of scenes. A woman, played by Deren herself, sees a figure go around the bend of a street, as she is heading toward a flight of stairs to her home. As she is about to unlock the door to her house, she drops the key. When at last she enters the house, she sees a table with two chairs, a loaf of bread with a knife, a telephone with its receiver off the hook. The woman goes up a flight of stairs to a bedroom, returns downstairs, and sits in a chair. She strokes herself gently, and as her eye appears in extreme close-up, the film begins to tell the same story again. Each retelling of the pursuit of the unknown figure and entry into the house—there are three such retellings in all—is initiated by Deren's gaze through the window. In each of the three repetitions, different elements are foregrounded. In one version, for instance, the mysterious figure on the road enters the house, and reveals a mirror in the place of a face; in another, the passage from the first floor to the upstairs of the house is made only with great turbulence and difficulty.

Narration itself is foregrounded in *Meshes of the Afternoon*, particularly insofar as the film turns further and further inward with each recasting of the story's "meshes," until there are four Maya Derens. In addition, the two most central repeated elements in the film are the quintessential narrative components of pursuing an other (the androgynous figure which disappears down the road) and crossing a threshold. Narration is also fragmented in the film, most obviously in the way Deren is presented initially. At the very beginning of the film, the only parts of her body visible are her feet and her hands, with the sense of her presence connoted rather by the shadows she casts as she moves down the road, and up the stairway to the house. There is a split vision from the outset, between what Deren sees and what we see of Deren. With the repetition of the initial event of *Meshes of the Afternoon*, Deren is designated simultaneously as narrator and as enigma, as subject and object of narration, but the elusive figure walking down the road remains unnamed, unidentified—specifically, remains unsexed. The objects foregrounded in the film, like the knife and the key, signal passage, the crossing of a threshold, whether the space separating inside and outside or the boundary between self and other.

The trajectory of the woman in *Meshes of the Afternoon* evokes a wide range of complex psychic questions, and the shape of the trajectory evokes much of the spirit and style of the "primitive" era of filmmaking. Deren herself is identified as both a dreamer and conjuror in a way that recalls two of the most common frames of the early cinema—the dreamer who awakens only to be confronted with a reality that contrasts brutally with the dream, and the conjuror who makes objects, including his own body, appear and disappear at will. The use of double exposure in the film to represent the multiplied personae of Maya Deren is also evocative, as Gunning suggests, of "primitive" filmmaking, and captures a sense of awe and wonder in the very representability of the woman's interior life. This evocation of the early cinema in *Meshes of the Afternoon* acquires a very specific gendered component, for the dream/fantasy frame of the film is interrupted twice by the man, played by Hammid. When the third Maya Deren approaches the sleeping woman, about to stab her, the woman awakens to find Hammid awaking her. Hence the appearance of the man seems to redraw the line separating dream and waking. If the pursuit of the ambiguous figure, as well as the constant folding of the event, suggests a threshold space, then the appearance of Hammid seems to mark the closing down of that threshold, and the attendant emergence of duality.

His appearance also signals a return to order, a designation of the space of the house as a dream space. That very polarity is again thrown into question when Deren reaches for the knife—now transformed from the flower, the object initially associated with the "other" in the first place—and stabs him. But "he" now is a mirror image, and the shattering of the mirror into fragments, dispersed on a beach, suggests the persistence of the narrative vision embodied by the woman—a narrative vision in which the polarities of self and other, of female and male, of dream and waking are fragile. The second ending of *Meshes of the Afternoon* tells another story. Now Hammid enacts the role of narrator, repeating the itinerary of Deren at the beginning of the film. His discovery of Deren in the house, with her throat slit and her body covered with seaweed, suggests the impossibility of that threshold space. As female and male, as the two sides of duality, then, Deren and Hammid enact, in these two endings to the film, two radically opposed narrative itineraries: the one which poses an endless movement between opposing poles, which opens up a threshold space between the dualities of self and other, and the other, certainly more "conventional," which asserts those dualities.

In other films by Deren, the realm of the "primitive" is evoked in ways that evoke the intersection between the feminine, the archaic, and the cinematic. As the female subject of *At Land* (1944), for instance, Deren emerges from the sea at the beginning of the film, and eventually discovers a meeting in progress inside a mansion, at which she gazes with all of the wonder of an Uncle Josh discovering the cinema for the first time, or an indiscreet bathroom maid peeking at forbidden scenes. *Ritual in Transfigured Time* (1945–1946) begins with two open doorways in a corridor, with Deren, now situated on the other side of the threshold, observed with awe by a woman in a scene that is quite evocative of "primitive" journeys down hotel corridors.[8] The realm of the "primitive" is given a particularly strong inflection of traditional femininity here. Once the woman crosses the threshold, she holds a skein of yarn while Deren winds it into a ball, and the rhythm of their motions creates a pattern of connection between them.

That the woman is black suggests, perhaps, the desire to rewrite the racist stereotypes of a film such as *What Happened in the Tunnel*; but it can suggest—much more problematically— the assumption of a patronizing desire for "racial harmony" or the appropriation of image of "exotic" femininity on Deren's part. While I do not think Deren's fascination with racial difference, as evidenced in this and other films, as well as in her writings, can be equated with the disturbing appearance of racist clichés of performance in Arzner's *Dance, Girl, Dance*, this does not mean her explorations of racial boundaries are not problematic in their own way.

Like most of Deren's films, *Ritual in Transfigured Time* suggests the trancelike state which so fascinated her in the dances of "primitive" culture. She herself made the connection between "primitive" dance and hypnoid states. Here, the representation of the winding of the yarn suggests—despite Deren's suspicions about Freud—another psychoanalytic association of the "primitive," recalling Freud and Breuer's assertion that "hypnoid states" often "grow out of the day-dreams which are so common even in healthy people and to which needlework and similar occupations render women especially prone."[9]

Undoubtedly the most persistent figure of the "primitive" in these films is the threshold —between dream and waking and man and woman in *Meshes of the Afternoon*, between nature and culture in *At Land*, between white woman and black woman in *Ritual in Transfigured Time*. The representation of the threshold taps the "primitive" in several senses of the word—as a mode of filmmaking, as a dream world apart from the reality of waking and spatial stability, and—most controversially in feminist terms—as a cultural realm to which women, it would appear, have privileged access. The female narrator in these films embodies a desire, a fantasy of narrative as a persistent movement, the creation of a threshold space.

Asparagus evokes those early films in which "primitive" narrators act out the pleasures of the cinema. Pitt's animated film depicts different stages of a woman's relation to a series of images, stages which take us from the interior of a house, to a city street, to a theater. The animation of the film creates a universe that is at once dreamlike, painterly, and childlike. The woman's imaginary world is most graphically portrayed in the tableaulike garden panorama that unrolls at the window in her house early in the film. Lush floral imagery is juxtaposed with a barren and somewhat dismal-looking asparagus patch. It does not require too much imagination to see here a rather brutal juxtaposition of female and male imagery, a juxtaposition that becomes a kind of running joke in the film. The female narrator's relationship to a world of dream, magic, and image-making suggests a reincarnation of the "primitive" narrator.

The psychoanalytic reference point is quite strong, since the process of narration in *Asparagus* draws upon the creation of dream images. The encounter of the female narrator of the film with a luscious world of imagery is like the transformation of dream thoughts into dream images in the dreamer, a process for which Freud used the term *primitive* ("All the linguistic instruments by which we express the subtler relations of thought—the conjunctions and prepositions, the changes in declension and conjugation—are dropped, because there are no means of representing them; just as in a 'primitive' language without any grammar, only the raw material of thought is expressed and abstract terms are taken back to the concrete ones that are at their basis").[10] In Deren's films, there is also an evocation of the state of dreaming. But in *Asparagus*, the specific relationship of women to the activation of dreams and imagination does not rely on the "feminine" defined in terms of traditional domestic activities—for instance, the winding of yarn in *Ritual in Transfigured Time*—but rather in terms of traditional sexual ones.

In the second section of the film, the woman narrator journeys to a theater where a claymation audience watches a spectacle of amazing special effects. The woman goes backstage, where she opens up a Pandora's box of images and sets them loose. The images float into the midst of the amazed audience; thus the woman transgresses the boundary line separating audience from spectacle. The world outside the theater is depicted as obsessed with sexual polarity, whether through phallic imagery (a gun shop, a sex store) or the storefront with two baby dolls, one on a pink blanket, the other on a blue one. The space of the theater thus becomes an other space, where the illusion of oscillation and fluidity is operative. In the concluding section of the film, the woman returns to the house, and the formerly resistant asparagus now not only yields to her caress but undergoes a series of fanciful transformations, from waterfall to colored sprinkles to stars. The images recall those images set loose in the theater. The narrator is certainly no longer an observer but an active participant, and a participant no longer concealed backstage as in the theater.

The connection between the woman and the asparagus is overtly sexual, becoming a fanciful rendition of a blow job. Throughout most of the film, the woman has been portrayed either as faceless or as the impression left in a mask which she dons to enter into the world at large. But in this final section of the film, the woman acquires at least one facial attribute: extremely red lips. At the very beginning of the film, the first asparagus motif occurs when the woman defecates into a toilet bowl. In one of many of a series of magical transformations in the film, the turds become asparagus stalks. Given the mouth and the sexual act as the film's conclusion, it would appear that one of the film's many fantasies is the rereading of the very notion of a psychic or sexual stage, since the conclusion of the film could be read simultaneously as "regression" (to an oral stage) or "development" to something of a "phallic" stage. While I suppose the film could be read as informed by penis envy, the fantasy of incorporation evidenced at the conclusion suggests a refusal of the very divisions, the "stages," that would make such a reading possible. The incorporation is quite literal, of course, but it is figurative as well, the sexual act becoming an exchange of the polarities of male and female imagery.

In other words, a fantasy of a threshold space informs *Asparagus*, and this fantasy of the threshold shares some similarities with the woman's journey in *Meshes of the Afternoon*. The three sections of *Asparagus* can be seen as a progression toward the fantasy of the incorporation of male into female at the film's conclusion, but the last two sections can also be read, along the lines of *Meshes of the Afternoon*, as a double ending. In other words, like *Meshes of the Afternoon*, *Asparagus* juxtaposes two narrative modes. The two endings of *Meshes of the Afternoon* suggest two different encounters between man and woman, as well as a juxtaposition of a conventional narrative resolution (the separation of dream and waking, male and female), with the persistence of narrative understood as a threshold space between opposing terms. In *Asparagus*, the two narrative modes are defined explicitly in terms of the position of the woman—in the one case a masked figure backstage who creates a different kind of spectacle, and in the other, a sexual being who becomes both active and passive, creator and recipient of sexual imagery.

The female narrator embodies a fantasy of movement, of transformation, whereby the imagery of "male" and "female" is interchangeable; thus it is a narration located in a hypothetical moment anterior to narration as a conquest of the other, evidenced in early films such as *A Subject for the Rogue's Gallery* and *What Happened on 23rd Street*. *Asparagus* appropriates, then, the metaphoric figure of the female voyeur in films such as *The Indiscreet Bathroom Maid*. If a condition of female voyeurism in early film is the pleasure of crossing the threshold, but in ways fundamentally different from the imposition of the law (in *A Search for Evidence*) or the conquest of the female body (in *A Subject for the Rogue's Gallery*), then the female narrator in *Asparagus* extends the possible fantasies of the threshold.

I turn now to three films in which it is not so much the representation of the female body per se that is central, but rather the narrative modes associated with traditional femininity. That these films are part of the history of French cinema (Akerman's film is Belgian, but is read largely within the context of French cinema defined in the broader terms of "French-speaking") situates differently their inquiries into "primitive" representation. The distinction between dominant and avant-garde cinema does not hold quite the same currency in a French context as it has in the American context, particularly since the rejection of narrative so central to the American avant-garde has not been a defining characteristic of French film. To be sure, it has been a recurring characteristic of French cinema to reject or revise considerably the narrative conventions of the American cinema. But this search for alternative cinematic forms has not entailed the dismissal of narrative, but rather its reconceptualization. Throughout the history of French cinema, and particularly at moments of crisis and transition, filmmakers have paid homage to, probed, and explored the "primitive" era. At certain moments within French film history, women filmmakers have appropriated forms of "primitive" narration, and have explored the links between the "primitive" and the feminine by staging tensions between different narrative modes.

Like many other films associated with the development of impressionism in France in the 1920s, Germaine Dulac's 1922 film *The Smiling Madame Beudet* attempts to convey inner, subjective states, in this case the inner frustration of a sensitive, musically inclined provincial woman who is trapped in a conventional marriage to a boorish husband.[11] From the outset, Mme Beudet's conflict with her husband is staged as a conflict of differing points of view: when they are invited to the opera, Monsieur Beudet conjures up an image of a group of happy singers, while Mme Beudet can only imagine an overbearing man bellowing to a woman crouched beneath him. While Dulac's film is technically more sophisticated than many films of the 1920s, it is characterized by a selective, foregrounded use of "primitive" narration.[12] For Mme Beudet fantasizes in a "primitive" mode. She is like the dreamers in early films who imagine fictional characters coming to life as they nod over a book, or like the conjuror in a Méliès film who makes threatening objects disappear—usually women, in Méliès's case; her husband, in the case of Mme Beudet.

As a dreamer, a fantasizer, Mme Beudet is portrayed in a far more complex way than are her fantasies.[13] In other words, a distance is created in the film between how the woman's fantasy life is represented and how she is portrayed in relationship to it. The depiction of Mme Beudet taps a wide variety of angles, camera distances, and lighting effects. The style of her fantasies and dreams tends, however, to be quite similar: she reads a magazine and imagines a character coming to life, drawing upon the kinds of superimpositions quite common in early cinema. She reads a poem and imagines one image after another—each shot in the straightforward, frontal style characteristic of early film—with no connection between them.

In Dulac's film, different narrative modes are juxtaposed with ironic effect.[14] The most obvious irony results from the juxtaposition of Mme Beudet's fantasy life with the equally "primitive," but even more limited, fantasy life of her husband. More significant is the interplay between two different narratives that constitute the overall structure of the film. On one level is the "primitive" narration that characterizes the points of view of the characters, and especially Mme Beudet. On another level is the narration of the film in a larger sense, involving crisis and resolution around the film's central event. Monsieur Beudet plays a "suicide game" in which he pulls an unloaded gun from his desk drawer and threatens to kill himself at moments of conflict and frustration. The turning point of the film is Mme Beudet's decision to load the gun.[15] Her plan misfires in more ways than one, however. For when Monsieur Beudet next pulls the gun from his drawer, he points it at her; and when he shoots it (harming no one), and discovers it was loaded, he foolishly assumes that his wife wanted to kill herself, and not him.

In a film so concerned with making visible the inner states of its characters, and of its heroine in particular, the absence of a shot actually showing Mme Beudet loading the gun—initiating some kind of narrative action—is particularly significant. The absence of such an image suggests a collision, within Mme Beudet, of two differing narrative modes—the "primitive" mode I have already described, and a more properly classical one, in the sense that the surreptitious "murder" of her husband requires the planning of just the kind of cause-and-effect actions that are central to the evolution of the classical mode of narration. The nonrepresentation of the significant action of loading the gun suggests the impossibility of Mme Beudet's position within that classical narrative mode.

However, this is not to say that The Smiling Madame Beudet brackets classical narrative altogether. Rather, the film represents the conventions of narrative resolution in order to problematize them. In the final image, we see the couple in the street, and Monsieur Beudet nods to a priest who passes. The representation of the outdoors, of the public sphere of the town, indicates a division between Mme Beudet's inner existence and the social universe that surrounds her. The film begins with standard "establishing shots" of the village in which the couple lives, although it becomes clear that there is no seamless fit between that social context and the inner world of Mme Beudet. Indeed, this is another dimension of Dulac's ironic narrative style, for the few shots of the outside world that occur suggest all the more forcefully the increasing distance between Mme Beudet and her surroundings.[16]

The final image of the film is the first time that Mme Beudet is actually seen outdoors, and she is framed by two men, their exchange occurring across her body. The image "cites" the conventions of the classical cinema—husband and wife reunited, order restored—in what is undoubtedly the most far-reaching irony of the film. For the supposed integration of Mme Beudet into the institutions of provincial life requires the failure of any narrative of her own. Like the narrators of the early cinema, Mme Beudet can conjure and dream isolated images, but she cannot construct a narrative. But Dulac, of course, can.[17] The Smiling Madame Beudet brings together a historical moment of the cinema with a particular mode of female consciousness, creating an encounter between the "primitive" cinema and the classical cinema, between a female imagination unable to break out of the duality of home versus public world, of isolated images versus complex narrative, and a more properly classical narrative which offers only the position of the obedient wife.[18] It is in the ironic juxtaposition of these modes that female narration takes shape.

Somewhat like filmmakers of the 1920s, the directors of the New Wave were interested in stretching the boundaries of narrative filmmaking, and they too entertained an ambiguous relationship to the conventions of the classical American cinema. Perhaps the most striking feature in the films of the directors associated with the New Wave was the consciousness of the history and theory of the medium that influenced their styles of filmmaking. Anecdotes of childhoods and adolescences spent at the Cinémathèque Française have become part of the standard histories of the period, and as is well known, the central group of filmmakers who formed the "core" of the Nouvelle Vague—Jean-Luc Godard, François Truffaut, Claude Chabrol, Eric Rohmer, and Jacques Rivette—all began their cinematic careers as writers and critics at Cahiers du cinéma.[19] Virtually all of the films of the New Wave—and especially those of Jean-Luc Godard—are films about film, about the particular nature of cinema as a form of representation. In keeping with the ambiguous relationship with American cinema that has informed so much French film practice, New Wave films that reflect upon the classical American cinema have received the most attention. But an equally important dimension of the films of these and other filmmakers of the period involves citations of, and inquiries into, the early years of film history.

Jean-Luc Godard's 1963 film Les Carabiniers, for instance, depicts two naive men whose departure to do battle for their king initiates them into a world where image and referent are split. When the two men return from the war, they display a series of "title deeds"— postcards depicting a wide range of department stores, women, and tourist attractions. The film features a first visit to the movies by one of its protagonists that recalls Uncle Josh at the Moving Picture Show. The program which Michel-ange watches shows a train, a family meal, and a woman bathing, all with exaggerated sound effects. Like Uncle Josh, Michel-ange is tantalized by the image of woman on the screen. After his efforts at peeking around the sides of the screen to get a better look at the woman bathing are unsuccessful, he then proceeds to tear down the screen. There is no rear-projectionist to confront Michel-ange, but rather an exposed brick wall and the continued projection of the film images over his astonished face and body.

In a different yet related way, François Truffaut's 1970 film *The Wild Child* (*L'enfant sauvage*) also cites the early cinema.[20] Based on Jean Itard's *Mémoire et rapport sur Victor de l'Aveyron* (1806), the film tells the story of the famous "wild child" found in the forest—his difficult access to the culture and civilization of France, and the role of his mentor, Itard, played by Truffaut himself. Throughout the film, Truffaut uses devices associated with the early cinema, such as iris shots, and eschews the use of techniques uncommon in the "primitive" era, such as close-ups; and he cites several "primitive" films, most notably the famous *Repas de bébé*, an early Lumière film showing Auguste Lumière and his wife feeding their child. Most notably, Truffaut draws an analogy between two kinds of relationships—his own relationship to the early cinema, and Itard's relationship to the zero degree of culture represented by Victor. Thus Victor is identified as "primitive" in both a cinematic and a cultural sense.

In both of these examples, the evocation of the early cinema serves to mark the passage of the individual—more specifically, the male individual—into realms of paternal authority, whether the comically defined (and never seen) "king" who distributes postcards as title deeds in *Les Carabiniers*, or the paternalistic figure of the physician who takes charge of Victor in *The Wild Child*. Agnès Varda's 1962 film *Cleo from 5 to 7* also "cites" the early cinema, in what appears—initially, at least—to be a gesture similarly engaged with "maturation," but now of a female figure. The protagonist of Varda's film is a mediocre but successful pop singer who embodies virtually all of the clichés of the stereotypical woman-as-object—she is narcissistic, childlike, and dependent on the reassuring images of those who surround her. The "5 to 7" of the film's title refers to the temporal trajectory of the film (actually more like 5:00 to 6:30 p.m.), the time spent waiting for the results of a medical examination which will show whether Cléo has cancer or not. Indeed, there is an obsession with time in the film. Cléo is extremely conscious of the passage of time until the test results will be ready, and the film marks off time in a series of thirteen segments, ranging from three to fifteen minutes long, each identified in titles flashed onto the screen with the name of a character or groups of characters attached.

It is tempting to describe the film in terms of Cléo's transformation from object to subject. Sandy Flitterman-Lewis, noting that in the film "relations of power are associated with vision," reads Cléo in these terms: "In assuming a vision of her own, Cléo assumes the power to direct her life, and the power to construct her own image as well."[21] There is no question that Cléo's passage in the film involves a literal discarding of many of the fictions of feminine identity —her blonde wig, her doll's house of an apartment, the substitute family within which she is forever the child. However, the scenario to which Cléo accedes is that of classical film narrative. At the conclusion of the film, Cléo strikes up a friendship with a young soldier about to leave for Algeria. While this is not exactly a typical Hollywood ending, it is nonetheless a girl-meets-boy, walk-off-into-the-horizon conclusion full of hope and optimism.

The threat of cancer is still real, but the fear has diminished; and the final segment of the film in which these changes occur offers the longest stretch of uninterrupted time. To be sure, it could be argued that the classical scenario is reproduced and defamiliarized simul-taneously, through the representation of and insistence upon the woman's relationship to it. But if *Cleo from 5 to 7* develops a critical reading of the relationship between women and classical film narrative, it is a reading that has as much to do with the narration of the film as with Cléo's transformation from female object into female subject. For underlying the apparently radical change in Cléo is a far more complex and contradictory process of narration, whereby two different kinds of narrating authorities intersect.

Like Dulac, Varda associates "primitive" narration with the traditionally female. It is not primarily Cléo who is designated a "primitive narrator," however, but rather a woman fortune-teller in whose apartment the film begins. In the film's "prologue," the woman card reader lays out a series of cards and interprets them. The entire cast of characters of the film, as well as its central events, is displayed in a series of still, static images. The card reader brings to mind the early Méliès film *Les cartes vivantes* (*The Living Playing Cards*), in which a (male) conjuror brings a series of playing cards to magical life. In Varda's film, however, the woman's presence is identified as wavering between the narrative authority of the conjuror and a superstitious belief in a fatalistic narrative agency beyond her powers of interpretation. The universe she inhabits is enclosed and claustrophobic, reminiscent of the Beudet apartment in Dulac's film (here, however, the husband is quite literally banished to the closet).

Given that Cléo's superstitiousness seems to be part of the feminine identity that is shed in the course of the film, it is tempting to regard this unnamed (and untimed) narrator as a presence that the film disavows. Cléo's superstitious nature is also revealed during a taxi ride later in the film, when another association of the "primitive" appears: a shop window reveals African masks, and a group of students—including one prominently displayed black man—surround the cab, terrifying Cléo. If the female fortune-teller is associated with "primitive" narration, the racial and racist stereotype here on display is an image with no narrative authority of its own. While it is tempting to assume that the stereotype emerges in order to indicate the limited state of Cléo's consciousness, it is equally possible that the "Africa" thus evoked is an exotic other for the film as well as for its protagonist.

A more direct citation of the early cinema occurs later in the film when Cléo goes to the movies. Raoul, the character with whom this segment is identified in the subtitles, is a projectionist who shows a short silent film comedy. A young man (played by Jean-Luc Godard) watches his loved one (played by Anna Karina) depart down the steps of a quay. When he turns to put on sunglasses, his gaze shifts to the opposite stairway where, unbeknownst to him, a different young woman—but who he thinks is his love—follows the same trajectory in a reverse field. A series of comic-tragic mishaps arrives, and the young man runs down the steps only to arrive too late to save his beloved. Back at the position at which the film began, he removes his sunglasses to wipe away a tear, and turns his head to discover that he had made a mistake, that because of his shift in position he had identified another woman's actions as those of his girlfriend. His "real" beloved is continuing to walk down the opposite stairway. He runs after her, and they embrace in the requisite "happy ending."

This re-created silent film is modern in very conspicuous ways, since it employs techniques of cutting, matching, and alternation of medium shots and close-ups that were quite alien to early filmmakers. That it is shown at sound speed increases the sense of "citation." However, the film's punchline relies on a use of time that is quite distinctly "primitive." Sequential events are repeated with a disregard for what have been, since the 1910s, "rules" of linear temporality. When the young man turns to wipe a tear, a temporal "mistake" has occurred, for he watches his lover depart as if the other intervening events had not occurred, as if no time had elapsed since she first began walking down the stairs.

The most frequently cited example of temporal overlap in the early cinema occurs in Edwin S. Porter's *Life of an American Fireman* (1903). From the interior of a room in which a woman and her child have collapsed from the effects of a fire, we see a fireman rescue the woman, and then return to rescue the child. The same action is shown again, but from the exterior of the house. As André Gaudreault has suggested, the repetition of the action of rescue from outside the house allows the representation of a climax: "on reaching ground, the woman implores the fireman to rescue her child still trapped in the room. Perhaps Porter added the last shot with the intention of showing us the mother's request." The motivation for this temporal repetition is the possibility of representing multiple perspectives. As Gaudreault says, "the simple copresence of two different points of view toward one single event justifies their successive presentation, which produces a repetition of the action and finally a temporal overlap that today can only astonish."[22]

In Varda's scene, there does not initially appear to be a real change of point of view, since Godard's young man is the focal point for both descents. The mistake in his perception occurs when he puts on dark glasses. The entire scene is filmed, it seems, as if shot through his dark glasses—the woman who departs down the stairs is black, for instance. But the filter of the dark glasses does not really determine the tint of the scene, since it is more properly described as an attempt to replicate a negative image—literally with costume and skin colors reversed, and figuratively with the heroine's sudden death replacing the couple's previous bliss. That race again emerges in the context of another kind of so-called primitivism, now one associated specifically with the history of cinema, makes it clear that race is central to the evocation of the "primitive" in the film.

But as with the racist stereotypes in Arzner's *Dance, Girl, Dance*, there is little to suggest that race is evoked in order to explore its construction in a critical way. The temporal repetition that would be motivated by a change in point of view in the early cinema is here motivated, rather, by the dualities of white and black, happiness and misery. As Claudia Gorbman has said, the silent film "works as a metaphor for Cléo's own dilemma of perception. Put dark glasses on (pessimism, superstition, anxiety) and you will see death, darkness, sadness; look by the light of day and you will find life, love, happiness."[23] But the allusion to early cinema provides a metaphor not just for Cléo's own development, but for the narrative of the film as well. For this evocation of the "otherness" of the "primitive" cinema suggests a pull toward another mode of representation, an affinity between Varda's own unorthodox use of temporality and the supposed "mistakes" of the "primitive" era. That pull, that affinity, complicate somewhat the seemingly smooth movement in *Cleo from 5 to 7* toward self-knowledge and subjecthood.

In the concluding segment of the film, Cléo and her new friend Antoine encounter the doctor, who confirms that Cléo does indeed have cancer. The prediction of the fortune-teller at the beginning of the film is confirmed, but it seems as though the doctor, a narrative authority associated with science, reason, and, need I add, masculinity, has replaced the superstitious female "primitive" narrator of the film's prologue. The diametrically opposed responses of Cléo appear to confirm this change: terrified and childlike at the beginning of the film, stoic and adult at the conclusion. However, there is a subtle irony in this apparent transformation, a suggestion that the enclosed, feminine world of superstition and "primitive" narration is not so easily separable from the bright light of science and the confident resolutions of classical narration.[24]

The force of the "primitive" narrator echoes not only in the actualization of her prediction, but also in a small gesture performed by the doctor. As he turns from Cléo and Antoine, he puts on his dark glasses in movements that echo very precisely Godard's movements in the short film that we have seen with Cléo in the movie theater. *Cleo from 5 to 7* is characterized by a considerably ironic narrative. The condition of Cléo's transformation would appear to be entry into a cinematic order from which any vestiges of the "primitive" are banished, whether in the form of narrative structures or female narrators who create cinematic equivalents of "living playing cards." However, the narrative of the film insists, rather, on the fold of the "primitive" into the classical, and the attendant impossibility of neatly separating the female object from the female subject. Yet while the film connects female subject and female object, the overlapping itineraries of the "scientific" (the doctor) and the "primitive" (the fortune-teller) suggest, just as forcefully, a distinctly unproblematized relation between black-and-white; indeed, the black remains as the unexamined projection of the white man's sunglasses, or the spectacle of a "primitive" mask.

In contrast to the contexts for Dulac's and Varda's films, there is no "movement," no "new Belgian cinema," no shared alternative tradition, of which Chantal Akerman's 1975 film *Jeanne Dielman, 23 Quai du Commerce, 1080 Bruxelles* is a part. No shared *cinematic* tradition, that is. Rather, one of the most important contexts for *Jeanne Dielman* is contemporary feminism. Akerman herself has said, "*Jeanne Dielman*, for instance, I wouldn't have . . . made the film in that manner, the idea wouldn't have been so clear, were it not for the women's movement."[25] Akerman's film responds more directly to a feminist context, one in which the notion of the "primitive" has surfaced in fairly controversial ways. From the resurrection of the pre-oedipal and the attendant child-mother bond in feminist psychoanalytic writing, to the insistence on the body in discourse in *l'écriture féminine*, to the conceptualization of a female aesthetic defined in so-called pre-aesthetic terms, contemporary feminism has been obsessed with the excavation of a space, an area, somehow prior to and therefore potentially resistant to the realm of the patriarchal symbolic. In *Jeanne Dielman*, Akerman taps this feminist

4. Chantal Akerman's *Jeanne Dielman, 23 Quai du Commerce, 1080 Bruxelles* (1975). Courtesy Anthology Film Archives; reprinted by permission.

preoccupation with the "presymbolic" and creates a dialogue between it and the supposedly "presymbolic" phase of the cinema, a dialogue that refuses any relegation of the feminine or of female desire to the status of the "pre-." In feminist terms, then, the "primitive" surfaces in *Jeanne Dielman* through the preoccupation with the mother-child bond, as well as with the rituals of everyday life.

Jeanne Dielman, like *Cleo from 5 to 7*, is preoccupied with time, and in particular with duration, repetition, and ritual. Although it makes no effort to represent Jeanne Dielman's states of consciousness and perception, as Dulac does with Mme Beudet, there is nonetheless a strong sense of lived duration in the film, an attempt to draw the spectator into the temporal framework of the protagonist. *Jeanne Dielman* is best known for its length—three hours and eighteen minutes—and its slow pace. For while the film does condense and elide time, it devotes extensive "real" time to the rituals of housework and everyday life. Most viewers watch *Jeanne Dielman* waiting for "something to happen." And while a climax eventually does occur—in the last fifteen minutes of the film—*Jeanne Dielman* demands nothing less than a revision of what is meant by "something happening." The film follows three days in the everyday routine of a Belgian widow in Brussels, played by Delphine Seyrig. Her routine includes prostitution, daily visits from regular male clients which are totally, obsessively integrated into the pattern of household chores. While documenting the gestures and rituals that make up Jeanne Dielman's everyday life, the film spends more time in the kitchen and the living room than in the bedroom, and it is not until the conclusion that we see Jeanne Dielman in the bedroom with one of her clients. The scene revealed is not just a scene of sex, but one of death: after Jeanne experiences what appears to be sexual orgasm, she kills her client.[26]

It should not be surprising that given its obvious affiliations with feminism, this film has become—as much as any other film made in the last twenty years—a feminist classic. Two issues in particular have emerged in the considerably extensive feminist commentary available on *Jeanne Dielman*. First, the film develops an aesthetic form equal to the task of the examination of women and the cinema undertaken by feminist film theorists. B. Ruby Rich describes the "filming degree zero" of Akerman's style, and Marsha Kinder emphasizes how Akerman "cultivates the unseen" and the "unheard."[27] That *Jeanne Dielman* can be read as a meditation on the very nature of the cinema has been noted by many critics, and of particular importance is the absence of the "reverse shot," the refusal to construct a fictional space along the conventional lines of seer/seen.[28] Hence, as Claire Johnston has argued, there is in *Jeanne Dielman* an "opening up of what suture attempts to fill."[29]

This is not to say that *Jeanne Dielman* can be read, in feminist terms, uniquely through its formal structure: indeed, most feminists who have written about this film foreground consistently the challenge it represents to any purely formal notion of alternative cinema. Second, feminist critics have drawn attention to the strong ambivalence in the film, the sense throughout of competing levels of agency, identification, and pleasure. The most obvious embodiment of ambivalence is Jeanne herself. Jayne Loader is quite critical of the film precisely for the reason that Jeanne's final action, the murder of the client, is presented so ambiguously.[30]

Others have found the ambiguous representation of Jeanne to be one of the greatest challenges of the film. Brenda Longfellow puts it this way: "Is she a hysteric or feminist revolutionary? Perhaps the only answer is both, and simultaneously so."[31] Laleen Jayamanne speaks in similar terms of the representation of housework in the film; noting Akerman's self-described "loving acknowledgement of women's household tasks. Jayamanne says that those tasks are "lovingly viewed at a distance because they also signify woman's absence; they are beautiful and lethal because they help her transcend her situation."[32] The ambivalence of *Jeanne Dielman* works in terms of its narrative structure as well. Janet Bergstrom has noted the split in the film between character and director, between two definitions of the feminine: "the feminine *manquée*, acculturated under patriarchy, and the feminist who is actively looking at the objective conditions of her oppression—her place in the family."[33] And Danièle Dubroux reads *Jeanne Dielman* in terms of the Freudian uncanny, with the film's sense of women's place rendered as both extremely familiar and extremely strange.[34]

This sense of ambivalence, of the uncanny, of the "beautiful and the lethal," reverberates throughout the film. Virtually every gesture and event represented is composed of a complex itinerary of pleasure and control, desire and repression. The orgasm is particularly significant in this context, but it is one instance in a long series of losses of control. It becomes clear that something has gone wrong in Jeanne's routine when, on the second day of the film, she leaves the cover off the soup tureen after putting the client's fee in, leaves her hair uncombed, burns the potatoes. So much has the film created a rhythm around the precise order of Jeanne Dielman's routine that these seemingly small disruptions are quite significant.

But what remains unspecified in the film is the exact source of the disruption. Perhaps the client on day two of the film stayed too long—but given the elliptical way in which the sexual encounters are shown, this is impossible to say with certainty. While day one of the film would appear to be the stable routine only disrupted on the following day, the letter from her sister Fernande in Canada seems to provoke disruption, particularly with Fernande's suggestion that Jeanne should think of remarriage. The letter ends with mention of a birthday present for Jeanne, and after Jeanne reads the letter aloud to her son, she wonders what the present might be. Jeanne is unwrapping the belated birthday package from Fernande when the doorbell rings on the third day, announcing her client. As a result, the scissors are left in the bedroom where they don't belong, soon to be grabbed as the murder weapon.

On the second day of the film, a neighbor of Jeanne's drops off her baby, whom Jeanne tends to for a short while. The neighbor—played by Akerman herself—is never seen, but when she returns to pick up the baby, we hear her voice as she asks Jeanne what she is making for dinner. She then proceeds to tell a humorous story about her own inability to decide what to buy at the butcher's. She decided to listen to what other women were ordering, but was uninspired, so when her own turn came she ordered what the woman before her had ordered. As a result, she was burdened with an expensive cut of veal, which her family doesn't even like. She continues to talk of her husband and her children. A sense of randomness dominates the woman's conversation, as she moves from one topic to another, and a sense below the surface of what she says of the enormous frustration of caring for her children and pleasing her husband.

Significantly, Jeanne stands at the door with her arm protecting the passage during the encounter, as if to ward off not only the possible intrusion of the neighbor but also the threat of randomness. When the neighbor asks Jeanne what she is making for dinner, Jeanne replies that on Wednesdays, she makes veal cutlets with peas and carrots. But later in the day, when the afternoon client leaves, he says he will see Jeanne next Thursday. One assumes that Jeanne regulates her clients with the same precision with which she regulates her choice of meals, so the mistake—if indeed it is a mistake—reads as one more possible cause for disruption. There may not be an exact and identifiable cause for the murder of Jeanne's client, but the threat of randomness, of an interruption which is not immediately regulated and defined within cycles of repetition and ritual, looms over the film from the outset.

Jeanne Dielman begins in the kitchen in the middle of the first day. Jeanne's routine is a model of synchronization: as the film begins, we see her preparing potatoes. The doorbell rings, and she greets a male client. Jeanne times her encounters precisely so that the potatoes that she and her teenage son will eat for dinner cook while she and her client are in the bedroom. After Jeanne shows her client out, she quickly and efficiently erases the traces of his presence. Here, as throughout the film, the camera occupies a stationary position, at approximately the same distance from Jeanne, in a medium-long shot. While the angles of the camera may change within each room, the shots are always paragons of symmetry, with Jeanne framed and defined very precisely by the objects that surround her.

There is little dialogue in the film, and what there is is usually conveyed in a stilted, stiff manner. Rather, it is the sounds of everyday life—water in the sink, heels clicking across the floor—which are exaggerated and which form the sonoric texture. While there are quite obviously cuts in the film, the individual shots are of long duration. Only the shots in the bedroom are significantly briefer than those of other rooms, thus emphasizing the somewhat forbidden quality of the room, even when it is a place to be cleaned up rather than occupied by sexual contact. Throughout *Jeanne Dielman*, virtually every shot focuses not only on how Jeanne is contained by her surroundings, but also on the passageways connecting and/or obstructing movements elsewhere—windows (through which only darkness is visible), archways, doors, curtains.

Put another way, the space of *Jeanne Dielman* is simultaneously claustrophobic and "open," or at least defined by the possibility of passage. The representation of space continues, then, the ambivalent quality characteristic of the film as a whole. So, too, is the representation of control that dominates the film from the outset marked by ambivalence. Jeanne's most obvious expression of control is the constant attention to switching lights on and off. Yet throughout the film, a neon light from the street outside flashes into the living room, its blue color and rhythmic flickering an intrusive presence in the space of Jeanne's home. If the style of the film appears to be as controlled and controlling as Jeanne's rituals, that style is disrupted as well.

Rooms are by and large represented with unchanging camera angles and distances, so as to create in the viewer a sense of the familiar not unlike that which characterizes Jeanne's routine. But sometimes angles change, just enough to make a room appear slightly different in one shot than in another. Most significantly, there is a change in mise-en-scène in the kitchen. Sometimes there is one chair at the kitchen table, and sometimes two, with no motivation or explanation as to why the change has occurred.[35] One is tempted to see in these "faux raccords," or mismatches, an homage to Godard, for whom such mismatches and refusals of continuity were deliberate subversions of classical technique. In *Jeanne Dielman*, however, the joke remains subtle, never called attention to in the way that Godard, for instance, in *Weekend*, inserts a written title announcing *"Faux raccord"* into the fabric of the mismatch.

The ambivalence which characterizes the representation of space and of control in the film characterizes the representation of Jeanne Dielman as well. Certainly, the film traces the restrictive conditions of housework, the dehumanizing effects of continuous labor and servitude, while it portrays Jeanne as an unmistakable compulsive. Yet it also produces an equally unmistakable sense of pleasure in the rituals of everyday life. Jeanne Dielman is observed, in other words, as both a symptom and a gesture, as an object to be studied at a distance and as a subject engaged in the pleasure of process. Given the extent to which the character of Jeanne occupies screen time in the film, it is perhaps tempting to read the narration in terms uniquely of her activities. But as the game of the disappearing chairs indicates quite emphatically, the representation of Jeanne's activities is only one part of the larger narrative of the film. The ambivalence of the narration acquires particular contours through the appropriation of "primitive" narration.

To be sure, the staging of "primitive" narration in *Jeanne Dielman* occurs, on one level, in the person of Jeanne Dielman herself. Silvia Bovenschen has used the term *pre-aesthetic* to describe the ways in which women's aesthetic impulses have traditionally taken shape in the forms of domestic arts, such as quilting; or personal decoration, such as make-up and costume.[36] In *Jeanne Dielman*, there is no object, pre-aesthetic or aesthetic, associated with Jeanne Dielman, but rather the gesture itself, constantly repeated and signifying both drudgery and a kind of meditative beauty. What is perhaps most strikingly "primitive" about the representation of the feminine in the film is that, like those gestures represented in the early cinema, they attach themselves to the devices of narrative closure only with great awkwardness and difficulty. In *Jeanne Dielman*, female narration is built precisely on that "difficulty," understood not as a lack but as a difference.

On a second level, the narration of *Jeanne Dielman*, however controlled and precise, evokes the early cinema by virtue of the absence of camera movement, the duration of the shots, and the camera distance. Noël Burch has categorized Akerman's rediscovery of the "primitive" mode of representation along the lines of contemporary film studies' attention to the exploration of early cinema in works of the avant-garde. But Burch draws here on Peter Wollen's well-known distinction between the two avant-gardes, one largely "formal" and resolutely antinarrative in orientation, and the other more directed toward political understandings of language and representation. As Burch puts it, the former is "outside" the institution, the latter on its "fringes." Most avant-garde films for which an affiliation with the early cinema has been claimed belong to the first category, but Burch suggests that the "other avant-garde, mainly European, has incorporated into its critical arsenal strategies which clearly hark back to the Primitive era."[37]

Jeanne Dielman exemplifies what Burch describes as the "Primitive camera stare," in which the camera "typically remains staring into space, unable or unwilling to move, when a character goes out of shot [. . .] and finally returns only after a long absence. . . ."[38] Noting that *Jeanne Dielman* incorporates the medium long shot and the front medium close-up central to the "primitive stare," Burch describes the film as

> one of the most distanced narrative films of recent years, recreating to a large extent the conditions of exteriority of the Primitive Mode (the sparseness of speech seems to be a further contributing factor here), positioning the spectator once again in his or her seat, hardly able because hardly enabled to embark upon that imaginary journey through diegetic space-time to which we are so accustomed, obliged ultimately to reflect on what is seen rather than merely experience it.[39]

Many critics have agreed with Burch's assessment of *Jeanne Dielman*, if not because of the specific affiliation of the "primitive," then at least because of the film's documentation of the woman's alienation. As I have suggested, however, I think that there is considerably more ambivalence in this film than claims to distance or alienation would suggest. The point is crucial not just in terms of the female narration of the film, but also in terms of the specific appropriation of the "primitive" that is performed. While I certainly agree that the film encourages one to "reflect on what is seen," I do not think reflection is opposed to experience, as Burch suggests. Rather, the appropriation of "primitive" narration engages a rethinking of the opposition between distance and identification.

Part of what distinguishes the appropriation of the "primitive" in *Jeanne Dielman* is not just the simultaneous inquiry into the "primitive" as it applies to both a mode of filmmaking and a mode of traditional femininity, but also the reverberations of the "scène primitive," the primal scene, in the film.[40] In *Jeanne Dielman* the components of the primal scene are quite obviously (and almost parodically) in evidence—the forbidden space of the mother's bedroom, and the accouterments of classical primal scene material, including drapes and thresholds. But there is a disjuncture between the visual components of the primal scene and its customary association with the male child. For Jeanne Dielman's son speaks the language of oedipal and primal desire in terms that are flat, obvious, and completely detached from any signs of narrative fascination.

Near the conclusion of the first day of the film, when Sylvain is in bed reading, he asks his mother about her first meeting with his father. Like virtually all extended "stories" told by the characters within the film, Jeanne rapidly and in monotone recounts her meeting with her future husband after the end of World War II, his loss of money, her aunts' (with whom she lived) initial enthusiasm and then opposition to their marriage. The questions which Sylvain poses suggest his own identification with his mother. He wonders how, if his father was ugly (as Jeanne's aunts insisted), she could make love with him; whether she would marry again if she were to fall in love; and finally—in one of the most curious exchanges between mother and son in the film—he says that, if he were a woman, he could not make love with someone with whom he was not truly in love. Jeanne's reply is one of many in the film that suggest repressed hostility: "How could you know? You are *not* a woman."

On the second day of the film, the possibility that Sylvain's emerging adolescence might be yet another source of disruption in Jeanne's routine is suggested more strongly, but once again, Sylvain's seeming identification with a woman's point of view is apparent. In a replay of the earlier scene—Sylvain again in bed, and Jeanne bidding him goodnight—he tells his mother that his friend Yan is becoming interested in women. It is clear that Yan's growing maturity (or Sylvain's perception of it) is putting a strain on their friendship. In a condensed narrative of a number of clichés of male oedipal development, Sylvain describes Yan as the source of his knowledge about a variety of sexual topics, from the equivalence between a penis and a sword (to which Sylvain protested that swords cause pain), to the sexual activities of parents, both for pleasure and for procreation.

Sylvain tells his mother that once he knew about sex, he called his mother in the night so that his father couldn't hurt her. Jeanne responds, in her typically laconic fashion, that he needn't have worried. The tangled web of the primal scene is picked up again on the third day of the film, but now it is Jeanne who tells a shopkeeper some details about her family past. Many years before, her sister Fernande—who seems, on each successive day of the film, to be an ever-increasing source of anxiety—spent three months in Belgium with her son John, who was younger than Sylvain but still bigger and stronger. While Fernande and John slept on the couch—presumably the same one that now serves as Sylvain's bed—Sylvain slept in the same bedroom as Jeanne and her husband.

Now it is crucial to remember that in the overall scheme of *Jeanne Dielman*, words and stories such as these are not given the foregrounded importance, as means of access to a privileged past, that they might be accorded in more classical films. Indeed, the process of flattening out speech and sound in the film stresses that the significance of everyday gestures is as great as if not greater than that of spoken language. Nonetheless, however downplayed the function of these lengthy narratives within the film, they are present, and are significant by virtue of their unconventional placement. Much of what is spoken in the film suggests a conventional psychoanalytic reading of the primal scene as an event, as a privileged cause, as the truth of a past. But there is something of a tease in this respect as well—significant details begin to be patched together, but never in a way that allows for a coherent scene to emerge. While Jeanne's son is certainly coddled, his every physical need attended to, his presence in the film never quite achieves the centrality one might expect, particularly given the evocations of primal scene material. Alongside the mother-son relationship, and frequently displacing it from center stage, are suggestions of another kind of primal scene, one informed by the tangled web of connections that inform the family, desire, and identification. In this rendition of the primal scene, in other words, the son's desire is displaced not only by the mother's—as the increasing significance of Aunt Fernande in the various "narratives" would suggest—but by the daughter's.

That *Jeanne Dielman* is a film made from the daughter's point of view has been suggested many times, both by Akerman's own comments and in critical readings of the film.[41] Akerman's literal signature (in the credits) to *Jeanne Dielman* is interesting in this respect. In *Je tu il elle*, Akerman's fictional name, Julie, is not given until the final credits, and the name inscribes the differing pronouns that constitute the text and address of the film. In *Jeanne Dielman*, Akerman signs her name "Chantal Anne Akerman." While there is no absolute rule for the use of middle names, they tend to signify—especially when they are not frequently used— family affiliation. But more obviously, the "Anne" is part of "Jeanne," a quite literal writing of the authorship of *Jeanne Dielman* as connected to the figure of Jeanne herself.

In the context of the present discussion, it is particularly significant that the daughter's perspective is not only a reversal—e.g., the daughter's primal scene in place of the son's— but also and especially a vantage point from which to revise substantially just what the primal scene is, both psychically and cinematically, for women. The most significant components of the primal scene that emerge in this context are, first, that the daughter's vision is necessarily intertwined with that of the mother, that there is no moment of pure distance or separation. Second, there is nothing autonomous about the tableau of the primal scene; rather, the bits and pieces of primal scene material, visual as well as verbal, lead to an ever-expanding narrative and visual scene, rather than the shock of a single spectacular crisis.

Jeanne Dielman recuperates "primitive" narration on three distinct levels—the feminine, the cinematic, the psychoanalytic—and maintains them in unwavering tension. Never, in other words, does one register totally subsume the others. The final representation of this tension is the seven-minute shot at the film's conclusion, during which Jeanne Dielman sits at the table in the living room, while the blue neon light continues to flash. During most of the film, and in keeping with the ambivalence that characterizes virtually every level, Jeanne wears a facial expression that sometimes seems to express compulsion and repression, and sometimes serenity and pleasure. The intrusion of randomness and the breakdown of her routine tilt the facial expression toward the former. But in the last shot of the film, more of the serenity has been recaptured.

It is impossible to draw a neat feminist conclusion, if by "conclusion" one means either a triumph over victimization or a condemnation of such an irrational solution as murder. To be sure, there is something in the way several threads are drawn together in the murder scene to suggest a resolution—the scissors, fetched to open the birthday present, are the female equivalent of the sword metaphorized as the penis by Sylvain and his friend; and if Sylvain imagines his father hurting his mother during sex, then Jeanne's attack is a brutal reversal of the son's imaginary scene. But the lengthy still shot at the film's conclusion deflates any such consolidation of narrative elements. One is left, rather, with the overarching sense of things unresolved, of levels of tension that cannot and will not resolve into coherent ends, of an ironic juxtaposition of narrative modes.

In all three of the French films just discussed, differences among women are central to the construction of female narration. The women whose names provide the titles of the films are symptoms, stereotypical products of patriarchally defined womanhood (the housewife in *The Smiling Madame Beudet*, the sex object in *Cleo from 5 to 7*, and a somewhat peculiar combination of the two in *Jeanne Dielman*), and female narration is the simultaneous investment in and distance from these women's activities. In other words, female narration in these films is a reexamination of the traditionally and stereotypically feminine, and an exploration of the position from which such a reexamination can take place without resurrecting the patriarchal dualities of repudiation or glorification.

In each of these films, the equation between "primitive" narration and female identity is largely a function of class: both Madame Beudet and Jeanne Dielman are bound by the rituals of domesticity as shaped by the expectations of a middle-class ethos, and Cléo's encounter with a "primitive" narrator, the female card reader, is the first of several cross-class encounters—culminating in her relationship with the soldier, Antoine—which shape her change in consciousness. The last two films to which I turn explore differences among women in a larger, cultural sense, and draw upon the associations of the "primitive" as they apply to the feminine, certainly, but more specifically as those associations intersect with anthropological definitions of the so-called primitive other. Too often, the phrase "differences among women" assumes a logocentric relationship between "West" and "East," or between "white" and "black," where the first term remains the norm. These films do not simply reverse the duality, but challenge its very foundations.

Trinh T. Minh-ha's *Reassemblage* is an examination and critique of the anthropologist's view of village life in Senegal. While the image track of the film "documents" the patterns and rituals of everyday life (with particular attention to the activities of women), there is no consistent or coherent narrative to emerge from the series of images. Rather, the filmmaker questions the very possibility of seizing the reality of Senegal through such a visual documentation. Hence, many of the images of the film are difficult to read. Close-ups of a human face, for instance, are placed in a discombobulating relationship to long, presumably "establishing" shots; other close-ups focus on a single body part—part of a face, or a breast—so that it is difficult to read the whole out of the part. Some images are deliberately out of focus; others are intercut with each other in such a way that any sense of continuity is disrupted. Documentary sound is also manipulated, with sound track and image track in a contrapuntal rather than synchronous relation. When rhythmic clapping sounds are heard, for instance, over an image of women pounding, they seem initially to be "natural," direct sounds; quickly, however, the image and the sound tracks are revealed to be separate and nonsynchronous.

The most obvious way in which *Reassemblage* critiques the tradition of anthropological filmmaking is in the use of the voice-over, spoken by Trinh herself. In much documentary filmmaking, of course, the voice-over is the primary means by which a coherent and supposedly objective perspective is assumed. From the outset, Trinh's voice functions as a self-conscious voice, one that questions constantly its own relationship to what is being shown and heard. Indeed, most of her comments are explorations of the significance of filming Senegalese life. It is an unexamined assumption of much anthropological filmmaking that the camera serves to document the "primitive" customs of "primitive peoples," and the voice-over is perhaps the most obvious embodiment of that desire. In *Reassemblage*, however, the voice-over becomes an embodiment of another desire, not just to critique the conventions of anthropological filmmaking, but to explore the possible connections between the filmmaker and the patterns that emerge from her observations of Senegal.

In other words, *Reassemblage* does not just critique the anthropological construction of the "other," for beyond that critique—or "near by," to use Trinh's words in the film ("I do not intend to speak about/Just speak near by")—is a renarrativization of the relationship between she who speaks and she who is spoken about, between she who looks and she who is looked at, one that draws upon another appropriation of the "primitive."[42] If *Reassemblage* critiques the appropriation of the "primitive," particularly insofar as the control of the "primitive" body relies on mechanisms similar to those used to represent the female body, it attempts simultaneously to read the "primitive" in a different, more complex way, resistant to the lure of an archaic femininity, a tribal past, or a one-dimensional "Third World" identity.

What I have described of the film thus far suggests that its "primitive" style has far more to do with a documentary tradition than with the early years of motion-picture history. For in documentary cinema, "primitive" technique can function as a marker of authenticity. As Trinh herself puts it, "It is, perhaps, precisely the claim to catch life in its motion and show it 'as it is' that has led a great number of 'documentarians' not only to present 'bad shots,' but also to make us believe that life is as dull as the images they project on the screen."[43] Much of the style of *Reassemblage* stretches the limits of anthropological observation, particularly through the relationship between the images and sounds of Senegal and the narrator's voice. Images which in another context might be signs of "authentic" observation—sights captured on the sly, or on the run, as it were—here are presented rather as markers of the difficulty and impossibility of ever capturing another on film. A frequently used technique in the film is the jump cut, and as Trinh herself has commented, "Recurrent jump cuts within a single event may indicate a hesitation in selecting the 'best' framing. They may also serve as rhythmical devices that disrupt spatial and temporal continuity, and suggest a grasping of things in their instantaneousness, in their fragility."[44]

Yet the technique of *Reassemblage* does evoke the "primitive" style in its historic as well as its generic dimension, particularly insofar as another recurrent technique is concerned—the use of stop motion, whereby a human or animal figure will suddenly disappear from the frame. This use of stop motion is far more evocative of the early trick film than of the authentic sloppiness of documentary cinema. A much-contested commonplace of film history is that the difference between documentary and fictional traditions can be traced back to the two lines of development suggested in France by the films of the Lumière brothers on the one hand, and those of Georges Méliès on the other.[45] The Lumière films were documentations of scenes of everyday life, while Méliès's films used the manipulative effects of the camera to create fantastic and supernatural effects. In *Reassemblage*, the sudden disappearance of human

5. A scene from Trinh T. Minh-ha's *Reassemblage* (1982). Courtesy Women Make Movies, Inc.; reprinted by permission.

figures from the Senegalese landscape suggests an affinity between the magician in Méliès's films and the narrator of *Reassemblage*—suggests, that is, a resurrection of the "primitive" style of early filmmaking in order to question and extend the accepted primitivism of documentary technique. Put another way, Trinh juxtaposes two kinds of "primitive" style, one which is readable within the tradition of documentary authenticity and one which is not. The "primitive" narration of the film seeks, then, not only to critique the conventions of the anthropological documentary, but also to reinvent another kind of narration, one which reconceptualizes the "magical" properties of the film medium.

Like most dualisms, the opposition between the "real life" subjects of the Lumières' films and the manipulated, fantastic subjects of Méliès's films masks a number of assumptions, particularly insofar as the truth-telling capacity of the cinema is concerned. *Reassemblage* does not assume the simple opposition of the Lumières and Méliès, of documentary and fiction, but rather seeks to inflect one notion of "primitive" filmmaking— "artless," capturing life "unawares"—with its presumed opposite—manipulative, magical—thereby putting the very opposition itself into question. Now in the appearances and disappearances so central to Méliès's magic films, it is a male magician who exercises his control and mastery over a world in which women tend more frequently than not to be the disappearing objects. If it is appropriate to describe Trinh's voice as the primary narrative perspective of the film, and if that voice acquires—by virtue of the various visual strategies associated with it—the function of a magical "primitive" narrator as well as a deconstructed anthropological one, then how are we to assess the gendered dynamics of the film?

At several points in the film, the female narrator tells anecdotes about the compulsions of whites to assign meanings to the observed experiences of Africans, meanings which are, of course, determined by white, Western notions of coherence and order. The narrator tells of a man and child who are dismissed by a "catholic white sister" for coming to the dispensary on Sunday, the day it is closed according to Catholic religion and therefore when its potential clientele should not presume to be in need of medical attention. Still another anecdote tells of an ethnologist who does not bother to actually listen to the music and stories of the people he has come to observe, since his tape recorder is on. If these examples serve to stress the extent to which colonial narratives impose their own framework on the experiences of others, they also function—somewhat ironically—as the most immediately readable and accessible "stories" within the film—that is, for a viewer trained and conditioned by classical film narrative.

But this is not to say that *Reassemblage* opposes these stories of Western "logic" with randomly selected images and words, for there is a very obvious process of selection that takes place in the film. Most of the film focuses, for instance, on the women of Senegal, with men most obviously present only at the beginning and the end. And the images which are repeated, as leitmotifs, are virtually all associated with women. Near the beginning of the film, the narrator says, "A film about what? my friends ask. A film about Senegal; but what in Senegal?" As she speaks, we see an image of a fire, an image that reappears several shots later. After these images of fire, the narrator tells of the association between women and fire: "In numerous tales/Woman is depicted as the one who possessed the fire/Only she knew how to make fire/She kept it in diverse places/At the end of the stick she used to dig the ground with for example/In her nails or in her fingers."[46] As she speaks, the accompanying image track shows men for the most part. But several images and lines of commentary later, the narrator repeats several lines ("She kept it in diverse places/At the end of the stick she used to dig the ground with for example"), and we see a woman holding a stick, shooing away a chicken. Such examples of apparent and immediate unity between image and sound are unusual in the film, and for a brief moment, one might perhaps read the impossible into the image—that is, see fire instead of a chicken, see the magical myth alluded to by the narrator instead of the documented reality before one's eyes.

A frequently repeated image in *Reassemblage* depicts women with sticks, whether digging, cleaning, or preparing food. Also repeated frequently are images of women's breasts, sometimes with babies nearby and sometimes not, but still suggestive of women's nourishing powers. The female body that emerges so centrally in *Reassemblage* is privileged to the extent that the entire film attempts simultaneously to question and to assume the maternal and nourishing properties of the female body. The film also examines the narrative modes irreducible to the traditions of either documentary or classical narrative filmmaking, modes which are associated with the rhythms and patterns of women's everyday lives. But there is little in *Reassemblage* to suggest that such a search for alternative ways of storytelling is the same as romanticizing the female body as an originary plenitude, as a wholeness to substitute for the fragmentation of "Western" experience.

One of the anecdotes told by the narrator describes a "man attending a slide show on Africa [who] turns to his wife and says with guilt in his voice: 'I have seen some pornography tonight.'" The images accompanying the voice show bare-breasted young women, and recall an earlier comment by the narrator: "Filming in Africa means for many of us/Colorful images, naked breast women, exotic dances and fearful rites."[47] But in both instances, something slips in the relationship between image and voice; the narrator uses the awkward phrase "naked breast women" (rather than "naked-breasted" or "women with naked breasts") and pronounces "pornography" with the accent on the wrong syllable (por-no-graph'-y, rather than por-no'-graph-y). Similarly, the narrator's voice assumes an affinity with those female voices whose words are repeated in the film in a kind of looping effect, thus assuming a rhythmic cadence. For Trinh's voice is too inflected with an accent to function as the transparent, overarching, "neutral" voice of documentary. The accent is not one typically associated with African speakers of English; thus, throughout the film, the female voice speaks as one who is not a part of Senegalese or African culture, but who is not a part of the tradition of white anthropological filmmaking either. Any presumed unity of the "Third World" disintegrates in the film, but at the same time the very division between the voice and the image suggests the possibility of another kind of observation, one resistant to the dualities of "West" versus "Third World."

The final section of Trinh's book-length study of feminism and postcolonialism, Woman, Native, Other, is entitled "Grandma's Story," and explores the significance of oral traditions of storytelling for women writers of color. "She who works at un-learning the dominant language of 'civilized' missionaries also has to learn how to un-write and write anew," she writes.[48] Reassemblage is a stunning demonstration of that process of "un-writing" whereby colonial notions of the "primitive" are demystified, certainly, but also where the very notion of a "primitive" mode of storytelling is reexamined in another light. Reassemblage is subtitled From the Firelight to the Screen. One could read in this subtitle the desire for a connection between the fire (which signifies a variety of aspects of women's lives in the film) and the cinema—for a cinema, that is, illuminated by the light of another experience. This is not to say that Reassemblage replicates the anthropological tradition it criticizes, but that it attempts another inflection, another pronunciation, whereby the "primitive" emerges not as the rigid duality of self and other but as the exploration of other modes of storytelling.

Like Reassemblage, Laleen Jayamanne's A Song of Ceylon critiques anthropological views of the "primitive," and takes the representation of the female body as its primary point of inquiry. But whereas Reassemblage refers to an entire tradition of anthropological filmmaking, A Song of Ceylon is much more specific in its reference to ethnographic definitions of the "primitive." The title of the film cites Basil Wright's 1935 British film The Song of Ceylon, which Jayamanne has described as "not pure ethnography [but] it has elements in common with an ethnographic enterprise, of rendering an 'ancient culture' visible as it enters the rapid transformations wrought by the colonial process of a plantation economy and international trade."[49] If Wright's film romanticizes Ceylon, the citation of the title in Jayamanne's film is an ironic displacement, both of a "name erased from the map of the world" and of the cinematic conventions which create the illusion of possession, whether of a culture, an experience, or a body.[50] And possession, in many senses of the term, is central to A Song of Ceylon. A Song of Ceylon is a rereading, or more precisely a performance, of a case study of Gananath Obeyesekere of a Sri Lankan woman, called Somavati in the text, who is possessed by demon spirits. The case study is a "psychocultural exegesis" of the woman's possession and subsequent exorcism. Obeyesekere's text is an exploration of "primitivism" understood in an anthropological as well as a psychoanalytic sense—anthropological insofar as the possession exemplifies ostensibly "primitive" beliefs in the relationship between the human and the spiritual world, and psychoanalytic insofar as Somavati's possession is also a function of her inability, or refusal, to contain infantile rage within the confines of "appropriate" female behavior.

Somavati's exorcism ritual is performed most literally in the spoken sound track to the film, which consists almost exclusively of citations from the case study. The inflection of the voice sets the components of the case study in a different relation to each other than is possible in the written text. To be sure, Obeyesekere includes in the case study lengthy quotations from the exorcism ritual, but these are always framed by his commentary. In the film, the different voices—and in particular the voice of Somavati, performed by Jayamanne herself—acquire more autonomy, and processes which remain subtle in the written text are more dramatically represented in the film. For instance, the first words spoken in the film are Somavati's description of her "spirit attacks": "My hands and feet grow cold; it is as if I don't possess them. Then my body shivers—shivers, and the inside of my body seems to shake. . . . This goes on and on . . . and if I hear someone talk I get angry. My rage is such that I could even hit my father and mother . . . this is how the illness starts."[51]

Somavati's voice acts out the words *shiver* and *rage*, so that one can practically feel a chill in the former word and anger in latter. But this performance of the text is no simple attribution of agency or authority to Somavati, for her voice is also quite literally "possessed" from the outset—a male voice accompanies hers, sometimes echoing what she says, sometimes completing a phrase that she begins. An example of this strategy occurs later in the film, when one of the more memorable utterances of the exorcism ritual is spoken: "Do you think I am a woman, ha! Do you?"[52] The female voice begins the phrase ("Do you think I am . . ."), but a male voice completes it (". . . a woman?"). Put another way, then, the voices of the film perform the contradictions of Obeyesekere's case study, on the one hand by identifying Somavati as a far more palpable, dynamic presence than she is in print, and on the other hand by embedding her speech within the speech of men.

If the spoken track to A *Song of Ceylon* performs and cites a specific ritual of possession, the image and music tracks explore other permutations of possession, and the film plays on "possession" in the collision of cultural meanings. More specifically, the Sri Lankan context of "possession" (i.e., spirit possession) finds its most striking "Western" echo in a series of poses, borrowed from film stills, denoting romantic possession. As Jayamanne explains, "the image track of the film is based on tableaux vivants constructed not from films but from looking at *film stills* of a selection of films. The film has tried to recreate certain classic postures and gestures of Western erotic and romantic possession taken from film stills."[53] These include poses of men and women in a series of romantic embraces, with an element of defamiliarization occurring through the stiff, tableaulike representations, or the casting of a transvestite in a woman's role; and a black-and-white sequence of fragmented body parts and frozen poses which cites Jean-Luc Godard's Une *Femme Mariée* (A Married Woman).

However, A *Song of Ceylon* does not set up a simple opposition between the visual and the aural, or between "Western" and "Asian" possession. The final performance within the film is a recital, where Schubert's "Litany for All Souls Day"—heard only in fragments previously in the film—is sung, in an example of what Jayamanne has described as "cultural hybridization."[54] For the participants in the recital, musicians as well as onlookers, are a combination of Western and Asian "types," and even the music itself is at times performed in such a way that the boundaries between Western and Asian music become tenuous. Similarly, A *Song of Ceylon* probes and stretches the gender polarities of possession. Somavati's desire to "play"—as uttered on the sound track—acquires a number of visual forms, particularly concerning various possibilities of rearranging the sexual hierarchy of male agent and female object. One of the most common motifs in the film is the "posing" sequence, in which the limbs of actors are manipulated by other actors (with often just an isolated arm visible), only to fall away in a kind of passive resistance to the gesture of control. The interchangeability of gendered roles here both amplifies and contradicts the play of voices on the sound track.

A *Song of Ceylon* is shot almost exclusively in the static, tableaulike images characteristic of the early cinema, and in the rare instances that camera movement does appear, it is—again, as in the early cinema—quite visibly motivated. But if Trinh's film critiques the way in which the "primitive" is captured on film in order to explore other possible formulations of "primitive" narration, A *Song of Ceylon* seems, rather, to eschew any such reappropriation. Put another way, one might argue that the "primitive" style of A *Song of Ceylon* has more to do with a postmodern mode of performance than with an exploration of the intersection between different associations of the "primitive." However, both *Reassemblage* and A *Song of Ceylon* embody a desire, not to repossess what Jayamanne has called "pristine cultural identities," but rather to redefine "primitive" narration as simultaneous connection with and distance from the female body.[55]

In A *Song of Ceylon*, the realm of the "primitive" is evoked by the disembodied voices which speak the tale of Sri Lankan possession, and by the visible bodies which may occasionally sing but which do not speak. The tale of possession collapses, in other words, into the tale of hysteria; "primitive" culture overlaps with the "primitive" body language of the hysteric. Indeed, Obeyesekere's case study is quite evocative of Freud's case history of Dora. Obeyesekere assumes, for instance, that if Somavati remained with her apparently sadistic husband, it is because she herself fits the profile of a masochist; in other words, if she is beaten by her husband she must like it—just as Dora, in Freud's view, must have welcomed the sexual advances of Herr K.[56] And like Dora, Somavati's body acts out what it cannot or will not speak.

While an impressive body of feminist psychoanalytic criticism has read Freud, Dora, and hysteria symptomatically, Jayamanne's approach is different, precisely to the extent that A *Song of Ceylon* performs the two registers of spirit possession and hysteria by insisting upon both their common denominator and their difference. This simultaneous connection and difference takes theatricalization, performance, and public spectacle as its central terms. Jayamanne describes part of her fascination with the case study as "the way in which 'my culture' dealt with hysteria in the form of a theatrical ritual, that is to say a public ceremony."[57] This is not to say, of course, that theatrical metaphors are alien to the description of hysteria; to the contrary. Josef Breuer's famous patient, Anna O., described one of her hysterical symptoms as her "private theatre": "While everyone thought she was attending, she was living through fairy tales in her imagination; but she was always on the spot when she was spoken to, so that no one was aware of it."[58]

Central to A *Song of Ceylon* in this context are the competing roles of private and public spheres in defining possession and hysteria. The film addresses how notions of the private and the public shape the cinema, particularly insofar as spectatorship is concerned. Catherine Clément has described the cinema as the "institutionalization of hysteria." In the context of the relationship between the cinema and the spheres of private and public life, this suggests a public spectacle far removed from the kind of public ritual Jayamanne describes, a spectacle—as Clément puts it—"without possible contagion."[59] But the relationship established in A *Song of Ceylon* between possession and hysteria inflects—and infects—one notion of a public sphere with the other.

In the different modes of performance in the film, the common denominator is virtually always the female body as "possessed," as "hysterical." When the elderly woman completes her song in the above-mentioned chamber-music scene, she collapses; the condition of performance is the inextricable connection between body and voice. "Primitive" narration in A *Song of Ceylon* is where possession and hysteria cross in the representation of the female body. If it is implied in Obeyesekere's case study that hysteria is cross-cultural, that the price of social interdiction is the division of the woman, then how are we to read Jayamanne's film, which itself returns constantly to the scene of possession as the scene of hysteria, and vice versa? In other words, is "cultural hybridization" just another name for psychocultural homogeneity? One of the key moments in the exorcism ritual as described by Obeyesekere is the chair episode. After Somavati and the two men performing the exorcism dance around a chair, one man "grabs Somavati by the hair and forces her down in front of the chair. He has a cane in his hand and with it directs the woman to crawl under the chair. She crawls under the chair on all fours. 'Get up—get to the other side,' says David. She crawls under the chair in the opposite direction This is repeated several times." Obeyesekere explains the significance of the chair episode as simultaneously the capitulation of the demons inhabiting Somavati to the superior gods represented by the men, and "Somavati's self-abnegation; she literally grovels in the dust at the feet of the priests, and later of the deities. She is broken, humiliated, made abject, and made pliable psychologically."[60]

The performance of this scene in the film displaces the resolution offered by the humiliation of Somavati. Instead, we see a body, dressed in a sari, wearing Cuban dancing shoes, dance atop the seat of a chair. The face and chest are invisible, and eventually the hands become a frenetic part of the dance. The dance itself begins as a rather mundane cha cha, but evolves into a most peculiar and disturbing sight, a frenzy of bodily gestures impossible to read—to "possess"—absolutely in cultural or psychoanalytic terms. At the same time, the dancer's body is difficult to read in terms of gender—is this another man impersonating a woman? Or a woman caught up in the frenzy of bodily excess? The desire of the film is precisely there—to imagine a body, not so much "free" of gender as absolutely unreadable in either/or terms. The film does not rescue the "primitive" body of possession and/or hysteria, nor does it collapse the one kind of "primitivism" into the other. Rather, the film *performs* the "primitive," sets the public and private versions of the body in tension with each other, and in so doing deinstitutionalizes cinematic possession and hysteria.

I began this chapter with two films which parallel the appropriation of early cinema by (male) avant-garde filmmakers, moved to three films which are more specifically narrative in their focus, and concluded with two films in which the very distinction between avant-garde and narrative is suspect, but more specifically which explore the cultural connotations of the "primitive" as what is repressed not only in patriarchal but also in some feminist notions of the subject. In other words, I have situated Trinh's and Jayamanne's films, if not as "last words" then at least as appropriate conclusions to the exploration of the "primitive" in the works of white, Western women filmmakers.

To regard *Reassemblage* and A *Song of Ceylon* as "continuations" of the projects central to the other films risks the flattening out of difference in the name of a "women's cinema" that assumes too quickly a universal, shared set of concerns. But to separate these two films from the rest involves another kind of risk, by placing the burden of the demonstration of cultural and racial difference on those women filmmakers to whom the descriptions "women of color" or "Third World" apply. In other words, a discussion of the cultural connotations of the "primitive" in films such as *Reassemblage* and A *Song of Ceylon* can evolve—however unconsciously or unthinkingly—from the assumption that these ramifications of the "primitive" apply only to *them*, to the "other woman" of white, Western feminism. But as the fascination with cultural "otherness" in Maya Deren's work or, even more problematically, the invocation of racial stereotypes in the context of "primitive" narration in *Cleo from 5 to 7* demonstrates, the lure of the "primitive" in women's cinema is also the lure of cultural constructions of the "other," and there is no guarantee that the displacement of the male subject simultaneously displaces his white skin or his Western assumptions.

Notes

1 Tom Gunning, "An Unseen Energy Swallows Space: The Space in Early Film and Its Relation to American Avant-garde Film," in John Fell, ed., *Film before Griffith* (Berkeley: University of California Press, 1983), pp. 357–358.

2 Maya Deren, "From the Notebook of 1947," *October*, no. 14 (Fall 1980). 29, 30.

3 Ibid., p. 37.

4 The notable exception is VèVè A. Clark, Millicent Hodson, and Catrina Neiman, *The Legend of Maya Deren*: A *Documentary Biography and Collected Works*, vol. 1, pt. I (*Signatures* [1917–1942]) (New York: Anthology Film Archives, 1985): vol. 1. pt. 2 (*Chambers* [1942–1947]) (New York: Anthology Film Archives, 1988). The approach taken by the authors is distinctly different, however, from most of the work that has characterized feminist approaches to women's cinema. See, for example, Lauren Rabinowitz's review of the first volume in *Wide Angle* 8, no. 3–4 (1986), 131–133.

5 Maya Deren, An *Anagram of Ideas on Art, Form, and Film* (Yonkers: The Alicat Book Shop Press, 1946); reprinted in Clark, Hodson, and Neiman. *The Legend of Maya Deren*. vol. 1, pt. 2, p. 565.

6 P. Adams Sitney analyzes the category of the "trance film" as it applies both to Deren's and Hammid's work, and to their influence on the subsequent history of the avant-garde film. See *Visionary Film: The American Avant-garde, 1943–1978* (1974; 2nd ed. Oxford and New York: Oxford University Press, 1979) chapters 1 and 2.

7 Eleanora Deren, "Religious Possession in Dancing," pt. 4 (previously unpublished), in Clark, Hodson, and Neiman, *The Legend of Maya Deren*, vol. 1, pt. 1, pp. 489–491. Parts 1–3 of the essay were published originally in *Educational Dance*, March–April, August–September 1942. The journal ceased publication before the last section was to appear.

8 P. Adams Sitney compares *Ritual in Transfigured Time* with Jean Cocteau's *Le Sang d'un poète* (1930), which is—in ways more explicit than Deren's film—a meditation on the primitive cinema, especially insofar as keyholes and hotel corridors are concerned. See *Visionary Film*, pp. 33–37.

9 Sigmund Freud and Josef Breuer, *Studies on Hysteria* (1893–1895; New York: Pelican, 1974), p. 64.

10 Sigmund Freud, "Revision of the Theory of Dreams," in *New Introductory Lectures on Psychoanalysis* (1933: New York: Norton, 1964), trans. James Strachey, p. 18.

11 For a detailed examination of the stylistic components of cinèmatic impressionism, see David Bordwell, "French Impressionist Cinema: Film Culture, Film Theory, and Film Style," Dissertation, University of Iowa, 1974, chapter 4 ("A Paradigm of Impressionist Film Style").

12 For a remarkably detailed study of French film production in the 1920s, see Richard Abel, *French Cinema: The First Wave, 1915–1929* (Princeton: Princeton University Press, 1984).

13 Richard Abel notes that the most significant difference between Dulac's film and the play by André Obey and Denys Amiel upon which it was based is precisely the representation of Madame Beudet's inner life. See *French Cinema*, p. 341.

14 Sandy Flitterman's analysis of *The Smiling Madame Beudet* focuses on how Dulac creates a textual system that works against the system of classical representation; see "Montage/Discourse: Germaine Dulac's *The Smiling Madame Beudet*," *Wide Angle* 4, no. 3 (1980), 54–59; and Sandy Flitterman-Lewis, *To Desire Differently: Feminism and the French Cinema* (Urbana: University of Illinois Press, 1990), chapter 4.

15 For an extended analysis of the scenes leading up to Madame Beudet's loading of the gun, see Flitterman-Lewis, *To Desire Differently*, pp. 102–112.

16 Sandy Flitterman discusses the disjunction between the two kinds of images in "Montage/Discourse: Germaine Dulac's *The Smiling Madame Beudet*."

17 For an analysis of Dulac's identification with Madame Beudet, see Wendy Dozoretz, "Madame Beudet's Smile: Feminine or Feminist?" *Film Reader*, no. 5 (1982), 41–46.

18 That Dulac's film functions as a critique of the institution of marriage has been pointed out by Abel, Flitterman-Lewis, and Dozoretz. See also William Van Wert, "Germaine Dulac: First Feminist Filmmaker," *Women and Film* 1, nos. 5–6 (1974), 55–57, 103; and Sandy Flitterman, "Heart of the Avant-garde: Some Biographical Notes on Germaine Dulac," *Women and Film* 1, nos. 5–6 (1974), 58–61, 103.

19 See James Monaco, *The New Wave* (New York: Oxford University Press, 1976).

20 See Natasa Durovicova, "Biograph as Biography: François Truffaut's *The Wild Child*," *Wide Angle* 7, nos. 1–2 (1985), 126–135.

21 Flitterman-Lewis, *To Desire Differently*, p. 283.

22 André Gaudreault, "Temporality and Narrativity in Early Cinema, 1895–1908," in Fell, *Film before Griffith*, p. 317.

23 Claudia Gorbman, "*Cleo from 5 to 7*: Music as Mirror," *Wide Angle* 4, no. 4 (1981). 40. See also Roy Jay Nelson, "Reflections in a Broken Mirror: Varda's *Cléo de 5 à 7*," *French Review* 56, no. 5 (April 1983), 740: "The little film-within-the film, in which a man commits a grotesque error because he is wearing dark glasses, provides a first lesson: the costumes we don to protect ourselves from exterior harm change our own perception of the outside world."

24 I believe this is quite close to Roy Jay Nelson's observation that "superstition and medical science are two contexts from which to view reality, and the film gives them equal validity. Whether or not the fortune teller's predictions 'come true' in the film depends upon the individual viewer's interpretation of them, and that interpretation is a function of his or her own mind set, of the context in which the film is viewed." See "Reflections in a Broken Mirror," p. 738.

25 Danièle Dubroux, Thérèse Giraud, and Louis Skorecki, "Entretien avec Chantal Akerman," *Cahiers du cinéma*, no. 278 (July 1977), 35.

26 It has always seemed "obvious" to me that Jeanne's response is unexpected orgasm. But Brenda Longfellow raises a question concerning Jeanne's response: "How do we read her contorted expression: one of pleasure or of pain, orgasmic or disgusted?" Longfellow reports these interesting results of a "random survey" of women who had seen the film: "the readings seem to divide, interestingly enough, according to the sexual preference of the spectator. For the lesbian spectator, Jeanne's response represents a flash of

consciousness and a frightening recognition of her own alienation, her own status as sexual object. For the heterosexual female spectator, the movement of the head and arm connote sexual pleasure, an eruption of the disordering possibility of desire against which Jeanne reacts with a gesture of violent negation." See "Love Letters to the Mother: The Work of Chantal Akerman," *Canadian Journal of Political and Social Theory* 13, nos. 1–2 (1989), 84.

27 B. Ruby Rich, "Chantal Akerman's Meta-cinema," *The Village Voice*, March 29, 1983, p. 51; Marsha Kinder, "Reflections on *Jeanne Dielman*," in Patricia Erens, ed., *Sexual Stratagems* (New York: Horizon Press, 1979), pp. 253, 255.

28 Ruth Perlmutter, "Feminine Absence: A Political Aesthetic in Chantal Akerman's *Jeanne Dielman, 23 Quai du Commerce, 1080 Bruxelles*," *Quarterly Review of Film Studies* 4, no. 2 (Spring 1979). On the self-reflexivity of *Jeanne Dielman* and other films by Akerman, see Rich, "Akerman's Meta-cinema."

29 Claire Johnston, "Towards a Feminist Film Practice: Some Theses," *Edinburgh Magazine: Psychoanalysis/Cinema/Avant-garde* (1976), p. 58.

30 Jayne Loader, "*Jeanne Dielman*: Death in Installments," *Jump Cut* no. 16 (1977), 10–12.

31 Brenda Longfellow, "Love Letters to the Mother: The Work of Chantal Akerman," 84.

32 Laleen Jayamanne, "Modes of Performance in Chantal Akerman's *Jeanne Dielman, 23 Quai du Commerce, 1080 Bruxelles*," *Australian Journal of Screen Theory*, no. 8 (1981), 107.

33 Janet Bergstrom, "*Jeanne Dielman, 23 Quai du Commerce, 1080 Bruxelles* by Chantal Akerman," *Camera Obscura*, no. 2 (Fall 1977), 117.

34 Danièle Dubroux, "Le familier inquiétant (*Jeanne Dielman*)," *Cahiers du cinéma*, no. 265 (March–April 1976), 17–20.

35 I confess that the first time I saw the film, I did not notice the "game" of the missing chair; and the second time I saw *Jeanne Dielman*, I "noticed" it but thought it to be my misperception. Having had the opportunity to see the film numerous times since, I am astounded that I did not notice it on first viewing. Is it possible that the creation of "order," of such precise and seemingly controlled framing and mise-en-scéne, is not only so strong but so seductive that blatantly disruptive details such as this pass unnoticed? In any case, in all of the writings that have appeared on *Jeanne Dielman*, I have seen only one reference to the missing chair. Laleen Jayamanne, in "Modes of Performance" (p. 110, n. 26), calls this a "visual joke," and notes, "The pleasure of noticing this reflexive joke (or bad continuity according to the codes of Hollywood) took my attention away from Jeanne/Delphine's actions and also served to denaturalise the naturalistic mise-en-scène." Noting that Babette Mangolte was the cinematographer for *Jeanne Dielman* as well as for Yvonne Rainer's *Lives of Performers*, Jayamanne suggests that "the way in which objects like chairs and tables are photographed in both films, within the overall structure, makes one attentive to these mundane objects which are usually devoured by the realist text."

36 Silvia Bovenschen, "Is There a Feminine Aesthetic?" *New German Critique*, no. 10 (Winter 1977), trans. Beth Weckmueller, 111–137.

37 Noël Burch, "Primitivism and the Avant-gardes: A Dialectical Approach," in Philip Rosen, ed., *Narrative/Apparatus/Ideology* (New York: Columbia University Press, 1986), p. 503. The essay by Peter Wollen referred to by Burch is "Godard and Countercinema: *Vent d'est*," *Afterimage*, no. 4 (1972).

38 Burch, "Primitivism and the Avant-gardes," p. 501. Burch's specific point of reference for this definition of the "primitive stare" is Andy Warhol's *Chelsea Girls*.

39 Ibid., p. 504.

40 For a discussion of how the style and structure of the film replicate the primal scene, see Perlmutter, "Feminine Absence," p. 132.

41 See, for example, Perlmutter, "Feminine Absence," and Longfellow, "Love Letters to the Mother."

42 Trinh T. Minh-ha, "*Reassemblage*—Sketch of a Sound Track." *Camera Obscura*, no. 13–14 (1985), 105.

43 Trinh T. Minh-ha, "Mechanical Eye, Electronic Ear, and the Lure of Authenticity," *Wide Angle* 6, no. 2 (1984), 63.

44 Constance Penley and Andrew Ross, "Interview with Trinh T. Minh-ha," *Camera Obscura*, no. 13–14 (1985), 90.

45 The most influential formulation of the opposition can be found in Siegfried Kracauer, *Theory of Film: The Redemption of Physical Reality* (New York and Oxford. Oxford University Press, 1960), pp. 30–36. See also Roy Armes, *Film and Reality: A Historical Survey* (Baltimore and Middlesex; Penguin, 1974), pp. 22–29.

46 Trinh T. Minh-ha, "*Reassemblage*—Sketch of a Sound Track," p. 105.

47 Ibid., pp. 107–108.

48 Trinh T. Minh-ha, *Woman, Native, Other* (Bloomington: Indiana University Press, 1989), p. 148.

49 Laleen Jayamanne, "Do You Think I Am a Woman, Ha! Do You?" *Discourse* 11, no. 2 (Spring-Summer 1989), 49.

50 Ibid., p. 50.

51 Gananath Obeyesekere, "Psychocultural Exegesis of a Case of Spirit Possession in Sri Lanka," in Vincent Crapanzano and Vivian Garrison, eds., *Case Studies in Spirit Possession* (New York: John Wiley and Sons, 1977), p. 249.

52 Ibid., p. 268.

53 Jayamanne, "Do You Think I Am a Woman?" p. 51.

54 "The visual dissonance is not only in the variety of clothes from different cultures worn by the actors but also in the juxtaposition of faces and bodies as they participate in a Western musical ritual. The ethnography here is one of cultural hybridization which if viewed negatively may be seen as one of dispossession of pristine cultural identities." Ibid., pp. 51–52.

55 Ibid.

56 See Sigmund Freud, *Dora: An Analysis of a Case of Hysteria* (1905; New York: Macmillan, 1963). Describing Herr K.'s advances to Dora. Freud writes (p. 43): "This was surely just the situation to call up a distinct feeling of sexual excitement in a girl of fourteen who had never before been approached."

57 Jayamanne, "Do You Think I Am a Woman?" p. 52.

58 Freud and Breuer, *Studies on Hysteria*, p. 74.

59 Catherine Clément, in Catherine Clément and Hélène Cixous, *The Newly Born Woman*, trans. Betsy Wing (Minneapolis: University of Minnesota Press, 1986), p. 13.

60 Obeyesekere, "Psychocultural Exegesis," pp. 276, 280.

THE 1960s EXPERIMENTAL CINEMA EXPLOSION

Introduction

Part Two is designed to offer the reader a glimpse into the fertile, festive, and politically charged arena of the experimental filmmaking communities of the 1960s. In bringing together interviews with the artists and contemporary criticism, this section provides signposts not only to the reader about the significant aesthetic practices of the filmmakers themselves but also to the ongoing theoretical debates and questions raised by the films of the time. Despite the buoyancy of the era, the emphasis on communality, and the tendency away from established norms, experimental filmmakers of the 1960s are clearly placed in competition and drawn into the battles of canon formation. For example, Juan A. Suarez champions Kenneth Anger's *Scorpio Rising* (1963) as the most representative film of the 1960s, while Suranjan Ganguly sees Stan Brakhage as the foremost living avant-garde filmmaker. Daryl Chin takes issue with the marginalization of Yoko Ono. Clearly, the egalitarian spirit of Mekas's "Notes on the New American Cinema" was utopic at best. In reading these essays and interviews, it becomes clear that, to experimental film, critical reception is as important as communal support.

Juan A. Suarez's "Pop, Queer, or Fascist? The Ambiguity of Mass Culture in Kenneth Anger's *Scorpio Rising*" contextualizes *Scorpio Rising* using queer theory and cultural studies as a site of the homoeroticization of pop culture icons, such as James Dean and Marlon Brando. Suarez concludes that Anger's film can be read in contradictory ways that allow for the appropriation and renarration of straight pop culture within a potentially subversive queer gaze. Similarly, Jerry Tartaglia, in "The Perfect Queer Appositeness of Jack Smith," finds an expression of queer visual thought in Smith's films. Jack Smith famously appropriated Hollywood icons, such as Maria Montez, and reveled in diva worship, camp, garish clothing, and veiled homoeroticism in *Flaming Creatures* (1963). Interestingly, Tartaglia argues that Smith differed from his straight peers in that he did not work in an oppositional manner toward Hollywood; instead, he reveled in mimicking it.

Suranjan Ganguly's "Stan Brakhage—The 60th Birthday Interview" refutes the myth that experimental cinema is essentially reactionary cinema in response to Hollywood. Brakhage discusses his influences (Marie Menken and Harry Smith, among others) and emphasizes the integrity of working by hand directly with the film. Ganguly discusses in detail Brakhage's hand-painted films and autobiographical films, as well as his trance films. In a discussion of *Window*

Water Baby Moving (1959), Brakhage discusses the politics of privacy. The film is a record of Jane Brakhage giving birth. Though Maya Deren and others critiqued Brakhage for his use of the male gaze in a woman's space, Brakhage explains that he wanted to be a part of a process forbidden to men.

In Kate Haug's "Interview with Carolee Schneemann," Schneemann explains that she made her groundbreaking feminist film *Fuses* (1964–1967) in response to *Window Water Baby Moving* because she was concerned about the sexual politics of a male filmmaker filming his partner giving birth. Schneemann agrees with Haug, who suggests that, despite feminism, sex is still the domain of men. She recalls how *Fuses* was criticized as pornography and initially dismissed even by feminist critics. Now widely celebrated as a film that reclaims sexuality from the point of view of the female, *Fuses* was misunderstood as pornography. Schneemann also links her feminist views to *Viet-Flakes* (1965), a political, call-to-action film against the war in Vietnam.

In "*The Flower Thief*: The 'Film Poem,' Warhol's Early Films, and the Beat Writers," Reva Wolf takes up the issue of negative criticism of the films of Ron Rice and Andy Warhol and concludes that Warhol and other experimental filmmakers of the 1960s used negative criticism to their advantage, just as the Beat poets Jack Kerouac and Allen Ginsberg had done. The critics who called Warhol's films "boring" and "bad" were flummoxed when Warhol simply agreed. Badness was absorbed in the identity of underground filmmakers, especially those associated with pop art who also championed the embrace of "mistakes" and willful disregard of norms of aesthetic artistry.

Daryl Chin, in "Walking on Thin Ice: The Films of Yoko Ono," examines the critical reception of Ono's works and credits her for challenging the formal and aesthetic concerns of Warhol. Yet, as Chin notes, Ono received little appreciation beyond a few critics. Chin champions the subversive, yet marginalized, films of Yoko Ono (many made in collaboration with John Lennon). Chin emphasizes the formal aspects of Ono's work, yet he notices that Ono's work is often rife with anger and rage.

Though known for her playfulness, Ono here, in "Yoko Ono on Yoko Ono," alludes to her own exclusion from the film canon. Already in 1970, Ono writes in defiance of what she terms the "aristocracy" creeping into the avant-garde. Ono's writing best captures her playfulness and rage. In response to criticism of her films made with Lennon as the work of "lolly-pop artists who are preoccupied with blowing soap bubbles forever," Ono cleverly retorts, "I thought that was beautiful," which could clearly be taken several ways. Ono seems undefeated: she predicts that in half a decade *No. 4* (1964) and films like it will define the 1960s as "not only an age of achievements, but of laughter."

Pop, Queer, or Fascist?

The ambiguity of mass culture in Kenneth Anger's *Scorpio Rising*

5

JUAN A. SUAREZ

Kenneth Anger's *Scorpio Rising* has often been regarded as the most representative film of the 1960s American underground cinema. Premiered in October of 1963 in the Gramercy Arts Theater, it quickly became a hit in the art cinema circuit, and was one of the very few underground movies to enjoy a successful commercial run.[1] To this day, it remains the most widely seen experimental movie of its time and the most frequently rented title in the repertoire of the Filmmakers' Cooperative. A "documentary" of sorts on the lifestyle of a motorcycle gang, it portrays motorcyclists cleaning and putting together their machines, lying about in their rooms, dressing for and attending a party, riding recklessly, and having an accident. As is the case with many other films by Anger, *Scorpio Rising* is deeply ambiguous, since it both glamorizes the marginal group's rebelliousness and seemingly condemns its self-destructive behavior.

Scorpio Rising consists of thirteen distinct segments scored to hit songs of the years 1961 to 1963. It is studded with pop culture icons and allusions that Anger brings up as sources of the biker subculture or as commentaries on it. At the same time, the film employs many thematic motifs and formal traits of the historical avant-garde, such as a fascination with technology, collage technique, and an interest in the "utopian" possibilities embedded in mass cultural forms. Like many other underground movies, *Scorpio Rising* pays tribute to the forms of mass culture which are the source of its imagery, and can therefore be seen as a self-conscious imitation of popular texts. Anger himself attests to this: "What *Scorpio* represents is me clueing in to popular American culture after having been away for eight years, because I had been living in France for that long."[2] "[C]oming back [to the United States] was like visiting a foreign country."[3]

Given the centrality of pop culture to Anger's film, this chapter will analyze *Scorpio Rising* as a movie about popular forms. In this respect, I intend to expand the critical views on Kenneth Anger's major film, views which have consistently underlined its debt to the European avant-garde cinema (Buñuel and Eisenstein frequently come up as creditors) and overlooked its engagement with the American pop vernacular.[4] This involvement consists primarily of the appropriation of popular youth culture forms from the 1950s and 1960s, such as rock and roll songs, the iconography of the motorcycle cult, comic books, and images of teen idols Marlon Brando and James Dean. Appropriation is dominated by a gay viewpoint that unveils meanings—such as homoerotic plots, or the proximity of eroticism and violence—which tend to remain displaced or muted in the straight uses of these forms.[5] Such gay desublimation of mass culture does not have an unambiguously liberating effect. The subtexts the film uncovers resonate with fascist oppression at the same time that they celebrate subversive pleasures and identities. I will show how such contradictory evaluation emanates from the dual implications of the biker and gay subcultures of the time (from which Anger's film borrowed iconography and point of view, respectively), both of which were widely regarded as "subversive," in a positive sense, and as dangerous or deadly. Ambiguity is also the result of the confluence in the film of two contradictory paradigms of mass culture: modernist condemnation, and pop celebration of its expressive potentials.

Before *Scorpio Rising*

Unlike Jack Smith and Andy Warhol, who started making films in the early 1960s, Kenneth Anger had been an experimental filmmaker since the early 1940s. Born in 1930 in Santa Monica, California, to a family connected to the Hollywood film industry (his grandmother had been a costume designer at Metro Goldwyn Mayer), he started shooting movies at age eleven,[6] and in 1947 became a consecrated director with *Fireworks*, a film whose unabashed homosexuality provided a moment of scandal for the postwar American art cinema. *Fireworks* portrays a young man's homoerotic dreams, in the course of which he obtains some sexual satisfaction from a muscular sailor and is later brutally beaten by a gang of the sailor's mates. *Fireworks* is an early compendium of Anger's aesthetics: the fascination with eroticism and death, the interest in gay iconography, and the unstable tone—by turns ironic and serious— recur in all his later films. Unlike most American experimental movies of the time, *Fireworks* became a cult piece in Europe; it was enthusiastically received at the 1949 edition of the *Féstival International du cinéma maudit*, celebrated in Biarritz, France, under Jean Cocteau's direction. Lured by a fan letter from Cocteau, Anger left America in 1949 for the supposedly wider social and intellectual horizons of Paris, repeating in this way an old gesture of the American intelligentsia.

During his European residency, Anger worked on a number of projects: among them, a film of Cocteau's ballet *Le Jeune Homme et la mort*; a feature-length adaptation of the French erotic novel *Histoire d'O*, of which only a few tests were run; and a documentary of Thelema Abbey, Sicily, place of residence of magus Alistair Crowley, one of Anger's intellectual heroes. These 1950s films are no longer available; they succumbed to bad storage conditions, to Anger's almost nomadic existence, or simply to his waning interest in them.[7] On several occasions, a dearth of funds forced Anger to leave his projects unfinished after filming only some fragments. Two incomplete films from this period are *Rabbit's Moon* (1955) and *Puce Moment* (1950). *Rabbit's Moon* was initially conceived as a feature-length project. Its characters and motifs derive from the *commedia dell'arte*, particularly as recreated in Marcel Carné's *Les Enfants du Paradis* (1945). The film's setting, an enchanted forest, is a reproduction of the background decor used in Max Reinhardt's version of *Midsummer Night's Dream*, in which Anger acted as the Princeling when he was six.[8] *Puce Moment* is also a fragment from a projected feature film on the everyday life of a retired Hollywood actress, and could almost be termed a failed *Sunset Boulevard*, which coincidentally premiered shortly after Anger stopped working on this film.

The extant footage shows a middle-aged woman languishing in a luxurious mansion, applying makeup, dressing up, and taking her hounds out for a walk.

The two 1950s films that Anger managed to complete are Eaux d'artifice (translated as Waterworks) (1953) and Inauguration of the Pleasure Dome (1956, recut several times afterwards). Eaux d'artifice shows a masked feminine figure in eighteenth-century costume fleeing through baroque gardens full of streams, ornate fountains, and statues, and bathed in spectral moonlight. At the end of the film the mysterious figure metamorphosizes into a fountain, a change conveyed through a series of dissolves that evoke the fluid passage of flesh into water. According to P. Adams Sitney, the film loosely recreates the final episode of Ronald Firbank's camp classic Valmouth, whose overwrought prose Anger conveyed through careful pans and zooms on running water, foliage, and statues.[9] Inauguration, shot in Hollywood during a brief stay in the mid-1950s, is a mythological masquerade acted by some of Anger's friends, among them bohemians and socialites Samson DeBrier and Anaïs Nin.[10] The film's dazzlingly arrayed characters incarnate such mythological deities as Isis, Shiva, Kali, Ganymede, and Dionysus, among others. In the film's minimal plot, they solemnly drink and get high, lust after a young apparition (the god Pan, according to Anger's notes), and laugh convulsively in their hallucinations. Sitney has argued that Inauguration of the Pleasure Dome occupies an important place in the history of American experimental cinema, since it signals the transition from the trance film, based on subjective impressions and dreams, to mythopoesis: the translation of movements of consciousness into archetypal, mythical forms.[11] From another perspective, however, both Waterworks and Inauguration belong fully in the tradition of decadentism and aestheticism, whose most important representative at the time was Jean Cocteau; they present precious characters in ornate settings, and evidence a fascination with demonism and artificial states of consciousness. These movies also show a self-conscious camp irony, present mainly in the excessive mise-en-scène, which undermines any pretense of seriousness.

As can be gathered from the foregoing descriptions, Scorpio Rising's plunge into pop culture is a departure from the themes and style of Anger's first phase. At the same time, however, the film replays two salient preoccupations of the early works: the deadly underside of (homo)sexual desire and the fascination with appearance and style.

Scorpio Rising's bikers recast the main theme of Anger's first film, Fireworks: the mutual implication of desire and death. The sailors in Fireworks are ambiguous objects of homosexual desire, whose presence leads first to arousal and then to punishment, intimating that desire yearns for an undoing, an inevitably violent self-shattering.[12] The unsettling mixture of desire and death also shapes Anger's anthology of scandal Hollywood Babylon. First published by J. J. Pauvert in France in 1960, Hollywood Babylon is a scathing look into the underside of Hollywood's glamour—the unheroic background of domestic violence, addiction, suicide, and unhappiness that surrounded some members of the film community behind the scenes. The book is based on the same duality that informs Fireworks and Scorpio Rising: stars, objects of desire, are also icons of death and destruction.[13] Like the sailors and Hollywood stars, the bikers in Scorpio Rising combine violence and eroticism. Early sequences of the film, such as the one edited to the song "Blue Velvet," spectacularize the bikers, who flex their muscles and pose for the camera in leather and chains. In addition to being objects of the camera's and the spectators' gaze, the bikers appear as objects of desire for each other; a series of eye-line matches construct a homoerotic circuit of looks in which the bikers seem to admire each other's bodies in several stages of dress or undress.[14] Well into the second half of the film, by the time such homoeroticism has been well established, the film starts presenting the bikers as a violent group bent on sadism and self-destruction. This becomes most evident in the sado-masochistic rituals of the song segments "I Will Follow Him" and "Point of No Return" and in the deadly crash of a gang member.

Another concern that connects *Scorpio Rising* to the earlier 1950s films is the emphasis on masquerade and appearances. *Inauguration*, *Rabbit Moon*, and *Waterworks* consist of loosely connected tableaux that showcase the characters' costumes and balletic movements. In this respect, they are more presentational than representational: rather than depict a narrative, they dwell on the process of staging and on precious settings, textures, surfaces, and gestures integrated into a loose storyline. Likewise, several sequences in *Scorpio Rising* show characters constructing their appearance in front of the camera, turning themselves into spectacles that tend to freeze the narrative flow. Yet while the theatrical excess of *Inauguration of the Pleasure Dome* or *Rabbit Moon* derives from high-culture traditions, such as fin-de-siècle decadentism, the styles portrayed in *Scorpio Rising* derive from popular sources: the motorcycle and gay subcultures, whose respective styles had specific resonances in the postwar social and historical contexts.

The Motorcycle Subculture and Youth Style

The motorcycle phenomenon started in California in the years following World War II and was triggered by the conjunction of a flourishing economy and postwar angst. The former gave working- and middle-class youths easy access to employment and disposable income, and with it, the material means to acquire and recycle motorcycles, clothes, music, and other commodities. Angst fed the murmur of discontent that can often be heard in their styles and practices. Hunter Thompson, author of the most thorough and extended study on the motorcycle subculture, characterized its origins as follows,

> The whole thing was born, they say, in the late 1940s, when most ex-GIs wanted to get back to an orderly pattern: college, marriage, job, children—all the peaceful extras that come with a sense of security. But not everybody felt that way . . . there were thousands of veterans who flatly rejected the idea of going back to their pre-war pattern. They didn't want order but privacy—and time to figure things out. It was a nervous, downhill feeling, a mean kind of Angst that always comes after wars . . . a compressed sense of time on the outer limits of fatalism. They wanted more action, and one of the ways to look for it is on a big motorcycle. By 1947 the state was alive with bikes. . . .[15]

Even for the youths who had not fought at the front, the postwar period brought on its own internal tensions, strictures, and regulations from which some escaped riding, forming groups cemented around machines and movement. Movement was a way to reject the reorganization and normalization of life after the war, with its conformist, settled lifestyle. In the social and ideological changes brought about by the end of the war, the bikers' constant drifting internalized the ideological instability and uncertainty of the period.

Bikers are one of the various forms of deviant youth culture that emerged in the postwar climate. As early as 1944, a host of documentaries (like the Time/Life movie *Youth in Crisis*), magazine articles, radio programs, and books (most notably, Robert Lindner's *Rebel without a Cause*), started spreading the impression that something had gone radically wrong with the country's adolescents. As the argument ran, lack of parental guidance and the violent atmosphere created by the war combined to turn juveniles into delinquents, whose lifestyles threatened fundamental American values, such as deferred gratification, cooperation, and family life. In this climate, so-called deviant youth culture consisted of a series of largely spontaneous formations which made visible an undertow of social discontent and expressed itself in violence or stylistic revolt—each acting as harbingers of the other.[16] Oppositional youth style, often allied to violence and delinquency, operated on received commodities, props of everyday common sense, practicality, and rationality. The first symptoms of stylistic rebellion emerged alongside violent resistance to authority in the 1943 zoot suit riots of New York and Los Angeles. In them, ethnic minorities (Hispanics in Los Angeles and blacks in New York) rioted against living conditions and the continued harassment of their communities by police and army personnel. The zoot suit, which young males in these communities had turned into a staple of their style, became, as a result of the riots, associated with protest and rejection of authority. The link between the zoot suit and rebellion was such that, after the riots of June 1943, the Los Angeles city council came close to passing an ordinance outlawing zoot suits citywide. The zoot suit consisted of a long, loose jacket with broad lapels and baggy pants pegged at the cuff, often adorned with a long, dangling watch chain. Both suits and watch chains were everyday commodities that members of these ethnic communities turned into signs of their difference from society. Cultural critic and historian George Lipsitz mapped the significations condensed in the zoot suits: the long, draped shapes and almost feminine ornamentation rejected the sober cut of conventional clothing; the conspicuous watch chain, a mere decorative item, mocked the connections between time and work schedules, discipline, and productivity; and finally, the zoot's sartorial excess (its ample, useless cut and flare) evoked its association with the culture of leisure. The zoot suit provided, in sum, "a means for creating a community out of a disdain for traditional community standards."[17]

The bikers can be seen as successors of the zoot-suiters in their use of style as a mark of outsidedness and dissent. Like other spectacular subcultures, they defined themselves largely through their appearance. And like the excessive figures of Anger's theatrical films, bikers turned "being" into an endless decking out intended to call attention to itself. Such self-reflexivity differed from the functionality and transparency of conventional style. To accentuate their difference from the mainstream, bikers dressed in leather and denim, gear that, besides being eminently practical in case of a wipeout, suggested the "open range" and their being untamed by social and communal ways. Their style was based on their interpretation of an all-American commodity: the motorcycle. Bikers did with motorcycles what hot-rodders and customizers did with cars: both cultures provided versions of their vehicles that contrasted with their "straight" functionalistic shapes. Their activities were centered around racing, riding and modifying their machines. Sober Detroit designs were transformed by the hands of expert customizers into demented shapes by adding chrome pieces, lowering the body of the vehicle, widening the mudguards, multiplying head and backlights, molding exhaust pipes into all sorts of shapes, adding tail fins and bubble tops. . . . For their part, motorcycles allowed for a smaller ornamental repertoire. Bikers favored heavy, stolidly built American-made machines such as Triumph, Indian, and Harley Davidson. They stripped these "irons" of much of their weight, added lights, mirrors, and chrome embellishments, and sometimes chopped their front axle to extend its length with the double purpose of defamiliarizing the machines and increasing their speed.

These manipulations were sharply described by Gene Balsey, a student at the University of Chicago who, in 1950, wrote an analysis of hot-rod culture for a seminar conducted by sociologist David Riesman.[18] Balsey interpreted hot-rod culture as an example of the autonomy of the consumer and of his or her ability to modify commodities through consumption, "despite the attempts of mass producers to channel consumption in 'respectable' directions." For Balsey, the souped-up cars of the hot-rodders (and the same could be said of the bikers' machines and style) were spontaneous and ingenious stylistic responses to the narrowness of industrial designs and by extension, of available social and professional options. As we will see, such manipulations of received images and commodities are structurally analogous to Scorpio Rising's gay decodings of everyday mass culture icons.

Rebellious youth styles problematized postwar ideological narratives, which postulated a fictitious national unity in opposition to the alien Communist threat.[19] By opening up cracks within such imaginary unity, oppositional youth cultures complicated the simplistic official dichotomies that pitted the United States against foreign threats. Neither alien invaders nor part of the social consensus, youth and other oppositional cultures presented dominant social ideologies with a limit to their legitimizing and naturalizing power. Many contemporary films, pulp novels, and comic books revolved around these troubling spots, attempting to exploit their energy and unmanageability for commercial profit and to contain their ideological scandals. Such popular forms were a privileged terrain of struggle between ideological containment, which worked to reassert official narratives of power, nationhood, and unity, and the dissonant expressions of youth style and resistance.

One of the best known popular genres where such a tug-of-war took place was the 1950s youth picture. Initially, such films as The Wild One, The Blackboard Jungle, and Rebel without a Cause, to name the most successful ónes, and later whole series of B-pictures on rock and roll (Rock around the Clock, Jailhouse Rock), motorcyclists (Motorcycle Gang), and delinquency (High School Confidential) both glamorized and popularized oppositional youth style and, at the same time, cautioned audiences against it by emphasizing its destructive underside. Hence, while popular films ended up by symbolically "punishing" youth subcultural forms, they also attributed to them a sense of autonomy, risk, and excitement. Popular texts like the motorcycle gang movie and the juvenile delinquent picture were thus internally split between condemning destructive outsidedness and glamorizing difference and transgression.[20] While transgression was expressed mostly through moments of spectacular style, condemnation was encoded in the narrative frames which tried to mediate the ideological threat of the bikers and other dissident subcultures. Attesting to a certain fascination with these popular styles, Scorpio Rising adopted, along with style bursting out of narrative bounds, the strategies of containment through which narratives set limits to such exuberant explosions of youth style. Anger's film then reproduced the same mismatch between attempted ideological containment and rebellion (or, in Robert Ray's words, between intent and effect) that characterized many commercial depictions of youth culture.

Bikers and Gays

Besides offering a popular transposition of Anger's modernist concerns, the bikers of Scorpio Rising deserve to be interpreted in terms of the filmmaker's interest in the iconography of homosexual desire, an interest already attested to by Fireworks. In this sense, Scorpio Rising shows Anger clueing not merely into popular culture at large, but more specifically into gay popular culture.

According to Hunter Thompson, the bikers' aura of danger and aggressiveness had made them popular icons in the sadomasochistic circuit.[21] The bikers' leather gear was, along with Nazi uniforms, a characteristic icon of the S&M aesthetic, and Anger's film does evoke such connections. However, the biker aesthetic was also attractive to a much larger sector of the subculture than those directly identified with S&M practices.

Images of bikers started cropping up in homoerotic physique magazines of the 1950s, the most popular of which was *Physique Pictorial*. *Physique Pictorial* started publication in the early 1950s. It was marketed as a physical culture magazine, but the insertion of models in elaborate fetishistic scenarios reveals a libidinal fantasy investment that can hardly be justified as interest in health and bodybuilding alone. The magazine was edited by Bob Mizer, who was also its main photographer and head of the photo studio Athletic Model Guild, source of the most widely disseminated gay erotica of the time. Started by Mizer in 1945 as an outlet of sorts for pictures of male models, the Athletic Model Guild soon found its most faithful constituency: male gay audiences. Guild's pictures were sold by mail order to those responding to advertisements in *Physique Pictorial*.[22] Bob Mizer's photos favored rough-looking, muscular men, many of whom, according to British painter David Hockney, had criminal records and earned their living modeling, sitting for artists, and hustling.[23] Many of Mizer's models were the human debris of the movie industry—handsome men who had moved to the area in search of a Hollywood career, and who, failing to land a job in the industry, ended up trading their beauty in less glamorous markets. For critic and historian Tom Waugh, Mizer's pictures evidence a shift in gay erotica away from the classical Greek decor and motifs which often favored androgynous adolescents as sexual ideals (an aesthetic best exemplified by the pictures of turn-of-the-century German photographers Wilhelm von Gloeden and Wilhelm von Pluschow), and closer to commonplace settings and rougher physical types.[24] Other symptoms of this shift are the works of contemporary gay photographer Al Urban; artist Tom of Finland, whose drawings gained wider circulation in America during the early 1960s; and Jean Genet's writings (first published in the English-speaking world by Grove Press) which also aligned homosexuality with roughness, everydayness, and criminality, and whose plots were often set in jails and the urban underworld. Of course, this gay iconography has an older history which can be seen in Walt Whitman's idolization of soldiers, field laborers, and workers, and, in a more elitist context, in Marcel Proust's character Baron de Charlus's weakness for "rough trade."[25] Both Whitman and de Charlus's tough boys are part of a tradition in gay culture that has received less pictorial representation than its Hellenic counterpart, since it lacked the artistic alibi of Greek classicism and was invested in eroticizing commonplace working-class motifs and milieus.

Mizer's photos often featured motorcycle punks as dominant figures in scenarios of bondage and discipline. While these images may have reflected Mizer's fantasy alone, its continued appearance in other facets of the subculture (in Eagle bars and as models for leather boys and for the 1970s clones) point to their wider gay appeal. Part of this attraction derived from the fact that the biker image contested conceptions of homosexuality disseminated by the popular culture of the time. The physicality of the biker contrasted with the effeminacy, frailty, and neuroticism attributed to homosexuals both in popular representations and medical and psychological discourses. The bikers also differed from a more genteel stereotype that emerged from within the subculture and that Richard Dyer has called the "sad young man": the vulnerable man who suffered helplessly in the dark, embodied for example, by Dirk Bogarde in the British film *Victim*, or, in a more closeted fashion, by Montgomery Clift's pin-ups.[26] The iconography of the "sad young man" was characterized by chiaroscuro lighting, interiors, averted gazes, and languid poses, and suggested being overpowered and confined, unable either to strike back or to escape. One can read in these secretive atmospheres the menace of the McCarthy gay-hunts, a menace corroborated by visual echoes from two main "paranoid styles": German expressionism and American film noir. By contrast to the physical and psychological confinement of the "sad young man," the biker imagery evoked movement, speed, and the open road. The bikers' aggressive stance offered a more empowering and affirmative gay icon that borrowed from spectacular forms of youth rebellion and replaced the besieged, passive look of the sensitive young man with a dire stylistic attack.

The uniformity, externality, and visibility of the biker image can be seen as instinctive attempts to form a community around an obvious and confrontational style. Images of sad young men stressed individuality, alienation, and isolation; they were in tune with contemporary characterizations of homosexuality as individual plight and personal pathology. By contrast, the biker image stressed a sense of commonality defined in terms of a shared style and de-emphasized individuation and subjectivism as bases of homosexual identification. *Scorpio Rising* exemplifies this shift; its focus on the group style of its multiple, interchangeable, and almost faceless protagonists is a sharp departure from the individualism and the subjectivism of the early *Fireworks*. Interestingly, this is also the time when sociological studies of deviance began to construct a paradigm of homosexuality that stressed the communal viewpoint and contravened the psychological models' emphasis on individual pathology. Deviance theorists and sociologists like Irving Goffman and Howard Becker took for granted a certain relativism in social and sexual mores. In their view, deviant identities developed as persecuted groups tried to establish their own social spaces and practices under the pressures of an antagonistic society. Homosexuality was not regarded by scholars of deviance as a failure to develop according to a normative oedipal trajectory (as American Freudianism claimed), but as an alternative form of socialization and commonality. Given their relativistic viewpoint, instead of proposing that homosexuals be cured and adjust to some psychologically based notion of "normality," sociologists of deviance advocated more acceptance and flexibility in social mores.[27] Gay-biker imagery encoded in an instinctive, untutored way the affirmation of difference, the depersonalization and de-individuation of marginality, and the stress on community that sociologists of the time were defending against the negative models of homosexuality-as-individual-disease legitimized by the psychological establishment.

Along with the emphasis on group style and the displacement of subjectivism, the hyper-masculine images of bikers implied an ironic detachment characteristic of camp. Anger's bikers, for example, represent masculinity as stylized drag or cosmetic facade, and therefore as far from natural or organic. The overabundance of phallic symbols in *Scorpio Rising* suggests that the masculinity of the bikers cannot be taken for granted, but had to be produced by insistent fetish-wielding. An example of this is the "Blue Velvet" song segment, in which, after putting on their leather and metal accoutrements, one of the bikers straddles a conical shape that points directly to his crotch. In case bulging muscles and macho poses did not bespeak masculinity strongly enough, it had to be underscored once more through this gesture. From another perspective, the fetishes may be a way to overcompensate for the specularization of the bikers, placed in what Laura Mulvey's characterization of visual pleasure has defined as a feminine position—objects of the camera gaze. In any case, the butch masquerade and fetishistic excess of the bikers' images contain strong doses of self-consciousness and artificiality; they contrast with the moral seriousness of the "sad young man," whose suffering is based on certain notions of authenticity and essentialism.

Scorpio Rising: Reading Mass Culture

Scorpio Rising's immersion in popular culture contrasts with the high cultural concerns and imagery of Anger's previous work. One reason for such a shift, as I have already suggested, is the extraordinary development of mass culture at the time when Anger made his film. *Scorpio Rising* appeared in a phase of American history characterized by the expansion of the electronic mass media and by an economic boom that increased consumer purchasing power across all social strata.[28] This period extends from 1945 to the present, and had one of its early peaks in the early 1960s, when *Scorpio Rising* was made, a time when television had reached near-ubiquity and other sectors of the media and entertainment industries were experiencing an enormous growth. Such developments came hand in hand with the vogue of Keynesianism, the most influential economic ideology of the 1960s, which was endorsed by the Kennedy administration. In contrast to classical economic theorists, who stressed production as the basis of economic growth, British economist Maynard Keynes, who developed his most

6. Kenneth Anger during the production of *Scorpio Rising* (1963). Courtesy Anthology Film Archives; reprinted by permission.

important insights during the 1920s and 1930s, maintained that increasing consumption was key to ensuring a stable economy with high levels of production and employment.[29] In keeping with these views, manufacturers developed sophisticated marketing and advertisement departments whose goal was to stimulate consumer demand.[30] A sharp increase in the quantity and quality of advertisement, coupled with the expansion of electronic media, made mass culture more pervasive than ever before. Such pervasiveness is born out by Anger's statement about the origins of Scorpio Rising's rock music score: "When I came back [from Europe], I spent the first part of the summer of 1962 at Coney Island on the beach under the boardwalk. The kids had their little transistors and they had them on."[31] The ubiquity of portable radios illustrates the extreme permeation of public spaces by the media and commercial culture. Art spaces seemed at the time equally permeable to mass culture, as in the early 1960s, some types of experimental art (pop and assemblage art are two examples) began to introduce popular artifacts into cultural domains like museums and art galleries, where they had traditionally been barred. We should also remember that popular forms had been, since the early 1950s, enacting some of the most subversive features of the historical avant-garde and high modernism. As an example, the biker and gay subcultures on which Anger draws in Scorpio Rising were interested in stylistic display and sexual ambiguity, issues which Anger had previously explored in modernist forms such as ballet and aestheticized cinema. But besides exploiting the subversive edge of some popular formations and iconographies, Anger's film also underlines their totalitarian menace.

Anger illustrates these paradoxical qualities of mass culture by appropriating popular images and artifacts and relocating them in his film. In doing so, he creates an open text which can be read in two nearly symmetrical, mutually contradictory ways. One of them equates mass culture with domination, and highlights its fascistic overtones; the other, in contrast with the former, stresses the anti-authoritarian openness and malleability of popular meanings—what cultural theorist John Fiske has recently called a popular economy of signification.

Before studying in detail how these two conceptions of mass culture traverse the film, I want to examine a sequence in Scorpio Rising that illustrates them both. This sequence corresponds to the fifth and sixth song segments, edited to Elvis Presley's "(You're the) Devil in Disguise" and Ray Charles's "Hit the Road, Jack." It shows a biker (Scorpio, in the film's credits) reclining in bed while reading the comics, and later on putting on his leather gear and preparing to attend a party. In the background, a television shows images of Marlon Brando in The Wild One. The walls of the room are crammed with posters, pin-ups, and film stills of James Dean—whose effigy also appears in cutaway shots to a plaque, an ashtray, a fan club diploma, and other star memorabilia. The biker's clothes and gestures mimic those of Dean and Brando, who embodied the ethos of youth rebellion in their 1950s films, and provided role models that oppositional youth subcultures such as the bikers eagerly identified with.[32] Mass-produced images determine Scorpio's looks, gestures, and stance, and can thus be said to erase his own identity and authenticity. From another point of view, these shots extend the gay spectatorial gaze that structures the film's early sequences to a number of mass cultural texts ranging from the songs of the soundtrack, to the comics ("Dondi," "Freckles and His Friends," "Li'l Abner"), to movie stars (besides the ones already mentioned, there are quick shots of Bela Lugosi and Gary Cooper). In this sense, the biker's mimicry should not be read as a blind reflex conditioned by the media, but as a defamiliarizing reading that "outs" the repressed homosocial and homoerotic significations of these specific popular texts.

The film maintains this ambiguity at every turn: the juxtaposition of Elvis's words "You look like an angel" to shots of a tough-looking boy lying in bed conveys the wit and exhilaration of deviant appropriation. But on the other side of wit, the noose hanging from the ceiling, skulls, some of the song's lines ("You're the devil in disguise"), and an insert of a newspaper clipping ("Cycle Hits Hole and Kills Two") suggest danger and violence. This is a paradoxical take: on the one hand, mass culture provides models for the construction of "deviant"—i.e., ideologically unmanageable—identities; on the other, the images appropriated and the process of appropriation itself contain a violence and negativity that recur throughout the film and explode in the Nazi imagery, death, and violence of its final sequences.

Totalitarianism and Mass Culture

The images of Nazism and sadism at the end of *Scorpio Rising* have proved particularly opaque to interpretation. At one level, *Scorpio Rising* suggests the closeness of homosexuality (of a sadomasochistic kind) and Nazism. The association had some historical grounding in the sexual scandals surrounding some high officials in the Nazi party, and was further supported by Nazism's misogyny and emphasis on male fellowship. The link between homosexuality and fascism was reinforced in psychoanalytic quarters by Wilhelm Reich's popular *The Mass Psychology of Fascism*. Although later discredited, Reich's theories influenced to a certain extent such sophisticated explorations of fascism in film as Pier Paolo Pasolini's *Salò* (1975), Luchino Visconti's *La caduta degli dei* (1969), and Bernardo Bertolucci's *Il Conformista* (1970).

The Nazi imagery in the film assimilates the bikers to Nazi troopers on the basis of their violence and gang-like structure. Sociological explorations of youth culture in previous decades have often turned to this comparison. Robert Lindner, whose influential study of juvenile delinquency, *Rebel without a Cause* (1944), became an obligatory point of reference in subsequent discussions of the topic, regarded criminal youth gangs (with their rigid hierarchies, leader-worship, and lust for violence) as embryonic fascist units. In view of the young outlaws' nihilistic and mutinous behavior, Lindner speculated that should they find a leader, the result might be fascism.[33] Two years after the publication of Lindner's book, the National Delinquency Prevention Society also echoed the concern that totalitarianism might infect the American outlaw youth.[34] The association of fascism and delinquency obeys the logic of postwar paranoia, which translated internal differences (those presented, for example, by gays, communists, and young outlaws) into threats to national boundaries. Hence the domestic problem of youth delinquency was transposed into one of borders and invasion—the threat of America falling prey to alien totalitarianism.

The presence of Nazi imagery and fascist icons in *Scorpio Rising* can be best explained as the film's commentary on mass culture.[35] From this perspective, the film relates the adoration of media and religious icons to the violence of fascism. Its overall trajectory depicts the slippage from the witty appropriation of mass cultural identities (the tough pose and leather gear of Brando on the TV screen) to the final outbursts of Nazi and sadomasochistic violence, which seem to be the result of the bikers' adoption of identities and styles disseminated by the media.

The connection between totalitarianism and kitsch is a recurrent trope in modernist left critiques of commercial culture. Both Clement Greenberg and Dwight Macdonald condemned kitsch for being a symptom of cultural poverty and a hollowing out of the critical and intellectual faculties which might eventually lead to totalitarianism. In the mid-1950s, Dr. Frederic Wertham based *The Seduction of the Innocent*, his well-known indictment of comic books, on the assumption that mass culture had the power to condition readers and consumers in an absolutist manner, outstripping the influence that schools, family, and other social institutions had over them.

The critique of mass culture as totalitarian force received its most influential and sophisticated formulation in the work of two members of the Frankfurt School: Max Horkheimer and Theodor Adorno. Conceived and written in the United States while in exile from Nazi Germany, Horkheimer and Adorno's *The Dialectic of Enlightenment* was a rigorous attempt to understand fascism within a streak of enslavement and domination intrinsic to the Enlightenment project. Fascism was thus, in their view, a latent condition of enlightened rationality (or in Adorno's terms, its dialectical negative), one that emerged most destructively in the Third Reich, but that could be spotted as well in triumphant moments of Western European Enlightenment. In different chapters of their book, Horkheimer and Adorno traced the undercurrent of Enlightenment-as-domination in the transition from mythic thought to reason, in the establishment of the proto-bourgeois notion of the individual in the myth of Odysseus, in the simultaneous emergence of Kant's enlightened ethics and de Sade's equally enlightened anti-ethics, in the ideology of antisemitism, and in the characteristics and social effects of the culture industry. In Adorno and Horkheimer's well-known formula, the culture industry was "enlightenment as mass deception"; it was based on the application of purposive rationality to the production of a totalitarian notion of culture devoid of real depth and complexity, integrated in the commodity market, and endowed with its own industrial infrastructure.[36]

The industrialization of culture results in three levels of totalitarianism. The first one is product standardization: "culture now impresses the same stamp on everything. Films, radio and magazines make up a system which is uniform as a whole and in every part" (120). Variations of and departures from the norm are not manifestations of creativity and autonomy, Horkheimer and Adorno argue, but commercial gimmicks intended to perpetuate the cycle of buying and selling. Second, the very apparati of culture, that is, the mass media, turn communication into a one-way activity: "The sound film . . . leaves no room for imagination or reflection on the part of the audience, who is unable to respond within the structure of the film" (126). Likewise, "[t]he inherent tendency of radio is to make the speaker's word, the false commandment, absolute" (159). Radio and film interpellate listeners, colonizing their own intimate spaces and precluding any opportunity to respond to the media messages. By analogy, the pervasiveness of television and pop culture icons in *Scorpio Rising* illustrates the oppressive ubiquity of mass cultural forms. Lastly, the culture industry exacerbates the commodity character of art products. Hence, for Horkheimer and Adorno, what is new about the culture industry is not so much its being a commodity, but its deliberate admission of this status (157). While in earlier historical times artists and creators resisted commodification by encoding into the work of art the contradictions between art's exchange value and its purposelessness, in late capitalism every feature of the art product works to facilitate exchange. And exchangeability entails a leveling of hierarchies between images and symbols, whose ability to circulate as commodities eclipses any other intrinsic qualities.

Scorpio Rising's mixture of high and low idols (of historical and mass culture figures) exemplifies the general equivalence and the flattening out of all images enthroned by the culture industry. By juxtaposing images of Hitler and Jesus with popular icons like Brando, Dean, Gary Cooper as the sheriff in High Noon, Bela Lugosi as Dracula, and several comic book characters, the film establishes an analogy between media myths and greater historical and religious myths. For example, the segment "He's a Rebel," crosscuts between Scorpio and a religious film on the life of Jesus, while the song's lyrics ("By the way he walks down the street") bind together the two "rebels." The editing of the scene cleverly applies Eisenstein's conflict of directions (both Scorpio and Jesus seem to be walking toward each other) to evoke a western-like showdown and to suggest, tongue in cheek, similarities between the two characters. The conflation of high and low icons in the film is made even more total because the high myths are incarnated in kitsch images (think, for example, of the image of Jesus reproduced in plastic statues, day-glo stickers, plaster busts, low-budget films, and Sunday school posters), which become in this manner as inauthentic and shallow as their mass media counterparts.

Throughout The Dialectic of Enlightenment, Horkheimer and Adorno highlight the continuity between the standardizing and de-individualizing work of the culture industry and Nazism. What Nazism does forcefully, the culture industry brings about by coaxing and solicitously recommending, yet the deep structure of domination is the same in both cases. In the context of a discussion on the power of advertisement, Horkheimer and Adorno state: "One day, the edict of production, the actual advertisement (whose actuality is at present concealed by the pretense of a choice) can turn into the open command of the Führer" (160). Fascism is thus the most extreme version of the culture industry and of the society it shapes—it is this society's outer limit and underlying structure.

In Adorno and Horkheimer's analysis, the totalitarian thrust of the culture industry works to eliminate authentic experience and autonomous individuality. In the same way that it colonizes the living space of consumers, the culture industry colonizes their minds, enthroning a false interiority whose points of reference, emotions, and ideas originate in media images. "The most intimate reactions of human beings have been so thoroughly reified that the idea of anything specific to themselves now persists only as an utterly abstract notion" (167). Individuality then becomes a reproduction of received clichés. In Anger's film, the images of the bikers copying each other's and their heroes' dress would seem to bear out Horkheimer and Adorno's critique: "the popularity of the hero comes partly from a secret satisfaction that the effort to achieve individuation has at least been replaced by the effort to imitate, which is admittedly more breathless" (155–156).

In a way, the culture industry's social conditioning prepares the masses of consumers for a totalitarian society, training them to respond in unison and to erase their own individuality. ("Fascism hopes to use the training the culture industry has given these recipients of gifts in order to organize them into its own forced battalions" (161)). The Nazi rally, where the masses are uniformed, lined up, and fully organized, literalizes the standardization imposed by the culture industry. Analogously, the stills of Nazi rallies in the last sections of Scorpio Rising are foreshadowed by the bikers' imitation of media images, as their mimicry contains the seeds of fascist uniformity.

The sadomasochism of the last sequences in the film can also be understood as an exacerbation of the violence involved in the adoption of borrowed identities, a violence that emanates from the retranslation and reformulation of subjectivity and experience in terms that are disconnected from community and autonomous thought, based instead on the oppressive flatness and one-dimensionality of the commodified images.[37] Such self-addressed violence is essentially masochistic, and defines for Horkheimer and Adorno the relations between consumers and mass culture.

> The attitude of the individual to the racket, business, profession, or party, before or after admission, the Führer's gesticulations before the masses, or the suitor's before his sweetheart, assume specifically masochistic traits. The attitude into which everybody is forced in order to give repeated proof of their moral suitability for this society reminds one of the boys who, during tribal initiation, go round in circles with a stereotyped smile on their faces while the priest strikes them. (160)

The sadomasochism of the last sequences of *Scorpio Rising* results from projecting introjected masochistic structures onto relations with others.[38] The "Torture" segment (the part of the Halloween party in which the "pledge" is manhandled in a prankish manner and doused with mustard) is a turning point in this respect: it follows Scorpio's ritual dressing in imitation of Brando and Dean and precedes the outright sadistic rituals of the (so-called, by Anger) "Rebel Rouser" scene. The goofy horseplay of "Torture" becomes increasingly sinister in subsequent song segments, which intercut shots of Scorpio desecrating a church with pictures of Hitler, footage of a Nazi rally, Nazi flags and swastikas, and references to sadomasochism—which include, in quick succession, close-ups of metal-studded boots, welts on a bare back, pictures of a suffering Jesus, and almost subliminal shots of the desecrator urinating into his helmet and offering it to someone off screen, in a combination of S&M routine and mockery of the eucharist.

After the sadism of the "Rebel Rouser" segment, masochism and self-immolation are the subject matter of the last section of the film, which features bikers riding at night through a city, scored to the Surfaris' "Wipeout" punctuated by the sound of roaring engines and screeching tires. The cyclists' antics become progressively more dangerous until one of them loses control of the machine and crashes. In these images, the sadism of the previous sequences appears introjected by the group and leads to self-annihilation in the final climactic shattering of man and machine. As an outcome of the erotic tensions built up through contemplation of the bikers' bodies and of ritualized violence, the crash almost has the character of sexual release. These last scenes also desublimate the violence that remained latent throughout the film, yet ready to burst to the surface. Ominous lines in such songs as "Fools Rush In," "My Boyfriend's Back," "You're the Devil in Disguise," and "Torture," together with the skulls that recur throughout the movie, spell a vague menace that takes concrete shape first in the gang's Nazism and sadism, and subsequently, in masochism and self-destruction. The shifts from the masochistic imitation of television images, to the sadistic desecration, and then to final self-annihilation suggest that sadism and masochism are inextricably entangled in the subject's relations with the culture industry and its products.

The Popular Economy

The foregoing reading makes *Scorpio Rising* into a visual counterpart of modernist critiques of kitsch. However, this reading does not resolve the ambiguity of the film, which also depicts mass culture as a site of dispute in which meanings are not fixed or imposed by media producers. While the culture industry's apparati may have totalitarian structure and intent, the texts they disseminate can be inflected and modified by specific audiences.

The use of pop love songs in the film exemplifies the mobility of popular meanings. While many of these songs are interpreted by male singers, and their implied addressees are women, they are edited to eroticized male images, a juxtaposition that contradicts the heterosexual romance of their lyrics. The opening sequence, cut to Ricky Nelson's version of "Fools Rush In," ends with a forward tracking shot on a muscular male chest encased in a leather jacket, while the singer blares "open your heart my love and let this fool rush in." Similar contrasts between sound and image track are the source of much of the humor in the film. Recall, for example, the well-known sequence edited to Bobby Vinton's "Blue Velvet," in which the velvet of the song transmutes into the blue denim and black leather of the images, while "she" becomes a series of tough-looking motorcyclists putting on their studded leather jackets, belts, chains, shades, and insignia. The section cut to Elvis's "(You're the) Devil in Disguise" can be analyzed along the same lines. Given Elvis's heart-throb status, the referent of such lines as "You look like an angel, you talk like an angel, you walk like an angel . . . but I got wise. You're the devil in disguise" is presumably a woman; however, the image track shows a boy who may be an angel only as a member of the notorious motorcycle club. In the shift, the erotic appeal distilled by the male vocalist is redirected to the leather boy. These examples typify the sorts of adjustments that male gay listeners may perform in order to anchor popular culture texts in their circumstances. Hence, rather than standardize listeners' reactions, the songs provide consumers with a chance to produce their own meanings, pleasures, and identities. In the case of *Scorpio Rising*, these pleasures emanate from ascribing gay significations to mainstream songs.

The production of gay subcultural pleasure and meaning then regulates the film's interpretations of popular texts. Through quotation and allusion, the film pulls a host of cultural icons into its own circle of homosexual desire. The insertion of images from *The Wild One*, for example, highlights the underlying homoeroticism of the almost all-male outlaw group in Laslo Benedek's film and Marlon Brando's pin-up appeal. Similarly, Anger underlines Dean's gay interest by placing his image within the regime of homoerotic looks and male display that characterizes the first half of the film. Anger's interpretation made visible the gay community's reception of Dean, whose screen persona as a sensitive, tortured outsider embodied some aspects of the subculture's self-image. In addition, Dean's performance in Nicholas Ray's *Rebel without a Cause*, in which he befriended Plato, arguably a gay character with Alan Ladd pin-ups in his high school locker, must have had enormous resonance with gay audiences.[39] (Perhaps Plato's character was a deliberate attempt to thematize an already palpable gay following garnered by Dean's performance in *East of Eden*.) Finally, rumors about Dean's homosexuality—rumors with which gay audiences of the time may have been familiar—might have furthered his eligibility as gay icon.[40] The brief inserts of comic book panels in the film are also charged with homoerotic connotations that might have remained invisible in a different context. Such is the case with the Li'l Abner cartoon showing two boys with their arms about each other under the title "The Sons Also Rise" (suggesting, in Ed Lowry's view, "the boys' arousal to erection");[41] or a panel of "Dondi" in which the eponymous character invites a handsome older man to see his room.

Such strategies of appropriation and contextualization illustrate a frequently unmapped force in mass culture: consumer agency. Popular agency operates on patterns of textual reception that both corroborate and modify the fetish structure of listening (and by extension, of popular culture consumption) theorized by Theodor Adorno.[42] As Adorno argued, popular listening is fetishistic—it operates as a transaction between songs and audiences which involves reified, mechanical, frozen musical phrases and lines, as well as contents and meanings that go beyond the merely aesthetic. They have to do with the social value of the cultural products—prestige, personal satisfaction, sense of belonging to the exclusive community of fans and connoisseurs, and so on. Adorno decried these surpluses in musical reception because they detracted from the autonomous character of the art work, and such autonomy was for him the only sphere of resistance to capitalist reification and control. These excrescences (or fetishes, in his terminology) introduced the work of art into the circuit of utility, exchange, and reification; they also occluded the structure (or non-structure, as the case might be) of the artistic whole.

But while Adorno's rejection of the fetishistic instrumentalization of cultural objects might be valid when applied to classical music—the original object of his critique—it cannot be unproblematically transferred to popular culture consumption, as he tried to do in the last part of his "The Fetish Character of Music" and in his writings on jazz. Contrary to Adorno's ideas, the circulation of popular texts is not based on autonomous contemplation but on a social contract based on utility, and utility requires the fetishization of listening (or viewing, or reading)—the reduction of songs and images to tokens for the exchange of (in John Fiske's words) "meanings, pleasures, and social identities."[43] Scorpio Rising fetishizes the popular texts it incorporates by subjecting them to a gay reading, but such fetishism does not entail a reduction of their meanings; on the contrary, it multiplies the chances of subordinate groups (the gay community, in this particular case) to express and promote their own pleasures and interests.

Scorpio Rising represents a highly articulate use of what cultural theorist John Fiske has called "the popular economy." A basic tenet of this economy is productivity: the "open" character of texts, which can be filled in, finished off by specific audiences in different contexts and for a variety of purposes. In the volatile economics of popular reception, significations are not stable or definitive; they are a function of the contexts in which they are integrated or of the purposes with which they are decoded. Popular texts act thus as catalysts for meanings and pleasures that audiences actualize according to their needs and desires.[44] In this sense, mass culture can provide an open terrain of contestation and resistance, where meanings are floating and relative, closed only in provisional ways by specific acts of reception. A great part of the exhilaration and wit of Anger's film comes precisely from this mobility of meaning, which allows for the inflection of popular artifacts with gay significations.

Scorpio Rising is therefore a complex, contradictory text: on the one hand it joins in a modernist condemnation of mass culture reminiscent of Clement Greenberg, Dwight Macdonald, Max Horkheimer and Theodor Adorno; on the other, it celebrates popular forms in ways that are characteristic of subcultural, militant gay postmodernism. While the film's overall movement reduces popular consumption to uniformity, violence, and death, singular acts of appropriation along the way point to the openness and political potential of popular texts. Such ambivalence toward pop culture extends also to the marginal identities and desires engendered in the act of short-circuiting mass cultural myths and icons; the glamour that characterizes outsider style and stance is at the same time problematized by the violence and negativity attendant on both.

After-Effects

Scorpio Rising's oscillation between the enjoyment of opposition and wariness at its possible failure is a function of its historical context. Poised between oppositional marginality and doom, subcultural and dissident communities of the time shared an analogous ambiguity. The bleakness of the film may have seemed unduly pessimistic in the "explosion of joy" (Tom Wolfe's words) of the early 1960s. However, by the end of the decade, which saw the escalation of the war in Vietnam, student revolts across the USA, the violent radicalization of some sectors of the counterculture, and the equally violent right-wing responses to liberal movements (manifested, among other events, in the assassination of leaders like Martin Luther King and Robert Kennedy), the overall trajectory of the film may have seemed an accurate metaphor for the fate of 1960s dissent and rebellion. At that time, *Scorpio Rising*'s transition from the affirmative expression of alienation to violent destruction resonated through many quarters of the counterculture and emerged in a handful of texts that expressed the exhaustion and paranoia of 1960s revolt.

Countercultural paranoia surfaced in such late 1960s commercial films as *Easy Rider*, *The Wild Bunch*, and *Bonnie and Clyde*, and in independent productions such as *El Topo*, a midnight hit of the time. All of these films sympathetically depicted the adventures of a group of outsiders and outlaws who end up being destroyed by repressive social forces. *Easy Rider* and *Bonnie and Clyde* are two cases in point. They signaled the breakthrough into mainstream filmmaking of young actors, directors, and sensibilities close to the counterculture. Both films depict the outlaws' aggressive marginality, estrangement from "straight" society, and subcultural values—associated with the drug world in *Easy Rider* and with crime in *Bonnie and Clyde*—in stories which culminated in their heroes' demise. They were self-conscious genre films which often commented on and revised the traditions they were reworking. *Bonnie and Clyde*, for example, quoted a number of visual motifs drawn from such art films as *Breathless*, *Citizen Kane*, and *Battleship Potemkin*, and, more important to my argument, from popular ones like *Golddiggers of 1933*, and the gangster genre. In turn, *Easy Rider* was less obviously allusive than *Bonnie and Clyde*, yet it also revised many motifs of popular genres like the Western (not the least of these revisions was reversing the direction of the journey from West to East) and incorporated several avant-garde techniques—the editing, for example, was reminiscent of Gregory Markopoulos and the rock and roll score harked back to *Scorpio Rising*. These quotations pointed to the fact that, as was the case with Anger's film, their sources were already existing narratives and icons. Their attitude toward their popular sources was analogous to *Scorpio Rising*'s: they partook of zest for rebellion encoded in mythologies and images from the media and popular culture, and of the paranoia that viewed destruction as the endpoint of difference and marginality. In this respect, these films were simultaneously an homage and an elegy to popular myths.

In more marginal cultural milieus, *Scorpio Rising*'s view of mass culture as a source of violence and manipulation was also echoed in the late 1960s and early 1970s in leftist ideology, more attuned to modernist suspicion than to the early 1960s paeans to the new sensibility. The mistrust characteristic of left media criticism was exemplified by (ex-leader of Students for a Democratic Society) Todd Gitlin's *The Whole World Is Watching*, and it underlay such political films of the time as Jon Jost's *Speaking Directly*, Robert Kramer's *Ice*, the Newsreel units' alternative media coverage, and Emile de Antonio's documentaries such as *Milhouse* and *In the Year of the Pig*. Across the Atlantic, an analogous animosity toward the established media and pop culture subtended post-May '68 film culture in England and France, spearheaded by Jean-Louis Comolli and Jean Narboni's programmatic "Cinema/Ideology/Criticism," which proposed ideological critique as the way to engage and disarm commercial cinema's complicit pleasures. This critical thrust found its cinematic expression in Chris Marker's documentaries and in the projects of Jean-Luc Godard and Jean-Pierre Gorin's Dziga Vertov group.

And yet, in a manner befitting its own contradictions, Scorpio Rising also foreshadowed less hostile engagements with mass culture on the part of subcultural, marginal, and/or oppositional groups. Its witty plunderings and outrageous readings of commercial culture texts were echoed in punk and in other style wars of the 1970s.[45] In addition, Scorpio's aggressive style foreshadowed contemporary forms of gay street culture, especially the leather, metal studs, butch posing, and other outer signs of radical gay difference deployed by 1970s clones and by such 1980s collectives as ACT UP and Queer Nation. Anger's influence also surfaces in the recent films and videos of such gay and lesbian artists as John Greyson's Moscow Does Not Believe in Queers (1986), The Acquired Dread of Sex Syndrome (1987)—an ironic remake of Luchino Visconti's Death in Venice in music video format—and The Pink Pimpernel (1990); John Goss's Stiff Sheets (1988) and Out-Takes (1989); Paul Wong's Confused (1986); Richard Fung's Looking for My Penis (1989); Bruce La Bruce's No Skin Off My Ass (1990); Julie Zando's I Like Girls for Friends (1987) and The Bus Stops Here (1990); Sadie Benning's Jollies, (1990); Tom Rubnitz's Wigstock, (1987), Made for TV (1984), and Drag Queen Marathon (1988); and Marlon Riggs's Tongues Untied (1989) and Affirmations (1989), the latter in music video format. These artists recycle popular images and narratives, imbuing them with subcultural significations. Like Anger's film, their texts freely mix original and borrowed footage and are stylistically heterogeneous, combining storytelling, direct cinema, interviews, mock advertisements, and music video formats. These videos and films partake of both activism and experimental culture. Although they have been screened in museums and galleries, many were originally produced for alternative television stations, such as Toronto's Deep Dish TV or the New York-based Paper Tiger TV, and have been regular fare at gay and lesbian film festivals across the country. These video works focus most often on explorations of gay politics and identities and AIDS-related issues. Their communal vocation is evident in their inventive engagement with commercial culture artifacts, an engagement which blurs politics and play, encoding and decoding, mainstream and marginal, while injecting gay significations into widely disseminated popular texts.

Hence, although Anger has tended to diffuse the gay connotations of Scorpio Rising,[46] this text has been an important influence on the cinema and cultural forms that emanated from the post-Stonewall politicization of the gay community. While remaining torn between the positive and negative connotations of the popular forms it assimilates, Anger's main film depicts a gay situationism of sorts, a deviation [détournement] or perversion (in both its etymological and sexual meanings) of popular objects that engenders a murmur of dissent. In this sense, its lessons are still used today in many quarters of the community, particularly in forms that try to meld politics with the affirmation of gay subcultural pleasures and identities—both of them perversely retrieved from the mass cultural forms which most often make them invisible.

Notes

1   J. Hoberman states "so avidly was this film absorbed by the media that one forgets that
    it was also avant-garde." "Once More with Anger," *Village Voice*, August 13, 1980.

2   "An Interview with Kenneth Anger," conducted by the magazine SPIDER, *Film Culture*, no.
    40 (Winter 1966), p. 68.

3   Cited in J. Hoberman and Jonathan Rosenbaum, *Midnight Movies* (New York: Harper, 1983),
    p. 56.

4   For a sample of such criticism, see the film's first reviews in *Film Culture* (Fall–Winter 1963,
    and Fall–Winter 1964), especially Ken Kelman, "Thanatos in Chrome," in the Fall–Winter
    1963 issue of *Film Culture*. See also Jonas Mekas's enthusiastic note on the film in his *Village
    Voice* column on November 14, 1963, reprinted in *Movie Journal* (New York: Macmillan, 1972),
    p. 108. P. Adams Sitney stressed *Scorpio Rising*'s place within the tradition of the American
    avant-garde cinema and within the rest of Anger's oeuvre. Perceptive as his criticism is,
    Adams Sitney rarely refers to the film's subcultural identity and belabors—too much, in
    my opinion—Anger's own conception of *Scorpio* as a conjuration of "Magick" (Anger's
    preferred spelling) forces. See "The Magus," *Visionary Film* (New York: Oxford University
    Press, 1979). More recent examples of discussions stressing *Scorpio*'s avant-garde
    aesthetics are Carel Rowe's *The Baudelairean Cinema* (Ann Arbor: University of Michigan
    Research Press, 1983), which dwells on Anger's connections to symbolism and
    decadentism, and his indebtedness to Eisensteinian montage; and Robert Haller, *Kenneth
    Anger* (Minneapolis: Walker Art Center, 1980).

5   For interesting discussions of Anger's film as a gay movie, see Ed Lowry's excellent "The
    Appropriation of Signs in *Scorpio Rising*," in *The Velvet Light-Trap*, no. 20 (1983), pp. 41–47;
    the sections on Kenneth Anger in Richard Dyer, *Now You See It* (London: Routledge, 1990),
    pp. 117–129; and Michael Moon, "A Small Boy and Others: Sexual Disorientation in Henry
    James, Kenneth Anger, and David Lynch," *Comparative American Identities*, ed. Hortense
    Spillers (New York: Routledge, 1991).

6   Kenneth Anger, "Filmography," *Film Culture*, no. 31 (Winter 1963–1964).

7   Other accounts maintain that *Histoire d'O* was seized by the French government because
    it featured the daughter of a government official. Robert L. Cagle, "Auto-Eroticism:
    Narcissism, Fetishism, and Consumer Culture," *Cinema Journal* 33, no. 4 (Summer 1994),
    p. 33, n.20.

8   Robert Haller, *Kenneth Anger*, pp. 15–16.

9   P. Adams Sitney, *Visionary Film*, pp. 102–103.

10 Samson DeBrier, "On the Filming of *Inauguration of the Pleasure Dome*," *Film Culture*, nos.
    67/68/69 (1979), pp. 211–215.

11 Another key filmmaker whose work also shows a parallel transition was Gregory
    Markopoulos. In Adams Sitney's scheme, Stan Brakhage's films represent the culmination
    of mythopoesis, as do Anger's *Scorpio Rising* and his later *Invocation of My Demon Brother* and
    Lucifer Rising. See P. Adams Sitney, *Visionary Film*, passim.

12 Along these lines, see the review by one of *Mattachine Review*'s editors, Richard Howard,
    "Homosexuality as a Vehicle for Masochism Symbolized in the Film *Fireworks*," *Mattachine
    Review*, 7, no. 7 (July 1961), pp. 6–9.

13 Kenneth Anger, *Hollywood Babylon* (San Francisco: Straight Arrow, 1975). In order to launch
    the first edition of his book in America, Anger took to the road with a multimedia "funny

Black Mass of a show," which included slides, film clips, music, dramatizations, and Anger's frantic performance as master of ceremonies. See Greil Marcus, "'Hollywood Babylon' on the Road," *Village Voice*, October 13, 1975.

14 As Richard Dyer states, "*Scorpio Rising* is intensely homoerotic but, apart from some lewd horse-play in 'Party Lights,' this is not so much in the form of sex acts as in the way the film invites us to look at these boys, as desirable", *Now You See It* (New York: Routledge, 1991). p. 125. Furthermore, as an avant-garde film, *Scorpio* was marketed and shown as a personal expression of its director; hence awareness of Anger's gender may have emphasized its homoeroticism.

15 Hunter Thompson, *Hell's Angels* (New York: Ballantine, 1981 [1966]). For a study of the British motorcycle subculture that integrates the perspectives of the British cultural studies school, see Paul Willis, *Profane Cultures* (London: Routledge, 1978).

16 "It is unclear what teenagers did in the very early 1950s . . . 'youthville' was absolutely nowhere in 1953. Within two years, things had changed. American youth were headlines uniquely their own: Juvenile Delinquency and Rock 'n' Roll." Richard Staehling's "From *Rock around the Clock* to *The Trip*: The Truth about Teen Movies," in *Kings of the Bs*, ed. Todd McCarthy and Charles Flynn (New York: Dutton, 1975), p. 220. For an excellent study of the social constructions of juvenile delinquency, the discourses surrounding it, and the frequent scapegoating it was subject to in the 1950s, see James B. Gilbert, *Cycle of Outrage* (New York: Oxford University Press, 1986).

17 On zoot suits, see George Lipsitz, A *Rainbow at Midnight* (New York: Praeger, 1981), p. 27, and "Cruising the Historical Block," in *Time Passages* (Minneapolis: University of Minnesota Press, 1987); and Stuart Cosgrove, "The Zoot Suit and Style Warfare," *History Workshop* 18 (Autumn 1984).

18 Gene Balsey, "The Hot Rod Culture," *American Quarterly* (Winter 1950), pp. 353–358.

19 For a reading of postwar culture as a tug-of-war between overall narrative "ideological" mediation and local attempts to escape such narratives, see Dana Polan, "Narrative Limits," in *Power and Paranoia* (New York: Columbia University Press, 1985). Some other limit cases to the "narrative's powers to naturalize and justify historical tensions" explored by Polan are labor politics, race relations, women's labor, and heterosexual relations.

20 In his study of the classical Hollywood cinema, Robert Ray states that this is a characteristic of the ideology of 1950s films, which evidence a mismatch between intent and effect. Robert Ray, A *Certain Tendency of the Hollywood Cinema*, 1930–1980 (Princeton: Princeton University Press, 1985).

21 Hunter Thompson, *Hell's Angels*, p. 114.

22 For a rather schematic history of Bob Mizer's enterprise and for illustrations of his art, see Timothy Lewis, *Physique: A Pictorial History of the Athletic Model Guild* (San Francisco: Gay Sunshine, 1983).

23 Cited in Stuart Timmons, "Wanted: Athletic Models," *The Advocate*, July 30, 1992.

24 For a succinct yet useful essay on American gay iconography, see Tom Waugh, "Photography: Passion and Power," *Body Politic*, no. 101 (February 1984). Representatives of such gay Hellenism in the nineteenth century are, for example, John Addington Symmonds, Oscar Wilde, Walter Pater, Lord Byron, Edward Carpenter, and, a generation later, E. M. Forster. See R. Jenkyns, *The Victorians and Ancient Greece* (Oxford: Blackwell, 1981); and P. Hahn, *Nos ancêtres les pervers* (Paris: Olivier Orban, 1979). On gay Hellenic icon-

ography, see also Bruce Russell, "Wilhelm von Pluschow and Wilhelm von Gloeden: Two Photo Essays," *Studies in Visual Communications* 9, no. 2 (Spring 1983), pp. 57–80.

25 Walt Whitman's "Calamus" is the most openly homoerotic section of *Leaves of Grass*, ed. Malcolm Cowley (New York: Penguin, 1959). *Time Regained* contains some humorous episodes involving de Charlus's fascination with young criminals and street toughs. In Proust, *Remembrance of Things Past*, trans. C. K. Scott Montcrieff and Terence Kilmartin. Vol. 3 (New York: Random, 1982).

26 Richard Dyer, "Seen to Be Believed: Some Problems in the Representation of Gay as Typical," *Studies in Visual Communication* 9, no. 2 (Spring 1983), pp. 2–19.

27 The classic works in this trend are Howard S. Becker, *Outsiders: Studies in the Sociology of Deviance* (New York: Free Press, 1963), and Irving Goffman, *Stigma: Notes on the Management of Spoiled Identity* (Englewood Cliffs, NJ: Prentice-Hall, 1963). For an overview of deviance theory, see Stuart H. Traub and Craig B. Little, eds., *Theories of Deviance* (Itasca, IL: Peacock, 1975). See also John D'Emilio, *Sexual Politics, Sexual Communities* (Chicago: University of Chicago Press, 1983), p. 142ff.

28 This follows the periodization of mass culture in modern America proposed in George Lipsitz, "Popular Culture: This Ain't No Side Show," in *Time Passages*, pp. 6–13.

29 For new-style Keynesian consumerism in 1960s America, see David Horowitz, "Capitalism and the Crisis of Abundance," *In the Marketplace: Consumerism in America* (San Francisco: Canfield, 1972). Christin J. Mamiya, *Pop Art and Consumer Culture* (Austin: University of Texas Press, 1992) is a fascinating study of the relation between pop art and the emergence of Keynesianism as official economic ideology.

30 The adoption of Keynesianism and the development of the advertising industry worked to instaurate Henry Ford's dream of linking mass production to mass consumption. The products of work would be absorbed by the market as props of leisure. This notion seemed to make leisure and consumption as necessary to the industrial machine as work itself, and suggested a dissolution of the distinctions between both. David Harvey, *The Condition of Postmodernity* (Oxford: Blackwell, 1989), pp. 125–141.

31 SPIDER, "Interview with Kenneth Anger," p. 69.

32 See Graham McCann, *Rebel Males* (New Brunswick, NJ: Rutgers University Press, 1992). See also Hunter Thompson, *Hell's Angels*, p. 90, where he quotes the responses of some bikers to the film when it first came out: "[*The Wild One* and Marlon Brando's role in it] gave the outlaws a lasting, romance-glazed image of themselves, a coherent reflection that only a very few had been able to find in a mirror".

33 Interestingly, Lindner attributed youth revolt to rebellion against a father wielding immoderate authority in the eyes of the son. A few years earlier, Adorno and Horkheimer had located the roots of authoritarianism in an opposite but equally problematic development of the father figure in contemporary German society. Writing separately, they argued that the authority of the father had been weakened while that of the state had increased. Concomitantly, the subjects' oedipal investment in the father as figure of opposition and identification was replaced by identification with the state incarnated in the person of the Führer. Consequently, the origin of the superego and of the subject's moral structure lay now not in autonomous familial and interpersonal relations, but in a "collective," "standardized" investment in the image of the Führer. The collective character of this process erases individuation and predisposes individuals to fascist uniformity. See Max Horkheimer, "The End of Reason," T. W. Adorno, "Freudian Theory and the Pattern

of Fascist Propaganda." Both in *The Essential Frankfurt School Reader*, ed. Andrew Arato and Eike Gebhardt (New York: Continuum, 1982); and Max Horkheimer, "Authoritarianism and the Family," in *Critical Theory* (New York: Continuum, 1981).

34 See James Gilbert, *Cycle of Outrage*, p. 42. Lewis Yablonsky, "The Violent Gang," *Commentary*, no. 30 (August 1960), pp. 125–130.

35 All other interpretations of *Scorpio*'s Nazi imagery I know differ from mine. P. Adams Sitney states that the film is mythographic; it "self-consciously creates its own myth of the motorcyclist by comparison with other myths: the dead movie star, Dean; the live one, Brando; the savior of men, Christ; the villain of men, Hitler. Each of these myths is evoked in ambiguity, without moralizing. From the photos of Hitler and a Nazi soldier and from the use of swastikas and other nazi impedimenta, *Scorpio* derives a Nietzschean ecstasy of will and power." (P. Adams Sitney, *Visionary Film*, p. 121.) One of the most clairvoyant critics of the film, Ed Lowry, attributes the film's fascism and self-destruction to the repression of the homoeroticism underlying the bikers, comics, Brando and Dean, and the many other icons that populate the film. Repressed homoeroticism thus expresses itself obliquely or else enacts a violent return in sadomasochism and fascism. (Ed Lowry, "The Appropriation of Signs in *Scorpio Rising*," *The Velvet Light Trap*, no. 20 [1983], pp. 41–47). Richard Dyer sees these icons as "wild, transcendent forces that convention represses. The point is that most people disapprove of them . . . their disapprovableness is a sign of their fitness for Magick invocation" (*Now You See It*, p. 129). Magick is Alistair Crowley's sort of magic, which Kenneth Anger recognizes as one of his major sources of inspiration. Part of the point of the film is to collide images and icons together with the purpose of liberating their latent meanings and identities—roughly, their Magick forces. And to sample one more opinion, David James states in his thorough study of 1960s avant-garde and alternative cinemas: "Though intercut images of Hitler imply that Scorpio's cult is fascist and his command is destructive, in general, the associations that accrue around him are unstable." *Allegories of Cinema* (Princeton: Princeton University Press, 1989), p. 153.

36 Max Horkheimer and Theodor W. Adorno. *The Dialectic of Enlightenment*. trans. John Cumming (New York: Continuum, 1972). Page numbers are given in the text.

37 In other words, mass culture does not falsify a "pure" pristine experience, since all experience only exists as a function of texts, as pure trace of signifiers. What Adorno and Horkheimer call attention to is what type of signifiers are used in making experience visible. The problem does not lie with the process of identity formation as such, which always entails a betrayal of a hypothetical "real" experience, but with the specific texts and images used in the process.

38 Freud's writings on sadism and masochism evolved, in connection with his views on instincts, from "Three Essays on the Theory of Sexuality" (1905), where he postulates a primary sadism linked to a will to mastery that is later introjected as masochism, to "The Economical Problem of Masochism" (1924), which proposes a primary masochism, residue of the death instincts and later externalized as sadism. Freud's difficulties in establishing the primacy of one or the other signal the fundamental mobility and fluidity of aggressive relations; these characteristics are illustrated by *Scorpio Rising*'s swift transitions between other-directed and introjected violence. "Three Essays on the Theory of Sexuality," *Standard Edition*, vol. VII; "The Economical Problem of Masochism," vol. XIX, trans. James Strachey (London: Hogarth, 1948).

39 The homoeroticism of their friendship was a source of concern for censors. Colonel

Geoffrey Stockley, successor of Joseph H. Hays as head of the MPAA Production Code Administration, wrote to Jack Warner: "It is of course vital that there be no inference of a questionable or homosexual relationship between Plato [Sal Mineo] and Jim [James Dean]." Cited in James Gilbert, *Cycle of Outrage*, p. 186. Vito Russo cites Stuart Steam, screenwriter of *Rebel*, saying that the Alan Ladd pin-ups are meant to suggest to the audience that Plato was "the faggot character." *The Celluloid Closet* (New York: Harper and Row, 1981), p. 110. For a gay reading of the film, see Christopher Castiglia, "Rebel without a Closet," *Engendering Men*, ed. Boone and Cadden (New York: Routledge, 1990), pp. 207–221.

40 Anger expatiates on these rumors in *Hollywood Babylon*.

41 Ed Lowry, "The Appropriation of Signs in *Scorpio Rising*," p. 45.

42 Theodor Adorno, "The Fetish Character of Music and the Regression of Listening," in *The Essential Frankfurt School Reader*.

43 John Fiske, *Television Culture* (London: Methuen, 1988), p. 313.

44 See John Fiske, "Popular Discrimination," in *Modernity and Mass Culture*, ed. James Naremore and Patrick Brantlinger (Bloomington: Indiana University Press, 1991), p. 110. See also "Conclusions" to *Television Culture*.

45 The best analysis of punk along these lines is still Dick Hebdige, *Subculture: The Meaning of Style* (London: Methuen, 1979). See also Stuart Hall et al. *Resistance through Rituals* (London: Hutchinson, 1976); Peter York, *Style Wars* (London: Sidgwick and Jackson, 1980); Dave Laing, *One-Chord Wonders* (Milton Keynes: Open University Press, 1985); and, on popular and street culture in general, Iain Chambers, *Popular Culture* (New York: Routledge, 1986).

46 On *Scorpio*, he stated: "In that film I'm viewing a certain phenomenon that was happening at that particular time. I don't see the film as a homosexual statement. I see it as a human statement." Cited in Robert Haller, *Kenneth Anger*, p. 6.

Stan Brakhage

6

The 60th birthday interview

SURANJAN GANGULY

Perhaps the best birthday gift Brakhage got when he turned 60 last year was the news that the Library of Congress had chosen *Dog Star Man* (1962–1964) for inclusion in the National Film Registry. But the gift came complete with price tag. Brakhage was expected to provide the internegative and print at a cost of about $6,000 which he can't afford. But did that get him down? No. In over forty years of filmmaking that has established him as the world's foremost living avant-garde filmmaker with an oeuvre of over 250 films, Brakhage has suffered all the vicissitudes—bureaucratic and otherwise—that can befall the independent filmmaker. And he's proved himself to be a survivor. Now he's learning to live with a new threat—not being able to even print his new work as costs spiral out of control.

The new work consists of films that Brakhage has made at the rate of six to eight a year since 1987 when his first marriage to Jane Collom ended in divorce. The break-up was decisive in more than one sense: it altered the very conditions of his filmmaking. Since 1964, for almost thirty years, Brakhage lived at Lump Gulch, 9,000 feet up in the Colorado Rockies, where he frequently photographed his family and his daily life in a series of films that celebrated "the glories of an undramatic present." All that changed with the divorce. At 54, living alone in a closet-size room in Boulder (he has been teaching film at the University of Colorado at Boulder since 1981), Brakhage was no longer sure whether he could make a film again. Then, in the same year he met Marilyn Jull, a Canadian, who had studied film at the Ryerson Polytechnic Institute in Toronto. They were married in 1989 and now have two children, Anton and Vaughn.

The films from 1987 are hard to classify, but they can be loosely grouped in relation to certain trends. At a number of points, Brakhage re-engaged with modes of filmmaking he had earlier abandoned for personal or philosophical reasons. Thus, the four-part collaborative Faust project (1987–1989), which Brakhage made with a group of young Boulderites, came as a surprise from one who had always upheld the sovereignty of the artist as maker. The project also led to a revival of interest in film sound which he had virtually written off as an aesthetic error. He was now ready to apply sound to film and experiment with electronic, instrumental and vocal music. There was also the reversion to story and narrative in the Faust films, another surprise, given Brakhage's avowed intention to prevent film from "being harnessed by the other arts." And, finally, Brakhage turned to psychodrama after many years, because it offered him a chance to confront the psychic drama of his own mid-life crisis. Thus, not only the

Faust films, but films like Nightmusic (1986), Confession (1986), Kindering (1987), The Dante Quartet (1987) and I . . . Dreaming (1988) are rooted in the events and emotions of this period, sometimes in a direct and confrontational ways as in Confession where Brakhage photographs himself and his private life, or more subtly as in Nightmusic, a thirty second hand-painted film about "the beauty of sadness."

But already by 1988 this phase was drawing to a close and Brakhage had begun a cycle of films inspired by Marilyn: Marilyn's Window (1988), The Child's Garden and the Serious Sea (1991) and Untitled Film (For Marilyn) (1992) in which there are allusions—especially in The Child's Garden—to earlier concerns with childhood, primal sight, the beginning of consciousness, and the phenomenological discovery of the world. It is in these films that Brakhage finally frees himself from "all melodramatic self-imaginings."

Brakhage was also at work on films that reflect his life-long obsession with modes of seeing, such as hypnagogic or closed-eye vision (optic feedback), moving visual thinking (the synapting of the brain which produces certain abstract shapes) and peripheral vision (what the eyes don't pay close attention to). Fireloop (1986) and Loud Visual Noises (1987) are hand-painted sound films that explore some of these processes. But the most extensive study of this subject resulted in a multiple series which Brakhage began in 1979 and completed in 1990: The Roman Numeral Series, The Arabic Numeral Series, The Egyptian Series and The Babylon Series. These films examine the nature of prelinguistic thinking out of which, Brakhage believes, arose the hieroglyphs of ancient cultures. To give some sense of the shapes and colors within this non-verbal, non-pictorial realm, Brakhage photographed with a variety of glasses, prisms, crystal balls and filters, making the films his most intense meditations on light. They also call to mind the structures of music—a visual music of light and color patterns.

Since then, Brakhage has used the camera less and less, preferring to paint on film, but without reference to his own life or his thought process or that of others. As he likes to say, film should be "about nothing at all," and in the very short films that he's now making, sometimes at the rate of four per month, there is a sense of an opening into the ineffable. This may prove to be the ultimate reversion in Brakhage's career: to zero and beyond.

Despite his qualms about video, Brakhage very kindly allowed me to record this interview on video tape. There were about six sessions, over ten hours of tape and a hundred page transcript.

Suranjan Ganguly: Why have you stopped filming your family?

Stan Brakhage: Only one-third of my work while living with Jane was frankly auto-biographical. That was fine because if I didn't make those films then we couldn't have held the marriage together, but in terms of what I've always been searching for, it was a passage through to other things. I don't film my family anymore partly because I think autobiography as a form is not good for film. It's very much on the record side of things—far too referential. Besides, I was never very interested in portraiture: very few of my films deal with people other than my immediate family or close friends. The big exceptions are The Pittsburgh Documents I made in 1971: deus ex, eyes and the act of seeing with one's own eyes; those were my social dramas of that period. But in general I've always tried to get at the qualities of being human. My portraits are often about people's blurred motions, or things that are around them. For example, in Dominion (1974) you mostly see a man's nervous movements reflected on his desktop.

Ganguly: Isn't it also true that Marilyn doesn't like to be photographed or filmed?

Brakhage: Yes. One of the reasons why Marilyn doesn't like to have her picture taken is because like me she senses some falsification in that process. Now, I could have gone on photographing myself and the children—done a series of self-portraits—she has never forbidden me, but it's just that my sense of the aesthetic has changed, and that's largely due to my conversations with her. Also, after the second marriage I felt a strong desire to *have* my life rather than photograph it. So now I feel the autobiographical mode is essentially finished in every other sense except that naturally whatever I make will have something of myself in it, but I don't want to be conscious of that—I'd rather just let it happen.

Ganguly: One of the reasons for filming your family and your daily life was to counter the influence of the other arts—especially drama—on film. Do you think you succeeded?

Brakhage: I underestimated the historical flypaper I was stuck in. I didn't realize until much later how people in their daily living imitate the narrative-dramatic materials that infiltrate their lives through the radio, TV, newspapers and, certainly, the movies. We went to the movies at least once a week and to plays, and I read a great deal to the children and they naturally acted out these things in their games . . . It was ironic that I who was an anomaly because I was working independently outside the studio system created for myself a situation that was akin to that of a studio. To that extent my work was tied to the whole history of cinema when I thought that wasn't the case. The films weren't free to grow aesthetically but dragged down by their subject matter. Despite all the evolutions of my film grammar and my inclusion of hypnagogic and dream vision, they were still tied to the more traditional dramatic-narrative framework. Moreover, while shooting I would ask Jane and the children to keep quiet or be still, very basic things, but that pushed everything back toward drama. And then, although they were used to being photographed, they knew, like most people, when their picture was being taken, and that became a factor in what they did before the camera.

Ganguly: But such moments were also important to your self-reflexive aesthetic.

Brakhage: Yes, I did everything I could to recognize such moments and include them. Very often people look directly at the camera and sometimes even flash a smile. Or I would include references to the fact that it was a film—flares, scratched titles, etc. *Dog Star Man* ends in a flare of sprocket holes . . . I believe most artists whose work has any lasting value to a culture put out warning signs like these to say this is not a window into reality but an art work. This is why painters sign their names on front of their paintings, or poets refer to the poem that's being written and to other poets. As Malraux said in *The Voices of Silence*, works of art speak to each other. And so there's a constant speaking to other filmmakers and filmmaking within my body of work.

Ganguly: Was it hard to see those films after their subject—the marriage—collapsed? Did they have the same relevance for you?

Brakhage: At first, I couldn't even bear to see snapshots of my previous life—I'd burst into tears. I was so twisted with agony that I couldn't even hold onto certain household objects, like a bunch of spoons because they reminded me of the destruction of that life. So I had some terrors about those films—that I wouldn't be able to look at them again. But I found I could, and what is more I could watch them with Marilyn—the films had achieved an aesthetic to that extent, and one that was vibrant enough to sustain me.

7. Stan Brakhage. Courtesy Anthology Film Archives; reprinted by permission.

Ganguly: How did the children react to being filmed?

Brakhage: For some certain films are very bothersome. For example, Crystal finds *Fifteen Song Traits* (1965) in which she is crying, very disturbing, and the fact that I filmed her at that point. I now believe that in photographing the children I was engaging them in a creative process, a trance process that was physically far more demanding than they knew. As a result, their childhoods were distorted in subtle and dangerous ways. I am very aware of this now. Also, when an artist mixes his working process with his daily life then there is a psychological imposition on other people who are involved. The children were not photographed continually—months or even half a year would go by—but there were long periods when there was some photography every day. It was more pervasive and in that sense more invasive of activities within the home which I now feel should be an area of privacy. There was an enormous invasion also of Jane and my privacy as well. So while I certainly achieved a better relationship vis-à-vis the children in the act of making those films than what I had inherited, it didn't go as far as I had hoped—all of which goes to show why that 29-year-old marriage, much celebrated in print and a constant point of reference within my art-making, finally collapsed.

Ganguly: In the Hollis Frampton Interview Jane actually complains of being used . . .

Brakhage: Hollis and I were both surprised by that claim. I think she felt used by the process coming through and directed by me, so I took her word for it then and still do now and feel condemned that a part of me couldn't see as well into her condition as it could with regard to the children. I must have been a terrible imposition on her. At the same time, I want to counterbalance this by saying that she always seemed very excited at being involved in the creative process, so I would invite her to look at the first edits and try to include her point of view in what I was making.

Ganguly: Still, it must have been an enormous challenge to be housewife and mother and also face the camera.

Brakhage: I think Jane was very much more a private person than she was permitted to be, not only vis-à-vis within the family, but with respect to the rest of the world. But she also seemed to enjoy the fact that people would come over and give her a lot of attention. Barbara Hammer even made a whole film on her in which Jane said she was a housewife and proud of the fact, so who's to know? There was that side of her which believed very strongly in being mother to her children and keeping house in that idyllic place. And I think what happened finally was that Jane increasingly felt that I was getting all the attention. And as the children began to grow up and she began to feel less enthralled being a mother, this fact began to hurt and disturb her deeply . . . After the Frampton interview I tried to represent her in ways she would recognize as being herself, and the first film that succeeded in doing this was *Hymn to Her* (1974). She also felt a close affinity with the last film I made with her—*Jane* (1986). And then there were her appearances in films like *The Loom* (1986) that moved her and satisfied her because she didn't feel used in them.

Ganguly: To be fair, did *you* ever feel used in the process of making those films?

Brakhage: I felt very used—ill-used—being given this burden of responsibility to stage-manage an unusually difficult family living situation at 9,000 feet in the mountains, subject to eight months of winter for a man who grew up a city boy. I was being used especially because I was inept in handling all that. It was hard to live there. I think I would have come to things that I have now come to very much sooner with a chance to better fulfill the intricacies of them. But there I had to split my personality . . . It's just so hard to live and I think the films show that. But still, it's all a gift—a gift of life and a gift of light, which are really one and the same. So despite it not being my kind of place, I had ecstatic moments up there. I was forced to open myself to the wonders that are available in the most difficult surroundings.

Ganguly: Wasn't it common in those days to refer to Jane as your Muse?

Brakhage: Many people thought she was the Muse and I found that to be utterly repugnant. For me the Muse is a persuasion. It often feels like a force in Nature that moves through certain people, but it should never be appropriated by human beings. At one point in history the Muses were called goddesses, now it would be more appropriate to call them manifestations of the unconscious, or perhaps along the line of Jung's "collective unconscious" to call them genetic manifestations that people shouldn't presume upon. Jane never called herself the Muse except as a joke, but she felt that what came through my work was really her doing although it was I who was mostly photographing and editing.

Ganguly: So whose films are they? In *Metaphors of Vision* you claim the term "by Brakhage" embraces the whole family, not just you.

Brakhage: Yes, and that was well meant. The films were collaborative works, but finally they belong to the Muse—not to me or to Jane or to the children. All of us were used in some evolution. When I associate the Muse with the unconscious I'm referring to the unknown. Those films came through me from the unknown. After we were divorced Jane told two of her friends that it was really she who made the films and that I was very good at following her orders. By that she meant she had been the real inspiration for the films she valued most, and I felt she was complimenting me for being extraordinarily sensitive to her inspiration. But the final result was extrinsic to any of us in as much as none of us could have conceived of them that way. And they came through with my style which is visible regardless of the subject matter or the techniques. I was the maker, for better or worse, and yet I wouldn't have been able to consciously make anything of any significance whatsoever. The only time I like to look at one of my films over and over again is when it is a product of this trance process.

Ganguly: And this trance process would extend to the editing of the film as well?

Brakhage: Yes, I would edit the material hoping to achieve an aesthetic ecology. That was always my intent without ever presuming to know whether I had succeeded or not, and I lent myself to that process in the most traditional ways—what you would normally expect from poets, painters, or composers—that their work is essentially under trance and largely alone in these final aspects of the making, even if they are working on a mural with people to help them. The impulse that distinguishes one mural from another comes essentially through one human being. I was trying to do that with film which was regarded as a communal art when I was growing up.

Ganguly: But before you would enter into a trance, you would consciously think about the film you were going to make?

Brakhage: I studied home movies as diligently as I studied the aesthetics of Sergei Eisenstein, and beginning with *Songs* (1964–1969) all the way to *Scenes From Under Childhood* (1967–1970). I turned to them for inspiration. But my films were different in that they were rooted in daily living rather than in the events that home movies tend to celebrate. What is embarrassing about certain amateurs is that they try to get everybody to jump around and act as if they were making a Hollywood movie which they can't. They are not showing the particularities or the *peculiarities* of their most mundane—i.e., "earthly"—surroundings and events. They would much rather photograph a staged birthday party than a normal day with their child . . . I believe if we don't really focus on where we live, then great dangers arise in human psychology, one of which is to live in a past that is utterly falsified by human thinking and project into a future that is utterly impossible. Or we get bored and need drama. So trying to stop the overwhelming influence of drama in film, I began to concentrate on the wonders that are under and on either side of our noses—more specifically the greatest movie in town if only we would look at it.

Ganguly: But at the same time you were turning that experience into myth, into . . .

Brakhage: True. By focusing on the particularities of our daily life I could provide for Jane and the children and myself an alternative to the strictures of traditional family living. So the impulse to make those movies—as practically everything in my work—arose out of a desperate living urgency to transform my sense of the constrictive family life. It was a need that Jane and I shared very vibrantly together. *Dog Star Man* is a good example—a myth which deals with the breadwinner—myself—being photographed by the wife, Jane (for the most part), climbing a mountain to chop down a tree, to bring home some firewood . . . That's the human story, spread out, all the way to the stars and down to the microscopy of the man's vascular system, with everything in between metaphoring various historical stages in this brief climb of a mountain. We needed that metaphorical distance.

Ganguly: But wasn't there a danger of taking that myth too seriously, of losing sight of the commonplace?

Brakhage: In one of her scrapbooks Jane describes herself as an ordinary goddess. She has now changed her name to Jane Wodening—which is the female version of the god, Woden. All this shows a predisposition to the goddess aspect of daily living, so both of us remained entranced by the most traditional, and, for myself, most dangerous presumptions of human existence on earth. All the same, there was a kind of glory and beauty to it. For a certain crowd in society we—the family—were like movie stars. We stood for certain ideals of the 1960s . . . As an orphan and as a multiply-abandoned child I respected the values of family living, and wished to assert their goodness and subvert what I felt was wrong. I wanted to create and sustain an inspired image of family living, and if those films inspire me today it is because there is a fair and honest representation of that image in them. I believe in those values, and thus run counter to some of the more virulent polemics of our time which would have it that family living is done for.

Ganguly: Whenever people talk about your vision of childhood in these films they go into a sort of rapture and invoke Wordsworth and Blake.

Brakhage: I think it's misleading to relate me to Wordsworth—I who had no childhood at all . . . I was after the emotional truth and the spiritual truth. And there was a tiny Weegee aspect to me too—only the bare truth, and sometimes I went out of my way to get that truth by photographing what normally you wouldn't photograph if you were making an idealized family living film. There's a lot of crying in my films of the children, of Jane and of myself. You see children being cruel to each other in ways that an amateur would never photograph.

Ganguly: And yet it all seems magical, the way you photograph the light and the house . . .

Brakhage: The films aren't idealized in a simple sense, but they are in the sense that's intrinsic to art. I'm trying to make a form representative of family living which is a little bit off of this earth. And as such those films sit there hanging in air. Looking at them you would think that everything was beautiful to those people . . . People who visited the cabin found it to be small, dark and cold, but in the films the house looks bigger and full of light. And that's because those films were inspired by the children and their growing up and having a childhood that was utterly different from mine, and the fact that I could give that childhood to them. I was translating that over into film emotionally. So people were shocked that from this grubby little cabin came a palace of visions.

Ganguly: There are moments in all these films that seem quite trivial and yet uncannily revealing.

Brakhage: I had read Freud's *Psychopathology of Everyday Life* where he discusses the verbal slips we make every day, and that was the time when I was intensely involved with representing common everyday occurrences. So I tried to capture those unconscious slips—"errors"—that can divulge hidden truths and tried to weave them into my work.

Ganguly: How did you go about doing this?

Brakhage: Sometimes while shooting I would consciously try to get at certain things that were revelatory, that were true slips. I would look for them and then during editing put them in a context where they would reveal something. They crop up all the time in *Scenes From Under Childhood*, and even more in the *Sincerity* series (1973–1980) and in the *Songs*. In the *Fifteen Song Traits* the footage of Crystal crying was shot when we were in Lexington, Kentucky. The first thing I shot on coming home—a week or a month later—was a caged canary. When the footage came back from the lab and I looked at it, I was astonished by the power of that cut. And it had less to do with the fact that here was a girl feeling like a caged canary than the toning between one shot and the other, and where and how the canary sits in relationship to her face, and so on. That was the beginning of that film, and I then began rummaging among past footage to find other things that I began to put together in editing.

Ganguly: How did some of your contemporaries respond to the family films, for example, the birth films?

Brakhage: Maya (Deren) was outraged at *Window Water Baby Moving* (1959) when I first showed it in New York because she thought I was intruding, exposing feminine mysteries that were inviolate, etc. I had not intended to do any such thing. In fact, I was in the room during the birth at Jane's insistence that I be present and be true to myself, and I could only be true to myself while working, i.e., filming the birth. But I still worry about what Maya said. I photographed childbirth so that I could be a part of the process which was forbidden to men. In fact, in those days men were *absolutely* excluded from any kind of participation. So I hoped the film would be a valuable source of inspiration in joining men and women together in the birth process . . . I once met a woman on the steps of the Boulder post office who told me that she suffered from a physical condition that made it very hard for her to give birth, but the film gave her courage and she finally did have a child. You can never be given a more meaningful compilment than that.

Ganguly: Do you think too much has been made of these films to the exclusion of your other work?

Brakhage: Yes . . . I'd like to mention here that people tend to overlook the two-thirds of my work which was *not* centered on family living and which through the 1960s and 1970s was prophetic, so to speak, of what I'm now mostly doing with film. The content of my current films is less mimetic and more "at one" with the unique possibilities intrinsic to film. I carried a camera with me and made films during lecture tours, in hotel rooms, in airplanes . . . I also made *The Text of Light* (1974) after months of sitting and photographing ashtrays in the office space of a friend, and it is much more pertinent to what I'm doing now than anything I did then when I was autobiographically trying to inspire people with my films about the ideals of the family.

Ganguly: And you were painting directly on film. In fact, your first hand-painted film goes all the way back to *Dog Star Man*. Are you still working in that mode?

Brakhage: Yes, very much so. I started painting on film primarily to create a corollary of what I could see with my closed-eye vision or hypnagogic vision because there was no way I could get the camera inside my head or create a photographic equivalent of those shapes streaming across my closed eyes . . . I tried all kinds of things—scratching on film, even baking it—but paint mixed with chemicals created certain shapes intrinsic to the organic cells of seeing itself. So paint seemed the main thing for me . . . Since then I've not only included hand-painted sections in my films but made whole films that are hand-painted to record different aspects of my hypnagogic feedback. And those films are the favorites of all my work. In fact, all I want to do now is paint on film.

Ganguly: What do you mostly paint with?

Brakhage: Acrylics, India inks, a variety of dyes and household chemicals. I've even done entire films with Magic Markers. I sometimes work with brushes, but it's mostly paint on fingers. I work very fast, applying the paints, then drying them and mixing chemicals to create certain patterns and shapes. To most people it would seem like the famous Montmartre donkey painting with his tail, but before the film is finished, every frame has been painted, and every passage interrelated to every other and an aesthetic ecology achieved.

Ganguly: How long usually are these films?

Brakhage: They can vary anywhere between nine seconds—*Eye Myth* (1972)—to twelve minutes—*Interpolations* (1992).

Ganguly: To get a second's worth of film time you have to paint 24 individual frames. For *Interpolations* that amounts to a mind-boggling 17,280 frames! How much do you throw away?

Brakhage: Some end up in the wastebasket, a few get clipped off into little strips that I frame or send to somebody—I've even sold a few . . . Yes, it's a lot of work, but there are people who believe it's all very simple, or it's work that's not important because it has no roots in psychodrama or neurosis . . . My biggest worry is: Am I degenerating? The danger with painting on film is that it could turn into decoration and when it does, I throw it away.

Ganguly: You've cited a number of influences on your hand-painting, among them Viking Eggeling, Walter Ruttmann, Len Lye, Oskar Fischinger, Harry Smith and Marie Menken. What about contemporary filmmakers like Gunvor Nelson and Carolee Schneemann who have both painted on film?

Brakhage: I've known Gunvor since the 1960s and always respected her work, but now it has evolved into an expression of thought process, and while she doesn't paint on film, she does paint over imagery, working with a frame at a time, and has created a combination of photographed imagery and painting, beginning with *Frameline* and leading to my favorite so far—*Field Study #2* which has affinities with my work being about remembrance which includes hypnagogic vision or moving visual thinking to counterbalance the dangers of nostalgia or sentimentality. I also have a great regard for Carolee who, dissatisfied with the male viewpoint of my *Loving* (1957) which was about her and James Tenney, made *Fuses* which more than any other hand-painted film is a truly visceral presentation of texture. She was also distressed by my use of paint in *Thigh Line Lyre Triangular* (1961)—she's a great oil painter—and I taking this to heart have evolved an aesthetic of paint-on-film which eschews "the painterly." It's like Orpheus in the Cocteau film when asked what is a poet replies, "Someone who writes but is not a writer."

Ganguly: Why are Eggeling and Menken so important to you? After all, they didn't work directly with the film strip.

Brakhage: Well, take Menken. It's true she didn't directly touch the film in that way, but she was a collage filmmaker, and she would handle her footage as if they were shapes and patterns she had painted, and weave them in according to their lateral motions. That, to me, is "hands-on" work . . . I think the more you're physically in touch with the material the more you become aware that you're smudging the passage of light, altering it by hand, and altering each frame, and every smudge reveals more of the light as you lessen it. And film, after all, is rhythmed light. So what matters finally is if you can *give in* to the light. That's the integrity of working directly with hands on film, which is also hands on light. I find that very inspiring. I'd like to mention Harry Smith here, Harry, who wanted to be a black magician in some sense and smudge the light in order to blot it out, came to a stage which can best be described as Jacob and the angel wrestling with the light. And at some point it became clear to him that despite everything he tried, the light was going to win. And Harry had the integrity to back off and put himself at service to humanity by recording with audiotapes and open himself to the phenomenological world and be a pure conduit of what could come through him and what he could put on tape. And he probably would have done the same thing with film if he could afford it. And I really respect that.

Ganguly: Two of your recent hand-painted films in the hypnagogic mode are *The Dante Quartet* and *Untitled Film (For Marilyn)*. What led you to make the Dante film?

Brakhage: Thirty years of reading all the translations in English of Dante's *The Divine Comedy*—I even tried to learn Italian at one point—as well as brooding on the Christian concept of hell, purgatory and heaven. The four parts are *Hell Itself*, *Hell Spit Flexion*, *Purgation*, and *existence is song*, and they appear in that order. It took me seven years to produce this nine minute film, but what is appalling is that you can see it today only in a postage size version.

Ganguly: Why is that so?

Brakhage: I wanted the dimensions of the film to match those of an Imax screen which is about three to four stories tall and half a city block wide. A film that would be like an enormous mural painting. I painted the four parts on different stocks—*Hell* and *existence is song* were done directly on IMAX film, *Purgation* on a worn-out 70mm print of *Irma la Douce* and *Hell Spit Flexion* on 35mm. But it proved too expensive to print them for Imax projection. I finally rephotographed the Imax and 75mm strips off a light box to achieve the 35mm and 16mm prints that are now in distribution. So I view it really as a sketch of the original film I wanted to make.

Ganguly: The real challenge must have been to find the hypnagogic equivalents of Dante's three-fold vision.

Brakhage: I made *Hell Itself* during the break-up with Jane and the collapse of my whole life, so I got to know quite well the streaming of the hypnagogic process that's hellish. Now, the body can not only feed back its sense of being *in* hell but also its sense of getting *out* of hell, and *Hell Spit Flexion* shows the way out—it's there as a crowbar to lift one out of hell toward the transformatory state—which is the third state—purgatory. And finally there's a fourth hypnagogic state that's fleeting and evanescent—a sort of heavenly feeling. I've called this last part *existence is song* quoting Rilke, because I don't want to presume upon the after-life and call it "Heaven." So what I tried to do in the quartet was to bring down to earth Dante's vision, inspired by what's on either side of one's nose and right before the eyes: a movie that reflects the nervous system's basic sense of being.

Ganguly: If *The Dante Quartet* contains something of your personal hell, *Untitled Film*, which is dedicated to Marilyn, seems full of that evanescent quality you just described as heavenly.

Brakhage: That's currently my favorite film, and how that happened was . . . I've always wanted to go to church with my children but churches don't like young children these days, so I've felt excluded from a full family participation. When I was in Helsinki about two years ago, I went to a Greek Orthodox Church, but its doors were locked, so I photographed through the window, and later began to paint on the film. The more I worked on it, the more I began to feel my church is right *here*, where I am with my family—the four of us gathered together in the name of something holy. And I believe in that.

Ganguly: Since this too is a quartet, what are the four parts?

Brakhage: The first and last parts have writing mixed with paint. The first one is public or social, a sort of outcry vis-à-vis the church and myself, and dominated by the straight line structures of the church, while the last part is a private invocation of myself and Marilyn, Anton and Vaughn, and then thanks to God. The two parts in between move from the one to the other. I think the hand-painted sections are the ultimate of all the *hypnagogic* painting I've ever done, and I think this will be my last hand-painted hypnagogic film. There's an intensity of feeling here that I've never achieved before.

Ganguly: What do the scratched words represent?

Brakhage: It's a way of saying thank you. By the end of the fourth part I'm so overwhelmed that I want to give thanks for the peace that has come with my discovery of this film church. At one point I felt so emotional that I wrote—"You"—but that didn't look right, and I felt I needed a small "y" since it was Marilyn whom I was addressing. Then that's followed by hand-painted passages of what I felt hypnagogically at the thought of her, and then I scratched Anton and Vaughn's names, and in the end there didn't seem anything left to do but write "Praise be to God."

Ganguly: Why is this going to be your last hypnagogic hand-painted film?

Brakhage: Well, what I create, after all, is only a corollary of the hypnagogic process and it bears no more relation to the actual thing than a painting does to a landscape. Besides, all my life I've been trying to pry film loose from all forms of usage, whether it's drama, illustration, propaganda, or modes of visual thinking. And now I've come to a point where I believe that if film reflects anything that's nameable, then that limits the fullest possible aesthetic of film . . . it's not film anymore. That's why I was on red alert when I first heard Whitman's praise of Shakespeare as a mirror held up to nature . . . Film should not refer to anything in the world, it should be a thing in itself. And my new hand-painted work tries to achieve this.

Ganguly: I now want to shift to the Faust films which were made just after the marriage ended and you were living in Boulder. It was your first collaborative project as well as your first sound film in many years. What made you revert to the dramatic-narrative mode which you had previously shunned?

Brakhage: I think I was seeking ground, going back to my beginnings, to psychodrama, sound and collaboration, which are all aspects of my early filmmaking. In that respect the Faust films certainly resemble the early psychodramatic works, especially *Blue Moses* (1962).

Ganguly: Was there any particular reason for choosing the Faust story?

Brakhage: Faust, for me, is *the* major legend of Western man. Some thirty five years ago I applied for a grant to do *Joe Faust*—a contemporary version—but I didn't get the money. The film I made in 1987 was about a young Faust who wishes to be old without having to grow old . . .

Ganguly: Why the reversal?

Brakhage: It made sense. I didn't want to go back in time nor relive my life, and the young people I knew then had no desire for eternal youth; in fact, they didn't expect to live very long. And no one typified this more than the man who played *Faust*—Joel Haertling, a composer and filmmaker, who lived in Boulder and had his own power-electronics group, Architect's Office. He was the contemporary Faust I had been looking for.

Ganguly: Who else worked on the film?

Brakhage: When I moved to Boulder, Joel introduced me to some very gifted young people, and we formed a group, "The Sunday Associates" and started an Arts Series with shows every Sunday at the Boulder Art Theater. They were my chief collaborators on *Faust*. By the time I made Part 2, word had got around that the mountain man and the family man was finished— prey to a bunch of Boulder hippies!

Ganguly: To what extent was this a collaboration? Was there a script you created together?

Brakhage: I would come back from a session and write a few lines which usually ended up on the narrative track. Mostly, I relied on the material people were giving me, and occasionally would ask them to do something twice. I was trying my best to draw on my own ideas of Faust and at the same time on whatever anyone could offer. I was going through a Godard phase— gathering people together to create the script and create the film . . . but despite all this collaboration, it still is a Brakhage film.

Ganguly: But by the time you get to Part 4, there is a falling off, a need to abandon this form . . .

Brakhage: By Part 4 I had to work my way out because I knew by then that I had to free myself from psychodrama, and from the dramatics of *Faust* itself, and inherit the landscape again. Part 4 is an obliteration by single frame of the memories of the past in the swell of the earth and in the desert. Also, by this time, I had met and fallen in love with Marilyn, and the film resulted from a road trip we took during which I photographed the landscapes of the west and the midwest. So in Part 4 there is no story really—but a going to the desert to rid myself of these "pictures" and encompass the whole spectrum of sky and earth and what lies beneath the two.

Ganguly: Another film resulted from that trip—the *Four Visions In Meditation* (1989–1991). Is that related to *Faust 4*?

Brakhage: It's a four part film with each part about 17 to 20 minutes long and it springs directly from *Faust 4*—in fact, the four parts are the fullest possible imaginable extensions of Part 4—what the mind can do as it turns back on itself.

Ganguly: You've said they were inspired by Gertrude Stein's "Stanzas in Meditation."

Brakhage: The basic inspiration is from the poem in which Stein tries to free words from reference and allows them to exist, each with a life of its own, within the jostling of all the words across the length of the poem. Thus "A" begins to take on a life of its own as the letter "A" or the sound "A" within the poem. You can wring a story from the life of "A" or "THE" or whatever word she introduces and repeats. But Stein didn't merely treat words as sounds. They have very live traits as they evolve, and I tried to create a corollary of that by photographing recognizable landscape.

Ganguly: The search for a new aesthetic is already apparent in *Marilyn's Window* which you made the year before and which is the first of a cycle of films inspired by Marilyn.

Brakhage: I think *Marilyn's Window* marks the beginning of everything that my *photographic* work has now evolved into. It was made when I visited her in Toronto and asked her to marry me. It was also just after my eye operation which had led to a lens implant in my right eye and given me a new sharpened vision . . . Marilyn had a room in her brother's apartment, and the view through the window was quite plain: three brick walls, a roof, things like that, but it seemed to me the whole world poured in through them. There's no way I can quite put that into words . . . I began to shoot with a fifty feet cartridge load camera, and later in the editing the sea suddenly rushed in. And I added other images, some hand-painted.

Ganguly: You like to call it your most perfect film . . .

Brakhage: Yes, it's the most perfect film given to me—in its rhythms, its shapes, but I didn't know it then nor did I aspire toward any such thing. There's no way you can plot or script such a film. And yet life provides these illuminations often in very mundane circumstances, like the view from the window of a room of the woman with whom I was falling deeper and deeper in love, and it's important to open oneself to these moments. Also, it was while making this film that I had a profound sense of how each object, each living thing is utterly unique, and the shapes they make on film are also unique, and so are the compositional relationships between the shapes. That recognition gave me a whole new sense of aesthetics.

Ganguly: And two years later you made A *Child's Garden and the Serious Sea* which, like *Marilyn's Window*, is about seeing the everyday world with new eyes, about discovering it for the first time again.

Brakhage: This is the longest film I've done which is not divided into parts or sections. It's symphonic in nature, but I made it at a time when I was also struggling to keep the consciousness of musical forms out of my work. While visiting Marilyn's parents on Vancouver Island, Victoria, I was deeply moved by her home and garden which hadn't changed much since she was a child. And there was the presence of the sea. I could even smell it from the garden. I had brought my camera hoping to film tide pools, instead I began to shoot the flowers in the garden, and the film grew out of those shots of the garden, the ocean, and a miniature golf course nearby. Anton was then about a year old and there is a brief shot of him crawling along the grass in the distance.

Ganguly: So is the film a child's perspective of the world?

Brakhage: Not a child's perspective but a metaphor of a child's emerging consciousness. In that respect the film goes all the way back to *Anticipation of the Night* (1958) to a major theme in my work: the primal sight of children and their first encounter with the adult world. But unlike *Night* where the loss of that vision is mourned, in *Child's Garden* there is an acceptance. The images of the adult world impinge on those of the garden and the sea, but I treat them as a kind of aberration which doesn't overwhelm the primal gift of the whole phenomenological world.

Ganguly: How was the film received?

Brakhage: Both *Marilyn's Window* and *Garden* have been misunderstood as an attempt to recreate Marilyn's childhood, of trying to see the garden through her eyes as she was growing up when I had no such intention. I have no illusions that people can see through somebody else's eyes except via aesthetics. We do not share each other's visions but a vision when it comes through an artist. To that extent the integrity or the ecology of a work of art can override the intrinsic differences between each of us.

Ganguly: Both films are silent, but around this time you had also begun to experiment with sound. And like so much of the work after the divorce, this too has its roots in *Faust*.

Brakhage: I think what pulled me back into a lot of sound-making was the same impulse, the need to go back to the roots of my filmmaking which lay in psychodrama. Sound is crucial for psychodrama principally because there's a lack of, what I would call, vision. What is psychodrama after all but the drama that's in the mind, and the extent to which you approach drama, even in the oblique way that I did in *Faust*, involves engaging with picture and continuity as well as a whole hierarchy of symbols. In the absence of vision, sound becomes a necessity to stitch the loose threads together and make it all bearable.

Ganguly: So you haven't essentially changed your position about sound being an aesthetic error in film?

Brakhage: No. Film is obviously visual, but Hollywood holds the opposite view, and the proof is that with most movies you can listen to the soundtrack and know what they are about without ever looking at them. For a long time only 2 per cent of my films were sound films because I felt sound interfered with seeing. Moreover, given the complex nature of my films, it was much harder to concentrate if the film had sound. But, at the same time, if I felt a film needed sound, I always included it.

Ganguly: Did you study music?

Brakhage: I was taught piano when I was 3 years old and living in Winfield, Kansas, and when I was 4½ I was singing solos because I had a high clear voice and could stay on pitch. And then I studied singing in Bisbee, Arizona, with a group of nuns who had taken an interest in my voice.

Ganguly: How did that happen?

Brakhage: There was a man in Bisbee, Arizona, who ran the local movie theater and he would go around photographing local events for a sort of Bisbee "March of Time" which he showed every week. He heard me singing in my backyard, photographed me and arranged a recording session. So I saw myself singing on screen and so did some nuns who felt I should have voice lessons. Later, at 8 or 9, I chose to join the St. John's Cathedral Choir at Denver and sang as a boy soprano soloist until my voice began to crack. I also studied the violin briefly and was in choirs all through school, but I was primarily a boy soprano soloist who sang at weddings and funerals and on the national radio and had quite a life as a musical prodigy.

Ganguly: Did you ever compose music?

Brakhage: No. I was never good with numbers, and composers have to be mathematicians in a sense. The only song I ever composed is a round (sings):

> The bear is fur
> The fur is bear
> The bear is walking everywhere
> Here, there, near, far
> Bear furrrr . . .

Ganguly: But quite early in your filmmaking, you began to experiment with electronic music.

Brakhage: I experimented with collage, or what was called "musique concrète," but I never kidded myself that I was a Goldstein or a Cage or a Varèse . . . After all, I'm not a painter or a composer—I'm a filmmaker, so when I collaged those sounds, I was creating a corollary of what I was doing in film, and I've never done it except for film. The earliest collage experiments are in *Daybreak and Whiteye* (1957) where I made compound soundtracks with very primitive tape recorders.

Ganguly: What about *Fire of Waters* (1965)?

Brakhage: Yes, that's another early example and perhaps the best since it's really a silent film and the three short sound pieces stand out in a vast sea of silence.

Ganguly: When did you first encounter electronic music?

Brakhage: I was a year out of high school and back from a nervous breakdown at Dartmouth College when I went to a record store, saw a strange label, put on the record and first heard the music of Edgard Varèse. And it transformed my entire life like the instant I first laid eyes on a reproduction by Jackson Pollack. Later I sought Varèse out in New York and he let me sit in on his music lessons at home for free since I couldn't afford to pay for them. At the same time I was incredibly lucky to have met John Cage and to be invited to some of his sessions and music soirees.

Ganguly: What did you learn from Varèse and Cage?

Brakhage: Primarily what I got from them was the inspiration to make silent film. I was especially attracted to the instrumental aspects of their recorded live-sound (for example, the hiss of tires on a wet street) and the fact that the sound could refer to the source of the recording (a passing car). This is a corollary of film because when you turn on the camera you automatically pick up reference. Even if you shoot totally out of focus, there is a certain quality of say a car's movement which even if reduced to a blob of hexagonal lens-reflecting light is usually recognizable as that of an automobile.

What Cage taught me was to recognize the "unscheduled disturbances in the atmosphere" as airplane pilots say when they hit an air pocket—disturbances that are routine in what we hear around us. And it's terribly important that these ambient sounds be recognized. I edited the A roll of *Dog Star Man* by chance operations inspired by Cage, and then I created superimpositions with the B roll and imposed metaphorical contexts (by conscious choice) in relation to the original chance operations. So I have consistently allowed these unscheduled disturbances to enter my work and exist in relation to the referential images. Cage continues to inspire me in that respect, and a good deal of my painting is based on chance operations.

On the other hand, Varèse was anxious to create sounds within a certain space so carefully that the flute noise which travels faster by a microsecond than the oboe noise would mix at a certain point in the room. When I first went to see Varèse he had maps of the Grand Canyon on his walls and was dreaming of a vast symphony of the universe where these slight delays of one sound texture or one pitch over another would converge in certain places and in certain ways . . . I was fascinated by that and also with how Varèse would allow a recorded sound into his work to serve as a musical instrument. Take the jackhammer with its electronic echoes in *Poème Electronique* or the waterdrop sounds that resound within the interpolations in *Deserts*, and consider how these references to the source of the sound are embodied within what is finally a pure sound aesthetic. That has taught me to resist the referent, to take on referential photography and contain it so that the references would not destroy the aesthetic of the film as a *film* experience.

Ganguly: When you made *Interpolations* last year, were you consciously thinking of Varèse?

Brakhage: They were originally inspired by the interpolations I just mentioned which were interwoven with the orchestral music of *Déserts* and which Frank Zappa later singled out and put on a recording. I had first heard them as single pieces, long before *Déserts* was completed, so when I made *Boulder Blues* and *Pearl's and* . . . last year—a peripheral vision film about Boulder—I thought of Varèse and of using five of my hand-painted strips as complete pieces of interpolations within the film's photographed content. I wanted them to exist as a counter-balance to the referential—the photographs of Boulder. I finally ended up with five films that go together so well in 35mm that I have not reduced them to 16mm. What went into *Boulder* were some handpainted strips in 16mm, so my *Interpolations* ended up not being really related to Varèse's *Déserts* or to anything I had originally in mind. They exist independently and constitute my longest hand-painted work.

Ganguly: Can you describe how you work with a piece of music?

Brakhage: Most people assume that I put on background music and then jam with vision or something! In fact, I never play music when I'm working on a film. I make visual corollaries of music and once even tried to cut a film exactly to a Bach fugue and the result was a disaster. On the other hand, there is a relationship between Messiaen's organ music and *Scenes From Under Childhood* and you can take *Mothlight* (1963) and see how it is related to a Bach fugue in the sense that the shapes of the wings and the recreated flight of the moth among the flowers has recurring colors which are melodic, and that the shapes themselves with their recurring actions are true to the overall sense of a Bach fugal integrity . . . In this sense, these are all pieces of visual music, and so are many of my hand-painted films. But now I very much prefer to set pictures to music, and it's usually the music that inspires me in the first place and the film comes out of that.

Ganguly: Who have you worked with mostly?

Brakhage: James Tenney was the first one to compose music for my films. For *Interim* (1952)—the very first film I made—he created a piano soundtrack inspired by Samuel Barber's *Sonata for Piano*. And we recently worked together again on *Christ Mass Sex Dance* (1991) which was made in very strange circumstances. I photographed the rehearsals of the Annual Boulder Christmas *Nutcracker Suite* hoping to make a children's film, but I ended up with imagery that had nothing to do with the *Nutcracker*. And the instant I got back the film from the lab I thought of Tenney's *Blue Suede* which is a collage of Elvis Presley's "Blue Suede Shoes" with the words broken up into a kind of sexual grunting, and it seemed perfectly suited to it, so I cut the film to the music.

Ganguly: What was the nature of your collaboration with Architect's Office?

Brakhage: Joel's group embodied for me a certain revitalization of ideals that had gone dead since the 1960s. Their music was built around communal ideas, so that musicians could retain their individual signatures while working together. And there was always room for chance operations. There were some extraordinary talents like Rick Corrigan who did the music for *Faust* Parts 1 and 4 and with whom I've collaborated on several films since. And there was Joel. I set *Kindering* (1987) to one of his pieces which combined his son's voice with tapes he had picked up at a yard sale—and it was all very beautifully integrated. He evoked for me a quality of childhood that I hadn't really felt for a long time, so I photographed my grandchildren with his music in mind and then edited the pictures directly to the music. I also set I . . . *Dreaming*, my self-in-crisis portrait, to his collage or "recomposition" of fragments of songs by Stephen Foster.

Ganguly: He also did some very innovative compilation tracks for your films about visual thinking and seeing.

Brakhage: Yes. I greatly admired Joel's collage abilities—he did an amazing track for my hand-painted film, *Fireloop*, in which I use fire as a metaphor for the light and sound process that accompanies moving visual thinking. He also did a compilation piece featuring music by groups like Tödliche Doris, Zoviet France, Nurse with Wound, and The Hafler Trio for *Loud Visual Noises*, my hand-painted film about optic feedback in response to sound. And he played Faust, collaborated on the music, and did the entire track for *Faust 2*.

Ganguly: I want to talk about one last sound film, *Passage Through: A Ritual* (1990). Why did you decide to juxtapose long stretches of black leader with a gamelan soundtrack?

Brakhage: The piece is by Philip Corner—*Through the Mysterious Barricades (After Couperin)*. After I heard the tape, I begin rummaging through two to three thousand feet of film which I had shot during the break-up of the marriage and put away. I was trying to pull out only what I could have shot *that* day and throw the rest out, and I ended up with about fifty feet . . . The film consists of mostly black leader with very brief shots of photographed objects that are usually unrecognizable. And I cut them to the music. So there are these long dark spaces of music with occasional flashes of imagery. It was one of the hardest films to edit since the challenge was to find the exact place where a particular image belonged. If I stretched some of those places ten seconds longer it would become absurd.

Ganguly: What were you really after?

Brakhage: I think it's a film about the dark night of the soul with moments of illumination that are intrinsic to my present, where I am *now*. In that sense, the film is very cathartic.

Ganguly: I noticed how despite the black leader, it's never completely dark.

Brakhage: There's a shimmering of light all through and there are little sprocket holes in the black leader that are like stars of light . . . The optic nerve-endings of the viewers interact all the time with this ephemera of light. The film proves that even with black leader you can't ever defeat the light.

Ganguly: I want to now change gears and talk about the 1960s, and I want to start with the fact that, unlike many of your contemporaries, you've been fairly critical of the rhetoric and ideology of that time.

Brakhage: I'll go so far as to say that the 1960s were very damaging to film as art, because of the assumptions many people had about film which were deflections from a pure opening to what film is and what film can be, and also because of assumptions of career which created an intense competitiveness that destroyed friendships among filmmakers. But more deeply than that, filmmakers went around lecturing so much that Hollis Frampton could quip quite reasonably that at some point the whole American independent film movement must have been up in the air, some were taking off, some were landing, and some were en route to talk about their work. Now the biggest problem lay in that talk, and I certainly did more of it than most, and as I flew into one antagonistic situation after another I naturally became defensive, and what I said very often got twisted and warped. That defensiveness created walls that I'm now beginning to dissolve . . . But it is also true that without the 1960s rhetoric none of the filmmakers' cooperatives would exist and their films would not be available for people to see.

Ganguly: There is a popular myth today that in the 1960s the battlelines were clearly drawn between Hollywood and the independents and that each wished the other dead. Was it really that antagonistic?

Brakhage: I personally never wanted to bring an end to the movies because I've always enjoyed the movies. That would be like patricide or matricide because I began at the movies, I went to the movies as a child, they were my babysitter, my parents, in fact. So I never had that wish. About Hollywood—it's one of the most powerful industries on earth, a massive shaper of opinion and feeling. You can bring on the independent filmmakers, and it's not David versus Goliath, but an electron on a flea on Goliath. No competition. There are those who suspected we were bacteria or viruses that were going to bring down the movies and they have had their rage . . . But during the 1960s the independents had an immense influence on Hollywood, then Hollywood went through a reactionary phase when it ceased being visual for a decade and retreated to the box dramas. But certain pieces of grammar remained because they were intrinsic to filmmaking and someone or the other discovered them because of his/her absolute necessity to express something that was unique to his/her personality.

Ganguly: Can you be more specific about the nature of this influence on Hollywood?

Brakhage: Long before colleges were renting my films with some regularity, advertising agencies were, and they were immediately mining them for quick tricks to make brief TV commercials. And a great variety of these tricks have become accepted cinematic convention. Take the hand-held camera which was always considered an aberration, a necessity of battlefield photography or something, but otherwise to be ignored. Hollywood's invention of the Steadicam was an attempt in some smooth way to emulate a body of work by me and others who took the camera in hand to try to get something of their physiology into their envisionment. And that's become a norm of very ordinary moviemaking. They, of course, missed the whole point by making it a Steadicam—by putting a machine between the cameraman's physiology and whatever he was shaping up as picture!

Ganguly: Hollywood also stole the flash frame from you and never bothered to own up.

Brakhage: Yes. Until I made a little tiny three minute film, Cat's Cradle (1959), the only usage film had for the flash frame was cheap lighting with the noticeable exception of Eisenstein who, influenced by Cubism, used brief frames to build up constructs. He would distort chronology and time to get the power, the energy of the brief cuts onto the screen. When I made Cradle, I used single frames of things previously seen as emblematic brain movie remembrances of the post operative in the present. Then Gregory Markopoulos saw that and got terribly excited and made Twice a Man which extended the grammar. The major thing about that film was its use of individual frames true to the memory process. Then much later Hollywood picked up on that in The Pawnbroker, then advertising agencies started to use it to subliminally prompt people into buying their products.

Ganguly: What do you think of the fact that Bruce Conner is now being called "the father of MTV?"

Brakhage: Perhaps the most blatant example of borrowing is Bruce Conner's work, imitated all the time on MTV. Conner was picking up standard clips from newsreel history and putting them in a psychological context. Here was a man brooding over his entire cultural gestalt. MTV turned his concept to crass usage . . . But to be fair, these stolen tricks have also formed a growth of visual possibilities, as well as a grammar, in fact, a structure for coherence in the movies which wasn't there before. And I think those who are devoted to that sort of thing are very worthy, and I would call some of them artists. To that extent independent film has served a function.

Ganguly: Who are these artists?

Brakhage: Tarkovsky was certainly one—an artist of the last of a certain kind of making. Kurosawa and Bergman in their old age . . . Bergman who always seemed to me visually very sloppy came into an integrity of vision in *Scenes From a Marriage*, I'll also give you the first five minutes of *Persona* which I think are quite free from any enslavement, just as I can give you in the same light the Last Supper sequence in *Viridiana*. As Man Ray once said to me on a bus ride in Brussels in 1958, "I've never seen a movie that didn't have at least thirty seconds of real film in it and I've never seen one that had much more." And that's true—there are always moments in films that are like whole visions in themselves.

Ganguly: To take a more recent example, you were quite taken by JFK.

Brakhage: I was struck by the editing. But there I was falling for the craft, and that's always dangerous. JFK doesn't sit in the head as an illumination like *Apocalypse Now* does. I think Coppola created a vision that is shimmering with light, and it doesn't matter to me that the plot collapses at the end. What interests me is his response to the light under those pained emotions about the war.

Ganguly: Scorsese seems the only one of that generation who has openly acknowledged the influence of the avant-garde on his work.

Brakhage: Yes, Scorsese is the only one who's gone out of his way to credit the inspiration he's had from my work, and Frampton's, and others. He's also the only one who's cared enough about film to actually fight for the preservation of film . . . But my caring for him is not along the line of light, he isn't really a light maker. In his case there is a love for film rhythm . . . It's almost as if he loves the behavior of the smudges that he puts between the viewer and the light, and they extend to the almost unseeable, the almost unphotographable slight shifts of the 120 or so odd muscles of the face. Between the noticeable dramatic lines of De Niro's face, there is a shimmering of some love of what film can be. And I think this is one of Satyajit Ray's greatnesses too. Certain people have so dwelt upon the human face— which as you know is not my forte—and they've done it in such a way that they've made an imprimatur on film that is revelatory of the truth of unseeable human feelings. They work in the ineffable of human expression.

Ganguly: Who are the other great light filmmakers?

Brakhage: I think in Tarkovsky light is always the first evident thing, that's why in *Andrei Rublyev* there is a real corollary between the painted icons and the people you see, and the "rhyming" factor in the film is the light and how it is framed. Tarkovsky gives us a surface of water, a pile of muck, and you see all sorts of objects, but what do they mean? Really it's the light feeling out the muck, and it highlights not just faces, but a veil around a bed, or a curtain or floorboards . . . What's so shocking about the milk getting spilt in *The Sacrifice* is that one has become intensely aware of the floorboards long before the milk falls on it and makes a solid pattern. There's a poet in Tarkovsky, a reverberation of his father, and something of that has gone over into light in his work . . . I see all of Orson Welles' work as a net of light, and what Tarkovsky has, Cocteau has too, some part of the energy that makes poetry with words. When I think of Cocteau, I almost think of Joseph Cornell. Cocteau almost made boxes in which the light is the main thing, how this box catches this light and these figures moving around in it. There's one box, and another box, and they're all set next to each other and they're translations of stage plays, but there's some vibrancy of light there . . . There's a quality of light whereby you know one filmmaker from another.

Ganguly: So for you the quality of light remains, as before, the distinguishing mark of a great film.

Brakhage: Some people use film so fully in its traditional senses that something of what film intrinsically is shimmers through a little bit in their work. Most of the names I've mentioned—all of them really—have nothing to do with what film intrinsically is, but out of their various dedications and needs they have allowed a little something of it to shimmer through. So I can both have movies with all their escapism and various knowledges of picture and at the same time have a little light shimmering through. Let's call it the Orson Welles syndrome—he tried to take all of Shakespeare—in the original and in a contemporary guise—and put it into film, and it's like a great net of Shakespeare caught in some light, and very often that light has some life of its own, but also as I watch Welles I'm aware that it's just caged light . . .

Ganguly: We were talking about the 1960s. How would you describe the current avant-garde film scene?

Brakhage: I have never seen anything like Peter Herwitz's films. There's something in his making that trusts rhythm, and his rhythming overrides everything else, including his dirt splotches and the scratchings that record his struggles to be true to himself. He is a constant inspiration to me. I also feel close to John Writer's work which I can't put into words because it is so unique. Then there is Andrew Noren. I feel a deep kinship with his opening to the light and making a whole film trusting the varieties of light and sustaining it for hours. And let me mention James Herbert who manages to photograph in very erotic conjunctions without verging on the pornographic—in that tension his work ceases to be referential and you are left with the aesthetic. And . . . Larry Jordan who works in ways similar to Harry Smith—with collage, animated collage figures, etc. His work began with traceries or engravings of lines which made a thin filament net of imagery through which light came. Over the years he has created through a combination of colors an almost direct reference to the sun, or to incandescence, to fire in some sense. I think *Sophie's Place* is one of the great few masterpieces of independent cinema. Larry belongs to my generation and continues to make films—one of the very few. And I'd also like to mention two other people. The first is Phil Solomon, who in the process of working with photographed imagery a frame at a time, not painting but using chemicals to crystallize into various shapes minute patterns along the line of his step-printing, has, like Gunvor Nelson, also created a counterbalance to what could become sentimental and nostalgic. And the second is Christine Noll Brinckmann. There is a quality in her work which is very much like some of Marie Menken's films except that there is much less obvious conscious mastery and more of that kind of trust of emotional continuity that one finds in Joseph Cornell.

Ganguly: These are all filmmakers with whom you share strong affinities. I'm curious about your enthusiasm for the work of someone like Michael Snow who belongs to a very different camp.

Brakhage: I feel a strong vibrancy with not only Michael Snow but also Bruce Elder and Ernie Gehr—in each case their work is distinct from anything I'd want to spend the rest of my life doing. I feel kin to Bruce with his forty hour epic film because it is premised exactly on the opposites of everything in my sense of making. I also feel kin to Michael for all the varieties of ground he has cleared that wasn't at all possible to me. I like *Presents* which is a much-despised film—the feminists jumped all over it—a film he made in the midst of his divorce and the rediscovery of his life; I'm in awe of the editing, the way he combined those images and left us a dictionary of the new grammar of independent filmmaking along the line of his own tortured search to find his new life. This is a deeply moving thing to me. But the pure aesthetic experience is *La Région Centrale* which has no humans in it; even its rocks finally become moving rhythms, and its sky and earth and the whole weave of it . . . And there's Ernie because his work leaves me speechless; while I detest the spartan rigidity of his forms, he's infused them with such feeling that his rhythms can be felt not only when there's a shot change, but in shapes and tones—he touches my nervous system at all times.

Ganguly: Given the fact that so many gifted filmmakers are at work, how do you explain the current apathy toward avant-garde film? What has killed the audiences? And where are the writers today?

Brakhage: For the art market it's simple—you can't treat a film as a precious object; anybody's print if it's well-made is equal to anybody else's well-made print. There is no way to corner the market on this, and even if you bought the original, you're buying rights that can easily be duplicated by other people. And you're saddled with this enormous problem of protecting and storing whatever you've bought and releasing it. You can't make a buck out of this . . . that's the problem. No millionaire can hang a film over his fireplace for any purpose whatsoever, so that has shown up the slavish business aptitude of practically every museum in the world. They're just not interested. Also, you're not going to get a case of whiskey for Christmas for being a critic and writing about a film. You're not even going to get printed because there's no business structure, there's no reward for anyone dealing with film as an art.

Ganguly: What about video? Does that hold out any hope for you?

Brakhage: Where video is an art it is like sand painting—now you see it, now you don't. It has no permanence, there is no way you can preserve it. What makes it even harder to accept it as an art is that the medium for looking at it is intrinsically hypnotic which is perfect for advertising, but lousy if not impossible for an aesthetic ecology. And its luminescent lighting actually sickens people. Then for a colorist like me it cannot hold any interest because it doesn't have any color—it's whatever color the set is when you twiddle the knobs. Where it also differs from film is that film has a base rhythm—a basic beat that can be 8, 16, 24, even 32 with Cinerama, and other rhythms play off against this base beat of still images changing.

But video is like a jel quivering variously. However, I will say that there is a kind of pulse to TV, but not a beat, so this doesn't mean it's preclusive of having a rhythm aesthetic ecology; it does have that but it's a muffled thing which is very off-putting for those who love film. So I really don't want to see a film on TV nor do I want to have anything to do with video filmmaking.

Ganguly: What now? More experiments with putting film to music?

Brakhage: No, I feel now I'll be working in modes where sound won't be needed. I think I've come to the end of my infatuation with music and film, and film being a close corollary of music. I have to now find out what it is that film can do that's purely film . . . As I said earlier, the truth of the matter is that I feel an increasing need to make something that has no title, that has no subject matter, that doesn't consciously draw on any of the other arts or even on the cells of the brain and the optic system and the modes in which I've worked for years . . . My main problem at 60 and for the last five years has been to get old *Dog Star Man* off my back, so that I can just start fresh and go on with what has been given to me to do. The whole grounds of my making have shifted and furthermore, I think they're shifting even more radically. I'm content with that. I've gone from "Brakhage" to "SB" which could be any old son-of-a-bitch to not signing the films at all. I think more and more I'd like to inhabit with great humility the position of anonymous . . . I'm not really that man who made those films in the past in any other sense than the aesthetic: the styles of rhythming that are intrinsic to my being, only now I hope I've cleared a great deal of the usages out of it, and it can just come through me. It has taken me a whole lifetime of hard work to get to the point of just making a film. The irony is that as I get there I don't know what to say about it. I now treasure those works about which people don't write anything or even remember having seen because those are films that exist in a realm which defies the verbal. They are films that are given over wholly to the unconscious.

Ganguly: Films like?

Brakhage: Like *Nodes* (1981) and *Matins* (1988). They are the kinds of films I would like to spend the rest of my life making—films that are, in the ordinary sense of the word, about nothing . . . And I'm getting there. I was just dabbling with paint when I made this new unnamed film, and I didn't even *think* that I was making a film. And that's very hard to achieve. Since I lost a nerve in my right hand my index and thumb fingers have become weak, so I painted this new film with my left hand and I think it's the best piece I've ever done with this hand. I'm encouraged by that—after all, the left hand is usually neglected; it began to come into its own when I began painting with my fingers, finding them more useful than brushes. Since I didn't use the left hand for my past work, it could be a more direct conduit for the feelings that are now in me—this was certainly the case with this film . . . Now and again something like this will slip through me that's got a mysterious, intangible quality to it like some of Cornell's films do, especially the Lorca Series (A *Legend for Fountains: Fragments*) inspired by *Poet in New York*. They have a certain is-ness that no map of the mind can decipher. They simply exist out there in the world, each film with a life of its own.

Ganguly: I'm intrigued by that word you just used—"nothing."

Brakhage: I don't know . . . It's very hard to be clear. This will sound like I'm mixing religion with life, but I didn't have a church to go to when several years ago I was stuck in Houston for six weeks. I was ill and at the bottom of my life. But I was able to go to the Rothko Chapel, and I wasn't going to a church but to these great paintings, and to me they were about nothing. They defied verbal description. And what I felt was distinct from a religious experience. They were also very free of any kind of autobiography, integral each in itself and in relation to each other in this surrounding aesthetic, so that I felt a sharpening of everything inside me and the need to survive. What I was having was an experience of *nothing*, and nothing exists—take John Cage's silence or the silence I once heard in a Kansas cornfield . . . I heard the dominant fifth in my ears and the beating of my heart. If something out there can be inspiring without manipulating a person without that being with reference to anything else in the world, be a thing in itself, then that seems to me an epitome of human making and experience.

Ganguly: Are you going to give up titles altogether in the new work?

Brakhage: I'm thinking of grouping some of these films in a series called, N*aughts* and others in a series called C*hartres*. But even that seems an intrusion, so at some point I hope I'll have the good sense to give up titles altogether. And the films will be "things" nobody can categorize verbally . . . I think of Michelangelo's "unfinished" sculptures in this respect which are so much more exciting to me than his D*avid* or M*oses*.

Ganguly: Why "Naughts?"

Brakhage: I don't really know what "naughts" means. When I call these films N*aughts*, I'm very conscious of the pun with "knots" which suggests a crossing of wires and the fact that I haven't quite got to where I hope I will someday.

Ganguly: And why the reference to Chartres?

Brakhage: Those are works that came out absolutely unexpectedly as a result of being at Chartres Cathedral in 1992 . . . I think the rest of my life will be profoundly affected by the several hours I spent there. When I was at the Beaubourg Center they even asked me whether I would be interested in coming back to photograph Chartres, and I said, yes, probably in a couple of years. It could happen and if it did then I would take a camera into Chartres and see what I could do, but what is wonderful is that I'm *already* at work on Chartres Cathedral without any grants or even consciously thinking that this is what I'm doing. Now I hope there will be more of these, or there will be more N*aughts*, or there will be something else that I won't be able to fit under either of those categories, and that finally all categories will collapse and I won't know what to do.

The Perfect Queer Appositeness of Jack Smith

JERRY TARTAGLIA

Those who are familiar with the writings of Jack Smith will recognize the inspiration for the title of this study in one of Smith's most notorious essays entitled "The Perfect Filmic Appositeness of Maria Montez," first published in *Film Culture* magazine in 1962 (Hoberman, 25–35). The article is ostensibly about Maria Montez, but in it Jack lays out the manifesto of his art, the expression of his vision, and the testament of his Queer soul. All of these are reflected in his personal identification with the failed actress and B Movie star, the "Queen of Technicolor," Maria Montez. Her films made for Universal Pictures included *Arabian Nights* (1942), *White Savage* (1943), *Ali Baba and the Forty Thieves* (1944), *Cobra Woman* (1944), *Gypsy Wildcat* (1944) and *Sudan* (1945).

Smith's obsession with Maria Montez as a movie diva was neither an isolated condition nor was it unique. Her films do enjoy a cult following even today, especially among gay men who came of age before and during the Stonewall era. That is especially so among Queers whose appreciation of languid acting, feeble plots, veiled homoeroticism (Sabu was a costar of three of the Montez films) and garish but fabulous sets and costumes mark them (or should I say us?) as followers of the "cult of the cobra." Now just to be absolutely clear about the regard in which Maria Montez was held among her professional peers, let me quote Robert Siodmak, the director of *Cobra Woman*: "*Cobra Woman* was silly but fun. You know Maria Montez couldn't act from here to there, but she was a great personality and she believed completely in her roles" (Vermilye, 17).

The worship of the Diva in her many forms has long been a part of Queer life. Most adopt the more conventional choices, such as the strong-willed women of 1930s and 1940s Hollywood: Bette Davis, Joan Crawford, Greta Garbo, Marlene Dietrich. There are also the Divas of Opera, of which there are two main camps with a multitude of sub-groupings: the principal duo are Maria Callas and Joan Sutherland. Then there are the pop singers and stars whose personae figure into the passing tastes of the Queer subculture. From Bette Midler whose shows at the Continental Baths in New York made of her an icon in the post Stonewall milieu to Donna Summer. And of course, there's Barbra Streisand, as well.

All of these women are emblematic figures for their Queer followers because each in their own character, or persona, or in their endeavor, represents the Other in a straight male world. As artists they all embodied the fancy-free creative life, suggested in films like *Auntie Mame* (1958), which starred Rosalind Russell, or *All About Eve* (1950) which featured Bette Davis in one of her most famous roles, or even in Puccini's *Tosca*. "They struggle through their lives in a world of straight men and the women who love them" (Tartaglia, *Remembrance*). They are the perfect screen onto which gay men of a particular generation could project their own struggle, alienation, and bold triumph in that same world of heterocentric domination.

Into this culture of Diva worship comes Jack Smith, with his movie queen, Maria Montez. Jim Hoberman, who was one of the people responsible for saving the Jack Smith legacy from the dumpster, is very accurate when he commented on this strange choice and how the Montez worship and Smith's film aesthetic go hand in hand: failure and trash meet despair. Hoberman says:

> the notion of Maria Montez as cinema goddess was campy to be sure—although Smith's *Film Culture* paean appeared two years before Susan Sontag would publish her "Notes on Camp" in the Fall 1964 issue of *Partisan Review* . . . In any case, just as Maria Montez ranked far below Maria Callas (for example) on the Diva Scale, so most of the secret-flix Smith celebrated in "The Perfect Film (sic) Appositeness of Maria Montez" were considerably more outré than those Sontag would cite. If these movies were junk, Smith never denied it: "Trash," he proclaimed, "is the material of creators." "The Memoirs of Maria Montez," first published in *Film Culture* in the heady aftermath of *Flaming Creature*'s spring 1963 release, suggests . . . a ritual set in a derelict movie studio. (In this case, the star is a decomposing corpse.) The trash heap is a recurring Smith trope. A collector of cultural detritus, a connoisseur of "moldiness," he was an aesthete with an acute sense of collapse and failure.
>
> (Hoberman, 17).

It was through this identification with Maria Montez in a campy Diva worship that Jack found the locus of his cinema.

In some very important ways, Jack Smith was significantly different from his straight male peers in the Underground film scene in New York. He wanted to mimic the Hollywood cinema of his childhood, whereas the others like Jonas Mekas, Ken Jacobs, Bruce Baillie, Hollis Frampton, and Tony Conrad worked in opposition to the aesthetics of Hollywood. Jack was different; he worked with a campy twist in counterpoint with the Hollywood forms and style. Smith himself said,

> I would like to point out that unlike my colleagues in the avant-garde cinema my experience and interests have been influenced not by literature or painting as much as by movies. I have tried to recreate the beauty and power of the secret raptures I first discovered in the Hollywood movies of my childhood. Maria Montez, *The Arabian Nights*, *Casablanca* and other "cult" films left me with an insatiable lust for a visceral fantasy that is both foreign and terrible
>
> (qtd. in Hoberman, 25).

Jack found his iconography in the B Movies of his youth—in Maria Montez—in the Hollywood of the 1930s and 1940s. But in a typically Queer way, he took the "worst" rather than the most "idealistic."

We need only remember that Frank Capra's *It's A Wonderful Life* (1946) was a product of the same era as Maria Montez; this was the mainstream vision supported by the audiences and practitioners of the dominant cinema. Jack Smith's vision of the 1940s was that of Queer alienation: the campy sensibility which turns straight images on their head, revising the paradigm, re-ordering not only the constructions of heterocentric dominance, but of the gay so-called subculture and its tradition of Diva worship. Smith's was an aesthetic quest to identify the gay image, and relocate it in a Queer landscape. Jack Smith was a vanguard filmmaker, a radical photographer, a seminal performance artist, a Queer saint. He maintained an intense, lifelong rapture conjured out of the frayed magic and glamour of a Hollywood that had come to camp out on the movie set of his own mind. The externalization of that tarnished magic and glamour, which obsessed him, enabled him to both exoticize and humanize a conservative American culture enamored with progress and bruised in its formation by economic speculation and cold war.

Jack Smith was one of the most accomplished and influential underground artists in the 1960s, 1970s, and 1980s, a key figure in the cultural history of Downtown film, performance, and art. From the late 1950s until his death from AIDS in 1989, Smith was chiefly recognized for his work in film and performance. Innovative and idiosyncratic, Smith explored and developed a deceptively frivolous camp aesthetic, importing allusions to B-Grade Hollywood films and elements of social and political critique into the arena of high art. Much less celebrated than the many people he inspired. Smith's multi-media influence is evident in the works of a broad segment of the American avant-garde. In film, his influence is evident in the work of Andy Warhol, Ken Jacobs, John Waters, George Kuchar, Scott and Beth B. In avant-garde theater and performance art, his hand touches Robert Wilson, Charles Ludlam, John Vaccaro, Cindy Sherman, and Richard Foreman. In his filmmaking, Smith created an "aesthetic delirium." Through his use of outdated film stock and baroque subject matter, he pushed the limits of cinema, liberating it from the straitjacket of "good" technique and "proper" behavior. In his best known film, *Flaming Creatures* (1963), characters cavort in a setting reminiscent of the court of Ali Baba. The film is a fantasy of Androgynes and Transvestites in which flaccid penises and bouncing breasts are so ambiguously equated as to disarm any distinction between male and female. In *Flaming Creatures*, Smith manages to combine the ornate imagination of his youth with the realities of adult fantasy.

Smith's second feature length film, *Normal Love* (1963), is something of a sequel. Unlike the black-and-white *Flaming Creatures*, it is shot in rich color, at outdoor locations including the swamplands of Northern New Jersey, and suggests the archetypal Gardens of the human imagination. The characters include a variety of 1930s horror film monsters, a mermaid, a lecher, and various "cuties" performed by a cast which included Mario Montez, Tiny Tim, Eliot Cukor, Tony Conrad, Diane DePrima, Beverly Grant, and John Vaccaro. Smith then created *No President* (1968), originally titled *The Kidnapping of Wendell Willkie by the Love Bandit*, in reaction to the 1968 Presidential campaign. It mixes black-and-white footage of Smith's creatures, with old campaign footage of Wendell Willkie, the 1940 Republican Presidential candidate. In addition to *No President*, Smith produced numerous short films and fragments of short films. Some of these include *Overstimulated* (c. 1960), *I Was A Male Yvonne DeCarlo* (1970s), *Scotch Tape* (1962), *Wino* (c. 1977), *Hamlet* (c. 1976), *Buzzards Over Baghdad* (1951), *Respectable Creatures*, and others.

Smith was both filmmaker and performance artist. After a period of about eight years (1961–1969) in which Smith showed the films in their completed forms in conventional film screening settings, he began to incorporate the films and his slides into the performances. He developed this technique in many of his performance pieces of the period: "The Tenant

8. A scene from Jack Smith's *Flaming Creatures* (1963). Courtesy Anthology Film Archives; reprinted by permission.

Landlordism of Lucky Paradise," "Exotic Landlordism of the World," "Dance of the Sacred Foundation Application," "Death of A Penguin," "The Secret of Rented Island," "Shark Bait of Capitalism," and "The Horror of Uncle Fish Hook's Safe." Smith created startling stage effects through the spontaneous rearrangement and interplay of recorded imagery on film and slides, with the live action on the "stage", editing and re-editing the film images on the spot, in the midst of the performance. This spontaneous editing, however, required a unique form of splicing in which he put together strands of camera original as well as printed material with masking tape (Tartaglia, 209). Thus Smith managed to create a unique version of the films for each performance.

In his book, *Deathtripping: The Cinema of Transgression*, Jack Sargeant describes Jack Smith as one of the filmmakers who paved the way, demarcating a terrain which others, like Richard Kern and Nick Zedd would later explore (Sargeant, 7–8). Jack Smith's cinema was transgressive, but it was also a cinema of transformation. Transgression can be transformative because it can propel the rebel out of the realm of the Normal and into the realm of the Queer. To break the rules is to announce that one is a self-declared misfit, and to occupy that position is to unleash upon oneself the projected fears of all of the "Normals", acted out through ridicule, attack, separation, and alienation. The purpose of all this psychological violence is to dissuade and distract the transgressor, pushing him/her back into the safety zone of predictable similitude: normalcy. And for the sexually different person, for the Queer, that "safety zone" is the closet.

There is, however, a second component in this transgressive process but it is only realized if the rebel consummates the violation of the ordinary, and passes through the violence of the separation. If that happens, the transgressor is transformed. This emergence from one world into another is reflected in a Spanish word for gay men, *Mariposa* (Butterfly) and in the German expression, *vom anderen Ufer* (from the other side) (Grahn, 37–38). But this transformation is understood differently by both the now transformed Queer, and by the mainstream Normals whom s/he has left behind. To the "great, outside, unwashed, heterosexual public," as Ondine once called them in my film *Lawless* (1977) positioned safely behind the self constructed metaphoric barbed wire fence which circumscribes and defines the heterocentric world view, to these, the Queer is viewed as either an outcast (if s/he has little or no social/economic status) or s/he is seen as an exotic individualist if there is some use that the mainstream can find for her life or work. But if the mainstream heterocentric culture allows the Queers for whatever reason, to enter into its fabric, it must occur within the constructs of the heterocentric world view of culture, values, and identity. In short, the Queer is allowed to enter the barbed-wire enclosed heterocentric compound but s/he must then occupy the space of the Other on the fringe of the Heterocentric Social Construction.

But that "fringe" is a great misnomer, as Judy Grahn pointed out in her study of *Another Mother Tongue*. Grahn describes human culture as a multitude of "interlocking worlds," with Queers living on the cusps of many of them (Grahn, 84). This leads to the inevitable Transgression of conventional values, the Transformation of the self, and the Transiting of the cultural boundaries. This threefold process is what I call "The Ontology of the Queer." Using the critical perspective of this Queer Ontology, we can turn to Jack Smith and his work in cinema and understand it in its *own* terms rather than straining to first sanitize it, de-sexualize it, and de-politicize it and then safely praise this Queer cinema as "a celebration of joy and innocence", as Susan Sontag once did (Sontag, 119). Or, as a handful of other commentators have done, only look to his film *Flaming Creatures*, simply because of the

transited across both roles, and often demanded that audience members help him as "volunteer" actors.

The next of the "Seven Deadly Transgressions" to consider are Gender Fucking and Mocking the Heterocentric. In his essay "Flaming Closets," originally published in the journal *October* shortly after Smith's death, Michael Moon offers readings of Smith's cinema which "short-circuit their relations to the heterosexualized representational regimes from which they derive" (Moon, 20). Further, Moon notes that it would be reductive to describe the work as simply a transvestite comedy, since cross-dressing is only one of the culturally enforced "police lines" which the film crosses (Moon, 20). We can see this expansion of cross-dressing into gender fucking in *Normal Love*. There is a scene in which the Werewolf pursues and captures the mermaid then slips and falls with her into the mud. It is both a moment of pre-meditated narrative rupture, to which I referred earlier, but it is also a moment of transit through multiple worlds of gender. The mermaid is played by Mario Montez, and the Werewolf by Eliot Cukor. Because of the narrative rupture (the accidental fall) which Jack leaves in the film, the narrative is not propelled forward into the next sequence, which would have been an abduction to who-knows-where. Instead, we watch as the Werewolf pours Coca-Cola on the Mermaid's face to clean off the mud. All through this action, Mario is desperately clinging to his wig, trying not to lose it and really destroy the scene by re-crossing the gender line in error. But the transgression of the narrative convention in which Jack allows the "mistake" to remain in the film plot is so jarring, that the viewer quite comfortably transits the worlds of human and fantastic creatures. We completely accept a trans-gendered piscatory vamp (a male mermaid) being abducted by a male victim of lycanthropy (a werewolf). But the scene reads quite naturally in the Queer landscape of the film, because there is a homoerotic underpinning upon which the layers of identity and gender are constructed.

In his writing, Jack referred to Normal (heterosexualism) as "the evil side of homosexuality." His film *Normal Love* can be read as a campy expression of this premise and there is an example of his Mocking the Heterocentric in the film. In *Normal Love*, the Cobra Woman, played by Beverly Grant, is pursued in an elaborate visual passage by the Mummy, played by Tony Conrad. The scene is thoroughly charming, seductive, and visually entrancing, with Beverly resplendent in green body paint, wearing ruby red shoes. It is so hypnotic, in fact, that the viewer forgets that a resurrected corpse is seducing and being seduced by the Cobra Woman. Thus, in *Normal Love* we ride the cusps of necrophilia, bestiality and heterosexuality, as Jack Smith beguiles us with the beauty and humor of his aesthetic, all the while making a subtle comment on the death worshipping heterocentric culture of violence and exclusion. Another example in which gender fucking becomes a mocking of the heterocentric norm occurs in Smith's short film *Hot Air Specialists*. Jack appears as Rose Courtyard—a sort of voluptuous alter ego who also turns up in another of his short films, *Song For Rent*. Rose is the object of the amorous attention of a rather wimpish looking man. The five minute film consists of Rose protecting her modesty, rebuffing the man's advances, and generally playing the role of a sexually proper heterosexual woman, determined to reject the man's interests. Smith's gender transiting performance rests squarely upon the border of credibility. In his gestures, eye contact and deportment on screen, he communicates to the camera, and to the audience, that he does not expect us to believe completely in his gender switch. Smith does want us to believe, but not in the switch, for to do so would disempower the performance. Rather than try to convince us of the verisimilitude of his drag, he would have us laugh at the act which is precursive to hetero sex: the Courtship, upon which Holy Matrimony itself is predicated.

The next of the "Seven Deadly Transgressions" is one of the more threatening to the cultural hetero hegemony: "Promoting the Homoerotic." How often have we heard the plea. "I don't mind it if people are gay; I just don't want them to flaunt their sexuality"? This is said while hetero-sexualism is actively flaunted in every arena of human culture. Smith's film No President is an answer to that normative compulsion. The secondary title of No President is The Kidnapping and Auctioning of Wendell Willkie by the Love Bandit. The plot of the film very loosely alludes to that story, using found footage culled from a campaign film from Willkie's unsuccessful run for the presidency against Franklin Roosevelt. In the footage from the campaign film, Willkie talks about all the good he's going to do for the farmers, and he opens and examines a corn cob. The images of the corn cob with a Vaseline jar reoccur later in No President, and the corncobs are also seen in I Was A Male Yvonne DeCarlo, Song For Rent, and in various Super 8 films Smith made. The corncob is a dildo, and as such it is an emblem of the single greatest perceived threat to heterocentric dominance: anal penetration of the male.

The homoeroticism continues later in the film, during the auction scene with the underground film actress Tally Brown, featuring poet Charles Henri Ford as a vampire in drag. During this scene, the "creatures" are posed in a tableau, and ogle a nude muscular young male. We are witness, in this sequence, to unashamed homosexual desire, and as film voyeurs, we share in the cruising of the hunky male as the drag queen vampire, using his/her hypnotic and silly stare, tries to lure the youth. The young man soaks his testicles in the vampire-queen's champagne glass, and after feigning disgust and horror, the vampire accepts the forbidden elixir. The action is so perfectly natural that we are hardly aware of the transgressive act which has just been represented on the screen, and we barely notice that we have crossed the boundary of the homoerotic. This campy yet visible homodesire serves to subvert the heterocentric gaze, and the concomitant imperative to interpret culture through it.

While some of the previously mentioned transgressions may be jarring to the heterocentric gaze, Smith's most anarchic structural device disorients all perspectives. A basic dramatic expectation in film and theater is that there will be a beginning, a middle, and an end. Smith denied his audiences even the satisfaction of this expectation. The live performances had no real beginning; Smith would usually arrive late, and integrate the process of setting up within the performance piece itself. The middle phase of the film or performance, in which one would expect development of structure through narrative structure, was also frustrated. Visual and performed material would be repeated and recycled. Actions would double back upon themselves, causing the audience to become unconsciously aware that they had seen certain scenes or sequences twice. The endings of Smith's theatrical pieces were equally ambiguous. Either the performance would go on interminably until everyone left the performance space, or it would end on an abrupt, dissatisfying note in which the viewer is denied the feeling of satisfaction which comes from dramatic resolution.

Overarching all of these ploys is Smith's own all-encompassing feeling of failure and despair. "What a horrible story!" he would exclaim during a performance. He did his best to make the audience see that the actors were inept, that the sets were amateurish and ugly, that the execution was a disaster, and that he himself was a failure in life and in art: a miscreant doomed to suffer the misery of oblivion. In an untitled videotape performance made around 1976, which is the only lip-sync recording of any of his performances, he repeatedly interrupts the action, asking the cameraman to turn off the camera. "The tape is already ruined," Smith moans. But the video camera continues to record the performance piece, as Jack sinks into deeper despair, utterly convinced of the "failure" of his staged spectacle. But watching the works of Jack Smith isn't supposed to be a normal experience. If we try to be open and accepting with his work, we'll be thwarted. We'll fester in a state of anxiety. We'll feel uncomfortable and begin to understand why he labeled so many experiences as "horrors." In short, we'll begin to share in the infamous Jack Smith paranoia. We'll feel the alienation which this Queer artist felt. We'll begin to understand what it means to be an artist whose aesthetic bars his own work from appreciation and acceptance.

Yet if we are open and accepting we will also find ourselves transported, in the last of these Seven Deadly Transgressions, into the Gay Elysium. This is represented by an eternal Halloween party, a never ending gay holiday (Grahn, 83). This Gay Elysium is a landscape in which all creatures are welcomed, and where the only exclusion is that of the divisive heterocentric gaze. Jack once wrote, "when you have police, everything looks queer" (Leffingwell, 35). Indeed, the elements of order, judgement and division are what separate us mere mortals from this other realm. It doesn't matter, then, if Smith's "creatures" do or do not fuck the "same" or the "different," because the divisions of the heterocentric are gone. And if we allow the normative, the heterocentric, and the exclusionary instinct to die, we can journey there, into the transformative landscape of Jack Smith's films and slides. There we can romp freely in the perfumed garden of perversity, savoring the aesthetics of trash with all of our fellow creatures, who, with us, are spun out of the stuff of the imagination, like the tales of Scheherazade. There we will find ourselves among the truthful, the glamorous, and the Queer.

Works Cited

Creekmur, Corey K. and Alexander Doty, Out In Culture: Gay, Lesbian and Queer Essays on Popular Culture. Durham, NC: Duke UP, 1995.
Grahn, Judy, Another Mother Tongue: Gay Words, Gay Worlds. Boston: Beacon, 1984.
Hoberman, Jim and Edward Leffingwell, Wait For Me At The Bottom Of The Pool: The Writings of Jack Smith. London and New York: Serpent's Tail, 1997.
Hoberman, Jim, Jack Smith and His Secret Flix. Astoria, NY: American Museum of the Moving Image: 1997.
Leffingwell, Edward, et al. Flaming Creature: Jack Smith, His Amazing Life and Times. London and New York: Serpent's Tail, 1997.
Moon, Michael, "Flaming Closets," October 51 (Winter 1989): 19–54.
Sargeant, Jack, Deathtripping: The Cinema of Transgression. London: Creation Books, 1995.
Smith, Jack, "The Perfect Filmic Appositeness of Maria Montez," Film Culture 27 (1962–1963): 28–32.
Sontag, Susan, "Jack Smith's Flaming Creatures," Against Interpretation. Delta, 1966: 94–99.
Tartaglia, Jerry, Remembrance. 16mm film, color, 1991, 6 minutes, distributed through Canyon Cinema.
—— Lawless. 16mm film, color, 1977, 60 minutes, distributed through Canyon Cinema.
—— "Restoration and Slavery," in Leffingwell, Edward, et al. Flaming Creature: Jack Smith, His Amazing Life and Times. London and New York: Serpent's Tail, 1997: 209–211.
—— Unpublished interview with Klaus Wyborny, February 1999.
Vermilye, Jerry, "Maria Montez, The Queen of Technicolor," Nostalgia Monthly 9 (September 1978): 17–20.

An Interview with Carolee Schneemann

8

KATE HAUG

Carolee Schneemann is a painter, filmmaker, and performance artist who began making films at 26. Her filmic work includes *Viet Flakes* (1965), *Fuses: Part I of Autobiographical Trilogy* (1964–1967), *Plumb Line: Part II of Autobiographical Trilogy* (1968–1971), and *Kitch's Last Meal: Part III of Autobiographical Trilogy* (1973–1978). In addition to her artworks, she has published several books including *More Than Meat Joy: Complete Performance Works and Selected Writings* (1979), *ABC, We Print Everything—In The Cards* (1977) and her feminist theory of art history, *Cézanne, She Was A Great Painter* (1974).

Fuses is a sexually explicit film shot by both Carolee Schneemann and her lover, Jim Tenney.[1] Schneemann not only employs an experimental production strategy; she also engages the material properties of film by baking it, painting it, and making its tenuous structure visible (such as including splices as visible facets of the film's montage). Her camera does not follow any systematic, narrative ordering. Rather the body interrupts the frame, avoiding diegetic storytelling and following an idiosyncratic pulse of gesture and musicality.

The film explores heterosexual sex from a variety of vantage points, disturbing the formulaic imaging of sex found in Hollywood cinema. In *Fuses* the sexual act is not driven by a sequence of events or in service of a linear plot. Instead, sex is shown as a continuous and spontaneous activity between two people. Their relationship to one another is determined by the dynamics of physical coupling rather than individual character development or extenuating social circumstance.

The exhibition history of *Fuses* is quite remarkable and underscores the film's radical nature. In 1969, it won a Cannes Film Festival Special Jury Selection prize and has had regular public screenings since its completion. Yet, it continues to be a controversial work. In Moscow, twenty years after winning at Cannes, it provoked a small riot and was censored for pornographic content.

I interviewed Carolee Schneemann on March 28, 1997 in her loft in New York City.

Kate Haug: To refresh you on my project, I am specifically studying *Fuses* (1964–1967), because I am looking at sexually explicit work made by women around the time of the women's movement. While I was watching *Fuses* the other day, I was struck by its beauty. It is so pivotal, for many reasons, in the history of experimental filmmaking. But, because it deals with sex, it has been left out of avant-garde film history and not really addressed by feminism. Is sex still the domain of men? Is that why it is so problematic for women?

Carolee Schneemann: Explicit sexual imagery propels the formal structure of *Fuses*. Initially, it was clear to me that people were so distracted by being able to have a voyeuristic permission to see genital heterosexuality that it would take them—if they ever came back to see it again— many showings before the structure was clear: the musicality of it and the way it was edited. *Fuses* is very formal in how it is shaped; that was crucial to making it have a coherent muscular life. Visualized erotic, active bodies deflect the very structures which shape montage: viewers are distracted by the simultaneity of perceptual layers *Fuses* offers.

Which is parallel to my own historic position. All my work evolves from my history as a painter: all the objects, installations, film, video, performance—things that are formed. But the performative works—which are one aspect of this larger body of work—are all that the culture can hold onto. That fascination overrides the rest of the work. It is too silly, but it is still kind of a mind/body split. If you are going to represent physicality and carnality, we can not give you intellectual authority.

Haug: As an artist, how do you see the work functioning beyond the sign of the body in terms of its formal structure?

Schneemann: Well, it is a risk, but it has always been a hope; I am a formalist and my influences are rigorous and keyed to a sense of historicity. The older artists who were really influential on my own sense of what work demanded were composers like Carl Ruggles and Edgar Varèse. There was this famous anecdote about Carl Ruggles keeping Henry Cowell[2] waiting when they were supposed to have lunch together at Ruggles's little Vermont school house. Cowell was standing at the door hearing this one dreadful piano chord over and over and over and he banged on the door and yelled: "Carl, what the fuck is going on in there? We're supposed to go to lunch!" And Carl yelled, "Wait, Henry wait! I am giving this chord the test of time." I took all that very seriously. What Bob Morris calls lag time, the delay that is involved with works that might bewilder cultural expectations by disrupting inherited principles. For instance, Cèzanne or Artaud—I came upon them in the early 1960s when they were still in a state of marginality. Virginia Woolf's writing was an immense influence for formal structure: reaching inside rhythms of the mind, the rhythms and linguistic motions of the phrase clarified as memory, as light, color—so that Woolf's nonlinear narrative is never literalized. I recognized the vision her writing opened to me when I was 15 years old, sitting on bales of straw in Vermont, dazzled by *The Waves*. With Cézanne, I studied the picture plane fractured into phrases of larger rhythms, contributing details; the body has to enter perception viscerally: each stroke is an event in pictorial space. These were my earliest influences, followed by Artaud, Beauvoir, Wilhelm Reich. Now people want to know about it. But it would not have mattered very much in the past years—whatever I said—many contemporary artists thought I was just doing something incredibly perplexing. Many of the men seemed to consider I was to be fucked or to be suppressed. And this is still more complicated because some men also fought for my work.

Haug: This opens up a whole gamut of issues. When you were just talking about your influences, I was thinking about the repetition in *Fuses*. Were you thinking of that repetition in terms of structure or narrative? Did you also consider it as a way to develop a type of play within the image? There is all this interplay between the layers within the images.

Schneemann: The different instrumental voices that Bach could weave and break apart in terms of a timbre, a pitch that had a certain weight and certain fracture . . . an instrumental clunkiness that would then suddenly reattract and reabsorb thematic elements and become ecstatic. In particular, I was submerged in the Bach Cantatas—form had an organic, strange, rhythmic dynamic that could conceptually and sensuously unravel in time; since film is in time, I was thinking about time structure. And about [Charles] Ives being able to layer a dissonant, discrepant montage of sound. Editing, I was thinking, "I am going to have a mass of blue and then this arm opens up and that breaks the reach towards the figure with three frames of yellow, the arm completes its gesture and a mass of blue dissolves into . . ." So I had all these crazy notes and that is how I would be editing and counting. There are beats . . . there are counts, frames of color, of gesture . . .

Haug: It's very much like you are painting with motion and composing with color.

Schneemann: With frames, it is almost like notes. So, yes, I am painting, but I am also time factoring. It is not just gestural. The gestures are subject to internal rhythms. Now, at the same time, these internal rhythms are definitely shaped by the fact that it is a self-shot film. Often I did not get back the film print I expected. If the camera was set on a chair or hanging from a lamp, the merge of the bodies might shift from the lens focus, and by chance the thirty-second wind-up Bolex camera would only capture my buttocks, or some area of all green . . . I would accept that as the film offering me the intercourse between the camera and my domestic space. I was always willing to adapt my explicit intentions.

I wanted to allow film to give me the sense that I was getting closer to tactility, to sensations in the body that are streaming and unconscious and fluid—the orgasmic dissolve unseen, vivid if unseeable.

Haug: What was your impulse to make *Fuses*? Were you making it in reaction to something?

Schneemann: Yes, it was in conversation with *Window Water Baby Moving* (Stan Brakhage, 1959). I had mixed feelings about the power of the male partner, the artist subsuming the primal creation of giving birth as a bridge between male constructions of sexuality as either medical or pornographic. Brakhage's incredible authenticity and bravery was to take this risk, to focus on what was actual and real, actually looking at the body's reality and leaving the protection of a constructed mythology. I know that Stan and Jane passed the camera back and forth, but I was still very concerned that the male eye replicated or possessed the vagina's primacy of giving birth. The camera lens became the Os, the aperture out of which birth was "expressed." The camera gave birth as he held the camera; this was metaphoric for the whole gendered aesthetic struggle in our friendship. You must understand in the early 1960s, the terminology, the analysis of traditional bias was completely embedded. I really wanted to see what "the fuck" is and locate that in terms of a lived sense of equity. What would it look like? Now I can reference a suppressed history of the sacred erotic. Brakhage's work touched into the sacred erotic. But we have to remind ourselves—that throughout the 1960s, only men maintained creative authority: women were muses, partners. Brakhage was unique in his willingness to focus on the actual birth. You must understand, there were no precedents that we knew of—only medical and pornographic models.

Haug: When you first showed *Fuses*, you showed it in 1967?

Schneemann: No, I showed it as I worked on it. 1965, 1966. People were seeing it in my studio, in process, and it was becoming an influence right away. That early. People weren't shocked—here was a visual construction which touched on the nascent nerve of "free expression," "open sexuality" . . .

Haug: When you were showing it, you were coming from this point of view that you wanted to take a look at "the fuck." You wanted to see what it looks like in a situation of equality. Were people able to read that at all when you would show it to them?

Schneemann: *Fuses* wasn't programmatic. The fuck was inseparable from an intimacy, an erotic generosity that was evident. Jim Tenney and I were together for thirteen years—an extraordinary and rapturous loving life together. As intellectual equals, Jim had full participation in the filming; his belief in my work situated his participation as both object and subject interchangeably. That was unique in 1965! Women would sometimes cry and say, "Thank you, thank you. This is the first time that I've seen a female genital and I'm going to be able to look at my own body! I'm going to look at my vulva!" Most of my contemporaries were pretty thrilled about the film. Others later admitted they considered it only "narcissistic exhibitionism." Some felt envy and displacement from the shameless pleasure. I remember many comments. There were objections to the cunnilingus sequence: "That went on too long." "We really don't want to see that." But others expressed feeling, "That was amazing to see. Yeah, that's what it's like."

Haug: That's one thing I'm really interested in. How has the reading of your work changed over the years? You have had this opportunity to see *Fuses* play in so many different audiences and also so many different theoretical contexts. When the film was originally being shown, it was a proto-feminist moment before the women's movement was actually consolidated or recognized as cohesive.

Schneemann: Well, it *was* outrageous and it was sometimes wonderful, salutary for many people. Reactions were mixed. It was usually the men who were most appreciative. They felt a released identification with the lyric, energetic partnering and the overt penis as a source of active pleasure; that the film focused the power of pleasured and pleasuring male sexuality. Did you find the Gene Youngblood article, the first review of *Fuses* ever? It was great. It says something like "a ninety-foot penis in cinemascope."

Haug: It was a surprise for me to read that, because it was so congratulatory, so excited about the work. It ran in contradiction to what I assumed public reaction would have been.

Schneemann: It is interesting to measure critical regard by male writers against its utter neglect by feminist film historians—which is what you mentioned previously.

Haug: That is why the screening history of *Fuses* is interesting; *Fuses* remained important through these different moments. When I talked to you originally, I was curious about that relationship to Laura Mulvey's essay.[3] It seems like *Fuses* really exemplifies so many of the different tenets of her particular argument. Even though her argument is directed towards Hollywood cinema, it is interesting that experimental cinema that doesn't base itself in relationship to the narrative is completely left out of that discussion. Your film is such a fine example of something that alters that relationship between the viewer and the . . .

Schneemann: *Fuses* was being shown in London, 1968, 1969 through the early 1970s when I lived there—as she began writing her film essays. Mulvey talked to me about the rupture *Fuses* made in pornography—how important *Fuses* was as an erotic vision. It was going to change the whole argument and discussion of filmic representation of sexuality and . . . then she couldn't touch it! Mulvey has never mentioned my films. But perhaps it was a touchstone behind critical theory for Mulvey. We were there at the same time, at the same moment, in parallel.

I showed *Fuses* first at the Round House for the "Dialectics of Liberation" conference in London in 1968 and at the Institute of Contemporary Art (ICA). I was pulled out of the film booth by the conference coordinator who told me that in case of immorality charges, he would *not* defend me. I was on my own. He *would* defend Stokely Carmichael, R. D. Laing, etc., etc. if their political transgressions were to be prosecuted. I felt incredibly alone, female, desired, and despised . . .

I ended up living in London for four years. One of the only ways that I could get any income at all was due to the curiosity around *Fuses*. Derrick Hill, a courageous independent distributor, kept getting me little showings for it. It was written about a lot; it was seen all over in London. I was on important censorship and pornography panels with editors, publishers, labor ministers.

Haug: In terms of feminism in the 1970s, did critics ever criticize you by saying that the film actually runs counteractive to a feminist political agenda?

Schneemann: You mean, did they ever ask if I was aware that I was internalizing male fantasies?

Haug: Did you ever get any reaction like that or were people generally supportive of it?

Schneemann: No, they were completely cowardly. They never told me. They never discussed that with me. Although I had terrible reactions to *Plumb Line* during a women's film festival. I was hooted. I mean, they wouldn't even look at it. All they saw was that traditional, all American guy's face in the opening sequence. Particularly the lesbian women, all they had to do was see that face and they started screaming. I crawled out of that showing on my hands and knees down the aisle to the elevator, trembling.

Haug: Obviously, as a practicing artist, you are aware of the history of the female nude. In fact, I was just reading something that you wrote in Moscow about *Fuses* being censored there; you refused to speak to the reporters at a press conference in front of an exhibit of oil paintings of female nudes. Being aware of the history of representation, how were you conceiving of yourself as a nude woman in your own film?

Schneemann: I had already done *Eye Body* (1963), the 36 *Transformative Actions For Still Camera*, where I posed the questions: Could I include myself as a formal aspect of my own materials? Could a nude woman artist be both image and image maker? Those were critical concerns at the time. I was constantly told that I shouldn't even be painting: "You're really good for a girl, but. . . ." My advisor said, "Don't set your heart on art because you're only a girl. . . . You're really good, kid, but don't set your heart on art." He was a second generation abstract expressionist and very sympathetic to me. I had naively anticipated a shared devotion, power, dynamic, energy that would envelop all dedicated artists to subsume, burn out sexual difference in creative pleasure and inclusion!

No, no. I had to get that nude off the canvas, frozen flesh to art history's conjunction of perceptual erotics and an immobilizing social position.

I was supporting myself when I first came to New York as an artist's model. I was lying naked listening to these terrible men, most of them really ruining their students' drawings . . . I had to listen to them say everything that would prevent the students from seeing fully and well. . . . Then I come back to the studio where the cultural message was, "You're incredible but don't *really* try to do anything." I would just pick up my hammer and start fracturing my materials with a full arm swing and focused aim. My work was about motion and momentum and physicality. The next step was to see what would happen if the body went in among my own materials. And would my rage at predictive rejection be supplanted by the gendered form exposed, displaced: active, present, and accusatory! Once I saw the images, I thought I had done something incredible with *Eye Body*, but I didn't know exactly what.

Haug: I think it is incredible that you saw the nude on the canvas as a direct challenge to your ambition to be an artist.

Schneemann: I had to wrest my body out of a conventionalizing history. I must say that poets in New York were very supportive of me. If the art world was always confused and ambiguous, my first solid insightful supportive response would be from poet friends, Robert Kelly, Paul Blackburn, Clayton Eshleman, Jerome Rothenberg, David Antin . . .[4] That was interesting. We formed a coherent conversation: the body as central to language, to image. Of course my partner, Jim, was always inspiring to me; our love gave me a coherent base. His close friends and musical collaborators Malcolm Goldstein, Philip Corner[5] were unwavering in their regard for my visual constructions, objects, performances.

Haug: Did you feel radically vulnerable when you were using your body that way?

Schneemann: Yes. Not because I was nude, but because the culture was going to trash this. I did not feel erotically or personally so vulnerable. I felt vulnerable for what my art statement was going to set off or close off.

Haug: On the one hand, you have this desire to be an artist. On the other hand, you are producing work which you know is highly controversial. It seems you would feel like you are taking an incredible risk; you know you are in a very combative situation.

Schneemann: It's not that I had a *desire* to be an artist. I'm in a very combative situation because I *am* an artist. Whatever an artist is or was, I was it. . . . This wasn't a choice, and that's different. It means you have a certain character structure.

Haug: How would you describe that character structure?

Schneemann: You have to make images or you're going to die, basically. That it is the most interesting, satisfying, compelling, necessary . . . like love and sex and breathing. Somebody somewhere recently wrote this variation on: "I don't know what great art is, but I know it when I see it"—"I can't tell what produces a great artist, but I know a real artist when I meet someone who has to create images or they imagine they'll expire."

Haug: In terms of a historical context, when you first started showing *Fuses* as a work in progress, who was your audience? Did you have discussions about the piece afterwards? What type of issues would come out?

Schneemann: Other artists in New York. The thing to do now would be to review my early phone book. I would just call everybody up and say I'm going to show what I've been working on and I would really like you to see it. When you are young and new in New York, everybody is interesting!

The really early showings I don't remember well. I think people were a little flabbergasted. Yes, they said some insulting things, too. A lot of them thought it was just a "narcissistic exhibition." I remember that. . . . So I was learning where the resistance would be and getting a sense that there was a lot of envy in the resistance.

Haug: I was just showing my work as part of a panel at UCLA. I attended another panel of women artists where the first audience question was "Do you find working with your autobiography self-indulgent?" I was struck by that question. Why is it that the first question about this work is whether or not it's self-indulgent? Will women making work about their experience always be accused of being self-indulgent and narcissistic? So it is interesting for me to now hear you say that people made the comments to you in the early 1960s. Could you speak to this? Do you think that this relates your teacher's comment, "Don't put your heart into art."?

Schneemann: If a man crosses a threshold to depict or engage a lived reality, he becomes a hero. To deal with actual lived experience—that's a heroic position for a male and a trivial exposure for a woman. A woman exploring lived experience occupies an area that men want to denigrate as domestic, encapsulate as erotic, arousing or supporting their own position. (Nurse, whore, waitress, dancer, mommy, sacrificial heroine: you always know equity is punishable by death in Hollywood culture—you can see it coming through the dust and clattering hoof beats . . .)

Culturally it has to do with the whole diminution of the feminine, what is female. We are so saturated with our own contradictory traditions and the degree of freedom that we have within these shifting traditions. It is hard for us to see where the deep hatred of the feminine still maintains its squirmy hostile boundaries.

Haug: I think that *Fuses* is an incredibly sexy film. I watched it right before I came to New York. I had only seen it in video. Then I saw it on film and it was like WHOA . . . this is one really hot film. . . . In your interview with Scott MacDonald, you say that *Fuses* is sexually political. Could you talk more about that description?

Schneemann: A depiction of woman's pleasure, authentic pleasure, created by herself of her lived experience is rare. In pornography, the pleasure is when the man comes all over her face, or her pussy is getting licked to the point where either she is going to be raw for the next week, or she already came, and we missed it. Because female orgasm *is* mysterious. There is still this dichotomous evidence—or reporting—on the difference between clitoral and vaginal orgasm. Those are crucial issues for me; experiencing two kinds of vividly different orgasms can place me in another kind of heterosexual closet among women who don't know what I'm talking about. I insist on the separateness, the distinctiveness, the various-ness of clitoral and vaginal orgasm. So *Fuses* opens up a sensory realm that people recognize in different ways and because it represents a lusciously privileged position—especially now with the counter-thrust examination of the abject, abused, scarred, repelled, sado-masocistic vocabulary of visual images. It is essential that women reveal their "privileged" position to counteract all the ignorance, stupidity, and denial of heterosexual interchange. But it is suspicious that male culture is so comfortable with the feminine brutalized-abject—the abuses of sexual experience, the erotic victim. And an abused body requires its defenses!

I just wanted to put everything in *Fuses* that seemed normal and ordinary. Then I edited sequences so that whenever you were looking at the male genital it would dissolve into the

9. Carolee Schneemann in performance. Courtesy Anthology Film Archives; reprinted by permission.

female and vice versa; the viewer's unconscious attitudes would be constantly challenged. You couldn't start to say. "That's disgusting!" or "I loved that!" before it became its equivalent.

Haug: One thing that I really enjoyed was I felt, when I was watching the film, that I would often get lost inside of the frame. That disorientation was what actually felt really sexual to me. I know that you have talked about your relationship to the frame. I was stunned at the intimate yet expansive sense of space, on a perceptual level for me as a viewer. A feeling of space that was intimate but yet very vast. Were you thinking about that at all?

Schneemann: Yes, and that's what that white section is. I wanted everything to suddenly drain into this open, indecipherable whiteness . . . like that orgasmic space where you are out beyond wherever you are. You don't know where you are. You don't know if it is his body or your body. I was wanting to move towards that kind of sensory place when the film goes all white. Actually, that is a snowstorm with cows in it. I was thinking of Altamira, something very ancient. I went out into the snowstorm naked, putting on a coat. It happened to have been some old scraggly fur coat so I was thinking about fur and animal and flesh and the heat of the coldness but sizzling in snow . . . let it all get white, emptied. And of course, aesthetically, that was a kind of crazy thing to do. I anticipated people would get bored and restless and say, "Oh, I see splice marks, what's happening, this looks speckled, it's not clean. . . ." My film is always dirty because of the way I edited with the cats moving around and the windows wide open.

So you seem like one of the ideal viewers. I'm wondering how much that has to do with your own sense of sexual pleasure and integrity in your own experience.

Haug: I think it does come from my own belief that pleasure is fundamental to any political paradigm. Often there are many elements, even within a liberal situation, working to repress pleasure.

Schneemann: It is very crucial to state here that for many women, pleasure is a defended territory where they can't take risks, because they have already been undermined, intruded on, abused. So if you are lucky enough not to have major psychic erotic damage done, then you can enter this arena of potential pleasure. But if damage has been done to you, this arena seems frivolous, dangerous, unprotected, and unrealistic. Yvonne Rainer used to say to me, "You make sexuality too easy." And I would say to her, "You make it too hard." We have been close friends since the 1960s, tugged by our aesthetic closeness and difference.

In the 1960s and 1970s, women rarely confessed sexual trauma to each other. Personal experiences would become encoded in work in ways that were often very bewildering, occluded to the artist herself, and to the audience. Why is this so cold? Why can't they touch? Why is this so oppressive? Why do I feel so much attraction but it's always repulsed? Why did my friend commit suicide?

Profound issues of hidden sexual abuse and victimization of the feminine really began to claim an explicit language and descriptive grasp in the 1980s. By the time I was teaching performance in Austin, Texas (1989), rape was finally out as a major traumatic component of women's experience that had to be addressed. Women who had been raped or abused were not doing films about pleasure! They might be constructing big voluptuous ceramic vase-like sculptures with knives thrust all through those hollowed out forms. I can facilitate enlarging the erotic vocabulary, but now we have to look at the specialness of being able to inhabit our bodies with confidence and freedom.

Haug: I think that it is really important to say. What is interesting is that at different moments in time, you have people working from different positions in their bodies. I think you're right in terms of the 1980s. There was this complete sense of urgency around issues of rape and sexual abuse. It is necessary for people to be able to discuss these issues and make work about it. It is very telling that the discussion of rape and sexual abuse had been repressed for so long.

Schneemann: It's a part of our suppressed, guilty male cultural history. When I started filming for *Fuses*, there was still an argument among some smart people, men, friends of mine, about rape; that women wanted to be raped, that it was good for them! That was still a commonplace piece of male philosophy! I remember the bitter arguments of women against this empathetic closure of the deluded men! The uncertainty of the men who doubted the pro-rape men. A bad dream. . . .

Haug: That seems so incredible . . . brutal to me that anyone could even argue about that. I come from a very different perspective since I was in college and high school during the 1980s and 1990s. That discussion was very much a part of my academic education. Also as a contemporary student of art history, I studied how the formal components of art can make the female body signify a form of docility. Which is why your work is so intriguing to me. It offers another perspective on women's sexuality; a sexuality that is in concert with physical pleasure.

In *Fuses*, you appear as someone who maintains your identity in a sexual relationship and through your sexuality. You are very strong within the film as an individual. It appears that you and James Tenney are partners coming together—having this life experience but also so strong in yourselves that you can be so generous with one another. So often we have these images of sexually active women as victims. You hardly ever see a representation of a woman's identity as something whole and autonomous and sexual . . . not victimized.

Schneemann: Well, two things. One is that whenever I collaborated, went into a male friend's film, I always thought I would be able to hold my presence, maintain an authenticity. It was soon gone, lost in their celluloid dominance—a terrifying experience—experiences of true dissolution. Frightening. Being in Brakhage's films *Daybreak* (1957), *Whiteye* (1957), and *Cat's Cradle* (1959), being in a Dwoskin film—almost every time—and we were friends. I thought it would be okay. It was not okay for me. I was never filmed at my own work. Stan in 1959 insisted I put on an apron to be filmed. Peter Gidal had me nude in a bathtub . . . I felt that whoever I really was had been obliterated and that they had *needed* to obliterate me. Just as in the "collaboration" with Bob Morris for *Site* (1964), I became historicized and immobilized. But it was a great adventure!

Haug: In relationship to the individuality between the two partners, the collaboration between you and Jim Tenney . . .

Schneemann: I wanted to also tell you: a linguistic sense. I had this sort of phallic sense— I wanted to penetrate the culture's suppressions with my body. But I wasn't sure it could do it. So I'm pretty content. They punished me in certain ways, but it is a very, very fortunate historic moment. We haven't been burned as witches. We don't have our genitals excised, we are not wrapped in chador. My images have been met by the unconscious needs, been sustained by the recognition of my culture. But my culture has not supported my work; I struggle to patch together grants, part-time teaching. I cannot afford to make new films or video works.

Haug: When I look at the work, I think that it is such courageous work to have happened at any time.

Schneemann: It's very schitzy for me. I'm getting appreciation twenty-five years later! I feel like I'm visiting somebody else's scene of the crime while producing my current art which is being neglected now—in its immediacy . . . lag time?

Haug: I want to ask this question about documentary film practice. Did you have the desire or impulse to document your experience? Were you thinking about documentary film as a practice at all when you made *Fuses*? Did that enter into your conceptualization of it as you were editing it?

Schneemann: Well, it is yes and no. I don't think of it as documentary. It's something different which has to do with a desperate desire to capture the passionate things of life. That can be very small things, very big. It can be war, it can be love, a cat whisker—but it's a sense of being a meeting, head-on, with some subject or material that can then become the process out of which a work develops. So it's kind of convoluted, the way I need to work: dream, research, hands into materials, the invocation of motive, necessity—what I must see. . . .

Haug: One thing I'm asking the filmmakers I interview concerns the lack of precedents. In your case, there are very few sexually explicit images by women that came before *Fuses*. I look at the work and think it signifies this very revolutionary moment; these images were circulating, they were being made. In a way it does leave a document, like any art object does. Also going on at this time, a new style of documentary practice was coming onto the scene . . . cinéma vérité. So I begin to think artists were also in concert with these more sociological aspects of filmmaking.

Schneemann: It's a proto-feminist issue again. I think it was influenced by the Vietnam war, by the civil rights movement. Documentary work begins to seize the actuality of lived experience in its contradictions and to start tearing away the horrible aggrandized mythology that comes out of the worst of self-righteous Amerikana. And the worst is replete with male over-determinations: reconstructive, heroic modes into which all troubled devious psyches fold and reemerge. A kind of reassuring hero monster in which the feminine is always just the mascot. If she's really good, she gets killed; if she's really bad, she gets fucked and killed. It doesn't leave us much room. Better put that apron back on even though you're stark naked!

Haug: I think what you are pointing to is that people in the 1960s were becoming conscious of the power of the image: the fact that images were being manufactured and made. This is especially true in relationship to your comment about the civil rights movement. I think images became a fundamental part of the political legitimacy of that movement.

Schneemann: You're right. We were being moved, we were being affected by images bringing information that was startling and taboo and terrible and made you convinced you had to do something. To enter the image itself! Activation as an intervention into the politics behind the revelatory images.

Haug: There seems to be a political expediency in the ability to take the medium into your own hands and produce images that had never been seen before.

Schneemann: Expediency . . . I would take that as a much latter day interpretation of a blind fierce moment. A wonderful moment. I was full of naiveté and conviction that we were going to change things. And everybody you met, as a young artist who just turned up in New York from Illinois or anywhere—everybody I met was definitely going to change everything—either in art, music, painting, sculpture, politics, economics, or farming. It was cumbersome as anticipation, as experiment. . . . Being able to hang out with Abby Hoffman, Janis Joplin, and Rauschenberg in the same night. Our world was completely charged up, charging. . .

Haug: You were speaking about people saying they wanted to change things. At that moment, were people thinking in terms of the establishment?

Schneemann: The arts were stultifying. My sense of it is that all the romantic domestic fantasies of the 1950s blew a foul breath in the cultural atmosphere which you could blow apart instantly. You came to New York and found a huge abandoned loft for $68 a month that nobody wanted to live in. We girls could teach each other wiring and plumbing, because one of us would have figured it out. You could engage all the adventurous courage you could possibly imagine you needed as an artist and as a promiscuous, adventurous girl wandering the New York City artist bars. Then you were impacted head on by an immense monstrous war coming—unconscionable, endless, and draining off our own generation. We had to fight that. There was no question about it. Each person of even slight political courage found a place as an activist.

Everyone was politically engaged. The phone was tapped, mail opened, we were grabbed at protests by undercover police. I spent several years teaching guys how to avoid the draft. I had my own ideas for psycho breakdown in the face of the military . . . and they always worked! I had a little training camp, my training sessions. Friends would bring their boyfriends and lovers to me. The guy would say, "I can't do it; I'm going to crack up, I'm going to go nuts, I'm going to kill the wrong person." And I said, "Fine, I think I can work with you on this." I was also training people how to encounter police brutality; how to fall, how to crawl, how to be conscious of where you were within the group, with peripheral police assault breaking into the group—in the back, in the front, and with one another. Total immersion in physical principles of sensitization as riot control.

Haug: I have read about your *Viet-Flakes* (1965) piece . . .

Schneemann: The need to explore the passionate feelings that had not been clarified, the need to see women give birth, the need for political action. Young artists didn't sit around making theoretical decisions to encapsulate subtle significations and signs. We'd just call each other to an action. We'd learned not to use the phone and we'd find a way to tell each other we had to do something. And then actions were spread through the whole community . . . a huge, sensitive wave. With my film *Viet-Flakes*, the kinetic theater performance *Snows* was built out of my anger, outrage, fury and sorrow for the Vietnamese—to concretize and elucidate the genocidal compulsions of a vicious disjunctive technocracy gone berserk against an integral, essentially rural culture. The grotesque fullfillment of the Western split between matter and spirit, mind and body, individualized "man" against cosmic natural unities. Destruction so vast as to become randomized, constant as weather. Snowing . . . purification clarification, homogenization, obliteration. . . .

Haug: It seems there was uniformity among people in the agreement that something should be done and something must be done and we will do it.

Schneemann: It was true. You smelled patchouli, you saw somebody who had mixed colors on their shirt and you gave the V-sign. But the dynamic in daily life was tense . . . the buzz word was "polarization." Some man would attack you with a knife and fork and try to stab you in the hand in an ordinary country diner if your guy's hair was long.

Now it's all mixed up. You can't tell what the mustache signifies, the long hair, short hair, tattoos, earrings, piercings, purple hair. Everybody is in each other's disguises. But in the 1960s, the coding was absolutely crystal clear. We helped one another with our recognizable symbols—Volkswagen bus! Yes! Dreadlocks, guitars, graffiti, the Beatles, Traffic, Hendrix, Joplin. You'd be out hitching on the highway somewhere, going from one demonstration to try to disappear and a Volkswagen van would always pull up. You'd *always* smoke some joints, and you'd always help each other go the next step. It was really quite extraordinary.

Currently the position of women in the 1960s has been presented in its worse aspect; the women were breeding machines, free sex machines. That's not the whole story at all. We were young women taking tremendous freedoms, maintaining self-definition and an erotic confidence in choosing partners, spontaneously in the firm expectation of great times to be won together.

Haug: That's one thing I'm really curious about. One of the more popular films reacting to that time is *Looking For Mr. Goodbar* (Richard Brooks, 1977). In that film, a young woman has a secret sexual life, but in the end, she gets killed. The culture as a whole could not absorb the idea of women's sexual independence. That is especially evident when I hear you saying that the 1960s and 1970s were actually a time when women felt confident, maybe, exploring their sexuality.

Schneemann: The waves of women artists, feminists, her energy building on radical politics of the 1960s. Of course, what you are describing is part of the male cultural clamp; the greater value of women's self determination pushes at very limited means, choices allowed by our society. You get all these films where the women are killed, the women are punished, or the women are vicious to men . . . (*Thelma and Louise*, the talismanic women's buddy film of the 1980s; they have to ecstatically commit suicide by accelerating their car over a cliff to escape male law and rule).

Haug: Then there can't be a sense of equality.

Schneemann: No. Hollywood's dominant myth production only envisions equity in which male symbology is diminished or overtly self-destructive. He loses power in equity. "Make love not war" becomes "get real"—back onto a crucial strand of re-action, re erected regressions.

Haug: I'm interested in this trajectory in feminism where feminism itself becomes slightly puritanical: what does that self-censorship produce on a political level?

One question I had specifically, in terms of the film itself, which is kind of a crude question. You don't have to answer it if it seems inappropriate. I noticed that some of the images of fucking seem animal-like to me—very lustful. The bodies are impulsive and there is a hard, rhythmic sense to it. Did you see that when you were making the film? How did it feel to put that next to . . .

I love that when it goes from this really hot and heavy sex and then these really tender moments with Jim Tenney. How did it feel to put those together like that? I don't think that had ever been done before.

Schneemann: Well, to me it felt completely ordinary and natural. Now I understand how very complex this is—for erotically uncertain viewers to accept this range of sensitivity *and* ferocity. I can only talk about my own experience. My partner's orgasm is really propulsive and it's fierce—his thrusting rhythms intensify my vaginal orgasm off into the ecstatic stratosphere. We just take off. With vaginal orgasm, you're blown out together at the same moment. It's big. Cosmic. I don't think I even got close to it in the film and that's a big regret. I could not capture the immensity of orgasm.

There was an approach. Of course, tenderness and sensitivity are part of that. In terms of cultural fragmentation and disease, dis-ease, the fact that sexuality has this full and complex range, you could say, "Touch tenderly, fuck fiercely." Both men and women have a great deal of contemporary confusion about phallic power, pleasure, and torment. The penis as a source of touching within, of friction, of momentum, is uniquely capable of giving rhapsodic pleasure, as well as being used as weaponry, brutality. So how do people address this crucial contradiction? How do they live that out in their own bodies? If a child or young woman has been raped or abused, what sort of trust, lubricity, receptivity, desire live in her vaginal walls?

Haug: I think that hearkens back to what you were talking about earlier in terms of personal experience with the body, with your own and others. The film does focus on male genitalia, but when I watched it, I felt I was seeing male genitalia for the first time on screen . . . the way it was filmed, filmed from angles that were so intimate. Once again, I felt the penis wasn't represented like a weapon. It seemed very friendly and happy. I think at one point you have this shot of his balls breathing.

Schneemann: The close-up on his testicles contracting. I have all these little sexual jokes in it . . . Tenney's "balls" testing on a little chair bordered with Christmas tree balls. Then I montaged a burning bush joke—there's a close-up of my "bush." Then the clouds over a silhouetted bush—the sun setting behind the shrub. I loved discovering those associations. Nobody saw those for years. I'd be the only person in the audience chuckling away. Like pussy/pussy—his hand on the cat and cut to his hand stroke on my pussy.

Haug: When you showed those images of the male genitalia how did people react to that? Did they see them as being playful?

Schneemann: They see many different things. Tenney has a curved penis when it's erect and that confused people. They wanted to know if it was *really* erect—technical questions. I didn't have close-up lenses so close-ups are a little fuzzily intimate. I never got a really beautiful cunt shot, which I've worked on since. That's how art builds on itself!

The fact that *Fuses* is filmed at home—the intimacy of lovers' own bedroom—I hope that there is a sense that there is no outside camera person. That's why the camera was part of our body. The cat Kitch watches with complete unrestrained interest. The cat becomes the filmic eye, a meta-presence inviting the viewers. The film follows lyrical seasonal changes that I wanted of where I still live. I wanted what was around us to be coming in and out of season, of frame, of focus, of flesh.

Haug: Why was that important to you in that film?

Schneemann: Just the ordinariness of surroundings in an intense erotic, domestic tactility . . . to allow the erotic continuum its domestic force instead of exaggerated, or glamorized, or artificial.

Haug: When I watched the film, it seemed like the sex was continual but inconsistent. I always have this feeling of erotic charge, but the type of eroticism that was happening was inconsistent. That goes back to the different rhythms of sexuality.

Schneemann: And also how different we are. Even with the same partner, every touch is always different but familiar. . . .

Haug: That is something else unique to *Fuses*, because most representations of sexuality don't acknowledge the variation of experience.

Schneemann: And they don't acknowledge that it goes on forever, which is where Barbara Hammer's important film *Nitrate Kisses* (Barbara Hammer, 1992) comes in.

Haug: In *Fuses*, the images of the body are fragmented; they are seen in a glimpse; there is interference of the body. That was one of the things that made it sexually charged. What were you thinking about in terms of creating a filmic image of the body?

Schneemann: As a painter, paint is the power of extending whatever you see or feel, of intensifying it, of reshaping it. So I wanted the bodies to be turning into tactile sensations of flickers. And as you said, you get lost in the frame—to move the body in and out of its own frame, to move the eye in and out of the body so it could see everything it wanted to, but would also be in a stare of dissolution, optically. resembling some aspect of the erotic sensation in the body which is not a literal translation. It is a painterly tactile translation edited as a music of frames.

Haug: That comes out of your formal training as a painter.

Schneemann: That's why it is collage, and cut and baked. I am also always radicalizing my materials. I have to be subversive with them so I am not repeating my same old habits. I have to be engaged so that some of it comes back with something that I might not expect from my material; that's why I risk it. That's why the original *Fuses* is so thick as a collage. It can't be printed! I never thought of that. It was a horrible shock, one of the worst. After three years of work, to be told by the film lab that *Fuses* in its collaged layers was too thick to run through the printer!

Haug: When you were talking about subverting your materials, I was thinking about your use of your own body. The body is literally inscribed with culture. You used your body as a medium. Were you thinking about subverting your body in some way?

Schneemann: I thought more that my body could subvert what was around me! It was a question· could I introduce the meanings of this body? To the extent that mine was an idealized body—could I make it insist on meanings conventionally resisted? Suppressed? And, by gum . . . once I got to *Interior Scroll* (1975), I was in deep shit!

Haug: You are taking this very patriarchal visual vocabulary, the female nude, and recreating it outside of that vocabulary. That is an amazing challenge for yourself. It is also a challenge to exhibit that vocabulary, because no one wants to read it. They search and search and search and there is this big . . .

Schneemann: It is much easier for this culture to read the abject. Consider the total economic neglect of my work—I keep saying this now, because I came out of the financial closet. I have still only sold two works to institutions in the United States of America in thirty years—only two works have ever been sold and one is a very small photo collage. Compare that economic history to any other contemporary artist who has been acknowledged as influencing, inspiring their culture. See if they have sold more than two things. . . .

    Well, what's the difference? Was I just a little too early? Or is it because my body of work explores a self-contained, self-defined, pleasured female-identified erotic integration? Is that what the culture can't stand? It *is* interested. It gets tremendous courage, vitality, and feeds itself off this material I provided. But it will not come back and help me. It's almost as if it's saying, "If you've got all that, go feed yourself!"

Haug: Do you think it's because your work is so personal? It's hard for me to use that word to describe it, because I feel the idea of the personal in terms of women artists, in terms of your work . . .

Schneemann: If it were only personal it wouldn't be iconic.

Let me just tell you one thing that came to mind recently. . . . The reason some of the men historians, archivists of my generation, are interested in my work now, or care about it, is because a whole generation of young women have brow beaten them and asked them over and over again: "Did you ever hear of Carolee Schneemann? Why aren't you reaching her work? Do you know anything about this work? You knew her? Oh, you were good friends? Oh, can we see her films? What do you mean 'they are not really films?' Can we see it and then let us think about that also? Oh, you think maybe they really are films? Oh, you think they're pretty marvelous. We think they are very marvelous. Can we see it again? Can we do our dissertation on it?" That's what's happened. I hear this all the time. The guys come with their tails barely waving saving, "Well, you know I really have to rethink this. My students are just nagging me about your work." They look sheepish.

Haug: To me it's like tragic comedy. What incredible patience. It's amazing to me that you were able to keep working through all this.

Schneemann: Well, that's what I mean about "you don't choose it." It's your own mania.

Notes

1   James Tenney (1934–), composer, conductor, and pianist long active in electronic and computer music.
2   Carl Ruggles (1876–1971), composer and painter, author of the influential article "American Composers on American Music." Edgar Varèse (1883–1965), French-born composer, known for electronic music and forging complex theories regarding music, noise, and acoustics. Henry Cowell (1887–1965), American composer, noted for using tone clusters and layering diverse musical influences.
3   Laura Mulvey, "Visual Pleasure and Narrative Cinema," in *The Sexual Subject: A Screen Reader in Sexuality* (London: Routledge, 1992).
4   Robert Kelly (b. 1935), American author; Paul Blackburn (d. 1971), American poet; Clayton Eshleman (b. 1935), American poet and editor of the journal SULFUR; Jerome Rothenberg (b. 1931), American poet, editor, and teacher; David Antin, performance poet/artist.
5   Malcolm Goldstein, composer specializing in innovative violin music; Philip Corner, composer, performer, who founded with Tenney the "Tone Bombs" concert series in the 1960s.

The Flower Thief

9

The "film poem," Warhol's early films, and the beat writers

REVA WOLF

Ron Rice's The Flower Thief (1960) was one of a cluster of experimental films to which Jonas Mekas—a poet as well as filmmaker, critic, and spokesperson for independent film—applied the label "film poem." The term was central to the conceptualization of film that Mekas developed in his writings, from his establishment of the journal Film Culture in 1955 through the mid-1960s.[1] For Mekas, the experimental filmmaker was a "poet" with all the connotations the word implied during this period: bohemian outsider, lyrical, anti-establishment, vital, truthful, free.[2]

Mekas used the term "film poet" because "poet" most fully signified a series of values that "filmmaker," "artist," "playwright," or other such career-defining terms did not. His application of the term fit into an artistic context in which poets regularly collaborated with visual artists, wrote plays, performed, and published magazines, and in the process became the central figures in avant-garde artmaking activities in all media, including film.[3]

The star of The Flower Thief, for example, was the poet Taylor Mead, and several of the central characters in another film that Mekas referred to as a "film poem," Pull My Daisy (1959), were poets, too—Gregory Corso, Allen Ginsberg, and Peter Orlovsky. Pull My Daisy, a 28 minute black-and-white film with narration by Jack Kerouac, was loosely based on the third part of Kerouac's unproduced play The Beat Generation[4] and was a whimsical portrayal of an ordinary day in the lives of a group of beat writers and their friends. The Flower Thief was inspired by this film,[5] and its documentation of the wanderings of Taylor Mead through cityscapes and landscapes of San Francisco evoked the spontaneous and adventuresome travels found in beat writings, especially in Kerouac's famous novel, On the Road, published in 1957.

It was against the backdrop of movies such as Pull My Daisy and The Flower Thief, and of Mekas's critical evaluations of them as "film poems," that Warhol began making films in the summer of 1963. In fact, Mekas's characterizations of the "film poem" have so much in common with Warhol's early films that it is as if Warhol employed them as a kind of blueprint for filmmaking.[6] For example, Warhol's use of his friends as actors and his practice of recording them engaged in activities that were part of their actual lives, in movies such as Sleep and the different versions of Haircut, correspond to the following assessment by Mekas, published in 1962, of The Flower Thief, Pull My Daisy, and a few other films:

Didn't Rimbaud write his *Illuminations* out of the burning, intensified reality of his own life? Such are the lives of the modern film poets. . . . In a sense, they don't have to "invent"; they just have to turn the camera upon themselves and their close friends, and it explodes into the pyrotechnics upon which no imagination could improve.[7]

In an earlier essay, of 1960, Mekas advocated inexpensive and technically simple filmmaking—the kind that Warhol later practiced—and used the production of poetry as an analogy to it: "Films will soon be made as easily as written poems, and almost as cheaply."[8]

This particular association of poetry with film has its source in the history of critical writing about experimental film—a history of which Mekas and Warhol were well aware. An important figure in this history was the poet and critic Parker Tyler, who years earlier had worked with Warhol's friend Charles Henri Ford on, among other things, *View* magazine. In 1958, Mekas published an essay by Tyler in *Film Culture*, in which Tyler called experimental film "Avant-garde or Poetic" and noted that when filmmakers worked without the apparatus of Hollywood and on small budgets, they were allowed "to do imaginative work that used the camera the way a poet uses his pen: as an instrument of invention."[9]

In another piece published in *Film Culture*, "Poetry and the Film: A Symposium," Tyler provided a synopsis of the history of film as poetry, tracing its origins to European films such as Jean Cocteau's *Blood of a Poet* (1930) and its evolution in American surrealist films of the late 1940s and early 1950s.[10] The symposium at which Tyler presented this synopsis was held in 1953 at Cinema 16 in New York, which was the first center for the screening of experimental film in the United States and a tremendous influence on Mekas's career.[11] The symposium was moderated by Willard Maas, who, like Tyler, was a strong advocate of the idea of film as poetry, while other panelists were adamantly against it.[12]

Mekas gave this 1953 debate new life by publishing the symposium proceedings in *Film Culture* ten years later, just when Warhol acquired his first camera. (In fact, Warhol possessed two copies of this particular issue of *Film Culture*.)[13] Warhol associated himself with this branch of experimental film by, for example, making a screen test of Maas as well as a movie of him and Marie Menken in their Brooklyn Heights apartment (though he was unsatisfied with this movie and therefore did not release it).[14] Typically, Warhol became part of a historical continuum—in this instance, of experimental film—by literally involving himself with its members through his artmaking process.

In one important way, however, Mekas and Warhol broke from this historical continuum: they rejected the mythological symbolism, extensive editing, and trick camera devices found in European surrealist films such as those of Cocteau, and their American inheritors, including films by Maas and even Jack Smith. The influence of Smith on Warhol has been often and correctly noted but has been overstated.[15] In fact, Mekas's analogy of film to poetry is perhaps most significant for Warhol's work in film because it concerns realism, which had no place in earlier conceptualizations of the "film poem." Mekas noted, writing in 1962, that only at present could filmmakers express social and personal truths "as freely as the poet with his typewriter."[16]

Indeed, the virtue that Mekas saw in seeking truth at any cost in his formulations of the "film poem" was precisely what drew him to Warhol's work in film. In his 1964 essay "On Cinéma Vérité, Ricky Leacock, and Warhol," Mekas extolled Warhol's work for the ways in which it embodied ideas he had already articulated in his discussions of film poetry:

It is the work of Andy Warhol . . . that is the last word in the Direct Cinema. It is hard to imagine anything more pure, less staged, and less directed than Andy Warhol's *Eat, Empire, Sleep, Haircut* movies. I think that Andy Warhol is the most revolutionary of all filmmakers working today. He is opening to filmmakers a completely new and inexhaustible field of cinema reality.[17]

Mekas had similar things to say about Warhol's *Chelsea Girls* (1966): "And one of the amazing things about this film is that the people in it are not really actors, or if they are acting, their acting becomes unimportant, it becomes part of their personalities, and there they are, totally real, with their transformed, intensified selves."[18] Here Mekas repeats, with only slightly different wording, his earlier description of the "burning, intensified reality" of the film poet's work.

Mekas's conceptualization of realism on film derives largely from beat ideas rather than from the European "film poem" tradition.[19] As we have seen, he valued *Pull My Daisy* for its sense of truthfulness. In its success in capturing life on the screen, this movie, according to Mekas, has the same feelings of "reality and immediacy" that are found in the first films made by Lumière.[20] Soon, Mekas would make exactly the same point about Warhol's films: "Andy Warhol is taking cinema back to its origins, to the days of Lumière. . . . [H]e records, almost obsessively, man's daily activities, the things he sees around him."[21]

The beat glorification of everyday reality had a strong impact on Mekas, and, likewise, had a direct, deep, and lasting impact on Warhol's development in film as well as other media.[22] Warhol's fascination with the beats was one facet of his attraction to poets, to poetry, and to all that the two represented in the United States of the 1960s. A consideration of the links between some of his early movies and the two beat films *The Flower Thief* and *Pull My Daisy* in the discussion that follows will serve as a springboard for assessing the broader significance of his interest in the beats.

Warhol met Taylor Mead just as the former was launching his career as a filmmaker. Warhol had by then seen *The Flower Thief*, which was extremely successful in the world of experimental film and in 1962 broke the attendance records when it was screened at the Charles Theater on East Twelfth Street and Avenue B, where Warhol regularly attended the film programs put together by Mekas.[23]

Warhol had also by this time acquired some of Mead's poetry (which, when they met, Warhol asked him to autograph).[24] Charles Henri Ford remembered that Warhol "was buying the poems of Taylor Mead. . . . [H]e just sort of put his finger on Taylor Mead at that time, when I hadn't even read him."[25] Mead's privately published *Excerpts from the Anonymous Diary of a New York Youth* (1961, 1962) contained much that would have appealed to Warhol: a brazen frankness about the author's homosexuality, an adoration of movie stars and other celebrities, humor, straightforward language, and an all-around outrageousness. In this book, Mead identified himself with the beats and made references to writers Lawrence Ferlinghetti, Ginsberg, Kerouac, and Orlovsky, and to "beatniks." Thus, when Warhol formed his initial involvement with Mead, he possessed a clear knowledge of Mead's image as a beat poet and a film star.

Mead accompanied Warhol, Malanga, and the artist Wynn Chamberlain to Los Angeles in the late summer of 1963 to attend the opening of Warhol's Liz and Elvis exhibit. The trip was a significant moment in Warhol's absorption of beat ideas. This absorption is especially

10. Six frames from *The Flower Thief* (1960). Courtesy Anthology Film Archives; reprinted by permission.

evident in the film he made in Los Angeles, starring Mead, and in the fact that the trip across country was made by car as a conscious "on the road" experience.

In the movie Warhol filmed while in Los Angeles, *Tarzan and Jane Regained . . . Sort of*, Mead plays Tarzan and Naomi Levine plays Jane (she also appeared in, among other experimental films, several of Warhol's *Kiss* movies of 1963–1964).[26] *Tarzan and Jane Regained* is unlike most of Warhol's early films in that the camera is not stationary, the film stock is in both black-and-white and color, and there is a soundtrack (which Mead recorded after the film was shot).

Mead's role as Tarzan is similar to his role in *The Flower Thief*: he clowns his way through jungle gyms, streets, the Watts Tower, and bodies of water, makes funny expressions in front of the camera, and dances while his swimming trunks are falling off. In the second half of the film, he acts as if he is rescuing a drowning doll, and the toy recalls the teddy bear he plays with in *The Flower Thief*.

Tarzan and Jane Regained . . . Sort of contains verbal and thematic links to Mead's poetry. The words "sort of" in the movie's title appear in *Excerpts from the Anonymous Diary*, in such passages as "what I think I wrote in/Ms. sort of" and "be free and easy / and open sort of."[27] Mead even mentioned Tarzan in his book, describing how in New York he went into a "subterranean toilet with one of the movies' Tarzans"; the Tarzan had a "big peter" and Mead, a "small one."[28] This passage has a parallel in Warhol's film, in a scene in which Dennis Hopper flexes his arm muscle, which is fairly large, and then Mead flexes his small one. (The inappropriateness of Mead's diminutive physique for the role of Tarzan contributes to the comedy.)[29]

Tarzan and Jane Regained opens with a view of the highway, along which the camera moves until it reaches the sign "Tarzana Rezeda next exit." Mead proposed that he play the role of Tarzan when he saw this sign.[30] Signs are a recurring motif in the movie. We see signs for Coca-Cola and other products at a race track, and a root beer sign at a little fast-food restaurant. The signs in the film parallel the subject matter of Warhol's paintings of Coca-Cola bottles, soup cans, and the like. As Warhol later explained about the 1963 trip to Los Angeles, "The farther west we drove, the more Pop everything looked on the highways. Suddenly we all felt like insiders because even though Pop was everywhere—that was the thing about it, most people still took it for granted, whereas we were dazzled by it—to us, it was the new Art. Once you 'got' Pop, you could never see a sign the same way again."[31]

But signs were not only "pop," they were also "beat," just as the act of driving across the country became, with the publication of *On the Road* (which was so popular that the paperback Viking Compass edition of 1959 was reprinted each year until 1963 and in several subsequent years),[32] the quintessential beat statement. Indeed, in a 1960 review of an exhibition at the Museum of Modern Art, the *New Yorker* art critic Robert M. Coates saw "traces of the Beat philosophy" in the use of commonplace objects by artists such as Robert Rauschenberg, who was a key model for Warhol in the area of visual art.[33] In *On the Road*, the narrator, Sal Paradise, sees the sign "USE COOPER'S PAINT" as he looks out the car window, and he spots a Coca-Cola stand in the Nevada desert.[34]

The opening scene of *Tarzan and Jane Regained . . . Sort of* on a Los Angeles road embodies the celebration of beat life that was behind Warhol's choice to go to Los Angeles by car rather than plane.[35] Warhol conceived of the trip as an event, not simply a means of getting from one place to another; "It was a beautiful time to be driving across America," he later wrote.[36] The presence of Mead made the trip an authentic beat experience, since he was a veteran cross-country traveler. As Warhol reminisced:

> When Taylor left his stockbroker job in Detroit, he had just fifty dollars in his pocket. "Kerouac's *On the Road* put me on the road," he said, "and Allen's *Howl*, which had just come out, had a big effect on me."
> Taylor was in San Francisco in '56 when the beat poetry scene got going. . . . He'd hitched cross-country five times by then.[37]

Taylor Mead, then, represented for Warhol a direct link to the beat life.

On the California trip, Mead gave a poetry reading at Venice Beach.[38] He claims that shortly before the reading was to begin, Warhol decided to be "cruel" and "tried to make me blow him."[39] What is interesting about this story is that Warhol's reported out-of-line behavior is altogether *in* line with the content of Mead's poetry. The opening of *Excerpts from the Anonymous Diary* reads, "I have blown / And been blown" (lines which consciously echo a segment of

Ginsberg's poem "Howl"), an activity that is mentioned throughout the book, as in the passage "Give me your poor, your tired—and let me blow them."[40] Warhol's sensibility did lead him to at times be extremely literal, especially when he wanted to provoke a person or an audience, and so if Mead's story is true, the request was likely Warhol's response to the content of Mead's writing. Put differently, Warhol was giving Mead the opportunity to live out his poetry.

Moreover, the "blow-job" enthusiast image that Mead painted of himself in *Excerpts from the Anonymous Diary* had by this time entered into the dialogues of the mimeograph publications. Ed Sanders, who had become friends with Mead and Ron Rice by 1962, described Mead in an author's biography in the August 1962 issue of his magazine *Fuck You* as the star of *The Flower Thief*, a poet, and a thinker, and then made reference to Mead's talent at that particular sexual act.[41] In another issue of the same year, Sanders again mentioned Mead in association with "blow jobs," in an advertisement.[42]

Just as Warhol's interest in Mead as an actor and poet led him to involve himself with Mead directly through the making of *Tarzan and Jane Regained* (and several subsequent films),[43] so his interest in more famous beat writers—Corso, Ginsberg, Kerouac, Orlovsky—led him to capture them on film. And, as he had done with Mead in the Tarzan and Jane movie, he placed these writers within a setting that deliberately recalled that of their prior film performances in the movie *Pull My Daisy*.

Warhol was familiar with *Pull My Daisy*, as he had been with *The Flower Thief*. He had even attended a special screening of the movie, the purpose of which was to dub it in French, with his friend, the filmmaker Emile de Antonio (who had been instrumental in distributing it in New York).[44] Jack Kerouac and the photographer Robert Frank, who did the cinematography for *Pull My Daisy*, were both at this screening.[45] The content of the movie was also easily accessible through an abundantly illustrated book about it that was published in 1961 and included the script of Kerouac's narration.[46]

Pull My Daisy is set in the loft studio of the painter Alfred Leslie, who, with Frank, was its director and editor. In the movie, Leslie's couch is a central locus of activity. At distinct moments, different groupings of people sit on this couch—for example, Ginsberg, Corso, and Orlovsky (who play themselves), or the bishop's mother (played by the painter Alice Neel), Ginsberg, and the bishop's sister (played by Sally Gross).

When Warhol included Corso, Ginsberg, Kerouac, and Orlovsky in *Couch* (1964), it was partly as an homage to *Pull My Daisy*. *Couch* consists of thirteen scenes, each the length of a 100-foot reel of film, of people doing various things on and around a couch at the Factory.[47] Warhol filmed several reels of the four beat writers all in one day, as a tape recording made during the visit reveals,[48] and then put only one of the reels in the movie, as the fifth scene.[49]

This scene was shot so that the couch is viewed from the side. Corso sits on it with a book in his hands as if to indicate his literary vocation. Someone else—it is often difficult to make out who is who due to the filming angle—is seated on the floor drinking beer from a can and then stands up and moves out of view. Another person, probably Kerouac, enters the frame and sits on the floor. Ginsberg soon enters the scene and sits beside him, in the foreground. We see him from the back, and the bobbing movements of his head suggest that he is chatting. The couch, beer can, book, and general animation of this scene all evoke the ambience of passages of *Pull My Daisy* such as the first few minutes, in which Kerouac's narration reads: "Gregory Corso and Allen Ginsberg there, laying their beer cans out on the table . . . falling on the couch, all bursting with poetry. . . ."[50]

To grasp the nature of Warhol's allusions to *Pull My Daisy* we must look at its position within his movie overall. *Couch* is extremely rich, even brilliant, in its meshing of references to the social world revolving around Warhol and to the history of film. The various sexual encounters that take place on the couch—which in some instances are either parodied or frustrated—bring to mind, as others have pointed out, the role of this piece of furniture in any number of Hollywood movies and in psychoanalysis.[51]

While *Couch* is thereby a recognition of establishment film, it at the same time encodes several key moments in the recent history of experimental film. A conspicuous reference to this other side of film history is embedded in the two reels of *Couch* just prior to the scene with Corso, Ginsberg, Kerouac, and Orlovsky. Here, we see Billy Name donning sunglasses while fidgeting with a motorcycle in imitation of the protagonist of Kenneth Anger's fascinating movie about a motorcycle gang, *Scorpio Rising* (1963).[52] Understood in this broader context, Warhol's evocations of *Pull My Daisy* become part of a kind of capsule history of film contained within *Couch*.

Warhol's inclusion of *Pull My Daisy* in this metahistory was his way of acknowledging its importance to his own work as a filmmaker. Like Warhol's early films, *Pull My Daisy* seemed spontaneous, even though it wasn't entirely (for this apparent quality, Mekas bestowed upon them all the label "realism").[53] It was filmed, as were many of Warhol's movies, in the studio of a painter who had branched out into filmmaking, and it was made by a group of friends and was about their lives. Jerry Tallmer observed in his introduction to the book *Pull My Daisy* that one reason he liked this film was because "it shows me people I know doing the things they do."[54] The film contained nuances of meaning, Tallmer intimated, that would not be fully comprehended by viewers who did not know the people in question.[55] It contained, that is, the kinds of "in-the-know" sub-stories that we have seen in such Warhol movies as *Haircut* or *Bufferin*.

The audio tape made during the production of the Corso, Ginsberg, Kerouac, and Orlovsky segment of *Couch* provides revealing glimpses of Warhol's endeavor to film these writers so as to provide a conceptual link to *Pull My Daisy*, and it also reveals that the dynamic that evolved between them in the filming process had a strong impact on the movie's final form. First of all, Kerouac, who could be quite difficult to work with—he had been banned from the set of *Pull My Daisy* after a fight with Alfred Leslie, and he had developed a tendency to behave outrageously[56]—was bent on taking over the role of director from Warhol. Meanwhile Warhol, although he exhibited some flexibility concerning the configuration of the set, kept grasping for control over his own movie in what seemed like a tug-of-war with Kerouac.

Three passages of the audio tape offer a vivid illustration of the way this tug-of-war played itself out:

Kerouac: What's the pro-ce-dure?

Warhol: Well, the movie's called *Couch*.

Kerouac: The movie's called *Couch*.

Warhol: Yeah. So it has to be on the couch.

Kerouac: It has to be on the couch. So nothing off the couch. Can't there be something off the couch?

Warhol: Yeah.

(An unidentified voice, possibly of Gerard Malanga, says that they can sit on the floor next to the couch, and Kerouac then says to one of his co-actors, "then you gotta get up.")

Warhol: Let's do the four of you just kind of getting up and off on the couch. It'd be very nice.

Kerouac: Getting on and getting off, and getting on and getting off, and getting on and getting off. The four of us, yeah. I think that'd be pretty mad. But there, it's gotta, sort of like, faster, faster, faster, faster. Now, are you game?[57]

(Warhol later asks if four of them would "just lie on the couch," and Kerouac says that he has to "take a piss" first;[58] when he returns from the bathroom he reports that it has two toilet bowls, which gives him the idea of using the superfluous one as a prop.)

Kerouac: Allen, bring the yellow john out. Allen, bring it out and sit on it. . . .

Warhol: No, no. It's a couch. This one's just going to be the couch. You're all getting up and off.

11. Gerard Malanga and Andy Warhol in the early 1960s. Courtesy Anthology Film Archives; reprinted by permission.

The first of these three interactions explains why Kerouac and Ginsberg are seated on the floor in Warhol's movie. In the second, as in the first, Kerouac takes Warhol's instructions and provocatively elaborates on them. It is intriguing to consider the ways in which Kerouac's idea that he and his coactors repeatedly and with increasing haste get on and off the couch relates at once to Warhol's art and to Kerouac's own interests.

The repetition is consonant with Warhol's painting method, while the speed is like that of comic actors in early silent films, and, of course, Couch was a silent film (although, ironically enough, since Warhol filmed his movies at sound speed, 24 fps, but screened them at silent speed, 16 fps, the resultant slowing of the action tends to imbue it with a sexily languid feeling that the speedy movements recommended by Kerouac would all but eliminate). Indeed, soon after Kerouac ordered his friends to ever more quickly get on and off the couch, he said to one of them (it is unclear to whom), "Now you look like Buster Keaton," and then laughed. All this reflected Kerouac's admiration for certain comedians of the early silent and talking films, whom he often mentioned in his fiction and in interviews.[59]

The exchange between Kerouac and Warhol concerning the toilet is perhaps the most revelatory regarding Warhol's filmmaking procedures. It demonstrates concretely how very mistaken is the commonly held assumption that Warhol's role as a director consisted of simply turning on the camera and walking away (even though he may have on occasion done just that).[60] This exchange, in which Kerouac endeavored to virtually be the director, shows that, on the contrary, Warhol was extremely engaged in the production of his films. Some input from the actors was acceptable (and often desirable), such as Kerouac's suggestion that they sit off rather than on the couch, but the basic scenario and visual composition were Warhol's, and he was capable of being insistent if someone—in this case, Kerouac—tried to change them.

The sense of general chaos that one gets from listening to the audio tape may well provide an explanation of why Warhol decided to film the beat sequence of Couch from the side of the couch in such a way as to obscure identities and actions. This peculiarity of the scene is often pointed out as a kind of perversity on Warhol's part.[61] Taylor Mead was not pleased with Warhol's cinematography on this occasion,[62] yet he later intuited that there was a reason for it: "[H]e wouldn't turn the camera around; he has his own ideas, and nothing would interrupt them. . . . He had a great integrity in a very funny way."[63]

It is quite possible—and certainly understandable—that Warhol refused to turn the camera around out of sheer exasperation with Kerouac's aggressive behavior, as a way to at once stay in control of his own film and get back at Kerouac for being uncooperative. (And it should also be kept in mind that in the distinct reels of film that make up Couch, the vantage point ranges from frontal to sharply angled, so that the side view is one in a sort of repertoire of viewpoints.)

In the years after the Couch filming, Ginsberg was the one figure in the group who remained in friendly contact with Warhol, probably in part through Ginsberg's associations with Malanga, Mekas, and the filmmaker Barbara Rubin. Ginsberg sat for a screen test, which was incorporated into the film Fifty Fantastics and Fifty Personalities (1964–1966) as well as into the book Screen Tests / A Diary, he stopped by the Factory occasionally, and he sang "Hare Krishna" on stage at a Velvet Underground performance in 1966.[64]

Ginsberg was drawn to Warhol's art because he could see in it an analogue to his own concerns. He once remarked,

I was interested in the Zen aspect of the taking of an object of ordinary consciousness or ordinary mind or ordinary use and enlarging it and focusing attention on it so that it became a sacred object or a totemic object, mythological. And that seemed very much parallel to the notion of a kind of attentiveness you get in Zen or Buddhist meditative attitude.[65]

It is worth noting here that already in 1964 Jonas Mekas had articulated the same connection between the ideas of the beat writers and Warhol's work in film. Mekas, referring to the "subtle play of nuances" in the films, wrote,

There is something religious about this. It is part of that "beat mentality" which Cardinal Spellman attacked this week. There is something very humble and happy about a man (or a movie) who is content with eating an apple. It is a cinema that reveals the emergence of meditation and happiness in man. Eat your apple, enjoy your apple, it says. Where are you running? Away from yourself? To what excitement? If all people could sit and watch the Empire State Building for eight hours and meditate upon it, there would be no more wars, no hate, no terror—there would be happiness regained upon earth.[66]

For his part, Warhol kept up with Ginsberg's activities and in 1966 accompanied Gerard Malanga to a reading by Ginsberg at Town Hall theater in New York.[67] Two decades later, he included Ginsberg in a literary "Portrait Gallery" published in Paris Review. Here, Warhol expressed his strong admiration for Ginsberg: "I love Allen's things. . . . He's such a great poet."[68]

This opinion evidently inspired a never-realized film project that had a direct connection to Ginsberg's poetry. In 1969, the New York Times reported that Warhol was planning to make a film in which Ginsberg would play the part of Walt Whitman.[69] The casting was extremely apt, since, aside from the fact that both poets had beards, Whitman was, for Ginsberg, a liberating spirit in terms of poetic language as well as sexuality.[70] Ginsberg himself often acknowledged this progeny, the most famous expression of which is his poem "A Supermarket in California" (1955). In this poem the speaker thinks about Whitman as he strolls down the streets and then has a vision of his nineteenth-century mentor in the supermarket: "I saw you, Walt Whitman, childless, lonely old grubber, / poking among the meats in the refrigerator and eyeing the grocery / boys."[71]

Warhol's film was to be set during the Civil War, with Whitman caring for wounded young soldiers. Whitman had in fact been a nurse during the war and wrote about the experience in a book of poetry, Drum-Taps (1865) (which in 1868 he added to Leaves of Grass), and in the prose notes Memoranda During the War (1875) (included in 1882 in the book Specimen Days).[72] In both these works, especially the latter, Whitman described the young age of many of the soldiers for whom he cared, and his affection for them.[73] (Whitman nursed soldiers on both sides of the conflict, a fact that resonated with the anti-Vietnam War protests of Ginsberg, which were at a high point in 1969 when the Warhol film idea was being considered.)

Apparently, Ginsberg's own attraction to handsome boys, which is embedded in his envisionment of Whitman's comportment at the supermarket, led him to seriously consider playing the role, when, in 1971, Warhol's film collaborator Paul Morrissey began to actively pursue the realization of the Whitman movie.[74] However, in the end, according to one account, the film studios (with which Warhol and Morrissey were by this time working in an endeavor to now produce commercial films) were unwilling to support such a venture,[75] while Ginsberg has stated that he decided not to play the role because he was busy and "I wasn't quite sure what they were going to do with Whitman. I didn't feel like making fun of Whitman."[76]

The idea of casting Ginsberg as Whitman exemplifies Warhol's penchant for seeing the relationships between and then weaving together into a tight fabric the artistic (Ginsberg's debt to Whitman's writings) and the personal (Ginsberg's interest in boys and political activities as echoing aspects of Whitman's biography). Ginsberg himself did not draw lines between the artistic and personal, and he shared this approach to creativity with other beat writers, especially Jack Kerouac.

Nowhere are the artistic and personal more intertwined in Kerouac's writings than in his novel *Visions of Cody*, which seems to have been a model for Warhol when, in the mid-1960s, he decided to write—or more accurately, to produce—his own novel. Warhol's *a: a novel*, published in 1968, was made up of audio tapes that he had recorded of Ondine in 1965. His idea was to record twenty-four hours of Ondine's life, but such a marathon proved to be an impossible feat and recordings had to be made on a few separate days.[77] Kerouac had introduced tape-recorded dialogue into fiction in *Visions of Cody*, of which the third part, "Frisco: The Tape," comprises his transcriptions of taped conversations primarily between Kerouac (who here goes by the name of Jack Duluoz) and Neal Cassady (who goes by Cody Pomeray). *Visions of Cody* has so much in common with *a: a novel*, ranging from its premise and structure to details of content, that it appears to have been the key literary model for Warhol's book.

Although Kerouac's novel was published in full only posthumously, in 1972, segments of it did appear during the late 1950s and early 1960s, the most extensive of which was a 120-page excerpt put out by New Directions in late 1959.[78] Since Warhol designed a number of jacket covers for New Directions from the early 1950s to around 1961, it is likely that he was familiar with this volume.[79] The New Directions limited edition excerpt was released just as Kerouac was reaching the peak of his publishing career, and it began to sell out by spring 1960.[80] Its rarity contributed to a curiosity about the volume as news of it spread by word of mouth and through its circulation among friends (for example, Padgett had given Berrigan a copy).[81]

When Warhol acquired his first tape recorder, probably in 1964,[82] an interest in using audio tapes for artistic purposes was stirring, in large part due to an awareness of Kerouac's experiments with them. William Burroughs, for instance, created several "cut-up" recordings during the 1960s,[83] and Jonas Mekas was by 1964 making taped diaries that were a counterpart to his "film diaries."[84] But only Kerouac used actual transcriptions of taped conversations with a friend as part of a novel.

Kerouac's undisguised deployment of his own life, and the lives of his friends—in all the disorderliness and minutiae of the everyday that is life—as the content of *Visions of Cody* corresponded to Warhol's conception of art, as John Tytell has aptly pointed out in his analysis of Kerouac's book.[85] The idea of creating characters was entirely alien to Warhol. The following anecdote told by Stephen Koch amusingly illustrates the fiber of Warhol's aesthetic:

> I once mentioned to Warhol that I was writing a novel, and he looked at me doubtfully, with his peculiar worried look. "But you need an awful lot of people for that, don't you?" I answered that I didn't really need a very large crowd. "Oh . . . oh . . . uh, you mean you just make people *up*?" A nervous incredulity spread over his face. I was speaking of a literally unimaginable artistic process.[86]

For Kerouac, as for Warhol, drug consumption was an important element in the actual process of making the tapes and in their content. Kerouac explained in the author's note preceding *Visions* that "The tape recordings in here are actual transcriptions I made of conversations with Cody who was so high he forgot the machine was turning."[87] The drug that Cody and Jack had taken (in addition to alcohol and marijuana) was Benzedrine (a form of amphetamine), as we learn in the tape section of the novel.[88] Likewise, Ondine's words in *a: a novel* were fueled by amphetamine, and the drug also became a topic of discussion in Warhol's novel.[89] Amphetamine seemed to produce an openness and a loquaciousness that were well suited to an art form based on conversation.[90]

In its overall structure, too, *a: a novel* has striking counterparts in *Visions of Cody*. In both, the end of the transcribed tapes (which in *a* is also the end of the novel) includes dialogue taken from the radio. Each draws on many of the same literary sources and most conspicuously on James Joyce's *Ulysses*: the second to last chapter of *a* is entitled "OND INE SO LILIQUY [*sic*]"; the second to last section of "Imitation of the Tape" in *Visions*—the chapter after "Frisco: The Tape"—contains a monologue that consciously emulates that found in *Ulysses*.[91] In both novels, furthermore, some of the same kinds of outside elements—notably telephone conversations and music—get recorded and transcribed as they affect, overtake, or interrupt the conversation.[92]

Woven into the dialogue in each novel are nonsensical word plays, or what in beat terminology was called "goofing."[93] Following are passages from *Visions* and *a*, respectively, that contain such word plays. Each passage ends with what seems to be a commentary on the senselessness of what is being said:

Cody: And merriment! No I said melliment, mellimist—
Pat: —I thought you said merriness—
Cody: . . . sepurious . . .
Pat: What, su*per*fluous
Cody: Superflous, that's it . . . wine has become superflous
Pat: Superious
Cody: Sup*eer*ious, that's the word
Everybody: What word?
Cody: Spoorious . . . spurious[94]

O—What would you, what symbol
     would you give a schlitz-
     monger?
Uh, sch . . .
T—Think of what it is. It's a spit,
     shit and split. (*Laugh*.)
     A monger is somebody who sells.
Sell, yeah.
T—Somebody who sells but like it's
     saying
     Schlitzmonger is like saying
     crap (*simultaneous conversation*:
     I—Did Drella do that? O—

No, I did them myself. You
know I'm very, I got lessons
from Allen Ginsberg y'know.
T— Bu it's saying it with spit, shit,
and split which is also divided in,
in, well it's uh ridiculous but.[95]

In both *Visions* and *a*, the consumption of drugs that was meant to produce uninhibited dialogue to fill up the tapes did not entirely work. On several occasions, the speakers became self-conscious about being recorded. Jack, for example, at one point in the conversation felt overwhelmed by the challenge of filling up an entire tape:

Jack: Wow, are you high now?
Cody: Yeah, I feel it
Jack: We got another big . . . long . . . sonofabitch to go!
Cody: Yeah . . . yeah . . . well not really
Jack: W-whole big reel—ass!
Cody: Yeah but that's nothing compared to all the things we can talk about, or say
Jack: Oh I'll—that can be solved easily
Cody: How?
Jack: Wal, by stopping it now (REEL ENDS)

(MACHINE BEGINS)

Cody: *(from a month-old tape)* [. . .][96]

And Ondine periodically insisted that Warhol turn off the tape recorder for a while: "let's relax 'cause we'll go crazy"; "Please shut it off, I'm so horrifying."[97] Thus, in each case the very act of recording conversation on tape affected the content of the conversation and thereby raised questions about all existing distinctions between authentic behavior and artifice.[98]

In addition, the taped dialogue was inevitably changed when it was transcribed for publication, due to the inflections produced in the process of turning sounds into written words. Such details as the parenthetical commentaries and the layout of the text on the page metamorphosed the dialogue. In the case of *Visions of Cody*, Kerouac made the transcriptions, but in the case of *a*, several people made them, and their typographical and other errors became part of the novel.[99] In this way, Warhol expanded on Kerouac's idea of using a tape recording as part of a novel, which he took to its logical conclusion by making an entire novel, as opposed to only one chapter, based on audio tapes.

Kerouac was unsuccessful in getting *Visions of Cody* published during his lifetime because parts of it were considered "obscene," and because of its radical format, particularly that of the tape transcriptions. Even his friends criticized the use of these transcriptions in the novel.[100] When Warhol adapted the same format for an entire novel, he created a sure formula for the negative criticism that his novel almost unanimously received.[101] (Warhol later said that he had wanted to write a "bad" novel, because doing something the wrong way always opens doors).[102]

The negative criticisms of the writings of the beats, like those of Warhol's work, were abundant and became part of the authors' cultural identities—that is, part of how the press presented them, and conversely, how they interacted with the press. A consideration of these cultural identities shows us that in addition to the connections between the beat writers and Warhol that are evident in specific works, such as *Couch*, the unrealized Walt Whitman film project, and *a: a novel*, there are connections of a general nature concerning public image. The most prominent of these connections are in 1) particulars of the artists' relationships with the mass media; and 2) a celebration of the commonplace that led numerous critics to deem the work "boring."

The beat writers—above all, Kerouac—received an enormous amount of attention, mostly negative, in the mass media during the late 1950s and early 1960s.[103] The fame, not to mention wealth, that these self-styled outcasts acquired was undoubtedly a model for Warhol in his unabashed quest for fame, which, as was true of the beats, came in the form of notoriety.[104] Several articles in the press attacked the fame of the beat movement. Somehow the critics failed to recognize that, by attacking this fame in high-circulation periodicals, they only fostered what they were attacking (and it is this kind of hypocrisy that Warhol in numerous ways brought to light in his work). A good example of such hypocritical reporting is found in a lengthy article that appeared in *Life* magazine in 1959, entitled "The Only Rebellion Around" and written by Paul O'Neil. O'Neil here stated,

> [The Beat Generation] is seldom out of the news for long. . . . Awareness of the Beat message is almost a social necessity today, and the name-dropper who cannot mention Beat Novelist Jack Kerouac (*On the Road*, *The Dharma Bums*), Allen Ginsberg (the Shelley of the Beat poets whose *Howl and Other Poems* has sold 33,000 copies) or Lawrence Lipton (author of last summer's best-seller, *The Holy Barbarians*) is no name-dropper at all. . . . [M]ost Americans . . . experience a morbid curiosity about them. All sorts of entrepreneurs have rushed in to capitalize on this fact.[105]

O'Neil's unflattering essay reached an especially wide audience because in addition to appearing in *Life*, it was disseminated through its inclusion in the paperback compendium *A Casebook on the Beat*, the first anthology of writings by and about the beats. Like *Life*, the *Casebook* targeted a broad audience. It contained a variety of opinions, positive and negative. An especially harsh negative vision of the beats was "The Know-Nothing Bohemians" by the extremely conservative Norman Podhoretz, who called attention to the media fascination with Kerouac especially: "[S]oon his photogenic countenance (unshaven, of course, and topped by an unruly crop of rich black hair falling over his forehead) was showing up in various mass-circulation magazines, he was being interviewed earnestly on television, and he was being featured in a Greenwich Village nightclub."[106]

Such reporting about reporting became, a few years later, standard fare in articles about Warhol. For instance, John Leonard, who had the ability to be more self-reflective than O'Neil or Podhoretz, explained in a *New York Times* article of 1968, "Warhol, a child of the media, is unfailingly courteous to their janissaries. Every impertinence, every ghoulish probe, is patiently endured, for he needs us as much as we need him."[107]

Shortly prior to the emergence of Warhol's symbiotic relationship with the media, strategies of self-promotion had been developing within the beat movement itself. The most conspicuous of these was the photographer Fred W. McDarrah's Rent-a-Beatnik business, which he started in 1960 and advertised in the *Village Voice*. McDarrah rented out his beatnik poet friends for parties, at which they would read their work and provide the desired "hip" atmosphere.[108] Such marketing from within a bohemian movement helped to pave the way for Warhol's self-promotion activities.[109]

The second way in which the public image of the beat writers was later echoed by Warhol concerns a glorification of the commonplace, and a resulting implied lack of discrimination between good and bad, right and wrong, high and low.[110] One of Jack Kerouac's most quoted statements, a reply to the question of what it meant to be beat, was that "We love everything. Billy Graham, the Big Ten, rock and roll, Zen, apple pie, Eisenhower—we dig it all."[111] Around five years later, when Warhol was asked by Gene Swenson what pop art is, he replied, in a concise variation on Kerouac's definition of beat, "It's liking things."[112]

Kerouac had also expressed this idea in On the Road, in which Sal Paradise says of a friend, "He began to learn 'Yes!' to everything, just like Dean at this time."[113] This terminology was taken over by Mekas in his description of Warhol's early films. Mekas is quoted in a 1964 Newsweek article as characterizing Warhol's films as "a look at daily activities like sleeping or eating. It's saying Yes to life."[114]

Both Kerouac's writings and Warhol's works were, because of their focus on the commonplace, repeatedly criticized—and also on occasion praised—for producing boredom in the audience. A 1959 review of Kerouac's novel Dr. Sax called the book "boring," while Herbert Gold, in his 1958 article "The Beat Mystique," lamented the beat life itself for being rooted in boredom.[115] Sure enough, one reviewer who discussed the "boredom" of Warhol's films related it to the lifestyle of the "hipster" (a term generally interchangeable with "beat"): "[T]he eight-hour 'Sleep' or 'Empire State,' in which unsteady cameras were simply aimed at their subjects, are the masterworks of a hipster subculture that is bored with life."[116] Repeatedly, the boredom of Empire, Sleep, and other early Warhol films was attacked.[117]

Warhol responded to such criticism by simply repeating it when he was interviewed. He would tell his interviewers, for instance, that his films were boring because he liked boring things. Thus he entered into dialogues with his critics—fascinating dialogues meriting a serious analysis of their own—just as he had with poets.

Notes

1 Early on in his career as a critic, Mekas used the term "film poem" to describe experimental film in, for example, "The Experimental Film in America," in Film Culture Reader, ed. and intro. P. Adams Sitney (New York: Praeger, 1970), 21–26 (first published in Film Culture 3 [May–June 1955]). This article contained a somewhat homophobic sentiment, which Mekas soon outgrew as is often noted.

2 An excellent study of the significance of the term "film poem" during the 1950s and early 1960s is found in David E. James, Allegories of Cinema: American Film in the 1960s (Princeton: Princeton University Press, 1989), 29–32.

3 It is also worth noting here the plethora of American poetry that either made film its subject or alluded in more subtle ways to film. For a general study of this phenomenon, see Laurence Goldstein, The American Poet at the Movies: A Critical History (Ann Arbor: University of Michigan Press, 1994).

4 Jerry Tallmer, introduction, Pull My Daisy, text by Jack Kerouac, film by Robert Frank and Alfred Leslie (New York: Grove Press; London: Evergreen Books, 1961), 17.

5 On this influence, see also J. Hoberman, "The Forest and The Trees," in To Free the Cinema:

Jonas Mekas and the New York Underground, ed. David E. James (Princeton: Princeton University Press, 1992), 116.

6   The one critic who has noted the connections between the idea of the "film poem" and Warhol's early films is Stephen Koch, who observed that these films, "speaking very roughly . . . belong in the stream of nonnarrative 'poetic' avant-garde cinema. . . ." *Stargazer: The Life, World and Films of Andy Warhol*, rev. ed. (New York: Marion Boyars, 1991), 19.

7   Mekas, "Notes on the New American Cinema," *Film Culture* 24 (spring 1962), in Sitney, *Film Culture Reader*, 101.

8   Mekas, "On Film Troubadours," in Mekas, *Movie Journal: The Rise of a New American Cinema, 1959–1971* (New York: Collier Books, 1972), 20 (first published in *Village Voice*, 6 October 1960).

9   Parker Tyler, "A Preface to the Problems of the Experimental Film," *Film Culture* 17 (February 1958), in Sitney, *Film Culture Reader*, 42.

10   Tyler, in "Poetry and the Film: A Symposium," *Film Culture* 29 (summer 1963), in Sitney, *Film Culture Reader*, 172.

11   Cinema 16 was founded in 1947 by Amos and Marcia Vogel and operated until 1963. On this establishment and its influence on Mekas, see James, *To Free the Cinema*, 6–7.

12   Willard Maas, "Poetry and the Film: A Symposium," in Sitney, *Film Culture Reader*, 176, 184. The other participants in the symposium were Maya Deren, Arthur Miller, and Dylan Thomas; the latter two objected strongly to the idea of film poetry. Another filmmaker involved with the Cinema 16 group, Hans Richter, asserted that all experimental film should be called "film poetry," in "Hans Richter on the Nature of Film Poetry," *Film Culture* 11 (1957): 5–7. For an analysis of Richter's essay within the context of the concept of the "film poem," see James, *Allegories of Cinema*, 29.

13   Archives Study Center, the Andy Warhol Museum. In this same issue of *Film Culture*, Mekas published his poem "Press Release," which begins with a list of filmmakers whom he characterized as "the film poets of America today" and draws attention to the lack of receptiveness to these "poets" by the public at large, asserting that it is, nevertheless, their work that will remain; *Film Culture* 29 (summer 1963): 7–8.

14   The film of Maas and Menken, and Warhol's dissatisfaction with it, were reported in John Wilcock, "The Detached Cool of Andy Warhol," *Village Voice*, 6 May 1965, 24. Maas also appeared, along with Menken, Malanga, and Edie Sedgwick, in a film called *Bitch* (1965); on this film, see Miles McKane and Catia Riccaboni, "Filmographie," *Andy Warhol, Cinema* (Paris: Editions CARRE and Centre Georges Pompidou, 1990), 256.

15   On Jack Smith's influence on Warhol, see, for example, Vivienne Dick, "Warhol: Won't Wrinkle Ever, a Filmmaker's View," in *Andy Warhol: Film Factory*, ed. Michael O'Pray (London: British Film Institute, 1989), 154. Warhol's divergence from the use of myth and symbol found in the films of Smith is pointed out in O'Pray, "Warhol's Early Films: Realism and Psychoanalysis," in *Andy Warhol: Film Factory*, 177.

16   Mekas, "Notes on the New American Cinema," *Film Culture* 24 (spring 1962), in Sitney, *Film Culture Reader*, 102.

17   Mekas, "On Cinéma Vérité, Ricky Leacock, and Warhol," *Village Voice*, 13 August 1964, in *Movie Journal*, 154.

18   Mekas, "Andy Warhol: 'The Chelsea Girls,'" *Village Voice*, 24 November 1966, 29 (first published in "Movie Journal," *Village Voice*, 29 September 1966). On the importance of the

concept of "realism" in Mekas's criticism, see John Pruitt, "Jonas Mekas: A European Critic in America," in James, *To Free the Cinema*, 52–56.

19 On the divergence of Mekas's aesthetic from that of the European "film poems" and likewise from that of the critic Parker Tyler, see J. Hoberman's 1995 introduction to Parker Tyler's book *Underground Film: A Critical History* (1969; reprint, New York: Da Capo Press, 1995), vii–x.

20 Mekas, "*Pull My Daisy* and the Truth of Cinema," *Village Voice*, 18 November 1959, in *Movie Journal*, 6. This review was occasioned by the premiere of *Pull My Daisy* at Cinema 16.

21 Mekas, "Sixth Independent Film Award" (1964), in Sitney, *Film Culture Reader*, 427.

22 The significance of *Pull My Daisy* for the work of Mekas and Warhol is noted in passing in Barry Miles, *Ginsberg: A Biography* (New York: Simon and Schuster, 1989), 258, while Rainer Crone has placed Warhol, in general terms, within the generation of the beats in *Andy Warhol: The Early Work 1942–1962*, trans. Martin Scutt (New York: Rizzoli, 1987), 15.

23 On Warhol's familiarity with *The Flower Thief*, see Andy Warhol and Pat Hackett, *POPism. The Warhol 1960s* (New York: Harcourt Brace Jovanovich, 1980), 35. The success of the film during its showing at the Charles Theater is discussed in Hoberman, "The Forest and The Trees," 117. Mekas wrote a favorable review of it, "Taylor Mead and *The Flower Thief*," *Village Voice*, 19 July 1962, in *Movie Journal*, 63–64. Mekas used the Charles Theater to show experimental film from 1961 to 1963; see Mekas, "Showcases I Ran in the 1960s," in James, *To Free the Cinema*, 323. Warhol stated that he often attended these screenings in *POPism*, 30.

24 According to Mead, "he had read my books before I met him and he asked to have them autographed. I was flattered by that because I really admired him." Taylor Mead and David Bourdon, "The Factory Decades: An Interview," *Boss* 5 (1979): 35. Warhol would also have known Mead's work through its publication in *Fuck You / A Magazine of the Arts*. Issue number 5, volume 3 (May 1963), containing Mead's work, is in the Archives Study Center of the Andy Warhol Museum.

25 Ford, interview with John Wilcock, in Wilcock, *The Autobiography and Sex Life of Andy Warhol* (New York: Other Scenes, 1971), no pagination.

26 For a summary of Levine's activities as an actress and filmmaker, see Sheldon Renan, *An Introduction to the American Underground Film* (New York: E. P. Dutton, 1967), 203.

27 Taylor Mead, *Excerpts from the Anonymous Diary of a New York Youth* (1961; reprint, New York: n.p., 1962), 33, 41.

28 Ibid., 2.

29 Regarding the casting for the Tarzan and Jane movie, Mead himself later observed, "I was a logical Tarzan, being opposite to the type," in his essay "Acting: 1958–1965," in Walker Art Center, *The American New Wave*, 1958–1967 (Minneapolis: Walker Art Center, 1982), 17.

30 Mead, telephone interview by author, 11 November 1991, tape recording.

31 Warhol and Hackett, *POPism*, 39.

32 Jack Kerouac, *On the Road* (1957; reprint, New York: Penguin Books, 1976), iv.

33 Robert M. Coates, "The Art Galleries: The 'Beat' Beat in Art" [review of "Sixteen Americans"], *New Yorker*, 2 January 1960, 60. A discussion of this review in relation to the work of Rauschenberg is found in Lana Davis, "Robert Rauschenberg and the Epiphany of the Everyday," in *Poets of the Cities: New York and San Francisco 1950–1965* (Dallas; Dallas Museum of Art and Southern Methodist University; New York: E. P. Dutton, 1974), 40.

34   Jack Kerouac, *On the Road*, 156, 182. Allen Ginsberg has aptly remarked that the pop material in books such as *On the Road* contributed to the emergence of pop art, in Peter Kadzis, "Interview: With Pen and Lens," *Boston Phoenix Literary Section* 38 (June 1991): 7. Taylor Mead himself has stated that he thinks the beat writers had an impact on Warhol; Mead and Bourdon, "The Factory Decades," 35.

35   Warhol recalled that he took this trip in order to see the United States and not because, as some people thought, he was afraid to fly; Warhol and Hackett, POP*ism*, 35. The car trip is attributed to a fear of flying by Mead in Mead and Bourdon, "The Factory Decades," 23, and by Victor Bockris (who also recognized the link to *On the Road*), *The Life and Death of Andy Warhol* (New York: Bantam Books, 1989), 135. It is amusing to consider here the fact that Jack Kerouac *was* afraid of airplanes; see Gerald Nicosia, *Memory Babe: A Critical Biography of Jack Kerouac* (1983; reprint, Berkeley and Los Angeles: University of California Press, 1994), 603.

36   Warhol and Hackett, POP*ism*, 35.

37   Ibid., 38–39.

38   Mead, interview by author, 11 November 1991, tape recording.

39   Bockris, *Life and Death*, 137.

40   Mead, *Excerpts from the Anonymous Diary*, 1, 2. For the passage in "Howl" that Mead here emulated, see Ginsberg, *Howl and Other Poems* (San Francisco: City Lights, 1956), 12.

41   *Fuck You / A Magazine of the Arts* 4 (August 1962): no pagination.

42   "Fuck You: The Talk of the Town," *Fuck You* 5 (December 1962): no pagination.

43   The other movies by Warhol in which Mead plays significant roles are: *Taylor Mead's Ass* (1964), *Imitation of Christ* (a segment of the twenty-five-hour film ****) (1967), *Nude Restaurant* (1967), and *Lonesome Cowboys* (1968).

44   Emile de Antonio's involvement with the distribution of *Pull My Daisy* is discussed in J. Hoberman, "Pull My Daisy / The Queen of Sheba Meets Atom Man," in Walker Art Center, *The American New Wave, 1958–1967*, 37.

45   This screening is described in Warhol and Hackett, POP*ism*, 31.

46   See this chapter, note 4.

47   This description is of the print I have seen of *Couch*, which belongs to Gerard Malanga and is the version discussed in Yann Beauvais, "Fixer des images en mouvement," *Andy Warhol, Cinema*, 98–100. Other versions of the film may have been screened. Richard Dyer describes the film as consisting of eight reels in *Now You See It: Studies on Lesbian and Gay Film* (London: Routledge, 1990), 155. In addition, a twenty-four-hour version of *Couch* was reportedly screened at the Factory; see McKane and Riccaboni, "Filmographie," 255.

48   Reel-to-reel audio recording, 1964, collection Gerard Malanga.

49   One of the reels shot on this day, of Corso, Ginsberg, Kerouac, and Mead, was lost, according to Warhol's account in POP*ism*, 240–241.

50   Kerouac, *Pull My Daisy*, 22.

51   The allusions in *Couch* to both Hollywood and psychoanalysis are noted in Bockris, *Life and Death*, 154. While the couch in this film refers to Hollywood, the kinds of sex that occur on it—between men, or a menage-à-trois of two men and one woman—show what Hollywood did not, as is noted in Beauvais. "Fixer des images en mouvement," in *Andy Warhol, Cinema*, 98.

52   On Warhol's interest in the film *Scorpio Rising*, and echoes of it in his 1965 movie *Vinyl*, see Paul Arthur, "Flesh of Absence: Resighting the Warhol Catechism," in O'Pray, *Andy*

Warhol: Film Factory, 151, and Gretchen Berg, "Nothing to Lose: An Interview with Andy Warhol," in *Andy Warhol: Film Factory*, 58 first published in *Cahiers du Cinéma in English* 10 [1967]).

53 On the *apparent* spontaneity of *Pull My Daisy*, see James, *Allegories of Cinema*, 92. An extensive account of the making of this film is found in Nicosia, *Memory Babe*, 582–585.

54 Tallmer, introduction to Kerouac, *Pull My Daisy*, 14.

55 Ibid., 15.

56 The incident on the set of "Pull My Daisy" and Kerouac's increasingly shocking behavior (fueled by alcohol) are described in Nicosia, *Memory Babe*, 584 and 571, respectively.

57 A few minutes prior to this exchange, Kerouac similarly instructs Ginsberg to "get up, move in, get up, move in; then we go faster and faster."

58 At this point in the dialogue someone, perhaps Warhol, suggested making a "piss" movie, to which Kerouac replied, "You can get that. But you need a light on it, right? Let's go. . . . But you have to do it fast."

59 See, for example, Kerouac, *On the Road*, 40 (on W. C. Fields) and 154 (on Groucho Marx). Kerouac included the Three Stooges, W. C. Fields, and the Marx Brothers among the figures to whom the roots of the beats can be traced in his paper "Is There a Beat Generation?" which he read at a forum of the same title, sponsored by Brandeis University and held at Hunter College Playhouse on 6 November 1958; *Jack Kerouac: "The Last Word"* (Rhino Records R4 70939-D, 1990).

60 The influential film critic and historian P. Adams Sitney contributed greatly to this incorrect assumption in his book *Visionary Film: The American Avant-garde* (New York: Oxford University Press, 1974), 409–410, in which he wrote that "Warhol made the profligacy of footage the central fact of all of his early films, and he advertised his indifference to direction, photography, and lighting. He simply turned the camera on and walked away." This viewpoint prevailed despite the fact that Jonas Mekas had attested, in an essay published four years prior to the publication of Sitney's book, that, through his own observations of Warhol working, he knew that Warhol was hardly an indifferent, passive filmmaker; "Notes After Reseeing the Movies of Andy Warhol," in O'Pray, *Andy Warhol: Film Factory*, 31 (first published in *Andy Warhol*, ed. John Coplans [New York: New York Graphic Society, 1970]).

61 See, for example, Miles, *Ginsberg*, 335.

62 See Warhol and Hackett, *POPism*, 240.

63 Taylor Mead, telephone interview by author, 11 November 1991, tape recording.

64 Ginsberg showed up at the Factory for a party to celebrate the opening of Warhol's flower paintings exhibit at Castelli Gallery in 1964, for the "Fifty Most Beautiful People" party in 1965, and during Bob Dylan's notorious visit there in 1966; see Warhol and Hackett, *POPism*, 87, 103, 150. On Ginsberg's performance with the Velvet Underground at the Dom, see Miles, *Ginsberg*, 387. Ginsberg's presence at one of the Velvet Underground's multimedia programs at the Dom was recorded by Jerry Tallmer in "Rebellion in the Arts: 5. Mixed Media," 1966 news clipping, Andy Warhol file, New York Public Library Theater Collection.

65 Allen Ginsberg, telephone interview by author, 13 December 1991, tape recording.

66 Mekas, "On Cinéma Vérité, Ricky Leacock, and Warhol," *Movie Journal*, 154–155.

67 A photograph by Nat Finkelstein of Malanga and Warhol at this reading is in the Archives Malanga.

68   I am grateful to Thomas Frick for calling my attention to Warhol's *Paris Review* literary "portrait gallery."

69   Kent E. Carroll, "More Structured, Less Scandalized Warhol Aiming for a Wider Playoff," *New York Times*, 7 May 1969: reproduced in Margia Kramer, *Andy Warhol Et Al.: The FBI File on Andy Warhol* (New York: Unsub Press, 1988), 54.

70   The relevance to Ginsberg of Whitman's poetry and celebration of love between men has often been pointed out. See, for example, John Tytell, *Naked Angels: Kerouac, Ginsberg, Burroughs* (1976; reprint, New York: Grove Weidenfeld, 1991), 223–226, 241–244.

71   Ginsberg, *Howl and Other Poems*, 23. "A Supermarket in California" remains one of Ginsberg's most often reprinted poems. It has appeared in collections ranging from *The New American Poetry: 1945–1960*, ed. Donald Allen (New York: Grove Press; London: Evergreen Books, 1960), 181, to *The Portable Beat Reader*. ed. Ann Charters (New York: Viking, 1992), 71–72.

72   See *The Portable Walt Whitman*, ed. Mark Van Doren, revised by Malcolm Cowley, with a chronology and bibliographical check list by Gay Wilson Allen (New York: Penguin Books, 1973), 216–294, 385, 411–484.

73   See, for example, "The Wound-Dresser," *Drum-Taps*, and "Boys in the Army," *Specimen Days*, in Van Doren, *The Portable Walt Whitman*, 226–229, 456–457.

74   In the poet Jim Carroll's slightly fictionalized diaries of actual events, he recorded that in 1971 Morrissey asked Ginsberg

> "to play the part of Walt Whitman, issuing aid and comfort, in every sense of the word, to the Union wounded (and any Rebels, for that matter, if they're cute enough)."
>
> "A lot of good-looking boys?" inquires Allen.
>
> "That's the way we work . . . that's our signature, Allen," Paul replies.
>
> "Sounds like fun," Allen is bubbling. "Any script written yet?"
>
> "Umm, not yet . . . but we'll send it to you soon . . . an outline at least. By the way, Jim, maybe there's some work for you . . . like writing dialogue, when we get to that stage. . . . maybe we can even use you as a soldier."

Carroll, *Forced Entries, The Downtown Diaries: 1971–1973* (New York: Penguin Books, 1987), 26. Ginsberg himself commented to his biographer Barry Miles, regarding his attraction to Warhol's Factory: "I was interested in the films, civil liberties, and the beautiful boys he had. . . . But they were unobtainable or in another realm of some sort." Miles, *Ginsberg*, 336.

75   Bob Colacello, *Holy Terror: Andy Warhol Close Up* (New York: HarperCollins, 1990), 61. According to Colacello, Paul Morrissey had proposed the Whitman film, which was to be a comedy, in spring 1971, and the attractive Joe Dallesandro, who was in several Warhol–Morrissey films of the late 1960s and early 1970s, was to play the wounded soldier whom Whitman, acted by Ginsberg, "nurses back to health."

76   Ginsberg, telephone interview by author, 13 December 1991, tape recording. Ginsberg also stated in this interview that Morrissey had called him to ask if he would play the role of Whitman, and that he was unsure whether the idea for the film was Morrissey's or Warhol's.

77   On the taping of *a: a novel*, see Warhol, *The Philosophy of Andy Warhol (From A to B and Back Again)* (San Diego: Harcourt Brace Jovanovich, 1975), 95.

78   *Excerpts from Visions of Cody* (New York: New Directions, 1959). For the other excerpts from

this novel that were published during the late 1950s and early 1960s, see A *Bibliography of Works by Jack Kerouac (Jean Louis Lebris De Kerouac): 1939–1975*, comp. Ann Charters, rev. ed. (New York: Phoenix Bookshop, 1975), 33, and Nicosia, *Memory Babe*, 593.

79 Four of the dust jacket designs that Warhol made for New Directions books are listed in *"Success is a job in New York . . .": The Early Art and Business of Andy Warhol*, ed. Donna M. De Salvo (New York: Grey Art Gallery and Study Center; Pittsburgh: Carnegie Museum of Art, 1989), 81, and a number of them are reproduced in Andreas Brown, *Andy Warhol: His Early Works 1947–1959* (New York: Gotham Book Mart Gallery, 1971), no pagination.

80 Nicosia, *Memory Babe*, 610.

81 See Ted Berrigan with Aram Saroyan and Duncan McNaughton, "The Art of Fiction XLI: Jack Kerouac," *Paris Review* 11 (summer 1968): 63.

82 Warhol, *Philosophy of Andy Warhol*, 94–95.

83 On Burroughs's use of audio tapes, see Robin Lydenberg, 'Sound Identity Fading Out: William Burroughs' Tape Experiments," in *Wireless Imagination: Sound, Radio, and the Avant-garde*, ed. Douglas Kahn and Gregory Whitehead (Cambridge: MIT Press, 1992), 409–437.

84 See, for example, Mekas, "On *Blonde Cobra* and *Flaming Creatures* (From My Tape Recorded Diaries), *Village Voice*, 24 October 1963; in *Movie Journal*, 101–103. On Mekas's "film diaries," see especially David E. James, "Film Diary / Diary Film: Practice and Product in *Walden*," in *To Free the Cinema*, 145–179. On the relationship between Mekas's notion of the "film diary" and the work of Malanga and Warhol, see my essay "Collaboration as Social Exchange: *Screen Tests / A Diary* by Gerard Malanga and Andy Warhol," *Art Journal* 52 (winter 1993): 62.

85 Tytell wrote that the events on the tape in *Visions of Cody* "are told in a manner anticipating Pop realism, with the graphic and relentlessly obsessive concentration on the ordinary that is seen in Warhol's movies. The catalyzing principle is Rimbaud's "*dérèglement de tous les sens*"; *Naked Angels*, 183.

86 Koch, *Stargazer*, 30.

87 Kerouac, *Visions of Cody*, with "The Visions of the Great Rememberer," by Allen Ginsberg (1972; reprint, New York: Penguin Books, 1993), ix.

88 See, for example, Kerouac, *Visions*, 155, 208.

89 Some examples are Andy Warhol, *a: a novel* (New York: Grove Press, 1968), 87, 198, 208–209.

90 On the idea that taking Benzedrine would produce an openness and honesty in communication, see Kerouac, *On the Road*, 42.

91 Critics have pointed out the connections of the individual novels to the work of Joyce. On the relationships between Joyce's writings and *a: a novel*, see, for instance, Sally Beauman, review of *a: a novel*, *New York Times Book Review*, 12 January 1969, 32. On *Visions of Cody* and the work of Joyce, see Nicosia, *Memory Babe*, 376.

92 There are even similarities in the details of the telephone conversations; compare, for example, Kerouac, *Visions*, 130, to Warhol, *a*, 36. For instances of music being played, see *Visions*, 135–136, and *a*, 57–58.

93 "Goofing" is defined by Kerouac in *Pull My Daisy*, 27.

94 Kerouac, *Visions*, 170. © 1972 by the Estate of Jack Kerouac. Reprinted by permission of Sterling Lord Literistic, Inc.

95 Warhol, *a*, 126–127. Ginsberg is also brought up by Ondine in another passage of the novel; see *a*, 96. Ondine frequented the same Bleecker Street bar as Ginsberg, the San

Remo, and it is possible that he met Ginsberg there or through one of his San Remo friends. On the San Remo, see Miles, Ginsberg, 127, and Warhol and Hackett, POPism, 54–55.

96   Kerouac, Visions (see n. 94 above), 220.

97   Warhol, a, 53, 264.

98   On this aspect of the tape recorded segment of Visions of Cody, see Michael Davidson, The San Francisco Renaissance: Poetics and Community at Mid-century (Cambridge: Cambridge University Press, 1989), 74. Regarding his use of the tape recorder, Warhol wrote, "You couldn't tell which problems were real and which problems were exaggerated for the tape. Better yet, the people telling you the problems couldn't decide any more if they were really having the problems or if they were just performing"; Philosophy of Andy Warhol, 26–27.

99   On this dimension of Visions of Cody, see Davidson, San Francisco Renaissance, 74. The process by which the tapes of a: a novel were transcribed is described in Warhol, Philosophy of Andy Warhol, 95, and Warhol and Hackett, POPism, 149, 287.

100   On the criticisms Kerouac received for using tape transcriptions in the novel, see Nicosia, Memory Babe, 387, 414.

101   The negative reviews of a included that of Sally Beauman (see this chapter, n. 91), Robert Mazzocco, "aaaaaa . . .," New York Review of Books, 24 April 1969, 34–37, and "ZZZZZZZZ," Time, 27 December 1968, 63. On the reception of a, see also Bockris, Life and Death, 243–244.

102   Warhol and Hackett, POPism, 287.

103   For example, there was a great deal of mostly negative writing about On the Road (but, as already noted, it was a great publishing success); on the criticism of Kerouac's novel, see Nicosia, Memory Babe, 556–557, 559.

104   I have considered this point in an abbreviated form in "Collaboration as Social Exchange: Screen Tests / A Diary by Gerard Malanga and Andy Warhol," 64. Ronald Sukenick has associated the "commodity component" of the beat movement with the "art publicity genius" of Warhol in Down and In: Life in the Underground (New York: William Morrow, Beech Tree Books, 1987), 112.

105   Paul O'Neil, "The Only Rebellion Around," in A Casebook on the Beat, ed. Thomas Parkinson (New York: Thomas Y. Crowell, 1961), 234 (first published in Life, 30 November 1959).

106   Norman Podhoretz, "The Know-Nothing Bohemians," in Parkinson, A Casebook on the Beat, 201–202 (first published in Partisan Review 25 [spring 1958]).

107   John Leonard, "The Return of Andy Warhol," New York Times Magazine, 10 November 1968, 32.

108   See Joseph Morgenstern, "Beatniks for Rent," in Kerouac and Friends: A Beat Generation Album, ed. Fred W. McDarrah (New York: William Morrow, 1985), 243–251 (first published in the New York Herald Tribune, 1 May 1960). The Rent-a-Beatnik advertisement that was run in the Village Voice and a Mad magazine parody of it are reproduced in Kerouac and Friends, 247, 284.

109   Ronald Sukenick noted that McDarrah's business foreshadowed a trend that would soon develop, in Down and In, 118.

110   Ginsberg has noted that the tape transcriptions in Visions of Cody presage Warhol's interest in commonplace objects, in "The Visions of the Great Rememberer," Visions, 409–410.

111   This statement was quoted, among other places, in Herbert Gold, "The Beat Mystique," in Parkinson, *A Casebook on the Beat*, 248 (first published in *Playboy*, February 1958), and by Bill Randle in the notes he composed to accompany the record he produced, *Readings by Jack Kerouac on the Beat Generation* (Verve LP #15005, 1960).

112   Gene R. Swenson, "What Is Pop Art?" ART*news* 62 (November 1963): 26.

113   Kerouac, *On the Road*, 126.

114   Mekas, quoted in Jack Kroll, "Saint Andrew," *Newsweek*, 7 December 1964, 103.

115   K. S. Lynn, review of *Dr. Sax*, by Jack Kerouac, *New York Herald Tribune Book Review*, 31 May 1959, as cited in Nicosia, *Memory Babe*, 588, and Gold, "The Beat Mystique," in Parkinson, *A Casebook on the Beat*, 247, 252, 254.

116   Joseph Gelmis, "On Movies: He Has Trouble Communicating Whether On or Off the Screen," *Newsday*, 8 December 1966. Probably in response to this article, Warhol brought up the question of boredom in his work in an interview that Gelmis later conducted with him; see Gelmis, *The Film Director as Superstar* (Garden City, N.Y.: Doubleday, 1970), 70.

117   See, for example, John Bernard Myers, "A Letter to Gregory Battcock," in *The New American Cinema: A Critical Anthology*, ed. Battcock (New York: E. P. Dutton, 1967), 139, and James Stoller, "Beyond Cinema: Notes on Some Films by Andy Warhol," *Film Quarterly* 20 (fall 1966): 38.

Walking on Thin Ice

The films of Yoko Ono

10

DARYL CHIN

> The key to Fluxus was that artists were killing individual egos. At least, that was how I interpreted it. But in New York artists have very big egos. I was never really antiart, but I was antiego. Postindustrial society will be a kind of egoless society is what I think. Many people now are giving up acquisitiveness in terms of money and material comfort; next stage is to give up acquisitiveness in fame. Of course, Fluxus people, including myself, are vain and do have ego, I know that. Is very, very hard.[1]
>
> Nam June Paik

Although Yoko Ono is one of the most famous people in the world, she remains one of the least known. Aside from her status as the widow of John Lennon, little seems to be known about her work, her ideas, her art. But her variegated career is finally getting serious attention. That, coupled with the controversies surrounding her public persona, makes Ono a particularly apt subject for an inquiry into a number of issues relating to art and the shifts that have occurred in the last two decades. The recent retrospective "Yoko Ono: Objects, Films," at the Whitney Museum of American Art, has provided the occasion for a reappraisal of Ono's art, but this reappraisal continues to be hounded by questions about her personal life and her artistic integrity barked by the mass media. The whole relation of Ono to the mass media is curious, because her films do not address the mass media directly. Rather, the aesthetic dialogue that her films engage in is that of avant-garde film.

Consider one of her most famous works, the film *No. 4* (1966). If you've ever heard anything about Ono's art, you've probably heard about *No. 4*, which consists of a series of close-ups of people's bare bottoms. There are, in fact, two versions of the film: a five-and-a-half minute version, which is included in the *Fluxfilm* program, the other an 80-minute version. Indeed, there may be other versions as well. In the 80-minute version, shots of 365 bare bottoms follow one another in rapid succession. The film is repetitive, with the image having very little depth of field. The film was shot with a camera attached to a treadmill: each subject would walk on the treadmill, while the movements of their bare bottoms were recorded. (The soundtrack consists of comments made while filming.)

An argument can be made that the perceptual nature of the film is enhanced by the lack of depth on screen: after a while, the image becomes less important, the shock value retreats, and the spectator starts to notice subtleties in the variations—as well as other aspects of the images, such as the film frame and even the screen surface. Paul Sharits (who also had a short film in the original *Fluxfilm* omnibus) once commented on Warhol's early films:

> Andy Warhol has demonstrated in his early work that prolongations of subject (redundant, "non-motion" pictures), because they deflect attention finally to the material process of recording-projecting (e.g., to the succession of film frames, and by way of consciousness of film grain, scratches and dirt particles, to the sense of the flow of the celluloid strip) . . . is perhaps as revealing of the "nature of cinema" as is consistent interruption of "normative" cinematic functions.[2]

In films like *Henry Geldzahler* (1964) and *The Thirteen Most Beautiful Women* (1964), there are simply "those close-ups where they did next to nothing," in Yvonne Rainer's description.[3] And so you become conscious of duration. The depletion of the subject matter makes the material conditions of the film process the actual subject, and an anti-illusionist attitude becomes the viewing vantage point. So it is with *No. 4*.

But for all the talk about the formal aspects of Ono's art, there's something else to discuss: her wit, and what it seems to mask. If Warhol focused his camera on faces, Ono (reversing his aims, both figuratively and literally) focused on anuses. And, of course, there is the obvious irony in terms of the sexual subtext of Warhol 's work, specifically in such "portrait" films as *Eat* (1963) and *Blow Job* (1963). Just as, in his way, Warhol subverted certain canons of the avant-garde film, so Ono takes Warhol as a paradigm and subverts (one might say inverts) his work. (As P. Adams Sitney pointed out, *Sleep* was a literal inversion of the "trance films," which were a genre of the avant-garde film, exemplified by Maya Deren's *Meshes in the Afternoon* and Kenneth Anger's *Fireworks*, films depicting the dreams and the impressions of the unconscious of a sleeping protagonist. Instead of showing the unconscious of his character, Warhol simply showed the sleeping protagonist.[4]) There is, of course, the stinging irony: whereas the faces in Warhol's films become his cinematic "objects of desire" (specifically in *Blow Job*, *The Thirteen Most Beautiful Women*, and *The Thirteen Most Beautiful Boys*, as those titles indicate), Ono presents a succession of anuses as an ironic comment on Warhol's strategy.

[. . .]

Another key Ono film is *Rape* (1969). In that film, a young woman is selected (seemingly at random) and followed by a crew. The title is figurative: there is no actual, physical rape in the film. Rather, the title refers to the idea of the girl's privacy being invaded; this violation is the film's rape. The film is a record of the encounter, as the girl, a foreigner in London, is at first hesitant, then flattered, then bewildered, finally frightened and angry. In a way, the film is a demonstration of Warhol's dictum that in the future everyone will be famous for 15 minutes, although this film stretches it out to more than an hour. The film can also be read as an exploration of Ono's own recent experience after her recent marriage to John Lennon, which had thrust her into exactly that situation where the paparazzi from the tabloids had begun to hound her. *Rape*, then, can be seen as an act of revenge, turning the tables on the public that had started to infringe on her privacy. But, of course, it's an unfair act of revenge, because the particular woman chosen didn't do anything to warrant this intrusion. So the film is a joke, but a curiously sour one.

The same might be said of *Fly* (1970). The film consists of extreme close-ups of a fly (actually several flies) moving across a woman's body, accompanied by a vocal score by Ono.

The music, which is highly expressive, provides a motivational narrative which the viewer can infer. But the film is problematic: the flies had to be chloroformed in order to ensure that they wouldn't escape, and their slow, hazy movements are the results of being drugged. Sure, they're only flies, but the idea of living things being "pressured" into performing links the film (conceptually) with *Rape*. This aspect of the work also points to the undercurrent of hostility behind Ono's whimsy. The flies aren't merely humiliated (as the woman in *Rape* is): they're destroyed. The final image of several flies gathered on the body is clearly parodic, meant to evoke the sinister images of Hitchcock's *The Birds*, but it's also sinister, considering how the flies got there.

Rape and *Fly* are films Ono directed in collaboration with Lennon. So, too, are *Apotheosis* (1970) and *Up Your Legs Forever* (1970). *Apotheosis* presents a situation, and derives its form and structure from that situation—Lennon and Ono in a balloon. The camera follows the trajectory as the balloon rises, and the movement of the camera is dictated by the movement of the balloon—from the mild hubbub of people surrounding the balloon as preparations begin to frames filled with the white of a cloud to the final image of the sky above the clouds. This last image was described by Jonas Mekas: "At that point, however, the balloon left the cloud, and suddenly the cloud landscape opened up like a huge poem, you could see the tops of the clouds, all beautifully enveloped by sun, stretching into infinity, as the balloon kept moving up above the soft woolly cloudscape."[5] *Apotheosis* is foremost a film about camera movement reminiscent of the work of Michael Snow, particularly *Wavelength* (1967) and ↔ (1969). That is, the imagery of the film is limited to the field of vision defined by the mechanism of the film's making. In *Wavelength*, that field is defined by a continual zoom. In *Apotheosis*, it's the view from the rising balloon.

For ↔ and *La Region Centrale* (1972), Snow modified and customized camera mounting devices in order to get the camera movements he wanted. In ↔ he controlled the panning of the camera on a tripod. In *La Region Centrale*, he combined a dolly and a crane that allowed continuous camera movement. Similarly, for *Up Your Legs Forever*, Ono needed a device that would pan up the different pairs of legs but would appear to be one long pan. She had the camera rigged so that every pan would be shot at the same speed. In *Up Your Legs Forever*, Ono performs at full stretch. The title is an obvious pun, playing on the phrase "up yours!" The repetitive nature of the imagery is grounded in the aesthetic ploys of duration, serial imagery, and stasis, which were such important concerns of the art movements of the period. There is also a sexual agenda at work in the film having to do with the representations of women in the media. (As an example, Mary Tyler Moore's first significant job in television was playing Sam, the answering service worker in *Richard Diamond*, shown only from the waist down.) Ono often turns the tables on her audiences, teasing them with a bland antagonism. Just think of the titles of some of her films: *Rape*, *Up Your Legs Forever*, *Erection* (1970). Put these titles on one bill, and the impression is one of titillation. But it's a joke. The "rape" of the title is psychological, metaphoric. The "erection" of the title (a film credited as directed by Lennon, in collaboration with Ono) is the construction of a building. If a woman can be judged in sexist terms as "a piece of ass," Ono creates a film that consists of "pieces of ass."

What can't be ignored is Ono's anger, her barely disguised hostility and rage. I think there are any number of factors operative here, some of which are sociological and psychological; others are aesthetic and philosophical. In terms of the latter, this was part of the avant-garde sensibility of the late 1950s and the 1960s, which gave rise to such art movements as Pop Art, Minimal Art, Conceptual Art, and, of course, Fluxus. The dance reviewer Don McDonagh, using Yvonne Rainer's *Terrain* (1963) as an example, wrote, "It was blunt, honest, puzzling, at times wearisome and, most importantly, it was different. Different because it wanted to pose a direct challenge to custom and didn't have the time to be subtle or polite."[6] That direct challenge to custom was one of the characteristics of the art from that period. And the compressed, pressure-cooked, compacted atmosphere of risk, camaraderie, and rivalry was always present—so that, in 1967, Ono could say of *Wavelength* that it was one of her favorite movies of the year and go on to parody and to subvert its formal qualities in *Up Your Legs Forever*.

But what if that challenge is ignored? What if a valid artistic challenge is defused by condescension or patronization? Let's take two examples: Carolee Schneemann's film *Fuses* (1967) and Simone Forti's 1961 dance concert 5 *Dance Constructions and Some Other Things*. (These examples are not chosen by chance. In her essay "Happenings: An Art of Radical Juxtaposition," Susan Sontag listed 12 artists as among the primary creators of Happenings in the United States; Ono and Schneemann were the women in the list. Forti's concert was presented at Ono's loft as part of a series of alternative performances during the spring and summer of 1961.)[7] In the San Francisco Cinematheque's journal *Cinematograph*, David James discusses how *Fuses* challenged traditional aesthetic and political trajectories. In particular, he details Schneemann's use of the forms defined by the Expressionist-oriented aesthetic of Stan Brakhage to extend and question those forms from a woman's perspective. James notes what happened: "*Fuses* became invisible, marginalized within and by the marginal cinemas of the time."[8] In his book *The Rise and Fall and Rise of Modern Dance*, Don McDonagh wrote about Forti, "In 1961 she moved to New York and in that year offered one of the most influential single concerts ever given by a dancer."[9] Yvonne Rainer (one of the performers in the concert) remembers the effects somewhat differently:

> Before her "retirement" Simone did complete her own "opus." It was *An Evening of Dance Constructions* at Yoko Ono's loft on Chambers Street (May 1961) and proved to be way ahead of its time. I sometimes wonder if more feedback would have prevented her retirement. As things then stood, it was as though a vacuum sealed that event. Nothing was written about it and dancers went on dancing and painters and ex-painters went on making painterly happenings and theater pieces. It would take another two and a half years before the idea of a "construction" to generate movement or situation would take hold.[10]

The effects of that kind of silence can be devastating. This can be seen in terms of the lack of discussion that Ono's major films faced. I've tried to indicate how her films challenged the formal and the thematic concerns of avant-garde filmmakers from that period, in particular, Warhol and Snow (who were also visual artists-turned-filmmakers). Yet, aside from Jonas Mekas and the late David Bienstock, there was no serious comment on her films, on the sly, mordant, subtle way she skewed the avant-garde film to admit a specifically feminine wit. Remember, during this period (1966–1971) Ono issued a statement that became notorious, "Woman is the nigger of the world." The conflation of racial and sexual politics to be found in that statement was (and still is, I think) shocking.

[. . .]

This subversive attitude was not unique to Ono; it was an attitude common to many of the avant-garde artists of the time, especially those artists who participated in Fluxus. The period of the late 1950s and the 1960s saw a veritable artistic onslaught, with many artists attempting to create works which would challenge and defy categorization. That's when Happenings, Events, things which people called Dance and Music that didn't seem like Dance or Music, or film screenings that turned into Expanded Cinema were produced and became notorious. In order to present these works, the usual categories of art spaces had to be flexible or redefined. That's why, during that period, there were a number of people whose art became a form of entrepreneurship, artists who organized concerts, exhibits, or performances, and numerous uncategorizable variations, e.g., concerts that became exhibits or exhibits that became performances. Yvonne Rainer, Steve Paxton, and Ruth Emerson went to the Judson Memorial Church and arranged dance concerts there, which became the Judson Dance Theater. Jonas Mekas kept moving his Filmmakers Cinematheque. Beginning with a concert meant to highlight a Stockhausen piece, Charlotte Moorman went on to organize the Annual Avant-garde Festivals. Moorman's only serious rival as an artist-entrepreneur-organizer was, perhaps, the late George Macuinas, the acknowledged center (words like "leader" and "head" seem inappropriate to a man who once listed himself under the heading Action Against Cultural Imperialism) of Fluxus.

What was Fluxus? In the simplest terms, it was an art movement that stressed conceptually-based art. (One of the earlier Fluxus works, the 1963 publication An Anthology, edited by La Monte Young and Jackson Mac-Low, included an essay entitled "Concept Art," by Henry Flynt. I believe this was one of the first times "concept" or "conceptual" art was proposed.) Often characterized as "neo-Dada" in intention and achievement, Fluxus was influenced heavily by the work of Marcel Duchamp and John Cage. (If the Judson Dance Theater can be said to have developed out of a series of composition classes given by Robert Ellis Dunn, so the U. S. component of Fluxus formed at classes John Cage gave at the New School in the late 1950s.) Many Fluxus artists were "intermedia" artists (a term coined by Dick Higgins), combining music, writing, and graphic art with performance. Fluxus artworks favored readymades, chance operations, and multiples. There was also a heavy dose of what— for want of a better word—I would call "whimsy." Some examples of that "whimsy":

Piano Piece for David Tudor #2
Bring a bale of hay and a bucket of water onto the stage for a piano to eat and drink. The performer may then feed the piano or leave it to eat by itself. If the former, the piece is over after the piano has been fed. If the latter, it is over after the piano eats or decides not to.

La Monte Young, October 1960

Direction
Arrange to observe a sign indicating direction of travel.
- travel in the indicated direction
- travel in another direction

George Brecht

Sun Piece
Watch the sun until it becomes square.

Yoko Ono, winter 1962

There is a "what if?" "why not?" "what the hell?" quality to a lot of Fluxus art, which can be attributed to the artists questioning the limits of art. What's art? What isn't? Ono once said that everyone could be artists, and everything could be art. There were Fluxus publications, Fluxus concerts, Fluxus films, Fluxus readymades, Fluxus multiples, Fluxus prints and graphics. Although Fluxus was very loose and very eclectic, gradually a profile emerged. In 1966, Macuinas drew a chart, "The Expanded Arts Diagram." (Macuinas was one of the first artists whose work consisted of lists, catalogues, and charts, a true postmodernist, although he'd probably hate that label.) On one end of the diagram were "Events/Neo-haiku Theater" (the Fluxus end) and the other "Happenings/Neo-Baroque Theater." In 1966, Ono described the distinction:

> Event, to me, is not an assimilation of all the other arts as Happening seems to be, but an extrication from the various sensory perceptions. It is not "a get togetherness" as most happenings are, but a dealing with oneself. Also, it has no script as happenings do, though it has something that starts it moving—the closest word for it may be a "wish" or "hope."[11]

Fluxus was a very loose amalgamation of artists, truly international and multicultural in its make-up. As an example: in 1963, Macuinas (a Lithuanian immigrant then living in New York City) sent a memo to Fluxus members or prospective members, i.e., artists whose works had been or might be distributed, exhibited, or performed in a Fluxus context. The list included George Brecht, Toshi Ichiyangi, Robert Filliou, Gyorgi Ligeti, Jackson MacLow, (Takehisa) Kosugi, Nordenstrøm, Ono, Benjamin Patterson, Nam June Paik, Robert Watts, Emmett Williams, La Monte Young, Dick Higgins, Allan Kaprow, Alfred Hansen, Claes Oldenburg, Richard Maxfield, and Stan Vanderbeck. In 1966, Macuinas called Fluxus a "collective"; the aforementioned *Fluxfilm* was made, with short segments by Brecht, Macuinas, Eric Andersen, Cheiko Shiomi, Watts, Albert Fine, Paul Sharits, Ono, John Cale, and Joe Jones; Peter Moore was the cinematographer for several of the films. It was in this context that Yoko Ono developed as an artist. In 1966, Ono went to London to participate in the Destruction in Art symposium. From that point, art history converges with the larger scope of cultural history.

Prior to the establishment of Fluxus, Macuinas had been the owner of the AG Gallery, one of the first (along with the Reuben Gallery and the Martha Jackson Gallery) to present performance works (usually called Happenings). In the milieu of the New York art world of the early 1960s, the artists who had met in John Cage's classes—Higgins, Al Hansen, MacLow, Philip Corner, Brecht—linked up with Macuinas, who was interested in an international perspective. To this end, they set up Fluxus tours in Europe, and contact was established between artists in the U.S., Europe, and Japan. Among the European artists who were associated with Fluxus were Ben Vautier, Filliou, Milan Knizak, Daniel Spoerri, and Joseph Beuys. The Asian component of Fluxus included Paik, Shigeko Kubota, Kosugi, Shiomi, Ay-O, Yoshimasa Wada, Yasunao Tone, the group Hi-Red Center, and, of course, Ono.

Like any subject tinged with nostalgia, this description may seem more idealistic that it was. Then, again, maybe not. About this same cultural moment, Rainer reflected,

> As I look back, what stands out for me—along with the inevitable undercurrents of petty jealousies and competitiveness—is the spirit of that time: a dare-devil willingness

to 'try anything,' the arrogance of our certainty that we were breaking new ground, the exhilaration produced by the response of the incredibly partisan audiences. . . .[12]

Perhaps appropriately, Ono has now recast her early Fluxus objects in bronze and justified this as a 1980s response to a 1960s aesthetic. There's some controversy about her revisionist strategy, but the films remain—without embellishments and without omissions—still challenging the predominant avant-garde aesthetic of the period and still providing an oddball feminist slant to some hoary aesthetic issues. One of my favorite pieces by Ono is *Sky Machine* (1967, not included in the Whitney show). It's a very elegant gumball machine, with plastic capsules inside, the kind that usually contain small "prizes," but, here, with nothing inside. Nothing, that is, except air—or, in the terms of the piece, "a piece of the sky." This could be a Duchampian ploy: the consciousness of demarcating a piece of the sky renders that piece of the sky part of a work of art. This could be a cynical commercial ploy: the artist saying that anything can be sold as art, even air. I think both meanings are within the parameters of the work, accounting for its particular humor and power. Ono's achievements as an artist (and her films, as with the films of Warhol, represent her art at its most impressive) show ingenuity, extreme irony, integrity, subversive wit, and a double-edged intelligence.

A section of my performance piece *The Future of an Illusionism* (1983) consists of a panel discussion on "alternative performance" since 1960. The panelists were Simone Forti, Alison Knowles, Charlotte Moorman, Carolee Schneemann, and Elaine Summers. At one point, Schneemann said, "Younger artists, who are struggling to find space and funding, are also all into marketing strategies. Or many of them are. They talk to me about being too sloppy and idealistic and having leftover attitudes from the '60s, because I haven't gotten together my networking."[13]

In the February 7, 1989, issue of the *Village Voice* John Perreault quotes Ono's comment on her decision to show her art after more than a decade:

For me it's moving forward. It's dispensing with that dream that my generation is carrying. We still have that inside of us. We can never forget that dream of revolution. We have that taste. In the future there will be an even more complex society. The 1960s was one of the stepping-stones. But we can't look back.[14]

Notes

1 Calvin Tomkins, *The Scene: Reports on Post-Modern Art* (New York: Viking Press, 1977), p. 207.
2 Paul Sharits, "Words Per Page," *Afterimage* (London), No. 4 (1972), p. 31.
3 Willoughby Sharp and Liza Bear, "The Performer as a Persona: An Interview with Yvonne Rainer," *Avalanche*, No. 5 (1972), p. 57.
4 P. Adams Sitney, *Visionary Film: The American Avant-garde* (New York: Oxford University Press, 1974), p. 409.
5 Jonas Mekas, *Movie Journal: The Rise of a New American Cinema, 1959–1971* (New York: Macmillan, 1972), p. 412.
6 Don McDonagh, *The Complete Guide to Modern Dance* (New York: Doubleday, 1976), p. 447.
7 Susan Sontag, *Against Interpretation* (New York: Farrar, Straus, Giroux, 1966), p. 264.

8 David James, "Carolee Schneemann's *Fuses* (1964–1967)," *Cinematograph*, No. 3 (1988), p. 38.

9 Don McDonagh, *The Rise and Fall and Rise of Modern Dance* (New York: Outerbridge and Drensthey, 1970), p. 190.

10 Yvonne Rainer, *Work* 1961–1973 (Halifax: Nova Scotia College of Art and Design, 1974), p. 7.

11 Yoko Ono, *Grapefruit* (New York: Simon and Schuster, 1970); 273.

12 Rainer, *op. cit.*, p. 8.

13 Daryl Chin, with Simone Forti, Alison Knowles, Charlotte Moorman, Carolee Schneemann, Elaine Summers, and Michael Kirby, "The Future of an Illusionism, Part II," *Heresies: A Feminist Publication on Art and Politics*, No. 17 (1984), p. 62.

14 John Perreault, "Age of Bronze: Yoko Ono at the Whitney," *Village Voice* (Feb 7, 1989), p. 30.

Yoko Ono on Yoko Ono

YOKO ONO

On *Film No. 4* (in taking the bottoms of 365 saints of our time)

I wonder why men can get serious at all. They have this delicate long thing hanging outside their bodies, which goes up and down by its own will. First of all having it outside your body is terribly dangerous. If I were a man I would have a fantastic castration complex to the point that I wouldn't be able to do a thing. Second, the inconsistency of it, like carrying a chance time alarm or something. If I were a man I would always be laughing at myself. Humour is probably something the male of the species discovered through their own anatomy. But men are so serious. Why? Why violence? Why hatred? Why war? If people want to make war, they should make a colour war, and paint each other's city up during the night in pinks and greens. Men have an unusual talent for making a bore out of everything they touch. Art, painting, sculpture, like who wants a cast-iron woman, for instance.

The film world is becoming terribly aristocratic, too. It's professionalism all the way down the line. In any other field: painting, music, etc., people are starting to become iconoclastic. But in the film world—that's where nobody touches it except the director. The director carries the old mystery of the artist. He is creating a universe, a mood, he is unique, etc., etc. This film proves that anybody can be a director. A filmmaker in San Francisco wrote to me and asked if he could make the San Francisco version of No. 4. That's OK with me. Somebody else wrote from New York, she wants to make a slow-motion version with her own behind. That's OK, too. I'm hoping that after seeing this film people will start to make their own home movies like crazy.

In 50 years or so, which is like 10 centuries from now, people will look at the film of the 1960s. They will probably comment on Ingmar Bergman as meaningfully meaningful filmmaker, Jean-Luc Godard as the meaningfully meaningless, Antonioni as meaninglessly meaningful, etc., etc. Then they would come to the No. 4 film and see a sudden swarm of exposed bottoms, that these bottoms, in fact belonged to people who represented the London scene. And I hope that they would see that the 1960s was not only the age of achievements, but of laughter. This film, in fact, is like an aimless petition signed by people with their anuses. Next time we wish to make an appeal, we should send this film as the signature list.

12. Yoko Ono. Courtesy Anthology Film Archives; reprinted by permission.

My ultimate goal in filmmaking is to make a film which includes a smiling face snap of every single human being in the world. Of course, I cannot go around the whole world and take the shots myself. I need cooperation from something like the post offices of the world. If everybody would drop a snapshot of themselves and their families to the post office of their town, or allow themselves to be photographed by the nearest photographic studio, this would be soon accomplished. Of course, this film would need constant adding of footage. Probably nobody would like to see the whole film at once, so you can keep it in a library or something, and when you want to see some particular town's people's smiling faces you can go and check that section of film. We can also arrange it with a television network so that whenever you want to see faces of a particular location in the world, all you have to do is to press a button and there it is. This way, if Johnson wants to see what sort of people he killed in Vietnam that day, he only has to turn the channel. Before this you were just part of a figure in the newspapers, but after this you become a smiling face. And when you are born, you will know that if you wanted to, you will have in your life time to communicate with the whole world. That is more than most of us could ask for. Very soon, the age may come where we would not need photographs to communicate, like ESP, etc. It will happen soon, but that will be "After the Film Age."

London 1967

On *Film No. 5* and *Two Virgins*

Last year, I said I'd like to make a "smile film" which included a smiling face snap of every single human being in the world. But that had obvious technical difficulties and it was very likely that the plan would have remained as one of my beautiful never-nevers.

This year, I started off thinking of making films that were meant to be shown in 100 years' time, i.e. taking different city views, hoping that most of the buildings in them would be demolished by the time the film was released; shooting an ordinary woman with her full gear—knowing that in 100 years' time, she'd look extraordinary, etc., etc. It's to apply the process of making vintage wine to filmmaking. This, in practice, would mean that as a filmmaker you don't really have to make a film anymore but just put your name (that is, if you so wish) on any film and store it. Storing would then become the main endeavour of a filmmaker. But then, the idea started to get too conceptual. That's the trouble with all my strawberries. They tend to evaporate and I find myself lying on the floor doing nothing.

One afternoon, John and I went out in the garden and shot *Film No. 5*, the smile film, and *Two Virgins*. They were done in a spirit of home movies. In both films, we were mainly concerned about the vibrations the films send out—the kind that was between us. But, with *Film No. 5*, a lot of planning, working and talking out things had preceded the afternoon. For instance, I had thought of making *Film No. 5* into a Dr. Zhivago and let it go on for 4 hours with an intermission and all that, but later decided to stick to a more commercial length of an hour (approx.). 8mm copies of the film are also available for people who'd like to have the film on their wall as a light-portrait. Also, we'll store some copies for the next century.

They say that in the corner of the world there is a man who sits and spends his life in sending good vibration to the world, and when a star twinkles, we are only catching the twinkle that was sent 1000 light years ago, etc.

Imagine a painting that smiles just once in a billion years. John's ghostly smile in *Film No. 5* might just communicate in a hundred years' time, or maybe, the way things are rolling, it may communicate much earlier than that. I think all the doors are just ready to open now. One light knock should do. It's just that there are still a minority group in the world who are afraid of the doorless world to come. They're just not sure how they can cope with it. But most of us know that doors are just figments of our imagination. The good thing is though, that law of nature that once you know, you can never unknow things, so the doors are going to disappear pretty rapidly, I think.

Some critic recently commented on us, John and I, as being lollypop artists who are preoccupied with blowing soap-bubbles forever. I thought that was beautiful. There's a lot you can do with blowing soap-bubbles. Maybe the future USA should decide their presidency by having a soap-bubble contest. Blowing soap-bubbles could be used as a form of swearing. Some day the whole world can make it its occupation to blow soap-bubbles.

Would they ever know that Johnny West and Yoko DeMille ate bananas together?

October 22, 1968

On *"Rape"*

Violence is a sad wind that, if channeled carefully, could bring seeds, chairs and all things pleasant to us.

We are all would-be Presidents of the World, and kids kicking the sky that doesn't listen.

What would you do if you had only one penis and a one-way tube ticket when you want to fuck the whole nation in one come?

I know a professor of philosophy whose hobby is to quietly crush biscuit boxes in a supermarket.

Maybe you can send signed, plastic lighters to people in place of your penis. But then some people might take your lighter as a piece of sculpture and keep it up on their living-room shelf.

So we go on eating and feeding frustration every day, lick lollypops and stay being peeping-toms dreaming of becoming Jack-The-Ripper.

This film was shot by our cameraman, Nick, while we were in a hospital. Nick is a gentleman, who prefers eating clouds and floating pies to shooting *Rape*. Nevertheless it was shot.

And as John says: "A is for parrot, which we can plainly see."

Yoko Ono
April 1969, London

PART THREE

STRUCTURALISM IN THE 1970s

Introduction

As P. Adams Sitney defines it, structuralism in experimental film is characterized by form and structure over narrative. He names three characteristics of structural film: the fixed camera, the flicker effect, and repetition without variation. Structuralism appeared in the late 1960s and was hailed by Sitney as a great new wave of experimental film. Sitney's essay "Structural Film," however, bespeaks the reality that even the most formal of artists often eludes generic classification. Sitney is a champion of purity, simplicity, and formalism. His use of the first person plural "we" suggests that he speaks for the filmmaking community or for *Film Culture* itself. Though Sitney is able to draw together such filmmakers as Andy Warhol, Peter Kubelka, Michael Snow, and Joyce Wieland, he is frustrated to find a structuralist film amongst the works of the great romanticist Gregory Markopoulos. Nevertheless, one can say that film form was much more important than narrative during the structuralist period, but one must also state that formalism is not necessarily the antithesis of romanticism. Indeed, many of the finest structural films are deeply personal and poetically romantic.

Take the case of Warren Sonbert, whose work is examined by Philip Lopate in "The Films of Warren Sonbert." Lopate notes that Sonbert's work is alive, humorous, and contemplative, even deeply spiritual. Sonbert's romantic attention to lighting and his formalist editing strategies of alternating a vertical shot with a diagonal shot would seem to be at odds. Yet they are not. Sonbert's diaries are formalist yet romantic. He does not frustrate audience pleasure, as Lopate notes.

In the "Warren Sonbert Interview" with David Ehrenstein, Sonbert deliberately draws the discussion away from Soviet editing theory to declare that in his own films, "each shot is a statement." For Sonbert, the independent film's greatness derives from the personal. The film reveals the filmmaker, Sonbert asserts, but more importantly his subjectivity, in the matter of what he decides to include and exclude in each film. Though Sonbert avoids direct discussion of his homosexual identity, he nevertheless displays pride in the personal, very intimate nature of his oeuvre. In fact, Sonbert states that his ideal audience would be one person at a time, reflecting his emphasis on intimacy, even as he discusses his formal production methods.

Structuralist filmmakers assumed that the audience for their films was to be an intimate, knowledgeable group of cineastes. In Scott MacDonald's "Interview with Michael Snow," Snow admits that he did not think that there was an audience for *Wavelength* (1967) beyond the cinematheque. Snow discusses the community of the cinematheque and the importance of the support and acknowledgement he received from his then wife, Joyce Wieland, and filmmakers Bob Cowan, Ken Jacobs, and Norman McLaren. *Wavelength* was highly influential upon its release. MacDonald and Snow discuss the changing critical reception of the film, as well as the reception of *Presents* (1980), which provoked much controversy because of its extensive inclusion of a nude female body. Audiences were hostile to the film, especially feminists, who were concerned about the objectification of the female body by the male gaze, as MacDonald notes. The lengthy interview also includes a discussion of Snow's background in music and painting, his collaboration with Joyce Wieland, and his famous *Walking Woman Works* series of films.

Zorns Lemma (1970) is the predominant subject of Peter Gidal's contribution to the volume, "An Interview with Hollis Frampton." Frampton found the progression from still photographer to filmmaker a natural and organic change because he sees cinema as a way of ordering still photographs. Frampton discusses the logic of his major work, *Zorns Lemma*, which begins with a blank section of film as a variety of voices (including those of Joyce Wieland and Twyla Tharp) read from the *Bay State Primer* (1800 edition) and Robert Grosseteste's eleventh-century text *On Light; or, The Ingression of Forms*. The second section consists of more than 2500 images, each exactly one second long, with no sound track of any kind. Each shot shows a word appearing on a street sign, on a wall, or as part of an advertisement. The final section is a long take of a couple and their dog disappearing into the depths of an idyllic snowstorm in the countryside; it represents the apotheosis of the film.

Frampton considered the film autobiographical; the still photographs used in the second section, for example, represent a homage to the filmmaker's past life as a gatherer of images. The deliberate, inexorable pace of the film is evident from the outset, but the systemic replacement of one image by the next becomes at once soothing and mesmerizing, leaving the viewer with a sense of a newly ordered universe. Frampton notes that his interest in words is directly related to his midwestern Protestant education. Though deeply formalist, he is keenly interested in audience response to *Zorns Lemma*, which often includes anticipation and laughter. Like many structuralists, Frampton likes to play with notions of time. For Frampton, duration is more important than narrative.

Structural Film 12

P. ADAMS SITNEY

Suddenly a cinema of structure has emerged. The dominant evolution of the American (and outlands') avant-garde cinema has been the pursuit of progressively complex forms; so this change of pace is unexpected and difficult to explain. Two points demand immediate clarity: first, what is the tendency towards complex forms?, and how is the structural cinema different? A view in perspective of the independent cinema over the past twenty years and, perhaps more pointedly in the work of those artists who have been outside of the sponsored cinema for more than a decade, will show the development of a cinematic language of *conjunction*, whereby diverse strands of themes are fitted together, or a language of metaphor, whereby the most is made of limited material. Those who have seen the whole work of Brakhage, Markopoulos, Kubelka, and Anger, for instance, will immediately grasp the concept of an "evolution of forms" by contrasting *Reflections on Black* to *The Art of Vision*, *Swain* to *The Illiac Passion*, *Mosaic in Confidence* to *Our Trip to Africa*, or *Eaux D'Artifice* to *Scorpio Rising*. In every one of these films, the early as well as the recent, the filmmaker attempts to make disparate elements cohere and to make cinematic architecture; yet in the later examples the themes (within each film) are more varied and the total more compact.

In the past five years nevertheless a number of filmmakers have emerged whose approach is quite different, although definitely related to the *sensibility* of those listed above: Tony Conrad, George Landow, Michael Snow, Joyce Wieland, Ernie Gehr, and Paul Sharits have produced a number of remarkable films *apparently* in the opposite direction of the formal tendency. Theirs is a cinema of structure wherein the shape of the whole film is predetermined and simplified, and it is that shape which is the primal impression of the film.

A precise statement of the difference between form and structure must involve a sense of the working process; for the formal film is a tight nexus of content, a shape designed to explore the facets of the material—the very title of Kubelka's first film, *Mosaic*, is an expression of this conscious aspiration. Recurrences, antithesis, and overall rhythm are the elements of the formal; in essence, a film whose content is, at root, a myth. In *Film Culture* Kubelka, Markopoulos, Brakhage, and to a lesser extent Anger, have discussed working processes, which share in common a scrutiny of the photographed raw material so that the eventual form will be revealed; their faith has been in editing. I exclude here of course certain recent films of Brakhage and Markopoulos made completely in the camera.

The structural film insists on its shape and what content it has is minimal and subsidiary to the outline. This is clearest in *The Flicker* of Tony Conrad and *Ray Gun Virus* of Paul Sharits where the flickering of single frame solids—in the former black-and-white, in the latter colors—is the total field.

Three characteristics of the structural film are a fixed camera position (fixed *frame* from the viewer's perspective), the flicker effect, and loop printing (the immediate repetition of shots, exactly and without variation). Very seldom will one find all three characteristics in a single film, and there are structural films which avoid these usual elements.

Origins

We find the sources of the three prevailing characteristics of the structural cinema in the immediate history of the avant-garde film. Andy Warhol made famous the fixed frame with his first film, *Sleep*, in which a half dozen shots are seen for over six hours. His films made a little later cling even more fiercely to the single unbudging perspective: *Eat*, forty-five minutes of the eating of a mushroom, *Harlot*, an eighty minute tableau vivant with offscreen commentary, *Beauty # 2*, a bed scene with off and on screen speakers for ninety minutes. For this, Warhol is one of the two major inspirations of the structuralists (he even used loop printing in *Sleep*, although Bruce Conner had done so more outrageously in *Report* a few months earlier). Yet Warhol, as a pop artist, is spiritually at the opposite pole from the structuralists. His fixed camera was at first an outrage, later an irony, until his content became too compelling and he abandoned the fixed image for a kind of in-the-camera editing. In the work of Ernie Gehr or Michael Snow the camera is fixed in mystical contemplation of a portion of space. Spiritually the difference between these poles cannot be reconciled. In fact, the antithesis of the structural film to the pop film (basically Warhol) is precisely the difference between Pop and Minimal painting or sculpture, where the latter grows out of and against the former. Here the analogy must end, because the major psychologies of structural cinema and minimal art are not usually comparable.

The second forefather of structural cinema is Peter Kubelka who made the first flicker film, *Arnulf Rainer*, in 1958, and who pioneered much of the field for the structuralists with his earlier minimal films *Adebar* and *Schwechater*. One could not really describe Kubelka as a filmmaker involved in the recently emerging structural tendency for several reasons: as an Austrian who created his films in a relative vacuum (seeing and caring for little but the work of Dreyer until late in his career) he would be outside the climate and mentality of the others; he is in the middle of his career while the others for the most part are beginners; and the direction of his work seems to be away from the structural into the more complex forms.

Ken Kelman suggested to me that the sensibility of the structuralists derives from the aesthetic of Brakhage. This is true to a certain extent—Brakhage more than anyone else has emphasized in print the primary importance of a visual cinema—but his films, until a very recent exception which I shall discuss, have been rhythmic rather than static. Actually if we are to seek a pioneer sensibility for the structural cinema it would be Robert Breer who literally founded the cinema of speed, single frame dominance, in the early 1950s. The effect of all of Breer's work is kinetic, as opposed to the static quality of the structural cinema. Nevertheless his work is the historical precursor of Kubelka's *Arnulf Rainer*, and subsequently an important link in the prehistory of our theme.

Examples

The structural film has appeared in filmographies where it was not to be expected. Were it not for three short films of Bruce Baillie, Gregory Markopoulos' *Gammelion*, and *Song 27*, *My Mountain* by Stan Brakhage a case might be made for a causal link among the new filmmakers of that area of cinema. These five works, all by artists in mid-career, indicate a general collective attitude has emerged. Its causes and meaning are obscure.

Perhaps the poetic form had reached such a sophistication in the complex works of Markopoulos, Brakhage, Anger, Kubelka, etc. (for certainly their forms more approximated the elements of poetry in this century than any other art) that these filmmakers wanted a new investigation of pure image and pure rhythm; or in other words, they sought to incorporate the aesthetics of painting and music (previously the domain of the animation filmmakers). No accident that Snow, Landow, and Wieland are also painters, Conrad a musician.

The films in their simplicity are easy to describe.

Bruce Baillie made his three structural films all at about the same time (1966–1967). *Show Leader* has one black-and-white shot of the filmmaker washing himself, nude, in a stream. Over the soundtrack he introduces himself to the audience. He intended this film as an epilogue or introduction to one man shows of his works and gives it without rent on those occasions. The shot and sound is loop printed to extend a few seconds into a couple of minutes. This unpretentious friendly film represents the structural cinema at its most casual.

All My Life is a one shot film and *Still Life*, Baillie's most sophisticated structural composition, is a one shot, fixed image film. The former is a pan shot in color across a fence trellised with roses and then up to the sky and telephone wires. It lasts as long as it takes Ella Fitzgerald to sing "All my life" on the soundtrack.

The title gives *Still Life* away: a fixed image of a tabletop floral arrangement, ash tray, and table objects; beyond the table, out of focus, is a room backed by windows. There seem to be figures in the far background: perhaps they are the men whose voices we hear on the sound, talking of Ramakrishna and apparently discussing a series of photographs of shrines in India. In the immediate background, just beyond the table, a female figure crosses the screen and returns later. Her costume is rich and elusive.

There is a metaphysics of irony; and the severe minimalization of Robert Indiana in a dumb felt hat taking 45 minutes to nibble a mushroom evokes it, especially when the camera doesn't budge. That's Warhol's *Eat*, a good instance of deadpan cinema. *Still Life* is a sweeter put-on; the humor is there, a particular form of Zen screwball native to hipper California, but also there is a sincere devotion to the apotheosis of space, the space framed within the camera field.

The overt principle of this film (and of some others we will discuss here, notably Michael Snow's *Wavelength*) is that the action or event is a function of the given space. It is not the floral arrangement that excites us in *Still Life*, but the whole field of action—the talking men, the passing female form, the flowers and the ashtray as constants—constitutes a single experience. Besides, the conscious concentration on a fixed quarter of space implies a conscious duality of the field—what happens, occurs either within or outside of the frame.

Again Warhol has explored this binary space, tongue in cheek, in *Blow Job* where the field of the frame, the subject's head, is obviously only the echoground for the title action. In *Beauty No. 2* an offscreen actor taunts Edie Sedgwick and her lover who are seen in bed. The idea of offscreen action as the focus of interest is certainly older than Warhol. Stan Brakhage first realized and pointed out that the major invention of Jerry Joffin, whose indescribable endless film is too seldom seen, was precisely the suggestion of significant action out of the camera's field. Brakhage himself utilized this principle in *Song 6*, an early anticipation of the structural film, in which a moth is seen dying against the flower pattern of a linoleum floor. It is sometimes center screen, but more often in a corner or just out of the screen. Since the moth is so close to the floor there is little sense of space. The linoleum is a backdrop rather, which becomes metaphorically an image of the veil of death because of the minimalization of the essential action—the moth death.

The importance of *Still Life* and the similar structural films is that the fixed camera electrifies a space, revealing in itself (not as a metaphor as in Brakhage or Joffin or as coy sideglancing as in Warhol). Within the context of Baillie's production the structural films can be seen as an outgrowth of the Japanese haiku form, a sensibility he had previously attempted with *Mr. Hayashi*, the portrait of a Japanese gardener, and with *Tung*, the negative "shadow" portrait of a girl walking. If the essence of haiku is the welding of two images into a synthetic mood, then in *Still Life* and *All My Life* Baillie has attained the form, with the union of picture and sound into an elemental structure.

Before continuing I must again allude to a technical antecedent in Warhol's work: the camera moving freely within the limits of a fixed tripod (right-left, up-down motions) and a zoom lens (in-out motion). This too is a manifestation of fixed space on a more intricate level. We saw it for the first time in *Party Sequence: Poor Little Rich Girl* and emphatically in the Marie Menken episode of *The Chelsea Girls*. When the tripod is fixed and the camera roams there is still a sense of minimalized space, less solid than in the fixed image, but more or less felt. *All My Life* is a pan or tracking shot, yet its structural monotone is apparent.

Michael Snow utilizes the tension of the fixed frame and some of the flexibility of the fixed tripod in *Wavelength*. Actually it is a forward zoom for forty-five minutes, halting occasionally, and fixed during several different times so that day changes to night within the motion.

A persistent polarity shapes the film. Throughout there is an exploration of the room, a long studio, as a field of space, subject to the arbitrary events of the outside world so long as the zoom is recessive enough to see the windows and thereby the street. The room, during the day, at night, on different film stock for color tone, with filters, and even occasionally in negative is gradually closing up its space as the zoom nears the back wall and the final image of a photograph upon it—a photograph of waves. This is the story of the diminishing area of pure potentiality. The insight of space, and implicitly cinema, as potential is an axiom of the structural film.

So we have always the room as the realm of possibility. Polar to this is a series of events whose actuality is emphasized by an interruption of the sine-wave blasting soundtrack with simple synchronized sound. The order of the events is progressive and interrelated: a bookcase is moved into the room, two girls are listening to the radio; so far we are early in the film, the cine-morning, the action appears random; midway through a man climbs the stairs (so we hear) and staggers onto the floor, but the lens has already crossed half the room and he is only glimpsed, the image passes over him. Late in the film, it's evening, one of the radio girls returns, goes to the telephone, which being at the back wall is in full view, and in a dramatic moment of acting unusual in the avant-garde cinema calls a man, Richard, to tell him there is a dead body in the room. She insists he does not look drunk but dead and says she will meet him downstairs. She leaves. The call makes a story of the previously random events. Had the film ended here actuality in the potent image of death would have satisfied all the potential energy built up before; but Snow prefers a deeper vision. What we see is a visual echo, a ghost in negative superimposition of the girl making the phone call, and the zoom continues, as the sound grows shriller, into the final image of the static sea pinned to the wall, a cumulative metaphor for the whole experience of the dimensional illusion of open space. The crucial difference between the form of Brakhage's *Song 6* and this film is that the *Song*, true to song form, is purely the invocation of a metaphor, while *Wavelength* uses a metaphor as the end of an elaborate yet simple structure whose coordinates are one room and one zoom.

I cannot evaluate Snow's earlier film *New York Eye and Ear Control* because the one time I saw it, it was projected silently. And that film is famous for its jazz soundtrack. Nevertheless, it is clearly a rudimentary aspiration to the principles of the structural film. In it, a cutout full size profile of a walking woman appears in a number of contexts with live action. From that one glimpse of the film I had, I would dare to say it is episodic, without development. Like Brakhage's *Song 6* it is an epistemological metaphor. What is particularly interesting is that, like Landow's *Fleming Faloon* which I shall soon describe, it is a first attempt to make a structural film by the filmmaker who later achieved that form, before the form had emerged.

A set of films by Ernie Gehr, *Wait* and *Moments*, work an area similar to that of *Wavelength* on a simpler level. Both are fixed tripod zoom structures, but the zoom movements are staccato and not the primary organizational principles of the films. Both are structured on rhythmic variations of the film stocks' exposure to fixed light sources. In *Wait* the source is a overhead lamp, giving the film a series of red dominant intensities. A couple are reading in a room. There is no sound.

Moments is another interior: a room with a cat and apparently someone in bed; yet the source of light is an outside window, in whose image we can see a firescape when the exposure is very low. The tones are bluish and again there is no sound.

Brakhage has of course used variations in exposure as formal elements of a film, but to the best of my knowledge, Gehr deserves the credit for first using exposure differences as the prime material of an entire film and for composing with the *f* stops as a rhythmic instrument.

Joyce Wieland, the wife of Michael Snow, has used loop printing for at least two kinds of structure. In *Sailboat* the loop gives an illusion of continuous movement as a boat sails from screen left and out of screen right repeatedly; in *1933* a single shot of a street taken from a high window with people rushing in fast motion and slowing down to normal motion (without a change of shots) is seen about a dozen times. Occasionally the title, *1933*, is printed over the entire shot, and between each set of repetitions there is white leader marked by different red flashes.

Of all the filmmakers included in this article Wieland is closest to Andy Warhol and the mentality of the pop film. In *Sailboat* the structural principle is clearly ironic, while *1933* is a pure and quite mysterious structural film. In *Catfood* she shows a cat devouring fish after fish for some ten minutes. There seems to be no repetition of shots, but the imagery is so consistent throughout—shot of the fish, the cat eating, his paw clawing, another fish, the cat eating, etc.—that it is just possible that shots are recurrent. There is no question but that Wieland has a unique talent. I doubt, though, that her strength will prove, in the future, to be in the arena of form. Already she has made *Rat Life and Diet in North America*, a facetious animalegory of political and economic repression in the United States and liberation in Canada! She's Canadian, by the way. The film is witty, articulate, and a far cry from all the other cute animal humanism the cinema has sickened us with in the past. Nevertheless it is a vital

13. Frames from Joyce Wieland's *Sailboat* (1967). Courtesy Anthology Film Archives; reprinted by permission.

extension of the aspect of her other films which runs counter to the structural principle: ironic symbolism.

I have had occasion to mention Stan Brakhage's work several times in these pages and to single out his *Song 6*. The nearest he has come to a structural film yet is his recent *Song 27, My Mountain*. To single out any single *Song* as a formal organism is to ignore the complex overall emerging form of *Songs* as a single homemovie serial, some of whose images and many of whose themes, sporadically recur. In fact, there will be an eight part coda to *Song 27*, five of which parts I've seen whose intricacies belong to the meta-serial film (a form I shall soon write about, but not now, which includes Markopoulos' *Galaxie* and Harry Smith's *Late Superimpositions*). Then, excluding the coda called *Rivers*, *Song 27, My Mountain* studies a mountain peak for thirty minutes, from a few different angles, with shots of clouds and a rainbow included.

How is this a structural film? The notes I have given so far describe a method of construction based on a fixed image, loop printing, and slight variations of this, and I have promised to discuss the flicker film. The minimalization of technique accompanies the minimalization of image in these instances, which is not strictly the case with Brakhage's mountain song.

The extreme concentration in Brakhage's film upon the mountain as durable energy—it survives several seasons, persistently emerges from engulfing clouds—creates a kind of tension and a sense of potential comparable to the most dynamic structural films, *Wavelength*, Landow's *Bardo Follies*, Markopoulos' *Gammelion*, and Sharits' N:O:T:H:I:N:G. The space of a mountain, an arrogant young Rockie at that, is not that of a room. Harry Smith once proposed that Warhol film Mt. Fuji with his fixed camera. The gesture would have been ironical and true to Warhol's world view: a diminishing of the energy of the subject. Brakhage has again shown his genius by moving the camera positions, allowing the seasons to change and thus finding the structure that would hold the terror of a field as big as a mountain.

In his recent lectures he has spoken of the growing influence of Dutch and Flemish painters over his compositional sense and has seen in Van Eyck especially an awareness for slight movements at the edge of the frame. Appropriately in *Song 27, My Mountain* the tension which a single shot could easily create over thirty minutes is sustained through a multitude of shots by careful coordination of the minute movements at the corners of the screen. He did not use a tripod, but he approximated the stillness of the tripod to make these tiny excursions more emphatic. Thus he keeps the unity of the image, thematically, and reaffirms the space of the film frame. The synthetic unity of these forces is his structure.

The most devout of the structural filmmakers and perhaps the most sublime is George Landow. His first film, *Fleming Faloon*, is a precursor of the structural tendency, though not quite achieved. The theme of a direct address is at the center of its construction: beginning with two boobs reciting "Around the world in eighty minutes", jump cuts of a TV newscaster, and image upon image of a staring face, sometimes full screen, sometimes the butt of a dollying camera, superimposed upon itself, sometimes split into four images (unsplit 8mm photography, in which two sets of two consecutive images appear in the 16mm frame) televisions, mirrored televisions, and superimposed movies are interspersed. Although I have seen the film many times, I could never find a structural principle after the opening, which Landow has called the prelude. *Fleming Faloon* is simply a series of related images.

The sensibility that created *Fleming Faloon*, a filmmaker more than any other non-animator devoted to the flat screen cinema, the moving grain painting, is the primary force in the structural film. Perhaps he actually invented it when he made *Film in which there appear sprocket holes, edge lettering, dirt particles etc.* He derived its image from a commercial test film, originally nothing more than a girl staring at the camera; a blink of her eye is the only motion, with a spectrum of primary colors beside her. Landow had the image reprinted so that the girl and the spectrum occupies only one half of the frame, the other half of which is made up of sprocket holes, frilled with rapidly changing edge letters, and in the far right screen half of the girl's head again.

Landow premiered this film as loop at the Filmmakers Cinematheque, calling it *This film will be interrupted after ten minutes by a commercial*. True to its title the film was interrupted with an 8mm interjection of Rembrandt's "Town Council" as reproduced by Dutch Master Cigars. A luscious green scratch stood across the splice in the loop, which gave it a particular tonality during that single performance, since only that identified the cycling of the loop, and contrasted with the red overtone of the image.

When the loop, minus the commercial, was printed to become *Film in which*, Landow instructed the laboratory not to clean the dirt from the film and to make a clean splice that would hide the repetitions. The resultant film, a found object extended to a simple structure, is the essence of a minimal cinema. The girl's face is static, perhaps a blink is glimpsed; the sprocket holes do not move but waver slightly as the system of edge lettering flashes around them. Deep into the film the dirt begins to form time patterns, and the film ends.

There is a two screen version of this film, projected with no line separating the two panels and with the right image reversed so that a synthetic girl, with two left hand sides of her face, is evoked between the two girl panels.

Bardo Follies, Landow's most sophisticated film, describes a kind of meditation analogous to the Tibetan *Book of the Dead*. The film begins with a loop printed image of a water flotilla carrying a woman who waves to us at every turn of the loop. After about ten minutes (there is a shorter version too) the same loop appears doubled into a set of circles against the black screen. Then there are three circles for an instant. The film image in the circles begins to burn creating a moldy wavering orange dominated mass. Eventually the entire screen fills with one burning frame, which disintegrates in slow motion in an extremely grainy soft focus. Another frame burns; the whole screen throbs with melting celluloid. Probably this was created by several generations of photography off the screen—its effect is to make the screen itself seem to throb and smolder. The tension of the silly loop is maintained throughout this section in which the film stock itself seems to die. After a long while it becomes a split screen of air bubbles in water filmed through a microscope with colored filters, a different color on each side of the screen. Through changes of focus the bubbles lose shape and dissolve into one another and the color filters switch. Finally, some forty minutes after the first loop the screen goes white. The film ends.

Structurally we have the gradual abstraction of an image (originally emphasized through loop printing) through burning and slow motion rephotography off the screen. The final images of air bubbles are metaphorical extensions of the process of abstraction. The entire opus is open to the interpretation suggested by the title, of the pursuit of the pure light from the "follies" of daily life. The viewer comes to see not the images of the earth, the girl on her flotilla, but the colors and tones of the light itself in a chain of purification.

In his latest work, *The Film that Rises to the Surface of Clarified Butter*, Landow extends the structural principle of the loop into a cycle of visions. Here we see in black-and-white the head of a working animator; he draws a line, makes a body; then he animates a grotesque humanoid shape. In negative a girl points to the drawing and taps on it with a pencil. This sequence of shots, the back of the animator, the animation, the negative girl looking at it, occurs three times, but not with exactitude since there is sometimes more negative material in one cycle than in another. Next we see (another?) animator, this time from the front; he is creating a similar monster; he animates it. Again we see him from the front, again he animates it. Such is the action of the film. A wailing sound out of Tibet accompanies the whole film. The title as well is eastern: Landow read about the film that rises to the surface of clarified butter in the *Upanishads*.

The explicit ontology of the film, based on the distinction between graphic (the monsters) two-dimensional modality and photographic naturalism (the animators, even the pen resting beside the monsters as they move in movie illusion), as a metaphor for the relation of film itself (a two-dimensional field of illusion) and actuality, is a classic perception implicit since the beginning of animation and explicit countless times before. Yet what film has been built solely about this metaphor? No other, I can recall. Landow's genius is not his intellectual approach, even though he would be among the most intelligent filmmakers in the country, which is simplistic, i.e. the variations on announcing and looking (*Fleming Faloon*), the extrinsic visual interest in a film frame (*Film in which there appear sprocket holes, edge lettering, dirt particles etc.*), a meditation on the pure light trapped in a ridiculous image (*Bardo Follies*), and the echo of an illusion (*The Film that Rises to the Surface of Clarified Butter*); his remarkable faculty is as maker of images; for the simple found objects (*Film in which*, beginning of *Bardo Follies*) he uses and the images he photographs are among the most radical, super-real, and haunting images the cinema has ever given us. Without this sense of imagery all of his films would have failed—as a few of his early 8mm works do. Because of this peculiar visual genius his work is the most consistently pertinent, on a spiritual level, of all the filmmakers considered here (excepting of course Brakhage and Markopoulos whose works are really tangential to the themes of this article).

The occurrence of a structural film among the works of Gregory Markopoulos is, to say the least, a surprise. His most outstanding contribution to the language of cinema has been the use of single-frame flashes in film narrative. But the whole point of this speedy image, which he confirms in his writing, was towards the elaborations of more complex forms, an articulation of simultaneity. Robert Breer was perhaps the true pioneer for the single frame film sequence (although of course, Eisenstein, Vertov and even Griffith had used rapid flashes in the past) and remotely the forefather of the structural film, certainly long before Kubelka or Warhol. His speed of imagery is quite opposite in effect to that of Markopoulos and his sensibility would be labeled more precisely "kinetic", along with Len Lye, his one equal.

It might be noted in passing that Breer too has created his most structural, certainly most minimal film during the past two years. It is 66, an animation of primary color shapes interrupting the stasis of the previous image shape. The film is still too much of a natural outgrowth of Breer's process and career to be considered an unusual deviation toward the structural. Yet much credit is his for developing speed of imagery as a sensibility and that, as much as Brakhage's attitude towards the plastic image, which Kelman believes is the root of the structural film, is a key point in the origin of the mode I am trying to define.

To return to Markopoulos, what is interesting in *Gammelion* is that it takes the shape of a flicker film and still remains a narrative. Perhaps a thousand times the screen fades into white and out again, creating the impression of a great winking eye. Sometimes the fades in and out are colored, sometimes not. After the first minutes of these slow blinks a single frame image is injected into the film; then a little later there are more, perhaps four or five frame shots. Until the very end *Gammelion* evolves as it began, a minimal narrative in a structural matrix.

For many years Markopoulos wanted to film *The Castle of Argol* of Julian Gracq and he chose Caresse Crosby's Roccasinabalda as the site. In 1963 I read a film script of some four hundred pages closely following the novel. This was while Markopoulos was editing *Twice A Man*. The project was postponed to make *The Illiac Passion* and never resumed in the original form. Yet when Markopoulos found himself in Italy in 1967 and with only enough money to purchase about two rolls of color film three minutes long apiece, he went to Roccasinabalda and filmed. He shot the entrance of the castle, the corridors, some rooms, the flag which is a black sun, a naked couple in the fresco, a spot of blood on the pathway. These are the elements of his narrative along with the sound of a trotting horse, some romantic music, Wagner I think, and the following lines from Rilke: "To be loved means to be consumed. To love means to radiate with inexhaustible light. To be loved is to pass away. To love is to endure." The details of the shooting experience can be found in issue 46 of *Film Culture* where Markopoulos has written "Correspondences of Smells and Visuals", the most revealing of all the articles I have read from him.

As we sit before *Gammelion*, we see the winking screen. The flashes are interruptions of the structure, as if the implanted narrative were taking place somewhere else entirely. Within the terms of Markopoulos' previous work the technique of fading in and out may be interpreted as a psychological distancing or phrasing of the images as in a remote memory. A few years ago he began to employ the fade as a formal device in *Eros o Basileus*, where it syncopates the rhythm of the long erotic tableaux. In spirit that film is close to *Gammelion* even though in mechanics they seem so opposite, the earlier being composed of the longest shots Markopoulos has ever taken and the later made up solely of flashes. The crucial difference of form concerns us here; for *Eros o Basileus* is a serial film and *Gammelion* structural.

By making *The Flicker* Tony Conrad brought a new clarity to Kubelka's *Arnulf Rainer*, which he had not seen. Both films are montages of black-and-white leader; Kubelka's is melodic and classical, with bursts of phrasing, pauses and explosions; the sound, white noise and silence, is likewise symphonic, sometimes synchronous with the image, more often syncopated;

Conrad built one long crescendo–diminuendo (*The Flicker* is four times as long as *Arnulf Rainer*) with a single blast of stereophonic buzz for the soundtrack.

Film Culture published a series of articles by and about Conrad in 1966 (No. 41). Here one finds the most articulate expression of the consciousness of structuralism of any published record of the filmmakers involved. In a letter to Henry Romney he wrote:

> So I always try to give an impression of serenity and repose whenever I work with extreme materials.
>
> A word on the subject of the static style and its place in art, since I have just implied a bias in this direction. The static seems to be regarded with some suspicion in the age of rock n' roll; although it is a basic dimension of all creative work, it easily gets labeled as exoticism or as very far out. Naturally this imagery is by that very fact a part of the picture, but I do not feel that static style can sustain itself on these alone as a thing in itself for very long. Like other "new" things, it has to incorporate itself as a tool into a moving stream of artistic creation. Among the current exponents of this style, I long ago sought out La Monte Young and I have felt that our long collaboration has proven unprecedentedly fruitful as a continuous evolving development. On the other hand I have never been able to cure myself of suspicions that Andy Warhol's static films, for example, are incurably opportunistic and basically devoid of the intrinsic interest or freshness that I feel to be the real challenge of static work.

. . . As I have elaborated earlier Warhol's form is something quite different, as becomes more and more apparent the more films he makes. Yet the use of the word "static" is a helpful guide to the difference between Conrad's *The Flicker* and Kubelka's *Arnulf Rainer*, and by extension a definition of the image in the structural cinema.

The structural film is static because it is not modulated internally by evolutionary concerns. In short, there are no climaxes in these films. They are visual, or audio-visual objects whose most striking characteristic is their overall shape.

Conrad's second film, *The Eye of Count Flickerstein*, begins with a brief Dracula parody in which the camera moves up to the eye of the Count; then, until the end of the film, we see a boiling swarm of images very similar to, if not made from, the static on a television screen when the station is not transmitting. Aesthetically, *Count Flickerstein* lacks the ambition of *The Flicker*, but it is not without visual interest.

Both Conrad and Kubelka have worked with the fundamental primitive energy of the flicker principle and it is obvious why they would use black-and-white film for this charge. Paul Sharits has made three color flickers, sensitive films, without the ecstatic power of either *The Flicker* or *Arnulf Rainer*, but he has done more than either of his predecessors to develop the formal potential of the flicker film.

Ray Gun Virus was his first attempt in this genre and it is the simplest. It is a splattering of colors. Its effect is distanced, a calm look at the modulations of rapidly changing color tones. In essence *Ray Gun Virus* is the base for both of Sharits' intricate structures, *Piece Mandala* and N:O:T:H:I:N:G. In *Piece Mandala* he elaborates themes of sex and self violence within the tissue of the color flashes. In this way he raises the dramatic power of the flickering colors by metaphor rather than visually. A mandala is a meditation wheel. Literally it derives its name from the Sanskrit etymology of "a circle". The film begins and ends the same way, with staccato stills of lovemaking, mostly of postures of entry, some cunnilingus, breast feeling. As the film progresses the color flashes grow longer, the stills more isolated, until in the middle of the work, there is the photograph of a young man's head; he is pointing a gun at his skull, animated dots outline the bullet's path. Then the film completes the circular form; the flashes grow shorter, the loving stills more excited. The film ends as it began with the flashing titles, Peace, War.

Before I had seen N:O:T:H:I:N:G I had a limited respect for Sharits' art. Now I can see the two films discussed above only as preparations for his one fully developed film. In N:O:T:H:I:N:G, the flashing colors have the sense of potential space-time that we noted in the fixed image structures of Baillie, Landow, Snow, and Markopoulos.

This film is much longer than the earlier two, about forty minutes, and to a much greater extent the colors group in major and minor phrases with, say, a pale blue dominant at one time, a yellow dominant at another. The colors tend toward the cooler shades. The ultimate aspiration of Sharits' cinema must be the synthesis of whiteness; because the natural effect of his blazing colors is a blending which will always tend towards a bleaching. In *Ray Gun Virus* the bleaching affected me as a weakness, but in N:O:T:H:I:N:G, the related contextual images and the sound, as well as the title, utilize the theme of evaporation (which is the converse of potentiality, which is the mode of all structural films). From the very beginning the screen flickers clusters of colors; the titles gradually flash on, the letters and colors separately, while the sound suggests a telegraph code, or chattering teeth, or the plastic click of suddenly changing television channels.

The first image interlude in the chain of color shows us a chair animated in positive and negative; it floats down screen, away into nothing, or the near nothing of the mutually exterminating colors. The interlude is marked with the sound of a telephone. The remaining and main body of the film is continually interrupted for short periods by the image of a light bulb, two dimensional like the chair before it, dripping its vital light fluid. From the first occurrence of this image until the last drop of bulb fluid has leaked out, a series of static beeps are heard, gradually spaced further and further apart. In the end we see only long passages of color clusters whose dominants are synchronized to the moos of cows.

In essence there are only three flicker films of importance, *Arnulf Rainer*, *The Flicker*, and N:O:T:H:I:N:G. The first is the most dynamic and inventive. The second is a splendid extension (who of those who knew Kubelka's film would have thought it possible?) into the area of meditative cinema. In terms of the subjects we have discussed here, it is Sharits' N:O:T:H:I:N:G that opens the field for the structural film with a flicker base. In all instances, even the overtly psychedelic use of the flicker by John Cavanaugh in *The Dragon's Claw*, the employment of color has diminished the basic apocalypse of the flicker and has worked it to an advantage. His latest film builds wave after wave of colors, each modulated by the minor of the spectrum, as a context of minimalization for his images.

Since I began this article a number of structural films have been premiered in New York. Most notable are Ken Jacobs' *Airshaft*, the films of Hollis Frampton, Morgan Fisher's *The Director and His Actor*; and I'm told his *Documentary Footage* would fit the genre. To this I should add that a number of structural films, some worse than others, were included in the Experimental Festival of Knokke-le-Zoute last year: Nekes' *Putput, Jum-Jum*, Mommartz' *Eisenbahn* and Thoms' *Bolero*. In the next years we can expect several more and inevitably both a climax and degeneration of the mode.

Interview with Michael Snow   13

SCOTT MACDONALD

Very few filmmakers have had as powerful an impact on North American independent cinema as Michael Snow. The impact of Snow's work—and of the breakthrough *Wavelength* (1967), in particular—is a function of the fact that Snow came to filmmaking, not with extensive experience as a moviegoer—conventional cinema never seems to have been of particular interest to him—but as an accomplished musician, painter, sculptor, and photographer, for whom the movie camera and projection space were new artistic tools to explore. While it was not his first extended film—that was *New York Eye and Ear Control* (1964)—*Wavelength* established him as a major contributor to the development of critical cinema.

In *Wavelength*, Snow demonstrated a new approach to cinematic space and time, and, at least by implication, declared his independence from the reliance on narrative in both conventional and independent cinema, as well as from the exploration of the personal that was characteristic of so many of the films of the 1960s. *Wavelength* defined a new kind of "plot," one closer to the geometric sense of the term than to its conventional meaning in film. Snow divided the focal length of his zoom lens into approximately equal increments and zoomed, at intervals, from the most wide-angle view of a New York City loft space to a close-up of a photograph on the far wall. The relentlessness of the viewer's journey across the loft is wittily confirmed by periodic nods in the direction of conventional narrative: near the beginning of the film, a woman (Amy Taubin) directs two men who move a bookcase into the space; they leave and the woman reenters with another woman; later, a man (Hollis Frampton) staggers into the loft and falls dead in front of the camera; he is discovered by Amy near the end of the film. This series of events allows *Wavelength* to critique the cinema's traditional reliance on story. While a mysterious death in a film would normally be a lynchpin for melodrama, in *Wavelength* the death is enacted precisely so that it can be ignored during the remainder of the film. Not only does the camera fail to stop for the death, the film overwhelms whatever interest we might have in the fledgling narrative by providing the eye and ear with continued stimulation of a very different order: as we cross the space by means of the periodically adjusted zoom lens, Snow continually changes film stocks, filters, and the camera's aperture, so that the loft becomes a visual phantasmagoria. And after the opening passage during which we hear "Strawberry Fields Forever" ("Living is easy with eyes closed") on Amy's radio, the sound of a sine wave increasingly dominates the soundtrack, ironically building toward the "climax" of our recognition that *this* film relentlessly refuses to conform to the "rules" engendered by the tradition of narrative cinema.

In the years since *Wavelength*, Snow has continued to make films that defy conventional expectations (and he has continued to work in a variety of other media). In film after film, he has explored the capabilities of the camera and the screening space and has emphasized dimensions of the viewer's perceptual and conceptual experience with cinema by systematically articulating the gap between the experience of reality and the various ways in which a film artist can depict it.

In *Back and Forth* ↔ (1969) the pan is the central organizational principle. The continual motion of the camera from right to left to right across the same classroom space (during the body of the film) becomes a grid within which Snow demonstrates the wide range of options panning offers. *One Second in Montreal* (1969) uses a set of still photographs of potential sculpture sites in Montreal as a silent grid within which Snow can focus on the viewer's sense of duration: we see each photograph in a single, continuous shot for a different period of time—at first for longer and longer, then shorter and shorter durations. *Side Seat Paintings Slides Sound Film* (1970) uses the repeated presentation of slides of early Snow paintings, filmed from the side of the auditorium in which they're projected, as a grid within which he can dramatize the "interference" created when artworks in one medium are reproduced in another medium. *La Région Centrale* (1971) extends Snow's interest in the moving camera. A complex machine designed by Snow enabled him to move the camera in any direction and at nearly any speed he could imagine as he filmed the wild, empty terrain north of Montreal: the resulting film immerses the audience for three hours ten minutes in an experience halfway between a landscape film and an amusement park ride. The epic *"Rameau's Nephew" by Diderot (Thanx to Dennis Young) by Wilma Schoen* (1974) uses a set of individual filmic actions to explore as many variations on the concept of synch sound as Snow could imagine. *Presents* (1980) compares different ways of composing film imagery with a moving camera. In *So Is This* (1982) Snow uses a grid of one printed word per shot to develop a fascinating exploration of the distinctions between reading a text and experiencing a movie. *Seated Figures* (1988) is a landscape film made up of repeated tracking shots of landscapes filmed from a camera looking vertically down from a position a few inches from the ground. And in *See You Later/Au Revoir* (1990) extreme slow motion transforms Snow's standing up and walking out of an office into a gorgeous motion study. Together, Snow's films provide one of avant-garde film's most elaborate critiques of cinematic convention. They are an inventive and productive artist's revenge on film habit.

While Snow remains known primarily as a filmmaker in the United States, he has continued to demonstrate that he is, above all, an *artist* for whom the cinematic apparatus is one of many sets of tools with which art can be made. Even during his most prolific years as a filmmaker (1964–1974), Snow maintained his interest and productivity in other media, and in intersections between media. The confrontation of audience expectations and assumptions so important in *Wavelength* and other films remains central in *The Audience* (1989), a set of sculptures commissioned by Toronto's new Skydome stadium: the individual characters in the two groupings of representational figures (baseball fans) confront the patrons entering the arena in a variety of provocative ways.

I spoke with Snow in Montreal twice, in early June 1989 and in late May 1990. The two sessions were combined into a single discussion.

Scott MacDonald: I want to start with *The Audience*. My guess is that people who know you solely or primarily as an avant-garde filmmaker will say the Skydome gargoyles are something new for you. I can even imagine somebody saying, "Oh, another formalist filmmaker selling out." And yet, on many levels, the gargoyles are in keeping with work you've done all along. From very early in your career, you've been drawn to the public arena and to the idea of confronting expectations. A central premise of the "Walking Woman" paintings, sculptures, and mixed media pieces was that they were located all over New York (and later other places), so that people—mostly people who hadn't planned on looking at or thinking about art— would be running into them. And, of course, film is a public arena, too. Your early films were powerful interruptions of what audiences had come to expect—even from what was then called "underground film." They remind me of the old gesture in Hollywood films of slapping people across the face to bring them out of a daze. When Pat [Pat O'Connor, MacDonald's wife] and I were driving in on the expressway the other day, our eyes were immediately drawn to the gargoyles (this is before I realized that the new work you had mentioned on the phone wasn't a film). Out of the whole panorama of the Toronto skyline we were noticing these funny things hanging out of the Skydome. Everything else is rectangles and planes, so this interruption in the city's geometry can't be ignored. Even at a considerable distance, the gargoyles confront the spectator. So, for me, this new piece seems very closely related to your early work.

Michael Snow: I think that's really true. The big departure in the new piece for some people, at least people who know my sculpture and gallery work, is that it's figurative. I haven't done that before, except with *The Walking Woman*, but *The Walking Woman* had a whole other kind of premise. In 1953 I did a painting called *Colin Curd about to Play*. It was one of my first big oil paintings. Colin Curd was a flute player I had met. The painting shows this person and a group of people, faces. It's rather Paul Klee-ish. The focus of the painting is the relationship between the audience and the artist or the audience and the work.

There's also some early sculpture, which people would generally call abstract, that includes the spectators. There's *Scope* [1967], which was originally shown in New York in the late 1960s. Actually, it's one of a series of sculptures I've continued. They're framers and directors of the spectator's attention. *Scope* is kind of a giant periscope on its side, an illusory straight ahead, made by a couple of right angles. If you look in one end, you see this tunnel and—if someone else is looking into the other end—another person at the end of the tunnel. There's also *De La*, a video installation work (owned by the National Gallery of Canada) which uses the apparatus I made to film *La Région Centrale*. The spectators are part of the image.

Another connection—though I didn't think about it at the time—is in *Seated Figures*, the film I made during the same period when I was working on the Skydome piece: the sound is the sound of an audience. The connection is obvious now, but when I made the soundtrack for the film, I was just trying to figure out what kind of sound was going to do the best job in connection with the imagery. So, yes, the Skydome piece is in some ways a continuation of my earlier work.

MacDonald: What originally drew you to film?

Snow: Confusion. I decided to go to art school from high school because I was given the art prize, which surprised me. I knew I was sort of interested in art, but I was still trying to figure out what to do, so I went to the Ontario College of Art to study design. I started to paint, more or less on my own. A teacher, John Martin, the head of that department, was very, very helpful (he's dead now). He suggested what books to read and made comments on my work. He was fantastic. He suggested that I put a couple of paintings in a juried show, put on by a group called the Ontario Society of Artists. This was a big group show that happened every year, for members and other people. I was still a student, but my two paintings got accepted. It was a big deal because a student had never been in the show. It was very encouraging.

I had already started to play music. During high school I had met a bunch of ne'er-do-wells and started to play jazz. It was a fantastic part of my life. At school I had been rebelling (mildly) against everything. But when I found music, I really found something. I started to play a lot, and a band formed, and by the time I went to O.C.A., I was playing occasional jobs. So I was simultaneously getting into music and into painting and sculpture, mostly painting. I was influenced by a lot of people: Matisse, Mondrian, Picasso, Klee. I liked Klee very much.

When I got out of O.C.A., I found a job in an advertising firm that did catalogues and stuff like that. And I was miserable and really terrible at the job. I made stupid mistakes. I thought, "Is this life on the other side of school?" So I saved what money I could and quit the job and went to Europe to find myself. I was miserable. Fortunately, I went with Bob Hackborn, who had been at O.C.A. with me. He was a drummer; we had played in some of the same bands. And some other musicians I knew at the time also went to Europe. I ran into some jobs with them, though not just with them: I played with the band at the Club Méditerranée (now known as Club Med), which had started just two or three years before. An amazing band. The guys were from French colonies or former French colonies like Guadalupe and Martinique—black guys studying dentistry in Paris. They were looking for a trumpet player and a drummer, and we were in Paris trying to figure out how to live on two hundred dollars for a year. . . .

MacDonald: Two hundred dollars?

Snow: That's about what I had.

I had started to play trumpet about three months before I went (I played piano before that) and knew a couple of tunes. Anyway, we did an audition. I played "Lady Be Good," one of the few tunes I knew, and these guys really liked it. So I got this job and went from Paris to Italy, where the Club Méditerranée had a place on the coast of Tuscany and another on the island of Elba. We were paid our board and drink tickets. They'd give us a book of tickets, so we were plastered every night.

I also traveled around during the year; I went to all the museums and churches. And I did thousands of drawings and some paintings, including Colin Curd about to Play. It's quite a big painting, at least for then, and for the circumstances.

When I came back, somehow or other, I was asked to exhibit some of the drawings I had made while I was away, along with Graham Koftree, another artist who had also been in Europe and was a friend of mine—at Hart House, a University of Toronto gallery. When the show was on, I got a call from a guy who said, "I'd be interested to meet you. When I saw your work, I thought that whoever did those drawings was very interested in film." In fact, I wasn't. I didn't know what he was talking about! I went to meet him and it was George Dunning, who later directed the Beatles film Yellow Submarine [1968]. He said, "Do you want a job?" I didn't know what the hell to do with my life. I told him frankly that I had no special interest in film, but I certainly would be interested to try and do something. He and some other people who had been at the National Film Board had just started a film company called Graphic Films, and he was hiring people whose main interest or training was so-called fine art. So I took the job.

I met Joyce Wieland there and we eventually married.

MacDonald: Had you been a film-goer as a kid?

Snow: No, not especially. That was a very strange observation on Dunning's part. In those drawings there is some inadvertent interest in movement. They're not futurist or cubist, but sometimes they include different positions of arms, of objects. Well anyway, he liked the work and saw something he thought could be applicable to film.

Graphic Films was the first company in Canada, or one of the first, to do television commercials. They were animated. Everybody, except for the cameraman, Warren Collins, was learning how to do the work. And it's hard! It was my introduction to film.

MacDonald: Your first film, A *to* Z [1956], is an animation.

Snow: It had nothing to do with the work. It was just that the camera was available and Warren Collins was willing to help me shoot. Some of the other people working there also made their own films: that's when Joyce got started.

Then Graphic Films collapsed. I had been playing music all along, occasionally with a guy named Mike White. He put a band together, and all of a sudden we got a hell of a lot of work. We were playing at the Westover every night for a year; this is 1961–1962. The band became quite popular, and the Westover brought in a lot of Dixieland stars. I was playing with the former Ellingtonians, Cootie Williams and Rex Stewart; and Buck Clayton, a really great trumpet player; Pee Wee Russell, a genius of a clarinetist. It was a fabulous job. We played in a lot of other places in Toronto, and sometimes in other parts of Ontario. And we made some records. I also started to play with my own groups occasionally because I had started to get interested in what were called "more modern" directions. I played Thelonious Monk pieces, stuff like that. And some of the musicians I met with the Mike White band asked me to play with them. I played with Jimmy Rushing, the great blues singer, in Detroit and a couple of places in New York State. There's a Film Board film, *Toronto Jazz* [1963], by Don Owen, that I appear in with my quartet (it's called the Alf Jones Quartet in the film, can't remember why— Alf was the trombone player).

It was a beautiful time for me. The music was wonderful and lots was happening. I was able to get to my studio every day to do painting and sculpture. During 1959 I had done a series of abstract paintings that I'm quite proud of. In them I gradually did this flip into working with the outline of a figure. *The Walking Woman* started in 1961.

MacDonald: Are those abstract paintings the ones in *Side Seat Paintings Slides Sound Film?*

Snow: Some that I did in Europe are in that film and some of the abstract ones. But I hope you wouldn't make any judgment of the paintings from their appearance in that film!

MacDonald: Things were going so well here. What drew you to New York?

Snow: Well, I had been following what was going on in New York very closely. For a long time, I had been moved (and still am) by the accomplishments of Willem De Kooning, Mark Rothko, Barnett Newman, Arshile Gorky, and Franz Kline. That's fantastic work, and I was carrying on my own dialogue with it, trying to define what I could do, what I could contribute, and after a while it seemed that doing this via magazines and occasional trips to the Albright Knox (in Buffalo) or to New York was not enough. I decided I should just get there. I was scared shitless, and Joyce was even more scared—so we went.

All during this period I kept thinking that in order to get somewhere and get something out of myself, I should make a choice. It seemed like the lesson was that Willem De Kooning *paints* and that's why it's so good. That's what he does; he does just that. And there's really a lot in that argument. So I tried not to play when I first went to New York. Mind you, I didn't know how I was going to make a living. It turned out that I did play a couple of times to make a couple of bucks, but basically, I was trying to get rid of music, to make it a hobby.

But when I got to New York, I had something I hadn't counted on, a contact with the most inventive music that was going on at that time, the "free musicians." I already knew about Ornette Coleman and Cecil Taylor. I had their records. But I met a guy named Roswell Rudd, a great trombone player, through a Dixieland clarinetist named Kenny Divern, another fabulous musician. I had a studio with a piano in it that I made available. There was no place for them to play, and the public antipathy was incredible. Cecil was considered a total nut. It certainly seemed that way the first time you heard him, but he was, and is, amazing.

Anyway, music wouldn't go away. But I was trying to be a painter. I was working on *The Walking Woman*, which, as you said earlier, involved works of many kinds in many places. A lot of it was what I call lost works: making things that were outside, in public spaces—on subways, in the street, in bookstores . . . it had a lot of range, despite the fact that it was concerned with this single outline.

The main thing I was trying to do was concentrate on visual art and get a gallery. I watched everything that was going on and gradually met people. That's when I met Hollis Frampton. I first noticed him at openings at Green Gallery. He was very noticeable! And he was at every opening. Gradually, I started talking to him, and at first I only knew that he was a photographer who was interested in art. I guess when I first met him he hadn't made any films.

MacDonald: When did you meet him?

Snow: Probably 1963, 1964. I went to New York in 1963.

MacDonald: In *The Walking Woman Works* you were putting the same figure in place after place, in serial fashion, which has a good deal in common with film. Were you conscious of that connection at the time?

Snow: Well, in the work itself there was a lot of sequential stuff. There are several pieces that are, say, four or five variations of the same figure. And, yeah, I did think there was something filmic about it. And then in 1964 I made *New York Eye and Ear Control*. I had had the idea for that film in Toronto.

When I first went to New York, I met Ben Park, who worked for one of the television stations I think, though he also produced films in a small way, I guess. I told him my ideas for *New York Eye and Ear Control*, and he said that he'd finance it. So we shot quite a bit of stuff, including a sequence of Marcel Duchamp and Joyce walking across the street, seen through a mask cutout of the Walking Woman. Anyway, Park finally decided against going ahead with the project and kept what I had shot. There wasn't too much enmity there, the film just stopped. Later on, I decided to try to do it myself.

MacDonald: *New York Eye and Ear Control* combines your fascination with music and *The Walking Woman Works*. It's as if you were learning how to work with film as a means of getting this other work down, but then, when you were done with that film, you were ready to be involved with film at a level comparable to what you'd achieved in music, painting, and sculpture.

Snow: Yeah, although *New York Eye and Ear Control* was interesting in itself. As far as I know, I invented the idea of putting art works—parts of *The Walking Woman Works*—out in the world, and then documenting the results in another work. The photographic piece, *Four to Five* [1962], was the very first time I did this, and the film expanded the idea. The business of making a work by documenting some action that you take hadn't happened yet, as far as I know, and I'm kind of proud of the priority of it. On one hand, *New York Eye and Ear Control* was another transformation of *The Walking Woman*, but I was also trying to work with the possibilities of the medium, especially with duration.

One of the things I wanted to do in the film was to bring two aspects of myself together. I used to refer to it as a classical side and a romantic side, or Apollonian and Dionysian. At the time, I felt I was rather schizophrenic. At any rate, the imagery is measured and calm, but beside it is this expressionist, romantic music. Most of the action is in the sound.

I already felt objections to the general use of sound in films, especially to the way music is subordinated to image. Even the greatest work of the greatest artist, J. S. Bach, is often used to set up a certain attitude in commercial films, and I've hated that for years. I wanted to do something where the music could *survive* and not only be support for the image. I think I accomplished that in *New York Eye and Ear Control*.

MacDonald: Was *New York Eye and Ear Control* shown a lot? At what point did you become part of the New York underground film scene?

Snow: Before Joyce and I got to New York, Bob Cowan was already there. He's from Toronto. In fact, he went to the high school I went to, Upper Canada College. And when Joyce and I went to New York on visits, we would see him occasionally. Sometimes we'd drive all night, and we'd park outside his place in Brooklyn and have a nap, then wake him up at eight o'clock. We used to get stoned and start driving, it was very nice. One time I drove all the way from Toronto to New York whistling Charlie Parker and Thelonious Monk tunes. But anyway, on one of these visits Bob said, "There's two friends of mine coming over with a film they just made. Do you want to see it?" And it was George and Mike Kuchar. They were nineteen. They had just made *A Town Called Tempest* [1963].

MacDonald: A wonderful film!

Snow: Their accents knocked us out. Anyway, we set up this little 8mm projector and showed the film. And Joyce and I were amazed. It was really, really inspiring. After that—it might have been through Bob—we discovered the Cinematheque screenings. When we were in Toronto, we didn't know there was a genre called "experimental film." We had seen Norman McLaren's films and not much else. When we were making our own films, we didn't feel like they were part of a big development. Anyway, we started to go to the Cinematheque and to meet people. Ken Jacobs was one of the first. And he was fabulous in those days, really an amazing man.

I was still saying to myself, "You should stop this and just do that, or you're just gonna be a dilettante all your life." I had thought that going to New York would clarify that. In fact, it didn't. I just kept on multiplying my interests.

MacDonald: You and Joyce were beginning to make films at the same time, and in one instance [*Dripping Water*, 1969] you did collaborate. Was there a reason why you didn't collaborate more often?

Snow: Our work was always independent. We discussed, and looked at work, and helped each other, but we never thought about doing things together. She had her own direction. She was affected by the Kuchar experience in a way that I wasn't. Their work was close to her sensibility in a lot of ways. I was very affected by A *Town Called Tempest* and their other films because I liked the freedom of it and the fact that George and Mike just went ahead and *did* it. It's wonderful, but it wasn't my kind of thing. I think it really opened up things for Joyce. She didn't imitate them, but she had a kinship with their work. I don't know whether you've seen any of her 8mm films, but they're really terrific. I don't know what's happened to them. She was going to get some blown up, but I don't know whether she ever did. When I was starting the first attempt at *Eye and Ear Control*, she was already shooting in 8mm.

MacDonald: Where does *Short Shave* [1965] fit into all this?

Snow: I did it before *Wavelength*, and after *Eye and Ear Control*.

MacDonald: It's a nice film.

Snow: You like it? I think you know I said in the Co-op Catalogue that it was my worst film. I saw it recently and I think it's good, too. I had worked with the Walking Woman concept from 1961 to 1967. I still had ideas for it, but I decided that it had to stop. And making that film, shaving that beard off, was part of trying to make the change. Actually, I had a big commission, the first I ever had—for Expo '67 in Montreal. And I decided that would be a nice way to end *The Walking Woman Works*. The Expo '67 piece grew out of the dispersed things that I'd done before, but this was more monumental, in stainless steel. There were eleven parts scattered all over the Expo area. They fit together, perhaps, in your memory; they couldn't all be seen together. So anyway, that was the last of *The Walking Woman Works*, except for her bow-out in *Wavelength*, which was shot in the same year: 1966. I finished it in January 1967.

MacDonald: Her appearance in *Wavelength* reminds me of Koko the Clown's appearances in some early Betty Boop cartoons: he's a star in the silent Fleischer Brothers' animations, but in the early Betty Boop sound cartoons, he becomes a bit player and moves into the background.

Wavelength has become a crucial film in people's writing about the history of avant-garde work. And yet, by the time you made it, you'd done a lot of work of a lot of different kinds, much of which is related to it. When you were making *Wavelength*, did it seem to you that it was pivotal, or was it just another of many comparable moments in your work?

Snow: It was very important to me. I spent a year thinking about it and making notes before I started shooting. I've always oscillated between an incredible lack of confidence and conceit. I was going through a stage where, as usual, I was trying to clarify myself and get rid of some of what I had been doing before. I was trying to make something that would benefit from what I'd done, but to work *in time* in a new way. What came to be *Wavelength* did feel like some sort of do-or-die thing. That's the kind of mood I was in. I wanted to prove something to myself. *Wavelength* was an attempt to concentrate a lot of stuff in one piece. I had come to feel that some of *The Walking Woman Works* had stretched. Individual works were strong, but others were just part of the series: if you didn't see the series, they didn't have strength in themselves. I wanted *Wavelength* to be very strong.

I don't know where the money came from because those years were pretty poor. But everybody else involved in the film scene, which was really tiny then, was scraping together a couple of cents to do a film. So I felt I could do it, too.

MacDonald: The idea of concentrating is interesting because a lot of the earlier work disperses outward. *Wavelength* is literally a narrowing in.

Snow: Precisely. You start with a wide field and move into this specific point.

MacDonald: How much did you envision the film in terms of its impact on an audience?

Snow: At that time, I didn't think there was an audience other than at the Cinematheque. When *Wavelength* was finished, I had a little private screening, which I thought might be the *only* screening. There's a nice photograph of the people who were there.

MacDonald: Who was there?

Snow: Richard Foreman and Amy Taubin, who were married then; Jonas [Mekas], Shirley Clarke, Bob Cowan, Nam June Paik, Ken and Flo Jacobs, a few others.

MacDonald: What was their reaction?

Snow: They thought it was good!

MacDonald: It's still a remarkable film. And it still works as an effective subversion of conventional film expectations. If I want to make my students furious, *Wavelength* is the perfect film. The duration of *Wavelength* has been much talked about. What kind of thinking did you do about how long *Wavelength* would be, and how you would control the duration? It's a long film for that period, particularly given the fact that no one had much money.

Snow: Well, it's hard to post facto these things. I knew I wanted to expand something—a zoom—that normally happens fast, and to allow myself or the spectator to be sort of inside it for a long period. You'd get to know this device which normally just gets you from one space to another. I started to think about so-called film vocabulary before I made *Wavelength*—with *Eye and Ear Control*. You know, what *are* all these devices and how can you get to *see* them, instead of just using them? So that was part of it.

And the other thing is that a lot of the work that I was doing, including the music, had to do with variations within systems. One of the pieces of classical music which I've always liked (I got one of Wanda Landowska's records of it in 1950) is J. S. Bach's *Goldberg Variations*, which is a statement of theme, followed by a number of variations (I'm oversimplifying). That was the basis of a lot of my work, like *The Walking Woman*. I wanted to make this film a unified unfolding of a number of variations with the zoom as the container for the variations. The process had to have a certain length of time. It could be fifty minutes and it could be thirty minutes—maybe thirty would be too short—but that's how I thought about it. I did want to make a temporal place "to stay in," as you've properly put it.

I'd noticed something like this happening in another way, in *Eye and Ear Control*. Sometimes when the music is at its most passionate or frenetic, there's a feeling of being in a space that's made by the continuity of the music and the picture. Other people might not feel this, but it gave me my first taste of a kind of temporal control I was able to elaborate in *Wavelength*.

MacDonald: Another thing that's very important in *Wavelength* is the way it deals with narrative. It sets up its direction, and what would be considered the conventional narrative moves in and out from the edges. Hollis Frampton comes in and falls dead and the camera just continues on its way. One is tempted to say, "There's no plot," and yet there *is* a "plot," in a number of senses, including the mathematical: you plot straight ahead on an axis toward

14. Frames from Michael Snow's *Wavelength* (1968).
Courtesy Anthology Film Archives; reprinted by permission.

the far side of the loft. At any rate, *Wavelength* comments on conventional narrative, especially on mystery and suspense.

Snow: Yeah, but you know, I had no background in that at all. I just wanted to set up a temporal container of different kinds of events. In the sections where you don't see anybody in the space, it becomes much more a two-dimensional picture. When it's peopled, it's a whole other thing. And the memory of the space seen one way affects our other views of it. The space and duration of the film allow for all kinds and classes of events. There is a life-and-death story, but on another level, the whole thing is sexual. And there are a lot of other considerations, like making a reference outside with the phone, having something come in from outside through the radio. There are all these different symbolic implications of the room. It can be the head, with the windows as eyes, and the senses feeding into the consciousness . . .

MacDonald: Or a camera with the windows as apertures . .

Snow: All those things. I was aware of a lot of them, and there are things I can see now that I didn't know about then, that's for sure. But a lot of it *was* conscious. A lot of the color effects weren't preconceived because I didn't know what the hell I was doing. Actually, Ken Jacobs was very, very helpful. He lent me the camera and he gave me some old rolls of stock. I used this stuff and didn't know what it would look like.

MacDonald: Over the years, the perception of *Wavelength* has changed. When I interviewed Anthony McCall, he mentioned that he was profoundly influenced by written descriptions of *Wavelength* when he made *Line Describing a Cone* [1973]. When he finally saw *Wavelength*, he discovered it was completely different from what had influenced him, and that he had developed a relationship to something that actually didn't exist.

Snow: In your mind, the shape of the zoom is the same as the shape of a projector beam. I was thinking about that at the time, too. All the imagery issues from still photographs, frames that are amplified in one direction, while the zoom narrows your view in the opposite direction. Maybe that's part of what he was thinking of.

MacDonald: What surprised him is that the zoom wasn't consistent, smooth, and even. In fact, *Wavelength* is a very rough film in many ways.

Snow: The zoom was hand done. The imagery was shot out of order. Originally I thought I might make the film without editing. Later, I realized I'd need to edit. I shot reel three and that had to be at a particular place on the lens, which I'd marked out. Then I shot reel one, then reel five. And I moved the zoom lens by hand, so it's very uneven. And I really like that a lot. There are cuts in the film, too, to get from reel to reel, and sometimes there's editing where I took something out. It's not a continuous zoom by any means. There's a lot of nuance to the fact that it was hand done, not in the tactile sense of, say, Brakhage's films, but as a nice by-product of the process.

MacDonald: There's a surprise at the end where viewers discover they're not going toward the photograph of the Walking Woman.

Snow: Well, there are a couple of mistakes at the end of *Wavelength*, because I had to move the camera. Almost all of the film was shot from a platform. I put the camera up high because

I figured that would provide a certain kind of view. But then to finish the zoom I had to move the camera down. I wanted to move it on the same horizontal line, but I made a mistake: it's a little off. This is toward the end where you've got the photographs sort of in the middle and an equal amount of space around them. Every time I see it, I think, Jesus, that's *bad* [laughter]. Sometimes I think it's good.

MacDonald: Well, it's what it *is*, now.

Snow: [Laughter] It certainly is.

MacDonald: I'm always struck by the textural dimension of *Wavelength*, by the variation in grain. In fact, there's so much to look at in the film that I'm amazed when it's called a minimal film.

Snow: Oh, I don't understand that at all. Every time I read that, I'm amazed—though it hasn't happened all that often. It's also described as a "conceptual" piece, sometimes. Certainly a lot of thinking went into it and I hope it provokes thinking, but that it's sometimes identified with the art style called "conceptual" seems peculiar, too.

MacDonald: You were friends with Taubin and Frampton at the time when you made *Wavelength*. Was there a reason beyond just knowing them and their being available that they show up in the film? Was Frampton's appearance related to his being a particular kind of artist?

Snow: No. They were friends and we had talked about what I was doing. I knew that Amy had acted, and I wanted an actress. She'd been in *The Prime of Miss Jean Brodie*, a popular Broadway play. Hollis volunteered. I was going around saying, "I want somebody to die for me," and he said, "Oh, I'*ll* do that."

MacDonald: When you first showed it to this small group of friends, they liked it very much. How was it received when it was first shown to a larger New York audience?

Snow: It wasn't shown in New York at first. You know what happened? When Jonas saw it, he said, "You know, you should send *Wavelength* to this festival coming up in Knokke-le-Zoute [Belgium, 1967]." But I didn't have enough money to finish the film: when I first showed it, the sound was on tape. I had decided I wanted to have the sine wave sound, the glissando, on reel-to-reel tape: it was better sound. But then I realized that was impractical, and if I wanted to show the film again I'd have to have an optical track. Anyway, Jonas—wonderful Jonas!—found the money to make this new print and he sent it to Knokke-le-Zoute and it won first prize, and all these things happened as a result.

MacDonald: Was *Standard Time* [1967] done as a sketch for *Back and Forth ↔*? In some ways they're very different, and yet when one sees them in succession, the question is almost inevitable since both center on the panning camera.

Snow: Well, no, because I didn't really know that *Back and Forth* was ever going to exist. *Standard Time* was exploratory. I wanted to find out about circular pans on a fixed base and about what happens at different speeds. And when the film was finished, I got the idea for *Back and Forth*. I decided I wanted to work with back-and-forth and up-and-down pans of a limited angle.

MacDonald: *Standard Time* has a diaristic element.

Snow: Yes. It's my home movie in the sense that that was where we were living—123 Chambers Street—and Joyce is in it.

MacDonald: I assume *Back and Forth* was scored but that part of it was exploratory.

Snow: Yes, that's right. Before I started shooting, I worked out the speeds with a metronome. I knew it would start with a medium tempo and slow down. And I guess that's the slowest point, actually. Then it would gradually speed up to its fastest and then cut to the vertical pans and finally slow down. I made these two sides to the tripod, so that when I panned, I couldn't go further than a certain point, which would define the arc I wanted. I tried making a little machine with a display motor, but it was uncontrollable, so I did it by hand.

My use of that space was similar to my use of the space in *Wavelength*: there's a difference in the space when there are people in it and when it's empty. Before shooting, I had set up places where certain kinds of things would happen, and I wanted them all to relate to the idea of back and forthness, or reciprocity, or exchange.

MacDonald: More fully than in *Wavelength*, every action that happens in front of the camera seems to be specifically referential to the process of the back-and-forth panning.

Snow: That's right. It's more integrated into one set of issues than *Wavelength*. I did *Back and Forth* during the summer of 1968. A number of artists were invited to Fairleigh Dickinson University in New Jersey over a period of a month. I decided to shoot it there in a classroom that had the interesting situation of being right on the street, so that would allow the imagery to be inside and outside, another kind of back and forth. *Back and Forth* was also shot out of order, depending on who was available when.

MacDonald: Both films start slowly and build to a kind of climactic fast motion, and then calm down during a denouement. This is particularly evident in *Back and Forth*. In fact, after the credits there's a passage of "reminiscence" about earlier moments in the film. Was that a conscious play on conventional narrative?

Snow: Well, no, though, as you say, the shape is climactic. *Wavelength* literally "cums" at the end: the last thing you see is liquid. I was and am interested in sex and so I suppose maybe that's the source of the shape, at least in those two films, though that's not the only way to think of that shape. As I told you, I really have no background in the development of narrative film and have never had any particular interest. I'm not consciously trying to subvert the movies. The structure you mention is just one way of moving in time, as far as I'm concerned.

The main problem with narrative in film is that when you become emotionally involved, it becomes difficult to see the picture as picture. Of course, the laughing and crying and suspense can be a positive element, but it's oddly nonvisual and gradually destroys your capacity to see. There's really no narrative in *Back and Forth*. There are isolated incidents that are called for partly by the kind of space you see, but no narrative connection between them.

MacDonald: *One Second in Montreal* followed *Back and Forth*. Whereas *Wavelength* and *Back and Forth* have often been called minimal, *One Second in Montreal* really is minimal: you subtract out almost everything except duration itself.

Snow: I have been influenced by reductive work—maybe that's not the right word. I like Mondrian a lot. And I like Donald Judd's first work. In fact, I had a piece from his first show.

In *One Second in Montreal* I wanted to concentrate again, and I was interested to see what it would be like to live through a film that, as purely as possible, had to do with duration. I didn't want what I put on the screen to be too interesting, which is a funny situation. I wanted each image to be different—otherwise there would be no measurement. But they couldn't be *too* different because I didn't want to have any peaks or checkerboarding of interest: I wanted the viewer to be aware of the time passing, of how long the shot was there. I finally decided on these bad offset-printing images I'd gotten years earlier for a competition to put sculpture in parks in Montreal. I'd put them away because I liked them, though I didn't know *what* I liked about them.

MacDonald: On a certain level they continue the idea in *Back and Forth* of making the figurative action that happens in front of the camera refer to the process of the film itself. The viewer is looking at spaces that are there because they're empty of what they're trying to draw into them. They're places where sculptures *could be*, just as the photographic imagery in your film is where action or event would be, were there any.

Snow: I suppose that's true, though you wouldn't know that from the film itself. They're just these bleak photographs of parks and public spaces. It is Montreal, but you don't need to know that either.

I think the film worked very well. And I think that people do recognize after a while what it's about. Yvonne Rainer told me one time that she got very, very fidgety as the shots got longer and longer, and was really mad. And then, when they started to go fast and the film ended, she was really mad that it ended. She wanted more. I'm happy that the film could do that. It's an interesting range of response that's *not* produced by an imitation of real life as in narrative film.

MacDonald: There was a period during the early 1970s when there was some acceptance of the idea that film is a temporal space within which you can meditate. This film has that dimension.

Snow: Also the silence is interesting. It's a silence that I don't think I've ever felt before in films. Sometimes silence is beautiful, and everybody's concentrating. That happens with some of Stan Brakhage's films. In this film the silence is almost meditational, partly because the snow-blanketed scenes have a mute quality. The imagery affects your feeling about the silence.

MacDonald: It's a pun, too, in that we're sitting in the audience "frozen" within this experience. In that way, *One Second in Montreal* prefigures *Seated Figures*.

Snow: I just remembered that originally I had the idea to mark the cuts with sound. I didn't, but I used that idea later in *Presents*.

MacDonald: *Dripping Water* is another reductive, "minimal" film, though it's more complex, more subtle than it first appears. It seems to be one shot long, but if you're watching and listening carefully, you realize that it's not a single shot. A drop of water sometimes doesn't make it to the sink, for instance. And a multilayered space is created outside the frame by the soundtrack.

Snow: I made the tape first as music. I just happened to notice this drip, and started to listen to it. And it's really fantastic. So I made a tape just to listen to that sound amplified.

The original tape was longer than the film. Mike Sahl, wonderful guy, a composer who at that time did a new music program on WBAI, played the entire tape on the radio. That dripping sound on the radio: fabulous! Joyce had the idea that maybe we should make a film of it.

MacDonald: There's an irony in the fact that *Dripping Water* announces that it's a collaboration of two filmmakers, and yet there's precious little to collaborate on.

Snow: We just set the camera up together; and I guess we put the dish into the sink together [laughter].

MacDonald: *Side Seat Paintings Slides Sound Film* has grown on me. It's a quirky film, but very interesting. If I remember the photographic piece *Glares* [1973] correctly, *Side Seat Paintings* has in common with it the idea that the process of recording something inevitably creates interference, which everybody normally labors to avoid, or at pretending it can be avoided. In *Side Seat Paintings* the many levels of interference, of distortion, become the primary subject of the work.

Snow: That's certainly true. I think you could say that representations are all abstractions from some original given, whether they're photographic or verbal or whatever. *Side Seat Paintings* is a Chinese box, one abstraction within another, within another . . . until you get a new form. I've always tried to make the recognition of exactly what's happening part of the experience of seeing a film. In this case, the projection of the slides of the paintings becomes the film, and I think it really *is* transformed into a film.

MacDonald: Of the films, *Back and Forth* seems the furthest from the other arts that have fascinated you. *Eye and Ear Control* combines music, painting, sculpture, photography *in* film. *Wavelength* has a musical element and, at the end, references to photography and *The Walking Woman*. By *Back and Forth*, you're really into film at a very intense level with, at most, vestiges of music on the soundtrack. Then with *One Second in Montreal*, you move back toward photography and with *Side Seat Paintings* you combine photography (in the slides) and painting and sound in a kind of artist's autobiography.

Snow: Yes. It's not exactly autobiographical, since you can't really see the paintings. It's really a redigesting or a recycling of earlier work. But it is true that other kinds of work come and go during various periods.

MacDonald: I think of *Side Seat Paintings* as autobiographical in the sense that, as a *visual* artist, you were first a painter, then a photographer, then a filmmaker. In the film, the paintings are recorded in the slides, which are recorded in the film. Did you and Hollis ever talk about the similarities between that film and *nostalgia* [1971]?

Snow: Well, actually *nostalgia* is more similar to A *Casing Shelved* [1970], a slide and tape piece, my only 35mm "film." It's a slide of bookshelves I had in my studio, loaded with all kinds of stuff. And the sound is a voice, my voice, discussing what's on the shelves from various points of view: what it is or what it was and where it came from. The bookshelf has many small things on it and the text is written to move your eyes around on this big image. There's a plan in the text that moves you over the whole space of the image, and through time, because some of the things and events referred to are recent and some are older. Some are art related and some are related to my so-called private life. But it is very autobiographical. And it's similar to what Hollis did in *nostalgia*, although there's no destruction involved.

MacDonald: What strikes me as similar in *nostalgia* and *Side Seat Paintings* is that both are look-backs at the past, and in both the earlier work is "destroyed." In yours the destruction isn't literal [actually, it isn't in *nostalgia* either, since only *prints* are being burned and since they're exhibited in the film before the burning "destroys" them], but because of the processes of recording those paintings have gone through, there's no way to know what they actually looked like: what we know is that we *can't* see exactly what they were.

Snow: That's interesting. And in both films, the works discussed are two-dimensional surfaces.

MacDonald: There's been a tendency, at least among some people I talk to, to think of you as an old-fashioned guy who has a problem accepting women and women's independence and that this problem is embedded in *Presents*.

Snow: Well, I am an old guy, but I've never had any problem accepting women's independence. In fact, I was very much interested in women's independence before this current wave of feminism. I was always very supportive of Joyce in her work. Everybody should have the possibility of going as far as they can with whatever they do. It's not an issue for me. However, exactly how "independent" anyone can be is a question we'd better not try to get into now.

MacDonald: I suppose it surfaced in the case of *Presents* because the film came out at a time when everyone was talking about the eroticized female body as the subject of the male gaze. This film seemed to rebel against that concern: it focuses in on a naked woman's body at the beginning, and then in the third long section where you jump from one shot to the next, naked women's bodies are used often. Were you addressing that issue or . . .

Snow: Yes, I guess I was. It was probably the first time I'd done something specifically as a means of entering a current dialogue. The way you said "rebel against that concern" is interesting. It reminds me of that horrifying phrase "politically correct." Is having *some* differences of opinion with *some* feminist/social theory "rebelling"? Is the "concern" so defined that it can't be discussed, only approved?

Looking for "what does this mean?" first and not experiencing what is happening in its sensual complexity is a terribly wasteful, ass-backwards way of experiencing my films or any other work of art. I have never made a work to convey *a* meaning. I work with areas of meaning and know that there are as many meanings as there are viewers. What is *there* in the concrete, phenomenological sense is of first importance. You seem to see all my other films, except this one, that way and I appreciate your observations. The problems here seem to be as much yours as the film's.

On one level I was asking the spectator to consider the relationship between separate, or seemingly separate, parts of this one film to each other, and in that light to consider the relation between the two parts of the human species. After the opening where the image, which is electronically shaped, focuses on the nude woman, there's a section that's totally staged: there's a fixed camera and the set moves. The longer, third section is the opposite of the first two in terms of what is done to make the image.

The first image sequence is made by shaping, molding, manipulating the entire frame. In the second, what was photographed was staged, constructed, the way a play or most narrative fiction films are made. The camera is fixed on a tripod and what one first reads as a series of side-to-side tracking shots is soon revealed as the opposite: the entire set is being moved. This sequence is audibly directed by the director. Then the camera dollies into the set, destroying it and knocking down a wall, which starts the third and longest section: a montage of images taken from life that's quasi-documentary and diaristic. It's important that I shot all these images: the surgery, May Day in Poland, the Arctic hunt, et cetera. All the shots are hand-held panning shots, the movement of the camera always being derived from an aspect of the scene: following a line, moving with, or against a motion. . . .

I wanted to make a dialogue between these systems. Aspects of the film are male: it's made by a heterosexual man. Some of this is conscious, for *this* film, and some of it's inevitable. Aspects of the film have to do with experiencing the inherent nature of the camera, and then, seeing with the camera within the different systems used in the film, which includes man seeing women with the camera. It so happens that I do occasionally lust and while I didn't try to shoot only that way, I do *see* women. I noticed in working on the film that women's magazines always have women on the cover, which is very interesting. There are a lot of photographs of women's magazines in the film. There's some so-called pornography. And there's some intimately personal stuff.

These images involve my sexual life as an artist in some respects, but they're interwoven with many, many other things that are all thematically announced in the first section. For example, the room is pink and the film gradually develops into a discourse on red: the symbolism of red, which, at least in the West, has to do with "stop" and red-light district, blood, sugar, passion—all those things and, of course, communism too. That's all in there. It demonstrates the multiplicity of readings there can be for any word or image.

The word "presents" has incredibly varied meanings and uses, including the use in zoological literature that females *present* to males. Biology is as important to the film as psychoanalysis. Entertainment advertising says So and So Presents Such and Such. I like that my title is an abstraction of this. It doesn't say who presents what, it says that "Presents" will be the subject of this film, so "presentation," then "re-presentation," is invoked. A mostly feminine use is: "is so and so presentable?" But of course the film is also "presents" or "nows," and also "gifts."

Interwoven with all *that* is this business about how things are made. There are three different ways of making things. You can shape something, squeeze material into a certain form. Or you can add this to that. Or you can subtract this from that. And those are the *only* ways you can make anything. The film is involved with those options, and with a latent aspect of them, which is the unfortunate truth that in order to make something, you have to destroy something else, or at least change its form. And that crisscrosses with the sexual themes in some ways, but again, it doesn't attribute any one way of making to one gender or the other. So much is interwoven in the film in so many ways that it's almost the opposite of *Wavelength*. *Presents*' references get wider and wider. It closes with the fading out of the red and a drum roll, which is either military or funereal, the death of the film.

MacDonald: I understand that *Presents* had some hostile audiences, at least at first.

Snow: One of the worst was at the Collective in New York, where some women were furious in a way I found really obtuse. One question was, "How come there's so much tits and ass in this film?" I was tempted to say, "I can tell from your voice that you are the possessor of tits and ass." The assumption seemed to be that tits and ass *can't be seen*. It was brought up that you *can't* photograph so-called pornography—for *any* purpose. That's amazing. I don't necessarily have anything against so-called pornography. I'm aware that there are aspects of it that are extremely questionable—involving children and cruelty for example—but I like, sometimes, some of what's called "pornography." I say "so-called pornography" because that's always a question, too. What do you mean by "pornography"? You mean it's what doesn't turn you on? Or what does? Another amazing question that night was, belligerently, from a male voice, "How come there's no men's asses in this film?" I thought the discussion at the Collective didn't have much to do with the film.

It's true that *Presents* was prompted by the debate about eroticism and the depiction of women that was going on. I had been thinking about those issues for quite a while.

I think it was at that Milwaukee conference [Cinema Histories/Cinema Practices II, held at the University of Wisconsin, Milwaukee, November 1982] that, after the screening of *Presents*, Christian Metz asked, with a certain amount of puzzlement, "What is the relationship between the two parts?" What I want that film to do is to force the spectator to *think* about the relationship between the two parts. All I could say to him was, "The relationship between the two parts is a splice." How *do* they relate? How are they part of the same organism? The point is that there are *a lot* of answers.

MacDonald: *So Is This* has been very useful for me—especially in thinking about the relationship of film experience and film criticism. Film criticism is almost always considered to be a *written* text about a *visual* experience. But there's an inevitable gap between what writing can communicate and the multi-dimensional experience of film. It strikes me that a lot of what passes for complexity in writing about film is interference that results from the inability of the word to really come to grips with the visual/auditory experience of film. *So Is This* is about these issues; it turns film onto language in the way that language is normally turned loose on film.

Early in the film you pay homage to independent filmmakers who have used text in inventive ways: Marcel Duchamp, Hollis Frampton, Su Friedrich. . . . Had you been thinking about working with text for a long time or did the recent spate of this kind of work inspire you?

Snow: I wrote the original part of that text around 1975 and made the film almost ten years later. It came out of the text for the Chatham Square album [*Michael Snow: Musics for Piano, Whistling, Microphone and Tape Recorder*, Chatham Square, 1975] and out of *One Second in Montreal*, as another way of controlling duration. Since then, I've been asked whether I knew Jenny Holzer's work, but I didn't at that time. The things she's done have some relationship, although there's no timing involved in her work, as far as I can tell.

MacDonald: *So Is This* is poetic justice for people who make a fetish of the ability to write and read sentences. Is that what you had in mind?

Snow: That's part of it, yes. Another thing is the business of using the art object, in this case film, as a pretext for arguments that the writer considers of more interest. That's valid in some senses, but sometimes it seems like a misuse of the stimuli, the film. It's as if you're producing these things for other people to advance their own interests and arguments.

MacDonald: The way in which text is used in *So Is This* makes a comment on language-based approaches to film. The formal design of showing one word at a time with the same margins, regardless of the size of the word, results in the little words being large, which of course grammatically they often are in the language, and the big words being much smaller. This is precisely the opposite of what a lot of academic writing does. At academic conferences, using complex vocabulary often becomes a performance. So Is This seems to critique that kind of linguistic performance with a different kind of performance.

Snow: It does, yes.

MacDonald: There's sometimes a tendency in academe to see filmmakers as laboratory animals who don't really know what they're doing, but whose doings can be explained by theorists. Have you read much theory?

Snow: I've read lots of Michel Foucault, Roland Barthes, Jean-François Lyotard, Jacques Derrida, Gilles Deleuze, Jean Baudrillard. Some of those people have become deified. I think Derrida is one of the most interesting.

Barthes's writing is unctuous. He seems often to be defining a new category of the object under observation, but when you start to examine what he says, you find that it isn't as essential as the revelatory tone of the writing suggests it is. And some of the ideas are really ludicrous. "The Death of the Author" [in Barthes, Image-Music-Text (New York: Hill and Wang, 1977, translated by Stephen Heath)] is this essay written by a very distinctive stylist, with a name, and *he* says that the individual writer is subsumed in the totality of writing, that there really is no writer. It's an arch little essay by a famous author! A lot of "theory" is like that. And in Barthes's A *Lover's Discourse*, the supposedly revolutionary tack is that there's no reference to gender. It's sex with no body. The book becomes this vapor of extraordinary style, perfume. *Mythologies* is interesting, but pretty strange, too.

There's a fashionable idea now, especially among academic theorists, that the person— or the subject, as they say these days—is totally culturally shaped. I don't believe that at all. I think somebody is born, that there is an organism that has functions. It can be twisted; it can be hurt; but there's still a specific person there. Every person is born with a certain complicated set of possibilities. Of course, there's a lot of breadth to that, but I don't believe that culture totally shapes the person. Individual people also shape culture, which is, after all, one of the functions of art. Those who have commented on the way in which dominant ideologies totally shape people often seem to assume *they've* been able to escape that process. Very mysterious!

Philosophy has been very important to me: Plato, Aristotle, Nietzsche, [Maurice] Merleau-Ponty, many many commentaries like Havelock's *Preface to Plato*. One of my favorite books is Heidegger's *Early Greek Thinking*. I've read everything by Wittgenstein, I think. Derrida is very interesting, a kind of Hegel/Mallarmé. Lacan is medieval Christian Zen. Laura Mulvey seems a university student in this context. Years ago I read a lot of Paul Valery and was quite affected by his writing, though sometimes he's arch in a way similar to Barthes.

My feminist reading is fairly wide. I've even read books by Andrea Dworkin! Joyce Carol Oates is terrific, Germaine Greer too. I like Fernand Braudel, Norbert Elias, George Steiner. I'm reading Mandelbrot on fractals and Jack Chambers's *Milestones* (on Miles Davis) right now. I read *October* and *Critical Inquiry* and other journals, and various art and film magazines. I've thought of my film work as a kind of philosophy.

The Films of Warren Sonbert   14

PHILIP LOPATE

I first saw the work of Warren Sonbert at a one-man screening around 1967, at a funny little theatre in the basement of the Wurlitzer Building on 42nd Street, where the Filmmakers Cinematheque then held forth. The program included his *Amphetamine*, *Where Did Our Love Go*, *Hall of Mirrors* and *The Tenth Legion*. Not a diehard fan of the New American Cinema but an occasional nibbler, who went to underground screenings out of an odd combination of civic duty and derelict voyeurism, always expecting the worst, or very little, I was almost jolted out of my chair by Sonbert's electric, bouncy, alive, humorous, roller coaster rides. The world was in them, the city-world, or let us say, to be candid and narcissistic about it, a world that felt like my own, a New Yorker in his early twenties: the ups and downs of that life, one moment crashing a fancy party and the next crossing a grimy 8th Avenue or yawning and waiting in line for a movie.

In addition to all the glitter and lights, there were ordinary lackluster moments as they so rarely appear in films about New York. I remember a shot of some college students gazing out the window of a lecture hall before their teacher had arrived, in *The Tenth Legion*, and thinking: How daring, he's letting us know that these young debauchees also have to go to school; there's something very touching about that.

And the films themselves were sexy. I don't mean to say that the actors took their clothes off, they didn't, but what was sexy was the extremely fluid way the movies were put together. The sound track of soul songs had something to do with it, but even more so the long hand-held tracking shots that followed in "real time" someone walking down corridor after corridor, or the merry-go-round shot that metaphorically described an attitude toward the cosmos as much as did Godard's swirling coffee cup. The shots took us over like a wet dream. It was as if Hitchcock's 360° turn around the lovers, Stewart and Novak, in Vertigo, that saturation of love and impossible yearning and doubt and fulfillment, had started to infiltrate *all* of Sonbert's images. It was a lover's cinema. The filmmaker was in love with the world, or was amused and saddened by it, so obviously that he had only to point his camera anywhere, it seemed, and it would fill up with feeling.

Another thing I liked about Sonbert's films: there seemed to be no conflict in him between narrative and non-narrative cinema. He was comfortably at home in the experimental cinema tradition, yet he was also a grateful offspring of Sirk and Borzage and Hawks. In his column Jonas Mekas had called Sonbert "post-Godardian," an interesting idea, but to me Sonbert was coterminous with Godard, in the romantic way he filmed images off of movie screens (paying tribute to *Contempt* and *North by Northwest*), in his choice of at-loose-ends character types, and in his "breathless" pace. Sonbert's plotless films felt narrative; though they told no story, they suppressed none either. Perhaps they were telling the story of life.

I found myself thinking a good deal about the people in Warren Sonbert's films. He was taking us behind the scenes and showing us the sort of young ambitious bohemians who were very much a part of 1960s urban chic. It was the world of boutiques and discos and art openings, Andy Warhol and Henry Geldzahler. These were not flower children but grant-getting types who wound long white scarves around soft black leatherjackets. King's Road and Portobello Road had left their mark on the fashions: mini-skirts and hot colors and synthetic rayons and sparkle dust and boots. When Susan Sontag defended young people in *Against Interpretation* by saying they wanted to look beautiful and what was so bad about that, these were the folks she meant. But Sonbert, engaged as his films are with fashion, did not, to his credit, photograph the subjects like *Vogue*. Instead he gave us the private moments of people we slobs in the audience were curious about. We saw both their scarlet blouses unbuttoned to the fourth button and their pimples and eye-bags of fatigue, or dirty-blonde hair that needed a washing. Moreover, they were filmed in context, in their apartment or on their street or relaxing with their friends, so that the very same person, like Gerard Malanga or Rene Ricard, who had been encouraged to project his personality as that of a fabulous monster in an Andy Warhol movie, would pop up in a Warren Sonbert film a week later looking very normal and scaled-down, sniffing at a painting in a gallery opening, one guest among many.

Sonbert seemed to be evolving a typology of Bohemia, filming his subjects in their haunts in somewhat the same way that August Sander approached his portrait of the German people by photographing subjects in their work-places. Like Sander, there was more than a hint of psychological astuteness and clinical objectivity in these portraits.

And there were moments when loneliness was allowed to enter. Someone would be lying on a bed, thinking, off somewhere in his mind, or waiting for his lover to return from the other room. Sonbert had a good way with couples: his *The Bad and the Beautiful*, consisting of several edited-in-the-camera portraits of twosomes, tells us everything we need to know about couple-love, the tenderness, the silly horsing-around, the compromises, the dead spots, the clinging to each other. It is a heartbreaking movie.

Though only an adolescent when he made these movies, Sonbert had the knack of creating an intensely elegiac mood about the present, as though he knew how quickly all these 1960s costumes and postures would fade. His titles and song choices ("Where did our love go?" etc.) accentuated the anticipated loss as much as the haunting camera tracks which seemed to be searching for the separated lover.

To sum up: these films were fluid, they were rough, mostly edited in the camera, they were highly poetic and charged with feeling, they gave us city life. And they swung.

A few years later, I dropped in at the Whitney Museum to see what Sonbert was up to in his latest work, *Carriage Trade*. This was a disappointment. Gone were the long duration takes, each shot now lasting only a second or two before giving way to the next. It was like a collection of postcards from around the world: vaguely amusing but finally cancelling each other out. I missed the long juicy sequences that established character and locale. Nothing had a chance to build. Gone also was the bouncy Supremes & Company soundtrack, replaced by austere silence. Probably I did not see the film intelligently enough; I think I would like it now, in the

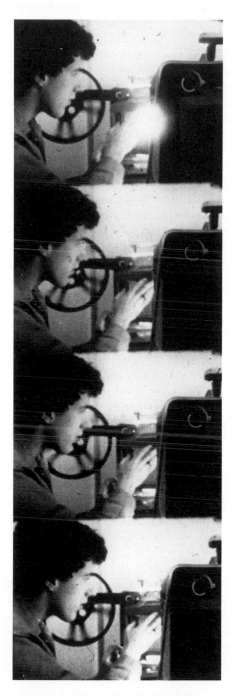

15. Warren Sonbert at Andy Warhol's
Factory in 1969. Photostrip by Wheeler
Winston Dixon. Courtesy of the author.

context of knowing where it would lead (*Rude Awakening* and *Divided Loyalties*), but at the time I reacted only as a disappointed art-consumer who does not want a beloved artist to change his style.

[Later, I was even more horrified to learn that the filmmaker had cannibalized *Tenth Legion*, which no longer exists, cutting snippets of it into *Carriage Trade*. I continue to think that Sonbert has an inaccurate under-estimation of his early films, wanting (like many artists) only to be identified with his recent mode and rarely showing or encouraging to be shown those youthful works, with the result that they exist for the most part only in people's memories. What a shame! If nothing else, Sonbert was one of the best historians recording that era.]

Rude Awakening (1976), his next movie, impressed me deeply. Though it was an extension of the style begun in *Carriage Trade* (short burst of images, no sound track), it took that method and refined it, tightened it, purified it. The film was a rigorously formed abacus of essences. Chamber music. It was obvious that this filmmaker knew what he was doing and had supreme control of his material. Also, Warren had made great technical strides as a motion picture photographer: his images looked burnished, classical. The lighting and color were more controlled. There were no more of those Abstract Expressionist-type accidents incorporated into the work, like the end-of-roll yellow blips or sudden light changes in his early films. He was after something else. As for his subject matter, he had gone beyond the bohemian scene (which was still included) to encompass more of the world: animals, children, workers, plants. The audience at Anthology Film Archives kept giggling and laughing appreciatively, but I was having an entirely different response. The film struck me as unflinchingly sad. (Another time, when my girlfriend saw it, she burst into tears—a response which understandably pleased Warren.) I wrote a brief note on the film for *The Thousand Eyes*, to help publicize its next showing:

> *Rude Awakening* is a dazzling funny, severe film which speculates about the value of human activity. Comparable in encyclopedic thrust to Vertov's ebullient *Man With the Movie Camera* it differs from that tradition in being more compressed, more *cutting*. Sonbert is fascinated with spectacle (ice follies, ballet, street fairs), with everyday labor (butcher shops, frankfurter stands) and recreation, but underneath all this motion one senses a futility. Like the shot of people thwacking each other with fake swords in the Renaissance Fair, the images express playfulness, energy, and impotence. They are held on the screen just long enough to bring us into a sense of comic contradiction: cutting used for undercutting. Each shot is another slice as harmless as a paper cut, but after a while one experiences the accumulated sadness behind all the joy and motion, and the title, *Rude Awakening*, becomes more fitting and darker in its double-edged irony. What sets Warren Sonbert apart from most other "non-narrative" experimental filmmakers, aside from his impeccable craftsmanship, is his ability to bestow the psychology of narrative cinema, of a Preminger or Sirk, onto his images of people. The connection between shots, even without a story-line, has an intuitive rightness that feels mysteriously syllogistic, though the fun is in knowing that much of this meaning may be audience projection while some may have been the filmmaker's intention. Sonbert lets you choose.

Warren's next work was *Divided Loyalties* (1978), which in some ways struck me as even stronger and tighter than *Rude Awakening*. It had great moments of humor, some breathtaking vignettes of human interaction, some lovely celebrations of the act of seeing. (It even has me in it for a few seconds.) The film is the ripening of a method and the successful proof of his new manner. Nevertheless, I think it must lead to a branching out into something else if Warren is to grow as an artist and not merely repeat himself.

I would like to spend the rest of this article by raising some nagging questions and doubts about Sonbert's latest film work.

First, a picky one: there is too much overlap and repetition in the two movies. Elevators, car trips, stage shows, be-ins, etc.—one film begins to look like the out-takes of the other.

Second, I wonder about the tight corset of the brief shot. Why must everything skip by in only a few seconds, like a still photograph, so that the moment you have "read" the scene, it is already being replaced? The editing principle behind *Rude Awakening*, which Warren once explained to me (I hope I'm not giving away any trade secrets), of alternating a vertical shot with a diagonal or horizontal or whatever in sets of four, while also alternating shots of people with shots of nature—this whole schema strikes me as arbitrary and barren. If the images in these two movies mysteriously connect, one with the other, it is probably in spite of this lines-of-force Eisensteinian editing formula. Here the 1970s influence of conceptual art, of grids and pre-conceived stencils applied to material, seems to have pushed Sonbert into a stiffer purity not always consonant with his gregarious talents. I prefer *camera-stylo*, to write with a camera whatever you're thinking.

Third, and perhaps most problematic, is the philosophy or "meaning" of these films. We start with the titles. *Rude Awakening* reveals the sardonic, partly sadistic whack which these amiable images, taken together, are meant to give. "Wake up! You're fooling yourselves!" Sonbert the teacher is administering his lessons on our bottoms: we are not to hope for lasting satisfactions, pleasure holds only a few seconds and then dissolves, a polymorphous flash that leads nowhere. A world-weary disappointment, a bitter choked laugh, lies over the images of people relentlessly busying and entertaining themselves. On the one hand, futility of endeavor; on the other hand, a tension which is raised but not permitted to be released. *Divided Loyalties'* title points to this unresolved (possibly irresolvable) tension: the urbanite's confusion of riches, unable to choose between too many parties and cultural events on the same night, politically, the inability to choose sides; romantically, the conflict from having several lovers, or bisexuality; geographically, not being able to make up one's mind where to live. As images on a film, it works itself out as one reality cancelling out another, without development.

The original title of *Divided Loyalties* was *Industrial Keys*. The young Orpheus is awakened rudely to a world in which industry holds all the keys, and even personal life has a manufactured, industrial quality, as Adorno would say. Warren Sonbert's films have always had a trace of sociological inquiry, and in *Divided Loyalties* one can almost make out the beginnings of a critique of modern society: from the furs and tuxedo set at the opening of San Francisco's opera season, to the mangy train tracks of the Chicago loop, to factories and impersonal glassed-in elevators. Collective action is also treated sardonically, in the gay lib parade sequences, as one more illusion or pretense to be punctured (we see a cemetery after a gay be-in). However, the mosaic technique as Sonbert (unlike Vertov) uses it does not take responsibility for direct political or social statements that can reasonably be attributed to the filmmaker. Indeed, we can assume nothing but a pileup of ironies which imply, in the worst circumstances, a shrug of indifference.

A frightening emptiness dogs these films. Perhaps their real programme is spiritual; and Sonbert is trying to induce a state of non-attachment, acceptance of the void, a pulling-down of vanity. The Buddhist text echoes him precisely: "Form is emptiness, and emptiness is form. Emptiness is not different from form, form is not different from emptiness." That may be the philosophy over the long haul, the twenty-year plan, but in the meantime what we are getting is not so much wisdom as the jaded sour dregs of sated youth. Warren needs to pause for a moment and catch his breath. Part of the problem with these films is that they have lost their geographical anchor. They are no longer rooted in the psyche of a place (like the earlier New York films) but wander everywhere. Sonbert has become a "citizen of the world." He can bring us back dancing bears from Berlin circuses and elephants from India, but the weariness of the travel begins to tell. The poet who tries to see everything ends up becoming a sort of globetrotting opportunist/journalist/tourist collecting mere *spectacle*, in lieu of knowing the life of the people around him, or what is in their hearts. He is everywhere curious, everywhere estranged. Nothing is allowed to deepen. It's all entertaining but empty, he reports back to us.

There is at the moment a great deal of support in avant-garde culture for art which wanders around in a sort of moebius strip; a floating lyricism coupled with a sort of punitive blockage of anything building to a climax. The sense of sterility in life (or of a mindless bubbling fecundity of no real issue, which comes to the same thing) leads some artists to affect a sniggling negation of human hopes and of anything adding up. Things just go round and round, everything's tacky, nothing's first-rate or authentic or real. . . . Ashbery says all that beautifully, combining a world-weary uncovering of cliché with a hunger for fresh perception. I'm not sure it's right to put all this on Warren's films, because he is such an entertaining materialist. But it's clear that even in his 'footloose early work there is that "life is just a hall of mirrors" claustrophobia, the endless walking down long halls that go nowhere, the merry-go-round symbol which can be seen in an ominous as well as a joyous light. There the circumscribed trap was expressed spatially; now it's more temporal (no one is allowed more than 15 seconds onscreen). And now it's more connected to a severe aesthetic that inhibits release.

When a young modern artist wants to do something new, he generally goes through a puritanical period where he tries to frustrate his audience's expectations of pleasure. This is understandable: the artist has to break the socialized boundaries of conventional catharsis, be it in films or music or literature, and search for greater rigor. But having done so, the artist, continuing to grow, often comes back to the realization that pleasure is not so bad after all, that the audience is not cheap to want release, and that the stock-and-trade of art is, in the long run, sensuosity and generosity. I am not saying that the news needs to be good, but at a certain point it needs to be ample, fullthroated, maybe even ragged the way Jean Renoir is ragged sometimes. A purity achieved too early can be a danger for a young artist.

I have no way of knowing what Warren Sonbert's future direction will be. He is still growing, he is extremely gifted and capable of anything, and I, as an admirer, wish him the heights. I daresay that Warren's films have not yet caught up with the full capacity for enjoyment and complexity of the man himself. When they do, we have something wonderful to look forward to.

Warren Sonbert Interview   15

DAVID EHRENSTEIN

David Ehrenstein: Have you done much theoretical reading about editing strategies? Eisenstein, Vertov . . .

Warren Sonbert: No, I haven't. A lot of it's been from seeing films like I did when I was a child, over and over again, which I don't do much now. I find I learn much more from music these days, listening to how a piece of music unfolds. New films don't move me much anymore, they seem eminently predictable.

Strangely enough before I'd made films I'd seen all the Eisenstein films, but I'd never seen Vertov or *Man With a Movie Camera* specifically until after I'd made *Carriage Trade*. And it was great—I totally loved it, totally embraced it. But it was because I realized that he was doing things along a line similar to what I had been doing. So it wasn't that he influenced me. Not exclusively so, because there's still a certain didactic element in Vertov, less so than in Eisenstein. There's more breathing space, more juxtaposition in Vertov than there is in Eisenstein.

Ehrenstein: Vertov felt that the camera was a scientific instrument to decode reality, to transform reality, and there are certain notions in the avant-garde like Brakhage's identification with the camera . . .

Sonbert: I think one of the pluses of independent filmmaking is that it does reveal the stance—psychological, physiological—of the filmmaker. How tall the person is, how he moves, what he sees, what he includes, what he excludes. Not just with the compositional frame, but also in the editing aspect. However, my main reason for making films is actually to set up arguments. Each shot is a statement, and I'm giving, virtually, *lines* that people should be able to follow. It's not that any shot can be used at any particular moment, they're not just drawn out of the air. There's a reason for the placement of everything in the film.

Ehrenstein: But your films aren't didactic at all. The viewer can always take everything somewhere else.

Sonbert: There are a certain amount of choices, ambivalences. Various meanings can be associated with the assembled shots. There is no one correct answer. There are several levels, hopefully. Puns, visual metaphors, points about cliches of language, even extending to the titles themselves. It's both very simple and very complex, and I like the tension between those two aspects.

Ehrenstein: There's a great difference between the editing style of the new film *Divided Loyalties* and the others. In *Carriage Trade* there was a sort of *weaving* of images, in *Rude Awakening* less so. Here there are moments where you have sequence shots which could turn into little narratives. Do you find yourself leaning towards the use of a certain kind of conventional narrativity?

Sonbert: Well, *Carriage Trade* was a six year project—stop and start. I'd go out and shoot a whole bunch of footage, and then sort of assemble it. Then I'd go out again and then totally rework the editing of the film *again*—take things out, add things in new places. It's a very leisurely, epochal, washing-over-you kind of film. It takes a while to unfold, and in a certain way it's not as immediately entertaining or enjoyable as maybe these later works are. In *Rude Awakening* I wanted to change that entirely and put a very strict grid/blueprint/mold over the whole work. It's very much influenced by what I would call "directional pulls," where either the composition within the shot, or the camera movement itself would be going either right-to-left or left-to-right, towards the end coming together in a sort of *centralizing* motif. But I would never have a moment in *Rude Awakening* where a figurative shot would be followed by another figurative shot, or close-up followed by a close-up and so on. In other words, it would be a close-up, wide angle, movement vs. still, abstract vs. figurative. I would realize, once this got under way, that I would need, for example, more abstract, non-figurative shots, therefore I would go out and film such things. In *Divided Loyalties* what I needed wasn't so much that, as more shots that had sinister elements. For example, there's a shot of a nude woman at night floating in a swimming pool. I went out and deliberately shot that, arranged that with some friends. But this film doesn't have so much of a strict grid on it, so there are brief sequences in which there's a cluster of similar shots, rather than jumping back and forth between widely different places. I wanted to combine the flexibility, the leisure of *Carriage Trade* with the strict grid of *Rude Awakening*.

There's a four-shot opening motif in this film as there is in *Rude Awakening*. In *Rude Awakening* the first four shots were the hardest to come up with, then there's a geometric progression. The next 12 shots took a little bit more time. But then things began to fall into place and the next 66 shots, let's say, would be very easy, and by the time I'd got what I needed I had this huge backlog of material to draw from. Sometimes I would have to sacrifice a really good beautiful shot for something that would fit better, where the characters would be going in a certain direction in a certain exposure which I needed more than what looked good for itself. It all has to do with the reverberations and the tensions between all the series of shots in the entire film. That's why I'm against stills for my specific works, because a still sometimes emphasizes something in the memory of someone looking at the image, and when they see it in the film, it gives it a prominence that is totally out of the context of the film. I really believe in film as building blocks. I guess, you could look at a piece of architecture and you could look at one stone of it, but it's not anything compared to looking at the totality.

Ehrenstein: Well, that's actually very close to Eisenstein.

Sonbert: Great, it's good to hear that he was on the right track.

Ehrenstein: There are a lot of echoes in *Divided Loyalties* of your earlier films. The subject matter: couples, groups. . . .

Sonbert: There are certain things that interest me, and that's what I film. People think that when they see new work of mine that I'm using out-takes from past films, things from seven, eight years ago. But I'll always go to the circus during a given period of filmmaking, or a parade, things that are out there on public display. But at the same time, the opposite of that—private, intimate things with friends, what they'll do at home, leisure, etc. Incidentally, the new project I'm working on now—the working title for which is *Noblesse Oblige*— is really reportage, things that are covered by the press, by the news media.

Ehrenstein: Is this because of your exposure to William Randolph Hearst in *Rude Awakening* and Jimmy Carter in *Divided Loyalties*?

Sonbert: There'll always be those sort of things in my films. But it has to do with what I've shot recently: in New York the Yankees ticker-tape parade and the 26 mile marathon beginning on Veranzano Bridge: here in San Francisco, the candlelight march for Moscone and Milk when they were shot, the various eulogies and congregations at City Hall. All of this is very six o'clock news material. I'm interested in very journalistic reporting, what is happening every day. I don't really like costume epics or futuristic films. I really think it's a filmmaker's duty to handle what's going on within a given period of history—what people are wearing, what their hairstyle is like. One of the aspects of *Carriage Trade*, for example, is that it takes place over six years. People who look one way at the beginning of the film look very different at the end of the film. The characters change.

Ehrenstein: You refer to the people in your films as characters, which is something some might find strange, seeing your films as falling under the heading of some species of documentary.

Sonbert: No, I don't think my films are documentary. They may have some aspects of it, or of newsreels or travelogs. There's always a narrative element. If you have people present, if you have a figurative image it always has a narrative element.

Ehrenstein: Do you think you're "capturing reality" in any way?

Sonbert: No, I don't know what that is.

Ehrenstein: In other words, do your films reproduce reality or do they *produce* reality?

Sonbert: Well, when I direct people to do things in my films it's always a joke, a parody of a serious situation in a regular narrative film. They're so exaggerated that they have to seem funny. In *Rude Awakening* there's a scene with all of my students at Bard, where we're all out on a field trip and everyone has a camera and is filming and I'm interweaving among them, and that's a sort of send-up of the narrative film. Also there's a getting away from the grid in the use of the match-cut. There's a scene of Douglas Dunn in his studio dancing. The first shot is of him swinging his arms and then cutting from there to a full frontal of him doing the same action. It's the only match-cut in the film.

Ehrenstein: Well, there's this scene in *Divided Loyalties*, too, of someone listening to some singers and then cutting back to his reaction.

Sonbert: Yes, there's a reaction shot, point-of-view. One takes these things and deals with them sort of gingerly, slyly, in the way that narrative films do. But I think it takes them to other levels than *just* that.

Ehrenstein: What do you think of narrative films? I mean, you like a lot of narrative films, take certain things from them. . . .

Sonbert: Well, it's a sort of growing up thing. I became interested in films because of certain narrative films I saw as a child. But it's hard to think of many narrative films made during the last 20 years that are really doing new things. The whole technical apparatus has become run-down and shoddy, the photographic process has really gone downhill. New is not necessarily better, and if you look at a really beautifully photographed Robert Burks film, there's no one today making narrative films that can get that richness, detail. They're so underexposed. And in editing there's not anything that hasn't already been done in, let's say, Hitchcock. Children today should go to films, they should fall in love with films, they should see the latest big spectacular, *Close Encounters*, *Superman*, go back again and again and maybe from that they will learn to love films. But I don't find I'm learning anything from it. I usually just get frustrated and mad at the whole corruptive experience.

Ehrenstein: But what about the avant-garde?

Sonbert: I prefer to use the word independent rather than "underground" or avant-garde or whatever. One person, one film interests me—a person who does everything on the film. But to tell you the truth, with a few exceptions what I like is mostly by people who are friends of mine [laughs], who will remain nameless to protect *me*. In any event, there are very few filmmakers nowadays whom I feel I can learn very much from. I'm interested in literature, in writing, in poetry, and in music.

Ehrenstein: How do you think independent films, your films, function in relation to film culture?

Sonbert: Well, that's more a problem of the audiences than the independent filmmaker's. The ideal way to see these films is one person at a time. Financially, economically, exhibition-wise it's an impossibility. These films are meant to be viewed the way one person would read a book or listen to a piece of music on earphones. It's a total solitary individual experience. You really shouldn't be aware of other presences, which movies as an entertainment form seem to thrive on and encourage. You can't react alone, you have to have the other reactions around you to feel safe, to feel secure. These independent films are not along those lines. They can work in huge theaters as well, but it's not the ideal way to see them.

Ehrenstein: Do you think that the way your films are getting shown, the audiences' experience is satisfactory?

Sonbert: No. First of all, that's not satisfactory; second the distribution of them isn't satisfactory; third of all what the filmmaker gets paid is not satisfactory. If a filmmaker spends six years on a single work, somehow he should be able to command prices that an artist who can whip out a canvas in a day gets paid for. The extreme disparity between what artists in painting make and what artists in film make is enough to send anyone who wants to be an independent filmmaker into a totally different vocation. You can't make independent films and make money. There's a whole area of teaching, or grants, or writing about film—the only other ways one can make money in this field—and they have their own individual drawbacks.

Ehrenstein: Do you feel that the avant-garde scene has changed very much since the years when you first became a filmmaker?

Sonbert: Well, they tell me that there are no new filmmakers, but in every class that I've given, either at Bard College or here at the San Francisco Art Institute, there've always been one or two new filmmakers whose work has been terrific. In this city there are two places to see these films. In New York maybe five or six, but it's only in the big metropolitan centers that there's any actual interest. This year the Whitney Biennial—every year they have painting and sculpture, this is the first year that film has ever been part of their catalogue or in their exhibition.

When I started seeing films it was a very exciting period in New York in the early and mid 1960s. People like Markopoulos, who has since renounced this country and gone off to Europe; Brakhage in Colorado, Jack Smith was making films, Warhol and the Kuchars were working. Now all these people are dispersed and there's no cohesive center for filmmakers. It just doesn't exist anymore—the whole independent syndrome.

Ehrenstein: All your films up to now have been silent. Do you ever think about the possibilities of making a sound film? The reason I ask is because I know of your love of music, especially opera. Do you ever see yourself working with sound in some way?

Sonbert: Well, actually I'd love to make a sound film, but I haven't been able to master the technical aspects of it yet. . . . That's just a joke, since I get that question at every film show. But I really feel that images are so much more clarified and ambivalent and really powerful if they can be just *seen* in and of *themselves*. Any soundtrack first of all imposes its own rhythm that sometimes people get boxed in by, or else the music *carries* the film along in a way that the visuals never would on their own. A soundtrack, I feel, is either redundant or has totally different concerns. The films *are* musical, I mean, it all has to do with how long a shot lasts. I always compare my shots to notes or chords. It does come from music, but because of that I can't *use* music. If you wanted to use any kind of music on it it would work— if you wanted to put a Mozart piano concerto on or the Rolling Stones—but that doesn't *mean* anything. It's much less than what goes into a shot itself—the exposure, the lines around the image, where the camera's placed. All these things are much more complex to me than sounds are.

Ehrenstein: In talking about filmmakers whose concerns are similar to your own, we've mentioned Eisenstein, Vertov. Who has influenced you on the independent scene?

Sonbert: Certainly Gregory Markopoulos. I was his protégé for a while and he did open up this entire new world of films for me. It's a crime that his films are not available to be seen today by people who want to make films or are interested in his films. What can be done about it I don't know. But he is one of the great filmmakers in independent film—really freeing film. Harry Smith, Marie Menken—these are major influences. I must mention Rudy Burckhardt, too, who has not been so much of an influence, but whose qualities and nobility were very impressive.

Ehrenstein: In seeing your films I get the feeling that you're *there* but not all the time. I never get the sense of the *direct* presence of the filmmaker.

Sonbert: All beginning film students, it's almost a mandatory thing, include themselves in the mirror with their camera. Like making it valid that they exist—identity crisis problems or whatever. I love that phrase, "second story man." I like the idea of being the invisible man, the eye of God, using a close-up focal length, being in a window looking out at people without their knowing that the camera's there. I like things to be very simple, very clear, very direct and I can do that best when the subject isn't aware of my presence or, at least, is relaxed.

Ehrenstein: But the results aren't like *cinéma-vérité*.

Sonbert: No. Absolutely not. I don't know what that means. It's the world that I'm constructing—that's the reality.

Ehrenstein: Well, to go to the other extreme—what about a filmmaker trying to remove himself as much as possible, like Snow?

Sonbert: Snow, I guess, has been the first person to do all these kinds of things, but structural cinema is one thing I have great problems with. The thing about those kinds of films is that they are unbelievably predictable in that after you see the first ten seconds you know what the next four hours are going to be. Films are like music and they have to be dense and kinetic. Elliot Carter is much more interesting than George Crumb or Terry Reilly and Steve Reich and all that work with repetition and small changes in a broad period of time, it interests me much less than rapid changes in a short period of time. The natures of the mediums of music and film lend themselves to sharp angular juxtapositions and changes. People, if they work at it, can have a tremendous capacity to consume both in listening and watching.

Ehrenstein: Getting back to the idea of your films having characters. I see that happening in *Divided Loyalties* more than in your other recent films.

Sonbert: The people in my films aren't really basking in the sun on the beach, they're actually out there doing something. We watch ten seconds of what people do all their lives—construction men or people in a bookstore. It tends to qualify the importance—or what Sartre might call "bad faith"—of people throwing themselves behind their own works. In a sense, it's a cruel touch of just showing glimpses of what people feel is very very important. It means something if people embrace, or if they give each other looks—the subtleties, the nuances in these films make up for the fact that they aren't blatantly involved with sex or violence. But the frown that one character might give another character to me is as tumultous as one character stabbing another in a narrative film.

Ehrenstein: What is *going on* in *Divided Loyalties*?

Sonbert: The films are never about anything or about nothing. *Carriage Trade* was about comparing different places, different people, different pastimes in different parts of the world, four seasons, four elements—really broad concerns. *Rude Awakening* continued along that line with things not working out, things not materializing, people having certain expectations, plans, input, and those *dissolving*. What does action mean, where does it get you? It doesn't get you anywhere. That's something about that in the first shot being this archer which is a pun on the Powell-Pressburger films, and the last shot which is a boy throwing sand in the air which is like the Sandman putting you to sleep. *Divided Loyalties* is about Art and industry and contemporary lifestyles like Gays in San Francisco, and I think all these things come in for a lot of criticism and a lot of almost scathing mischievous sly treatment.

Ehrenstein: Like the shot of the guys embracing followed by a shot of a graveyard, which for some people may seem too obvious.

Sonbert: Well, in one sense it may be obvious. You know, "All is vanity." These beautiful bodies will eventually be dust. But what follows after that—you just can't take it from A to B without including C as well. It changes with all the things that are surrounding them. There is a shot of sheep getting clipped and another of sitting ducks on ice. It's people being exploited and not really knowing it. It's both embracing everything and being unbelievably critical of it at the same time.

Ehrenstein: One of the great limitations of film is in what Godard talked about in *Ici et Ailleurs*—"each shot must wait in turn for the next." But in your films, I think you've found a way of getting around that.

Sonbert: Right. I don't really like direct abrupt cuts. I generally like to have what I call "bridge" shots or "cleansing the palate" shots, "after dinner mint" shots. Something very non-specific, neutral—mostly having to do with architecture, flora and fauna, usually non-figurative non-human shots. An undertow before the next wave sweeps over you.

Ehrenstein: Another thing I find in your work, and in this you have a lot in common with Tati in *Playtime*, is that often some very straightforward figurative action that's going on—someone getting out of a car—is seen in a very abstract non-figurative way.

Sonbert: Sometimes there is a gesture of a character—the image is still, and the character reaches his arm left to right—very often there will be a jettison movement—a moving vehicle going in that direction—a spasm of energy. So that physical, contained gesture erupts into movement that's totally disconnected from it.

Ehrenstein: Like one moment in *Divided Loyalties*, a player throws a frisbee and it almost seems to generate another shot.

Sonbert: I guess, it's nothing new. A lot of people had done it before—I came to their work after sort of settling into my own. More influence on the narrative level in film than Tati probably would be Sirk. Giving symbols multiple levels of meaning, none really excluding the other but enriching one another. A famous quote of his, "a director's philosophy is his camera movements and lighting." What he did within that context was very staggering and beautiful—much more impressive than anyone else working at that time. I also like his subversive quality.

Ehrenstein: Sternberg?

Sonbert: His work is very very voluptous. He's one of the few directors who worked in narrative film who did exactly what he wanted to do—not commercially minded and a real autocrat, tyrant or whatever.

Ehrenstein: He said that he tried to make his compositions so perfect that they'd work if the film were projected upside down.

Sonbert: That's not far from the attitude I have. I generally work with my original rather than getting a work print. I don't feel so much the sanctity, holiness of every frame.

Ehrenstein: You've spent a number of years on three films. Do you see yourself accelerating your production speed?

Sonbert: Well, one of the reasons is that I have to feel close to what I actually want. If I have enough of a backlog of material then I'm set to go. But it is a question of being in different places and different times and letting several years elapse to allow for this. Sometimes the images evolve through people that I know—I have a job somewhere, a date with a friend, a certain event. Generally, when I'm in new circumstances, new surroundings, I feel most at ease to shoot. I'm based wherever my editing equipment is—at the moment that's here, in San Francisco. What happens when I get towards the end of a project, I shoot a roll and I know immediately, the first time through: well, those are the three shots I'm going to use. So I don't have to throw things out, really, because I already know what I'll need.

Ehrenstein: There've been some recent articles about diary filmmaking.

Sonbert: I don't understand—people have said that I make diary films. I'm totally adamant that I *don't* make diary films. Diary films always imply that it's just like it came out of the camera. I think that that's too limiting and the whole point of editing—it's like not using depth of field if you're doing renaissance painting or not taking into account different aspects of a musical piece. Webern introduced the whole idea of combining the horizontal and the vertical in music, and what I want to do is to have the narrative and structural levels complement one another—reinforce one another.

Ehrenstein: Do you feel an affinity with the New York poets? A lot of your films involve what might be described as urban sentiments.

Sonbert: Well, a lot of them are good friends of mine, and I am attracted to urban living.

Ehrenstein: O.K., then, this is the time for the real interviewer's question. What do you think about *your* work in relation to the time in which you're living?

Sonbert: It's in many ways like striking out at what is presented to people. I mean, we saw a movie last night [Philip Kaufman's 1978 re-make of Don Siegel's 1956 *Invasion of the Body Snatchers*]—if this passes as a classic of its kind, a great work, it would be disheartening if one didn't do something to slash out against it. Something that's poetry rather than something that's really degrading, dehumanizing entertainment. There's so much junk around, there's so much crap. Webern talked about this—about how there's so *much* junk, why not produce *less*, something really scaled down and perfected. A small contained body, that really says it all. And I do like to turn people on, I'm a great believer in . . . it's a split between shaking people up and making them feel *central*. It's definitely a criminal act—going against the grain. It's giving people what they do not expect, almost what they would rather not hear about. It's taking people to different places. It's not patting them on the back. If you have a work and no one boos it, there's something wrong. Although I don't go out of my way to do these things. I just follow my own needs and wants and desires. Do I sound too megalomaniacal?

Ehrenstein: Oh, no.

Sonbert: Well, I am. I think all artists have to be solipsistic, very exclusive. I said this at a dinner party the other night and no one knew what to make of it: I'm for French literature, German music, and American movies.

An Interview with Hollis Frampton

16

PETER GIDAL

Peter Gidal: What do you consider *Zorns Lemma* to be about?

Hollis Frampton: Well, I can tell you what the film came out of, and how it reached its present form . . . I first began using a movie camera at the end of Fall of 1962. At that time I was being systematically forced into cinema in a way by my still work. I'd been working for a long time in series, sometimes long series, and there were things that began to trouble me about the still series. Such as, if you have a bunch of photographs that you believe cohere even in book space, let alone on a gallery wall or something like that, there's no way to determine the order in which they're seen, or the amount of time for which each one is seen, or to establish the possibility of a repeat . . . so that had already made me think of the film. As a kind of ordering and control, a way of handling stills.

Gidal: So the control element is time?

Frampton: Yeah. Then at the same time I was thinking a lot about the standard paradoxes about photography. You have all these spatial illusions, tactile illusions even, whereas there is a cultural reflex somewhere to believe that when you're looking at something it's real. Let's say. Even if that is the impression you're assembling only from the barest of abstract kind of thing . . . and at the same time the thing is undeniably absolutely flat, it doesn't have impasto, it has nothing, it is perfectly superficial, it only has an outside. That paradox seemed to me most strongly embodied in some stills I had made of words, environmental words, where the word as a graphic element that brought one back to reading (and being conscious of looking at a mark on a surface) emphasized the flatness of the thing. And at the same time the tactile and spatial hints that were compounded with it, the presence of the word within the image, were full of illusion. So that I'd begun to make a bunch of these still photographs. And I thought, "Well, I'll make them into a film", and I shot better than 2000 words in 35mm still. With the idea that I was going to just put them on a stand and shoot them. And I did a little of that as a matter of fact. It's perfectly dead.

It was simply going absolutely noplace. . . . Well, that's how the thing began, as a concern with that spatial paradox or set of spatial paradoxes, and the kind of malaise that it generated as you get farther and farther into it. There still are a few of those original black-and-white photographs. They all have some real object lying on top of it. The oldest one is the word "fox", from the old Brooklyn Fox theatre, that I think is the first one I made . . . dark blue sky, some little straw flowers or paper flowers on top of it as a memento to the sentimental nature of the occasion.

Gidal: Before you go on about your concerns in *Lemma* could you briefly, fairly descriptively, give an idea what *Lemma* itself is?

Frampton: Can I describe it?

Gidal: Yeah, and then go on to the conceptual thing which led to the actual film. To some degree first give a clarification of the film itself.

Frampton: Well that's easy. There are 3 parts, first part is 5 minutes long, soundtrack with no image, a woman recites in a schoolteacherly voice 24 rhymes from the Bay State Primer which was designed to teach late eighteenth century and early nineteenth century children the alphabet. The primer is oriented towards death, towards accepting authority, a kind of rote learning in the dark, I suppose. The second section opens with an enunciation of the Roman alphabet itself, with as little context as possible. The letters are made of metal, actually they were typed on tin foil and photographed in one-to-one closeup. That's how it developed.

Gidal: I was wondering about that.

Frampton: Yeah, they weren't cast.

Gidal: They look like huge cast, 3, 4 feet tall, silver. . . .

Frampton: In the body of the second section, the main section of the film, which is 45 minutes long, there are 2,700 one-second cuts, one second segments, 24 frame segments, of which about half consist of words; the words were alphabetized. The reason for alphabetizing them really was to make the order of them as random as possible, that is to say to avoid using my own taste and making little puns out of them or something like that, much as the encyclopedists of the Enlightenment thought they could somehow categorize all human knowledge or a large part of it under the initial letter of the name of the subject. So that it just happens that quaternians are found in volume so-and-so under "Q"—it's crazy when you think about it. As it is, it does generate some intelligible phrases, some odd pairings anyway. Let's see, there's a kind of Hart Crane line early on that reads "nectar of pain", there's a phrase of Victorian pornography, "limp member", which sticks out like a sore thumb, a limp thumb or something—straight out of *My Secret Life* or *A Man and a Maid*. Well, that happens of course—the words were mostly, not all of them but mostly, shot from the environment. They're store signs, posters and so on. And one finds out very quickly that very many words begin with "c" and "s" and so forth, very few begin with "x" or "q". One quickly begins to run out of "q's" and "x's" and "z's". What happens here is that essentially one is using a chance operation. What always happens when using a chance operation is that along with generating some things that you want it also generates holes. Fate has problems. It's always true. And one has to think a great deal more about the holes, having taken care of the operations. Well, I don't know at what point the notion of substituting other images for words as they disappear in each alphabetic slot supervened. Particularly, I first thought all the images would be different. It would be what John Simon called (fake German accent) "Just a jumble of imaches". . . . And for quite a long time I held that notion of the film. The greatest bulk of time was really shopping in Manhattan for the words themselves. I can't say I did it day after day for seven years, but I did it for seven years, and I shot actually four times as many words as I used, as well as duplications. The word "shot" comes up again and again; I think I used the word "shot" five times. From which to choose essentially. Some just didn't work out for one reason or another. Rather than make 1,350 entirely separate shots. I didn't want to use stock footage. I could achieve essentially the same degree of randomness by using 24 and by dissecting them, exploding them, and once that occurred to me, the possibility of developing an iconography . . .

Gidal: As separate . . .

Frampton: Yeah, as separate from the words and what they were doing and so forth, presented itself. From then it was easy, I did shoot some images that I did not use in fact. There's one image I remember of sawing wood, sawing a board, that I tried several times to get together. Many of the images are in some sense sculptural, to do with kind of generative acts concerning three-dimensional space rather than two-dimensional space.

Gidal: But each image is one second long, and substitutes. So the time sequence, the time span is the same, whether the image is visual or verbal-visual.

Frampton: Yes, that's right. They're all one second. Well, in fact they're not all one second. I suppose I should talk about this: all my work contains mistakes, presumably every-body's work contains mistakes, and sometimes I find them out when I'm doing them, and lock into them one way or another, sometimes I find them out later. Some people think the whole thing is a mistake. But if you think about any long and comparatively ambitious work, it always contains errors of some kind or other. *Divine Comedy* contains metric errors where Dante got locked into the text and had to, you know, fight his way out of it; maybe it doesn't come off so well. . . . So I decided deliberately to incorporate a series of kinds of errors.

Gidal: A system of errors.

Frampton: Right, so that I'd know where they were, since they were gonna be there anyway. And at the moment I won't go into that, but there is one class of metrical errors. There are 12 images which are 23 frames long and 24 which are 25 frames long. And I did not generate those myself. The person who was helping me cut the footage down into one second lengths determined by his own chance operations where they were, and cut them.

Gidal: Still, but even when it happens, I mean I noticed the "errors" while watching the film again. Still, it comes over very clearly that it's one second segments. You feel a certain tension at moments when it breaks. But not to the point of mystification where one thinks, "Is it a second or not?" It's basic that each time piece is one second.

Frampton: But then that's an elastic interval. It depends a lot on how much there is to see in the frame. I mean, some of them are very simple and very graphic, where you almost start to get bored, 24 frames. . . . There are others where there's at least a suggestion that if you saw one second over fifty times it would still be frantic. Your eyes would be crawling around the frame trying to get the stuff out of it. . . .

But to get on with the description of the thing: finally, all the words are replaced by images. The last one is "c" which is a red Ibis flapping its wings in the Bronx zoo, which is seen for only one second in the entire hour of the film.

Gidal: I think many people leave thinking whether or not the images totally substituted. It's not a sense of completion. There is completion but not that total sense of completion.

Frampton: Yeah, well it depends . . . some people play that part of the film as a game. Some audiences were playing it so much they were waiting to see which would go out next and what would replace it and so forth. And when finally the "c" does substitute in the last cycle of the film, there have been cheers, and so forth (giggling, laughter, etc.). Then finally there's a section 10 or 11 minutes long in which a man, woman and dog walk from very near foreground to a distance close to 400 yards across a field of snow and disappear at the end into pine woods. It is for all intents and purposes a continuous take. In part, it's not; it's a shot of five 100 feet rolls, and suggestions of fogged ends are left in, and it's dissolved, so . . . if you're at all into the materiality of film, it suggests several times that it's about to end, then it dissolves into a new image, then finally goes out to white. There's a track on the last part which consists of six women's voices reading a text by Robert Gros-tet or Grosse-teste . . . who was a bishop of Lincoln. A text called "On Light, or the Ingression of Forms", which is a beautiful medieval Latin treatise which is variously translated. Translated, vulgarized by me, then cut down to about 620 words. It's read pocketed. At the rate of one word a second. And the text itself I think is apposite to film and to whatever my epistemological views of film are. The key line in the text is a sentence that says, "In the beginning of time, light drew out matter along with itself into a mass as great as the fabric of the world." Which I take as a fairly apt description of film, as the total historical function of film, not as an art medium but as this great kind of time capsule, and so forth. It was thinking on that which led me later to posit the universe as a vast film archive which contains nothing in itself and presumably somewhere in the middle, the undiscoverable centre of the whole matrix of filmthoughts, an unfindable viewing room in which the great presence sits through eternity screening the infinite footage.

Gidal: Screening unshot negatives.

Frampton: Well, what have you! Is it then the infinite intelligence which in the act of doing the screening imagines the images into the frame and they reflect back into the projector? One can make a whole religion out of this thing!

Gidal: We're trying.

Frampton: I plan to have more to say about that. That's my metaphor because I'm a filmmaker. I mean Borges has a wonderful story called "The Library of Babel" in which the entire universe has been transformed into a library of books. And while conjecturing about the actual structure of the library he manages to reconstruct the entire history of human thought. In terms of this one metaphor, I'm not so much in sympathy with books as Borges is, so that this cinematic metaphor seems to be more poignant; more meat.

Gidal: But if you're talking about Borges. I find important and beautiful in Lemma the fact that it's non-mystificatory, that it isn't labyrinthine at all, and that on one level, for me at least, it denies logic and function. In that sense it's really an anti-calvinist film. . . .

Frampton: Oh, I'll go along with that.

Gidal: And you're substituting visual templates for verbal ones. Considering the cultural system we're brought up in, really you're setting up a defunctionalized system. Let's face it: the word. "First there was the word." And if you are going to fuck up the word in some cases in

16. A scene from Hollis Frampton's *Zorns Lemma* (1970). Courtesy Anthology Film Archives; reprinted by permission.

Lemma with a non-linear image, you are making a non-hierarchical system which is already blowing the whole game.

Frampton: Absolutely. Let me tell you a bit more what this film is for me. A couple of people spotted it too. The film is for me a kind of cryptic autobiography, in a way. I have the kind of standard mid-Western American Protestant education in which you do learn by precept and by rote in the dark. And it was, although perhaps not to that kind of puritanical extent, authority-ridden and death-saturated, and so forth. Presumably, everybody, well I won't say everybody, many of my contemporaries or peers have very much the same kind of experience. It was highly oriented to words. And even to words only in the most superficial denotative kind of way. This is where one could call it Calvinist as well.

Gidal: Definitely.

Frampton: Part 2 really has a great deal to do with something that happened to me somewhere between the ages of 20 and 30, 32, 33, something like that, a decade and a half that I've spent largely in New York. If you think about it, it represents a kind of long dissolve, a very attenuated and skippy dissolve, from primarily verbal to primarily nonverbal concerns: the last part in the film, also of course the middle section, was all shot in Manhattan, pointedly urban, in one way or another, in its visual style: a conglomeration, a glutination of successive visual styles which are imitated in the individual shots. This is still very much distancing itself from, in one way or another, renaissance space, that sort of urban rectilinearity. Then finally the last part turned out to be prophetic. Simon Field wrote to me in the summer of 1970—at least I think it was him—and asked me whether the film was autobiographical, and whether the last part of the film had something to do with some kind of gesture of leaving the city, as a lot of New York artists were doing. And at the time of the film's making I had not left. I thought of it in January 1970 on a farm a friend of mine had just got 25 miles from where my place now is. I was out in the country looking for a place. And it turned out to be prophetic.

Gidal: The second segment of the film already hints at that, by ending with earth air fire water.

Frampton: Sure. Very much so.

Gidal: What you should perhaps talk about is that it isn't just leading to getting out, moving in one direction; what I find so important is precisely that some images are linear in their substitution for letters, like tying a shoe, peeling an orange; others are not. And not in any specific order. Although the last are earth air fire water, then the third segment is walking out to the snow, the final feeling of the whole film, of the final structure of the film as such, doesn't leave one with that feeling. Doesn't leave me with a narrative notion of the filmmaker leaving the urban environment. It leaves me much more with a system, a new system of alphabet. A self-contained serial.

Frampton: OK. I might want to get back to that later. I suppose I do most of my work in such a way that I supply a certain amount, I make a kind of container, and for the rest of it the film, the work, generates its own set of demands and its own set of rules and finally if possible— and this is I think the very oldest kind of idea, not new at all—it consumes itself, uses itself up, leads to a stasis of some sort. I can't say precisely how the . . . well one begins to do something. . . . I get to a point where I've done as much as I know how to do. OK. So I then wait, and after a while something comes. What I tend to do is wait around for some kind of insight into how to do the next thing, you know, where does the insight come from? I don't know where it comes from, I'm not here to make explicit appeals to the muse or the angels, or what have you.

But it wasn't simply a question of, say, getting more and more ambitious and wanting to order larger and larger amounts of material. There are ways of doing that. But to find some way they would order themselves, that would have something to do with it, that would seem appropriate to my feeling. And my feeling is something which is partly genetic and has been generated partly by my own understanding of the medium and also the more distant tradition of the art that has moved me specifically, which may be genetic too. There are some things that appeal to you and some things that don't. I guess I, in some sort of way, know that some of those Egyptian things in the British Museum are great sculpture, but I mean I am unmoved by granite colossi. I may at the age of 70 be moved by granite colossi. I may have been moved by them at the age of 5.

Gidal: But that's the ultimate test, though, in that sense. What we're talking about, the structural part: you can have a worked out structure, a construct, even to the point of substituting certain images for words, that whole business, and it still can be a terrible film or a great film. That's the thing.

Frampton: Yes, the degree of rationality involved in something is no guarantee at all. It's like sincerity. Sincerity presumably is some kind of *sine qua non*; it doesn't guarantee a goddamn thing. Most art is sincere and most art is bad. Perfectly rational. . . .

Gidal: That's the problem of talking in art-critical terms. One may be rationalizing all one wants and a film doesn't work. That aspect one can't deal with easily.

Frampton: I remember being one time on the third floor of the permanent collection of the Museum of Modern Art in New York and passing by Matisse's *Maroccans*, and there's a little old lady standing enraptured in front of it. A young girl went by, glanced at it, went on to Rouault, German Expressionist stuff, the Picassos, the whole tour of the third floor, and YES she came back around and the little old lady was still standing enraptured in front of the Matisse. And she said to her, obviously stunned, "45 minutes ago I was here and you were standing here and you're still standing here, what is it that you see in this painting?" And the little old lady said "Ah, my dear, it's plain that it requires a trained sensibility". She wasn't insulting her. She was saying she had not reached that level of spiritual organization.

Gidal: And verbalization.

Frampton: Well, if you understand that phrase in its depth. Aristotle talks somewhere of six kinds of intelligence. And we've whittled it down to one kind of intelligence, right, goodness, being able to talk, to write something which is like talk. Being articulate. That leaves five kinds of intelligence as recognized by Aristotle shivering in the cold. Well, one of the kinds he talked about was *techne*, which is the kind that lets people make things, presumably good things. Well, we get *technical* from that. We say, "That's merely technical." But he didn't mean it as pertaining to craft, he meant it as the whole faculty of mind that makes it possible for a Brancusi to be able to march up to a billet of bronze and get the "Bird in Space". Whereas if I march up, whatever my powers are, to the same billet of bronze I get a pile of filings, essentially. Yet all, to my knowledge, Brancusi had to say in his whole life about sculpture was ten sentences. Something like that. None of which is what your art reviewer would recognize as rational.

It is obvious again to a person of trained sensibility or disciplined sensibility that Brancusi was an intelligent man, and we're not dealing here with a dumb or even a crafty Rumanian peasant. We're talking about an individual of extraordinary intelligence. So that you see . . . if each of us have six kinds of intelligence we could call a, b, c, d, e, f, then I make something with intelligence "a" that is intended to be apprehended by you with intelligence "a". Something on channel "e" intended to be apprehended on channel "e".

Gidal: But it's the *crossings* that are interesting. That's why *Zorns Lemma* works.

Frampton: Well, OK, I mean they have wide penumbras. You don't dial the station by pressing a button. Presumably you're receiving on all channels all the time. Maybe I used the wrong figure. Here I am trying to use metaphor from radio rather than a cinema metaphor; a cinema metaphor is richer. I mean, we think of it as pictures with sound, but film has this whole tactile channel as well, this whole level of being so real you could touch it.

Gidal: And duration, which nothing else has.

Frampton: Yeah.

Gidal: I mean, your film has pieces of time, whether they're visual or verbal. The tensions come basically from the piece of time.

Frampton: I like your word "duration". That's a word which means something. When you say "time", you're floundering. . . .

Gidal: Of course.

Frampton: Duration is how long something lasts.

Gidal: From point a to point b.

Frampton: Something that is concretely measurable by counting the number of frames on the strip.

Gidal: The other thing is that it's not narrative. Point "a" to point "b" in *duration* as opposed to narrative. Because everything moves forward in time. That's an important distinction.

Frampton: OK. What about time? Since so much of my work seems to deal with notions of time—it's something I've thought about. What are these views of time? There's time as the universal solvent. We're dropped on the surface of the tub, which is corrosive. We slowly rot away and sink down and disappear. Or: there's time as an elastic fluid. The frog Tennyson leaps into the elastic fluid and creates waves which ultimately joggle the cork Eliot. Or, in Eliot's view, the elasticity travels in both directions: tradition and individual talent. Eliot of course says that Eliot has changed Tennyson and that is clearly true. Or: there is the DNA model of time, the spiral in which it's possible in four dimensions to have every turn of the helix cross every other turn of the helix within one lifetime or some other finite thing. Or: Pound's view of time: the continuous co-presence of everything. That is essentially the view of time that the generation of the 1980s comes down to.

Gidal: And then there's Beckett's view of time which could be the continuous co-presence of nothing.

Frampton: Which still amounts to the same thing. I don't know . . . there is anyway this— what would you call it?—this incubus that settles over any attempt to think about time, time being itself a phenomenon like gravitation, radiation or what have you. There's a problem with that. That is, that phenomena are directly sensible and the intellect can devise direct ways to measure them. "32 feet per second per second" is an expression about gravitation. Which leads me to suspect that time is not a fiction, you know, but simply without being a phenomenon nevertheless a kind of intellectable condition of perceiving all other phenomena.

Gidal: An unavoidable . . . *thing*, really.

Frampton: Well, but I mean it is the condition under which other phenomena proceed. I mean, if you say 32 feet per second per second then we're talking about rate and total duration and so forth; we're talking about conditions, or a condition under which gravitation can be spoken of.

Gidal: So how does that relate back now to *Zorns Lemma*? I mean, specific instances of pieces of time, which means also pieces of space. . . .

Frampton: I think very specifically in *that* film I have made the cut in duration (the pointed sense of the passage of time) explicitly, a condition of perceiving everything that's going on in the film. That's one view of the matter. Of course, I've gone on with this black-and-white thing—the new films—to elaborate other possible views. . . .

ALTERNATIVE CINEMAS, 1980–2000

Introduction

The contributions in Part Four point the reader toward the alternative cinema of the late twentieth century. Though these essays address only a handful of the myriad experimental filmmakers and their communities, they nevertheless give an idea of just how rich and broadly developed alternative cinema practice has become. Foster's interview and Holmlund's essay demonstrate the importance of lesbian communities in experimental film; Gibson's essay alludes to the growing communities of African-American women filmmakers, and Kobena Mercer's essay touches on the significance of black gay men's filmmaking communities. In addition to the rise of identity-oriented communities, the distribution venues of Women Make Movies, Inc., the Sankofa and Black Audio Visual Collective, Electronic Arts Intermix, and Frameline Films have had a significant impact on the ability of alternative voices to be heard.

Identity politics surfaced as the predominant force in both film criticism and alternative film practice in the late twentieth century. Gays, lesbians, bisexuals, transgendered and nonwhite filmmakers, previously ignored, scorned, and omitted, began to speak out and band together to form alliances to support one another, help one another find financing and distribution, and, perhaps most significantly, document and explore identity issues. Barbara Hammer, for example, found a need to resuscitate and document lesbian history through the means of experimental film. In an interview with Gwendolyn Audrey Foster, "Re/Constructing Lesbian Auto/Biographies in *Tender Fictions* and *Nitrate Kisses*," Hammer explains that she needed to document lesbian existence (especially that of older women) in *Nitrate Kisses*. Hammer speaks of the importance of knowing about other lesbian directors and women directors in history. She also discusses the relevance of lesbian communities among the digital world, stressing the viability of the web for community making.

Chris Holmlund's essay, "The Films of Sadie Benning and Su Friedrich," is equally concerned with documentation. Holmlund looks at the films of Sadie Benning and Su Friedrich as experimental autobiographical ethnographies, or documentaries, specifically "dyke documentaries." Holmlund notes that, as women and lesbians, both Benning and Friedrich began to make experimental films and videos as a response to feeling excluded from mainstream films and filmmakers.

As Gloria J. Gibson concludes in her essay, "Black Women's Independent Cinema," black women filmmakers found support and community in a loosely connected California-based alliance known as the "LA Rebellion." Gibson discusses works by three black women filmmakers, Ayoka Chenzira, whose *Hair Piece* (1984) contemplates African-American identity politics through the prism of hairstyling; Julie Dash, whose *Illusions* (1983) deals with passing in Hollywood; and Kathleen Collins, whose *Losing Ground* (1982) explores a black woman professor's search for meaning in cultural identity. Though Gibson carefully points out that the experiences of black women are certainly not homogenous, she does find striking similarities among the works she examines. Gibson notes that all these women, despite their different backgrounds, classes, and unique self-definitions, select themes that highlight sociocultural issues.

Both Isaac Julien and Marlon Riggs place at the center of many of their films the complexities of identity politics. Kobena Mercer, in his essay "Dark and Lovely Too: Black Gay Men in Independent Film," addresses the paradoxes of race, sexuality, and representation in Julien's experimental films, including *Territories* (1985), *Looking for Langston* (1988), *This Is Not an AIDS Advertisement* (1988), *The Attendant* (1992), and *Frantz Fanon: Black Skin, White Mask* (1996). Born in Britain, Isaac Julien was associated with the black independent collective Sankofa Films. In 1988, Julien took the experimental filmmaking and documentary communities by storm with his homage to Langston Hughes, the black, gay Harlem renaissance poet. Mercer also discusses Marlon Riggs, who also used independent experimental film to explore and perform gay blackness and black gayness. Beginning with *Ethnic Notions* (1986), *Affirmations* (1998), and *Tongues Untied: Black Men Loving Black Men* (1991), Riggs took on established notions of identity only to problemize them as much as he celebrated them. *Tongues Untied* revealed the total absence of blacks in gay media and film festivals and the near erasure of African-American gay subcultures. Before he died in 1994, Riggs completed another powerful independent film that also took up identity issues. In *Black Is . . . Black Ain't* (1994), he directly challenges the notion that queer blacks are not really part of the black community. Riggs also confronts the complexities of identity within black culture, which traditionally has been defined from outside and has suffered because of the divisions between light and dark skin in black society. Kobena Mercer's essay about *Looking for Langston* and *Tongues Untied* concludes with a reexamination of postmodern dismissals of authorship. Mercer argues that who the filmmaker is ultimately *does* matter, and a filmmaker's cultural, social, racial, and sexual identity matter. As with the films of Marlon Riggs and Isaac Julien, Mercer insists that it is not enough to celebrate difference; we must also continually scrutinize the inherent assumptions we base on identity politics.

As stated in the volume introduction, Part Four of this book in no way represents the entirety of current alternative film practice. Instead, we hope to offer some sense of the exciting and developing work being made despite distribution problems and financial woes. The rise of identity politics in the 1980s has led to a number of communities that support one another and ultimately has led to the distribution of groundbreaking experimental films and videos.

Re/Constructing Lesbian Auto/Biographies in *Tender Fictions* and *Nitrate Kisses*

17

GWENDOLYN AUDREY FOSTER

Filmmaker Barbara Hammer's *Tender Fictions* (1995) and *Nitrate Kisses* (1992) work to re/construct lesbian autobiographies and histories. Both are highly experimental feature films that interweave archival footage with personal documentary "evidence" of lost and found lesbian history. Since the late 1960s, Hammer has been making personal films which combine the evocative and the performative in a haunting blend of images and sound in a style which is uniquely her own. I corresponded with Barbara Hammer about her latest work over a period of some time; here is an edited transcript of our give-and-take correspondence. In all of her works, Hammer is most interested in the creation of lesbian biography and autobiography, and it is these questions which she addresses in her first feature films. At once sexy, erotic and confrontational, Hammer's work operates at the margins between truth and fiction, memory and history, opening up a web of discourse for a new conceptualization of lesbian auto/biography.

Gwendolyn Foster: It seems like the central theme of *Tender Fictions* is the constructedness of biography, autobiography, and the self. At the beginning of the film, you introduce the theme that you wanted to write your own biography before one is constructed for you. I'm fascinated by the way that you dance around this question in all its complexities; the way you almost immediately introduce performative selves and performativity as a means to self construction. For example, at the beginning of the film there is a sequence in which you are dancing on the star of Shirley Temple at the Hollywood Walk of Fame. At once, you destabilize the notion of an integrated self that is constituted through the manifestation of the cult of the individual. You intertwine your selves with those of Charlie Chaplin, D.W. Griffith, Shirley Temple and others. You also use the voices of critics such as Helene Cixous, Sue-Ellen Case, Roland Barthes, Trinh T. Minh-ha, Barbara Smith, and many others. I wonder if you would elaborate on the idea of construction of selves?

Barbara Hammer: First, let me say that it has been over two or three years that I began the research on "autobiography" that helped me with ideas and ideology on that subject. I think each of the writers I quote, each of the cultural heroes I show or quote or refer to, are all the different constructions I hang on the skeletal scarecrow of the "self," "the constructed self." For instance, the quotes in *Tender Fictions* about D.W. Griffith came from his Memorial Service at the Masonic Temple on July 27, 1948. Charles Brackett's words are used on behalf of the Motion Picture Academy and the entire industry. As a pioneer of lesbian avant-garde cinema, I sympathize and identify with Griffith, as one of the pioneers of American narrative cinema.

As Brackett wrote, "I'm afraid it didn't ease his heartache very much," talking about the Academy Oscar Griffith received in 1936, during dark days for him. "When you've had what he'd had, what you want is the chance to make more pictures, unlimited budgets to play with, complete confidence behind you. What does a man full of vitality care for the honors of the past? It's the present he wants and the future."

Now, you may wonder why this quote has resonance for me? I am 57 years old, have made over 77 films and videos, am full of creative ideas and projects for new work, yet I had to take a full time teaching job to insure myself of health insurance, basic needs, and a social security monthly income. Real basic stuff. This is just an example. The use of "he," the application of the moustache over the Griffith soundtrack, further increases the identification. Perhaps the self is made of the cut and paste applications from historic and contemporary culture as much as anything. Today I awoke with the idea that I should go to my studio everyday that I work cross-dressed as a man. What are the power implications that the gender construction would lend to the work?

Foster: In *Tender Fictions* you create new ways of looking at truth and its constructedness in autobiography and biography, yet you are careful to point out that history and biography are important political tools; that for example, when you looked back through your mothers, so to speak, you saw no lesbians. You underscore this point with a very touching and playful use of sound and voice. When we hear you singing a fragment, "looking for lesbians" it strikes me as a stunning use of humor for an important political statement. This might be a good place to begin talking about your use of humor and strategies of opposites to make the viewer/listener want to look again. In an interview with Trinh T. Minh-ha that I did, she talked about how some audiences did not seem to be able to approach her films with a sense of humor. I wonder if that happens with your films and I wonder what you think about using humor as a performative political strategy?

Hammer: Humor in a film leads to instant gratification for the filmmaker when she is sitting in the audience. No one has talked about "receptivity theory" in regards to the *maker* as audience member in an audience community. When I hear laughter or giggles or murmurs at junctures in *Tender Fictions* and other films that I enjoyed, laughed out loud at while editing. I am rewarded, pleased, feel connected to the community that is my audience. Similarly, when the film falls flat, and I am greeted with silence, I feel anxious, not sure that the film has been read with the intention with which it was made.

Humor is a great way to make a point. I like to pleasure myself while working, so it was with great surprise and joy that I found the over 30 year old black-and-white super 8mm roll of a kitten playing with my exhusband's penis. Yes, it was directed!

Filmmaking can be such hard work. When you work as an independent using your own resources or limited grant monies, you are spending time that is your life. I want to enjoy myself as much as possible within the limited time and resources I have, even with a life expectancy of 84. If I am working on a subject that is not humorous, I want to feel deeply.

Foster: I'm interested in your theories about performative gestures between lesbian couples, and how lesbian couples develop a complementary set of movements and gestures.

Hammer: I thought that was so funny, to notice the carefully precise back and forth movement in the footage I found of Sally Cloninger and Marilyn Frasca in their motorboat on the Puget Sound. I noticed that within my own relationship I was sensitive to the nuances of body gestures of my partner and myself; nuances that I didn't have with my friends. I imagine if someone were filming Florrie Burke and myself today they would find in the footage the same careful acuity of sensitivity to emotional/intellectual variations of each of us to the other. This borders on the phenomenon of couples picking up each others' habits, ways of wording phrases, even laughter patterns. And, of course, the ultimate is finishing your partner's sentences. "Till death do us part," but it may be sooner, if sentence completion sets in!

Foster: Another section in which you cut together a performance of your cross-dressing with a voice-over describing an entirely different, if related, scene strikes me as an enactment of the slippage in biography itself, between the referent and the signifier. You also embed the notion of multiplicity in the voice-overs which are sometimes read by two or more people of different genders. You have, in post-production, changed the pitch of your voices so that we can no longer "read" gender and we are confronted with our own participation in what Kate Bornstein calls "the cult of gender." You move across subjectivities here and elsewhere. Aren't you, in a way, enacting the call for politicization of location in the words of, for example Barbara Smith, whom you quote as saying, "White feminists and lesbians should render their own histories, subjectivities, and writing complex by attending to their various implications in overlapping social discursive divisions and their histories"?

Hammer: The voice is my own but the frequencies are changed. I first used this technique (of course, Laurie Anderson used it long ago) myself in a performance at The Women and Technology Conference in April, 1994 at the Yerba Buena Gardens in San Francisco. In a live performance I noted in my script arrows going up or down (up for feminist theorists, down for male cultural analysts, and normal for my "I stories") and I gave it to the sound person with instructions to lower or raise the frequency according to my directions. This was so successful with the audience (laughter, again), that I incorporated the technique throughout the film as a way of using theory and poking fun at it at the same time.

When I repeat the story of driving around the world on a motorcycle and use a different pronoun with every telling, I am suggesting the patriarchal incorporation of power and words. I heard that the "she" pronoun carried less significance in the story than the "he," and that when I used the first person singular, "I," there was a greater suggestion of truth-telling. All these attached conditions interest me. This is the cultural baggage, be it a pronoun or a moustache.

Foster: I wrestled with the question of the role of biographer as I was writing an encyclopedia of women directors. I must admit I reexperienced a sinking feeling when you talked about biographers telling other/s stories in *Tender Fictions*. I was highly aware of constructing selves, highlighting one thing over another, putting things in a positive or negative light, trying to write women directors into a history which has traditionally excluded them. These women had extraordinarily complex lives, as we all do, but I had to look at them primarily as filmmakers.

To some extent I see a parallel in your story of your selves. You include a section on your father and another on your mother. I'm sure you were thinking about the politics of telling another's story and you do fascinating and moving things with their stories. In the section on your father, who is remembered as being many things, including suicidal, you demonstrate the constructedness of truth and biography by having his photograph framed and reframed with mattes that a hand moves in the frame. In the sections on your mother, you capture the elusiveness of the truth or truths of her existence. According to the film's multivalent planes, she was either a product of her times, which demanded women act in horribly confined ways and/or she was a woman who controlled her own destiny and own self. Your work with the dualities of constructions of selfhood here is profound; between the culturally defined self of the televisual and fashion culture, and the self-defined person. Are you working toward a self that can be experienced across subjectivities and therefore a different way to look at the familial construct?

Hammer: Definitely, and the placement of the individual within the community is important here. I see myself as defined and defining myself along side of and sometimes within the burgeoning feminist movement of the late 1960s and early 1970s. These were formative years for me as an artist as well as a political woman. If the rising surge of lesbian/feminism hadn't been happening at that time, I don't think I could have identified myself as one (a lesbian/feminist) without the community. I have always read that a biographer needs to look at the context of an individual's life; but looking back on mine it seems even more profound. More like a tribal context, something we read about in some African cultures where the individual (as such) isn't even a construction. He or she is there only as part of a long tradition that includes ancestry, tribal rites and histories, etc. In many ways, I can see those of us participating in the early culture-making of women who were self-defining, as part of a tribe/community. That's the new family. The "old" family, the "natural born killers," is to be understood, then, left. A few hinges will remain but they are easily seen and so accounted for as the woman springs into her newly defined being (this takes years of course and is a slow-motion spring!).

Foster: I love the way you weave in a reference to *The Flower Thief*, a classic Queer film by Ron Rice. It is one of the incidences that we know may not be "true" (but by now we are questioning whether or not it matters if everything be factual). This is how I read it, and of course every viewer constructs their own truth(s). You tell a story about being in an audition and not doing well and being shamed by having to wear a sign that says, "I am a flower thief." It made me think of the "classic" Freudian case, the one referred to as the "Child is Being Beaten" scenario and of course all the Freudian baggage of childhood; questions of safety, pain, pleasure, and punishment. But by bringing in the reference to Ron Rice, it moved your subjectivity into context with an icon of queer 1960s freedom; therefore I read it as you having control over the memory, control over the manner in which you wish to reexperience the memory. I was wondering if you were working around this, and were you doing something different in the "I saw a meese" sequence, in which the child Barbara Hammer is forever associated with a tale that is retold in your family, until it becomes as much a part of one's self as a name?

Hammer: In editing I find tremendous control, ability to shake things up, reconfigure and by doing so, make references to my own thievery as well as Ron Rice's. Memory is reconfigured through context and this is important. I recently saw a show at The African Museum here in

New York. The Luba use a memory board to attempt to make exact recall of historic events and figures. The board is carved with raised symbols, beads are attached, a few human figures are carved (standing in for gods and goddesses). They remember through touching. I don't know if these locators affirm an exact and ongoing retelling as I believe they are meant to do, or if each history-teller embellishes or in some way interprets the event/figure/icon from their particular frame of reference. What do we have here in the West as locator boards? Scrapbooks, but mainly, snapshots. Snapshots in the form of photographs or in the form of stories. When the "meese" story gets attached to "Barbara memories," the yoking of personhood and familial story become a kind of tribal family memory. This is a bump on my memory board.

Foster: In *Tender Fictions*, you utilize several quotes having to do with post-modern experiences of truth, memory and subjectivity. You have a voice-over from Helene Cixous, "Her speech even when theoretical or political, is never simple or linear. She draws her story into history." You include another voice-over from Roland Barthes, stating "The one who speaks is not the one who writes and the one who writes is not the one who is." One of the most profound quotes, however, is from Barbara Hammer: "I is a lesbian couple." Can you place this in the context of your developing theories and experiences as a postmodern filmmaker?

Hammer: As a developing postmodern filmmaker, I must give credit to the many, many literary sources as well as my own lived experience that prompted the statement "I is a lesbian couple." The statement that continues to make me uneasy and confirms my emotional ambivalence to, perhaps, any definition. The chapter "A Signature of Autobiography: 'Gertrice/Altrude'," by Leigh Gilmore in *Autobiography and Questions of Gender* as well as Biddy Martin's "Lesbian Identity and Autobiographical Difference(s)," in *The Lesbian and Gay Studies Reader* were especially important to me. In all my research, these were the only two essays on lesbian autobiography I could find. Shocking.

So "I is a lesbian couple" addresses the dilemma of self-naming and polarities. Since taking a class at UCLA in my undergraduate years on "Ethics," I have been perplexed by the "idea" that one cannot understand 'freedom' without constraint. Similarly, if one accepts the 'genital definition of lesbian' (Tee Corinne), rather than the intellectual definition (T. Grace Atkinson), one knows one's lesbian self in relationship. There are a whole lot of selves, however, that are unknown in relationships and continue to be important functioning, creative, artistic and other parts of play that exist outside of the couple. This has yet to be addressed in essay literary form, but I address it in my film with all the material, and image/sound conjunctions, that come before the introduction of "the couple." As a postmodern filmmaker, I draw from everything I see and read and taste and hear and smell and hold and delight and suffer from and with and more.

Foster: You problematize the notion of an essentialized, easily defined notion of lesbian vs. hetero, butch vs. femme, self vs. models, etc. It seems to me that you continue to transgress boundaries; that one of your goals as an artist is to confront and to challenge and to celebrate. How do you manage to combine a celebratory energy with a radical political energy and how can we continue the work (and the play) of *Tender Fictions*?

Hammer: I do take on goals like confrontation, challenge and celebration. The challenge for me is to find the boundaries (my own as well as community limits, systems rules, institutional demands) and then confront them. Confronting these constructed boundaries and deconstructing them is hard political work made possible through play or fun. Take any problem as a challenge and turn it into play while you confront it and you find out you are having fun, celebrating your life energy. Hey, what else is it about?

Ask yourself these questions: what is it I am afraid of? How has this fear been constructed? And, by whom? Then what am I going to do about it? How can I turn it into play? *The Lesbian Primer* or *How To Return to My Pre-adolescent Roots and Reclaim my Pre-heterosexual Self* by Barbara Hammer.

Foster: That's an important concept. Let's talk about your pre-heterosexual identity.

Hammer: I call my pre-heterosexual identity the years up until 13, or more like 15, when I became acutely aware of my interests in the adventures of having boyfriends. Of course, the heterosexist training and cultural conditioning started with my name and from day one, I'm sure. However, what I'm talking about is the time when a girl thrives on just being herself in all her fullness with imagination galore, fear unknown, and turning a blind eye to prescriptive behavior. That was my life until 14 or 15. I lived without a mind to "femininity," restrictive clothing, ideas on what a girl should or shouldn't do. Even when I became interested in "boys," I chose the ones who were rebels, older than me, and sometimes out of school. During high school and college there is such pressure to date, to attract men, that I can imagine even the hardiest of girls in the 1950s trying to conform to some precast mold of docility, etc. So, when I became a dyke, at the ripe old age of 30, I felt like I was back inside the "old" me of 13 and now I could keep on growing. It felt like a continuum that had been broken was restored. It felt absolutely great and still does.

Foster: *Nitrate Kisses* begins with some words from Adrienne Rich about the importance of recovering what has been "unnamed." Both films deal with the issue of loss, recovery and retrieval of lost histories and narratives of lesbians, gays, bisexuals, and "others." Going back even further in your work you were already, of course, exploring these issues. I'd like you to elaborate on that and talk about how you came to this material, particularly the sections on Willa Cather.

Hammer: It wasn't easy. Everything at the Cather Foundation was "under covers," but I found a sympathetic person there who pointed me in the direction of some articles she Xeroxed for me, and a host of archival photographs that included the ones I eventually purchased for use in the film. I had a thick biography of Willa Cather by James Woodress, yet I could not find "lesbian" in the index. This was the initial impetus that eventually became the beginning of *Nitrate Kisses*. After Sharon O'Brien published her biography on Cather, I felt better.

I attended a lecture Sharon O'Brien gave at the New York Historical Society. When I asked her about her courage in writing of Cather's hidden sexual preference, she gave the frank answer that she had no intention of doing so and was going to continue the tradition of secrecy until she talked with William Curtin, who absolutely knew Cather was gay from first-hand knowledge and who encouraged her to publish the lesbian facts.

Foster: I am especially drawn to the beginning of *Nitrate Kisses* in which you perform an active and living biographization of Willa Cather. Living here in Nebraska, I am familiar with the way many literary biographers, teachers, historians and Nebraskans in general choose to erase her lesbianism lifestyle. What I am struck by is how you turn this appalling situation around and make her history alive again. I'm interested in the way that you bring out the

17. Barbara Hammer. Courtesy Anthology Film Archives; reprinted by permission.

visual evidence—what should be quite obvious evidence, photographs of her cross-dressing as a young girl, calling herself Will, the testimony of her lifelong lesbian relationship—but instead of simply stating these things as fact you reenact them in a way, onscreen. How did you arrive at the strategy of exposing the uncovery/recovery process?

Hammer: Traditional cinema uses a story line of ever changing events to keep audience interest. This is boring because it is so programmed and predictable. Experimental cinema presents film in a new and changing light either through content, formal concerns, or exhibition practices and awakens me to myself, stimulates my ability to perceive, gives me pleasure of process and imagination. That's why I like to watch it and why I like to make it. I don't have to be a historian, or an expert on Cather, to let the film give the viewer the distinct experience of what it is like to investigate, to look for traces, to uncover and find forgotten or misleading paths. I try to make an experimental cinema of investigation. The viewing audience become the archeologists, the historians, piecing together the fragments, feeling the emptiness of blurred and overexposed film, seeing through the scratches of dated emulsion, and finding the memories to recover their own history. For if one history is lost, all of us are less rich than before.

Foster: In this same section on Willa Cather, you use the visual image of torn photographs of Willa Cather that, for lack of a better word, "regenerate." You intercut this with on-the-road footage in which you go searching for the lesbian Willa Cather. Would you say this is in some ways comparable to what you are doing in *Tender Fictions* with auto/biography? I'd like you to elaborate on your feelings about how we can use experimental cinema to regenerate.

Hammer: Experimental cinema for me knows no scripting. Filming can take place through adventure, or chance proceedings, but develops with energy when "a way is found." I filmed the torn photographs in forward motion, but because I had put the camera on the copy stand incorrectly, the images came out backwards, making the photos being put back together rather than torn apart. I liked this much better than my original more traditional idea and incorporated it as is with glee. This was a metaphor for the copy-and-paste and put-the-puzzle-together method of creating the film, of finding the lost lesbian history of Willa Cather. It was similar to the road trip from Lincoln, Nebraska to Red Cloud where I looked and saw only horizon lines and a broken down building as sites for Willa Cather. Ultimately, Willa Cather is a place in the imagination and represents the many lives that have been lost through a false but codified history.

Foster: Both *Nitrate Kisses* and *Tender Fictions* feature the use of multiple narrators. One sequence that struck me as particularly self-reflective and performative was the section in which we hear a female voice-over intercut with what I assume is the male voice from a recording that one would hear at the Willa Cather home. This authoritarian voice gives us the "official" biography of Willa Cather and she is treated almost as an ethnographic subject. Naturally, the official version tells us nothing about Willa/Will that has to do with her sexuality. In this sequence, I get a sense that you are asking the viewer to participate in the regenerative process of the recovery of lesbian history, no?

Hammer: The tour guide's voice that you hear with the photos of Willa Cather's home in Red Bank is even further removed than you think! The guide's voice is piped in from a pre-recording and as visitors walk through the house a different sequence is played. It was very funny. The feminist author who visited Willa's home herself and who wrote a book on mid-western women, Sandy Boucher, is the other voice you hear telling the story that hasn't been told. I believe we need multiple voices to present multiple viewpoints. As light can be defined neither by particle or wave theory, it seems to me varying phenomena need different approaches. There is no reason we can't hold several "truths" to be self-evident.

Foster: Both *Tender Fictions* and *Nitrate Kisses* are political call-to-action films. In addition to all the other things that you accomplish with these works you encourage, demand, and insist that lesbians write their own stories. You also have a website that is a communal lesbians biography in the making. When you reach the site, you are asked to participate in the rewriting of Lesbian/Gay/Bisexual/Transgendered history. What has the response been?

Hammer: The response to *The Lesbian Cyberspace Biography* has been exciting. A few weeks ago I received a posting from a young woman in Korea who was in her late teens and who felt that she was a lesbian, but had so far found no place to explore these feelings. That was a good feeling for me, to find a way to communicate with someone with that need. I want to go deeper with the website, have more interactivity, more visuals. I want to hyperlink the stories, images, and countries. I want to print out the material and post it in a gallery space with a computer setup ready for visitors to enter in more data.

Foster: What are the political implications of someone, like myself, who, though bisexual or heterosexual, is not of the lesbian community; how do you feel about non-lesbians working in the field of recovery and regeneration of lesbian history?

Hammer: A person who describes her/himself as a non-lesbian would have difficulty in understanding and interpreting cultural innuendoes, just as lesbians from different generations can easily make errors of interpretation by not knowing the coding, the subtleties, the distinctions that are generational differences. Anyone can be a lesbian, but I still agree with identity politics, in that difference is best illuminated by those members of the self-inscribed group.

One of the more challenging ideas that has come from the internet is the possibility and practice of assumed identities. These "masked" selves can be heroes, personifications of inanimate objects, or project sexualities. Anyone can be a virtual lesbian in cyberspace. This is so different from the 1970s, when we limited our identity to particular women who wore particular clothes and hairstyles and who practiced a particular type of sexuality. There is such strength and sureness now in identity practices around sexuality that the door can be opened, the reins loosened, that the sexual horse can canter into the field without fences. I hope that metaphor didn't run away in all its freedom! If everyone can be a virtual lesbian then there are no non-lesbians and everyone can work in the recovery of marginalized peoples, their history as well as their contemporary contributions to late twentieth century politics, economics and culture. Of course, I still think Tee Corinne's "genital definition" of lesbian practice is criteria for the card-carrying type. Do I contradict myself? Well, well.

Foster: In *Nitrate Kisses* there is a recovery of a tremendous outpouring of lesbian testimony, especially that of older lesbian women. There is a lot of hot sex and eroticism and playfulness between these women that makes the film, again, a performative vehicle. Your camera-eye finds pleasure in the beauty of age itself, as well as the retelling and staging of lesbian auto/biographies. This film must draw a strong response, especially from older lesbian women, but I am sure all women. I watched it with a friend of mine who is gay and he could not stop talking about the beauty of these scenes. I think he liked them even more than the scenes of gay male sexuality and storytelling. I want to ask you: what has the response been from various different members of different communities?

Hammer: I have admired older women since I came out at 30. The wrinkles and loose skin tell me about experience that goes beyond my own. Everything can be eroticized, and it is especially exciting to take the more maligned physical features of aging and find them erotic. When various people think they are complimenting me with a "You don't look 57," I respond to the ageist remark with "This is what 57 looks like."

The [images] of the older women making love [have] been universally the most talked about and impressive [scenes] of the film. This surprised me. I didn't make these images to create the amount of attention that they have drawn. In fact, it was late in the editing process when I realized that I was leaving out an underrepresented sexuality. I had included black-and-white couples, s/m sexual practices, sex between women of color. I am conscious that as members of lesbian communities, gay communities, we also sometimes marginalize and leave out the history of many members of our own communities. I saw that I had left out old lesbians.

I'm glad you see the older women making love as performative, as, indeed, it was. Many viewers immediately "believe what they see" and inscribe notions of relationship longevity onto these bodies. In fact, these two women had never had sex before. They were friends and were willing to be directed by me in the shoot. One of them is bisexual and the other is a lesbian. So stop it girls and boys! Stop reading in the narrative you want to see, the myth-making propaganda slipped into your bedtime reading materials.

This response of seeing these women as a stable couple who continue their erotic practices is very common. Another response was from two young women, perhaps in their late teens, who left the film as soon as the sexual expression of the older women appeared. I confronted them in the lobby of the theater and asked why. They weren't able to articulate their feelings. I flashed on the thought that they might have seen the women as their mothers and this was the greatest taboo: don't watch your parents having sex. When I suggested this might be the cause of their discomfort, they agreed.

Gay men are often amazed and provoked in different ways than women at the older couple. Gay culture is vastly different from lesbian culture. There is such an emphasis placed on the fit and youthful-looking body. Some guys just can't even imagine that two old gals could go to town in this manner and that the camera could so lovingly celebrate their wrinkles. Hey, when does lesbian culture get to influence gay and heterosexual culture?

I am very interested right now in the construction of the closet, both by deceased female artists who were lesbian or bisexual by the contemporary institutions that "protect" or "represent" the artists and their work. I think I have to understand the contextual historical situation of the period of time in which these artists lived and practiced artmaking before I can make statements, judgments, or anything of the like. That means I have to talk to cultural historians and read people like Lillian Faderman, Jennifer Terry, Terry Castle and Adrienne Rich to increase my knowledge. It is more difficult to find historical societies, museums and individual art collectors who allow a contemporary sexual reading of the artists whose work they own. This I fear is blatant homophobia and it is also based on economics. I think it is feared that if the photographer is considered to be a lesbian, her work will be worth less.

Foster: As you know, my special area of interest is women filmmakers. I'm especially interested in recovering the history of early women directors. I find it really frustrating to deal with the erasure of sexualities in these cases, especially because looking through the photographic record and reading the biographies of and around these early women directors it seems obvious to me that there was a strong lesbian community directing and writing in the 1910s and 1920s. Everyone knows that Dorothy Arzner was lesbian, but I think there were many many more lesbians and bisexual women working in Hollywood at that time. I sure hope someone is writing a book called *Queering Hollywood*, because I think it is so important to recover as much L/G/B/T sexual history as possible. And what about cases where, such as that of Willa Cather, certain lesbians go to extreme measures to hide their sexuality from the public and from historians? For example, it is strongly rumored that Ida Lupino was involved in a long term lesbian relationship. I guess this gets us into the politics of outing?

Hammer: The "politics of outing"? On that topic, I'm reading *The Sewing Circle: Hollywood's Greatest Secret: Female Stars Who Loved Other Women* by Axel Madsen. We don't consider politics involved in the uncovering of an ancient Scythian tomb, an archeological site, where a slave to a prince is found buried next to his master. Surely our "interpretation of class strata" can be of no less interest and importance than "our interpretation of sexual preference." Must we find two female skeletons entwined in embrace before we might tentatively be led to the important historic definition of these two women as lesbians? Do Willa and Edith have to be buried on top of one another before their importance and particular lifestyle is credited?

Foster: I found the images of decay and loss equally compelling in *Nitrate Kisses*. For example, I wanted to discuss the black-and-white images of rubble that are reminiscent of World War II documentaries. The tracking shots along the rubble reminded me of the loss of the history of sexualities as well as the constant war our society wages against sexuality, especially Lesbian/Gay/Bisexual/Transgendered people and practices. I was struck by the element of performativity in these strong images. You lay them as a bed under the voices of women and men who talk openly about their coming out and living in the world as lesbians and gays. It has a transformative effect. Do you generally pre-plan this sort of idea, or do you do this more intuitively in post-production?

Hammer: I was living in a home in the Oakland Hills that was nearly destroyed by the catastrophic Berkeley-Oakland fire in October, 1991. Many people lost their lives or their life work in this fire. When I drove through the rubble a few days after the fire, I felt a terrible loss. A loss that could have been my own loss of work.

I think a distinguishing characteristic of my films is that they all come from deeply-felt personal experience. An image will have personal resonance for me and I will use it. I trust that there will be enough of a collective reading of the emotional text in the image to be useful, to propel the forward movement of the film.

In the editing as well, there are many personal meanings that I hope are understood. For example, in the older woman section, a dyke historian, Frances Doughty, is commenting on how people will inscribe history if there is a blank background. The image is of a naked older woman's back without clothing. To me that is the background onto which we viewers inscribe meaning: the lesbian body.

This work is not pre-planned. I find meaning through the process of making. I use intuition to guide the research, filming and editing of picture and sound. In these films I did not use a script, and only wrote the script afterwards from the completed film so that translations for subtitling could be made in Germany, France, Japan and Taiwan.

By the way, I have just finished my first feature film script, *Nothing Could Be Worse Than Two Dykes in Menopause*, and I'm looking for a producer. It's a romantic comedy. Kathleen Chalfont, the great Broadway actor, is interested in one of the leading roles!

Foster: Great title! In *Nitrate Kisses* you cover so much political territory in such a brief period of time: Passing, coding, the history of the Village and Christopher Street, issues of lesbians and gays of color, pulp novel culture, butch/femme and beyond, coming out, being closeted, sexuality, etc. Would you elaborate on how you manage to cover so much in such depth and complexity?

Hammer: There is so much covered in so little time because the lesbians I interviewed who were in their 60s, 70s and 90s had so much to say, they had so much lived and felt experience. I only intercut four stories, each one rich with dense references. My idea was not to make a definitive film on any one of these issues, but to make a film about how history is made. Questions of who makes history and who is left out: the processes of history-making is the subject matter of *Nitrate Kisses*.

Foster: In *Nitrate Kisses*, while we are watching images from an early experimental gay film, *Lot in Sodom*, a man speaks on the soundtrack about the complexity of sexuality and sexual categorizations. I think he speaks for a lot of us when he says that the categories don't always work, in fact they are boxes that few people fit. This brings up the unnamable again, and it is important to note that this is lyrically demonstrated or performed by the experimental film we are watching. Neither are easily explained. Both subjects are difficult. What would your position be on categorization?

Hammer: On categorization, I was teaching my Feminist Film Seminar last week at The Museum School of Fine Arts in Boston, when an African-American student said she felt it as demeaning to have her work put in the context of a Black Film Festival or a Woman's Film Festival. Films made by men were not put into a White Film Festival or a Men's Film Festival. That's the catch. We get the screenings, but we're categorized. People think of my work as lesbian. I think of my work as experimental or documentary or now, dramatic, or any combination of the genres. Some of the work deals with lesbian representation, some of it is purely formal, some of it confronts death or the fragility of film. Categorization is unidirectional, linear and un-lifelike. Stop it.

Foster: I would like to ask you to discuss the importance of the sequence in *Nitrate Kisses* dealing with the Motion Picture Production Code of 1930. In the film you run the text of the code as a crawl title over anal interracial sex. This strikes me as a performance of transgressive activism which works on a number of important levels. Not only is this funny and politically and sexually charged, but it has a visceral effect on the viewer that takes me back to what we were talking about earlier: the unnamable. The text is scored with an opera, and there are again multiple voices speaking about how the code itself was designed to work against "The Mixing of the Races" and a host of other social taboos, including homosexuality. This sequence has elements of the performative documentary, it reads like a post-modern opera, erotica with commentary, a poem. How would you describe this sequence?

Hammer: In selecting the four separate couples who would have explicit sexual relations in the film, I searched for couples that historic or contemporary lesbian, gay, bisexual and transgendered communities might censor. We have our own issues about acceptability and presentability. No community is without its own censoring phenomenon. I chose old women, an S/M leather couple, two tattooed and pierced women of color, and the black-and-white gay male couple to represent some areas of experience the gay community, itself, might censor.

The most exciting element in the gay male scene was the beautiful shape of the rounded butts of different color, almost an abstract shot that went on and on. The Motion Picture Code completely forbid representation of "mixed races" on the screen for twenty five years. I was making this film with NEA monies and trying very hard to not self-censor in the conservative time when the agency was under attack. The sequence became a perfect metaphor. The scripted code rolls up the screen and makes the viewer choose between looking at the beautiful sexuality or read the fascinating "no-no"s in the code. The code acts as a jailer to the image; we must see the underrepresented, the disallowed, through the bars of censorship. I, as a filmmaker, must make the invisible, visible.

The operatic references come from the late and great experimental filmmaker Warren Sonbert, who directed me to *Don Carlos*, and suggested that the love songs between the Don and his best man could be appropriated and seen as "gay." The two women of color make love to a duet between Octavian, a young gentleman dressed as a woman and often played by a female on the stage, and The Marschallin, Princess Werdenberg in *Der Rosenkavalier* by Richard Strauss.

Foster: Another postmodern technique you use is the inclusion of texts themselves as images. Trinh T. Minh-ha, Su Friedrich, Sadie Benning and many other experimental filmmakers use this strategy. I love how you integrate a long quote of Michel Foucault, whose words almost read like a battle cry. He called for us to free ourselves from repression and he said it would take what amounts to a full-scale overthrow of dominant ideologies. That we must transgress laws, lift prohibitions, and, perhaps most importantly, reinstate pleasure. This is exactly the kind of art you are performing and generating, both in yourself and in the audience. What is your philosophy when it comes to the role of the artist and the need to create "a new economy of power" (in the words of Foucault)?

Hammer: Artists should unionize! Artists should form their own code of ethics; have our own organization much as physicians and lawyers do. We should use our physical presence in demonstrations, our monies to make political announcements. We should make a general attempt to raise the consciousness of the American public about the profession of artmaking, the necessity of imagination, and the life-giving source art is to the individual and society. When I first moved to New York City, I would feel I was a part of a profession when I was out and about in the city. I saw other artists on the street, collecting materials, posting their mail, buying supplies. I felt like a cultural worker, which is exactly what I am. There is a visible community of artists in New York. That community has never received the recognition and support it deserves from the general society. It is time to demand it and to organize.

Foster: Finally, I have not really talked to you about your influences, and perhaps even more importantly—who you are influencing in the artistic and filmmaking, and performative community? I am thinking of figures going back to Alice Guy Blaché, and up through Marie Menken, Gunvor Nelson, Jonas Mekas, Sadie Benning, Marlon Riggs, Chantal Akerman, Trinh T. Minh-ha, Barbara and so many others.

Hammer: I began to make films in my late 20s and it wasn't until I was 30 that I enrolled in college courses in filmmaking. There I saw for the first time *Meshes in the Afternoon* (1943–1944) by Maya Deren. I saw a cinema of difference, a cinema of woman. I felt that there was a blank screen in terms of women's cinema and I could try to begin to fill it. There were very few experimental film classes at San Francisco State University where I received my M.A., so it wasn't until I moved to New York City and saw the work of Marie Menken at The Anthology Film Archives that I was taken with the vigor and freshness of her films. I researched her life and films at the Archives. I had felt for a long time that "art was energy," and here it was exemplified in the extraordinary and unpretentious physical and perceptive films by Marie. Gunvor Nelson's films, especially her early films, used symbolic imagery that influenced me. There is one image of a bicycle tied to a tree, wrapped round and round by a rope, that I will never forget. Yvonne Rainer and Trinh T. Minh-ha challenged me to regard the possibilities of "a thinking cinema," a more complex viewing experience that challenged and engaged the audience intellectually.

I was aware after I made *Dyke Tactics* in 1973 that something unusual had happened. I projected it at Film Finals at San Francisco State University. Several professors ran up to me afterwards with exclamations and congratulations. Later, I was told that this was the first lesbian lovemaking film made by a lesbian. Connie Beeson confronted me when I repeated that statement, and said that she was the first with her film, *Holding*. *Holding* did precede *Dyke Tactics*, and is a beautiful film. Connie told me she identified as a bisexual, so I continued to think the pronouncement was right on. Now, I don't think "firsts" are THE important thing. Simultaneous invention, cultural constructions, the sexual liberty that was "in the air" all contributed to the making of both of our films.

I was aware that there had been none or little lesbian filmmaking before me because I looked for it and couldn't find it. I strongly felt that Maya Deren was bisexual, and later study has confirmed this, but at the time there were no biographies on her life. I decided quite intentionally that I would put my life on film (of course, in my own manner), so that at least one lesbian's life in the twentieth century would be known. Today I can laugh at that presumption: 1) that what we see on the screen could be considered "true" and "a life" and 2) there is a wonderful flood of lesbian, dyke, queer film now.

The entrance of The Independent Television Service on the scene made a major difference for me. There was an opportunity for major funding that would allow me to envision a much larger project than I had up to this point. In my first grant application to ITVS (one I did not get nor have I been funded by them up until now), I wrote expansively, researched a large project of "searching for lost lesbian and gay culture," and proposed a budget to match the project's scope. In my usual manner, I couldn't wait to see if I were funded, but began to shoot almost as soon as I had conceptualized the ideas.

Immediately upon finishing the grant application I left for a tour of Germany and France with my films. In Hamburg, Berlin and Paris I borrowed Super 8mm cameras, hunted out the only source of black-and-white Super 8mm films, cajoled transportation from my hosts, and began to film. By then I had found I didn't enjoy "touristic" travel and was much happier pursuing research even when I was on a screening tour. The days were intense, but I like them that way.

It wasn't until I began teaching Feminist Film Seminars that I found the forgotten history of the first narrative filmmaker in the world, Alice Guy Blaché, and the two hundred films she made in her lifetime. Barbara Kruger's use of text has always amazed me, especially the last show she had at the Mary Boone Gallery in Soho where the floor, walls and ceilings were covered with her astounding red, black-and-white image text. I felt as if I were entering a feminist church of the twenty-first century when I walked into the space that day. *Reassemblage* was the best film I saw in 1985. Trinh T. Minh-ha's sound/image cutting introduce a third space in film, the floating space between the soundtrack and the picture that does not have to correspond exactly, but that works as a "third track," an area of disruption, an "unsettling." Today I recommend the freely moving narrative in the optically-printed masterpiece, *Chronic*, by the young filmmaker Jennifer Reeves.

There are artists who achieve a certain level of recognition with a particular body of work and who spend the rest of their artmaking re-doing, re-fining, re-thinking that work. That seems the "easy way out." Artmaking for me is a commitment to a lifetime work of exploration and process. I could continue to make the optically printed work of the 1980s (*Optic Nerve*, *Endangered*, *Sanctus*), but I chose to attempt a longer form, a more documentary form, a form that used text as image (*Nitrate Kisses*, *Tender Fictions*). With the feature narrative *Nothing Could Be Worse Than Two Dykes in Menopause*, I would like the opportunity to direct and bring a narrative vision of issues around aging and commitment to a large screen near you!

The Films of Sadie Benning and Su Friedrich

18

CHRIS HOLMLUND

> To what extent can the particular serve as illustration for the general? . . . What generalizations are appropriate? What categories can serve to facilitate understanding and the acceptance of difference rather than diminish our receptivity to the unique in the name of the typical, reducing difference to the measure of otherness . . .?

I begin with this quote from Bill Nichols's "'Getting to Know You . . .': Power, Knowledge, and the Body"[1] because the questions he raises haunt the terms around which my essay revolves: autobiography, ethnography, and "dyke doc." How are "unique," "typical," "particular," and "general" to be linked to "self"—the basis of autobiography? Or to "subculture" and "culture"— the primary foci of ethnography? What of "lesbian" and the more militant "dyke," especially when they are used as adjectives, as in "lesbian autobiography," "lesbian ethnography," or "dyke documentary"? For me, and also for Nichols, posing such questions has both practical and theoretical implications: as Pierre Bourdieu underlines, aesthetic definition is tightly connected to class distinction, as much a matter of rank as of difference.[2]

To ground my discussion, I ask these questions of three of Sadie Benning's videos and two of Su Friedrich's films. I choose to look at works by these two women primarily for two reasons: because both make creative experimental documentaries that combine autobiographical and ethnographic features and because often, though not always, their work is programmed and distributed as "lesbian."

The better to gauge the impact of Benning's and Friedrich's dyke documentaries *as* dyke documentaries, I first rehearse how autobiography, ethnography, and lesbian have been theorized with respect to self and other, culture and subculture, in literature and film. At the end of this section I argue that Benning's videos and Friedrich's films are often described as "lesbian" autobiographies or ethnographies because they articulate concerns about coming out and kinship shared by many lesbians and gays today.

In the two middle sections of this essay I offer close readings of Benning's *Me and Rubyfruit* (1989), *Jollies* (1990), and *Girl Power* (1992), and Friedrich's *First Comes Love* (1991) and *Rules of the Road* (1992). Since one of my goals is to convey in words something of the ingenious composition and flair for storytelling that characterize their work, I do not at this point restrict my discussions to whether and how autobiography meets ethnography and girls meet girls.

In the conclusion I return to the question of disciplinary boundaries, looking at how critics and audiences variously perceive the "dyke" of these "dyke docs." My desire here is to emphasize how much social context determines textual content in contemporary documentaries—like these by Benning and Friedrich—that marry autobiography to ethnography and "dyke" or "gay" or "queer") to "doc."

Of Definition and Distinction

The "classic" definition of literary autobiography might well be that proposed by Philippe Lejeune, for whom autobiography is a "retrospective prose narrative that someone writes concerning his own existence, where the focus is his individual life, in particular the story of his personality."[3] In literary autobiographies, author, narrator, and protagonist coincide; the author's signature frequently operates as the guarantee of identity. Defining films and videos as autobiographical is more tricky because, as Elizabeth Bruss cautions, one must distinguish between cinema "eye" (the body behind the camera) and cinema "I" (the body in the film), and differentiate between (usually) single author of a book and (often) collective "auteur" of a film.[4]

Both visual and print autobiographies, however, take the "constitution of identity . . . [to be] the genre's characteristic, even defining, goal."[5] This identity is necessarily fictional, culturally bound, and other-dependent, "grounded in the signs of one's existence that are received from others, as well as from the works of culture by which one is interpreted."[6] Many now argue, therefore, that the "autobiography" label is the result of a "pact' between author and reader or spectator, a pact whose terms are thoroughly mediated by culture.

Ethnography would seem to be a necessary part of studies of why, when, and how literary or cinematic works are categorized as autobiographical. Yet for a long time ethnographers refused to discuss autobiography, in part because they took the "normative subjects of ethnographic inquiry" to be "non-western people doing non-western things."[7] Ethnographic "truth" was held to reside in "raw data" collected in an apparently "authorless" fashion. Ethnographers working in film advocated a "plain" film style composed of long takes, sync sound, whole acts, whole bodies, no scripts, and little editing.[8]

Many contemporary ethnographers, however, find presumptuous the idea that the everyday activities of "non-western people doing non-western things" might somehow contain and even "articulat[e] . . . social meanings,"[9] and preposterous the premise that all cultures can be "understood, on their own terms" or "studied as original wholes."[10] There is, instead, growing *theoretical* agreement—concrete studies are rare—that one must ask how ethnographic films are used, by whom, and general *theoretical* recognition that, as James Clifford says, "there is no single general type of reader [or spectator]."[11] Many agree moreover, with Judith Okely that "contrary to the expectation that an autobiography which speaks of the personal and specific should thereby elaborate uniqueness, autobiographies may . . . evoke common aspects."[12]

To speak of "lesbian" autobiography or "lesbian" ethnography is, of course, only to complicate further the question of what might be considered unique, typical, particular, or general in autobiography or ethnography. As Biddy Martin says:

> The *lesbian* in front of *autobiography* reinforces conventional assumptions of the trans-
> parency of autobiographical writing. And the *autobiography* that follows *lesbian* suggests

that sexual identity not only modifies but essentially defines a life, providing it with predictable content and an identity possessing continuity and universality . . . It is to suggest that there is something coherently different about lesbians' lives vis-à-vis other lives and . . . something coherently the same about all lesbians.[13]

Martin does not mean, of course, that it is impossible or undesirable to write, or to write about, "lesbian autobiography" or, I would add, "lesbian ethnography." But the problems she raises do underline the need for studies that situate themselves geographically and historically with as much precision as possible, while acknowledging that the definitions they proffer are provisional.

At present in the United States, two key concerns emerge from lesbian autobiographies and ethnographies: coming out and kinship.[14] Bonnie Zimmerman and Martin, for example, both talk about "community," and Martin explicitly discusses "family" and "home" in autobiographical writing by lesbians of color. Both emphasize the roles that coming out plays, agreeing that, while all autobiography restructures the past, "such re-visioning may be particularly essential to the formation of lesbian identity."[15] Anthropologist Kath Weston also conceives of coming out as fundamental, arguing that "at this historical moment, a lesbian or gay identity [is] realized as much in the course of the telling as the feeling or the doing."[16] She contends that coming-out stories restructure the past to accord with the present and reformulate the present as an advancement over the past "to counter the implication that being gay transforms a person into something alien, deviant, or monstrous."[17]

Crucially, Weston situates current debates about gay marriages and families within, rather than on the margins of, broader historical transformations of kinship. She challenges conventional definitions because "to assert that straight people 'naturally' have access to family, while gay people are destined to move toward a future of solitude and loneliness, is not only to tie kinship closely to procreation, but also to treat gay men and lesbians as members of a nonprocreative species set apart from the rest of humanity."[18]

Sadie Benning and Su Friedrich strike similarly self-assured, "uppity" poses in their "dyke docs." Like Weston, Zimmerman, and Martin, both reflect, as "out" lesbians, on marriage and family in their work. Both draw on past experiences, somehow inscribe their voices and bodies, and variously position lesbian and other subcultures in relation to a dominant heterosexual culture. To use Bill Nichols's formulation, both thereby "blur boundaries" between subjectivity and objectivity, autobiography and ethnography, and thus extend how documentary is defined and "queers" are seen.[19]

"Benning on Benning"—and Beyond

Several of Benning's nine videos are overtly presented as coming-out narratives.[20] Though almost half (New Year, Living Inside, Me and Rubyfruit, and If Every Girl Had a Diary) are recounted primarily in the present, all contain references to Benning's past, and three (Welcome to Normal, A Place Called Lovely, and Girl Power) even incorporate home movies of baby Sadie. All are narrated, largely in the first person, by Benning herself. All feature close-ups and extreme close-ups of Benning's body, and most are shot in her room, literally enacting what Paul John Eakin calls the "connection between personal space and the concept of self" so important to autobiography.[21]

But Benning also positions her "self" as representative of a larger group, fluidly composed of other young lesbians, alienated teens, riot grrrls. Her expressive, highly personal videos acquire polemical, quasi-ethnographic resonance in consequence. Everywhere, for example, the in-your-face presence of Benning's body challenges the idea that, because lesbians love women, lesbians are somehow men.[22] Throughout her work she insists that she likes being a woman and is *not* a man, though she is quite willing to dress as one: in *Jollies* she shaves her face; in *It Wasn't Love* she acts the part of a bearded gangster; in *Girl Power* she intercuts a picture of herself, with an identical haircut and shirt, between two halves of a Matt Dillon pinup poster. At other moments she adopts stereotypically female roles: in *It Wasn't Love* she becomes a cigarette-smoking vamp in blond wig and heavy makeup; in *Girl Power* she imagines she is Blondie, Joan Jett, and every member of the Go-Gos.

Especially combined with Pixelvision's grainy images, tinny sound, and inescapable box frames, Benning's stress on fantasy and gender performance highlights the constructedness of her autobiographies: though Pixelvision practitioners and theorists often comment on the apparent "infantilism inherent in the form,"[23] Benning's seemingly casual video style is the result of "boiling down . . . hours and hours of tape."[24] All the videos contain intertextual references: clips from old movies and television shows, snatches of songs by famous pop artists or lesser known bands; headlines and photos from pulp magazines and newspapers; drawings, paintings, product labels; Benning's own printed and typed messages. Together these function both as autobiographical extensions of her own voice and as ethnographic reflections on a world where racism and homophobia are ubiquitous, and "private" and "public" have become interpermeable categories.

Benning's third tape, *Me and Rubyfruit*, is the first of her "dyke docs" to signal itself as such, and literally served as her coming-out story.[25] The title assumes viewer familiarity with Rita Mae Brown's comic bildungsroman about coming out in the South, *Rubyfruit Jungle*. The rest of the video continues the imaginary dialogue of "me *and* Rubyfruit," as Benning and a fictional "girlfriend" exchange comments via intertitles and voice-over monologue. Pirated snatches of hit (heterosexual) songs link teenage lesbian to adult heterosexual love. As Benning paints it, however, heterosexual marriage seems dull: "Yeah, I'll get married and wear an apron like my mother. Only my husband will be handsome." Does "husband" here mean girls can be husbands too? The next few lines of dialogue certainly suggest as much: "Why don't you marry me? I'm not handsome, but I'm pretty." In comparison with hetero-sexual marriage, lesbian love is exciting if—or because—illicit. Though lesbian marriage may be limited to "FANTASY," as Benning proclaims in block letters, it is unquestionably glamorous: "We'll kiss like in the movies, and then we'll be engaged." In a scenario familiar to many lesbians and gays, imagination and, crucially, action "queer" both Hollywood and kinship.

Jollies, Benning's fifth tape, continues her tongue-in-cheek look at her own sexual "history," but in this video marriage is not even mentioned. Benning's deadpan narration begins after a credit sequence performed by naked Barbie dolls. Over extreme close-ups of her eye, ear, nose, and mouth, she says: "It started in 1978 when I was in kindergarten. They were twins and I was a tomboy." She turns toward the camera and, revealing braces on her teeth, continues: "I always thought of real clever things to say like . . . like . . . I love you." A shock cut to Diane Arbus's photo of twin girls, then pans up Benning's hairy leg and over a Mr. Bubbles bottle ironically underscore her youth and the absurd excitement of childhood crushes, especially of a lesbian crush on twins.

Benning mentions two episodes with boys, but describes both in such distanced, even anticlimactic terms that she highlights how unimportant these heterosexual encounters were—and are—to her. The last part of Benning's coming-out story is no less parodic, but reconfigures passion in that, like other coming-out narratives, it paints homosexual identity as an underlying "truth." In direct address Benning tells of exchanging phone numbers with another girl. Then a trumpet blast hails a printed text: "THAT NIGHT I FOUND OUT I WAS AS QUEER AS CAN BE." The final credits, "SPECIAL THANKS TO DEBBIE DAVIS," are accompanied by a woman singing "You give me what I want when I want it." Masks and pans create a strobe-light effect over the words "DEBBIE DAVIS." As in *Me and Rubyfruit*, Hollywood glamour is claimed for lesbians and lesbianism, suggesting that Debbie Davis just might be a star on a par with Bette Davis.

Like many of Benning's earlier tapes, *Girl Power* reflects on unhappy childhood and adolescence. Here, however, Benning consciously portrays herself and her (now visible) girlfriend as "out" young lesbians within a riot grrrl subculture. For Benning, *girl* is "a strong word," especially when it is preceded by the adjective *bad*.[26] Not coincidentally, then, the video begins with "thanks to bad girls girls girls everywhere." Images of "bad girls" of all ages follow, including a home movie of Benning as drooling toddler and new footage of Benning as young adult. "MOM" is tattooed on her lower lip; in the penultimate image "GIRL LOVE" is stenciled on her knuckles. Periodically, written texts flash our warnings like "Violent Youth/Fierce and Furious"; "Ashamed/Ridiculed/Denied/Fucked with/Fuck/You/Man/Hear/ Me/or Die."

Clips from documentary films and television shows—an atomic bomb blast, rockets firing, the Rodney King beating, a homophobic diatribe delivered by American Nazi Party leader George Lincoln Rockwell—are intercut with footage shot in Benning's room. In voice-over, Benning says, "In my world, in my head, I was never alone. It was at school, with my father, and in my own culture that I felt most alone." Her juxtaposition of imaginary and "real" spaces subtly critiques and redefines both culture and community.

The final printed texts and credits are accompanied by a Bikini Kill song whose beat, mood, and lyrics echo Benning's images, editing, and narration: "We're Bikini Kill, and we want Revolution! . . . All the doves that fly past my eyes, have a stickiness to their wings. . . . HOW DOES IT FEEL? IT FEELS BLIND. . . . WHAT HAVE YOU TAUGHT ME? NOTHING."[27]

Throughout *Girl Power*, however, Benning's connections of individual girls to girl groups testify to the existence of different community and kinship networks. As the tape ends, Benning cautions us that this is only "the end/for now": "this has been a continuing work in progress/beware be alert/watch out/for/girlpower the movie."

Though nowhere more overtly than in *Girl Power*, in all these "dyke Girl docs" refrains common to contemporary lesbian and gay lives emerge from the intricate rhythms Benning composes using her own life, among them portrayals of coming out as culmination and revelation, protests against injustice, and quests for community and kinship. In these videos, girls love girls, autobiography marries ethnography, and personal expression acquires political resonance.

Su Friedrich's Sidewalk Soliloquies

Where Benning insists in her videos on the formation/revelation of a visible and audible lesbian "self," Friedrich does not usually deal directly with the personal and public ramifications of coming out in her work. Several films, including *First Comes Love* and *Rules of the Road*, instead focus on marriage and families, subtly expanding kinship to include lesbians as well as heterosexuals.[28]

Stylistically, too, Friedrich's films, and especially her latest films, are quite different from Benning's videos. Shot in 16mm, both *First Comes Love* and *Rules of the Road* make use of the greater depth of focus, clarity of image, and variety of field that film affords. Although both include popular songs, unlike Friedrich's earlier films neither makes extensive use of intertitles or employs excerpts from other films or television shows as a way to distinguish—and link—subcultures and mass culture.

Intriguingly, *First Comes Love* and *Rules of the Road* represent divergent points on the autobiographical–ethnographic continuum. *First Comes Love* is the most clearly "ethnographic" of all Friedrich's films: in it Friedrich studies heterosexual marriage ceremonies from a position literally and figuratively on the sidelines. Thanks to its first-person voice-over narration about personal experience, *Rules of the Road* is, in contrast, Friedrich's most "autobiographical" work to date.

First Comes Love is composed of three elements: (1) intercut black-and-white footage from four different weddings; (2) fourteen musical selections; and (3) a two-part scrolled text that Friedrich calls "a surprising public service announcement" (the first part lists 120 countries where lesbian and gay marriage is forbidden; the second credits Denmark with being the first country to legalize same-sex ceremonies).[29] In classic ethnographic fashion, Friedrich's camera chronicles each wedding ceremony from "arrival scene" to departure. Less classic, however, is the way she shoots and edits these ceremonies: hers is clearly not the stance of an "objective" scientist. Studied pans, close-ups on accessories rather than faces, and editing that follows gestures rather than bodies make identification of or with an individual bride or groom difficult. The constant intercutting among limousines, flowers, handshakes, back slaps, hugs, and kisses instead emphasizes how much time, money, energy, and enthusiasm are poured into heterosexual wedding celebrations.

In the midst of such widespread approbation, the "PSAs" about the illegality of lesbian and gay marriages stand out starkly. Whip pans, zooms, and rapid editing register a range of emotions toward a ceremony from which lesbians and gays are excluded. The musical selections—all rock, soul, or country hits—also provide nuanced commentary, thanks to Friedrich's juxtaposition of each song against the others, and each song against the images. Though all the lyrics are somehow about love, attraction, or sex, many also convey exclusion, loss, and loneliness. The last song, Willie Nelson's haunting "You Were Always on My Mind," plays as altar boys sweep up rice from the church steps. The juxtaposition prompts questions: Why do people marry? Will these marriages last? At the very end, Nelson's ballad still in the background, Friedrich dedicates her film "for Cathy," adding a personal note to the film's commentary on the exclusion of lesbians and gays from legally sanctioned marriage ceremonies.

In many ways, of course, *First Comes Love* is more *about* heterosexuals than about lesbians. Nevertheless, it is also a documentary *by* and *for* lesbians; as Friedrich jokingly puts it, her film is about "rites and wrongs."[30] By not being visibly or audibly present, she rejects traditional autobiographical subjectivity and at the same time declines the "plain film style" characteristically associated with ethnographic objectivity. In *Me and Rubyfruit*, Benning also refuses to accept that marriage is a heterosexual institution off-limits to lesbians; *First Comes Love*, however, seeks to broaden the meaning of marriage by, as Leslie Kossoff says, "gently yet forcefully asking you to deal with questions of commitment and love and the public announcement of them."[31]

Rules of the Road continues to "queery" kinship, though Friedrich's personal investment is more clearly in evidence since the film is basically about her relationship to, breakup with, and mourning for her lover. The first of Friedrich's films to be shot in color, *Rules* opens with images taken from inside a moving car. Then, in close-up, a woman's hands hold a deck of Greyhound bus playing cards; lay out the film's title, one letter at a time; shuffle the cards; and spell out "by" and "Su Friedrich."

Offscreen, Friedrich tells how her girlfriend celebrated Thanksgiving alone with her brother and his girlfriend one year because she thought her brother would "be uncomfortable if she brought along her own girlfriend." She returns home in "a big old beige station wagon . . . a 1983 Oldsmobile Cutlass Cruiser, a sensible family car," which her brother has helped her to acquire. Suddenly, beige station wagons—parked and moving—appear everywhere. For the rest of the film, Friedrich's camera hunts them out, panning, tracking, and zooming restlessly. These street scenes are intercut with shots of the hands playing solitaire, moments of black, and a few black-and-white images of a woman rowing. Gradually they make sense as the spaces within which Friedrich searches for, and flees from, the car and lover she has lost.

Descriptions of road trips are illustrated by images shot from a moving car. Some trips are lyrically depicted: "When I was driving, I felt as though I was carrying her in my arms, away from the relentless, claustrophobic city towards an unpredictable and generous expanse of forest or ocean. I wanted to give her that. And I wanted to be with her when she got there." Others involve horrible fights with her lover, fights much like those Friedrich says she witnessed as a child from the backseat of her family's car.

After the breakup, Friedrich imagines what it would be like to turn the corner and see her ex. Quick cuts of different station wagons moving in different directions, followed by blurred, out-of-focus swish pans visually underline her fear that she will not be able to distinguish her lover's car from other station wagons. The constant zooms in to close-ups on license plates are finally explained: in a world full of beige station wagons "ready to surprise me at every turn," Friedrich protects herself from chance—though not entirely undesired—encounters with her former girlfriend by looking at license plates.

Especially at the beginning of the film, the songs heighten the offbeat humor of Friedrich's descriptions and delivery. Subsequent selections briefly translate Friedrich's confidence in her relationship, but the musical selections in the last half of the film are all about anger, loneliness, and bereavement. The last, Randy Travis's "Hard Rock Bottom of Your Heart," plays as the car carrying Friedrich and her camera heads out of New York City. The lyrics convey the ache and emptiness she feels: "I need your love, I miss it./I can't go on like this/It hurts too much."

Though Friedrich's chosen family has dissolved, and though she has lost her access to the quintessential family car, her lover's station wagon, she *is* leaving town again, together with another woman whose hands we see on the steering wheel. Over the course of the film, moreover, cars, not just queers, have come to seem like family members.[32] While station

18. A scene from Su Friedrich's *Rules of the Road* (1993). Courtesy Anthology Film Archives; reprinted by permission.

wagons may temporarily have become metaphors of mourning, they—and every other vehicle—now hold out the promise of a "family" open to all, a family of used car owners:

> The first time I laid eyes on the car, I was disappointed by its homeliness but consoled by the thought that it was unique . . . Consequently I was surprised to find that there are many thousands of them on the streets of New York. Almost overnight I went from barely noticing their existence to realizing that I lived in a world swarming with station wagons. By becoming the owner of one, she seemed to have been initiated into a special clan. And by sharing the car with her, I felt I had become an honorary member of that same family.

The film ends on a hopeful note, with Friedrich making plans to buy her own used car. Retrospectively, we realize that the very first images of the film display the choices she now sees: a pink Vespa, a little red sedan, a dark blue jeep. As *Rules of the Road* closes, "girl" may thus have lost "girl," but Friedrich will soon be back in the driver's seat, following the same "rules of the road" as everyone else. Though *Rules of the Road* is more clearly autobiographical than *First Comes Love*, they share the ethnographic conviction that "self," "love," "kinship," and "culture" should not, cannot be construed as solely, or exclusively, heterosexual.

For Fun and Fantasy

Friedrich and Benning both began making experimental films and videos, respectively, because as women and as lesbians they felt excluded from mainstream movies.[33] Now successful independent artists, both feel keenly the responsibility of representation. Both therefore seek to make their work accessible, but not just to lesbian and gay audiences. Reversing the liberal heterosexual line on queers, Benning says of *Girl Power*: "Most of my friends are straight. We can't, like, shut people out because some girls like men. So what? That's what makes them happy. As long as nobody's being abused or hurt, why exclude anyone?"[34] Friedrich describes *First Comes Love* in terms that are similarly inclusive, yet transformative: "The film doesn't attempt to defend—or discredit—the institution of marriage. Instead, it . . . raises questions about how the double standard regarding marriage affects both gay and straight couples."[35]

But authorial intent does not sufficiently answer the questions of definition and distinction with which I began this essay. How, when, and by whom are the "dykes" of Benning's and Friedrich's "dyke docs" perceived as unique, as typical, as particular, or as general? Who describes their works as autobiographical or ethnographic? Why? Do critics and audiences acknowledge Benning's and Friedrich's openness to others?

Over fifteen years ago, Annette Kuhn signaled the need to take into account "the institutional contexts within which documentaries are produced" in discussing questions of reception and representativeness.[36] Certainly exhibition, marketing and distribution are key to how lesbian and gay experimental documentaries are seen. Unlike, for example, the gay male experimental documentaries of the 1950s and 1960s, which were usually labeled "experimental" rather than "gay" because they were addressed to and received within art world contexts, Benning's and Friedrich's work is explicitly programmed and billed as "lesbian" at many festivals and in most catalogs, though it is also exhibited and distributed without that label. Not surprisingly, therefore, of the twenty-two reviews of *Me and Rubyfruit*, *Jollies*, *Girl Power*, *First Comes Love*, and *Rules of the Road* indexed as of January 1995, two-thirds are based on screenings at lesbian and gay festivals.[37] Moreover, since Benning and Friedrich refer at length to lesbian issues, include their own bodies or voices or both as markers of lesbian "authenticity" and "identity," and speak openly of and to other lesbians in their work, all twenty-two reviews at some point describe this work as lesbian. In contrast, most critics of Friedrich's earlier films did not usually write about their lesbian content, imagery, and address "except when a veritable constellation of features [were] present, among them: (1) verbal and/or visual representations of lesbian sexual acts, combined with (2) a simultaneous if not necessarily synchronous representation of lesbian issues on both image and sound tracks, for 3) the bulk of narrative time."[38]

Nevertheless, though critics acknowledge the "dykes" of Benning and Friedrich's "dyke docs," *how* they are seen varies a great deal. Most critics as well as most students to whom I have shown these works easily label them autobiographies, diaries, or confessions. Occasionally critics place both women's work in a tradition of personal films, diary films, or psychodramas.[39] Except in the case of *First Comes Love*, however, almost no one discusses these works as ethnographies. In twelve of fifteen interviews and reviews, moreover, no mention is made of Benning's consistent condemnation of homophobia, racism, and sexism, and no recognition is given to her general concern with young people and women. It is as if "autobiography" were understood solely as the inscription of a self-absorbed subjectivity uninvolved with others.[40] Only in the case of *First Comes Love* do critics applaud Friedrich's even-handedness and openness, perhaps because they view the film as "ethnographic" and therefore as "objective."

As my textual analyses show, however, neither Benning nor Friedrich presents lesbian identities as singular, unchanging, or exclusionary. Necessarily, therefore, lesbian and gay spectators are not automatically or as a block "better" spectators of their works. As Benning points out, although lesbian and gay teens devour her work, in part because they recognize in it their own experiences, thoughts, and feelings, "the gay community is just as anti-youth, sexist, and racist as any group; sometimes they're even more scary and conservative, trying even harder than straight people to fit in."[41] That these "dyke docs" are experimental works of course only complicates matters: as Friedrich says, "being a lesbian doesn't automatically make a woman more sophisticated about art, or less desirous of the big-screen-color-love-story-with-a-happy-ending."[42]

When I teach and program these works as autobiographies, ethnographies, or "dyke docs," I worry, I confess. Will describing them as autobiographical induce some viewers to think of the unique solely as singular or exceptional? Will labeling them ethnographic diminish "our receptivity to the unique . . . in the name of the typical?"[43] As a critic and a teacher, I try not to assume that what is said or written afterward equals all that is seen. But because gays are so often excluded from families and so invisible unless they come out, I do insist (especially if no one else does) in post-screening discussions on the impossibility of simple definition or clear-cut distinction where both "dykes" and "docs" are concerned, and I stress the crucial roles production, distribution, and exhibition play in shaping reception.

Because Benning and Friedrich so skillfully mix humor and pathos, imagination and advocacy in their work, however, many audience members become "queer readers," able, willing, even eager to savor erotic desires and acknowledge family resemblances that may or may not be part of their own experiences.[44] For these spectators, fun and fantasy help loosen strict definitions and nuance sharp distinctions. There are times, after all, when lexical precision matters less than shared emotion, as Sadie Benning demonstrates at the end of *It Wasn't Love*:

> And yet, in that parking lot, I felt like I had seen the whole world. She had this way of making me feel like I was the goddamn Nile River or something. We didn't need Hollywood. We were Hollywood. . . . It wasn't love, but it was *something*.

Notes

Thanks to Chris Cagle, Cindy Fuchs, Su Friedrich, Paul Harrill, Chuck Kleinhans, Chon Noriega, and Paige Travis for comments on earlier drafts.

1 Bill Nichols, "'Getting to Know You . . .': Knowledge, Power, and the Body," in *Theorizing Documentary* ed. Michael Renov (New York: Routledge, 1993), 176.
2 Bourdieu is not concerned with autobiography or ethnography per se, but is broadly interested in the connections among class, educational background, and aesthetic perception. See Pierre Bourdieu, *Distinction: A Social Critique of the Judgement of Taste*, trans. Richard Nice (Cambridge, Mass.: Harvard University Press, 1984).

3 Philippe Lejeune, "The Autobiographical Pact," in *On Autobiography*, trans. Katherine Leary (Minneapolis: University of Minnesota Press, 1989), 14. The question of time is in many ways crucial to autobiography. Lejeune, for example, maintains that autobiography plays at creating the illusion that producer-work-consumer exist at the same time (126).

4 Bruss goes so far as to claim that "there is no real cinematic equivalent for autobiography." See Elizabeth Bruss, "Eye for I: Making and Unmaking Autobiography in Film," in *Autobiography: Essays Critical and Theoretical* ed. James Olney (Princeton: N.J.: Princeton University Press, 1980), 296–297. For a critique of Bruss, see Michael Renov, "The Subject in History," *Afterimage* 17.1 (1989): 4.

5 Paul John Eakin, *Touching the World: Reference in Autobiography* (Princeton, N.J.: Princeton University Press, 1992), 67.

6 Janet Varner Gunn, *Autobiography: Toward a Poetics of Experience* (Philadelphia: University of Pennsylvania Press, 1982), 31.

7 Marcus Banks, "Which Films Are the Ethnographic Films?" in *Film as Ethnography*, ed. Peter Ian Crawford and David Turton (Manchester: Manchester University Press, 1992).

8 Other prescriptions include a minimum of voice-over narration, the use of subtitles for indigenous dialogue, the employment of a wide-angle lens, an avoidance of close-ups, and a preference for in-camera editing. See, for example, Banks, "Which Films Are the Ethnographic Films?," 122–124; Peter Ian Crawford, "Film as Discourse: The Invention of Anthropological Realities," in *Film as Ethnography*, 77; and David MacDougall, "Complicities of Style," in *Film as Ethnography*, 93–94.

9 Dai Vaughan, "The Aesthetics of Ambiguity," in *Film as Ethnography*, 107.

10 Asen Balikci, "Anthropologists and Ethnographic Filmmaking," in *Anthropological Filmmaking: Anthropological Perspectives on the Production of Film and Video for General Public Audiences*, ed. Jack R. Rollwagen (Chur: Harwood, 1988), 33.

11 James Clifford, "On Ethnographic Authority," in *The Predicament of Culture: Twentieth-Century Ethnography, Literature and Art* (Cambridge, Mass.: Harvard University Press, 1988) 37. For a succinct discussion of contemporary debates and silences around ethnographic film, see Bill Nichols, "The Ethnographer's Tale," in *Blurred Boundaries: Questions of Meaning in Contemporary Culture* (Bloomington: Indiana University Press, 1994), 63–91.

12 Judith Okely, "Anthropology and Autobiography: Participatory Experience and Embodied Knowledge," in *Anthropology and Autobiography*, ed. Judith Okely and Helen Callaway (London: Routledge, 1992), 7.

13 Biddy Martin, "Lesbian Identity and Autobiographical Difference[s]," in *Life/Lines: Theorizing Women's Autobiography*, ed. Bella Brodski and Celeste Schenck (Ithaca, N.Y.: Cornell University Press, 1988), 78.

14 Coming out was, of course, also a crucial component of 1960s and 1970s activism. Weston argues that kinship has emerged as a political concern in the 1980s and 1990s as a result of the number of lesbians having children, the rise in gay marriages, and the horrifying percentage of gay men living with and dying of AIDS. See Kath Weston, *Families We Choose: Lesbians, Gays, Kinship*, (New York: Columbia University Press, 1991).

15 Bonnie Zimmerman, "The Politics of Transliteration: Lesbian Personal Narratives," *Signs* 9.4 (Summer 1984): 667.

16 Weston, *Families We Choose*, 66.

17 Ibid., 79.

18 Ibid., 22–23. For further discussions of lesbian and gay marriages, see Becky Butler, *Ceremonies of the Heart: Celebrating Lesbian Unions* (Seattle: Seal Press, 1990), and Suzanne Sherman, ed., *Lesbian and Gay Marriage* (Philadelphia: Temple University Press, 1992).

19 See Nichols, *Blurred Boundaries*, especially 1–16 and 63–91.

20 The expression "Benning on Benning" is taken from Chris Chang, "Up in Sadie's Room," *Film Comment* 29.2 (March/April 1993): 8. Benning began making videos at age 16 when her father, experimental filmmaker James Benning, gave her a Pixel-vision camcorder for Christmas. Titles include *A New Year* (1989), *Living Inside* (1989), *Me and Rubyfruit* (1989), *If Every Girl Had a Diary* (1990), *Jollies* (1990), *Welcome to Normal* (1990), *A Place Called Lovely* (1991), *It Wasn't Love* (1992), and *Girl Power* (1992).

21 Eakin, *Touching the World*, 101.

22 In *Welcome to Normal* Benning admits that when she was younger, "I didn't know I could love women without being a man." She was known by her middle name, Taylor: "I talked like a boy . . . dressed like a boy, played with the boys. My best friend . . . a boy . . . was paranoid to tell the rest of the neighborhood his best friend was a girl, so he told everybody I was a boy and I just went along with it." Benning's first girlfriend, at age eleven, knew she was a girl. When they broke up, "the whole neighborhood found out I was a girl. I got ridiculed for the next two years, and during high school I was treated so *awful*." Cited in Elise Harris, "Baby Butch Video," *Queer World*, Nov. 15, 1992, 33.

23 Jonathan Romney, "Honey I Shrunk the Kit," *New Statesman and Society* 6.278 (Nov. 12, 1993): 34.

24 Roberta Smith, "A Video Artist Who Talks through a Keyhole," *New York Times*, March 28, 1993, H33.

25 One by one, Benning brought her friends into her room and showed them her tape as a way of declaring her sexual identity to them. See Ellen Spiro, "Shooting Star," *Advocate* 563 (March 26, 1991): 68, and Karl Soehnlein, "Lights, Camera, Lesbian," *Outweek*, Dec. 12, 1990, 49.

26 See Kim Masters, "Auteur of Adolescence," *Washington Post*, Oct. 17, 1992, D7.

27 Thanks to Chris Cagle for Bikini Kill's lyrics.

28 Only *Damned If You Don't* (1987) deals directly with coming out. Friedrich's other work includes *Cool Hands, Warm Heart* (1979), *Gently Down the Stream* (1981), *The Ties that Bind* (1984), *Sink or Swim* (1990), and *Lesbian Avengers Eat Fire Too* (1993, codirected with Janet Baus). *Scar Tissue* (1980) and *But No One* (1982) are not in distribution.

    For a discussion of autobiographical elements in *Gently Down the Stream, The Ties that Bind, Damned If You Don't*, and *Sink or Swim*, see Chris Holmlund, "Fractured Fairytales and Experimental Identities: Looking for Lesbians in and around the Films of Su Friedrich," *Discourse* 17.1 (Fall 1994): 16–46.

29 Publicity blurb written by Friedrich.

30 Ibid.

31 Leslie Kossoff, "History in the Making," *Gay Community News*, Sept. 1–14, 1991, 7.

32 I owe this idea to Paige Travis, who argues: "Both visually and through the narration, Friedrich treats cars like a valuable member of the family. In fact it's possible that the real main character of *Rules of the Road* could be the 1983 Oldsmobile Cutlass Cruiser the narrator comes to love and depend on." Paige Travis, "The Undeniable Connection between Cars and Family in Su Friedrich's *Rules of the Road*," unpublished ms., April 1995.

33 Friedrich says she used to dislike narrative film "partly because I'm a woman (I saw a lot of films about interesting male characters and stupid female characters) and at times because I couldn't identify with the romantic line of the films." Cited in Scott MacDonald, "*Damned If You Don't*: An Interview with Su Friedrich," *Afterimage*, May 1988, 10, and *A Critical Cinema*, vol. 2 (Los Angeles: University of California Press, 1990), 306. Benning describes Hollywood movies as "totally fake and constructed to entertain and oppress at the same time—they're meaningless to women, and not just to gay women." Cited in Smith, "A Video Artist Who Talks through a Keyhole," H33.

34 Masters, "Auteur of Adolescence," D7. Elsewhere, however, Benning does say she makes her videos largely for young lesbian and gay audiences. See, for example, Spiro, "Shooting Star," 68.

35 Publicity blurb written by Friedrich. Friedrich discusses her approach to experimental film in Su Friedrich, "Radical Form/Radical Content," *Millennium Film Journal* 22 (1989–1990): 118–123.

36 Annette Kuhn, "The Camera I: Observations on Documentary," *Screen* 19.2 (1978): 81.

37 Indexes consulted include *Film Literature Index*, the *General Periodicals Index*, and the *National Newspaper Index*.

38 Holmlund, "Fractured Fairytales and Experimental Identities," 33.

39 Friedrich's earlier work is sometimes positioned in terms of *cinéma-vérité* and structuralist materialist film as well. Simon Field, "State of Things," *Monthly Film Bulletin* 54 (Jan. 1987): 4–6; Lindley Hanlon, "Female Rage: The Films of Su Friedrich," *Millennium Film Journal* 12 (1982–1983): 79–86; Bruce Jenkins, "*Gently Down the Stream*," *Millennium Film Journal* 16–18 (Fall/Winter 1986–1987): 195–198; and Scott MacDonald, *Avant-garde Film: Motion Studies* (Cambridge: Cambridge University Press, 1993), 102–111.

   MTV and, more rarely, Benning's father, James, are cited as influences on her work. Benning herself insists that "people on the street, music, everyday images, my mom, how I was raised, way more influence how I work and think than other artists. . . . People I hate influence me a lot; I'm influenced by people that are just total assholes." Cited in Harris, "Baby Butch Video," 63.

40 Reviews of Friedrich's earlier work contained similar oversights. See Holmlund, "Fractured Fairytales and Experimental Identities," 34.

41 Harris, "Baby Butch Video," 63.

42 Su Friedrich, letters to Chris Holmlund, Dec. 10, 1991, and Oct. 4, 1992. Of course many experimental filmmakers also "ghettoize" lesbian work. Benning describes her father's reaction: "My dad said to me, 'You know, I'm really worried that all your work is just going to be on one subject,' and I was like, 'Yeah, my life.' He makes [experimental] films. What are his films about? They're about his life. It just so happens that his sexuality isn't something that people are going to label or talk about or say, 'He's the heterosexual artist.'" Cited in Harris, "Baby Butch Video," 68. Friedrich says of the experimental film world: "In this old boys' scene there's this assumption that if you're speaking from the point of view of a minority, what you're saying does not have any bearing on their lives, and they can't learn anything from it—which is ridiculous. We spend all our time looking at straight films." Cited in Soehnlein, "Lights, Camera, Lesbian," 48.

43 Nichols, "'Getting to Know You . . .'" 180. Such misreadings probably occur, as Kath Weston argues, because "homosexuality in the U.S. is now most commonly understood as an identity that infuses the entire self [and, I would add, that distinguishes homosexuals as

a group] as opposed to an activity in which any self can participate" (Weston, *Families We Choose*, 24).

44 On "queer readers," see Alexander Doty, *Making Things Perfectly Queer: Interpreting Mass Culture* (Minneapolis: University of Minnesota Press, 1993), especially 1–16.

Black Women's Independent Cinema

19

GLORIA J. GIBSON

> When images of African-American women are depicted on the screen by someone outside our culture, it is a projection of that filmmaker's mind—not an expression of our reality. The films I make are from a Black aesthetic and from an African-American woman's reality.
>
> Julie Dash

Black women independent filmmakers are emerging as one of the most vibrant, influential groups of contemporary cultural artists. Through their interpretations of black women's racial, sexual, and class status in white society, and of the sexism prevalent in the black male community, these "cultural storytellers" provide new perspectives on varied personal, sociocultural, and emotional relationships of black women's communities. Specifically, their works, drawn from the diverse experiences of black women's lives, promote exploration of self, attack racial polarity, instill racial and female pride, and encourage individual and collective activism.

Focusing on three representative films, *Hair Piece: A Film For Nappy-Headed People* (Ayoka Chenzira, 1984), *Illusions* (Julie Dash, 1983), and *Losing Ground* (Kathleen Collins, 1982), this analysis demonstrates (1) how past and present attitudes and behaviors toward black women have helped formulate certain tenets of the black feminist movement; (2) how selected films function within a black feminist cultural ideology to communicate aspects of African-American female sociocultural identity; and (3) how elements of a black feminist cultural ideology in films can serve as a catalyst to promote audience introspection and change.

Black Feminist Cultural Ideology

Art does not develop in a vacuum; its metamorphoses result from a melding of personal/cultural history, values, and norms. Moreover, art communicates a specific ideology derived from one's sociocultural identity. Bill Nichols states, "Ideology is how the existing ensemble of social relations represents itself to individuals. It proposes obviousness, a sense of 'the way things are' within which our sense of place and self emerges."[1]

Deborah Gray White explains the implications of this concept of ideology formation to the oppression of African-American women from the earliest days of slavery: "Black in a white society, slave in a free society, women in a society ruled by men, female slaves had the least formal power and were perhaps the most vulnerable group of antebellum Americans."[2] Their experience as female slaves contributed to their lack of self-identity as historical racism and the racial polarization of the sexes continues to define the "place" of black women in society despite the women's movements.

The ideology of black women's art developed in response to the complexities of black women's interpersonal relationships. Given the history of black women and their invisible or negative position within the dominant white patriarchal society, black women artists frequently infuse their work with didactic messages exposing racial and sexual inequities by pointing to aspects of their lives that are lost in the stereotypes and narrow roles allotted them in the mass media.[3]

Black feminist scholar Michele Wallace notes, "It is necessary to realize that the voices of black feminism in the U.S. emerge today from a long tradition of structural 'silence' of women of color within the sphere of global knowledge production."[4] African-American women filmmakers collectively as well as individually voice their personal and cultural realities based on "the shared belief that black women are inherently valuable, that [their] liberation is a necessity not as an adjunct to somebody else's but because of [their] need as human persons for autonomy."[5] Stemming from black feminism the philosophical core of which is the desire for complete recognition and understanding of black women's life experiences as valuable, complex, and diverse, the films of black women function as a cultural microcosm. They provide narratives that relate to historical occurrences and conditions, beliefs and values that are germane to black women. Consequently, their cinematic frames challenge decades of "structural silence" levied against African-American women.

Although black feminist cultural ideology manifests itself within film narratives in several ways, I want to concentrate on only two components: first, the eradication of racial and sexual distortion and myths concerning black womanhood.[6] The silver screen has consistently presented grossly distorted, patriarchal visions of black women since its inception. From *Birth of a Nation* (D. W. Griffith, 1915) onward, the character, morals, and physical stature of black women have been maligned in white cinema. In addition, while a few black male filmmakers have incorporated women's issues into their works, for the most part they have not unraveled the historical tensions that have contributed to a lack of self-fulfillment experienced by many black women.[7] Therefore, a dire need exists to dispel myths and "half-truths."

The second means by which black feminist cultural ideology manifests itself in films is through characterizations of black women conceived and projected by black women filmmakers themselves. Most important, the images are situated within a cinematic context to explore black women's sociocultural identity and the environmental forces that have shaped their self-concepts. As the narratives progress the filmmakers underscore the psychological maturation and self-awareness the characters undergo as their personal and/or cultural consciousness is transformed. From these films emerge black women characters that represent "cultural" heroines whose qualities of "heroism" exemplify the values of black women artists.

Perhaps the most dynamic element utilized by these women to restructure and convey the complexity of black women's existence is narrative theme, especially when understood as a concept within a cultural milieu. Viewed as chronicles of African-American experiences, theme becomes a powerful and indispensable agent to dramatize the characters' consciousness-raising process. Black women independent filmmakers hope that all audiences will understand how the characters' maturation and subsequent empowerment on the screen can function to strengthen their own personal knowledge and consciousness.

Hair Piece: A Film for Nappy-Headed People

Hair Piece: A Film for Nappy-Headed People is a hilarious animated satire that traces historically the "hair problem" among black people and questions the relationship between beauty and ethnicity. Hair Piece goes beyond a discussion of black hairstyles and fads to an examination of the cultural values that have accompanied those hairstyles. Chenzira's film functions as an important work because, "on the one hand it shows a political commitment and an ideological lucidity, and is on the other hand interrogative by nature, instead of being merely prescriptive."[8]

Chenzira, in the opening sequence, uses voice over to communicate the value system operating before the black power movement. The narrator equates "bad" nappy hair with unattractiveness and charges that it is a major contributing factor in black women's inability to attract men or find and keep a job. Clearly the standard of beauty was constrictive, dictated by white "mainstream" society. Long, straightened hair was the imposed icon and many black women and men believed conformity to or an approximation of white standards would translate into social acceptance in white America.

Music reinforces the voice-over's message. The film begins with a blues melody to punctuate the dilemma of nappy hair and to capture the low self-esteem ingrained into the fiber of black consciousness. Still, as the voice-over and blues accentuate the feelings of inferiority that shackled many African-Americans, Chenzira's visual images portray diversity among the penciled faces of black women moving across the screen, faces only. The visual complexity is intensified as she integrates photographed faces of black women, once again faces without hair. The women are noticeably different shades of "black," subtly pointing out that although African-American women share "blackness," their individual stories may contain unique experiences based on skin color and hair texture.[9]

The animated character begins her yarn. "For years there have been many approaches used by colored women, Negro women, and black women in dealing with what is commonly referred to as the 'hair problem.'" Thus Chenzira grounds her script within a historical context as the labels "colored," "Negro," and "black" convey different cultural icons and an evolving self-awareness. Colored is a label that conjures up the image of subservience, but the Negro, especially the "New" Negro of the Harlem Renaissance, suggests assertion, polite assertion of one's rights, and black connotes strength and aggression as black people demanded and fought for their freedom in the 1960s. Thus the "hair problem" reflects historical eras, the politics of black America, and issues of self-identity, self-esteem, and cultural awareness.

The animated narrator then briefly discusses Madame Walker and the Afro hairstyle. While the narrator delivers these lines, animated women wearing natural hairstyles move across the screen. They are followed by a still of Angela Davis displaying her powerful Afro symbolizing resistance and liberation. On the soundtrack, James Brown bellows, "With yo bad self, say it loud, I'm black and I'm proud."

19. Ayoka Chenzira's *Hair Piece* (1984). Courtesy Women Make Movies, Inc.; reprinted by permission.

Through the film Chenzira briefly surveys the solutions African-Americans have ingeniously adopted to disguise or eliminate the true nature of their hair, including wigs, permanents, and the straightening (hot) comb. In the sequence highlighting perms the "male-sounding narrator" begins to "preach" about the miracle of permanents. His rhetorical style imitates the speech/song mode of the black folk preacher. However, the dream of long hair, promised by the *white* cream to *colored girls*, turns into a nightmare as the female animated character returns to report that she had a perm and her hair performed for a while, but then fell out. Once again, the dream is deferred and feelings of despair and unattractiveness resurface.

In the final scene, however, Chenzira dramatizes that exploration and affirmation of self can bring about a keener sense of one's personal and cultural identity. The narrator states, "If you have problems with your hair, perhaps the comb you use was not designed with your hair in mind." She continues over a still photo of black women wearing "natural" hairstyles including Afros, cornrows, and dreadlocks, "Perhaps now it's time to allow your hair to come into the full beauty of its own rebelliousness." During this climactic scene, the "cute" narrator's voice modulates to a powerful delivery, singing, "Give me something real, something that won't fade in the light of day," and the comical one-dimensional cartoon imagery transforms into a still photo of "real" black women wearing natural hairstyles.

Hair Piece functions as participatory, not escapist, art. Two levels of involvement emerge. First, black audience members laugh and "talk" to the film characters. In many cases, however, the laughter is a mask for suppressed anxiety or pain. Consequently, the second level of participation becomes personal confrontation. As the laughter fades, audience members begin thinking and discussing aspects of self-awareness and self-definition that reveal the film's function as a catalyst for introspection. The emphasis on filmmaking and film viewing shifts from an activity of entertainment to one of personal growth and pride while audiences follow Chenzira's identification of damaging, erroneous myths and attitudes about African-American identity and then affirms and celebrates black womanhood and African-American beauty.

Illusions

Like Chenzira's, Julie Dash's keen sense of racial and sexual oppression provides the undergirding structure for her film Illusions. Set during World War II, the black-and-white work examines various levels of illusion, including that which surrounds racial identity and the presentation of history. "This story is about Mignon Dupree, a black woman who appears to be white; Ester Jeeter, a black woman who is the singing voice for a white Hollywood movie star; and the power and the use of the film medium—three illusions in conflict with reality."[10] Dash dramatizes how the film industry, perhaps more than any other institution, has sown seeds of racism and sexism. Individually and collectively, one-dimensional stereotypes have promoted "homogeneous" imagery ignoring diversity. Dash demonstrates that film has the potential to become an influential mechanism to document and communicate black history, women's history—to be an inclusive history rather than continue to be illusionary, presenting a dysfunctional misrepresentation of reality.

Dash's goal to "demythify and demystify" cinema is presented in the opening credits. The film title is overlaid in white over a coiled reel of black film. In the following frames a shining, twirling white object moves from the background to the foreground in a sea of black. It appears to be an Oscar, the symbol of cinematic excellence. The female narrator's voice begins, "In the beginning was not the shadow, but the act and the province of Hollywood is not action but illusion."[11]

Illusions, however, functions as more than an attack upon Hollywood. It seeks to alert audience members to the seductive influence of cinema as it promotes "shadows" rather than the "acts" by denying or ignoring the diversities of black life. Dash is careful not to generalize, but specifically singles out Hollywood cinema, thereby establishing lines of demarcation between Hollywood and independent productions.

After a brief clip of newsreel footage from World War II, Dash presents the setting of the film, National Studios, and the central character, Mignon Dupree. Her suit is black-and-white, sculpted to depict a "double V."[12] Throughout the film Dash ingeniously colors Illusions with black-and-white—black-and-white film stock, a black-on-white, white-on-black suit, black or white woman. As the audience is presented with a full view of Mignon, the camera reveals another symbolic prop. She wears a hat with a veil.

The veil or mask is a recurring symbol incorporated in black film and literature. It was scholar W. E. B. DuBois, however, who almost a century ago attempted to penetrate the psychological dimension of the veil, stating, "The Negro is born of a veil, and gifted with second sight in this American world—a world which yields him no true self-consciousness but only lets him see himself through the revelation of the other world."[13] The veil of Mignon Dupree functions not only as a shield that masks her true identity, but also as a barrier she must eventually overcome. Transcending the veil becomes the broader issue Dash addresses.[14]

Mignon is determined to structure her "visibility" by communicating realistic objectives for the film industry, although her boss, Mr. Forrester, is strictly concerned with finances. Her present assignment is to salvage their current film production, in which the audio and visual elements are out of sync. They cannot reshoot because the white singer is out of the country entertaining military troops. The solution is to bring back Ester Jeeter, the black singer who performed the original soundtrack, to perform a reverse lip sync.[15]

As Ester carefully watches the screen to match word for word the white singer's lip movements, Mignon appears distressed, seemingly convinced that now the visual imagery is out of sync. Her face fills with anguish at the gross appropriation of Ester's talent. Dash then divides the screen into three parts to juxtapose illusion with reality—at the top of the screen the white singer, in the foreground Ester, and in the center a reflection of the white technician in the sound booth. They all appear to be in close physical proximity to each other, but actually they are quite distant in the realization of their contribution "to the shadow."

After Ester saves the film, Mignon calls her mother. It is from this conversation that audience members gain greater insight into her ambition and true identity. Mignon explains that she wants more out of life and does not conform to the "traditional" mold of a woman. This line of discussion is interrupted by an apparent question from her mother regarding her racial disguise. Mignon replies, "They didn't ask and I didn't tell them." Dash then moves the camera in for a close-up shot of a small poster on the wall of the phone booth. It reads, "I am *so* an American—no matter what race, creed, or religion." Ironically, the poster has some, but not full, relevance to Mignon and Ester. Once again the dream is deferred.

The perplexity of Mignon's life intensifies in the next scene as she brings contract papers for Ester to sign. She immediately recognizes Mignon's true racial identity and embraces her as a sister. Ester functions as a pivotal character in Mignon's life. Their relationship develops and strengthens as they fantasize about goals and aspirations they fear will never materialize. Although both women are wounded by racism, they use each other as a support system. The two women illustrate how female bonding can ultimately provide self-healing and inner strength. Moreover, their relationship dramatizes that "for women, the need and desire to nurture each other is not pathological but redemptive, it is within that knowledge that real power is rediscovered."[16] Mignon's and Ester's relationship serves as a symbol of and a paradigm for female bonding.

In the final scene of *Illusions*, Lieutenant Bedsford discovers Mignon's true racial identity. Because of her heightened self-esteem, Mignon has the personal strength to "fight back." She proudly admits she is not ashamed of her race. Mignon then delivers a searing indictment against the film industry and biased, inaccurate historical accounts, stating, "I never once saw a film showing 'my boys' fighting for this country. Your scissors and paste methods have eliminated my participation in the history of this country."

As the camera moves in for a close-up shot Mignon is symbolically seated behind Mr. Forrester's desk. A voice-over reveals her heightened consciousness. "We would meet again, Ester Jeeter and I, for it was she who helped me see beyond shadows dancing on a white wall; to define what I had already come to know, and to take action without fearing. Yes, I wanted to use the power of the motion picture, for there are many stories to be told and many battles to begin."

Illusions presents a holistic image of an African-American woman and the effects of her social and cultural environment. Despite negative circumstances, Mignon emerges as a heroine. Dash molds a character who is not afraid to face her fears. Mignon recognizes the social forces that she must combat, and she also recognizes and values genuine friendship. These attributes closely conform to those Claudia Tate ascribes to heroines created by black women writers.[17]

Dash's film conforms to and promotes the concepts of black feminist cultural ideology. She uses film as a context in which to reexamine history, reminding audiences that "scissors and paste" are sometimes used to erase the contributions of African-Americans, while at other times their talents are exploited or expropriated. Dash's cinematic reinterpretation of history articulates not a chronology of facts, but a period in the developing consciousness of two African-American women. The eradication of "illusion" and the presentation of "authenticity" regarding racial identity and the effects of history become the dominant message of the film. *Illusions*, however, is not a film of despair and despondency. The spiritual center, the very essence of the film, communicates the power of self-awareness and maturation.

Losing Ground

Kathleen Collins's film *Losing Ground* continues the theme of self-affirmation. Collins, however, produces a cinematic narrative that examines the importance of self-definition to the maturation process. Creatively she dramatizes the concept that change results from introspection and from an awareness that external stimuli such as sociocultural history, values, and norms have an impact upon the perception of self.

Briefly recounted, *Losing Ground* explores a black woman professor's quest for a more complete identity. Collins summarizes her persona: "She is an exceptionally intelligent woman, in many ways trapped by her intelligence—trapped into not being able to explore other areas of herself." Sara Rogers, a philosophy professor, is married to an artist who is outgoing and sometimes irrational. She is the antithesis of her husband.

Collins seeks to dramatize the transition of a woman from "emotional frigidity" to self-awareness and empowerment. The path to this "new self" for Sara is subsequently realized through searching for ecstasy and embracing her own psyche. Initially, however, Sara views herself strictly as a professional to the extent that she denies certain aspects of her own "womanhood." Consequently, in some ways she emulates personality traits generally attributed to men: she is analytical, cold, and sterile. Collins conveys this by employing medium shots throughout the film. These revealing shots capture Sara's personal environment and her disengaged interactions within it. For example, the audience first meets Professor Rogers as she is lecturing to her class on existentialism. Most class members fight to stay awake or rock to the beat of their walkman. Amusingly, however, she rambles on with her lecture on the existential movement.

Dr. Rogers's class must prepare an analysis of Jean-Paul Sartre's Play *No Exit* (1944). Yet, paradoxically, it is Sara who personifies the quest for existentialism as she wrestles with the meaninglessness of her life. Sara's present "realm of existence" consists of her sterile life as an intellectual and a wife—both personally unfulfilling. So she embarks on a mission to intellectually research the notion of ecstasy, a concept that implies the ability to *feel* emotional exaltation.

As a scholar she searches meticulously for concrete facts on her research topic by visiting the library, her mother, the church, and a spiritual reader. As she explores her topic, Sara actually yearns, not for information on ecstasy, but for the experience of ecstasy. She subsequently discovers that she has lost touch with her own spiritual essence. It is not until she conducts an introspective analysis of herself that the impetus to seek what she is missing surfaces.

A series of incidents and conversations precipitate Sara's awakening from "emotional somnambulism." The culmination of her quest for self-affirmation occurs, however, when she believes her husband Victor is having an affair with his Puerto Rican model. She then decides to star as "Frankie" in a student's film project entitled "Frankie and Johnny." This is Sara's first step in confronting her emotionless state. Paralleling the songs lyrics, her frustration with herself and Victor builds to a climax when Victor vigorously flaunts his relationship with the model:

Sara: There you go taking your thing out in front of me. It's uncalled for, for you to sling your little private ecstasies in my face.

Victor: This is not one of your classes, don't lecture to me.

Sara: Don't fuck around then! Don't you take your dick out like it was artistic—like it's some goddamn paint brush. Maybe that's what's uneven—that I got nothing to take out.

Sara has been suffering in silence, but no more. On the one hand she is jealous of Victor's ability to experience ecstasy and is angered at the means by which he achieves it. Sara questions if ecstasy is achieved only by "taking something out." Is it strictly a male privilege? Collins captures the irony in Sara's life. She feels emotionally fragmented and frustrated by restrictions she has placed on herself. In her thoroughly exasperated state she calls her mother on the way to the film set.

Sara: I'm on shaky ground.

Mother: That's not the kind of feeling you'd like.

Sara: That's what Victor loves about me; that there's no chaos anywhere.

Mother: That's the quality in you that even I admit to counting on.

Sara: Mama . . . (*silence*)

Sara has functioned as a dependable "pillar" for her students, mother, and husband—a pillar that now crumbles under severe pressure. She must determine how she will resolve her personal relationship with her mother, her husband, and, most important, herself.

Collins employs a blues folk ballad and the film-within-a-film technique to conceptualize Sara's emotional experience. "Frankie and Johnny" serves as a microcosm of Sara's world. It becomes the "stage" in which Sara explores her inner self through a film exploring someone else's experience. Most important, the "Frankie and Johnny" blues ballad resides in the oral tradition of black folklore and music and within the film to elucidate aspects of the overall cinematic narrative.[18] In addition, the blues ballad has historically functioned as a vehicle to confront life on a personal basis as it explores intimate situations in detail. The blues provides the ideal cultural context for Sara's examination of self and transforming consciousness because the text and structure in many instances represent a cultural icon communicating sexual empowerment.[19]

Sara, like Frankie, rebels. In the final scene of *Losing Ground*, the student director is filming the climactic scene of "Frankie and Johnny." Sara is dressed as Frankie, low-cut top, skirt with a slit, hair down and blowing in the wind. As the director gives final instructions, Victor arrives at the set. In this provocative scene, Frankie points the gun to kill her lover, Johnny. On another level, it is Sara pointing the gun at Victor and her previous life. Collins uses a medium close-up shot to allow the audience to experience the mental anguish Sara is undergoing. As the saxophone plays the theme music of "Frankie and Johnny," the student director shouts out, "OK, Frankie . . . raise the gun . . . take your time and when it feels right . . . blow him away."

Frankie fires, Johnny falls. As the bullet explodes it is Sara's previous psychological state that is shattered to reveal a new person. Paradoxically, Sara fires and Victor also symbolically falls. Coffins moves the camera to a close-up of Victor's face, also filled with anguish. They both understand that if their relationship is to survive, there must be change. Collins moves the camera back to Sara, still pointing the gun. She ends the film with stark, naked silence— only the reverberation of the gunshot is heard. If, when, and how Sara and Victor will mend their relationship is not answered. The only clear message is that Sara has discovered something about herself that was previously lost.

Collins dramatizes a concise message—introspection is the path to empowerment. In an article published posthumously, she admits, "While I'm interested in external reality, I am much more concerned with how people resolve their inner dilemma in the face of external reality."[20] Losing Ground encourages women to develop the inner resources they need to cope with greater social forces. Furthermore, it conforms to the basic principles identified by Jan Rosenberg in what she terms "feminist issue films": "The themes in issue films delineate the shared, socially structured limitations, oppression, and discrimination which women suffer as a group. The recordings of such experiences are compressed cinematic simulations of the consciousness-raising process."[21] Collins's objective is to uncover perplexing ironies demonstrating that "through conflict we get to see something about people, and realize something about them and ultimately about ourselves."[22]

Synthesis

In one sense, Hair Piece, Illusions, and Losing Ground are three very different films because the experiences of black women in America are not homogeneous. Collins and Dash focus on highly privileged women, certainly middle class; Chenzira is more pluralistic and inclusive and transcends class. Sara's identification with Frankie and Mignon's with Ester take them out of upper-class privilege. The films demonstrate that differences existed and exist in the lives of African-American women and in the lives of the filmmakers translating everyday experiences into cinematic narratives.

On another level, however, striking similarities among these films suggest a cinematic message forged from common ingredients of black womanhood. Moreover, aspects of black feminist cultural ideology, which provide the undergirding structure contributing meaning, stem from a shared sociocultural history. Consequently, one of the major threads that permeates black feminist cultural ideology and the films of Dash, Chenzira, and Collins is the need for women to understand themselves in the totality of their sociocultural environment.

Chenzira, Dash, and Collins demonstrate that confrontation with self and others, is, in fact, intrinsic to growth and inner strength. As the film characters confront their problems, they, in essence, help eradicate prescribed images of self and they forge their own unique self-definition. Thus these films dramatize the resilience of black women who seek creative solutions as they confront and overcome personal and historical tensions.

These films also demonstrate that women should function as reflectors for one another. That is, in their reciprocal relationships they should be able to share their feelings, insights, and fears. Sisterhood and female bonding become important ingredients for survival. Therefore, these films, and others, function as participatory art suggesting a paradigm for personal and collective introspection and activism. Unlike mainstream film, which frequently promotes a "living happily ever after" formula, films by black independent filmmakers frequently isolate the necessary personal skills needed to interpret and confront issues in everyday life with the hope that a heightened sense of self will lead to individual and collective empowerment.

Each of the films presented here addresses the multiplicity of life's issues that converge with African-American women's historic and contemporary experience. Cinema becomes a form of expression that allows filmmakers to present their personalized vision of culture. Most often, black women independent filmmakers select themes that highlight sociocultural issues, not only promoting education, but also personal awareness and activism. Black in a white world, woman in a man's world, Dash, Chenzira, and Coffins affirm their existence and present and control their image, thereby dignifying "blackness" and "womanhood."

Notes

1 Bill Nichols, *Ideology and the Image* (Bloomington: Indiana University Press, 1981), 1.
2 Deborah Gray White, *Ar'n't I a Woman: Female Slaves in the Plantation South* (New York: W.W. Norton, 1985), 15.
3 See the following for discussions of how black women's music and literature convey poignant sociocultural messages. Billie Barlow and Lisa Miller, "Women's Music: Activism and Artistic Expression," *Iris: A Journal about Women*, no. 15 (Spring–Summer 1986); Barbara Christian, "Trajectories of Self-Definition," in *Conjuring: Black Women, Fiction, and Literary Tradition*, ed. Marjorie Pryse and Hortense J. Spillers (Bloomington: Indiana University Press, 1985).
4 Michele Wallace, *Invisibility Blues: From Pop to Theory* (New York: Verso, 1990), 242.
5 Combahee River Collective, "A Black Feminist Statement," in *This Bridge Called My Back: Writings by Radical Women of Color*, ed. Cherríe Moraga and Gloria Anzaldúa (New York: Kitchen Table: Women of Color Press, 1983), 212.
6 Because black women's cinema still exists in a developmental stage as an emerging tradition, new and dynamic theoretical foci to analyze the films are at an equally embryonic phase. Several approaches such as "womanist perspective," "black feminism," "Afrocentric feminism," and "Third World feminism" are beginning to surface in the analysis of black women's film. See Mark A. Reid, "Dialogic Modes of Representing Africa(s): Womanist Film," *Black American Literature Forum* 25 (Summer 1991): 375–388; "Black Feminism and Media Studies," upcoming issue of *Quarterly Review of Film and Video*; Trinh T. Minh-ha, "Questions of Images and Politics," in *When the Moon Waxes Red: Representation, Gender, and Cultural Politics* (New York: Routledge, 1991).
7 The following films by black men address the complexity of black women's lives: Haile Gerima's *Bush Mama*, Billy Woodberry's *Bless Their Little Hearts*, and Bill Gunn's *Ganja and Hess*.
8 Trinh T. Minh-ha, *When the Moon Waxes Red*, 149.

9   Intraracial prejudice is addressed in *Color* by Warrington Hudlin and Denise Oliver and *School Daze* by Spike Lee.

10   *Black Camera: Catalog for the Black Filmmaker Foundation*, (New York, 1982), 11.

11   This statement is a direct quote from Ralph Ellison's *Shadow and Act* (New York: Random House, 1964), 276.

12   The double V philosophy was promoted by many blacks during World War II. Blacks fought for victory in Europe against fascism. They felt that this monumental effort would subsequently result in victory at home against racism.

13   W. E. B. DuBois, *The Souls of Black Folk* (Chicago: A. C. McClurg, 1903), 7.

14   Trinh T. Minh-ha gives a slightly different interpretation of the veil: "If the act of unveiling has a liberating potential, so does the act of veiling. It all depends on the context in which such an act is carried out. [To replace the veil] is to reappropriate [one's] space or to claim anew difference, in defiance of genderless hegemonic standardization" (151). It should be noted that Mignon never replaces the veil in the film, but she does defy hegemonic, patriarchial standardization.

15   Ester's voice is really that of Ella Fitzgerald. Dash adds another level of illusion, only with a cultural foundation.

16   Audre Lorde, "The Master's Tools Will Never Dismantle the Master's House," in *This Bridge Called My Back*, 98.

17   See *Black Women Writers at Work* (New York: Continuum, 1988), xxiv.

18   See Kathryn Kalinak, "Music as Narrative Structure in Hollywood Film" (unpublished Ph.D. diss., University of Illinois, 1982), 2.

19   Hazel Carby, "It Jus Be's Dat Way Sometime: The Sexual Politics of Women's Blues," *Radical America* 20, no. 4 (1986): 21.

20   David Nicholson, "A Commitment to Writing: A Conversation with Kathleen Collins Prettyman," *Black Film Review* 5 (Winter 1988–1989): 12.

21   Jan Rosenberg, *Women's Reflections: The Feminist Film Movement* (Ann Arbor: UMI Research Press, 1983), 55.

22   Nicholson, "Commitment to Writing," 14.

Selected Video/Filmography

Anita Addison: *The Secret Space* (1981); *Savannah* (1989), 30 min; *Sound of Sunshine, Sound of Rain* (1983). Addison Productions.

Madeline Anderson: *Integration Report* I(1960), 24 min.; *I Am Somebody* (1970), 30 min. Indiana University.

Camille Billops: *Suzanne, Suzanne* (1982), 25 min.; *Older Women and Love* (1988), 28 min.; *Finding Christa* (1991), 55 min. Women Make Movies.

Carroll Parott Blue: *Varnette's World: A Study of a Young Artist* (1979), 26 min.; *Conversations with Roy deCarava* (1984), 28 min.; Smithsonian World Series: *Nigerian Art—Kindred Spirits* (1990), 58 min. Produced by WETA and the Smithsonian Institute. First Run.

Ayoka Chenzira: *Flamboyant Ladies Speak Out* (1982), 30 min.; *Hair Piece: A Film for Nappy-Headed People* (1984), 10 min.; *Secret Sounds Screaming: The Sexual Abuse of Children* (1986), 30 min.; *Five out of Five* (1987), 7 min.; *Zajota and the Boogie Spirit* (1989), 20 min. Women Make Movies.

Kathleen Collins: *The Cruz Brothers and Miss Malloy* (1980), 54 min.; *Losing Ground* (1982), 86 min. Mypheduh Films.

Julie Dash: *Four Women* (1978), 7 min.; *Illusions* (1982), 34 min.; *Praise House* (1991), 30 min.; Women Make Movies; *Daughters of the Dust* (1991), 30 min. Kino International.

Zeinabu irene Davis: *Crocodile Conspiracy* (1986), 13 min., *Recreating Black Women's Media Image* (1987), 28 min. Third World Newsreel. *Cycles* (1989), 17 min.; *A Powerful Thang* (1991), 58 min. Women Make Movies.

Elena Featherston: *Visions of the Spirit: A Portrait of Alice Walker* (1989), 58 min. Women Make Movies.

Alile Sharon Larkin: *Your Children Come Back to You* (1979), 27 min.; *A Different Image* (1982), 51 min. Women Make Movies. *Miss Fluci Moses: A Video Documentary* (1987), 22 min.; *Dreadlocks and the Three Bears* (1991), 12 min. Alile Productions.

Michelle Parkerson: *But Then She's Betty Carter* (1980), 53 min.; *Gotta Make This Journey: Sweet Honey in the Rock* (1983), 58 min.; *Storme: Lady of the Jewel Box* (1987), 21 min. Women Make Movies.

Dark and Lovely Too

20

Black gay men in independent film

KOBENA MERCER

We are in the midst of a wildly creative upsurge in black queer cultural politics. Through political activism and new forms of cultural practice, we have created a community that has inspired a new sense of collective identity among lesbians and gay men across the black diaspora.

The recent work in film and video by Isaac Julien and Marlon Riggs emerges from and contributes to the movement and direction of these new developments. I will begin by framing Riggs's *Tongues Untied* and Julien's *Looking for Langston* in the specific context of black lesbian and gay cultural politics, in order to open up a discussion on questions of difference and identity in the general context of contemporary struggles around race, gender, and sexuality. In this sense, what is important about black lesbian and gay cultural politics is not simply that we have created a new sense of community among ourselves—although the importance of that cannot be emphasized enough—but that our struggles make it possible to arrive at a new perspective on political identity and imagined community at large.

To invoke a couple of well-worn metaphors, we have been involved in a process of "making ourselves visible" and "finding a voice." Through activism and political organization, from large-scale international conferences to small-scale consciousness-raising groups, black lesbians and gay men have come out of the margins into the center of political visibility. One need only point to the numerous service organizations created in response to the AIDS crisis—or more specifically the crisis of indifference and neglect in the official public health policies of countries such as Britain and the United States—to recognize that our lives are at the center of contemporary politics. Such activity has created a base for collective empowerment. If I think about my own involvement in a small collective of gay men of African, Asian, and Caribbean descent which formed in London in the early 1980s, what was so empowering was precisely the feeling of belonging which arose out of the transformation from "I" to "we."

It was through the process of coming together—communifying, as it were—that we transformed experiences previously lived as individual, privatized, and even pathologized problems into the basis for a sense of collective agency. This sense of agency enabled us to formulate an agenda around our experiences of racism in the white gay community and issues of homophobia in black communities I think I can generalize here to the extent that the agenda of black lesbian and gay struggles over the past decade has been shaped and defined by this duality, by the necessity of working on at least two fronts at all times, and by the difficulty of constantly negotiating our relationship to the different communities to which we equally belong.

For this reason, rather than conceptualize our politics in terms of "double" or "triple" oppression, it should be seen as a hybridized form of political and cultural practice. By this I mean that precisely because of our lived experiences of discrimination in and exclusion from the white gay and lesbian community, and of discrimination in and exclusions from the black community, we locate ourselves in the spaces *between* different communities—at the intersections of power relations determined by race, class, gender, and sexuality. What follows from this is a recognition of the interdependence of different political communities, not completely closed off from each other or each hermetically sealed like a segregated bantustan but interlocking in contradictory relations over which we struggle. If you agree with this view, then it has important implications for the way we conceptualize the politics of identity

We habitually think of identity in mutually exclusive terms, based on the either/or logic of binary oppositions. As black lesbians and gay men we are often asked, and sometimes ask ourselves: which is more important to my identity, my blackness or my sexuality? Once the question of identity is reduced to this either/or dichotomy, we can see how ridiculous and unhelpful it is; as black lesbians and gay men we cannot separate the different aspects of our identities precisely because we value both our blackness and our homosexuality. It is this contrast between both/and against either/or that is at stake in the problem of "identity politics"—in the pejorative sense of the term.

We are all familiar with the right-on rhetoric of "race, class, and gender," so often repeated like a mantra to signify one's acknowledgment of the diversity of social identities at play in contemporary politics. What is wrong with the "race, class, gender" mantra is that it encourages the reductive notion that there is a hierarchy of oppressions and thus a hierarchy of "doubly" or "triply" oppressed identities. What often occurs when different communities try to come together is a tendency to use our differences as a means of competition and closure in order to assert who is more oppressed than whom. In this way, difference becomes the basis of divisiveness, encouraging group closure in the competition for resources, rather than the recognition of the interdependence of our various communities. This is because identity is assumed to be an essential category, fixed once and for all by the community to which one belongs—a view which ignores the fact that we very rarely belong exclusively to one homogeneous and monolithic community and that, for most of us, everyday life is a matter of passing through, travelling between, and negotiating a plurality of different spaces. Black lesbians and gay men are not exempt from the worst aspects of such categorical identity politics. But precisely because of our hybrid legacy, drawing on the best aspects of our dual inheritance from both black struggles and lesbian and gay struggles of the 1960s and 1970s, we might arrive at a better appreciation of the politics of identity which begins with the recognition of difference and diversity.

Let me put it like this: the literary work of writers such as Audre Lorde, Joseph Beam, Essex Hemphill, Cheryl Clarke, and Assoto Saint—to name only a few—has been absolutely essential to the process of finding a voice and creating community. Through their stories we have transformed ourselves from objects of oppression into subjects and agents busy making history in our own right. Such narratives have been indispensable to the formation of our identity. As Stuart Hall has put it, "Identities are the names we give to the different ways we are positioned by, and position ourselves within, the narratives of the past."[1] But what we find in their work is not the expression of one singular, uniform, homogeneous, black lesbian or gay male identity that is at all times identical to itself. Rather we find stories that narrate our differences and the multiplicity of experiences lived by black lesbians and gay men. We find that black lesbians and gay men do not all speak in one voice. To me, this suggests the recognition of the possibility of unity-in-diversity, and implies a skeptical disposition towards categorical identity politics. Such work suggests that we give up the search for a purified ideal type or a positive role model of political correctness, because it teaches us to value our own multiple differences as the very stuff of which our queer diasporic identities are made.

Insofar as these issues inform the interventions that Isaac Julien and Marlon Riggs have made in independent film, it is important to situate their work in relation to the question of identity. Namely, that identities are not found in nature but historically constructed in culture—or to put it another way, *identity is not what you are so much as what you do.* Black queer cultural politics has not expressed an essential identity that was always already there waiting to be discovered, but has actively invented a multitude of identities through a variety of activities and practices, whether organizing workshops and fund-raising parties, lobbying and mobilizing around official policies, writing poems, publishing magazines, taking photographs, or making films.

Finding a Voice: Independent Cinema and Black Representation

Tongues Untied and *Looking for Langston* share a number of similarities: both are the "first" black independent productions to openly address black homosexuality, because prior to now such issues have been avoided or omitted from black independent cinema; both tell our stories of the experience of dual exclusion, being silenced and being hidden from history. And, taking all this into account, both have won similarly enthusiastic responses from various audiences around the world, and have received numerous awards and prizes.

At the same time, these two works could not be more different in style and approach. Whereas *Tongues* foregrounds autobiographical voices that speak from the lived experiences of black gay men in the here and now, and emphasizes the immediacy, direct address, and in-your-face realism associated with video, *Langston* speaks to black gay experience by tracking the enigmatic sexual identity of one of the most cherished icons of black cultural history, Langston Hughes, whose presence is evoked through music, poetry, and archival film to create a dreamlike space of poetic reverie, historically framed by images of the Harlem Renaissance of the 1920s. To put it crudely, the contrast in aesthetic strategies turns on the difference between a video which embodies the values of documentary realism and a film which self-consciously places itself in the art cinema tradition.

Rather than play one off against the other, I want to use these differences to underline my point about the plurality and diversity of identities among black gay men. From this perspective we can recognize the way in which both Julien and Riggs participate in a similar cultural and political project that concerns the struggle to find a voice in the language of cinema, which, up to now, has treated the black gay subject as merely an absence, or present only as an object of someone else's imagination. In this sense, Julien and Riggs deepen and extend the critical project of black independent cinema: to find a place from which to speak as a black subject in a discourse which has either erased and omitted the black subject, or represented the black subject only through the mechanism of the stereotype, fixed and frozen as an object of someone else's fears and fantasies. However, between them, the two works also challenge and disrupt certain assumptions within black independent cinema itself, and in this way their strategies bring to light an important paradox about race and representation which parallels the problem of identity in political discourse.

Both Julien and Riggs are independent practitioners, which is to say that the conditions of production in which they work are distinct from the conditions that obtain in the commercial film industry, in which production, distribution, and exhibition are monopolized by private corporations, mostly centered in Hollywood. Yet, as James Snead has pointed out, the term independent is something of a misnomer, since such practitioners are highly dependent on the role of public sector institutions, not only in the funding of production, but in terms of the subsequent distribution and exhibition of films regarded as "noncommercial."[2]

Indeed, public funding is a key condition enabling both works. *Tongues* was financed by a range of grants from various foundations and institutions, including a Western States Regional Fellowship from the National Endowment for the Arts, and *Langston* was funded principally by the British Film Institute and Channel Four Television, both of which have an official mandate and responsibility to support work from and about social constituencies underrepresented in film and television.

Although such public sector institutions have shaped, influenced, and sometimes curtailed the renewal of black independent film in the 1980s, there are salient national differences in the conditions of independent practice. Whereas Julien's film is a Sankofa production and emerges from a context in which collective methods have flourished in the British workshop sector, which includes Black Audio Film Collective, Ceddo, Retake, and other groups, mostly in London,[3] Riggs directs his own independent production company, based in Oakland, and works on an individual basis, as do most black practitioners in the United States—from Julie Dash and Haile Gerima to Charles Burnett and Michelle Parkerson—where the independent sector is more dispersed.

It is significant, however, that, at the point of exhibition, both *Tongues* and *Langston* have been shown twice on public television, on PBS in the United States and on Channel Four in Britain. This is significant, not simply in making the works accessible to a broader range of audiences, but in terms of the responsibility of public television—as opposed to commercial cinema—to represent the underrepresented. This can be seen as the locus of a particular problem in the politics of representation that all minority practitioners encounter, namely, that representation does not simply denote a practice of depiction but also has the connotation of a practice of delegation, in which the minority practitioner is often positioned in the role of a representative who speaks for the entire constituency from which he or she comes. Elsewhere, I have discussed this problematic as the "burden of representation" which black artists and filmmakers have had to negotiate once they gain access to the apparatus of representation.[4]

In a situation where the right to representation is rationed and regulated, so that minorities experience restricted access to the means of representation, there is often an assumption on the part of funding institutions and an expectation on the part of audiences that they should "speak for" their particular community. This is felt and lived as a real dilemma for artists and practitioners themselves, as Martina Attille, formerly of the Sankofa Collective, put it in relation to the making of *The Passion of Remembrance* in 1986:

There was this sense of urgency to say it all, or at least to signal as much as we could in one film. Sometimes we can't afford to hold anything back for another time, another conversation or another film. That is the reality of our experience—sometimes we only get the one chance to make ourselves heard.[5]

What has emerged in the "new wave" of black independent film during the 1980s, particularly in the British context, is the awareness of the impossibility of carrying this burden without being crushed by it. It is impossible for any one individual to speak as a representative for an entire community without risking the violent reductionism which repeats the stereotypical view within the majority culture that minority communities are homogeneous, unitary, and monolithic because their members are all the same. It is impossible for any one black person to claim the right to speak for the diversity of identities and experiences within black society without the risk that such diversity will be simplified and reduced to what is seen as typical, a process which thereby reproduces and replicates the logic of the racist stereotype that all black people are, essentially, the same.

Julien and Riggs both recognize these pitfalls in racial representation, and what is remarkable is that through entirely different aesthetic strategies they enact a film practice which refuses to carry the burden of representation, instead opening it up to displace the assumptions and expectations contained within it. To examine how they do this I want to focus first on the articulation of multiple voices in *Tongues Untied* and then turn to the gaze and looking relations as articulated in *Looking for Langston*.

Dialogic Voicing in Documentary Realism

One of the adjectives most frequently invoked in response to *Tongues Untied*, especially among black gay men, is "real": we value the film for its "realness." A cursory historical overview of black independent cinema would reveal the prevalence of a certain realist aesthetic which must be understood as one of the privileged modes through which black filmmakers have sought to contest those versions of reality inscribed in the racist discourses of the dominant film culture. As a counterdiscourse, the imperative of such a realist aesthetic in black film, whether documentary or drama, is to "tell it like it is." What is at issue in the oppositional or critical role of black independent cinema is the ability to articulate a counterdiscourse based on an alternative version of reality inscribed in the voices and viewpoints of black social actors.

Tongues is congruent with the tradition of documentary realism in black film culture, as it foregrounds a range of autobiographical voices that dramatize the power of witness and testimony. Through the authority of their own experiences, black gay men come to voice as primary definers of reality. As Riggs has said in a recent interview:

We live in a society in which truth is often defined by your reflection on the screen. . . . But you don't really live and you're not really somebody until you're somehow reflected there on the tube or in the theatre. . . . What films like *Tongues Untied* do, especially for people who have had no images of themselves out there to see, is give them a visible and visual representation of their lives.[6]

20. Marlon Riggs's *Tongues Untied* (1989). Courtesy Anthology Film Archives; reprinted by permission.

In this sense, the "realness" of the work concerns the desires and expectations of a black gay audience who decode it. But in terms of the aesthetic strategy in which it is encoded, such "realness" is an effect of the consistent use of direct address, whereby in place of the anonymous, impersonal, third-person narrator which tends to characterize the documentary genre, individuals tell their stories directly to the camera, creating the space for an interpersonal dialogue that is simultaneously confessional, affirmative, and confrontational. Its "realness" consists not simply of the accuracy or veracity of its depiction of the experiences of African-American gay men—through poetry, rap, drama, dance, and music—but through this dialogic mode of address which brings the spectator into a direct relationship with the stories and experiences that find their voices.

Of the four cinematic values associated with documentary realism—transparency, immediacy, authority, and authenticity—*Tongues* seems to emphasize the latter through Riggs's presence, as he tells his life story, which serves as a thread connecting the multiple components of the video: from the poems performed by Essex Hemphill, Steve Langley, and Allan Miller, and the scenes in which the homophobic voices of a black preacher, an activist, and various black entertainers conspire to silence, ridicule, and intimidate, to the eroticism of a tender embrace between two lovers, and scenes showing rallies and Gay Pride marches. The emphasis on authenticity, honesty, and truth-to-experience through personal disclosure is underlined by Riggs's visual presence at the beginning, where he appears nude: a gesture of exposure not only suggesting the vulnerability of revealing one's own life through one's story but also establishing the framework of personal disclosure that guides the work as a whole.

It is precisely the achievement of *Tongues Untied* that its realism foregrounds such authenticity without recourse to the master codes of the documentary genre, in which the function of the impersonal voice-of-God narrator seeks to resolve all questions raised, tie up all loose ends, and explain everything as the narrative inexorably moves towards the movement of closure. *Tongues* displaces this function entirely: there is no unifying voice-over, nor indeed any single voice privileged in a position of mastery, explanation, or resolution. In terms of his own presence, Riggs does not speak as a representative whose individual story is supposed to speak for every black gay man; rather, he speaks as one voice among others, each of which articulates different experiences and identities. He does not seek to typify some unitary and homogeneous essence called "the black, gay, male experience" by presenting his story as the only story or the whole story; rather, he speaks from the specificity of his own experience, which, because of the presence of other voices and stories, is not generalized or typified as such.

This kind of dialogic voicing assumes crucial importance for a number of reasons. First, by contrast, it highlights the degree to which black independent cinema has often inadvertently replicated the problem of exclusion by reproducing the monologic voicing of the master codes of documentary realism, in order to authorize its own counternarratives. Furthermore, because he does not privilege any one voice as the source of authority, Riggs highlights the degree to which those voices in black cinema that claim implicitly to be representative, and to speak for the entire black race, very often tend to be only the voices of black men, whose heroic and heterosexist accents often exclude the voices of black women and black gay men. In this sense, *Tongues* can be said to challenge the heterosexual presumption that so often characterizes the documentary realist aesthetic in black cinema.

To contextualize this issue, one might point to the dual role of Spike Lee as director and narrative character in *Do the Right Thing*, where he is positioned, along with the other main young black male protagonists, as the embodiment of the Bedford-Stuyvesant community itself, pitched into antagonism with white society across the battle lines of race and ethnicity. By making the implicit claim to speak for the condition of young black men in the urban U.S. (in terms of both the narrative structure and the marketing of the film), Lee seems to replicate the all-too-familiar stereotype of the "angry black man" consumed with rage about the politics of race and racism on the streets, to the exclusion of any other politics, such as his sexual politics between the sheets.

The second reason why the dialogic voicing of *Tongues* is important has to do with its awareness of the multidimensional character of the political. In this sense its "realness" has to do with the acknowledgment that real life is contradictory—"home is a place of truth, not peace," as Riggs comments at one point. In the autobiographical sequence, as he narrates his first kiss and being bussed to a nearly all-white school in the South, Riggs's narrative presence is framed by the concatenation of abusive epithets—"punk," "motherfuckin' coon," "homo," "nigger go home"—spat out at rhythmic intervals that underline the interplay of racism and homophobia, experienced at one and the same time. It is this awareness of a dialectic in the politics of race and sexuality that is maintained throughout the work by virtue of its dialogic strategy. *Tongues* does not seek to reduce, simplify, or resolve the lived experience of real antagonism but is constantly vigilant to the complex effects of contradiction —particularly as these enter into the interior space of our own relations with each other, our intimacy, and our aversion.

If the work refuses facile notions of "internalized oppression," it equally rejects the reductive tendency of the current discourse of endangered species in which black men are seen as victims and nothing but victims. Such questions concerning the contradictions through which black masculinity is lived are forcefully raised, but rather than provide the false security of easy answers, the strategy of direct address brings the viewer and audience into the dialogue as active participants who share an equal responsibility in the search for answers. By invoking a certain answerability on the part of the audience, what the film gives is not a neat resolution to the contradictions of the real, but a range of questions for the audience to take home.

If all this sounds terribly earnest, I should emphasize that the irreverent humor of *Tongues Untied* is absolutely crucial to the subversive force of its dialogic strategy. More to the point, the element of playfulness and parody, like the aesthetics of dialogic voicing, is thoroughly embedded in the oral tradition of African-American cultural expression. As the Lavender Light quartet pleads in the tape, "Hey, boy, can you come out tonight?" *Tongues* shows that its tongue is firmly in cheek in this appropriation of black pop acappella from the doo-wop tradition of the 1950s. Like the freaky-deke ritual on the killing floor of the dance halls of the 1930s, the Oaktown ensemble engaged in the electric slide and the beautifully stylized boys caught vogueing in New York City underline the affirmative role of black expressive culture— and the contributions black gays have made to the renewal of its expressive edge. As elements of black queer subcultural ritual, such dance forms enact a performative body politics, in which the black body is a site both of misery, oppression, and exploitation, as well as of resistance, transcendence, and ecstasy.

Moreover, considering the dialectic of appropriation as a constitutive feature of diasporan culture—in the case of vogueing, for instance, how black gays appropriate the poses of white female models in glossy fashion magazines to create a stylized dance form, are then appropriated in turn by white performers such as Malcolm McLaren and Madonna—*Tongues Untied* performs a doubly critical role in its affirmation of black gay pleasures. On the one hand, by reinserting black gay subcultural style into the expressive context of the African-American cultural tradition as a whole, it refutes the premise that gayness is a "white thing." On the other, by recontextualizing such styles in the lived experience of black gay men, it brings to light the extent to which our pleasures may be misappropriated by white audiences, who are nevertheless fascinated and perhaps even, in some sense, envious of them. Let's face it, who wouldn't want to be a member of the Institute of Snap!thology? "Don't mess with a snap diva!" If you want the politically correct party line, please stay at home and dial 1-900-Race-Class-Gender instead.

Looking Relations: Allegories of Identity and Desire

In turning to Isaac Julien's *Looking for Langston*, I want to develop the theme of appropriation as a figure in diaspora culture. This is important, not simply because of the stylish way in which the film appropriates art cinema conventions, but more fundamentally because it is impossible to understand the formation of black British identities, gay or otherwise, without a recognition of the way in which different signs have been appropriated and re-articulated to construct new forms of political identity and imagined community in this specific context.

Here I would emphasize "imagined" in Benedict Anderson's term "imagined community,"[7] because without the notion of a collective historical imagination, how could we understand why a black British filmmaker whose parents migrated to London from St. Lucia would choose to make a film about a black American writer from Kansas City?

If one thinks about the naming of the black subject in postwar Britain, it becomes necessary to reiterate the theoretical view that subjectivity is indeed socially constructed in language. What we see are not simply different names used to designate the same community but the historical becoming of such a political community in and through a struggle over the signifiers of racial discourse. The displacement of the proper name—from "colored immigrants" in the 1950s, to "ethnic minorities" in the 1960s, and to "black communities" in the 1970s and 1980s—vividly underlines the point that social identities are not just there in nature but are actively constructed in culture. Of course, this did not just happen in the realm of language alone, since a whole range of nondiscursive practices have constituted Black Britain as a domain of social and political antagonism. Nevertheless, it is crucial to acknowledge the material effects of symbolic and imaginary relations.

For over four hundred years in Western culture, the sign /black/ had nothing but negative connotations, to say the least. However, we have also seen that the signifying chain in which it was equated with negative values was not totally closed or fixed. In the U.S. context during the 1960s, the term /black/ was disarticulated out of the negative chain of equivalence in racist discourse, and rearticulated into an alternative chain of equivalences as a sign of empowerment, indicated by the shift from Negro to Black. In Britain during the 1980s something similar happened, inspired and influenced by the black American example, as blackness was disarticulated out of one discursive system and rearticulated into another, where it became a sign of solidarity among Asian, African, and Caribbean peoples, and functioned as a term of a politically chosen identity rather than a genetically ascribed one. The cultural politics of the black diaspora thus highlights a deconstructive process in which the central signifiers of racist ideology, based on the binary opposition of white/not-white, were rearticulated to produce a new set of connotations in one and the same sign.

It is an awareness of the multi-accentual character of the sign that informs the critical project of black British workshops, such as Sankofa and Black Audio Film Collective. And this awareness is not merely the result of an engagement with difficult poststructuralist theories, but something achieved through a practice of trial and error and open-ended experimentation inscribed in their productions, such as *Territories* (1985) and *Handsworth Songs* (1986). *Looking for Langston* continues the critique of racial representation signalled by those earlier works, but deepens and complicates it by extending it into the domain of fantasy. I would argue that the film is not a documentary search for the "truth" about Langston Hughes's ambiguous sexual identity so much as an investigation into the psychic reality of fantasy as that domain of subjectivity in which our desires and identifications are shaped. The film is as much a meditation on the psychic reality of the political unconscious—which concerns the imaginary and symbolic conduits of the diaspora, through which black Britons have sought to symbolize our political dreams and desires in part through identifications with black America and black Americans—as it is a poetic meditation on the psychic and social relations that circumscribe our lives as black gay men.

This double reading is suggested by the ambiguous sense of time and place evoked by the montage of music, poetry, and archival imagery across the film's monochrome texture and stylized art direction. Characters inhabit the fictional milieu of a 1920s speakeasy, where tuxedoed couples dance and drink champagne, celebrating hedonistic pleasure in defiance of the hostile world outside. It is this outside that intrudes at the end of the film when thugs and police raid the club only to find that its denizens have disappeared, while 1980s house music plays on the soundtrack almost like a music video. The multilayered texture evoked by the ambiguity of past and present, outside and inside, fact and fantasy, thus allows more than one reading about what the film is looking for. I want to focus on only two possibilities: an archeology of black modernism and an allegory of black gay male desire. Langston Hughes is remembered as the key poet of the Harlem Renaissance and has come to be revered as a father figure of black literature, yet in the process of becoming such an icon, the complexity of his life and the complexity of the Harlem Renaissance itself has been subject to selective erasure and repression by the gatekeepers and custodians of "the colored museum." Hughes is remembered as a populist, public figure, but the enigma of his private life—his sexuality— is seen as something better left unaddressed in most biographies, an implicit gesture of denial which buries and represses the fact that the Harlem Renaissance was as gay as it was black, and that many of its key figures—Claude McKay, Alain Locke, Countee Cullen, Wallace Thurman, and Bruce Nugent—were known to be queer, one way or another. Looking for Langston engages with and enters into this area of enigma and ambiguity, not in order to arrive at an unequivocal answer embodied in factual evidence, but to explore the ways in which various facets of black cultural life are subject to psychic and social repression, from within as well as without.

As an archeological inquiry, the film excavates what has been hidden from history, not only the fluidity of sexual identities within the black cultural expression of that period, but the intertwining of black culture and Euro-American modernism. Just as official histories of modernism tend to erase and selectively repress the work of black artists, official versions of the Harlem Renaissance narrative tend to avoid the sexual politics of the "jazz era." Yet the film suggests that it was precisely the imbrication of race and sexuality that underpinned the expressive and aesthetic values of the cultural practices of that time—from Picasso's Demoiselles d'Avignon to Josephine Baker, for instance. But Looking for Langston is not a history lesson: the point of archeology is not to research history for its own sake but to search for answers to contemporary dilemmas, in this case the need to historicize the hybrid domain of black British cultural production in the 1980s and 1990s.

The film looks for Langston, but what we find is Isaac. Not so much in an autobiographical sense, but in terms of a self-reflexive awareness of the multiple influences that inform his artistic choices and methods. The desire to unravel the hidden histories of the Harlem Renaissance serves as an emblem for an inventory of the diverse textual resources which have informed the renascence and renewal of black artistic and cultural practices in contemporary Britain. From this perspective, one might describe the film as a visual equivalent of a dialogue with the different cultural traditions from which Isaac Julien has invented his own artistic identity as a black gay auteur.

This view is suggested by the promiscuous intertextuality which the film sets in motion. Alongside visual quotations from Jean Cocteau, Kenneth Anger, and Jean Genet, the voices of James Baldwin, Bruce Nugent, Toni Morrison, and Amiri Baraka combine to emphasize the dialogic and hybridized character of the text. In this "stereophonic space," in Barthes's phrase, Julien acknowledges the importance of the Euro-American avant-garde as much as the importance of black American literature as textual resources which black British artists have used in the process of finding their own voices. It is significant, therefore, that the film articulates theory and practice not in terms of didactic prescription but in terms of enacting a translation of cultural studies into cultural politics. This reflexive enactment of cultural theory is implicit in the role played by Stuart Hall in the film, who performs the voice-over narration, as his presence suggests that the intellectual practice associated with British cultural studies now informs Julien's filmic practice as a black gay auteur.

There is another aspect to this intertextuality that concerns what the film is looking for in the more literal sense. Its languid, dreamlike texture seduces the eye and its avowed homoeroticism solicits the gaze. Issues of voyeurism, fetishism, and scopophilic obsession arise across its sensual depiction of beautiful black male bodies. But the film does not simply indulge the pleasure in looking; it radically problematizes such pleasure by questioning the racial positions of the subject/object dichotomy associated with the dialectic of seeing and being seen.

Here the key motif is the direct look, whereby the black subject looks back (whether as auteur or character) and thus turns around the question of who has the right to look in order to ask the audience who or what they are looking for. This motif appeared in Julien's first film made with the Sankofa Collective, *Territories*, in the context of a confrontational, and somewhat didactic, inquiry into the objectification and fetishization of black culture as framed by the white gaze. In *Langston*, however, by virtue of the seductive and invitational direction of the textual strategy, he achieves a more penetrating insight into the structures of racial and sexual fantasy, precisely by setting a trap for the gaze and by the provocative incitement of our wish to look.

It is significant that the ghost of Robert Mapplethorpe is present in this staging of the look. This occurs not so much in the scene in which a white male character leisurely leafs through *The Black Book*—while Essex Hemphill reads one of his poems pinpointing the reinscription of racism in white gay culture—but in terms of a set of aesthetic conventions, such as fragmentation and chiaroscuro lighting, which the film employs to punctuate its incitement of our pleasure in looking. In this way, Julien's strategy of promiscuous intertextuality appropriates a range of visual tropes associated with white artists like Mapplethorpe to lay bare the way in which race determines the flow of power relations through the gaze in complex and ambivalent ways.

Hence, in one key scene an exchange of looks takes place between the actor who may be interpreted as "Langston" (Ben Ellison) and his mythic object of desire, a black man named "Beauty" (Matthew Baidoo). This provokes a hostile, competitive glare from Beauty's white male partner (John Wilson), who makes a grand gesture of drinking more champagne. As he turns away to face the bar, Langston drifts into a daydream. In this sequence, Bruce Nugent's poem "Lillies and Jade" is read, over images that portray the Langston character searching for his lost object of desire in a field of poppies. At the end of his reverie, Langston imagines himself coupled with Beauty, their bodies entwined on a bed as if they have just made love. It is important to recognize that this coupling takes place in fantasy, because it underlines the loss of access to the object of desire as being the very source of fantasy itself. Moreover, it shows how race enters into the vocabulary of desire: as the object of both the black and the white man's gaze, Beauty acts as the signifier of desire as his desirability is enhanced precisely by the eroticized rivalry between their two looks.

It is here that the trope of visual fetishism found in Mapplethorpe's photographs makes a striking and subversive return, in close-up sequences set in the nightclub, intercut with Langston's daydream. From Langston's point of view, the camera lovingly lingers on the sensuous mouth of the actor portraying Beauty, with the rest of his face cast in shadow, like an iris shot in the silent movies. But, as in Mapplethorpe's images, the strong emphasis on chiaroscuro lighting invests the fetishized fragment, or body part, with a compelling erotogenic residue. The "thick lips" of the Negro are hypervalorized as the iconic emblem of Beauty's impossible desirability. In other words, Julien takes the risk of replicating the racial stereotype of the thick-lipped negro precisely to reposition the black subject as the desiring subject, not the alienated object, of the look. Like the image of the two men entwined on the bed, which recalls the homoerotic photographs of George Platt Lynes, yet also critiques them, it is only by intervening in and against the logic of fetishization in racial representation that Julien is able to open up the ambivalence of the psychic and social relations—of identification, object-choice, envy, and exclusion—inscribed in the brief relay of looks between the three men. Of each of these, I would draw attention to envy—wanting the object possessed by the Other—not only because it informs the kind of scopic obsession that Mapplethorpe works upon, suggesting that the white subject sees blackness as an enviable quality, but because as Julien recodes it, turning the fetish inside out, he points to the way that intraracial relations among black men themselves also entail feelings of rivalry and envy at the very basis of our identifications with each other.

I have focused on this particular moment because it strikes me that there are important formal similarities between Julien's strategy of working in and against the logic of racial fetishism and that of Nigerian-British gay photographer Rotimi Fani-Kayode, whose work is also inflected by a dialogic engagement with problems raised in Mapplethorpe. In contrast to the isolation effect in Mapplethorpe's work, whereby only one black male nude appears in the field of vision—a device that encourages a fantasy of mastery—in Kayode's work, such as *Technique of Ecstasy*, black men's bodies are coupled and contextualized to evoke an eroticism that seems to slip out of the implied power relations associated with the interracial subject/object dichotomy. Kayode creates an Afrocentric homoerotica precisely and perversely by appropriating conventions associated with the Eurocentric history of the fine art nude.

What Julien and Kayode share in common is not so much the fact that they are both black gay male artists, but that as artists they both use an intertextual strategy of appropriation and rearticulation in order to signify upon, and thus critique, the dominant regime of racial and sexual representation but without negating, denying, or disavowing the reality of the fantasies that give rise to such representations. Rather, by virtue of working in and against the master codes that regulate and govern the stereotypical, they begin to unravel what takes place at the borderlines between the psychic and the social, between fantasy and history.

In this brief discussion of *Looking for Langston* I have emphasized the formal dimension of its aesthetic strategy in order to draw attention to its enunciation of an allegory of desire, which is the source of its emotional resonance, not just for black gay men but for others in the audience as well. Although it is not the only available theory of desire, psychoanalysis suggests that desire is always about loss: our search for pleasure, the search for a significant other, is about the attempt to recover a state of fusion, wholeness, or nonseparation, which can never be fully retrieved. In so far as this lost object of desire can never really be found, the search for pleasure inevitably entails frustration, privation, and despair.

The achievement of *Looking for Langston* lies precisely in the way it shows how desire and despair run together, and thus how desire always entails rituals of mourning for what is lost and cannot be recovered. There is a sense of mourning, not just for Langston, buried in the past under the repressive weight of homophobic and ethnocentric narratives, but mourning for friends, lovers, and others lost to AIDS here and now, in the present. There is mourning, but not melancholia: as Langston himself says at the end of the film, "Why should I be blue? I've been blue all night through." Just like the multiple allusions of the term "blue," the textual strategy of the film as a whole creates an evocative "structure of feeling," in Raymond Williams's sense, that speaks not only to black gay men—although I can think of no other film which has laid bare our desire and despair in quite the way that it has—but to any desiring subject who has experienced the blues.

I want to conclude with a brief discussion of the issue of authorship, because the work of Marlon Riggs and Isaac Julien urges us to rethink questions of identity and agency that many thought were dead and buried with the poststructuralist argument concerning the "death of the author." That these are among the first cinematic texts authored by black gay men means that it really *does* matter who is speaking. We can all live without the return of Romantic notions of creative genius, which always placed the author at the center of the text—resembling the godlike figure of the "universal intellectual" who thought he had an answer for everything—but we need to revise the notion that the author is simply an empty, abstract function of cultural discourse through whom various ideologies speak.

The welcomed development of postmodernism that accompanied the collapse of the grand narratives and the decentering of universal Man was that it revealed that the subject who had monopolized the microphone in public culture—by claiming to speak for humanity as a whole, while denying that right of representation to anyone who was not white, not male, not middle-class, and not Western—was nothing but a minority himself. If postmodernism simply means that the era of modernism is past, then hurrah! The pluralization and diversification of public space, where a variety of subjects find their voice and assert their right to speak, has only just begun. As black gay artists, "specific intellectuals" who speak from the specificity of their experience, Riggs and Julien, like other black lesbian and gay artists, have actively contributed to the cultural and political terrain of postmodernism.

Precisely because their work is so important, we should do more than merely celebrate. Above all, we should be deeply skeptical of a certain assumption embedded in categorical identity politics that would argue that these films are of aesthetic and political value *because* their authors are black gay men. Throughout this paper I have drawn attention to the formal strategies in *Tongues Untied* and *Looking for Langston* because I want to resist the conflation between artistic value and authorial identity that so often arises in debates on emerging artists. The problem here is not simply that bad works get celebrated alongside good ones but that constructive criticism is inhibited by the fear of being seen to be politically incorrect: if it is assumed that a black film is necessarily good because a black person made it, any criticism of the film is likely to be read as an attack on the very person who made it rather than on the film that was made.

Analogously, we are familiar with that rhetorical strategy of categorical identity politics in which a statement is prefaced by the adjectives that describe one's identity—for example, "As a black gay man, I feel angry about my place in the world." The statement may be entirely valid, but, because it is embedded in my identity, it preempts the possibility of critical dialogue, because your disagreement might be interpreted not as a comment on what I say, but as a criticism of who I am. So, in relation to *Tongues Untied* and *Looking for Langston*, I would adopt an anticelebration position, because I want to emphasize that these rich, provocative, and important works do indeed "make a difference" not because of who or what the filmmakers are, but because of what they do, and above all because of the freaky way they do it.

Notes

1 Stuart Hall, "Cultural Identity and Cinematic Representation," *Framework*, no. 36 (1989) pp. 68–81; reprinted in Jonathan Rutherford, ed., *Identity: Community, Culture, Difference* (London: Lawrence and Wishart, 1990) p. 225.

2 James Snead, "Black Independent Film: Britain and America," in Kobena Mercer, ed., *Black Film/British Cinema*, ICA Document 7, (London: Institute of Contemporary Arts, 1988) p. 47.

3 Sankofa Film and Video Collective comprises Isaac Julien, Maureen Blackwood, Nadine Marsh Edwards, and Robert Crusz. It was formed in 1984 in London with the aims of developing an independent black film culture in the areas of production, exhibition, and audience discussions. Under the aegis of the ACTT Workshop Declaration, the Collective has been funded from a variety of sources, including the Greater London Council, the British Film Institute and Channel Four. For background information on their work, and that of the Black Audio Film Collective, see interviews in Coco Fusco, ed., *Young, British and Black*, (Buffalo: Contemporary Hallwalls Arts Center, 1988).

4 See Kobena Mercer and Isaac Julien, "De Margin and De Centre," introduction to *Screen* vol. 29 no. 4 (Autumn, 1988) pp. 2–10, and Kobena Mercer, "Black Art and the Burden of Representation," *Third Text*, no. 10 (Spring, 1990) pp. 61–78.

5 Martina Attille in Jim Pines, "The Passion of Remembrance: Background and Interview with Sankofa," *Framework*, no. 32/33 (1986) p. 101.

6 Marlon Riggs in Ron Simmons, "Tongues Untied: An Interview with Marlon Riggs," *Black Film Review*, vol. 5, no. 3 (1989); reprinted in Essex Hemphill, ed., *Brother to Brother: New Writing by Black Gay Men*, (Boston: Alyson, 1991) p. 191.

7 See Benedict Anderson, *Imagined Communities: Reflections on the Origin and Spread of Nationalism* (London: Verso, 1983).

Select Bibliography

Acker, Ally (1993) *Reel Women: Pioneers of the Cinema, 1896 to the Present*, New York: Continuum.

Banes, Sally (1993) *Greenwich Village 1963: Avant-garde Performance and the Effervescent Body*, Durham, N.C.: Duke University Press.

Battcock, Gregory (1967) *The New American Cinema*, New York: Dutton.

Berg, Gretchen (1967) "Nothing to Lose: An Interview with Andy Warhol," *Cahiers du Cinéma in English* 10 (May): 38–42.

Bobo, Jacqueline (ed) (1998) *Black Women Film and Video Artists*, New York: Routledge.

Bourdon, David (1989) *Warhol*, New York: Abrams.

Bowser, Pearl, Jane Gaines, and Charles Musser (eds) (2001) *Oscar Micheaux and His Circle: African-American Filmmaking and Race Cinema of the Silent Era*, Bloomington: Indiana University Press.

Brakhage, Stan (1989) *Film at Wit's End*, Kingston, N.Y.: McPherson.

Breitrose, Henry (1960) "Films of Shirley Clarke," *Film Quarterly* 13.4: 57–58.

Bresson, Robert (1975) *Notes on Cinematography*, Jonathan Griffin (trans) New York: Urizen.

Brown, Robert (1964) "Interview with Bruce Conner," *Film Culture* 33 (Summer): 15–16.

Brunsdon, Charlotte (ed) (1986) *Films for Women*, London: BFI.

Burckhardt, Rudy (1983) "Warren Sonbert," *Film Culture* 70–71 (Winter): 176.

Bute, Mary Ellen (1954) "Abstronics," *Films in Review* 5.6: 263–266.

Canyon Cinema (1992) *Canyon Cinema Catalogue No. 7*, San Francisco: Canyon Cinema.

Castle, Ted (1980) "Carolee Schneemann: The Woman Who Uses Her Body as Her Art," *Artforum* 19.3: 64–70.

Charnov, Elaine (1998) "The Performative Visual Anthropology Films of Zora Neale Hurston," *Film Criticism* 23.1: 38–47.

Chin, Daryl (1989) "Walking on Thin Ice: The Films of Yoko Ono," *The Independent* (April): 19–23. Reprinted in this reader.

Collins, Patricia Hill (1990) *Black Feminist Thought: Knowledge, Consciousness, and the Politics of Empowerment*, London: HarperCollins.

Curtis, David (1971) *Experimental Cinema: A Fifty-Year Evolution*, New York: Delta.

de Lauretis, Teresa (1984) *Alice Doesn't: Feminism, Semiotics, Cinema*, Bloomington: Indiana University Press.

Dixon, Wheeler Winston (1995–1996) "Maureen Blackwood, Isaac Julien, and the Sankofa Collective," *Film Criticism* 20.1–2: 131–143.

Dixon, Wheeler Winston (1997) *The Exploding Eye: A Re-Visionary History of 1960s American Experimental Cinema*, Albany: State University of New York Press.

Dixon, Wheeler Winston (1998) "Performativity in 1960s American Experimental Cinema: The Body as Site of Ritual and Display," *Film Criticism* 23.1: 48–60. Excerpted in the introduction to this reader.

Dyer, Richard (1990) *Now You See It: Studies on Lesbian and Gay Film*, London: Routledge.

Ehrenstein, David (1983) "Warren Sonbert Interviewed by David Ehrenstein, December 1978," *Film Culture* 70–71 (Winter): 185–196. Reprinted in this reader as "Warren Sonbert Interview."

Export, Valie (1988–1989) "The Real and Its Double: The Body," *Discourse* 11 (Fall–Winter): 3–27.

Field, Simon, and Peter Sainsbury (1972) "*Zorns Lemma* and *Hapax Legomena*: Interview with Hollis Frampton," *Afterimage* 4 (Autumn): 44–47.

Filmmakers' Cooperative (1967) *Filmmakers' Cooperative Catalogue No. 4*, New York: New American Cinema Group.

Flitterman-Lewis, Sandy (1990) *To Desire Differently*, Urbana: University of Illinois Press.

Foster, Gwendolyn Audrey (1995) *Women Film Directors: An International Bio-Critical Dictionary*, Westport, Conn.: Greenwood.

Foster, Gwendolyn Audrey (1997a) *Women Filmmakers of the African and Asian Diaspora: Decolonizing the Gaze, Locating Subjectivity*, Carbondale: Southern Illinois University Press.

Foster, Gwendolyn Audrey (1997b) "Barbara Hammer, an Interview: Re/Constructing Lesbian Auto/Biographies in *Tender Fictions* and *Nitrate Kisses*," *Post Script* 16.3 (Summer): 3–16. Reprinted in this reader as "Re/Constructing Lesbian Auto/Biographies in *Tender Fictions* and *Nitrate Kisses*."

Foster, Gwendolyn Audrey (ed) (1999) *Identity and Memory: The Films of Chantal Akerman*, Trowbridge, U.K.: Flicks.

Foucault, Michel (1973) *The Birth of the Clinic: An Archaeology of Medical Perception*, A. M. Sheridan Smith (trans) New York: Pantheon.

Ganguly, Suranjan (1994) "Stan Brakhage—The 60th Birthday Interview," *Film Culture* 78 (Summer): 18–38. Reprinted in this reader.

Gibson, Gloria J. (1994) "Aspects of Black Feminist Cultural Ideology in Films by Black Women Independent Artists," *Multiple Voices in Feminist Film Criticism*, Diane Carson, Linda Dittmar, and Janice R. Welsch (eds) Minneapolis: University of Minnesota Press: 365–379. Reprinted in this reader as "Black Women's Independent Cinema."

Gidal, Peter (1976) "An Interview with Hollis Frampton," *Structural Film Anthology*, Peter Gidal (ed.) London: BFI: 64–72. Reprinted in this reader.

Goldberg, Marianne (1987–1988) "The Body, Discourse, and *The Man Who Envied Women*," *Women and Performance: A Journal of Feminist Theory* 3.2: 97–102.

Gordon, Bette (1990) "*Variety*: The Pleasure of Looking," *Issues in Feminist Film Criticism*, Patricia Erens (ed) Bloomington: Indiana University Press: 418–422.

Gronau, Anna (1987) "Avant-garde Film by Women: To Conceive a New Language of Desire," *The Event Horizon: Essays on Hope, Sexuality, Social Space, and Media(tion) in Art*, Lorne Falk and Barbara Fischer (eds) Toronto: Coach House and Walter Phillips Gallery: 159–176.

Haller, Robert A. (2001) *Galaxy: Avant-garde Filmmakers Look Across Space and Time*, New York: Anthology Film Archives.

Hammer, Barbara (1993) "The Politics of Abstraction," *Queer Looks: Perspectives on Lesbian and Gay Film and Video*, Martha Gever, Pratibha Parmar, and John Greyson (eds) New York: Routledge: 70–75.

Hart, Lynda (1993) "Identity and Seduction: Lesbians in the Mainstream," *Acting Out: Feminist Performance*, Lynda Hart and Peggy Phelan (eds) Ann Arbor: University of Michigan Press: 119–137.

Haug, Kate (1998) "An Interview with Carolee Schneemann," *Wide Angle* 20.1: 20–49. Reprinted in this reader.

Hill, Jerome (1972) "Brakhage's Eyes," *Film Culture* 52 (Spring): 43–46.

Hoberman, Jim (1981) "Three Myths of Avant-garde Film," *Film Comment* 17.3: 34–35.

Hoberman, Jim, and Edward Leffingwell (1997) *Wait for Me at the Bottom of the Pool: The Writings of Jack Smith*, London: Serpent's Tail.

Hoberman, Jim, and Jonathan Rosenbaum (1983) *Midnight Movies*, New York: Harper and Row.

Holmlund, Chris (1997) "When Autobiography Meets Ethnography and Girl Meets Girl: The 'Dyke Docs' of Sadie Benning and Su Friedrich," *Between the Sheets, In the Streets: Queer, Lesbian, and Gay Documentary*, Chris Holmlund and Cynthia Fuchs (eds) Minneapolis: University of Minnesota Press: 127–143. Reprinted in this reader as "The Films of Sadie Benning and Su Friedrich."

hooks, bell (1992) *Black Looks: Race and Representation*, Boston: South End.

Horak, Jan-Christopher (1996) "The First American Film Avant-garde, 1919–1945," *Lovers of Cinema: The First American Film Avant-garde 1919–1945*, Madison: University of Wisconsin Press: 14–66. Reprinted in this reader.

Jacoby, Roger (1976) "Willard Maas and Marie Menken: The Last Year," *Film Culture* 63–64 (Winter): 119–124.

James, David E. (1989) *Allegories of Cinema: American Film in the 1960s*, Princeton: Princeton University Press.

Jameson, Fredric (1990) *Signatures of the Visible*, New York: Routledge.

Juhasz, Alexandra (ed) (2001) *Women of Vision: Histories in Feminist Film and Video*, Minneapolis: University of Minnesota Press.

Kotz, Liz (1993) "An Unrequited Love for the Sublime: Looking at Lesbian Representation Across the Works of Abigail Child, Cecilia Dougherty, and Su Friedrich," *Queer Looks: Perspectives on Lesbian and Gay Film and Video*, Martha Gever, Pratibha Parmar, and John Greyson (eds) New York: Routledge: 86–102.

Kruger, Barbara (1988) "Sankofa Film/Video Collective and Black Audio Film Collective [at] the Collective for Living Cinema," *Artforum* 27.2: 143–144.

Kuhn, Annette, with Susannah Radstone (eds) (1994) *The Women's Companion to International Film*, Berkeley: University of California Press.

Lippard, Chris (ed) (1996) *By Angels Driven: The Films of Derek Jarman*, Westport, Conn.: Greenwood.

Lopate, Phillip (1983) "The Films of Warren Sonbert," *Film Culture* 70–71 (Winter): 177–184. Reprinted in this reader.

MacDonald, Scott (1992) "Interview with Michael Snow," *A Critical Cinema 2: Interviews with Independent Filmmakers*, Berkeley: University of California Press: 51–76. Reprinted in this reader.

Malanga, Gerard (1967) "A Letter to Warren Sonbert," *Film Culture* 46 (Autumn): 20–21.

Malanga, Gerard (1988) "Working with Warhol," *Art New England* (September): 6–8.

Mayne, Judith (1990) "Revising the 'Primitive,' " *The Woman at the Keyhole: Feminism and Women's Cinema*, Bloomington: Indiana University Press: 184–222. Reprinted in this reader as "Women in the Avant-garde: Germaine Dulac, Maya Deren, Agnès Varda, Chantal Akerman, and Trinh T. Minh-ha."

McCreadie, Marsha (1983) *Women on Film: The Critical Eye*, New York: Praeger.

Mead, Taylor (1998) "Notes on *The Flower Thief*," *Anthology Film Archives Program Notes* (January–February): 2–5.

Mekas, Jonas (1962) "Notes on the New American Cinema," *Film Culture* 24 (Autumn): 6–16. Reprinted in this reader.

Mekas, Jonas (1972) *Movie Journal: The Rise of the New American Cinema*, New York: Collier.

Mercer, Kobena (1993) "Dark and Lovely Too: Black Gay Men in Independent Film," *Queer Looks: Perspectives on Lesbian and Gay Film and Video*, Martha Gever, Pratibha Parmar, and John Greyson (eds) New York: Routledge: 238–256. Reprinted in this reader.

Moore-Gilbert, Bart, and John Seed (eds) (1992) *Cultural Revolutions: The Challenge of the Arts in the 1960s*, London: Routledge.

Mulvey, Laura (1975) "Visual Pleasure and Narrative Cinema," *Screen* 16.3: 6–18.

Myers, Louis Budd (1967) "Marie Menken Herself," *Film Culture* 45 (Summer): 37–39.

Nicholson, David (1986) "Conflict and Complexity: Filmmaker Kathleen Collins," *Black Film Review* 2.3: 16–17.

Ono, Yoko (1970) "Yoko Ono on Yoko Ono," *Film Culture* 48–49 (Winter/Spring): 32–33. Reprinted in this reader.

Rabinovitz, Lauren (1991a) "The Meanings of the Avant-garde," *Points of Resistance: Women, Power, and Politics in the New York Avant-garde Cinema, 1943–1971*, Urbana: University of Illinois Press: 13–36.

Rabinovitz, Lauren (1991b) "The Woman Filmmaker in the New York Avant-garde," *Points of Resistance: Women, Power and Politics in the New York Avant-garde Cinema, 1943–1971*, Urbana: University of Illinois Press: 1–12. Reprinted in this reader.

Renan, Sheldon (1967) *An Introduction to the American Underground Film*, New York: Dutton.

Rice, Ron (1983) "Note from Ron Rice to Jonas Mekas," *Film Culture* 70–71 (Winter): 100–111.

Sargeant, Jack (1997) *The Naked Lens*, London: Creation.

Schimmel, Paul (1998) *Out of Actions: Between Performance and the Object 1949–1979*, Los Angeles: Museum of Contemporary Art.

Shaviro, Steven (1993) *The Cinematic Body*, Minneapolis: University of Minnesota Press.

Sitney, P. Adams (1969) "Structural Film," *Film Culture* 47 (Summer): 1–10. Reprinted in this reader.

Sitney, P. Adams (1979) *Visionary Film: The American Avant-garde 1943–1978*, 2nd ed, Oxford: Oxford University Press.

Smith, Gavin (1998) "Toy Stories: Sadie Benning Interviewed," *Film Comment* 34.6: 29–31, 33.

Suarez, Juan A. (1996) "Pop, Queer, or Fascist? The Ambiguity of Mass Culture in Kenneth Anger's *Scorpio Rising*," *Bike Boys, Drag Queens, and Superstars: Avant-garde, Mass Culture, and Gay Identities in the 1960s Underground Cinema*, Bloomington: Indiana University Press: 141–180. Reprinted in this reader.

Tartaglia, Jerry (2001) "The Perfect Queer Appositeness of Jack Smith," *Quarterly Review of Film and Video* 18.1 (Fall): 39–53. Reprinted in this reader.

Taubin, Amy (1995) "Warren Sonbert, 1947–1995," *Village Voice* June 20: 48.

Tyler, Parker (1969) *Underground Film: A Critical History*, New York: Grove.

Wolf, Reva (1997) "*The Flower Thief*: The 'Film Poem,' Warhol's Early Films, and the Beat Writers," *Andy Warhol, Poetry, and Gossip in the* 1960s, Chicago: University of Chicago Press: 125–148. Reprinted in this reader.

Youngblood, Gene (1970) *Expanded Cinema*, New York: Dutton.

Index